Christian Homburg,
Sabine Kuester
and **Harley Krohmer**

MARKETING MANAGEMENT

A Contemporary Perspective

Christian Homburg,
Sabine Kuester
and Harley Krohmer

MARKETING MANAGEMENT

A Contemporary Perspective

McGraw-Hill Higher Education

London Boston Burr Ridge, IL Dubuque, IA Madison, WI New York San Francisco
St. Louis Bangkok Bogotá Caracas Kuala Lumpur Lisbon Madrid Mexico City
Milan Montreal New Delhi Santiago Seoul Singapore Sydney Taipei Toronto

Marketing Management: A Contemporary Perspective
Christian Homburg, Sabine Kuester and Harley Krohmer
ISBN-13 978-0-07-711724-5
ISBN-10 0-07-711724-7

McGraw-Hill Higher Education

Published by McGraw-Hill Education
Shoppenhangers Road
Maidenhead
Berkshire
SL6 2QL
Telephone: 44 (0) 1628 502 500
Fax: 44 (0) 1628 770 224
Website: www.mcgraw-hill.co.uk

British Library Cataloguing in Publication Data

A catalog record for this book is available from the British Library

Library of Congress Cataloging-in-Publication Data

The Library of Congress data for this book has been applied for from the Library of Congress

Acquisitions Editor: Rachel Gear
Development Editor: Jennifer Rotherham
Marketing Manager: Alice Duijser
Senior Production Editor: James Bishop

Cover design by Adam Renvoize
Printed and bound in Spain by Grafo

ISBN-13 978-0-07-711724-5
ISBN-10 0-07-711724-7

Dedication

To our families with love

Brief Table of Contents

Detailed Table of Contents

Detailed Table of Contents Continued

Detailed Table of Contents Continued

Detailed Table of Contents Continued

Preface

Today's markets have become increasingly difficult environments for most companies. Challenges arise from a variety of changes taking part in many different domains impacting the behavior and conduct of customers, competitors and other important stakeholders such as suppliers and channel partners. In this changing landscape companies have to be smart and able to address customer needs in a way that makes them purchase their offerings and – more importantly – that satisfies customers' genuine needs so that satisfaction and loyalty result. If there is one business discipline that can help companies to accomplish this goal – it is marketing. Marketing can greatly facilitate an understanding of markets and its players to create value for both customers and the company.

Marketing management, however, is not an easy task. It is neither easy for the practicing manager nor is it easy to convey for academics involved in teaching marketing management. The challenges and issues that students of marketing and marketing managers face are often misjudged as simplistic, and proposed solutions do not fully account for the complex nature of the problems that marketing is able to solve. In writing this book we set out to be a companion for all those who appreciate the important and crucial role that marketing can play in creating value for companies and companies.

Although we had discussed the idea for the book for a long time the final decision to get down to writing was made when the market spoke in very clear terms to us that such a book was indeed needed. Faculty, students and marketing practitioners desire a contemporary textbook suitable for an undergraduate or graduate level course featuring concepts, cases and examples. The knowledge that we poured into this volume has been honed during many years of experience in teaching and practicing marketing. While we concentrate on conceptual foundations and practical applications, we do so without glossing over some of the important theoretical and also formal details that have been established in the marketing discipline. This understanding helps to get to the bottom of things and to grasp the complex nature of the challenges that marketing is able to address.

In making this book we used a four-pronged approach which offers:

- a comprehensive orientation
- a comprehensive theoretic foundation
- an international scope, and
- a practical orientation.

The **comprehensive orientation** of this textbook is evident in the fact that we thoroughly examine all the essential perspectives of marketing, including the marketing strategy, marketing mix, and the specific contexts of marketing (e.g. B-2–B marketing and international marketing). We also provide an elaborate discussion of the issues in marketing implementation. This applies, for example, to the presentation of the aspects of human resources management that are relevant to marketing.

Furthermore, this book provides a **comprehensive theoretic foundation**, which is demonstrated by the theoretical aspects discussed throughout the entire book. Moreover, additional theoretical issues are discussed in the Appendix.

Our book also has an **international scope**, which is particularly illustrated by our inclusion of international market research studies that have been published in important journals of the marketing discipline (for example, *Journal of Marketing* and *Journal of Marketing Research*). In our examples and case study material we also describe companies from various markets and geographical settings including Europe, North America and Asia.

The book also offers a **practical orientation**. Our goal is to impart knowledge that is highly relevant to actual business practice. A strong emphasis on the company-internal facets of marketing is crucial to achieving this practical orientation. By now, it has become sufficiently well known that intelligently designed marketing concepts often fail in practice due to internal company problems.

Above all, our intention was to write a **contemporary textbook** that provides up-to-date and current insights into all relevant topics important for marketing management. We welcome the reader to this new volume. We sincerely hope that reading Marketing Management is as enjoyable as it was writing it.

Christian Homburg
University of Mannheim

Sabine Kuester
University of Mannheim

Harley Krohmer
University of Berne

Guided Tour

Learning Objectives

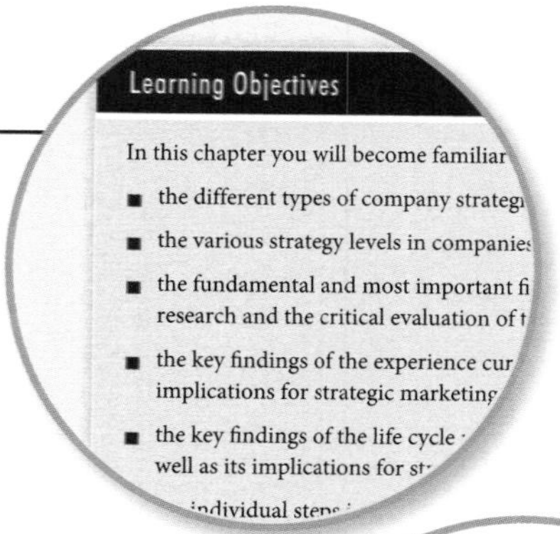
Learning Objectives
In this chapter you will become familiar
the different types of company strateg
the various strategy levels in companie
the fundamental and most important fi
research and the critical evaluation of t
the key findings of the experience cur
implications for strategic marketin
the key findings of the life cycle
well as its implications for st

At the beginning of each chapter you will find a list of learning objectives that highlight the main points you should be familiar with after studying each chapter.

Focus on Marketing

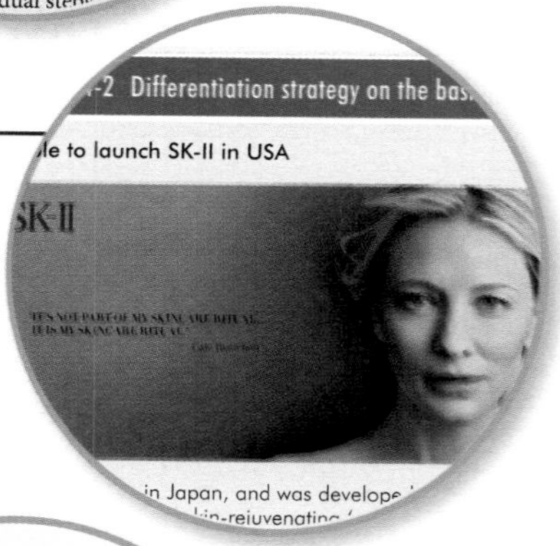
-2 Differentiation strategy on the bas
le to launch SK-II in USA
SK-II
in Japan, and was develope

These boxes provide additional practical examples to highlight the application of concepts, and encourage you to critically analyze real-world issues.

Key Terms

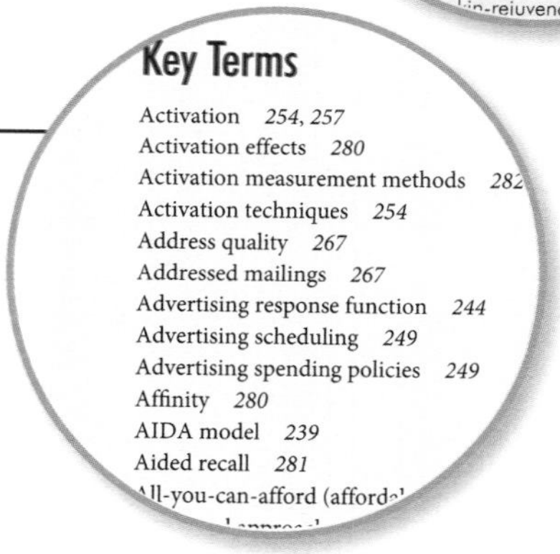

These are highlighted in the text with a summary at the end of each chapter so that they can be found quickly and easily. An ideal tool for last-minute revision or to check definitions as you read.

Figures and Tables

Each chapter provides a number of figures, illustrations and photos to help you to visualize key theories.

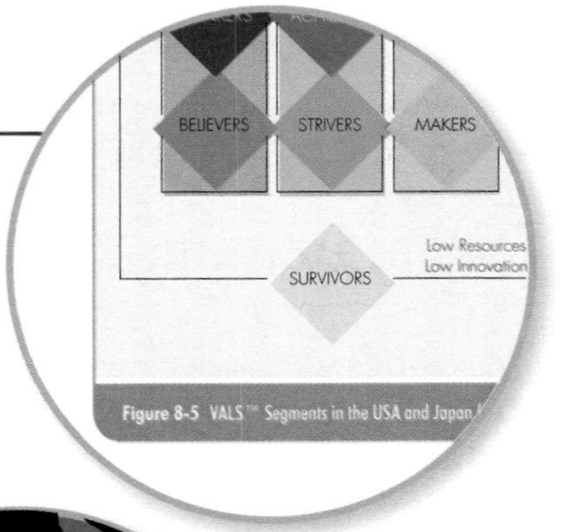

Cases

Each chapter concludes with a case study and a longer case concludes each part. These up-to-date examples encourage you to apply what you have learnt in each chapter to a real life marketing situation. You can test yourself by trying out the discussion questions that follow.

References

Each chapter contains a full list of references so that, if you wish, you can continue to research in greater depth after reading the chapter.

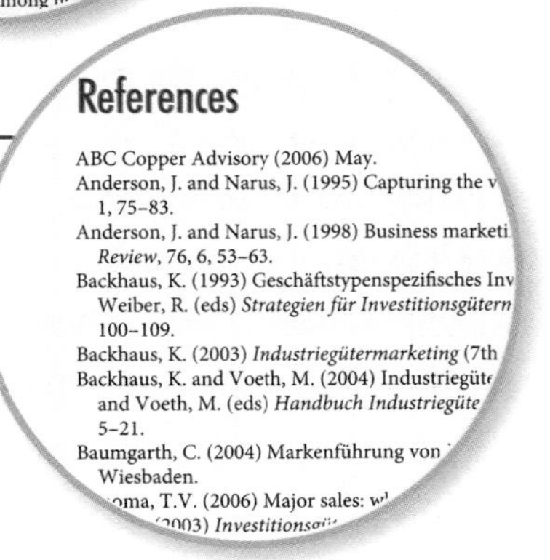

Technology to enhance learning and teaching

Visit www.mcgraw-hill.co.uk/textbooks/homburg today

Online Learning Centre (OLC)

After completing each chapter, log on to the supporting Online Learning Center website. Take advantage of the study tools offered to reinforce the material you have read in the text, and to develop your knowledge of marketing management in a fun and effective way.

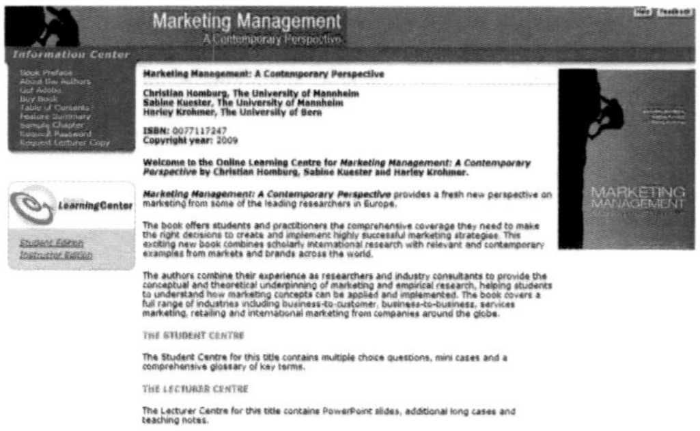

Resources for students include:

- Mini cases & review questions
- Glossary
- Weblinks
- Self-test multiple-choice questions

Also available for lecturers:

- Instructor's Manual
- PowerPoint presentations
- Additional cases
- Guidance on using cases
- Case notes
- Guide answers to questions in the book
- Additional tasks, problems & exercises

Custom Publishing Solutions

Let us help make our **content** your **solution**

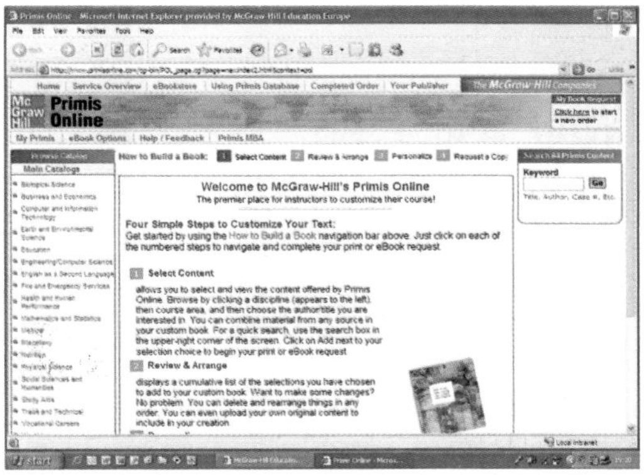

At McGraw-Hill Education our aim is to help lecturers to find the most suitable content for their needs delivered to their students in the most appropriate way. Our custom publishing solutions offer the ideal combination of content delivered in the way that best suits lecturer and students.

Our custom publishing program offers lecturers the opportunity to select just the chapters or sections of material they wish to deliver to their students from a database called Primis at www.primisonline.com.

Primis contains over two million pages of content from:

- textbooks
- professional books
- case books – Harvard Articles, Insead, Ivey, Darden, Thunderbird and BusinessWeek
- Taking Sides – debate materials.

Across the following imprints:

- McGraw-Hill Education
- Open University Press
- Harvard Business School Press
- US and European material.

There is also the option to include additional material authored by lecturers in the custom product – this does not necessarily have to be in English.

We will take care of everything from start to finish in the process of developing and delivering a custom product to ensure that lecturers and students receive exactly the material needed in the most suitable way.

With a Custom Publishing Solution, students enjoy the best selection of material deemed to be the most suitable for learning everything they need for their courses – something of real value to support their learning. Teachers are able to use exactly the material they want, in the way they want, to support their teaching on the course.

Please contact your local McGraw-Hill representative with any questions or alternatively contact Warren Eels email: warren_eels@mcgraw-hill.com.

Visit www.mcgraw-hill.co.uk/textbooks/homburg today

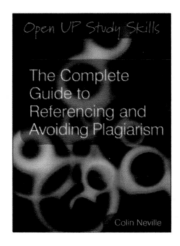

Acknowledgements

Authors' acknowledgements

Many people have contributed to shape the content and structure of this book. It is therefore our great pleasure to thank those who contributed and supported us in the process to write this book, especially Dr. Nikolas Beutin, Torsten Bornemann, Barbara Broermann, Dr. Mathias Droll, Silke Heß, Melanie Krämer, Katja Leschnikowski, Christine Lenz, Klaus Miller, Sophie Nietfeld, Bettina Nyffenegger, Thomas Rilling, Isabel Rist, Monika Schuhmacher, Dr. Mathias Staritz, Viviana Steiner, and Sabine Winkelmann. We thank Barbara Broermann and Silke Esser who supported us in the preparation for the launch of the book.

We would also like to express our gratitude to our team of staff and students who have helped us in typing, editing, and preparing the manuscript. Our very special thanks go to Jan Allmann, David Blatter, Christian Buchmann, Inna Buyun, Pascal Chatelain, Claudia Grigull, Martina Guggisberg, Alexander Hahn, Silvia Hribar, Vitali Kasmil, Sandra Kettler, Maren Kuhlmann, Julius Mantel, Christine Melcher, Sarah Müller, Lisa Neuhaus, Velizara Radeva, David Rings, Stephen Schandelmeier, Kristina Schmidt, Maike Siedentopf, Tereza Toneva, Arnd Vomberg, Angelika Wallis and Tomas Walter.

We also thank Nils Henne for help on the cover design.

Thanks to Jennifer Rotherham, Caroline Prodger and James Bishop at McGraw-Hill for their editorial support.

Christian Homburg, Sabine Kuester and Harley Krohmer

Publishers' acknowledgements

Our thanks go to the following reviewers for their comments at various stages in the text's development:

Fatimah Moran, University of Staffordshire
Charlene Gerber Nel, University of Stellenbosch
Magrit Nostor, Aarhus Business School
Henry Robben, Nyenrode
Antti Vassinen, Helsinki University
Mette Praest Knudsen, University of Southern Denmark
Hans Stubbe Solgaard, Copenhagen Business School
Tim Williams, Sheffield Hallam University
Johanathan Vickers, University of Northampton
Jan Møller Jensen, Roskilde University
Michael Flynn, University of Gloucestershire
Anna Lund Jespen, University of Southern Denmark
Neeru Malhotra, University of Aston
Sven Weel Jensen, Vitus Bering
Stefan Roth, University of Kaiserslautern
Daniel Baier, University of Cottbus
Hartmut Holzmüller, TU Dortmund
Ove Jensen, Otto Beisheim School of Management
Bernd Helmig, University of Fribourg
Marcus Schoegel, University of St. Gallen

About the Authors

Christian Homburg is the President of the Mannheim Business School and professor of marketing at the University of Mannheim in Germany. He also serves as co-chair of the marketing department and as the director of the Institute for Market-Oriented Management (IMU). His research interests include market-oriented management, customer relationship management and sales management. Christian Homburg is founder and chair of the advisory board of the management consultancy Professor Homburg & Partner.

Sabine Kuester is professor of marketing and the co-chair of the marketing department at the University of Mannheim in Germany. Her research includes competitive marketing strategy, innovation management, international marketing and marketing management. She also serves as Director of the Institute for Market-Oriented Management (IMU) at the University of Mannheim.

Harley Krohmer is the director of the Institute of Marketing and Management and chairperson of the marketing department at the University of Berne in Switzerland. His research interests include marketing strategy, market-oriented management, brand management, marketing and sales organization, sales management and international marketing.

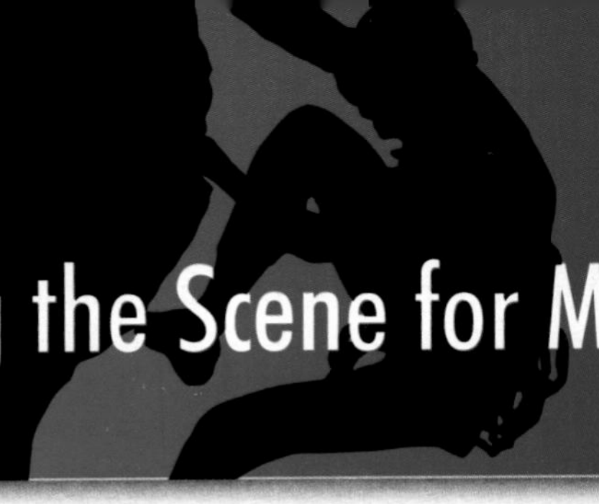

CHAPTER 1

Setting the Scene for Marketing

Contents

Learning Objectives

In this chapter you will become familiar with:

- the characteristics of markets, different types of markets, and how markets can be differentiated from one another
- the historic development and various facets of marketing
- the various perspectives of marketing
- the general structure and orientation of this book.

Today's markets have become increasingly difficult environments for most companies. Challenges arise from changes in technology such as the convergence of information and communication technology, and from intensifying globalization. In particular, developments on the technological front and the rise of the internet have changed the customer and competitor landscape. Customers today are much better able to search for and obtain information that helps them to make intelligent buying decisions. Industry boundaries have become increasingly indeterminate as companies from different industries merge or partner, or as firms combine the knowhow of multiple industries. In this ever changing environment companies have to be smart and able to address customer needs in a way that leads them to purchase their products and – more importantly – that satisfies customers' genuine needs so that satisfaction and loyalty are the result. This is where marketing plays a crucial and vital role. Marketing helps firms to understand markets and to craft offerings that contribute to their performance. In this sense marketing is not seen as an isolated function of business but it is *the* function of business (see Haeckel 1997 and Focus on Marketing 1-1 on the changing role of marketing in this context).

But marketing is not an easy task, and good marketing is carefully planned, devised and executed. A critical question, then, is how marketing should be designed in order to provide greatest value to companies, customers and other important stakeholders (such as channel partners and suppliers).

This book will help you to obtain an understanding of the challenges that marketing has to master and how marketing management can contribute to creating superior customer value.

Focus on Marketing 1-1 On the role of marketing in a changed world

The future of marketing: from monologue to dialog
Until a few years ago, marketing was a monolog. Marketers invested time, talent and money to broadcast messages designed to correspond with each stage of a theoretical buying cycle: awareness, research, consideration, testing, negotiation and transaction. The past two years have witnessed the first examples of true two-way marketing 'conversations' between customers and some of the world's leading consumer brands. Driven by a confluence of innovation, competition and big shifts in consumer behavior, the dialog between brands and their customers is replacing the traditional marketing monolog.

1.1 Markets as Focal Points of Marketing

The term 'marketing' is derived from 'market' and 'to market', which highlight the great significance that markets have for marketing. Two facts make this especially evident:

1 markets define the framework for marketing practiced by companies – the customers, competitors and other stakeholders present in a market shape the scope of marketing activities to a major extent

2 the significance of markets is demonstrated by the fact that within the course of their marketing activities, companies strive to actively exert a controlled influence on the behavior of both customers – or potential customers – and competitors to the benefit of the company and its stakeholders.

We **define a market** as any place where supply meets demand, thus leading to the formation of prices. Supply and demand can meet at a physical location (e.g. in a store or at a trade fair) or at a virtual location (e.g. on the internet or by telephone).

The following stakeholders have an important influence on market activities:

- buyers
- companies
- sales partners
- public institutions
- lobbyists.

Buyers function as customers in the market. From the standpoint of a company, buyers are considered **customers** if they buy the company's products or have previously bought a product from the company at least once. Buyers and customers make purchases to satisfy needs. A **need** is a subjectively perceived deficiency or lack that the buyer wants to remedy (see also 'customer needs' in the Appendix). Examples include basic human needs such as food, clothing and educational requirements. Within the context of a broader understanding of the concept, the term 'need' can extend to deficiencies that the buyer has not (yet) perceived, often referred to as latent needs.

Not to be confused with a need is **demand**, which results from a need. Demands are objectively quantifiable and are addressed by a customer buying the corresponding product. Demand is thus associated with the willingness to pay to fulfill a need. Buyers tend to cover their demand with those products or services that can best satisfy their needs and thus offer the greatest benefits (customer benefits).

An important differentiation with regard to marketing is the distinction of buyers into end customers (i.e. individuals) and organizational customers (e.g. business-to-business and corporate customers) or public institutions. Marketing that is oriented towards individual end customers is often referred to as **consumer goods marketing**. Typical products exchanged in consumer goods markets are entertainment products such as MP3 players or DVDs, food and beverages, holiday packages, clothing and cars. Marketing directed at organizational customers is called **business-to-business marketing** (B2B marketing) (for more on this distinction, see Chapter 10). Products that are being exchanged in business-to-business markets include fleet cars, office supplies, raw materials, production facilities and energy. Public institutions can be governmental agencies or non-profit organizations such as charities or academic institutions.

Companies compete in the market with their products (physical products and services) to win the favor of the buyers. A company therefore has to identify and monitor other companies already active in the relevant market (current competitors) as well as possible future companies (potential competitors). Companies strive to sell their products as successfully as possible, in order to secure the profitability and sustainability of the company in the long term (for a detailed discussion of the various company objectives, please see Chapter 2). To realize this objective, companies deploy different marketing strategies and marketing instruments.

When selling their products to buyers, companies often cooperate with **sales partners**, e.g. intermediaries or brokers (see Chapter 7). Sales partners play an important role in the market environment and particularly in the success of a company. Accordingly, crucial to the success of a company is the challenge of selecting suitable sales partners and cooperating with them in long-term business relationships.

As stakeholders, public institutions (in addition to their potential role as buyers or suppliers of products) also exert a regulatory influence on the market environment. For instance, the government issues and enacts legal regulations and enforces compliance with them. Examples of this include legal requirements regarding the design and content of advertising and promotional activities. Along with general regulations, industry-specific regulations also have to be mentioned here. For example, marketing by pharmaceutical companies is usually very strictly regulated (e.g. with respect to reimbursement for pharmaceutical products).

Besides the various stakeholders, the different **types of markets** are also of interest. Markets can, for example, be classified according to the following criteria.

- *Classification by types of goods sold* – we distinguish markets for consumer goods, business-to-business goods as well as services: consumer goods are primarily intended to satisfy the needs of private end customers. Industrial and business-to-business goods are sold to organizations (e.g. companies, associations, public administrative offices) (for more about the marketing of business-to-business goods, see Chapter 10). Services refer to economic exchange activities that create essentially non-physical output (see Section 11.1 for a definition and Chapter 11 for a general discussion of services marketing).
- *Classification by degree of internationality* – we distinguish local markets, regional markets, international markets and global markets. The specific characteristics of international marketing are discussed in Chapter 12.
- *Classification by distribution of power* between buyers and companies – here we distinguish buyers' markets and sellers' markets: in contrast to sellers' markets, buyers' markets are characterized by a dominance of the demand side over the supply side. This constellation can result from an oversupply or lack of demand and will force the companies to become more customer-oriented. Today, most markets in industrialized and developed economies tend to exhibit features of buyers' markets.

From a company perspective, it is important to define at which markets (and thus at which customers and competitors) the marketing strategy and activities should be aimed. This is called the **market definition**. Market definition describes the structuring of a market, and defines the relevant market area.

Various criteria can be taken on board when defining the relevant market, including the following:

- *companies* – definition of the market based on groups of companies, for example, firms in a certain industry or economic sector (e.g. the 'chemicals market' as a market served by chemicals companies)
- *products* – definition of the market based on certain products or product lines (e.g. 'market for long-distance travel')
- *buyers* – definition of the market based on certain buyers or groups of buyers (e.g. 'market for price-sensitive students')
- *needs* – definition of the market based on certain needs or need categories on the part of the buyers (e.g. 'market for leisure time recreation and entertainment').

In business practice, several of these categories are often combined when defining the market. This book embraces the view that markets should, first and foremost, be defined based on buyers and their needs. A market definition that centers exclusively on products can be

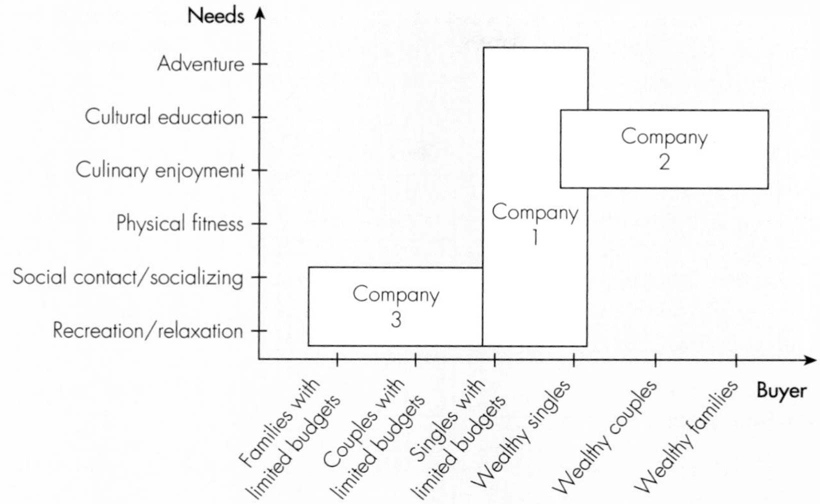

Figure 1-1 Market definition using the example of three companies in the tourism sector

problematic if the products fulfill needs that can also be met by other types of products. If, for example, a financial services provider speaks of a 'market for life insurance' as well as a 'market for equity funds', it is obvious that a problem can arise, since in part, both products aim at meeting the same customer need (retirement savings and pension funds). Another problem associated with a solely product-oriented market definition is that it can lead to a market perspective that is too narrow in scope. A well-known example of this is the company failures of American railroad companies (see Levitt 1960). The railroad companies had based their market definition on the 'market for railroad services' (product-based definition) and not on the underlying customer need (mobility). The consequence of this myopic product-oriented market definition was that new competitors such as bus companies and airlines, which in some cases could better meet the same need for mobility, were totally ignored (see also Section 2.1 for the issue of 'myopia' (Levitt 1960) in defining the business mission). Figure 1-1 shows an example of market definitions based on needs and buyers.

1.2 Development and Scope of the Marketing Concept

After discussing the market in Section 1.1 as the focal point for describing marketing, we will examine the concept of marketing in this section. First, however, we will take a look at the historical development of the concept.

Marketing activities such as the development of new products or pricing decisions have certainly been playing a role in market transactions for several centuries (see Dixon 1981). However, since the systematic investigation of marketing on the basis of scientific considerations did not start until the beginning of the twentieth century, we will be limiting our discussion to this time span (for an in-depth examination of the historical development of marketing, see Bartels 1951; Fullerton 1988; Jones and Monieson 1990; Mason 1995; Webster 1992; Zinkhan and Pereira 1994).

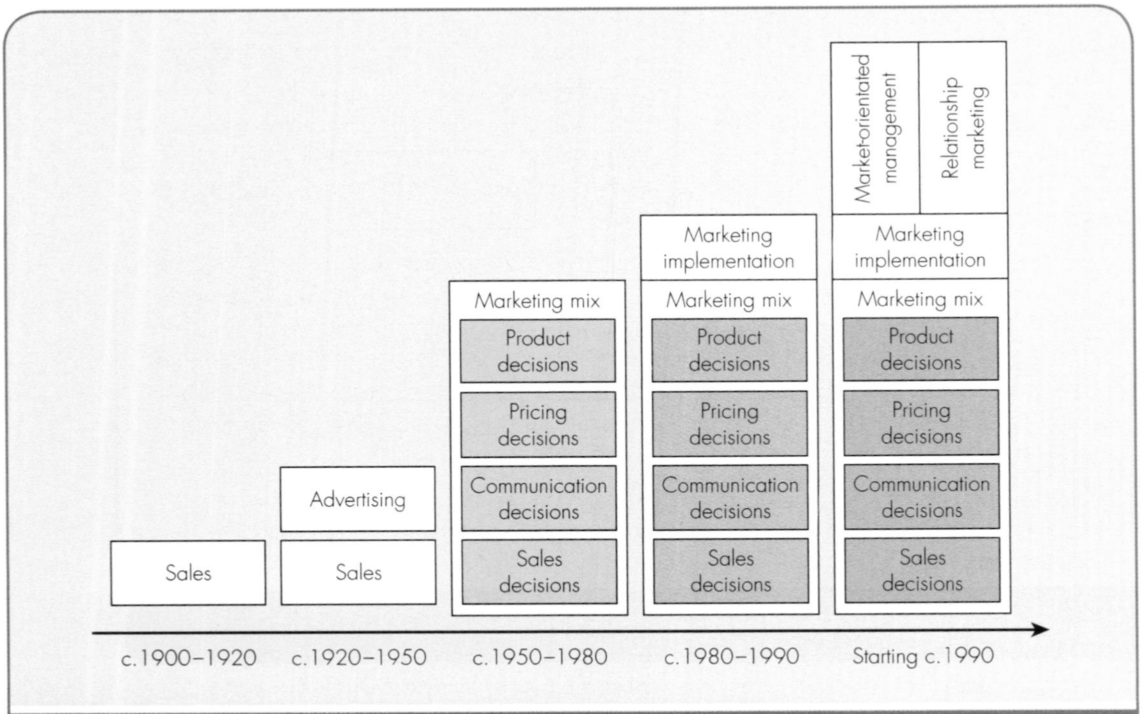

Figure 1-2 Historical development of the marketing concept

In general, the definition of marketing has become significantly broader over the course of time (see Figure 1-2). The early phase of marketing's development was characterized by the idea that it was very much associated with sales. The primary focus here was the task of selling the company's products in the market. At the beginning of the twentieth century, this concept of marketing was communicated in marketing courses at universities (for an overview, see Bartels 1951) and in the first marketing publications (see Nystrom 1915; Shaw 1912; Weld 1916). This limited conceptual approach was particularly due to the fact that at that time most markets tended to be sellers' markets (see Section 1.1). In many companies, the marketing function was thus considered less important than other functions within the company (e.g. production).

In the period that followed, the sales concept of marketing was expanded to include the aspect of advertising. Starting in the 1920s, the principles of marketing were defined in textbooks and monographs in the USA, with a strong focus placed on **sales and advertising** (see Hotchkiss 1940; Maynard *et al.* 1927; Vaile and Slagsvold 1929). In the 1930s and 1940s, the concept of marketing was developed further to only a limited degree as a result of the worldwide economic crisis and the Second World War.

The renewed growth of the world economy in the 1950s and 1960s provided a new impulse for the development of the marketing concept. During that time, the so-called **marketing mix** was defined (see McCarthy 1964; McKitterick 1957), which integrated the existing concept of marketing as advertising and sales into a broader system of classifying marketing activities – today commonly referred to as the 'four Ps':

1 product decisions (**P**roduct)
2 pricing decisions (**P**rice)
3 communication decisions (**P**romotion), and
4 distribution decisions (**P**lace).

This expanded concept of marketing still remains relevant today (see van Waterschoot and van den Bulte 1992).

In recent years the discipline has witnessed a shift to issues addressing **marketing implementation** (e.g. company-internal organizational issues, performance/success benchmarking and monitoring). The growing attention paid to these implementation issues called for a more multi-disciplinary viewpoint combining marketing with other business disciplines such as organizational behavior or finance (for an overview, see Workman *et al.* 1998).

This implementation perspective focuses predominantly on those departments or units of the company that are involved in marketing tasks. Contrasting with this, a new approach addresses the question of to what extent a company should be managed as a market-oriented organization. The concept of marketing as **market-oriented management** had already been articulated and discussed in the 1980s. However, a more intensive analysis of this topic was not conducted until the 1990s (see Becker and Homburg 1999; Homburg and Pflesser 2000; Jaworski and Kohli 1993). Aspects related to market-oriented management will be discussed in Part 4 of this book.

Parallel to the emphasis on market-oriented management, customer relationships increasingly gained more importance and attention from both marketing practice and theory. The basis of this perspective is the awareness that the establishment and sustainability of (profitable) long-term customer relationships pose a central challenge to marketing. The term **relationship marketing** is also used in this context (for further discussion of the development of relationship marketing, see Berry 1983; Grönroos 1990, 1995). The main implication of this approach (both in terms of research and company practice) is that the frequently observed focus on individual transactions with customers is replaced by a focus on long-term business relationships.

Against the background of the development just described, various approaches to defining marketing have emerged (for an overview, see Cooke *et al.* 1992). There are basically three approaches here.

1 *Activity-oriented definitions* characterize marketing as a bundle of market-driven activities practiced by companies focusing on the creation and delivery of value to customers, and the management of customer relationships. Activity-oriented definitions of marketing are thus closely connected to the concept of the marketing mix.

2 In contrast, *relationship-oriented definitions* are rooted in the logic of relationship marketing. Here the objective of marketing is to establish, maintain and strengthen relationships with customers. For example, Grönroos (1990, p. 5) defines marketing as follows: 'Marketing is to establish, maintain, enhance and commercialize customer relationships (often but not necessarily always long term relationships) so that the objectives of the parties involved are met. This is done by a mutual exchange and fulfillment of promises.' One objection to be mentioned here is that the formation of long-term customer relationships is not necessarily a marketing objective for every company. It is certainly possible for a company to concentrate on realizing isolated transactions with occasional customers without ever investing in long-term relationships.

3 A third approach is established by *management-oriented definitions* of marketing, which focus on managing the company from a market perspective. They particularly concern the degree to which the company's decisions are guided by market-oriented considerations (see also Part 4). From our viewpoint, the main contribution of this approach is that it introduces the issue of the company's internal situational factors for market-related activities. This creates the basis for incorporating aspects of market implementation and market-oriented management within the scope of marketing.

Along these lines, it should be noted that these three approaches to defining marketing are complementary: each definition covers an important aspect of marketing. In view of this background, we formulate the following **integrative definition of marketing**: 'Marketing has a company-external and company-internal facet.'

- With regard to the company-external aspects, marketing comprises the conception and implementation of the market-related activities that are practiced by a company and geared towards buyers or potential buyers of its products (physical products and/or services). Such market-related activities include the systematic acquisition of information about market conditions as well as the design of the product portfolio, pricing, communication and sales.
- In terms of the company-internal aspects, marketing refers to creating the necessary prerequisites and conditions within the company in order to facilitate the effective and efficient implementation of the market-related activities. In particular, this includes the management of the entire company in line with the concept of market orientation.
- Both the external and internal approaches to marketing aim at designing and structuring customer relationships so that company objectives can be achieved.

We would like to point out that this definition integrates both the external (market-oriented) activities of a company as well as the creation of the internal conditions necessary to achieve market success. With respect to internal conditions, in addition to company-wide market-oriented management, this also includes, for example, the design and structure of the marketing organization and marketing control (see Part 4 of this book for a perspective on implementation). Moreover, it is important to emphasize that we are not implying that the establishment of long-term customer relationships inevitably has to be the key marketing objective. Instead, we are stressing the need to design and structure customer relationships in order to best support the achievement of company objectives such as improving profitability, increasing market share, and the long-term sustainability of the company's competitive advantage. In practice, this objective can be pursued when companies focus on long-term relationships with high-potential customers. However, there are also conceivable situations, for example, in which investments in long-term customer relationships do not prove economically viable (for a related discussion, see Chapter 9).

1.3 How this Book is Structured

The book is structured in four parts (see Figure 1-3):

- Part 1 discusses the strategic perspective of the company (Chapters 2, 3 and 4)
- Part 2 pertains to the marketing mix instruments (Chapters 5, 6, 7, 8 and 9)
- Part 3 focuses on marketing in specific contexts (Chapters 10, 11 and 12)
- Part 4 investigates aspects of marketing implementation (Chapters 13, 14, 15 and 16) and concludes with a discussion of issues of market-oriented management (Chapter 17).

In Part 1 we will discuss the basic and long-term alignment of the company's market development – the **strategic perspective** of the company. Strategic decisions are usually crucial for the success of a company. Their revision requires major effort and is associated with high risk. The formulation of marketing strategies must also be based on a systematic and thorough analysis of the company environment.

In this part, we will first describe the basic concepts with regard to understanding the marketing strategy, and the impact that these concepts have on success (see Chapter 2). This will be followed by a discussion of the key aspects, tools and models related to the analysis of the initial strategic situation (see Chapter 3). This strategic analysis represents the first step in the strategic planning process, with the analysis particularly focusing on the global company environment, the market (customers and competitors) as well as the company itself. Finally, the formulation, evaluation and selection of alternative strategies will be dealt with as further steps in the strategic planning process (see Chapter 4).

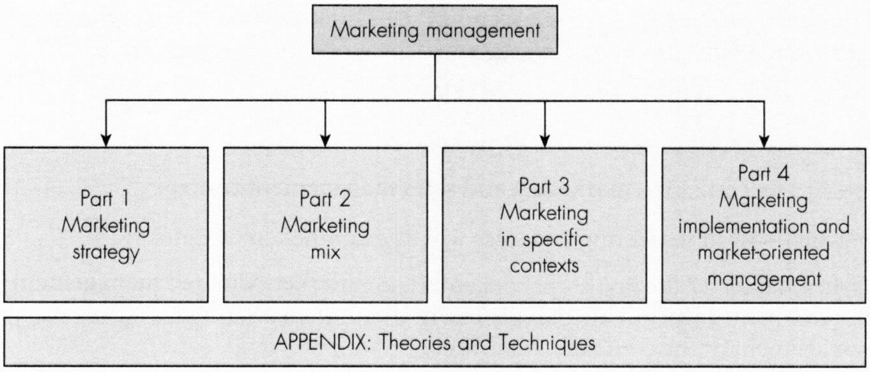

Figure 1-3 Structure of the book

The marketing strategy is implemented by systematically deploying the marketing instruments, which are described in the context of the **marketing mix** in Part 2 of the book. In designing the marketing mix, the marketing strategy is translated into concrete activities.

The marketing mix comprises the following four components.

1 *Product decisions* (see Chapter 5): concerned with all decisions related to the current and future product range. Here we will discuss decisions regarding product innovations as well as products that are already established in the market, including branding.

2 *Pricing decisions* (see Chapter 6) deal with all decisions concerning the price that customers have to pay for a product. To facilitate the understanding of the relevant decisions we will discuss classic pricing theory as well as behavioral pricing.

3 *Sales decisions* (see Chapter 7) cover decisions about acquisition activities aimed at the marketplace and decisions related to distribution logistics. Acquisition activities are geared towards acquiring new customers and generating sales. Distribution logistics focus on the structure and design of the physical distribution of goods.

4 *Communication decisions* (see Chapter 8) concern all decisions regarding the company's communication in the market. The company can use various tools to communicate including, for example, media advertising or online marketing.

In the chapter on the role of **customer relationship management** in the marketing mix (see Chapter 9) the focus is on the two most relevant issues in customer relationship management: customer satisfaction and customer loyalty. We propose a range of tools for customer relationship management within the individual marketing instruments discussed in Part 2 that can help to establish customer satisfaction and loyalty.

Part 3 of the book will deal with marketing in specific contexts. These contexts are determined by the activities of a company in a specific economic sector or by the internationality of the marketing activities. We will differentiate between three contexts, describing the special requirements each has in terms of marketing:

1 Chapter 10 will explain **business-to-business marketing**

2 in Chapter 11, **services marketing** will be addressed first; we will also elaborate on the specific characteristics of retail marketing

3 finally, Chapter 12 will present a discussion of **international marketing**.

In contrast to the previous chapters, Part 4 of the book deals with the company-internal conditions, i.e. the second facet of our marketing definition (see Section 1.2). This **implementation-related perspective** primarily addresses those company departments that support marketing tasks:

- Chapter 13 will address aspects of the **marketing and sales organization**
- **information systems** in marketing and sales will be discussed in Chapter 14
- subsequently, Chapter 15 will attend to **marketing and sales management control**
- **human resource management** in marketing and sales will be examined in Chapter 16.

Following on from this, in Chapter 17 the book will concentrate on **market-oriented management**, focusing not only on the company departments that primarily attend to marketing tasks, but also on the market-oriented management of the company as a whole.

The book concludes with an Appendix that includes information on theories and techniques. This Appendix serves as an additional source of information on theories and marketing research techniques that are not covered in greater depth in the book itself.

Key Terms

References

Bartels, R. (1951) Influences on the development of marketing thought, 1900–1923, *Journal of Marketing*, 16, 1, 1–17.
Becker, J. and Homburg, C. (1999) Market-oriented management: a systems-based perspective, *Journal of Market Focused Management*, 4, 1, 17–41.
Berry, L. (1983) Relationship marketing, in: Berry, L., Shostack, G. and Upah, G. (eds) *Emerging Perspectives of Service Marketing*. Chicago, 25–28.
Cooke, E., Rayburn, J. and Abercrombie, C. (1992) The history of marketing thought as reflected in the definitions of marketing, *Journal of Marketing Theory and Practice*, 1, 1, 10–21.
Dixon, D. (1981) The role of marketing in early theories of economic development, *Journal of Macromarketing*, 1, 2, 19–27.
Fullerton, R. (1988) How modern is modern marketing? Marketing's evolution and the myth of the 'production era', *Journal of Marketing*, 52, 1, 108–125.
Grönroos, C. (1990) Relationship approach to the marketing function in service contexts: the marketing and organizational behavior interface, *Journal of Business Research*, 20, 1, 3–12.
Grönroos, C. (1995) Relationship marketing: strategic and tactical implications, *Management Decision*, 34, 3, 5–14.
Haeckel, S. (1997) Preface, in: Lehmann, D. and Jocz, K. (eds) *Reflections on the Futures of Marketing*. Cambridge, ix–xvi.
Homburg, C. and Pflesser, C. (2000) A multiple-layer model of market-oriented organizational culture: measurement issues and performance outcomes, *Journal of Marketing Research*, 37, 4, 449–462.
Hotchkiss, G. (1940) *An Outline of Advertising: Its Philosophy, Science, Art, and Strategy*. New York.
Jaworski, B. and Kohli, A. (1993) Market orientation: antecedents and consequences, *Journal of Marketing*, 57, 3, 53–70.
Jones, D. and Monieson, D. (1990) Early development of the philosophy of marketing thought, *Journal of Marketing*, 54, 1, 102–113.
Levitt, T. (1960) Marketing myopia, *Harvard Business Review*, 38, 45–56.
Mason, R. (1995) Interpersonal effects on consumer demand in economic theory and marketing thought, 1890–1950, *Journal of Economic Issues*, 29, 3, 871–881.
Maynard, H., Weidler, W. and Beckman, T. (1927) *The Principles of Marketing*. New York.
McCarthy, J. (1964) *Basic Marketing: A Managerial Approach*. Homewood.

McKitterick, J. (1957) What is marketing management?, in: Bass, F. (ed.) *The Frontiers of Marketing Thought and Science*, Proceedings of the December 1957 Teachers Conference of the AMA in Philadelphia, Chicago, 71–82.

Nystrom, P. (1915) *The Economics of Retailing*. New York.

Shaw, A. (1912) Some problems in market distribution, *Quarterly Journal of Economics*, 26, 3, 706–765.

Vaile, R. and Slagsvold, L. (1929) *Marketing*. New York.

van Waterschoot, W. and van den Bulte, C. (1992) The 4P classification of the marketing mix revisited, *Journal of Marketing*, 56, 4, 83–93.

Webster, F. (1992) The changing role of marketing in the corporation, *Journal of Marketing*, 56, 4, 1–17.

Weld, L. (1916) *The Fundamentals of Marketing*. New York.

Workman, J., Homburg, C. and Gruner, K. (1998) Variations in the organization and role of marketing: findings from an international field study of manufacturing companies, *Journal of Marketing*, 62, 3, 21–41.

Zinkhan, G. and Pereira, A. (1994) An overview of marketing strategy and planning, *International Journal of Research in Marketing*, 11, 3, 185–218.

PART 1

Laying the Groundwork: Shaping Marketing Strategies

Contents

CHAPTER 2

The Key Aspects of Marketing Strategy

Contents

Learning Objectives

In this chapter you will become familiar with:

- the different types of company strategies and marketing objectives
- the various strategy levels in companies and how they relate to each other
- the fundamental and most important findings of PIMS (Profit Impact of Market Strategies) research and the critical evaluation of the PIMS Project
- the key findings of the experience curve model and the critical evaluation of the implications for strategic marketing
- the key findings of the life cycle model, the critical evaluation of the life cycle model, as well as its implications for strategic marketing
- the individual steps involved in the process of developing marketing strategies.

A principal element of the marketing management process is the strategic setting in which it takes place. Companies need a broader road map that defines their conduct over a longer period of time. This planning process is described by the strategic aspects of marketing. To fully appreciate these strategic aspects it is essential to understand the concept of marketing strategy. Therefore, we will first address the basic idea of the marketing strategy concept. In addition to the definition of the concept, a particular focus in Section 2.1 will be the importance of marketing strategy and how it is integrated into the company. Section 2.2 will then discuss the fundamentals of strategic success factor research, where we will present three 'classic' approaches to researching the success factors of marketing strategies. Finally, in Section 2.3, we will describe the strategic marketing planning process.

2.1 An Initial Overview of the Marketing Strategy Concept

This chapter introduces the concept of marketing strategy. We will start this introduction by describing the different **objectives** organizations may pursue. As Figure 2-1 illustrates, these objectives can be described on different levels of the company. Many companies establish a **business mission** that consists of the long-term objectives related to the nature and purpose of the company. The business mission therefore provides a framework for all company activities and also aligns the various objectives at lower levels of the pyramid shown in Figure 2-1.

The business mission of an internet-based financial services company may be phrased as follows: 'Our vision is to be the world's most innovative information service provider'. The business mission for a management school may be 'Our school's mission is to provide quality lifelong learning for future leaders in business'. Business missions should pave the way for the long-term development of a company but should never constrain it. This 'marketing myopia' can be avoided when companies define their businesses along the lines of customer needs (and not products) as has long been advocated by Levitt (1960) (see also Section 1.1).

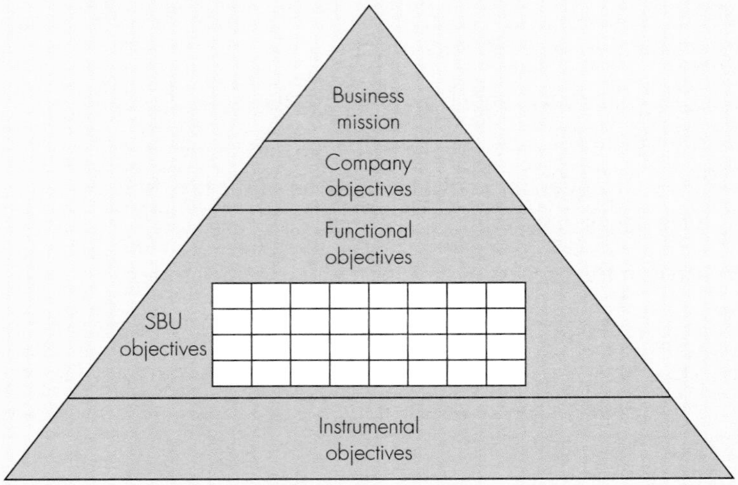

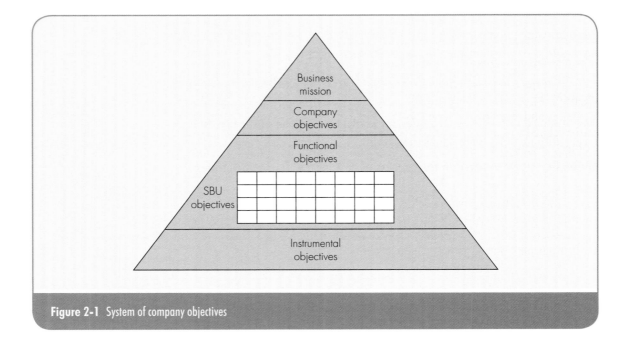

Figure 2-1 System of company objectives

On the second level, we distinguish the overall **company objectives**, where we differentiate between financial and non-financial goals. Financial objectives include, for example, realizing a sufficient return on investment (ROI), achieving suitable dividends and increasing shareholder value. Non-financial objectives, for example, can refer to attaining a high degree of customer satisfaction, developing an image as an attractive employer, and creating or maintaining the company's innovativeness. (For detailed information concerning customer needs and customer satisfaction, please refer to the Appendix.)

The next level comprises the functional objectives and the **strategic business unit (SBU) objectives**. Frequently, companies are divided into SBUs when they serve multiple markets. Each SBU has its own profit/loss responsibility, for which, in turn, objectives have to be set. A strategic business unit is an organizational unit within a company that has its own business and market mission along with a certain strategic decision-making autonomy. SBUs that have profit responsibility, often called 'profit centers', represent a sort of 'company within a company'. The goals of a profit center correspond with the company objectives to a large extent.

Realizing the company objectives demands the achievement of a large number of **functional objectives**. Consequently, the company objectives can be accomplished only with contributions from the various functional areas within the company, such as marketing, human resources, management, finance, production, and research and development. In the production area, the objective could be, say, to increase product quality. For the finance department, the intention could be to reduce capital costs.

The relationships between the functional objectives and the goals of the SBUs are presented in the form of a matrix like that shown in Figure 2-1. The strategic autonomy of an SBU implies that it is independently in charge of at least some functional areas (see Homburg *et al.* 1999). For example, the SBUs of a company can have their own marketing departments or research and development departments. If the SBUs autonomously undertake practically all functions, the SBU objectives are superordinate to the functional objectives. In this case, each SBU has its own functional objectives. Often, however, it can be observed that some functions (including marketing) are centralized in companies to a certain extent, and thus geared towards cross-SBU objectives and activities.

For the marketing area, we distinguish between the three categories of objectives:

1. marketing objectives related to potential
2. marketing objectives related to market success
3. financial marketing objectives.

We can assume that the fulfillment of these different categories of objectives is linked by a causal chain (see Figure 2-2). **Marketing objectives related to potential** are those objectives that refer to the prerequisites and important drivers for market success. For example, a high market share (objective related to market success) based on a high degree of customer satisfaction (marketing objective related to potential) can arise from the repeated buying behavior of satisfied customers.

Marketing objectives related to market success refer to the essential factors that impact the success of a company or of SBUs on the basis of actual customer behavior. The focus on actual behavior distinguishes this category of objectives from the marketing objectives related to potential, the former being more concerned with the realization of the potential. Common goals in company practice are, for example, increases in market share or sales.

Financial marketing objectives describe the targeted performance of a business along conventional economic success factors, such as turnover, profit and return on sales (see Figure 2-2). The fulfillment of such financial marketing objectives is significantly (but of course not exclusively) influenced by achieving the objectives related to market success (for more on this see for example the explanation

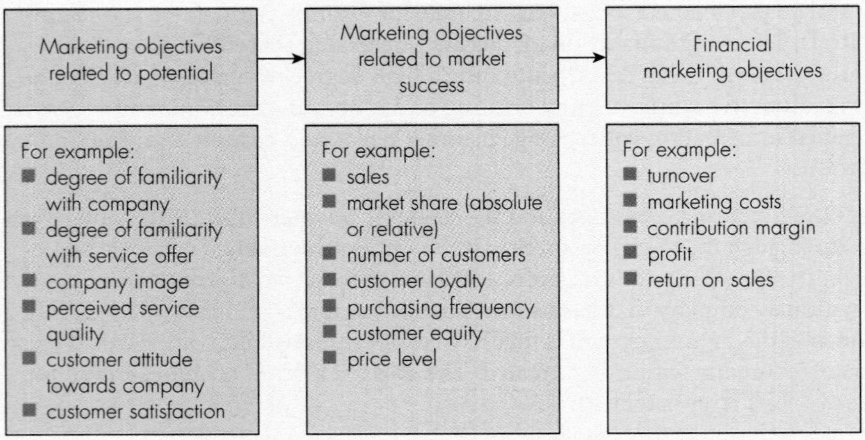

Figure 2-2 Systematization of the marketing objectives of a company

on the positive relationship between market share and profitability in Section 2.2.1, and on the link between market success and economic success in Homburg *et al.* 2008, and Homburg and Pflesser 2000).

Frequently, an overall analysis of the marketing objectives is less helpful than a breakdown of these objectives by specific customer or product groups. With regard to financial marketing objectives, it is interesting, for instance, to know what contribution margin a certain product generates (see also Section 5.3.3). Equally, such a disaggregated view of the other categories of objectives is often beneficial. Objectives associated with customer satisfaction or loyalty in a segment comprising strategically significant customers can be more relevant than those pertaining to a less important customer segment.

Finally, **instrumental objectives** (the lowest level in Figure 2-1) are derived from the functional objectives, and are the most tangible and specific company goals. Functional objectives from a marketing standpoint are mostly concerned with the individual components of the marketing mix – that is, objectives related to the:

- product decisions (see Chapter 5)
- pricing decisions (see Chapter 6)
- sales and distribution decisions (see Chapter 7)
- communication decisions (see Chapter 8)
- decisions regarding customer relationship management (see Chapter 9).

The way functional objectives impact instrumental objectives can be illustrated by the following example. A company can set the marketing objective to improve customer satisfaction. This objective, in turn, affects the instrumental objectives of the marketing mix. With respect to product decisions, the company could strive for high-quality products with excellent design and functionality. Communication decisions could then aim to establish an image of superior quality and excellence in design. Sales decisions could target the development of a selective sales and distribution network with qualified intermediaries that could help to provide the necessary consulting services for customers.

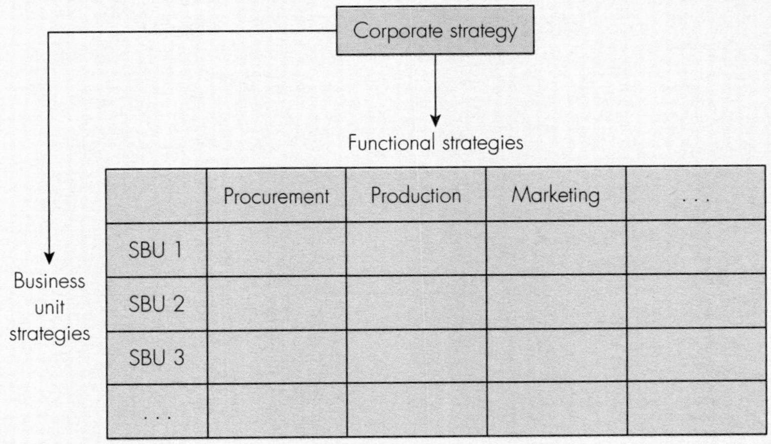

Figure 2-3 Differentiation of strategies according to level in the organization

When formulating strategies, it is important to consider at which level in the corporation the strategy is aimed. Here we distinguish corporate strategy, business unit strategy and functional strategy (refer to Figure 2-3 and, with regard to how these strategies are interconnected, see Morgan *et al.* 2000; Sharma 1999; Varadarajan and Clark 1994; Varadarajan *et al.* 2001).

The **corporate strategy** defines the basic orientation of the company and involves a long-term planning horizon (e.g. for the next five years). Key aspects of the company strategy include:

- to determine the strategic alignment of the overall company, taking into account the purpose of the company
- to establish the central financial and non-financial company objectives
- to define the relevant markets and the strategic business units
- to distribute the resources across the strategic business units
- to define the scope of action for strategic measures in the respective business units and functional areas
- to develop and explore the strategically relevant resources and capabilities of the company.

The **business unit strategy** defines the competitive measures to be applied in a specific market or business sector. For example, a company operating in the energy sector and in the financial services sector will need to establish different business unit strategies for these distinct markets. For companies that are not divided into SBUs, the differentiation between the corporate and business unit strategy is not relevant. Similarly, **functional strategies**, which define the strategic alignment of certain functions in the company, are derived from both the corporate strategy and, if applicable, the business unit strategies (see Figure 2-3).

The question then arises as to how the marketing strategy is positioned within this strategy framework. In this context, there are three divergent approaches (see Figure 2-4). In the first – more traditional – approach, the **marketing strategy** is interpreted as one of several functional strategies. It is thus seen as on a par with the other functional strategies. In this case, the corporate strategy represents the framework for formulating the marketing strategy. Consequently, the marketing

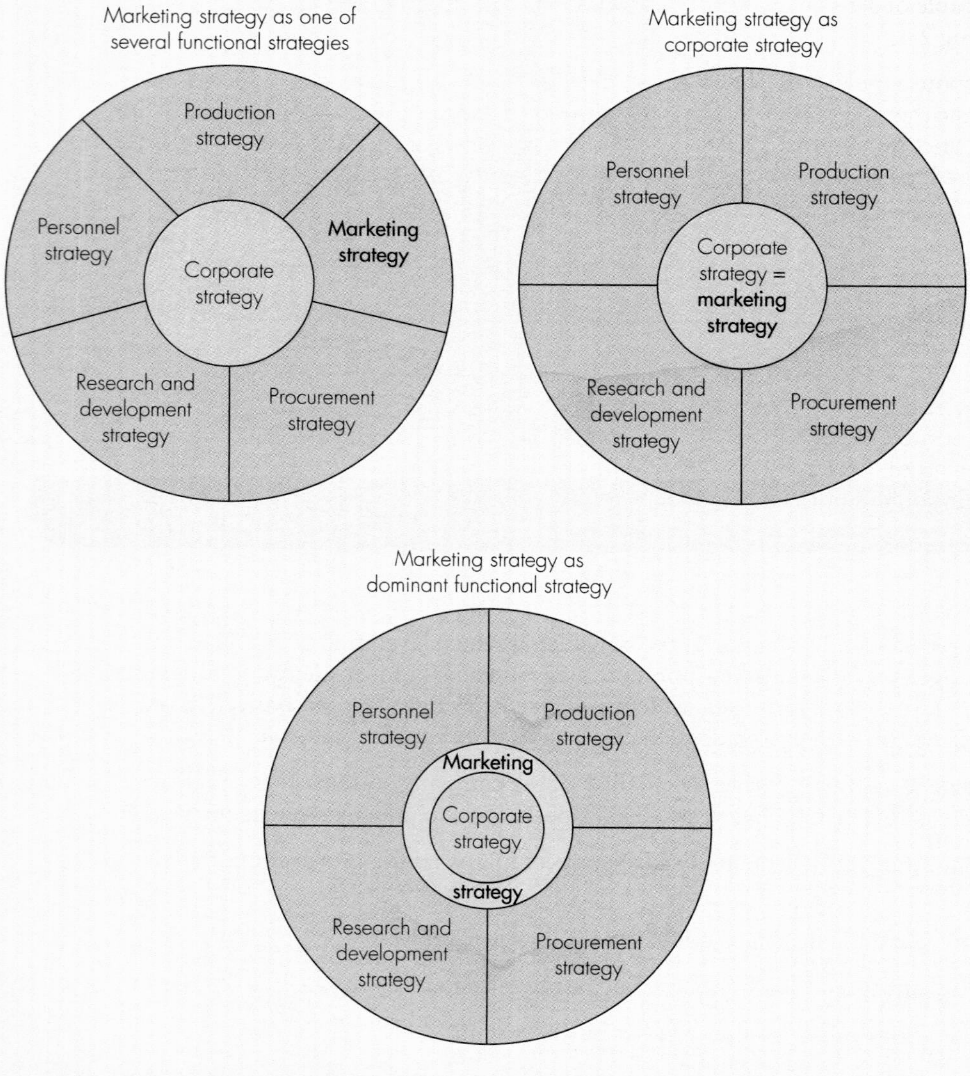

Figure 2-4 Different approaches to classifying the marketing strategy

strategy is primarily concerned with strategic questions regarding the use of the marketing instruments (for a discussion of these strategic aspects, see Cravens 1999; Lambin 1997).

The second perspective places the marketing strategy on a considerably higher level. Some companies even equate marketing strategy with **company strategy**. In this case, the definition of the company philosophy and strategic objectives constitutes the main tasks of strategic marketing.

A third approach views the marketing strategy as a **dominant functional strategy** that plays a key role especially when compared to the other functional strategies (see Varadarajan and Clark 1994). The practical relevance of this approach has been shown in empirical studies, which document the marketing area's central role with respect to strategic issues in the company (see Homburg *et al.* 1999). For an example of a company where marketing is a dominant functional strategy, see Focus on Marketing 2-1.

In this book we espouse the view that marketing strategy is primarily a dominant functional strategy. We assume that marketing strategy, in addition to its relevance to the strategic design of the marketing function, is also a key element of the corporate strategy (also see Figure 2-4). The various facets related to the content of a marketing strategy will be described in more detail in Section 4.1.

Focus on Marketing 2-1 Nestlé – marketing as a dominant functional strategy

Nestlé develops a taste for marketing

An article of February 2005 in the *Financial Times* explains how the world's largest food company has put marketing at the heart of its growth plans in a bid to reach more than a billion first-time consumers of manufactured products.

Nestlé's headquarters are based in Vevey, a small town in French-speaking Switzerland, overlooking the snow-topped peaks of the Haute-Savoie Alps and the serene waters of Lake Geneva. Peter Brabeck, chief executive and chairman-designate of the world's leading food company, enjoys the view from his office.

The company's most senior marketer, Ed Marra, is on long-term leave fighting severe illness, so Mr Brabeck, 61, has stepped into his position. It is very revealing that the marketing task is delegated upwards in Nestlé, as it is a clear indication of how fundamental marketing and brands are to the company. The company has an annual marketing budget of $2.5bn, which is used to promote its large product portfolio. The company boasts 8,000 products, of which there are up to 20,000 variants.

'We are a branded consumer good company,' says Mr Brabeck. 'Marketing is important because it is the engine of growth and brands play a key role in this.'

Mr Brabeck is ideally positioned for his temporary role, as he himself was formerly a marketer. He confesses he was frustrated by the peripheral role played by marketing in the company in the past. In a 'matrix organisation' structure, where managers with responsibilities for specific functions overlap with local market management, he felt that accountability could be blurred. 'We had marketing to one side. It was responsible for some innovation but it wasn't responsible for country performance.

'They would talk about returns on investment on advertising instead of returns on business investment. For too long marketing was just one part of the business.'

Mr Brabeck set about tackling the challenge facing him. The company has seven strategic business units – dairy, beverages, ice cream, confectionery, food, pet care and food services. He decided to make his head of marketing responsible for all of these business units.

Each unit is responsible for research and development, production expertise and systems control. They also establish a global business strategy, from which regional business strategy evolves. This then forms the starting point for business strategies at a local market level. In this way, marketing strategy is at the very heart of all of Nestlé's activities.

Source: Benady 2005.

2.2 The 'Classics' of Strategic Success Factor Research

The success factors of the relevant markets should play an essential role when formulating the marketing strategy. Strategy research and strategic marketing research focus on the investigation of such success factors. In this section, we will present three approaches that can be called the 'classics' of strategic success factor research. Even if some of their findings are too general when viewed from the current state of knowledge, these approaches are still vital in terms of a fundamental understanding of strategic marketing issues.

In this section we will discuss the PIMS project (Section 2.2.1), the experience curve model (Section 2.2.2) and the life cycle model (Section 2.2.3).

2.2.1 The PIMS Project

PIMS Research: Basic Information and Findings

For a long time, the **PIMS project** (Profit Impact of Market Strategies) was the best-known study used in success factor research. The central objective of this study was to obtain insights about the factors that influence the business success of an SBU.

The roots of the PIMS project date back to the 1950s. At that time, the US company General Electric began to establish a database for collecting the data essential to characterizing the strategic competitive position of individual SBUs. The PIMS database was subsequently maintained and managed by the Strategic Planning Institute (SPI). At its peak, it comprised data for more than 3,000 SBUs, representing several hundred companies from a broad range of industries.

The data collected in the database relate mainly to five areas:

1 characteristics of the business environment (long-term and short-term market growth, price trends, number of customers, buying frequency and volume)

2 competitive position of the strategic business unit (market share, relative market share, relative product quality)

3 characteristics of the production of goods and rendering of services (investment intensity, degree of vertical integration, capacity utilization, productivity)

4 budget allocation (budget for advertising, marketing and sales promotions, budget for personal selling)

5 SBU strategy (changes with regard to variables such as relative price, relative marketing expenditures).

In addition, performance data such as return on investment (ROI), return on sales (ROS) and cash flow were summarized.

The various studies based on the PIMS data have identified the following three key influencing variables affecting ROI (see Buzzell and Gale 1989):

1 investment intensity

2 relative market share (as compared to the three largest competitors)

3 relative product quality (as compared to the three largest competitors).

These variables affect the ROI in different ways. **Investment intensity** has a negative impact on the ROI. This effect was explained as follows: high investment intensity forces a company to strive for a high utilization of its expensive capacities. Often, companies feel forced to secure sales through low prices and/or cost-intensive marketing measures, which can have a negative impact on profitability.

In contrast, the **relative market share** has a positive impact on the ROI. This positive relationship is predominantly explained by economies of scale, which indicate that firms with large market shares (i.e. with large output quantities) can operate at lower costs than competitors with lower market share. This concept is closely connected to the experience curve model (see Section 2.2.2), which advances the idea that SBUs with a high market share can benefit from experience-related cost advantages. This *relation between the relative market share and profitability* became the focus of a controversial discussion in later works (see, for example, Szymanski *et al.* 1993).

Contrasting with this, the positive impact of **relative product quality** on the ROI is largely undisputed. This effect can be explained on the one hand by the attainment of higher prices on the basis of superior quality. On the other hand, high quality can also contribute to limiting hidden costs, such as high costs of complaint management and costs of correcting errors.

Critical Evaluation of the PIMS Project

In the literature, the PIMS project came under criticism (see the overviews in Ramanujam and Venkatraman 1984) mainly along three aspects:

1. regarding the data basis
2. regarding the analysis and the methodology
3. regarding the derived strategy recommendations.

Table 2-1 summarizes the most significant points of criticism in each area (for a more thorough discussion of these points, see Buzzell 2004; Farris and Moore 2004).

Some newer studies account for some of the criticism. Some have, for example, reviewed the PIMS results with respect to intercultural validity (see Kotabe *et al.* 1991). According to a survey of US, German and Japanese managers, most found the PIMS results to be applicable, albeit with country-specific accentuation (see Kotabe *et al.* 1991).

The critique summarized in Table 2-1 illustrates that it is necessary to be prudent when using PIMS findings for strategy formulation. Nevertheless, in our opinion, the fundamental importance of the PIMS approach for the empirical research of success factors is indisputable.

Table 2-1 Summary of criticism of the PIMS project

Data basis	Analysis/methodology	Strategy recommendations
▪ Evaluation of individual variables (e.g. relative product quality) is subjective ▪ Short-term examination of individual variables despite long-term conceptual orientation ▪ Inadequate representation of less successful SBUs, non-US SBUs, smaller SBUs and SBUs from the service sector	▪ Empirical correlations do not necessarily imply causation ▪ Interdependencies between explanatory variables may be neglected ▪ Multiple regression analysis not suitable for the investigation of complex dependency structures, such as causal chains	▪ Too narrow orientation on ROI as success factor ▪ Neglect of potential synergies between the individual SBUs within a company ▪ No consideration of features and issues specific to certain industries

Table 2-2 Empirically determined cost reductions when doubling accumulated volume for various product types (adapted from Simon 1992, p. 184)

Product type	Cost reduction %	Product type	Cost reduction %
Electric stove	11.7	Television set	20.0
Automobile	12.0	Industrial air-conditioning system	20.0
Home air-conditioning system	12.3	Electric razor	23.0
Washer-dryer	12.5	Integrated circuit	27.8
Gas stove	17.2	Semiconductor	40–50

2.2.2 The Experience Curve Model

Experience Curve Model: Basic Information

Compared to the PIMS method, the **experience curve model** takes a much more narrow approach. The model is based on the development of costs of products over time and on the notion that the more often a task is performed the lower the costs of performing this task become. More specifically, this effect leads to a reduction in costs depending on the amount of 'experience' accumulated over time (as measured by accumulated volume).

Studies performed by the Boston Consulting Group (see, for example, BCG 1972) found that, with each doubling of the accumulated volume of a product over time, a reduction of value-added costs (including administration, marketing, distribution and manufacturing) of 20 to 30 per cent could be realized. (Table 2-2 shows an overview of the cost reductions achieved in various sectors and Figure 2-5 a graphical representation of the experience curve.)

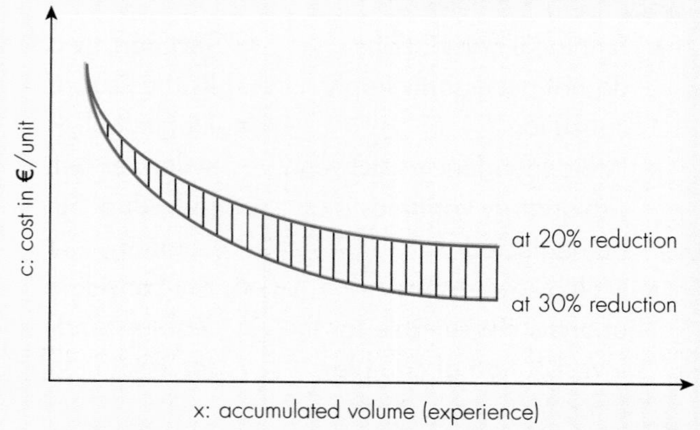

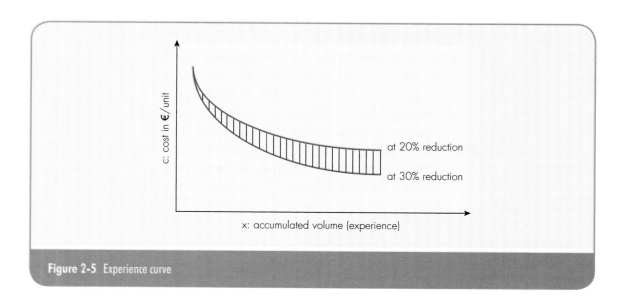

Figure 2-5 Experience curve

A primary reason for the potential cost reduction implied by this model is **learning effects**: the principle of the learning curve is based on the idea that companies can successively gather experience (measured by the accumulated volume) when producing and marketing a product. This then leads to a reduction of costs and/or increases in productivity.

Critical Evaluation of the Experience Curve Model

The experience curve model has been critically evaluated. One point that makes the performance assessment of products especially difficult is that this assessment requires a product with a consistent identity over a longer period of time. This is difficult for many product categories, especially for those that are subject to rapid changes (e.g. technology or fashion goods).

The experience curve model has limited implications for strategic marketing, as it is restricted to one influencing variable of economic success (i.e. costs). Therefore, direct strategic implications based on this model can be problematic and should be considered only with caution. Despite this limitation, however, a few suggestions can be derived from the model.

The relevance of the experience curve model for strategic marketing depends to a great extent on the **characteristics of the market environment**. For example, the more the customer's purchase decision is driven by price, the more relevant the concept becomes: if the price sensitivity on the part of the customer is low, the importance of cost for business success may not be very pronounced. Moreover, the relevance depends on the life cycle phase (see Section 2.2.3) and the growth of the market: a significant increase in the cumulative volume is more feasible in new or fast-growing markets than in established, stagnating markets.

The principal strategic recommendation based on the experience curve model advocates that companies should strive for a high market share in order to gain a cost advantage over the competition. This can especially be applied when new products are launched in the market – for example, with low prices ('penetration pricing', see Section 6.1). Another approach for implementing volume-oriented and cost-oriented strategies is the standardization of products. This also demonstrates one of the key disadvantages of such a strategy: with widespread standardization, companies tend to be less capable of responding to the specific requirements of various market segments.

In summary, the experience curve concept is a simplified model that describes the potential cost developments of products. It emphasizes the need to continuously assess unrealized cost reduction potential and to seek ways to explore this potential. The primary strategic implication of the model is that a high market share on the part of the company can constitute considerable cost advantages. Whether it is relevant for marketing strategy greatly depends on situational factors.

2.2.3 The Life Cycle Model

The Basic Idea of the Life Cycle Model

The **life cycle model** is based on the idea that products go through several life cycle phases, each characterized by different sales and profit potentials. A typical life cycle model is shown by drawing sales (in units or monetary value) over time. Commonly, the model is depicted by an S-shaped curve showing a slow initial uptake in sales followed by a subsequent acceleration and finally a slowdown of sales (see Figure 2-6).

In general, four phases can be distinguished in the life cycle model:

1 introduction

2 growth

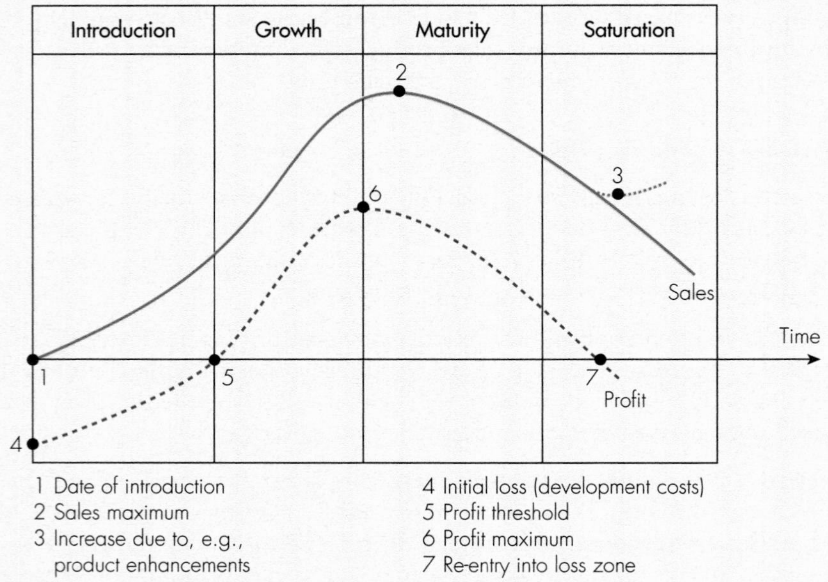

Figure 2-6 Sales and profit curves according to the life cycle model

3 maturity
4 saturation.

In its classic form, the life cycle model refers to a product or a product category. However, the underlying mechanisms are also applied to entire markets or industry sectors. In this context, we refer to the **market life cycle** or the **industry life cycle**. The individual phases in this cycle can be characterized by means of market conditions, such as market growth, market potential or market share distribution (see Table 2-3). An analysis of these factors also facilitates the identification of the life cycle phase that currently applies to an industry sector or market.

Two important points of the **product life cycle** (PLC) are the turning points. Golder and Tellis define them as takeoff (1997) and slowdown (2004). The takeoff marks the transition from the introductory stage to the growth phase as shown in Figure 2-6. At this point, sales experience a sharp increase. The slowdown, on the contrary, is the transition from the growth stage to the maturity state. Here a noticeable decrease in sales usually occurs. The knowledge of the different phases and the transitions from one phase to the other is especially important for managers since they need to plan resource deployment in line with sales development (e.g. the need to plan production capacities, inventories, advertising and sales activities, as well as distribution, accordingly) (see also Montaguti *et al.* 2002). Golder and Tellis's (1997) work indicates that takeoff for product categories does not occur soon after market introduction but the period until takeoff rather spans several years.

Critical Evaluation of Life Cycle Model

The life cycle model has been criticized because – in its classic application – it uses *time as the only variable for explaining sales*. In view of the wide range of variables that influence the sale of a product (e.g. marketing activities, customer behavior, seasonal fluctuations), it is obvious that this model simplifies reality to a large extent. Against this background, it is not surprising that actual, empirically observed sales curves frequently do not correspond to the commonly assumed

Table 2-3 Characteristics of market life cycle phases

Criterion \ Life cycle phase	Introduction	Growth	Maturity	Saturation
Market growth	Increasing growth rate	Steeply increasing growth rate	Stagnation, negative growth rate towards end of phase	Negative to strongly negative growth rate
Market potential	Difficult to determine; realization of small percentage of potential demand	Still considerably difficult to estimate market potential mainly due to price reductions	Limited market potential	Very limited market potential, frequently only demand for replacement
Market share	Not feasible to estimate market share development	Market share distributed under growing number of firms	Market share concentrated in the hands of a few companies	Increased concentration and consolidation as weak competitors are eliminated
Stability of market share	Strong fluctuation of market share – high volatility	Consolidation of market share	High degree of stability, fluctuations mostly due to exit of competitors	
Number of competitors	Small	Number of competitors reaches maximum	Exit of competitors that do not possess competitive advantage	Number of competitors is further reduced
Customer loyalty	Hardly any loyalty towards companies	Certain degree of customer loyalty, while alternatives are frequently explored	Relatively high degree of customer loyalty	
Entry barriers	In general, entry barriers do not exist; entry depends on financial capacity, technical knowhow and the willingness to take risks	Market access difficult (established companies use cost reduction potential); as a rule, entry feasible when market niches (beachheads) can be created	Market entry increasingly difficult because of growing 'experience' of competition; market share can be increased only at the expense of competitors	In general, companies do not have incentives to enter a stagnating market
Technology	Technological innovation as a prerequisite for tapping into new markets	Product and process improvements	Familiarity with market requirements; streamlining of production and distribution processes	Well-known, widespread and stagnating technology

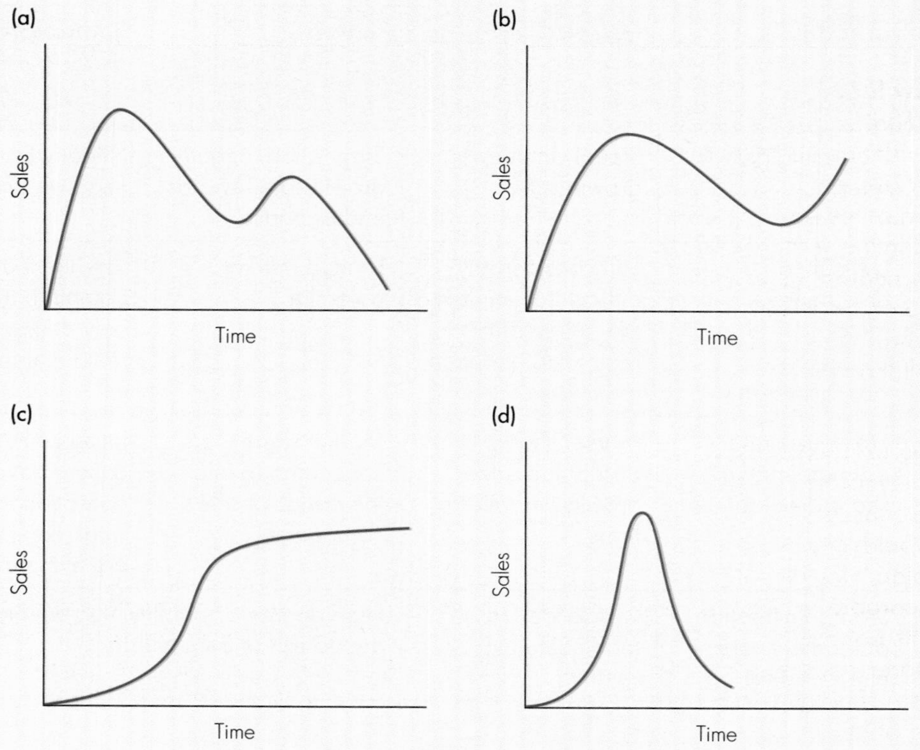

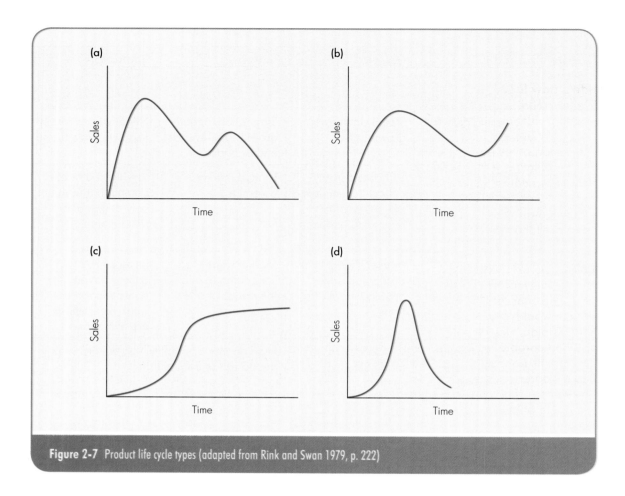

Figure 2-7 Product life cycle types (adapted from Rink and Swan 1979, p. 222)

S-shaped curve as depicted in Figure 2-6 (see Easingwood 1988; Rink and Swan 1979). Figure 2-7 illustrates alternative forms of product life cycles. Section (a) shows a situation in which the product (or product category) experiences multiple takeoffs before its decline; in section (b) the product experiences a sharp initial increase before sales decrease without leveling-out; section (c) illustrates a rather long growth phase (with a sales situation characterized as a plateau); and in section (d) there is both a strong increase and a sudden decrease of sales.

Another point of criticism arises when the sales curve is viewed as exogenous in a sense that it cannot be influenced by management. This perspective is not consistent with the fundamental approach of stimulating sales through marketing management activities. For instance, there are numerous examples demonstrating that companies have succeeded in boosting the sales of a product during the maturity phase with product variations (see also Focus on Marketing 2-2). Golder and Tellis (1997, 2004), for instance, found empirical support that market penetration and price predict the timing and duration of product life cycle stages. Thus, managers might be able to influence takeoff through price reductions as they increase the likelihood that the product takes off.

Research by Kuester and Robertson (2005) and Montaguti *et al.* (2002) also supports the argument that managers can actively manage the life cycle by reducing takeoff time. Their proposed strategies include, for example, market penetration strategies, product compatibility and product pre-announcing prior to launch.

Focus on Marketing 2-2

Nintendo's new look

An article from *Forbes*, July 2006, suggested that videogame industry executives may have wanted to push the 'reset' button at the end of 2005. It was a disappointing year – their games consoles neared the end of their product life cycles, customers held off buying new titles, and gamemakers felt the effects.

But while Sony's and Microsoft's boxes were considering expensive high-definition disc players and complex processors, Nintendo decided that [its] new machine would take a different tack. Perrin Kaplan, vice president of marketing and corporate affairs for Nintendo of America, felt their new console could help move Nintendo from its position as the steady third player in the American gaming market. Nintendo had never had a clearer opportunity to differentiate itself to American audiences, or more broadly in the rest of the world. Originally named the Revolution, their new console was eventually launched under the brand name of Nintendo Wii.

Employing a radical new interface and games designed to appeal to hard-core gamers and nontraditional audiences alike, the Wii is described on the Nintendo website as the console that 'returns gaming to simpler times while innovating game development at the same time. The unique Wii Remote gives parents and grandparents a chance to play games with their children. It gives gamers and traditional non-gamers a chance to share the same experiences in this new generation of gaming.'

Kaplan described 2005 as the 'year we saw consumers get savvy'. He explained that 'they want to experience new innovative software. We have seen this challenge grow over the past year as the console market has seen some decline. The industry library shows a plethora of the same type of games – and while many of them are popular, all good things run dry after a while.'

'Nintendo also offers a new controller that allows users to move hand, arm, wrist or body to control the game. If you were playing a fishing game, before you would just press buttons on a controller held in both hands in front of you. With this, you can move your arm back and forth and cast your bait. It senses depth. As someone who doesn't spend hours per day gaming, I was thrilled with the experience. We're also offering what we call the 'virtual console' – the ability to download nearly every kind of Nintendo game going back to the original Nintendo Entertainment System through the GameCube. We think there is an untapped nostalgia market: Gamers who grew up and cut their teeth on these older games could come back.'

In its first five months of its launch, the Wii sold 5.84 million units. This has steadily grown, and in the first six months of the 2008 fiscal year, 7.33 million units of Wii hardware were sold worldwide.

Sources: Consolidated Financial Statements, Nintendo Co. Ltd, 25 October 2007 (http://www.nintendo.com/corp/report/2QFY2008.pdf), Rosmarin, R., Nintendo's new look, *Forbes*, 2 July 2006 and the Nintendo website, 11 April 2008 (http://www.nintendo.co.uk/NOE/en_GB/systems/about_wii_1069.html).

Despite its limitations, the life cycle model has significant implications for strategic marketing. The statement that, as a rule, all products have a **limited life span** is of fundamental significance. It implies that companies need to continuously assess their offer and redesign products and services – for example, through product innovation or differentiation (see Sections 5.2 and 5.3). Taking on board the implications of the life cycle concept companies should, therefore, continuously monitor the product portfolio and aim for a portfolio with a balanced mix of products in the various phases (see, for example, Urban and Hauser 1993).

For the different life cycle phases, statements can be formulated with respect to strategic objectives and behavior (see Rink and Swan 1987; Table 2-4). These fundamental statements provide companies with a certain degree of orientation with regard to the practical strategic alignment of their marketing activities in different life cycle phases.

In summary, the life cycle model simplifies reality to a large extent. Sales curves very often show different patterns than the basic model (see Figure 2-7). Therefore, an application of the concept

Table 2-4 Typical strategic behavior in the various life cycle phases

Phase / Strategic issues	Introduction	Growth	Maturity	Saturation
Market-related objective	Market is being established	Market penetration	Maintenance of market position	Leveraging of market position
Target market range	Test markets	Domestic/ international	Multinational	Differentiated
Product decisions	Narrow product range, frequently only one basic product model	Relatively narrow product range, frequently one product technology	Extensive product range, several variants and brands	Reduced product range, unprofitable product variants are discontinued
Pricing decisions	Price level tends to be at the lower end in order to increase market share	Price level tends to be at the higher end	Differentiated price levels, willingness to grant larger price discounts (e.g. trade discounts)	Differentiated price levels with tendency towards lower end
Communication decisions	Communication very intense, geared towards innovators	Communication intensely aimed at establishing a high level of product awareness and a positive product image	Communication intensity tends to decrease; establishment of brand loyalty	Communication tends to be less intense
Sales and distribution decisions	Selective distribution, quick development of sales and distribution system	Intensive sales and distribution		Selective distribution, unprofitable sales and distribution channels are discontinued

as a forecasting tool is problematic. Implementing strategic recommendations derived from the life cycle model can lead to 'self-fulfilling prophecies' and to incorrect strategic market decisions. This is the case, for example, if highly profitable products in their maturity phase are eliminated prematurely or no longer promoted, even though they would have been able to maintain their position for a considerable period of time if supported by suitable marketing activities.

Despite these critical points, the life cycle model is an important model for supporting strategic marketing decisions.

2.2.4 Beyond the 'Classics': Further Findings of Strategic Success Factor Research

Having discussed the 'classics' of strategic success factors research in Sections 2.2.1 to 2.2.3, we will now address the further findings of strategic success factor research. There are currently a great number of conceptual and empirical studies that aim to determine companies' strategic success factors. These studies have been summarized in a number of meta-studies (see, e.g., Varadarajan and Jayachandran 1999). In general, these meta-studies demonstrate that key success factors definitely exist. However, it has to be stated that success factors should not be viewed as automatic mechanisms in the sense that a company need only adhere to these success factors in order to be successful. Rather, it is important to take the specific situation of the individual company into account.

So far, the following key success factors have been examined.

- In general, product quality has a positive impact on success (see, e.g., Capon *et al.* 1990). In particular, it positively affects the profitability of a company by means of a higher market share (see Phillips *et al.* 1983).
- In principle, a higher market share leads to the increased profitability of a company (see, e.g., Szymanski *et al.* 1993).
- The basic strategic alignment of a company affects its success, with the cost leadership strategy, differentiation strategy and a combination of the two all being considered successful (see Campbell-Hunt 2000).
- Market entry order (e.g. pioneer vs follower) also affects company success, especially with regard to market share (see also Szymanski *et al.* 1995). (See section 5.3.4 for market entry order issues).
- Finally, the market orientation of a company increases its success (see Cano *et al.* 2004). (see chapter 17 for more on the concept of market orientation).

2.3 The Marketing Strategy Development Process

The strategic perspective of marketing is best discussed when displaying the process by which marketing strategies are developed. This process is shown in Figure 2-8.

Accordingly, the first step of the process consists of an **analysis of the initial strategic situation**. This analysis includes the overall company environment (e.g. trends in political and legal framework conditions that have an impact on marketing), markets addressed by the company (e.g. changes in the behavior of customers or competitors) and the situation of the company itself (e.g. developments in customer loyalty and market share). This provides the information basis that is needed to design marketing strategies. Chapter 3 contains a detailed description of the process used to analyze the initial strategic situation and the methods that can be used when doing so.

Subsequently, the actual **strategy is formulated**. It refers to aspects such as customer segments targeted, desired customer benefits and the design of the marketing mix.

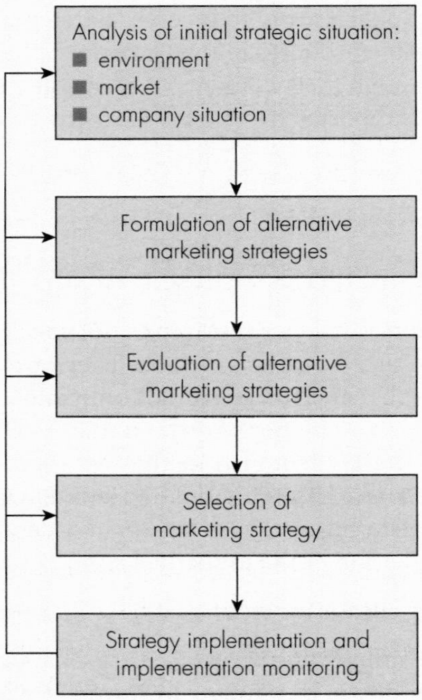

Figure 2-8 Process of strategy development in marketing

Further steps in the process are the formulation, evaluation and selection of an appropriate marketing strategy. Chapter 4 puts a focus on the central questions and concepts of the formulation of marketing strategies.

The last step in this process is concerned with **strategy implementation** and monitoring of this implementation, which may once again lead to the analysis of the environment, the market and the company situation. A discussion of these aspects will not take place within the scope of the strategic perspective of marketing, but rather in connection with the aspects related to implementation (see Part 4).

At this point, we would like to emphasize that the process illustrated in Figure 2-8 looks structured and deliberate. Examples of strategy models that do not have such a systematic character can also be found in the literature. For example, it is frequently mentioned that strategies are the result of numerous small steps (incremental). In his 'grassroots' model of strategy formulation, for example, Mintzberg (1989) assumes that strategies develop like 'weed in a garden' and are not grown like 'tomatoes in a greenhouse'. According to this theory, strategies are often dismissed and replaced by emerging strategies that were not planned. These emerging strategies evolve through a learning process in the course of a company's history, with individual projects turning out to be particularly successful and therefore setting the trend for the company. In general, in company practice a mix of both rationally planned and incremental strategy development can be observed.

Summary

In this chapter, we introduced the marketing strategy concept and reviewed the conceptual foundations of the process of strategy formulation. Objectives – the foundations of strategy formulation – can be related to different levels of the company, ranging from the business mission to instrumental objectives. Specifically, in the marketing area, objectives pertain to potential (such as customer satisfaction), to market success (such as customer loyalty) and to economic success factors (such as turnover and profit). Based on the different objectives, strategies are also related to different levels of the company. Corporate strategy, which defines the basic orientation of the company, serves as a presetting for the lower-level business unit strategies and functional strategies. In this framework, the marketing strategy can be interpreted as a dominant functional strategy that also constitutes a key element of the corporate strategy.

The fundamentals of strategic success factor research were presented subsequently to guide the process of strategy formulation. The key insights generated by the PIMS project, the experience curve model and the life cycle model were discussed and complemented by more recent findings. These indicate that, in particular, product quality, market share, the strategic alignment of the company, entry order and a company's market orientation positively impact success. Finally, we presented the process of strategy development, which consists of the analysis of the initial strategic situation, the formulation and evaluation of alternative marketing strategies, and subsequently the selection and implementation of a marketing strategy.

Case Study: Nothing Lasts For Ever – Subtle Reminders for Consumers from Gillette

In 1998, Gillette introduced a new high-tech razor that took $750 million and more than five years to create. One of the features of the new product that Gillette promoted was surprisingly low-tech. Gillette had introduced a blue strip that fades to alert users that it is time to replace the blade. But does the blade really need to be thrown away when Gillette says it does?

Not surprisingly, Gillette and other companies that employ similar features defend these reminders. They argue that they provide valuable information about whether a product is delivering optimal performance. This could be true up to a point. However, these in-built warnings are also an ideal way to prompt their customers to replace goods, such as razor blades that fade, or toothbrushes whose bristles change color, more frequently than they would otherwise. This of course results in higher sales of the manufacturer's product.

In an article from the *New York Times*, Tom Vierhile, general manager of Marketing Intelligence Services, commented that 'these companies are all competing in very mature markets. They have got to invent strategies to increase user rates. If you double the throwaway rate, you double sales.'

Case Study (Continued)

Marketing experts say that these types of gimmicks largely benefit the manufacturer, but by trying to shorten a product's life cycle, companies also want to promote proper use of their product. If consumers use goods as they are intended, they are less likely to complain about an overused product that is failing to perform. This ultimately protects brand loyalty too.

Source: adapted from: Where nothing lasts forever: subtle reminders for consumers on replacing products, by Canedy, D. (from the *New York Times*, 24 April 1998 © 1998 *New York Times*).

Discussion Questions

1. Evaluate the measures Gillette takes against the background of the life cycle phase of its razors.
2. What are other measures Gillette could have taken in this life cycle phase?
3. What is the main implication of the life cycle model and what are weaknesses of this concept?

Key Terms

Analysis of the initial strategic situation *31*
Business mission *16*
Business unit strategy *19*
Characteristics of the market environment *25*
Company objectives *17*
Company strategy *20*
Corporate strategy *19*
Dominant functional strategy *20*
Experience curve model *24*
Financial marketing objectives *17*
Functional objectives *17*
Functional strategies *19*
Industry life cycle *26*
Instrumental objectives *18*
Investment intensity *22*
Learning effects *25*
Life cycle model *25*
Limited life span *30*
Market life cycle *26*
Marketing objectives related to market success *17*
Marketing objectives related to potential *17*
Marketing strategy *19*
Objectives *16*
PIMS project *22*
Product life cycle *26*
Relative market share *23*
Relative product quality *23*
Strategic business unit (SBU) objectives *17*
Strategy implementation *32*
Strategy is formulated *31*

References

Benady, A. (2005) Nestlé tries a new flavour of marketing, *Financial Times*, 22 February, Circulation 30629.

Boston Consulting Group (1972) *Perspectives on Experience*. Boston, Mass.

Buzzell, R. (2004) The PIMS program of strategy research: a retrospective appraisal, *Journal of Business Research*, 57, 478–483.

Buzzell, R. and Gale, B. (1989) *Das PIMS-Programm*. Wiesbaden.

Campbell-Hunt, C. (2000) What have we learned about generic competitive strategy? A meta-analysis, *Strategic Management Journal*, 21, 2, 127–154.

Canedy, D. (1998) Where nothing lasts forever: subtle reminders for consumers on replacing products, *New York Times*, 24 April © 1998 *New York Times*. All rights reserved. Used by permission and protected by the copyright laws of the United States. The printing, copying, redistribution, or transmission of the material without express written permission is prohibited.

Cano, C., Carrillat, F. and Jaramillo, F. (2004) A meta-analysis of the relationship between market orientation and business performance: evidence from five continents, *International Journal of Research in Marketing*, 21, 179–200.

Capon, N., Farley, J. and Hoenig, S. (1990) Determinants of financial performance: a meta-analysis, *Management Science*, 36, 10, 1143–1159.

Cravens, D. (1999) *Strategic Marketing* (6th edn). Chicago.

Easingwood, C. (1988) Product life cycle patterns for new industrial goods, *R&D Management*, 18, 23–32.

Farris, P. and Moore, M. (2004) *The Profit Impact of Marketing Strategy Project: Retrospect and Prospects*. Cambridge.

Golder, P.N. and Tellis, G.J. (1997) Will it ever fly? Modeling the takeoff of really new consumer durables, *Marketing Science*, 16, 3, 257–270.

Golder, P.N. and Tellis, G.J. (2004) Growing, growing, gone: cascades, diffusion, and turning points in the product life cycle, *Marketing Science*, 23, 2 (Spring), 207–218.

Homburg, C., Pflesser, C. (2000) A multiple-layer model of market-oriented organizational culture: measurement issues and performance outcomes, *Journal of Marketing Research*, 37, 4, 449–462.

Homburg, C., Kuester, S. and Lueers, T. (2008) Shareholder value orientation of the firm: conceptualizing the construct and analyzing its performance outcomes. Working paper, University of Mannheim.

Homburg, C., Workman, J. and Krohmer, H. (1999) Marketing's influence within the firm, *Journal of Marketing*, 63, 2, 1–17.

Kotabe, M., Duhan, D. and Smith, D. (1991) The perceived veracity of PIMS strategy principles in Japan, *Journal of Marketing*, 55, 1, 26–41.

Kuester, S. and Robertson, T.S. (2005) Winning the take-off battle, *European Business Forum*, 20 (Winter), 45–48.

Lambin, J. (1997) *Strategic Marketing Management*. London.

Levitt, T. (1960) Marketing myopia, *Harvard Business Review*, July–August.

Mintzberg, H. (1989) *Mintzberg on Management*. New York.

Montaguti, E., Kuester, S. and Robertson, T.S. (2002) Entry strategy for radical product innovations: a conceptual model and propositional inventory, *International Journal of Research in Marketing*, 19, 21–42.

Morgan, R., McGuinness, T. and Thorpe, E. (2000) The contribution of marketing to business strategy formation: a perspective on business performance gains, *Journal of Strategic Marketing*, 8, 4, 341–362.

Phillips, L., Chang, D. and Buzzell, R. (1983) Product quality, cost position and business performance: a test of some key hypotheses, *Journal of Marketing*, 47, 2, 26–43.

Ramanujam, V. and Venkatraman, N. (1984) An inventory and critique of strategy research using the PIMS database, *Academy of Management Review*, 9, 1, 138–151.

Rink, D. and Swan, J. (1979) Product life cycle research: a literature review, *Journal of Business Research*, 78, 7, 219–242.

Rink, D. and Swan, J. (1987) Fitting business strategic and tactical planning to the product life cycle, in: King, W. and Cleland, D. (eds) *Planning and Management Handbook*. New York.

Rosmarin, R. (2006) Nintendo's new look, *Forbes*, 2 July.

Sharma, S. (1999) Trespass or symbiosis? Dissolving the boundaries between strategic marketing and strategic management, *Journal of Strategic Marketing*, 7, 2, 73–88.

Simon, H. (1992) *Preismanagement: Analyze, Strategie, Umsetzung* (2nd edn). Wiesbaden.

Szymanski, D., Bharadwaj, S. and Varadarajan, P. (1993) An analysis of the market-share-profitability relationship, *Journal of Marketing*, 57, 3, 1–18.
Szymanski, D., Troy, L. and Bharadwaj, S. (1995) Order of entry and business performance: an empirical synthesis and reexamination, *Journal of Marketing*, 59, 4, 17–33.
Urban, G. and Hauser, J. (1993) *Design and Marketing of New Products* (2nd edn). Englewood Cliffs, NJ.
Varadarajan, P. and Clark, T. (1994) Delineating the scope of corporate, business, and marketing strategy, *Journal of Business Research*, 31, 2/3, 93–105.
Varadarajan, P. and Jayachandran, S. (1999) Marketing strategy: an assessment of the state of the field and outlook, *Journal of the Academy of Marketing Science*, 27, 2, 120–143.
Varadarajan, P., Jayachandran, S. and White, C. (2001) Strategic interdependence in organizations: deconglomeration and marketing strategy, *Journal of Marketing*, 21, 1, 15–28.

CHAPTER 3

Analysis of the Initial Strategic Situation

Contents

Learning Objectives

In this chapter you will become familiar with:

- the different factors that need to be evaluated when analyzing the initial strategic situation within the scope of the global company environment
- the procedures applied in early warning systems/early intelligence systems, forecasting methods and scenario techniques
- the key aspects to be considered when analyzing the initial strategic situation within the scope of the market
- the key methods and models that can be applied to analyze markets
- the different factors to be evaluated when analyzing the initial strategic situation within the scope of the company situation
- the most important methods that can be used for analyzing the company situation.

The development of marketing strategies should be based on a thorough analysis of the initial strategic situation of a company. In this section we will focus on this type of analysis.

The key objectives of such an analysis are the identification of facts, conditions and changes (particularly those that are related to the company environment) that have an impact on the marketing strategy. Another major objective is the identification of strategic opportunities and risks.

First, Section 3.1 will give an overview of the most important issues and methods involved in analyzing the initial strategic situation. Sections 3.2 to 3.4 will then provide detailed information with regard to the analysis of the environment, the market and the company. In each of these three sections, we will first formulate central questions that will serve as guidelines for a situational analysis. Subsequently, we will discuss selected models and methods that can facilitate and support the analysis in the individual areas.

3.1 Issues and Key Methods in Analyzing the Initial Strategic Situation

The analysis of the initial strategic situation focuses on three areas (see Figure 3-1). These are:

1 the analysis of the global environmental factors (macroenvironment)

2 the analysis of the market conditions (microenvironment)

3 the analysis of the company situation.

In terms of **global environmental factors** (macroenvironment), an analysis of the initial strategic situation should identify present and potential developments in society, macroeconomics, politics, law and technology that have or will have an impact on the marketing strategy. For example, the climate debate has had an impact on companies' conduct via increased public awareness of environmental issues and also via changed legislation in some industrialized countries.

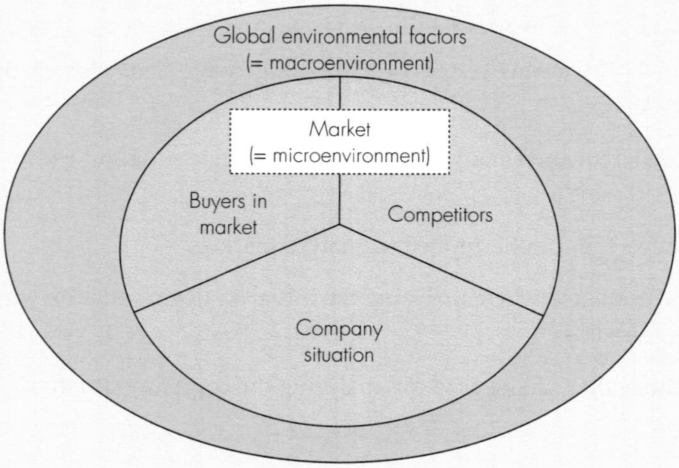

Figure 3-1 Areas relevant for the analysis of the initial strategic situation

In addition to general market characteristics (such as estimated market growth), an **analysis of the relevant market** (microenvironment) focuses in particular on changes in the needs and the behavior of **all buyers in the market**. An evaluation of the **competitors** plays another key role in this area. For example, a company in the industrial goods sector might become aware of an increasing trend among buyers to discontinue in-house maintenance of their production equipment and outsource this activity to service companies with the appropriate knowhow. This can change customer requirements and result in increasing demand for technical services in addition to the supply of tangible products. When formulating their marketing strategy, industrial goods manufacturers need to examine whether they intend to cater to the increased demand for services.

When **analyzing the company situation**, it is especially important to focus on customer-related aspects. In contrast to the market analysis, this analysis does not consider all buyers in the market as a whole, but specifically the customers of the company. In this context, an evaluation should be conducted regarding, for example, whether changes in customer loyalty can be observed. Another key aspect is the situation of the company within the competitive environment.

In the following sections, we will formulate central questions that can be used as guidelines for the analysis of each of the three areas: microenvironment, macroenvironment and company situation. We will also discuss important models and methods that can support a strategic analysis in the individual areas. Table 3-1 provides an overview of these models and methods.

Table 3-1 Key models and methods for analyzing the initial strategic situation

Area of analysis	Models/methods
Global environmental factors (= macroenvironment)	■ Early warning systems/early intelligence systems ■ Forecasting methods ■ Scenario techniques ■ PEST analysis
Relevant market (= microenvironment)	■ Market research methods ■ Competitive structure model ■ Strategic groups model
Company situation	■ Value chain analysis ■ Benchmarking ■ Consistency matrix of competitive advantages ■ SWOT analysis

3.2 Scanning the Scene: Analysis of the Global Company Environment

3.2.1 Central Questions

The general framework for the design of the marketing strategy is provided by the **global company environment**, which typically cannot be influenced by an individual company. The global company environment comprises the following areas: society, macroeconomics, politics, law and technology (see Table 3-2).

Table 3-2 Central questions for the analysis of the global company environment

- Which general developments in society are relevant for formulating a marketing strategy?
- Which general macroeconomic developments are relevant for formulating a marketing strategy?
- Which general political developments are relevant for formulating a marketing strategy?
- Which general legal developments are relevant for formulating a marketing strategy?
- Which general technological developments are relevant for formulating a marketing strategy?

The question concerning **developments in society** is considered to be relevant for most companies, as these developments affect the vast majority of buyers in the market. This central question relates to changes in general values, attitudes and norms in society, including aspects such as work, leisure time, consumption, environmental protection, dietary and nutritional habits, and health, as well as family and relationships. Focus on Marketing 3-1 illustrates how changes in customer values and attitudes will influence the luxury goods industry in the future (for detailed information concerning values and lifestyle, and attitude, please refer to the Appendix).

Focus on Marketing 3-1 An example of the changing market environment

The new laws of luxury marketing

For decades, the golden rule of the luxury business was elegant, consistent and highly effective: don't ask consumers what they want – tell them what they need. But according to recent Bain & Company interviews with chief executives at a score of luxury's top performers, times are changing. Indeed, as luxury comes of age as a truly global industry, the leaders are following new rules that put consumers in charge of growth. Adapting winning techniques from the broader consumer products marketplace, they're developing deep consumer insights in a manner new to the luxury marketplace.

What factors undergird this shift? For one, the luxury sector no longer consists primarily of small, family-based businesses. It's a full-fledged global industry. Second, consumers are changing. By 2020, the chief characteristic of consumers will be empowerment, according to Bain research. The consumers of the future will have more discretionary income, less time and more choices, and will display wholly new spending patterns, depending on age, geography and wealth.

They will also exhibit 'crossover' buying behavior – as low-end consumers reach for the occasional luxury item, and those at the high end seek inexpensive basic goods. In this environment, mass market retailers' attractive alternatives to luxury products – like designer knockoffs from H&M, and Target's private-label designer offerings – could threaten luxury companies' growth and profits. Luxury makers need to take pains to offer consumers a clearly differentiated experience, particularly in newer luxury markets like China.

The top quintile of consumers will also increasingly value their time and leisure over their money, and reward businesses that recognize this. They will value products and services that are tailored to lifestyle and life stage needs. And they will expect a more engaging customer experience, with an appreciation for variety. For premium makers of luxury goods, consumers will increasingly redefine just what constitutes value for the money.

Source: Rigby *et al.* 2006.

Macroeconomic developments are mostly of equal importance. Here, for example, changes in population size and structure (e.g. number of households, age distribution), economic growth, household income, public and private spending are predominant issues. Focus on Marketing 3-2 describes important demographic changes in Japan.

Focus on Marketing 3-2

Hey, big spender

A shift in a country's demographic can have wide-reaching implications for society, but can also create opportunities for new products to be developed.

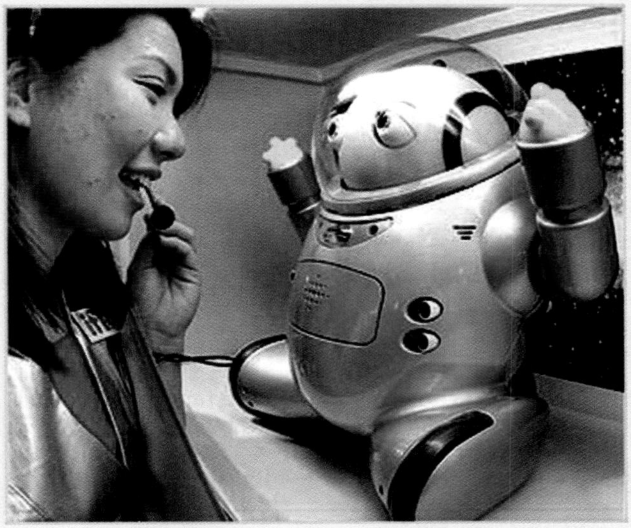

Take the example of Japan. By 2015, it is estimated that one in four of all Japanese, or 30m, will be over 65. Already, more than 25,000 Japanese are over 100, and that number is set to rise fast. Japan's big baby-boom generation is just about to retire from the workforce and the average life expectancy, now 82, is growing by almost 2.5 years every decade. An article in *The Economist* (12 March 2005) commented that:

'These changes are causing a good deal of hand-wringing among policymakers contemplating a growing burden for the state and for a shrinking workforce. But it is also causing a good deal of hand-rubbing among businessmen, who see older Japanese as a source of profit.'

The change in the average age of the population creates a number of challenges, including the need to provide affordable care for a growing number of elderly. A great majority of these older people may still be able to live at home, but may no longer be living with their children. At the present time, the political climate in Japan is considered to be averse to immigration, so it is unlikely that bringing in cheaper, foreign nurses and carers would be a popular option.

The Economist goes on to explain how Japanese businesses, true to form, are developing suitably high-tech responses to this problem:

'Increasingly, the development work on robots is designed either to assist the old with physical functions such as bathing or lifting things, or to monitor health and well-being. A government report [2005] guessed that annual demand for 'service robots', i.e. those not used for manufacturing, could top ¥1 trillion ($8.4 billion) by 2015, and the elderly are likely to be among the biggest customers.'

Source: adapted from Hey, big-spender, *The Economist* (2005), 377, 8455, 59–60 (12/3/2005).

Some **political developments** (e.g. changes in the labor market, employment and environmental protection policies) as well as the associated **legal developments** (e.g. changes to laws and regulations) affect all companies in the economy, while others affect only single industries and sectors. Deregulation in industries such as the airline or telecommunications sector have had a significant impact on all industry players, while companies outside these particular markets were, generally speaking, unaffected. Many airline and telecommunications companies, respectively, have changed their approach to the market as a consequence.

Technological developments (e.g. in the areas of biotechnology, information and laser technologies, microelectronics and robotics) can both offer new opportunities and pose significant risks that need to be considered when formulating a strategy (see Christensen *et al.* 1998; Oliver 1999). Most prominently, the fundamental changes in the information technology sector significantly affect the formulation of a marketing strategy in many industries, since they can lead to the emergence of new markets, competitors and market rules (see Yoffie 1996). One example is the **increasing utilization of internet technology**, which comes with many opportunities and risks for companies. As far as opportunities are concerned, the internet facilitates tapping into new business sectors and markets, attracting new customer segments as well as establishing a more direct approach to customers and providing them with more and better information (for an overview on the effects of increasing internet use, see, e.g. Parasuraman and Zinkhan 2002; Varadarajan and Yadav 2002). One risk for companies arising from internet technology is increasing transparency for customers, who can obtain quick and inexpensive information about prices and product weaknesses. This increased transparency strengthens the position of buyers (see, e.g. Smith 2002).

3.2.2 Selected Methods

The following tools and methods are particularly suited for an analysis of the global company environment. They can give support for the early detection of changes in the environment:

- early warning systems/early intelligence systems
- forecasting methods
- scenario techniques
- PEST analysis.

It should be pointed out here that these methods can also be used for the purpose of market analysis (see Section 3.3).

The key objective of an **early warning system/early intelligence system** is the timely detection of significant changes in the company environment. These systems potentially help companies to account for such changes as early as possible when formulating a marketing strategy. While early warning systems focus on the detection of potential risks, early intelligence systems are additionally concerned with the identification of new opportunities.

The importance of an early warning system with regard to the success of a marketing strategy is based on the fact that – as a rule – a significant period of time passes between the formulation of a marketing strategy and its implementation in the market. If a change is detected too late (i.e. when it is already evident in the market), the company's adjustment in marketing strategy will usually lag behind. Early warning systems and early intelligence systems are based on the key assumption that significant changes (discontinuities) in the environment do not occur abruptly, but are frequently preceded by 'weak signals' (see Morris 1997). **Weak signals** refer to largely qualitative information from the company environment, which indicates discontinuities and helps to anticipate them.

In order to detect these signals, early warning systems/early intelligence systems make use of either special indicators (indicator-based early warning systems/early intelligence systems) or general information from selected information sources (information-based early warning systems/early intelligence systems).

Indicator-based early warning systems/early intelligence systems use a (usually relatively small) number of leading indicators that help to forecast future developments (e.g. macroeconomic benchmarks such as labor market trends and household spending, as well as indicators of confidence such as the purchasing manager's index or consumer confidence indices). **Information-based early warning systems/early intelligence systems** use information sources that are specifically useful for the detection of weak signals (e.g. studies conducted by research institutions and trade associations, publications by government authorities or political parties, or articles on technological developments published in the specialist press).

While early warning systems and early intelligence systems tend to make relatively general statements with regard to future developments, **forecasting methods** provide more concrete information. Forecasting methods are concerned with an estimation of unknown situations and as such they aim to describe future developments as precisely as possible (in the form of forecasting statements).

With **qualitative forecasting methods** the company can develop estimates concerning future developments based on the experiences and knowledge of experts. These methods are particularly suited to forecasting environmental factors and developments for which there is no sufficient historical data available for a formal mathematical forecast, or that cannot easily be quantified.

A frequently applied qualitative forecasting method is the **Delphi method** (see Figure 3-2 for the process involved in Delphi interviews). With this method, experts are interviewed (mostly in written form) in several rounds about their opinion on future environmental developments. After each

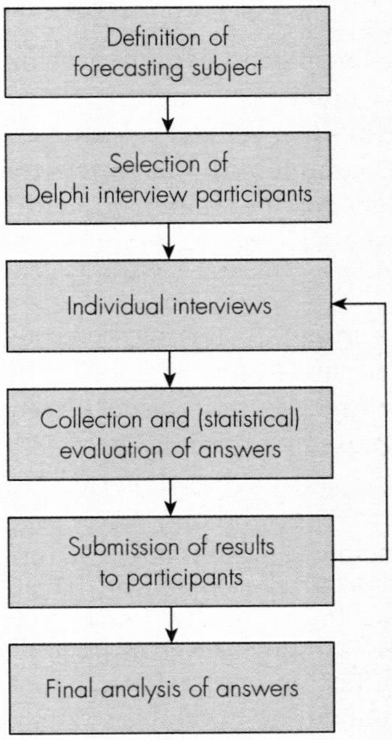

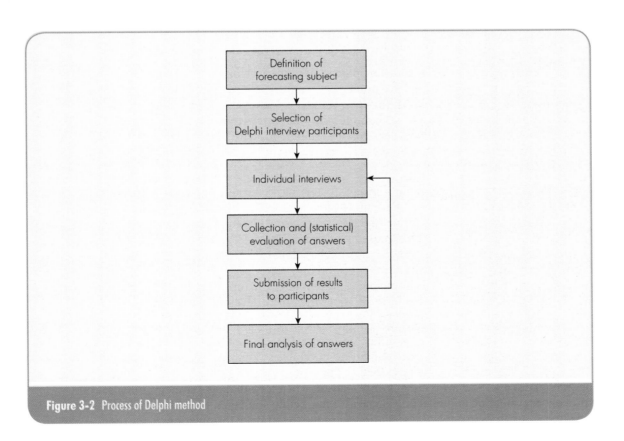

Figure 3-2 Process of Delphi method

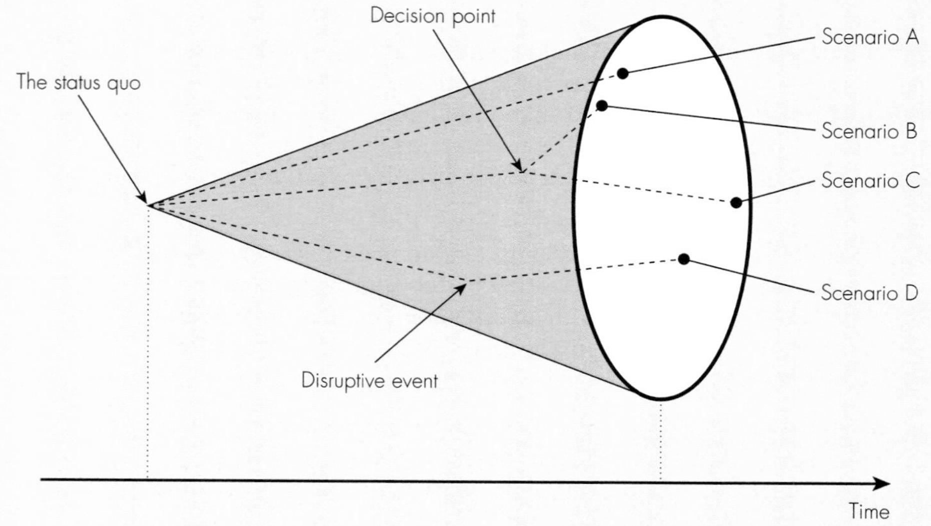

Figure 3-3 Scenario funnel

round, the participants are informed about the overall results on the basis of all interviewees and, against this background, are requested to re-evaluate and, if applicable, modify their opinions from previous rounds. This procedure is used for the purpose of having the experts re-evaluate extreme (and possibly unrealistic) forecasts, so that the process ideally converges to a group opinion.

While most forecasting methods generate only one potential future development, **scenario techniques** outline several potential future developments (scenarios), thus making the method particularly important for industries in which the environment evidences strong discontinuities – as is the case, for example, in the media and telecommunications sectors today. In addition to describing scenarios, the scenario analysis also provides statements with regard to their probability of occurrence (for more details on the scenario technique, see Linneman and Klein 1985; Phelps *et al.* 2001; Schoemaker 1995).

The **scenario funnel** illustrates the underlying concept of creating scenarios (see Figure 3-3): as a rule, developments in the near future are predetermined to a large extent by present conditions (the status quo). The further we look into the future, the wider the spectrum of potential developments, so that the possible deviations from the status quo can be graphically represented as a funnel. This approach provides various scenarios that are extrapolated based on trends and disruptive events (see Figure 3-3). For example, extrapolating a present trend may result in Scenario A. This trend can change when decisions are being taken resulting in Scenario B or C. Disruptive events (i.e. changes in environmental factors such as technology) can also alter the future development (Scenario D).

With regard to the application of the scenario technique in strategy formulation the company can either develop strategies for each scenario identified or develop a strategy for only one scenario (lead scenario). For the latter option the objective should be to develop a strategy that provides sufficient flexibility with regard to the other scenarios, so that a change of strategy is still feasible if the lead scenario does not take shape. Scenarios are not only relevant when formulating a strategy, but also during the process of evaluating and selecting alternative marketing strategies. Royal Dutch Shell was one of the first companies to apply the scenario technique for strategy formulation. Since then it has strongly advocated this approach (see Focus on Marketing 3-3).

Focus on Marketing 3-3 The birth of scenario planning

Scenario planning at Royal Dutch Shell

Thirty years ago, Pierre Wack, a French oil executive with a personal affinity for Indian mystics, realized that strategy as it had been practiced – straight-line extrapolations from the past, forecasts captured in three-ring binders – did little to frame the choices that would define the future. The true role of strategy was to describe a future worth creating – and then to reap the competitive advantages of preparing for it and making it happen. Strategy, in other words, was about telling stories.

Under Wack's influence, Royal Dutch Shell learned the art of strategy as storytelling – creating scenarios about the future. Scenarios are carefully crafted tales that link certainties and uncertainties about the future to the decisions that must be made today. Scenario planning – or 'scenario thinking', as Wack called it – has made Shell an industry leader.

Scenario planning has spread from Shell to other corporate giants. Companies have learned how to frame the future by describing bookend scenarios, stories that offer vastly different trajectories and starkly opposing outcomes.

In the summer of 1970, a delegation from the Club of Rome paid a visit to the System Dynamics Group at MIT's Sloan School of Management. The Club had a request: Help us predict the future of the world.

World3, the MIT computer model, digested 120 variables before calculating that within 20 years the planet would run out of oil.

But a funny thing happened on the way to the future: The prediction turned out to be wrong, largely because in 1973, the oil industry suffered a different catastrophe – one that computer modeling could never have foreseen, but one that Pierre Wack was thinking about.

While World3 was crunching numbers, Wack was presenting a series of stories about possible futures to senior Shell executives. In one scenario, an accident in Saudi Arabia led to the severing of an oil pipeline, which in turn decreased supply. That created a market reaction that increased oil prices, allowing OPEC nations to pump less oil and make more money.

The tale spooked the executives enough to make them reexamine their assumptions about oil price and supply. Was OPEC preparing to increase oil prices? What would be the implications if they did? As a consequence, when OPEC announced its first oil embargo Shell handled the challenges better and faster than the competition. Within two years, Shell moved from being the world's eighth biggest oil company to being the second biggest. Scenario planning had earned its stripes.

Source: Wylie 2002.

Another method for the analysis of the global environment is the **PEST analysis** (also referred to as STEP analysis). The following factors are important in this regard:

- political (e.g. tax policy, tariffs)
- economic (e.g. GDP growth, inflation)
- social (e.g. population growth, health consciousness)
- technological (e.g. R&D intensity, use of the internet).

Including legal, environmental, educational and demographic factors, the approach can take various forms (e.g. PESTLE, STEEPLED).

Table 3-3 Initial strategic situation: central questions when analyzing the market

I. Buyers/customers in the market
- Who are the customers in the market?
- What are the different customer segments in the market?
- What are the basic requirements of the customers?
- How will the basic customer requirements change?
- What changes in customer behavior can be expected?

II. Competitors in the market
- Who are the relevant competitors in the market?
- How likely is the market entry of new competitors and the market exit of existing competitors?
- How will the general competitive conduct change in the market?
- How strong are the market positions of the individual competitors and what changes can be observed in this regard?
- What particular strengths and weaknesses characterize the individual competitors?
- What strategies do the individual competitors pursue?

III. General market characteristics
- How large is the market volume, the current market growth and the estimated future market growth?
- What is the current profit situation of the companies in the market and how will it develop in the future?
- How foreseeable are changes with regard to the stakeholders in the market (not including buyers and competitors, e.g. with respect to the intermediaries)?

3.3 Assessing the Microenvironment: Analysis of the Relevant Market

3.3.1 Central Questions

The analysis of the **relevant market** (microenvironment) is an essential prerequisite for the successful formulation of marketing strategy. Three analytical areas are at the forefront of this interest, and Table 3-3 lists the strategic central questions regarding the analysis of buyers/customers, competitors and the general market characteristics.

The analysis of **buyers/customers in the market** focuses on all buyers present in the relevant market – thus both the current customers of the company as well as potential customers. An important initial question is who is actually present in the relevant market and – related to this – which customer segments can be distinguished in the relevant market. At this point, it should be noted that the identification of customer segments is the basis for deciding whether the company intends to pursue the market development differentiated according to the different customer segments (see the explanation on differentiated market development in Section 3.3.2). If customer segments are sufficiently distinct, such a differentiated market development is recommended.

Furthermore, the basic customer needs and customer behavior are also essential for formulating the marketing strategy. If necessary, this examination has to be differentiated by market segments.

In this context, not only current but also future developments are of particular interest (i.e. changes in customer requirements or behavior such as increased demand for services).

A second set of questions when analyzing the market refers to the analysis of the **competitors in the market** (for an in-depth discussion of competitor analysis, see Day and Wensley 1988). This analysis should be initiated by an identification of the company's competitors. Another key question when formulating the marketing strategy pertains to the potential market entry of new competitors. Here it is of primary importance for the company to evaluate whether new competitors are able to make forays into the market. If this seems to be likely, a proactive response needs to be formulated (e.g. by establishing customer loyalty programs, see Chapter 9).

In connection with the entry of new competitors, it has to be mentioned that a 'blurring' of industry boundaries can be observed in some markets. One example of this development is the merger of telecommunications and information technology. Another important issue is the degree of competitive intensity in the relevant markets.

The final question related to competition in Table 3-3 addresses the **individual competitors**, not the competition as a whole. The question concerning the market position of competitors refers to their success with regard to the marketing objectives related to potential and market success as well as financial marketing objectives (see Section 2.1). The issues here deal with competitors' reputation and image as perceived by the customers, the market shares, the attained customer satisfaction and loyalty, as well as the question of how profitable individual competitors are. In addition to examining the actual situation, the anticipation of changes in the market position (e.g. market share gains by a competitor) is also of particular relevance.

In contrast, the questions concerning a competitor's strengths and weaknesses aim more at internal aspects. They call for an evaluation of factors that form the basis for the current market position of the competitor. Skills of employees, cost position, strength of the distribution network, financial resources (e.g. liquidity, access to additional capital), patents as well as technological knowhow are a few examples of such aspects.

A third set of questions refers to the **general market characteristics** and comprises, for example, questions related to the size of the market and the development of market growth. The analysis of the profit development in the market is a very important aspect, especially since it enables statements about the future behavior of competitors. For example, if the competitors in a market are highly profitable, new competitors are potentially lured and can be expected to enter this particular market.

3.3.2 Selected Methods

In this section, we will first discuss market segmentation as a method used in customer analysis. We will then examine the Five Forces Model of competitive intensity and the Strategic Groups Model. These models are relevant for the second set of central strategic questions regarding competition (see Table 3-3).

In general, **market segmentation** covers two aspects:

1. identification of market segments differentiated according to specific criteria (task of marketing research)
2. development and implementation of segment-specific marketing strategies (how should segments be developed?).

In this section, we will focus on the first aspect.

Market segmentation refers to the process of dividing a market into distinct (sufficiently homogeneous) groups of customers that are similar with respect to particular aspects (such as their needs). Market segmentation is one of the most fundamental concepts in marketing and can be regarded as a dominant concept applied in company practice. A crucial issue is the selection of segmentation criteria.

If effective marketing strategies are to be developed and implemented on the basis of the segmentation results, segmentation should meet the following requirements.

- **Behavioral relevance**: there should be clear differences with respect to customer behavior (especially buying patterns) between the segments.
- **Accessibility/responsiveness**: the members of the segment should be accessible and responsive to marketing campaigns and promotions.
- **Clear differentiation**: the segments should be clearly distinguishable.
- **Measurability**: the criteria on which the segmentation is based (size or purchasing power) should be measurable.
- **Stability over time**: the segmentation should have a certain degree of stability over time with regard to both the segment structure (number and type of segments) and the affiliation of the individual buyers to the segments.
- **Economic feasibility**: it should be possible to develop the segments with reasonable economic effort. This means that a large number of segments with a low demand level in some segments should be avoided.

The segmentation criteria can be applied alone or in combination with one another. Depending on which criteria are used, there are five basic segmentation approaches:

1 sociodemographic market segmentation
2 geographic market segmentation
3 psychographic market segmentation
4 behavioral market segmentation
5 benefit market segmentation.

Of these approaches, **sociodemographic market segmentation** is widely used in marketing practice as the necessary information for the criteria is usually readily available and measurable. Furthermore, segments resulting from sociodemographic segmentation are easy to access. Demographic and socioeconomic criteria can either be applied separately or in combination. For example, in the personal banking sector, segmentation can be based on customer age, marital status and income. Focus on Marketing 3-4 describes sociodemographic segmentation in the global market for furniture.

Market segmentation based on geographical characteristics is referred to as **geographic market segmentation**. Here we distinguish macrogeographic and microgeographic segmentation. Macrogeographic segmentation categorizes buyers by, say, country or city (place of residence of private customers or headquarters of corporate customers). In a microgeographic segmentation approach – which is mostly applied for private end customers – residential areas within a city can be the basis for developing segments. The microgeographic form of segmentation is based on the idea that customers with similar social status, lifestyle and buying patterns live in similar microgeographical areas.

With **psychographic market segmentation**, segments are identified on the basis of lifestyles, personality characteristics or attitudes. Psychographic segmentation has a high degree of behavioral relevance, particularly in the case of high-involvement products (e.g. cars, medical equipment) (see Haley 1985). Another advantage lies in its relatively high stability over time. Nevertheless, the implementation of psychographic segmentation is associated with high expenses (see Kamakura and Wedel 1995).

Focus on Marketing 3-4 Ikea – targeting the global middle class

An article in *Business Week* in 2005 neatly describes Ikea by stating that 'perhaps more than any other company in the world, Ikea has become a curator of people's lifestyles, if not their lives.'

Ikea provides a 'one-stop sanctuary for coolness' at a time when consumers face a plethora of choices for everything they buy. The Ikea store is described like 'a trusted safe zone' – meaning that people can enter and immediately feel that they are a part of a like-minded global tribe, united on various fronts including cost, design and their attitudes to environmental issues. Starbucks and Virgin do a good job at developing a similar feel, but Ikea is widely regarded as the company that is most successful at creating this unique experience.

The Ikea concept has plenty of room to expand as currently the retailer accounts for just 5% to 10% of the furniture market in each country in which it operates. Their CEO, Anders Dahlvig, feels it is important that 'awareness of our brand is much bigger than the size of our company'. That's because Ikea positions itself as far more than just a retailer of furniture. It promotes a lifestyle that customers all over the world embrace. The association customers make with Ikea brand is described as 'a signal that they've arrived, that they have good taste and recognize value'.

Right now, Ikea hosts 410 million shoppers a year in its 226 stores in Europe, Asia, Australia, and the US. However, it also has new markets to explore – consumers in the rapidly growing economies in China and India for instance. As long as customers from Moscow to Beijing and beyond keep striving to enter the middle class, there will be a need for Ikea.

Interestingly, the global middle class that Ikea targets share buying habits as well as values. As the article explains, 'The $120 Billy bookcase, $13 Lack side table, and $190 Ivar storage system are best-sellers worldwide . . . Spending per customer is even similar. According to Ikea, the figure in Russia is $85 per store visit – exactly the same as in affluent Sweden.'

Source: adapted from Capell *et al.* 2005.

Figure 3-4 depicts an example of psychographic market segmentation as applied by a catering business. By evaluating customers according to their attitude towards food (vertical axis) and according to their willingness to experiment (horizontal axis) the company derived six distinct segments.

Behavioral market segmentation identifies actual behavioral patterns, especially the buying or consumption patterns of customers. Very common in company practice is segmentation based on customers' price sensitivity (e.g. differentiation between premium buyers, price-conscious buyers and price-aggressive buyers). This type of segmentation is often useful as such buying patterns help to clearly differentiate between different groups of buyers (e.g. in the airline industry economy travelers exhibit marked behavioral differences when compared to business travelers). However, behavioral segmentation does not explain *why* certain buying patterns can be observed.

Benefit segmentation, on the other hand, uses causal variables – as opposed to descriptive variables – to group customers. Haley (1968) first proposed the idea that customers should be grouped according to the principal benefit sought from a product or service. At its core, this segmentation approach focuses on the question of *how* people assess the different benefits a product offers. In practice, the analysis of the customer's benefit assessment is often conducted by conjoint analysis (for more on 'conjoint analysis', see Appendix).

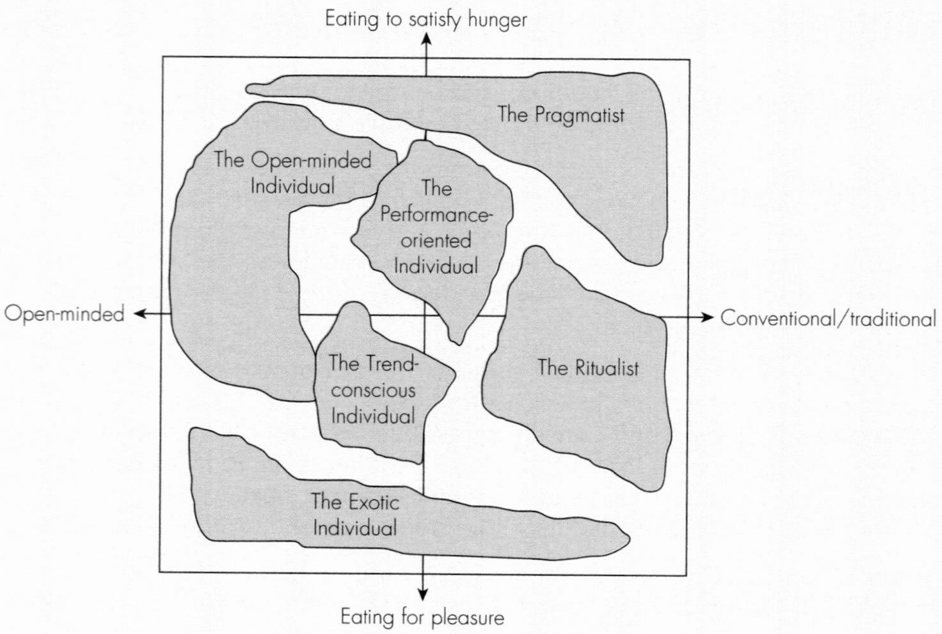

Figure 3-4 Example of a psychographic customer segmentation of a catering company

Benefit segmentation can be illustrated by the example of a railroad company (see Table 3-4). In this example, three segments with different benefit structures were identified. For instance, in the segment 'minimize travel time' customers rated the criteria 'travel time' with 64.2%, whereas this was a less important criterion for the price-sensitive segment (only 17.1%).

Table 3-4 Benefit segmentation illustrated for customers of a railroad company (adapted from Perrey 1998, p. 187)

Benefit criteria	Description	Minimize travel time	Price sensitive	Comfort-oriented
Service	Cleanliness, food and beverage services/catering	2.9%	5.0%	**45.1%**
Furnishings and features	Seat comfort, entertainment, work areas/options	4.6%	8.6%	25.0%
Price	Absolute price in €	23.7%	**60.7%**	4.8%
Travel time	Frequency, delays, speed	**64.2%**	17.1%	9.5%
Social benefits	Waste disposal, disabled accessible	4.6%	8.6%	15.6%

Importance of benefit category rating

This type of segmentation is very relevant for companies as benefit considerations play a key role in buying decisions. In practice the accessibility of the segments can be problematic – frequently, the identified segments have to be described by means of additional segmentation criteria (e.g. demographic or socioeconomic). It should also be noted that the effort and expense involved in developing benefit-based segments is substantial, particularly if a conjoint analysis needs to be conducted.

To summarize, geographic or sociodemographic methods of segmentation do not reflect the underlying needs of customers but their advantages lie in their ease of implementation (accessibility of segments) and low costs. In contrast, psychographic, behavioral and benefit segmentation demonstrate a higher relevance with regard to buying patterns but the identified segments are more difficult to address. The goal conflict between behavioral relevance and accessibility of segments is referred to as the '**dilemma of market segmentation**' (see Bonoma and Shapiro 1984).

Finally, we need to distinguish market segmentation in business-to-customer (B2C) and business-to-business (B2B) markets as there are some important differences (see also Chapter 10). Figure 3-5 shows that some of the criteria applied differ depending on this distinction.

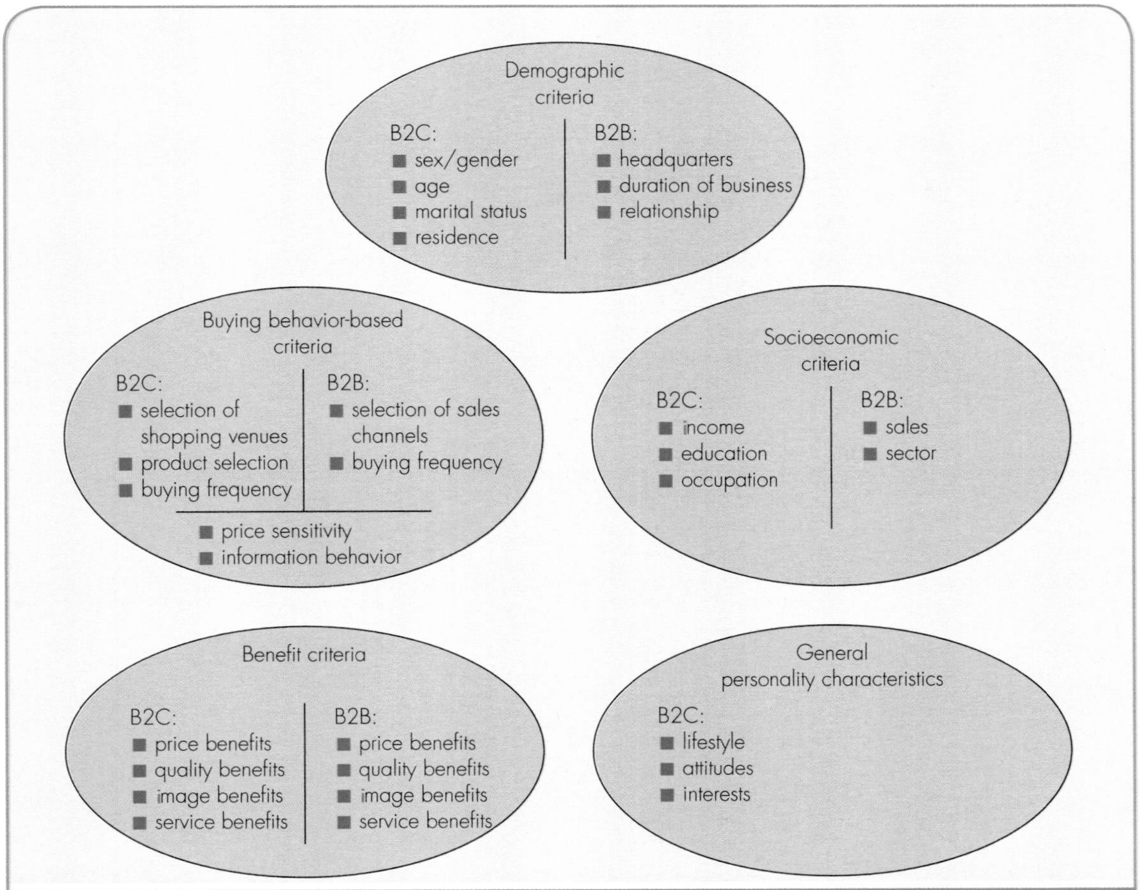

Figure 3-5 Overview of types of segmentation criteria (see Homburg *et al.* 2003)

After discussing market segmentation in the context of customer analysis, we will present two models used by companies within the scope of **analyzing the competitive environment**. These models are:

- the Fives Forces Model, and
- the Strategic Groups Model.

The **Five Forces Model**, developed by Porter (1980), analyzes five forces that determine the attractiveness of an industry. This well-known model considers the following five factors:

1. intensity of rivalry among existing competitors
2. bargaining power of customers
3. bargaining power of suppliers
4. threat of new entrants
5. threat from substitute products.

Figure 3-6 shows an overview of the relevant aspects of each area.

This model, which is based on concepts developed in industrial organizations, represents a classic approach for strategic market analysis. A significant advantage of this model is that it does not restrict the market analysis to the currently existing structures (e.g. the examination of the competitors currently present in the market), but provides a comprehensive analysis of the potential

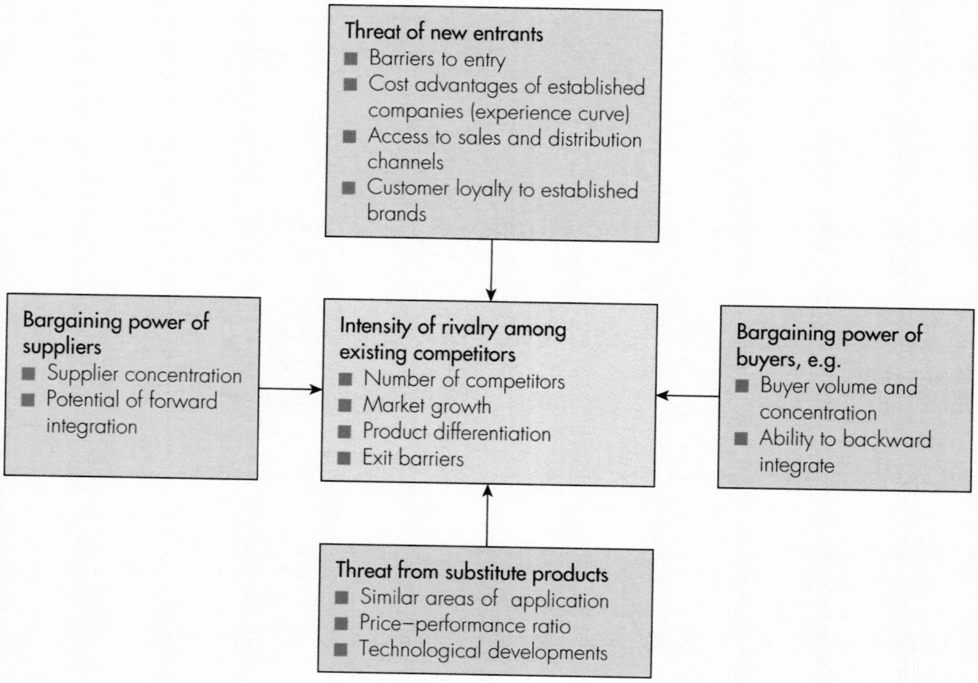

Figure 3-6 The Fives Forces Model (Porter 1980)

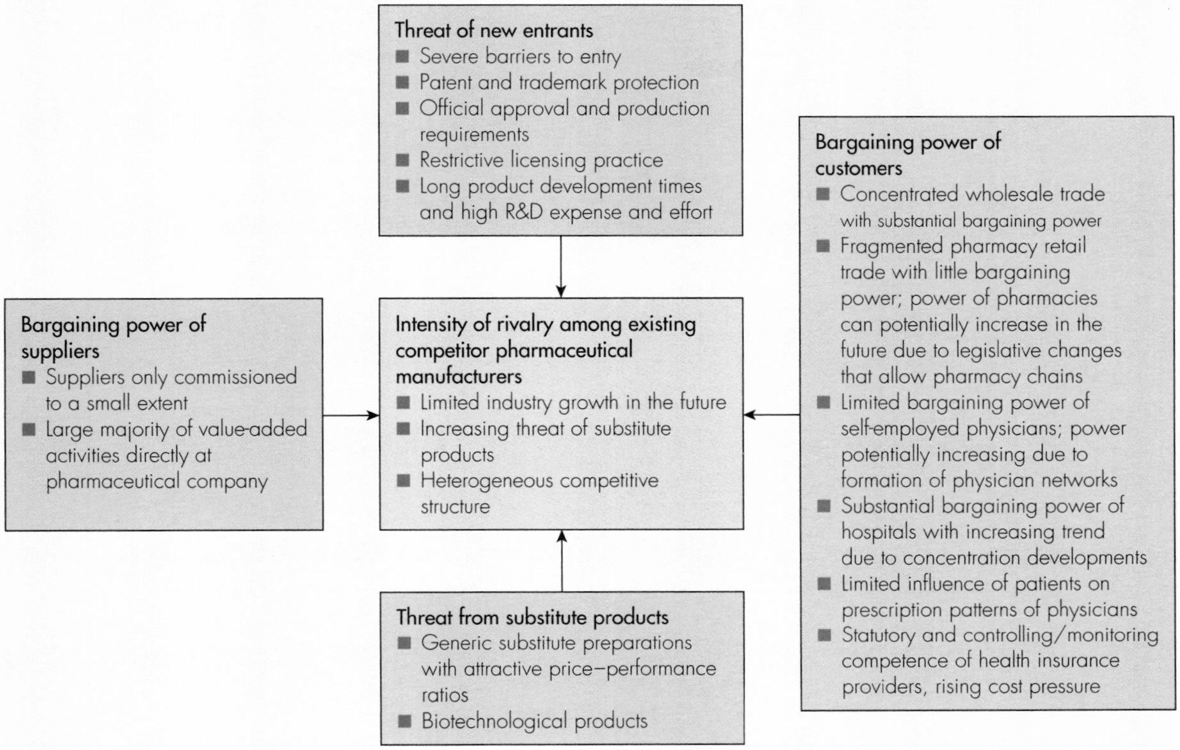

Figure 3-7 Five Forces Model for the pharmaceutical industry in Germany (adapted from Molitor 2000)

influencing factors on market development. The focus is therefore also on strategically relevant questions that are frequently inadequately addressed during the formulation of marketing strategies (e.g. the assessment of the threat of substitute products).

Figure 3-7 shows an application of this model for the pharmaceutical industry. The model facilitates the systematic collection and identification of those forces that have an impact on the profit potential and ability of pharmaceutical firms to serve their customers. These forces have to be taken into account when formulating the marketing strategy.

Another approach based on Porter's (1980) work, which can serve as a tool for systematic market analysis, is the **Strategic Groups Model**. This model is based on the assumption that firms within an industry are usually not homogeneous but differ in the strategic choices that they make (e.g. production, diversification, product differentiation or pricing), even if they pursue a common goal of long-term growth and profitability. This model classifies competitors in strategic groups with each group consisting of firms that are very similar in their corporate strategy. The groups thus show different results from their economic activity (such as profitability).

To illustrate this model, we examine a strategic group analysis in the mechanical engineering industry (see Figure 3-8). In this case, strategic groups are formed by considering two variables: extent of product range and net output ratio. Net output ratio refers to the extent to which a

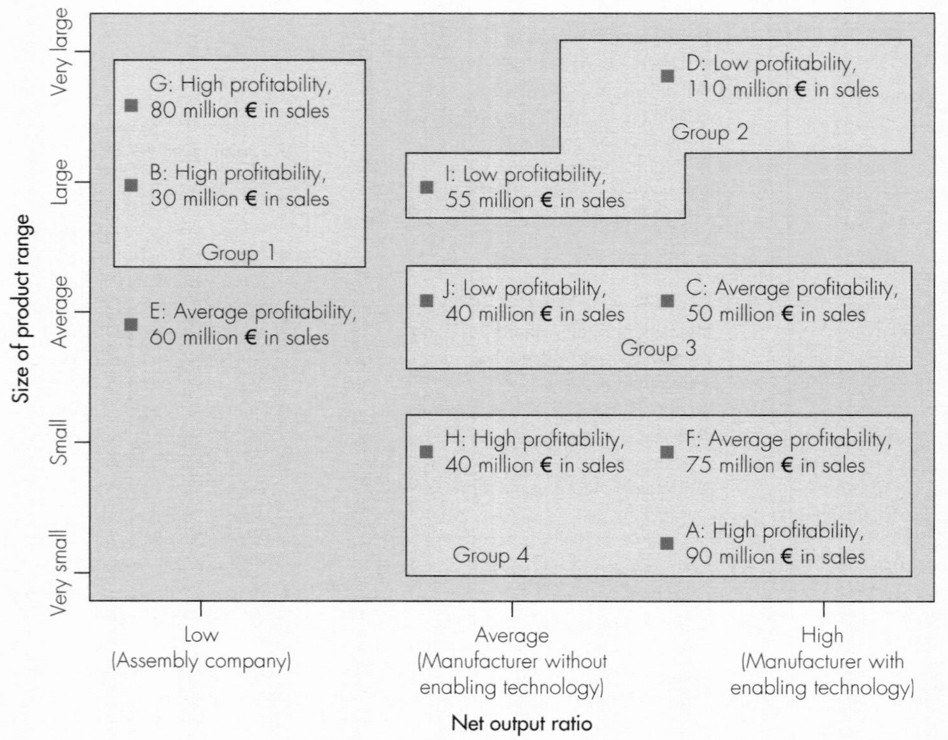

Figure 3-8 Example of an analysis of the strategic group structures of ten mechanical engineering companies (adapted from Homburg 1992, p. 85)

firm buys preliminary products (e.g. raw materials) or intermediate products (e.g. components) in the market as opposed to producing them in-house. Assembly companies have the lowest net output ratio (they purchase finished products and make only small adjustments) and manufacturing companies such as original equipment manufacturers (OEMs) have the highest net output ratio. Four strategic groups emerge from combining these two dimensions (see Figure 3-8):

1. assembly companies with a broad to very broad product range (Group 1)
2. manufacturers with a broad to very broad product range (Group 2)
3. manufacturers with a medium-sized product range (Group 3)
4. manufacturers with a small to very small product range (Group 4).

It is important to point out that firm profitability differs in the identified groups: the highest profitability is observed in Groups 1 and 4, while the lowest profitability is observed in Group 2. This finding illustrates the main objective of strategic group analysis: to explain differences in profitability between competitors in the same industry.

Focus on Marketing 3-5 illustrates an example of a strategic group in the oil industry.

Focus on Marketing 3-5 Example: a strategic group in the oil industry

Playing the game in its own strategic group

For a company in such an old, dirty business as providing oil-field services, Schlumberger Ltd has made its mark in a decidedly newfangled way. The industry leader has maintained its position for most of its 80 years by being far and away the most technologically advanced player in the game.

Today, its menu of services for Big Oil is broader than that of such peers as Halliburton Co. or Baker Hughes Inc. Schlumberger can do everything from sizing up the geology of a site to assisting directional drilling to extract oil, from managing information about reserves and production for super-majors such as Shell Oil Co. to cementing the holes on a completed well.

With oil and gas prices at record levels and exploration budgets bulging, Schlumberger's revenues and profits are surging.

Demand for its high-margin services has propelled the New York company into the No. 5 spot on the *Business Week* 50 this year.

Last year, the company's R&D budget was $506 million – substantially more than any of its competitors, according to brokerage A.G. Edwards Inc. 'Schlumberger has the clear leadership position and is very committed to maintaining that,' says analyst Poe Fratt.

With easy-to-find oil scarce, Big Oil companies are looking to expensive and risky exploration projects deeper in the sea, and Schlumberger technology can improve the chances that wells will find substantial oil or gas reserves.

It's inevitable that another downturn will visit the energy sector, but expect Schlumberger to keep doing what it knows best.

Source: Morrison 2006.

With respect to the application of the Strategic Groups Model in strategic analysis, the following aspects should be noted.

- The knowledge regarding which strategic group can obtain the highest profitability in an industry is obviously key to the design of both the marketing strategy and the corporate strategy as a whole. In the example above, Company D can consider switching to another strategic group to improve profitability.
- Moreover, such an analysis provides a company with a more structured picture of the competitive environment. Here, a differentiation can be made between the competition within one strategic group (intragroup competition) and the competition between companies affiliated with different strategic groups (intergroup competition).
- To a certain degree, strategic group analysis also supports the analysis of the future strategies of the competitors (e.g. if Company D in our example strives to change to a different strategic group in the future by greatly reducing the size of its product range).

3.4 Reading the Market's Mind: Analysis of the Company Situation

3.4.1 Central Questions

When formulating a marketing strategy it is also essential to analyze the **company situation**. There are three focal points within the scope of the company analysis, which are described in Table 3-5:

1 the analysis of the company's situation with regard to the buyers in the market

2 the analysis of the company's situation with respect to the company's own customers

3 the analysis of the company's situation with regard to the competitive environment.

When addressing each of these focal points, the current situation, differences between the various market segments as well as changes in the situation over time should be analyzed.

The analysis of the **company's situation with regard to the buyers in the market** focuses on all buyers – regardless of whether or not they are customers of the company. Two key aspects are the company's image and degree of awareness of both the company and its products. Low levels of awareness can emphasize the need for proactive market development (e.g. by intensifying communication). Moreover, positive image and high awareness among buyers who are not yet customers signal a potential for additional sales. The company can tap into this potential – for example, by intensifying acquisition of new customers.

The questions concerning the **company's situation with respect to its own customers** are guided by the marketing objectives related to potential, market success and financial success (see Section 2.1). In particular, the consideration of customer satisfaction, customer loyalty and untapped sales potential are essential issues when formulating the marketing strategy. Finally, the question of how profitable the company is in developing individual customers and customer segments is relevant too.

Table 3-5 Initial strategic situation: central questions when analyzing the company situation

I. Company's situation with respect to buyers/customers in the market
- What image do buyers have of the company and its products/brands?
- Among buyers, what degree of awareness has been achieved by the company and its products/brands?

II. Company's situation with respect to its own customers
- How satisfied are the customers with the company's services and products?
- How loyal are the customers to the company?
- To what extent does the company reach its customers in terms of the existing sales potential?
- What price level does the company attain with its customers?
- What is the level of customer profitability and what is the level of profitability of individual products with regard to different customers?

III. Company's situation in the competitive environment
- What is the company's (absolute/relative) market share?
- What are the company's strengths/weaknesses as compared to the competition?
- To what extent does the company have sustainable competitive advantages that are both relevant to and perceived by customers?

A central aspect in the **analysis of the company's situation in the competitive environment** addresses the company's **competitive advantages**. This refers to the company's performance relative to competitors and the ability of individual firms to outperform competitors in one or several aspects. Michael Porter (1980) had early pointed out the need for companies to build competitive advantages. In order to be relevant, however, competitive advantages accrue if:

- they are based on attributes relevant and important to customers
- they can be perceived by customers
- they are sustainable over time (i.e. they should not have the potential to be quickly or easily adopted or imitated by competitors).

Competitive advantages can particularly be explained by the resource-based view of the firm (see Barney 2002). This concept focuses on idiosyncratic and difficult-to-copy resources that are controlled by a firm. The exploitation of these resources can give rise to the competitive advantages discussed above.

Further sources of competitive advantage are **core competencies**. This concept is very closely related to the idea of the resource-based view of the firm (Barney 2002). Prahalad and Hamel define core competencies as 'the collective learning in the organization, especially how to coordinate diverse production skills and integrate multiple streams of technologies' (Prahalad and Hamel 1990, p. 82). Core competencies can basically be obtained in any step of the value chain. Their key characteristic is that they can be leveraged across the entire corporation and can thus be used in multiple business units and for the production of different products. Therefore they are especially relevant in the context of diversification strategies. Focus on Marketing 3-6 illustrates the concept of core competencies.

Focus on Marketing 3-6 Illustration of the concept of core competencies

Consider 3M's competence with sticky tape. In dreaming up businesses as diverse as 'Post-it' notes, magnetic tape, photographic film, pressure-sensitive tapes, and coated abrasives, the company has brought to bear widely shared competencies in substrates, coatings, and adhesives and devised various ways to combine them. Indeed 3M has invested consistently in them. What seems to be an extremely diversified portfolio of businesses belies a few shared core competencies.

In the core competencies underlying them, disparate businesses become coherent. It is Honda's core competence in engines and power trains that gives it a distinctive advantage in car, motorcycle, lawn mower, and generator businesses. Canon's core competence in optics, imaging, and microprocessor controls have enabled it to enter, even dominate, markets as seemingly diverse as copiers, laser printers, cameras, and image scanners.

Source: Prahalad and Hamel 1990, pp 82ff.

The formulation of a marketing strategy should be based on the existing competitive advantages. If competitive advantages cannot be identified, the marketing strategy should necessarily facilitate their establishment. But, as pointed out before, it is not only important to establish a competitive advantage; in addition, marketing strategy has to be particularly geared towards its sustainability over time (Barney 2002). This proves to be increasingly difficult to achieve as more and more industries become unstable and unpredictable. Product design and life cycles shorten, established technologies are readily available while new ones emerge, and market boundaries are increasingly indeterminate. As a result, established firms reposition themselves, unexpected outsiders enter the market, competition rapidly escalates and competitive advantages erode fast. This situation, where markets are in constant disequilibrium and change is permanent, is referred to as **hypercompetition** (D'Aveni 1995). Market success can no longer be based on one sustainable competitive advantage but needs to build on a series of temporary advantages instead. In hypercompetitive markets the fastest player is in the best position. Therefore, in this environment proactive disruption of one's own competitive advantage, creativity, speed and flexibility are key success factors.

Against this background, so called **dynamic capabilities** are of vital importance for a company. Teece *et al.* (1997) define dynamic capabilities as 'the firm's ability to integrate, build, and reconfigure internal and external competences to address rapidly changing environments'. This concept is similar to the concept of core competencies but places more emphasis on the dynamic aspect of competition.

Kim and Mauborgne (2004, 2005) have introduced the concept of the **blue ocean strategy** to deal with hypercompetition. In their view, markets can be divided into red and blue oceans: red oceans represent the existing markets with clearly defined industry boundaries and companies striving to beat the competition in terms of an increased share of the existing demand. On the other side, blue oceans display all the markets not yet existent. Here, demand is created rather than being subject to rivalry. Blue ocean strategy refers to creating uncontested market space and making the competition irrelevant, either by inventing new industries (e.g. eBay) or by altering the boundaries of existing industries (e.g. Cirque du Soleil merging the circus and theater industries). A common feature of blue ocean strategies is that they neglect the traditional trade-off between differentiation and low cost. Additionally, blue ocean strategies are based upon core competencies while at the same time companies pursuing blue ocean strategies do not use the competition as a benchmark. As such, Kim and Mauborgne's concept is challenging the idea of competitive advantages. Further examples of blue ocean creations are Dell's built-to-order PCs and Ford's introduction of the Model T in 1908, since both involved unprecedented customer experiences.

3.4.2 Selected Methods

Market research plays a key role in the analysis of the company situation (for detailed information on 'market research' please refer to the Appendix). For instance, indicators such as the image and level of awareness of a company on the part of the buyers as well as customers' satisfaction and loyalty can be evaluated in market research studies (e.g. with 'surveys', see Appendix). The profitability of customers and products is determined on the basis of company-internal sales and cost information.

In the following, we will briefly discuss three concepts that can facilitate an analysis of the company situation:

1 value chain analysis

2 benchmarking concept

3 strengths, weaknesses, opportunities and threats (SWOT) analysis.

Value chain analysis was introduced by Porter (1980). This type of analysis identifies sources of customer benefits and thus potential competitive advantages rooted in individual company activities. Possible competitive advantages are the relative cost position and differentiation with regard to the competition (see Section 4.1.2). In order to identify these advantages the company's business process is separated into a series of value-generating activities, which is referred to as value chain (divided into primary and supporting activities – see Figure 3-9). The firm's profitability depends on how well and efficiently it can perform these activities and in doing so it can create 'value added' for its customers (and realize the profit margin depicted in Figure 3-9). Value chain analysis thus assumes

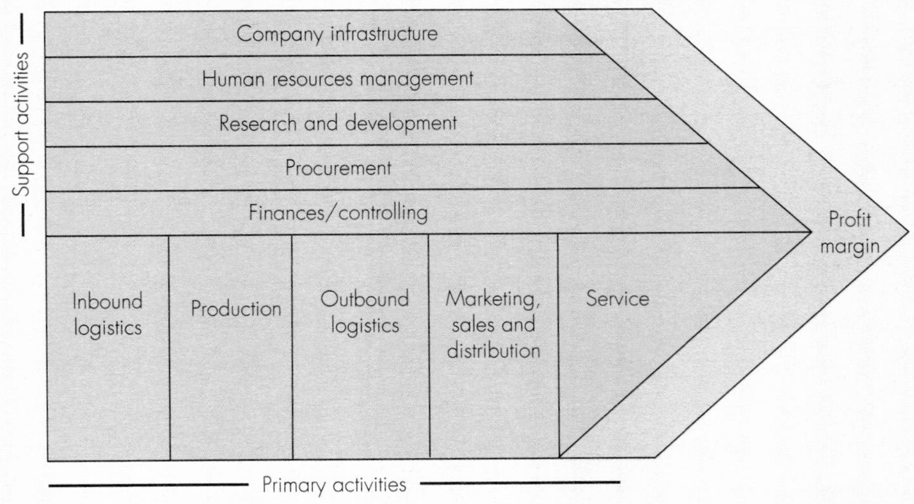

Figure 3-9 Value chain of a company (adapted from Porter 1980)

that each of these activities has the potential to establish a competitive advantage vis-à-vis the competition. At each level of the value chain, resources and core competencies can be analyzed (see Barney 2002). Consequently, the value chain represents a systematic approach for the identification of actual or potential sources of competitive advantage.

Within the value chain model, activities are categorized into primary and support activities. In addition, the profit margin is recorded as the difference between created value and incurred cost (see Figure 3-9).

Value chain analysis examines the individual activities with regard to the extent that they represent added value to the customers and their level of influence on the cost position of the company. On the one hand, such information can identify those activities that should be eliminated by the company. This can emerge in particular in situations where high costs yield only marginal benefits. Second, such information can be used to decide whether these activities should be carried out by the company itself or by external partners (outsourcing).

Another approach to analyzing the company situation is **benchmarking**, which can particularly be applied for analyzing the company's situation in the competitive environment. During the course of the analysis, companies can evaluate various aspects of their business by means of standardized benchmarks. Of particular interest is a comparison with 'best practice' companies. This comparison can identify approaches for improving the company's own performance relative to that of the competition.

Both benchmarking and value chain analysis are tools that extend far beyond marketing; they can also provide input and ideas for the design of corporate strategy. From a marketing aspect, benchmarking, for example, can address delivery processes (e.g. delivery times), customer service activities (e.g. response times), as well as sales and distribution activities (e.g. cost aspects).

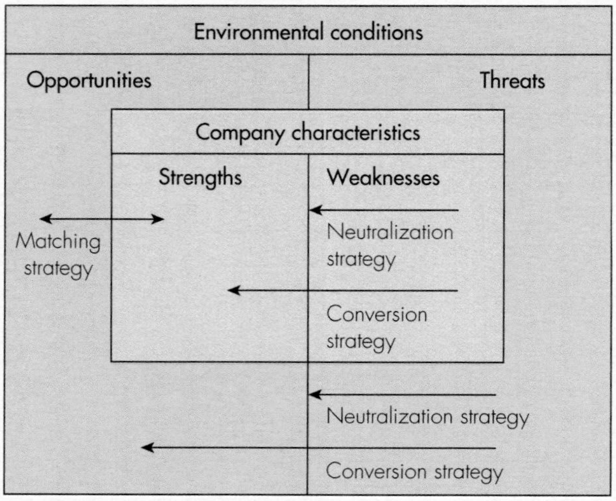

Figure 3-10 The concept of SWOT analysis (adapted from Piercy 1992, p. 260)

On the whole, it can be said that the benchmarking concept may contribute to an analysis of the company situation, with a special focus on analyzing the company's situation in the competitive environment. Advantageous here is the fact that the company's situation is evaluated on the basis of a comparison with the actual situation of the competitors and therefore aims at a high level of objectivity. However, benchmarking should not be overemphasized within the scope of a strategic analysis as it applies more to an optimization of operative efficiency than to the strategic orientation. A strong reliance on benchmarking may lead to companies copying other companies rather than creatively searching for innovative approaches to serve the market (ultimately, this can lead to competitive mediocrity).

SWOT analysis (the analysis of **S**trengths, **W**eaknesses, **O**pportunities and **T**hreats) primarily addresses the company situation but can be viewed as an integrated approach that combines analyzes of the macroenvironment, microenvironment and the company, as examined in this chapter. In particular, the company-external opportunities and threats are compared to the company-internal strengths and weaknesses (see Piercy 1992; Sudharshan 1995).

Based on this comparison, a structured development of marketing strategies can take place. Two strategy types are differentiated: **matching strategies** aim to seize an opportunity through a company-internal strength; in contrast, **conversion/neutralization strategies** address weaknesses or threats and aim to convert weaknesses/threats into strengths/opportunities or at least neutralize weaknesses/threats. Figure 3-10 illustrates this principle for the design of marketing strategies.

The main benefits of SWOT analysis are its simplicity and integrative nature. During the course of a strategic analysis, the method systematically guides companies through the process of reconciling external opportunities and threats with internal strengths and weaknesses.

Summary

In this chapter, we focused on the analysis of the initial strategic situation, the first step of the strategy development process as outlined in Chapter 2. The analysis of the initial strategic situation deals with three areas: global environmental factors, market conditions and the company situation. The analysis of the global company environment focuses on developments in society, macroeconomics, politics, law and technology. The aim is to proactively detect and predict changes in these fields in order to align the marketing strategy accordingly. Methods suited to analyzing the global company environment include early warning/early intelligence systems, forecasting methods and scenario techniques.

The analysis of market conditions includes buyers/customers in the market, competitors and general market characteristics. One important method for customer analysis is market segmentation. Market segmentation aims at dividing markets into homogeneous subgroups of customers that are similar with respect to particular aspects, such as sociodemographic variables or behavioral patterns.

With regard to the analysis of the competitive environment, the Five Forces Model and the Strategic Groups Model were discussed. Whereas the Five Forces Model incorporates several factors influencing the current and prospective market structure, the Strategic Groups Model investigates the strategic choices of groups of competitors, and their economic outcomes.

Subsequently, we discussed methods that help to analyze the company situation with respect to the buyers in the market, the company's own customers and the competitive environment. Important instruments here are value chain analysis, benchmarking and SWOT analysis. The objective of value chain analysis is the identification of sources of customer benefits rooted in individual company activities. With the help of this method, activities that do not provide 'value added' can be detected and possibly eliminated. Benchmarking refers to a comparison of different aspects of the company with other, 'best practice', companies. Finally, integrated SWOT analysis merges the analysis of the global environment, market conditions and the company situation in order to derive marketing strategies that take into consideration the strengths and weaknesses of the company, as well as the threats and opportunities of the environment.

Case Study: Zara, a Spanish Success Story

In a recent article from CNN, a Harvard researcher stated that 'Zara . . . has turned control over garment factories into a competitive advantage.' How has this been possible?

The Spanish firm Zara, owned by Inditex the fashion distributor, is unique in many ways. As of April 2008, it has more than 1,100 shops in 68 countries worldwide but has never run an advertising campaign. Zara sells clothes but also designs and makes them. As it makes the clothes itself, it can react quickly to changing market trends. Zara's retailing rivals Gap and H&M can take up to nine months to get new lines into their shops, whereas Zara takes just two to three weeks. Its success has led to it being described as 'possibly the most innovative and devastating retailer in the world', by LVMH [Louis Vuitton Moët Hennessy SA – an international group with over 50 luxury brands] fashion director Daniel Piette. This exciting new model has been described as one that 'breaks all the rules of the apparel industry as it has developed over the last two decades', that is, to 'contract out all production and spend obscene amounts to advertise your brand'.

All of Zara's operations are co-ordinated from the company's headquarters on an industrial estate in Sabon-Arteixo, outside La Coruña in Spain. Its success lies in it retaining complete control of every part of its business, from design to production, and finally, to distribution. By managing the entire process from factory to shop floor, Zara can react swiftly to the ever-changing trends that appeal to its fashion-conscious customers, providing a 'newness' and exclusivity that has taken Europe by storm.

Case Study (Continued)

The process begins with a team of over 200 designers, responsible for the creation of the original design for the item of clothing. The cloth is then selected and cut, and sent on for sewing to co-operatives and workshops based in northern Portugal and the surrounding area of Galicia. The clothes are finished off at La Coruña before being shipped out twice a week to all its shops. Shoppers addicted to the Zara brand know exactly when the deliveries will be scheduled to arrive at their local branch. Some dedicated customers even turn up before opening time on delivery days to be the first to pick up the latest lines!

The Zara shop managers also play a key role in this process, as they report back every day to designers in La Coruña on what has and has not sold in their stores. In just a few days the feedback can be used to decide which product lines and colors are kept, which are altered, and whether new lines need to be designed. All this happens incredibly rapidly, and as well as being very responsive to customer needs, the system is also very efficient as it means the company can keep its stocks low and keep costs down. Zara's design team produce a staggering 11,000 different designs every year, and the designs that appear are directly related to the demands of its customers.

Sources: Zara, a Spanish success story (http://edition.cnn.com/BUSINESS/programs/yourbusiness/stories2001/zara/), 6.7.2007, and www.inditex.com; image from www.inditex.com.

Discussion Questions

1. Outline the steps involved in the analysis of a company's initial strategic situation.
2. Illustrate Zara's competitive advantage within the apparel industry on the basis of a value chain analysis.

Case Study: Molecular Weight – BASF and the Chemical Industry

An article from *The Economist* from November 2006 explores the unique business complex of BASF in Germany and how its premises comprise one of its key competitive advantages.

In German, the BASF headquarters is known as the *Verbund.* Jürgen Hambrecht, the chief executive of BASF, describes his company's sprawling complex of pipes, towers and storage tanks as the 'ultimate business cluster'. Covering an area of over ten square kilometres (four square miles), it is the biggest integrated chemical site in the world.

Case Study (Continued)

The article describes the site's efficiency as legendary. The key to this efficiency is extracting the last drop of value from every chemical reaction that occurs on the premises. It makes use of the numerous by-products from each process that in other places are often sold or shipped to another factory for further processing. At the *Verbund*, the remainder of one process is used to make something else, often just a few hundred metres away.

As *The Economist* states, this saves BASF a fortune:

'Compared with having, say, 70 separate factories some 100km apart, BASF calculates its cluster enjoys annual savings of €300m ($380m) in logistics, €150m in energy and €50m in infrastructure.'

In the wider business context, chemical companies can find they are vulnerable to changes in the price of raw materials. BASF hopes to gain some protection using a cluster effect, by investing directly in these raw materials – for example, as long ago as 1969 it bought Wintershall, an oil producer, which has proved to be a useful hedge against the ever-increasing prices of oil.

The Economist points out some dangers inherent in BASF's tactics however, as it recognises that the 'conglomerate-building' approach of the *Verbund* could lack the flexibility to cope with rapid market changes. But BASF could vary the concept to overcome this, by creating a radical new 'virtual' *Verbund*. This could take the form of 'a large chemical site where a number of independent companies could voluntarily work together to achieve the same economies of scale, but use different processes as market conditions change'.

Source: Molecular weight – BASF and the chemical industry. © The Economist Newspaper Limited, London 04/11/2006. Image from BASF website www.corporate.basf.com.

Discussion Questions

1. Outline the steps involved in the analysis of a company's initial strategic situation.
2. Select appropriate tools for each of these steps and analyze BASF's strategic situation within the chemical industry.

Key Terms

References

Barney, J. (2002) *Gaining and Sustaining Competitive Advantage* (2nd edn). Upper Saddle River.

Bonoma, T. and Shapiro, B. (1984) Evaluating market segmentation approaches, *Industrial Marketing Management*, 13, 4, 257–268.

Capell, K., Sains, A., Lindblad, C., Palmer, A.T., Bush, J., Roberts, D. and Hall, K. (2005) Ikea, *Business Week*, 3959, 96–106.

Christensen, C., Suarez, F. and Utterback, J. (1998) Strategies for survival in fast-changing industries, *Management Science*, 44, 12, 207–220.

D'Aveni, R.A. (1995) Coping with hypercompetition: utilizing the new 7Ss framework, *Academy of Management Executive*, 9, 3, 45–57.

Day, G. and Wensley, R. (1988) Assessing advantage: a framework for diagnosing competitive superiority, *Journal of Marketing*, 52, 2, 1–20.

Economist, The (2005) Hey, big-spender, 377, 8455, 59–60.

Economist, The (2006) Molecular weight – BASF and the chemical industry, © The Economist Newspaper Limited, London 04/11/2006, 80–81.

Haley, R.I. (1968) Benefit segmentation: a decision oriented tool, *Journal of Marketing*, 32, 3, 30–35.

Haley, R.I. (1985) *Developing Effective Communications Strategy: A Benefit Segmentation Approach*. New York.

Homburg, C. (1992) Wettbewerbsanalyze mit dem Konzept der strategischen Gruppen, *Marktforschung & Management*, 36, 2, 83–87.

Homburg, C., Schäfer, H. and Schneider, J. (2003) *Sales Excellence: Vertriebsmanagement mit System* (3rd edn). Wiesbaden.

Kamakura, W. and Wedel, M. (1995) Life-style segmentation with tailored interviewing, *Journal of Marketing Research*, 32, 3, 308–317.

Kim, W.C. and Mauborgne, R. (2004) Blue ocean strategy, *Harvard Business Review*, 82, 10, 76–84.

Kim, W.C. and Mauborgne, R. (2005) *Blue Ocean Strategy: How to Create Uncontested Market Space and Make the Competition Irrelevant*. Boston, Mass.

Linneman, R. and Klein, H. (1985) Using scenarios in strategic decision making, *Business Horizons*, 28, 1, 64–74.

Molitor, H. (2000) *Absatzsystem, Wettbewerb und Marktbearbeitungsalternativen bei verschreibungspflichtigen Arzneimitteln*. Berlin.

Morris, R. (1997) *Early Warning Indicators of Corporate Failure: A Critical Review of Previous Research and Further Empirical Evidence*. Ashgate.

Morrison, M. (2006) Free-flowing technology, *Business Week*, 3978, 70.

Oliver, R. (1999) Strategy in the biotech age, *Journal of Business Strategy*, 20, 6, 7–10.

Parasuraman, A. and Zinkhan, G. (2002) Marketing to and serving customers through the internet: an overview and research agenda, *Journal of the Academy of Marketing Science*, 30, 4, 286–295.

Perrey, J. (1998) *Nutzenorientierte Marktsegmentierung: Ein integrativer Ansatz zum Zielgruppenmarketing im Verkehrsdienstleistungsbereich*. Wiesbaden.

Phelps, R., Chan, C. and Kapsalis, S. (2001) Does scenario planning affect performance? Two exploratory studies, *Journal of Business Research*, 51, 3, 223–232.

Piercy, N. (1992) *Market-Led Strategic Change: Making Marketing Happen in Your Organization*. Oxford.

Porter, M. (1980) *Competitive Strategy*. New York.

Prahalad, C.K. and Hamel, G. (1990) The core competence of the corporation, *Harvard Business Review*, 68, May–June, 79–91.

Rigby, D., Chen, A., D'Arpizio, C. and Jilla, C. (2006) The new laws of luxury marketing, *Harvard Business Review China*, 4 January.

Schoemaker, P. (1995) Scenario planning: a tool for strategic thinking, *Sloan Management Review*, 36, 2, 25–40.

Smith, M. (2002) The impact of shopbots on electronic markets, *Journal of the Academy of Marketing Science*, 30, 4, 446–454.

Sudharshan, D. (1995) *Marketing Strategy*. Englewood Cliffs, NJ.

Teece, D.J., Pisano G. and Shuen, A. (1997) Dynamic capabilities and strategic management, *Strategic Management Journal*, 18, 7, 509–533.

Varadarajan, P. and Yadav, M. (2002) Marketing strategy and the internet: an organizing framework, *Journal of the Academy of Marketing Science*, 30, 4, 296–312.

Wylie, I. (2002) There is no alternative . . . , *Fastcompany*, 60, July, 106.

Yoffie, B. (1996) Competing in the age of digital convergence, *California Management Review*, 38, 4, 31–53.

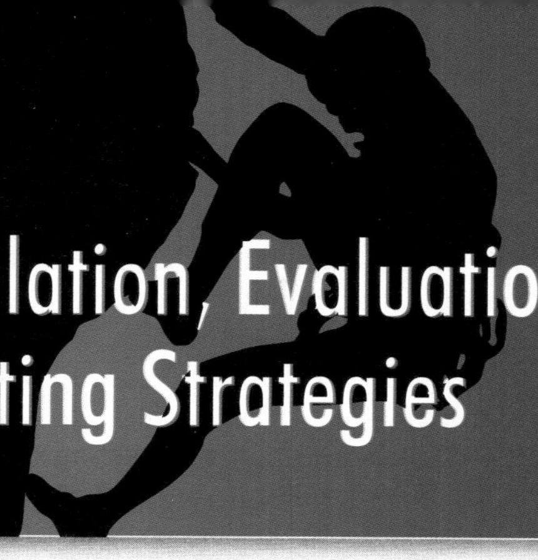

CHAPTER 4

Formulation, Evaluation and Selection of Marketing Strategies

Contents

Learning Objectives

In this chapter you will become familiar with:

- the different aspects to be taken into consideration when formulating a marketing strategy
- the basic design options within the various aspects of a marketing strategy
- the most important portfolio models for supporting the formulation of marketing strategies
- the key criteria that should be applied in the evaluation of marketing strategies
- the options for applying formal decision-making models when selecting marketing strategies.

In accordance with the strategic planning process discussed in Chapter 2, and following the situation analysis presented in Chapter 3, this chapter describes the steps for formulating and evaluating strategies, and selecting suitable strategy alternatives. **Strategy formulation** takes into account aspects such as the objectives that are being pursued, the targeted customer group(s), the intended customer benefits to be offered and the basic design of the marketing mix. In Section 4.1, we will first define the concept of marketing strategy by outlining central questions that a marketing strategy is supposed to provide answers for. Subsequently, in Section 4.2, we will present concepts that can support and facilitate the formulation of marketing strategies. In Section 4.3 we will close this chapter with some concluding remarks.

4.1 Central Questions for the Formulation of Marketing Strategies

In order to structure the discussion of marketing strategy, we introduce a set of key questions that need to be addressed in the course of formulating a marketing strategy. Figure 4-1 provides an overview of these key questions. The following sections will discuss each of these questions in more detail.

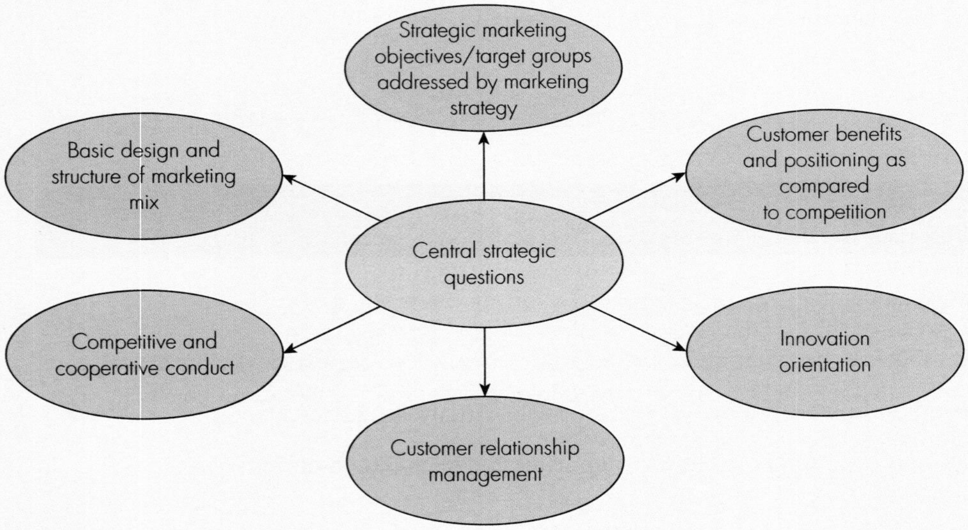

Figure 4-1 Central questions for formulating marketing strategies

4.1.1 Where do we go from Here? Questions Regarding Strategic Marketing Objectives and Target Groups

These central questions deal with the issue of **what** should be achieved (strategic marketing objectives) and **which** customers should be reached (target groups of the marketing strategy). Table 4-1 provides a list of the most important questions in this respect.

Table 4-1 Central questions concerning strategic marketing objectives and the target groups of the marketing strategy

- Which market segments should be developed by the company and what priorities should be set for the individual segments?
- How should the marketing resources be allocated with regard to developing existing customers and acquiring new ones?
- What marketing objectives related to potential should be achieved for all market segments/for the individual segments and by what particular point in time?
- What marketing objectives related to market success should be achieved for all market segments/for the individual segments and by what particular point in time?
- What marketing objectives related to financial success should be achieved for all market segments/for the individual segments and by what particular point in time?

The first question concerns the issue of **which market segments should be developed** (see Section 3.1 for how to identify market segments). To this end, we have to distinguish different coverage strategies (i.e. the company needs to choose between complete or partial market coverage). In the case of partial market coverage, the company restricts itself to the development of selected segments. Complete coverage implies the targeting of all identified segments.

Once the company has identified the segments it intends to target, it has to tackle the question of the **priority with which the individual market segments should be developed.** This is necessary as companies have limited resources and some segments are more attractive than others. Portfolio methods (see Section 4.2) can explore this question.

A second question related to the target group(s) addresses the distribution of the marketing resources with respect to the **development of existing customers** and the **acquisition of new customers.** According to the concept of customer relationship management (see Chapter 9), optimizing business relationships with existing customers should be the focus of market development. Research shows that the acquisition of new customers is considerably more costly than maintaining existing ones (for an overview of this approach, see Reichheld and Sasser 1990).

The recommendation to focus on existing customers is plausible, and studies have proven that this marketing strategy can be successful (see e.g. Blattberg and Deighton 1996; Capon *et al.* 1990; Reichheld and Sasser 1990). However, a company needs to spend a certain portion of its marketing resources to acquire new customers. This is especially important in the early phases of the market life cycle (see Section 2.2.3). It is also possible that the sales potential of existing customers has essentially been saturated, so that significant growth potential can be explored only by acquiring new customers. In pursuing both – the development of existing customers and the acquisition of new customers – the most attractive customers should be treated as a priority. The customer portfolio and the customer lifetime value (CLV), for example, can assist in prioritizing individual customers and customer segments (see Chapter 9).

Subsequent to these considerations, the *specific marketing objectives* need to be determined. Here, the differentiation between marketing objectives related to potential, market success and financial success (see Section 2.1, Figure 2-2) can be applied. As Table 4-1 shows, these objectives should be defined for both the market segments as a whole as well as for the individual segments. The more dissimilar the individual segments and the more differentiated the company's approach to developing the segments, the more important is this differentiation by market segment.

4.1.2 In the Catbird Seat? Questions Regarding Customer Benefits and Positioning Relative to the Competition

A second category of key strategic questions is related to the general decision of what customer benefits should be created and to the company's basic strategic positioning relative to the competition (see Table 4-2). These two questions reflect the relationships in the 'strategic triangle' (see Figure 4-2).

With regard to the question of **what customer benefits the company should create**, it should first be emphasized that, in principle, customer benefits arise when **customer needs are satisfied** (for a discussion regarding 'customer needs', refer to the Appendix). Here it is crucial that the benefits sought from a particular product or service are based on genuine and actual customer needs, and that the company is able to (at least partially) satisfy these needs. In this context, different customer benefits can be offered for different segments (especially when segments vary greatly in terms of customer needs).

It can be helpful to categorize **benefits** with respect to the question of which benefits to offer. In this context, we differentiate two types of benefit: core benefits and additional benefits.

Core benefits relate to fundamental aspects of the company's products and services. They result from satisfying the basic customer needs with regard to a specific product or service offer (see Anderson and Narus 2003). **Additional benefits,** in contrast, arise from the offer of additional services and features extending beyond the basic needs of customers. Here, a need on the part of the customer exists as well, but the customer does not necessarily expect that need to be met by the company. For example, a customer of a car repair shop expects the car to be repaired and to run smoothly (core benefit). An additional benefit can arise if, say, the car repair shop provides the customer with a rental car for the duration of the repair job.

In order to compete effectively in the market, companies must provide core benefits. This can be regarded as the minimum prerequisite for serving a market. Even though additional benefits are 'add-ons' providing these can be an important basis for a differentiation strategy.

Table 4-2 Central strategic questions concerning customer benefits and positioning as compared to the competition

- What benefits should the company offer its customers?
- What competitive advantages is the company striving for?

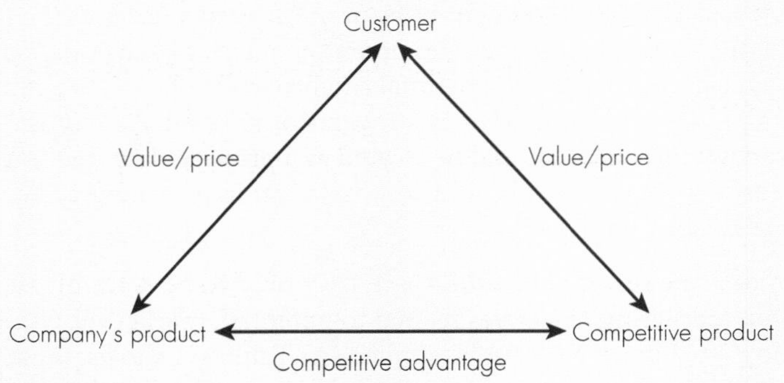

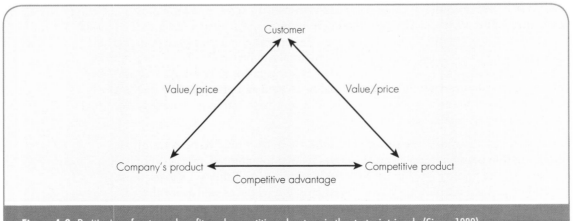

Figure 4-2 Positioning of customer benefits and competitive advantage in the strategic triangle (Simon 1989)

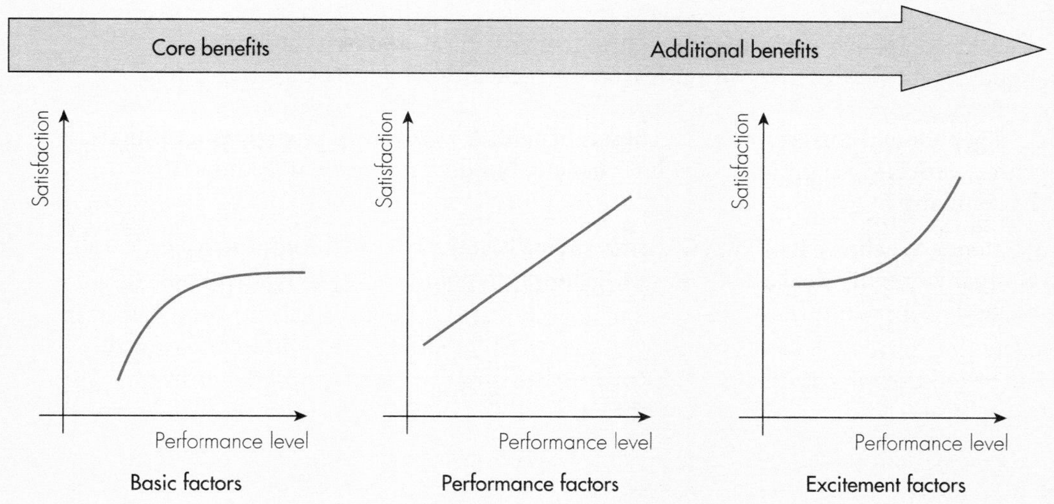

Figure 4-3 Customer satisfaction effects in relation to various performance factors (adapted from Oliver 1997, p. 152)

Depending on whether a core benefit or an additional benefit is achieved, company services and products are differentiated into **basic factors, performance factors and excitement factors**. These factors are characterized by a different impact of the performance level on the overall satisfaction of the customer (see Figure 4-3). Accordingly, with basic factors, a low performance level leads to dissatisfaction, while a high performance level does not result in a high degree of satisfaction since customers expect a high performance level. However, in the case of excitement factors, a high performance level leads to high customer satisfaction (for more on 'customer satisfaction', see Appendix), while a low performance level does not lead to dissatisfaction, since the customer does not have any strong expectations with regard to this performance level. When formulating the marketing strategy it is therefore of importance to assess which of the additional services and features constitute excitement factors for customers.

We can identify various other types of benefits (see Anderson *et al.* 1993; Anderson and Thomas 1997; Anderson and Narus 1998; Ulaga 1999), including those listed below.

- **Functional benefits** originate from the basic functions of the product and are associated with its benefit. Mobility is the functional benefit of a car.
- **Economic benefits** also result from the product features. A car provides an economic benefit if it is fuel-efficient.
- **Process-related benefits** arise from easy procurement or business processes that facilitate company–customer interactions. For example, many car dealers will offer to pick up the customer's car if it needs to be repaired.
- **Emotional benefits** emerge from the positive feelings and emotions evoked by a product, for example the pride owners take in their luxury cars.
- Like emotional benefits, **social benefits** are also associated with positive feelings. A social benefit results when other people admire the owner of a prestigious car.

The question of **competitive advantages being pursued** relates to how the company wants to differentiate itself relative to its competitors. As already discussed in Section 3.4.1, a competitive advantage refers to the company's performance relative to competitors and to its ability to outperform competitors. In view of the relationship between customer benefits and competitive advantage, it is important to note that a performance feature can serve as a basis for a competitive advantage only if it generates a corresponding customer benefit. A widespread phenomenon is that performance features generate a significant customer benefit, but do not represent a competitive advantage for the company.

How a company intends to achieve its competitive advantage is at the core of the **competitive strategy** of the company or individual SBU. Figure 4-4 shows a typology of the basic (generic) competitive strategies.

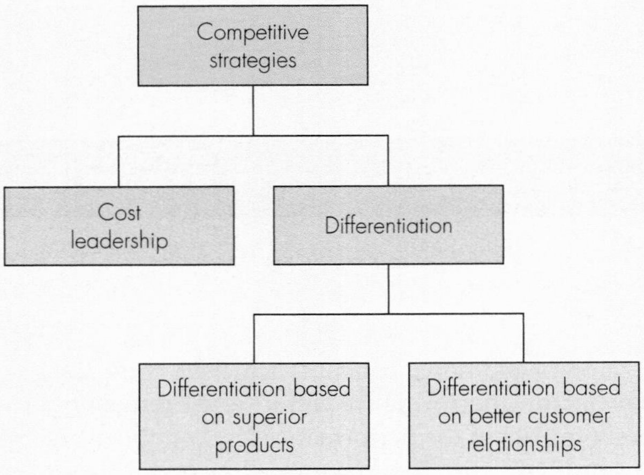

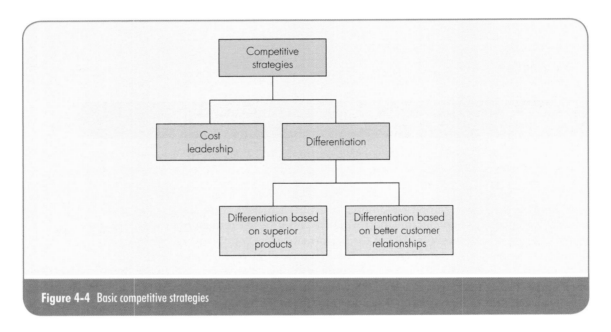

Figure 4-4 Basic competitive strategies

The **cost leadership** strategy aims at efficiency of operations in order to achieve the most favorable cost position within an industry (see Porter 1980; Treacy and Wiersema 2003; see also Focus on Marketing 4-1 for an illustration). Such a position allows the company greater flexibility in terms of pricing (i.e. the company can offer its products at prices lower than its competitors and win market share in doing so). In addition to a low price, extensive standardization of products and utilization of efficient sales channels are typical characteristics of cost leadership.

In contrast, a **differentiation** strategy aims to achieve superiority for the company based on the performance of its product offer (see Hagel and Singer 1999; Porter 1980; Treacy and Wiersema 2003). A differentiation strategy offers a broader range of strategic options as compared to the cost leadership strategy. In general, there are two types of differentiation strategy:

1 differentiation on the basis of superior products

2 differentiation on the basis of superior customer relationships.

Differentiation on the basis of superior products (Hagel and Singer (1999) term it 'product leadership') aims to design the company's products so that they are perceived by customers as being unique and superior in comparison to those of the competition (for an illustration of this type of strategy, see Focus on Marketing 4-2). The perception of superiority does not necessarily have to be grounded on objective performance features (e.g. product reliability), but can be based on subjectively perceived performance advantages (e.g. brand image). Typical characteristics of a market development based on this strategy include intensive brand management and unremitting innovation.

In contrast, **differentiation on the basis of superior customer relationships** focuses on the company's customer relationships. The basic concept of this strategy is to establish and maintain long-term, stable customer relationships. Typical characteristics of a market development based on this strategy include thorough analyzes of individual customer needs, a high degree of customization in sales and customer relationship management, as well as training initiatives geared towards securing and improving the customer orientation of employees.

Focus on Marketing 4-1 Example of a cost leadership strategy

Making every gallon count

When it comes to pinching pennies, few full-fare airlines can match American. During his long tenure as American Airlines' chief executive, Robert Crandall loved to boast that his decision to remove a single olive from passengers' dinner salads saved $40,000 a year.

Thanks in part to a flurry of initiatives that the company believes will slash fuel consumption by roughly 3% this year, vs 2004 – a seemingly trivial amount that nonetheless represents more than $220 million in annual savings at current prices – the Fort Worth-based carrier is likely to emerge as one of the few airlines to turn a profit. Energy-saving measures run the gamut from the surprisingly simple, like removing unused service galleys to reduce the weight of the plane, to the supremely sophisticated, such as using algorithms to help pilots use less fuel while in the air. As a result, American estimates it will consume 110 million gallons less than in 2004. As fuel costs began to soar after Hurricane Katrina, American installed 'winglets' on all of its 737s and many of its 757s.

Those are devices that, when attached to the wings, help reduce drag and increase range. Robert W. Reding, senior vice-president of technical operations for American, estimates this move alone is saving between 100,000 and 140,000 gallons annually per aircraft.

Then American made an exhaustive review of the interior of its planes, scrutinizing 'anything that doesn't provide value,' Reding says. First, American ripped out one of the food-service galleys in some planes and replaced it with four extra seats. Next, Reding's team analyzed the amount of potable water carried to make coffee and flush the toilets. Their finding: Forty-seven gallons was far more water than was being used on most flights. Gradually, American cut by half the amount of water it carries on its MD-80s.

American's ability to cut its fuel bill is paying off. Wall Street analysts now expect American and AMR to generate a profit of better than $200 million in 2006 on roughly $22 billion in revenues, after losing a cumulative $8 billion since 2000.

Source: Foust and Grow 2006.

Empirical studies in the field of strategy research have shown that combined competitive strategies aiming at a balance of differentiation and cost aspects can be more profitable than 'pure' competitive strategies. In view of this, the **ability to combine the different strategy types** becomes important. Here the idea is that it is possible to simultaneously realize cost leadership and differentiation (see Sheth and Sisodia 1999). Such combined strategies are called **hybrid competitive strategies**.

Focus on Marketing 4-2 Differentiation strategy on the basis of superior products

Procter & Gamble to launch SK-II in USA

SK-II launched 20 years ago in Japan, and was developed, according to a legend propagated by P&G, by a monk who discovered skin-rejuvenating 'pitera' after noticing workers at a sake factory had unusually soft hands from the yeast used for fermentation. P&G acquired SK-II as part of Max Factor in 1991 and it caught the fancy both of former Chairman-CEO Durk Jager and current Chairman-CEO A.G. Lafley, who formerly headed P&G's Asian business.

In the past decade, SK-II has grown at compound double-digit rates as it expanded into Taiwan, Korea and Hong Kong. Since its UK launch, the brand has grown globally at a 16% annual clip to $400 million, Mr Lafley said at a recent investor conference.

Price is almost no object to 'age-defying' SK-II consumers, said Patrick Hansson, Geneva-based brand manager for SK-II in Western Europe.

The most avid spend as much as $10,000 a year on their twice-daily ritual of creams, lotions, cosmetics, masks and cleansing cloths. Average SK-II consumers in the UK may spend $2,000 a year – more than 10 times what an average US family spends on all P&G brands combined.

In the UK, where the brand was introduced in 2000, SK-II launched solely in two Selfridges stores; three years later it is in only about a dozen more stores in that chain, along with Harrods and Fraser.

In contrast to the typical big-budget mass-market P&G launch, SK-II marketing is a low-risk, low-budget, high-service affair that really does build the brand one consumer at a time. First purchases come only through a 'consultant' who performs an individualized skin analysis in one of SK-II's elaborate stores within stores and follows up with a handwritten note. Database-customized mailings drive most new SK-II product launches in the UK, Mr Hansson said.

Source: Neff 2003.

Mass customization is such a hybrid competitive strategy combining both the differentiation and cost leadership strategy. Mass customization refers to the cost-efficient production and marketing of products tailored to the individual requirements of a few customers (in extreme cases, this may be a single customer). The term 'customization' reflects the strategy of differentiation, while 'mass' and the associated large-volume production reflect the cost leadership strategy (for more on mass customization, see Focus on Marketing 4-3).

Focus on Marketing 4-3 Different examples of mass customization

The customized, digitized, have-it-your-way economy
The excerpt below is from an article from *Fortune* magazine in 1998, about customization.

'A silent revolution is stirring in the way things are made and services are delivered. Companies with millions of customers are starting to build products designed just for you. You can, of course, buy a Dell computer assembled to your exact specifications. And you can buy a pair of Levi's cut to fit your body. But you can also buy pills with the exact blend of vitamins, minerals, and herbs that you like, glasses molded to fit your face precisely, CDs with music tracks that you choose, cosmetics mixed to match your skin tone, textbooks whose chapters are picked out by your professor, a loan structured to meet your financial profile, or a night at a hotel where every employee knows your favorite wine. And if your child does not like any of Mattel's 125 different Barbie dolls, she will soon be able to design her own.

'Welcome to the world of mass customization, where mass-market goods and services are uniquely tailored to the needs of the individuals who buy them. Companies as diverse as BMW, Dell Computer, Levi Strauss, Mattel, McGraw-Hill, Wells Fargo, and a slew of leading Web businesses are adopting mass customization to maintain or obtain a competitive edge. Many are just beginning to dabble, but the direction in which they are headed is clear. Mass customization is more than just a manufacturing process, logistics system, or marketing strategy. It could well be the organizing principle of business in the next century, just as mass production was the organizing principle in this one.'

In the ten years since the article was written, how have customized or tailored products taken off? How has this been affected by new technologies?

As an example of how far customization has come, at the BMW website in 2008 (www.bmw.co.uk), you can configure your choice of any brand new BMW with different trim, paintwork and alloy wheels online. At McGraw-Hill's Primis website (www.primis.com), your professor can search all the publisher's textbook content to select the chapters, articles or cases he or she wishes you to read for your marketing module! Consider other examples of successful customized products – mass customization has certainly come a long way.

Sources: Schonfeld, E. (1998) The customized, digitized, have-it-your-way economy, *Fortune*, 28 September, 138, 6, 114–124; www.bmw.com; www.primis.com.

4.1.3 What's the News? Questions Regarding Innovation Orientation

Another category of key strategic questions concerns the innovation orientation of a company or strategic business unit. Table 4-3 lists the key questions.

Table 4-3 Central strategic questions concerning innovation orientation

- How should the company set priorities for the development of new products and markets?
- Which technologies should be used and further developed, and to what extent?

The key question is concerned with the company's **innovation orientation**. In principle, a company can **innovate in products** and also **innovate in markets**. Four alternative strategies emerge from combining these two options, which can be integrated into Ansoff's (1965) Product-Market Growth Matrix (see Table 4-4).

Table 4-4 The Product-Market Growth Matrix (adapted from Ansoff 1965, p. 109)

	Existing markets	New markets
Existing products	Market penetration	Market development
New products	Product development	Diversification

1 With the **market penetration** strategy (existing products, existing markets), the company concentrates on markets already served and products currently being offered. This strategy thus exhibits the lowest degree of innovation.

2 The **product development** strategy (new products, existing markets) focuses on developing products in the same markets the company is already catering to (for a detailed discussion of new product development, Section 5.2).

3 With the **market development** strategy (existing products, new markets), the company's established products are marketed in new geographic markets (internationalization), in new market segments or by establishing new sales channels.

4 With the **diversification** strategy (new products, new markets), new products are offered in markets where the company had no presence before. This strategy exhibits a high degree of innovation.

The Product-Market Growth Matrix has important strategic implications. First, it formulates different growth strategies along the line of an innovation orientation. Second, the concept illustrates the risks inherent in the different strategies. Market penetration has a low risk, product development and market development have an intermediate level of risk, and diversification is a risky strategy. Third, the matrix can also be regarded as a portfolio of strategies and, in line with the basic idea of a portfolio, the notion of a balanced Product-Market Growth Matrix should be emphasized. No company can survive by pursuing only market penetration as the Product Life Cycle Model indicates that products will eventually reach maturity (see Section 2.2.3). Companies need to innovate in products and markets and – consequently – in both to survive in the long run. In order to do so, companies need a strong focus on innovation orientation, as is the case described in Focus on Marketing 4-4. Focus on Marketing 4-5 highlights a market development strategy.

Focus on Marketing 4-4 Example of innovation orientation

The world is your lab
How do you build an innovation culture? Try carrots.

3M has long awarded 'Genesis Grants' to scientists who want to work on outside projects. Each year more than 60 researchers submit formal applications to a panel of 20 senior scientists who review the requests, just as a foundation would review academics' proposals. Twelve to 20 grants, ranging from $50,000 and $100,000 apiece, are awarded each year. The researchers can use the money to hire supplemental staff or acquire necessary equipment.

Source: McGregor *et al.* 2006.

Focus on Marketing 4-5 Market development strategy at Nokia

Nokia connects

It wasn't hard for Wang Ninie to decide on a mobile phone. In early March the twentysomething Beijing entrepreneur saw a golden Nokia handset with a flower pattern etched into the trim, one of the company's 'L'Amour' line of high-end designer phones. Wang knew she had to have it. More than any other handset maker, Nokia Corp. has connected with the likes of Wang and their billions of countrymen. In both China and India, the Finnish company is the top brand.

Nokia's sales in China jumped by 28%, to $4.5 billion. The region today is the company's biggest market, accounting for 11% of global revenues, compared with 8% in the US. In India, Nokia has a 60% share, with sales last year of about $1 billion. By 2010 the company expects India to be its No. 2 market.

Nokia isn't letting up: On Mar. 11 it opened its first Indian factory, a $150 million facility near the southern city of Madras that will turn out as many as 20 million inexpensive phones annually both for the local market and for export. And the company is doubling the size of its plant in the Chinese city of Dongguan, near Hong Kong.

The two Asian giants are of fundamental importance for Nokia. The company that can control Asia's Big Two will have a lead in the global handset wars. Today, China is the world's No. 1 cellular market, with some 400 million users and growth last year of 20%. While India is far smaller, with just 81 million users in February, handset sales are expected to double this year and total users could hit 500 million by 2010.

Since 2002, when India's cellular market took off, Nokia has drawn on its China experience to consolidate its lead. In 2004 the company launched two India-specific models, which included a flashlight, dust cover, and slip-free grip (handy during India's scorching, sweaty summers). Nokia introduced software in seven regional languages for non-Hindi speakers and added ring tones of patriotic songs such as the nationalist hymn India Is the Best. 'We invested when the market was nothing,' says Robert Andersson, who oversees manufacturing, sales, and marketing at Nokia. 'We have been able to harvest the fruits of that commitment in the last four years.'

Source: Einhorn *et al.* 2006.

4.1.4 All Strings Attached? Questions on Customer Relationship Management

A fourth category of central strategic questions is concerned with the aspects of customer relationship management. A primary element here is the management of existing customers to optimize customer satisfaction – a key prerequisite for customer loyalty (for a discussion of 'customer satisfaction', please refer to the Appendix). As far as company objectives are concerned, customer relationship management (we will also use the term 'relationship marketing') aims at the optimal design of the customer relationships of a company. Of special relevance are the establishment and maintenance of **long-term business relationships**, which can be associated with numerous potential advantages for the company, such as:

- sales-related advantages
- cost-related advantages.

In terms of **sales-related advantages**, sales volumes generated with a customer can increase over the course of a business relationship. If a company gains an increasingly better understanding of the customer's needs in the course of a relationship, it can use this information to create an improved offer for the customer. Furthermore, the customer may increase their share-of-wallet with the company. Cross-selling and reduced price sensitivity of customers are additional advantages of successful customer relationship management (see also Chapter 9).

Cost-related advantages can arise from a decrease in information and coordination expenses required for maintaining the business relationship (i.e. transaction costs are reduced – for more on 'transaction cost theory', see Appendix). In light of the fact that the acquisition of new customers is generally very costly (see Hart *et al.* 1990; Reichheld and Sasser 1990), a potential cost-related benefit of long-term business relationships is that they can reduce the necessity of costly new customer acquisition activities.

Accordingly, the objective of customer relationship management is the establishment of **customer loyalty**. As a rule, an essential prerequisite for customer loyalty is a sufficient level of customer satisfaction. The strategic orientation of these customer relationship management activities can be derived from the answers to the central questions shown in Table 4-5.

Table 4-5 Central strategic questions concerning customer relationship management

- For what should customer loyalty be established? The company, company employees, products or brands?
- Which customers/customer groups should be targeted in loyalty-building programs?
- How (i.e. via which reasons for loyalty) should customer loyalty be ensured?
- Which instruments can be used to secure customer loyalty?

The first central question regarding customer relationship management refers to which object the customer loyalty should refer to. In principle, customers can be loyal to companies, persons, products or brands.

With respect to the second central question, concerning which **customers/customer groups** should be targeted in terms of developing loyalty, it should be pointed out that prioritizing the individual market segments (already discussed in the first central question in Chapter 3) is particularly important when defining customer relationship management activities.

A further central question in customer relationship management addresses how to ensure customer loyalty. At the core of this question are the fundamental factors driving customer loyalty. When formulating the marketing strategy, a company has to determine which **reasons for loyalty** should be promoted and to what extent. Four basic reasons for customer loyalty are especially relevant (see Meyer and Oevermann 1995):

1 **psychological reasons for loyalty** comprise customer satisfaction, personal relationships and customer habits (psychological reasons for loyalty also include, e.g., loyalty to a specific brand, see Fournier 1998)
2 **economic reasons for loyalty** arise if the business relationship is designed so that it is economically disadvantageous for the customer to switch to another company due to high switching costs
3 **technical/functional reasons for loyalty** exist if there are technical dependencies, and switching to another company is associated with difficulties of availability or problems of compatibility
4 **contractual reasons for loyalty** exist if the customer is bound to the company for a certain period of time due to a contractual agreement and thus, for legal reasons, cannot switch to a different company (e.g. a contractual tie with a provider in the telecommunications market).

A fourth question inquires about the instruments that should be used to secure customer loyalty. A detailed description of the available tools and instruments will not be presented here. For more information, please refer to Section 9.2 in Part 3 of this book, which discusses the marketing instruments of customer relationship management.

4.1.5 In Good Company? Questions Regarding Competitive and Cooperative Conduct

A fifth category of central strategic questions regarding the formulation of marketing strategies tackles a company's conduct towards other companies (see Table 4-6). The focal point here is on strategic considerations concerning the competitive and cooperative conduct of a company.

Table 4-6 Central strategic questions concerning competitive and cooperative conduct

- How should the company generally interact with its competitors?
- With which companies, and with what objectives, should the company cooperate within the scope of the market development, and how should the cooperation be structured and designed?

The first question relates to how the company should generally interact with its **competitors**. In the course of their market development, companies are frequently confronted with competitor actions that go beyond the normal 'day-to-day business'. A differentiation between cooperative actions and threatening behavior can be made in this context. Cooperative actions on the part of a competitor do not have a negative impact on the company's achievement of objectives. For instance, price increases by a competitor can be interpreted as cooperative since they can enable the company to increase its own prices. Threatening behavior, on the other hand, can negatively affect the company's ability to achieve its objectives. For example, the launch of a new product or price reductions on the part of the competition can diminish the company's profit.

The best way to respond to the competitive activities has to be decided on a case-by-case basis. The marketing strategy can provide only general response patterns. For example, a strategic guideline can define how aggressively a company tends to react. The extent to which a company can forecast probable competitor activities and respond to them proactively before they are actually implemented (e.g. price reductions prior to an expected new product launch by a competitor) is also decisive.

Of particular relevance are threatening actions on the part of competitors. If a company is threatened by another competitor, four basic **competitive reactions** have been observed (see Kuester *et al.* 1999, 2001):

1 ignoring the activity
2 cooperating with the competitor
3 counterattacking
4 switching to different markets.

If the competitor has not yet carried out its threatening actions, but is expected to, the company can try to defend itself (see Bowman and Gatignon 1995; Gatignon *et al.* 1997; Kuester *et al.* 1999, 2001). A range of **defence mechanisms** can be taken into consideration when formulating the marketing strategy (also see Bain 1956; Gruca and Sudharshan 1995). The company can use product, price, communication and sales, as well as customer relationship management instruments, to fend off threatening competitor behavior.

Another key question concerns **cooperative conduct** and thus the issue of which companies should be cooperating in the market development process. In this context, a **strategic alliance** refers to a formal business relationship between two or more companies that established a cooperation with common objectives (e.g. development of technologies or markets). The cooperating companies remain legally independent and regulate the cooperation in the specified areas through more or less formal contracts. By contrast, the legal independence of the participating companies changes in the case of a **merger** or **acquisition**. In a merger, two or more companies build one entity by giving up their previous legal existence. With an acquisition, a company buys out one or more other companies or parts of companies and the acquired companies lose their legal independence. Acquisitions can be voluntary (with the consent of the target company) or involuntary (referred to in this case as hostile takeovers).

When discussing cooperative conduct it is important to focus on the intended objectives of the companies involved. The following potential objectives exist in this context (see Barney 2001; Gulati 1998; Varadarajan and Cunningham 1995):

- joint creation of market entry barriers for other competitors
- reciprocal access to knowhow and other resources
- easier market access and sales synergies
- expansion of the service range and/or filling gaps in the product range
- leveraging cost-cutting potential in the form of economies of scale and experience curve effects (see Section 2.2.2)
- risk management.

There are three possible forms of cross-company cooperation.

1 In **vertical cooperations**, companies positioned at different levels of the value chain work together. An example here is the strategic alliance between an insurance firm (as product supplier) and a company in the financial services sector.
2 **Horizontal cooperations** refer to collaborations between companies positioned at the same level of the value chain within the same industry. In this case, the cooperating companies are thus (potential) competitors. An example here would be an alliance between airlines.
3 In **lateral cooperations** (also called diagonal cooperations), companies in different industries work together. Such cooperations are created, for instance, between companies whose markets are merging due to technological developments (e.g. acquisition of a software company by a telecommunications provider).

In addition to this general description of potential forms of cooperation, strategic alliances can also be categorized in terms of marketing aspects. Table 4-7 shows a classification of strategic alliances categorized by the most dominant marketing instrument.

Table 4-7 Differentiation of strategic alliances categorized by the dominant marketing mix instrument

Form of alliance	Possible focus of cooperations	Examples
Product alliance	■ Granting of a manufacturing license for another company ■ Bundled marketing of complementary products of both partners ■ Joint new product development or market launches	Joint development of new medications by pharmaceutical companies
Communication alliance	■ Joint usage of communication tools, possibly with a common advertising message	Joint sponsorship of a sports event
Distribution alliance	■ Joint utilization of sales channels, field or customer service organizations ■ Joint activities in logistics	Inventory of a trade company is managed by a manufacturer
Price alliance	■ Joint pricing activities on the part of several companies	Joint discount systems, cross-company price bundling
Customer loyalty alliance	■ Joint customer loyalty activities by companies	Joint bonus systems of airline, car rental and hotel companies

4.1.6 All Well Mixed? Questions Regarding the Marketing Mix Design and Structure

The final category of central strategic questions deals with the basic design and structure of the marketing mix (see Table 4-8). There are two different categories of question in this context: those that relate to the general design and structure of the marketing mix, and those that concern the basic alignment of the individual components of the marketing mix.

A key question addressing the general design and structure concerns the degree to which the **market development is differentiated** for individual market segments. In other words, this question addresses the positioning of a company between the two extreme points of a completely standardized market development across all segments and a completely customized development of each individual market segment. In fact, if the market development is strongly differentiated for the different segments, the key questions related to the design and structure of the marketing mix should be answered on a segment-specific basis.

As noted above, the question regarding the company's **product–price positioning** is related to the general design and structure of the marketing mix. The basic options for design and structure related to the decision about the positioning are shown in Figure 4-5. Price and performance are the two attributes that help to construct this two-dimensional matrix. The attribute 'performance' relates to non-price marketing instruments. Both price and performance are assessed qualitatively or quantitatively relative to the competition (for 'multi-dimensional scaling' as a general technique for positioning analysis please refer to the Appendix). In the diagonal depicted in Figure 4-5 a consistent positioning can be achieved, with relative price and relative performance at corresponding levels. In company practice, strategic positioning in this diagonal area is frequently applied. Moreover, companies that want to increase their market share or penetrate a new market often choose a positioning with a particularly favorable price–performance ratio.

Table 4-8 Selected central strategic questions concerning the design and structure of the marketing mix

Central questions regarding marketing mix design and structure
- To what extent should the market development between the individual customer segments be differentiated during the course of market development?
- How should the company's product–price positioning be designed?
- How large should the marketing budget be and how should it be allocated to the various marketing instruments?
- What interaction effects between the various marketing instruments or various products have to be taken into consideration?

Selected questions regarding product decisions
- How broad and detailed should the company's product range be?
- What quality level does the company want to achieve with its products?
- What types of product innovations are the focus of the company's innovation activities?
- How should the company's brand(s) be structured and positioned?

Selected questions regarding pricing decisions
- What price positioning should the company strive for in relation to the competition?
- When setting prices, how should costs, competitor prices and customer benefits be prioritized?
- To what extent and by means of which criteria should the company pursue price differentiation?
- To what extent and by means of which criteria should the company grant discounts, rebates and bonuses?

Selected questions regarding communication decisions
- What communication objectives and target groups should the company focus on?
- How large should the communication budget be and how should it be allocated to the individual communication instruments?
- What communication messages should be particularly emphasized?
- How should the success of the communication be monitored?

Selected questions regarding sales decisions
- Should the products be directly or indirectly sold?
- Should just one sales channel or several sales channels be used?
- How should the various sales channels be defined?
- What criteria should be used to select the sales partners?
- How should the activities be distributed between the company and its sales partners?

'Premium' positioning is based on high-quality products and services, while 'economy' positioning is based on low prices. This process is essentially similar to the cost leadership strategy (see Section 4.1.2) and is often associated with high volume (thus, also referred to as 'price–volume strategy').

Another question is concerned with the overall **marketing budget**. In connection with budget decisions, a relevant issue is how to allocate the budget to the individual marketing mix instruments.

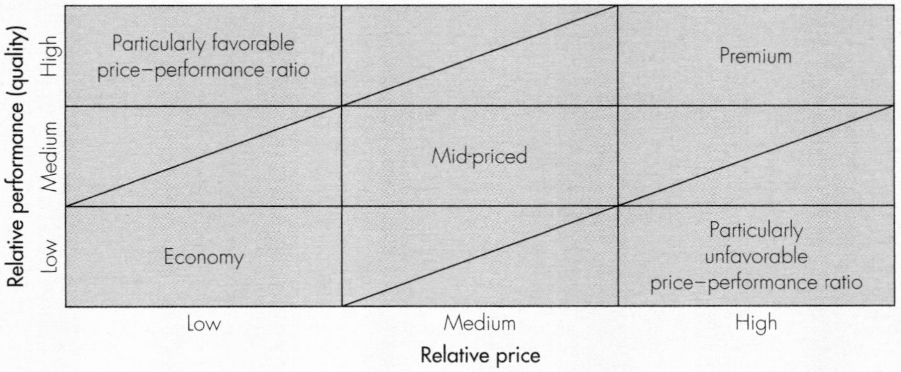

Figure 4-5 Basic design of product–price positioning strategies (see Simon 1992, p. 64)

4.2 Supporting Concepts for the Formulation of Marketing Strategies

After describing the different facets of a marketing strategy, this section will discuss a number of concepts that can play a supporting role in the formulation of marketing strategies. It should be mentioned in this context that some of the concepts presented within the scope of strategic analysis (see Chapter 3) can also be relevant here. This applies, for example, to SWOT analysis (see Section 3.4.2). However, the models discussed in Chapter 3 focus more on analytical aspects, whereas the concepts in this section explicitly aim at generating **recommendations for marketing management**.

We will introduce the following concepts:

- the strategic gameboard
- portfolio techniques.

The **strategic gameboard** is a qualitatively oriented creativity technique that describes the nature of competition in an industry. To this end, two fundamental questions are asked: 'Where does competition take place?' (referring to market segmentation) and 'How is competition shaped?' (referring to the business system). With regard to the first question, the development of a niche or, alternatively, the entire market can be considered. The second question takes into account competition according to old rules vs competition according to new rules as strategic options. These dimensions result in a matrix that identifies four basic strategies (see Figure 4-6).

The analysis focuses on finding ways that allow for radical realignments of the competitive landscape (see Kerin *et al.* 1990). New rules can be realized through innovation or by reconfiguring the rules of competition in the entire market. Striving to rewrite the rules of competition is called a **new game strategy** (see also 'blue ocean strategy' in Section 3.4.1). An example of this strategy is the approach of a mechanical engineering company to provide customers with the option of leasing machines instead of buying them. This offer, when first introduced, led to a reconfiguration of competition. Competitors were no longer primarily focused on product performance and price, but to a great extent on financing and service concepts.

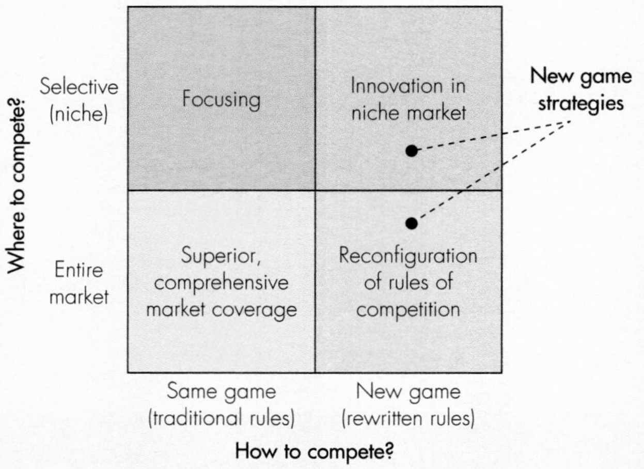

Figure 4-6 The strategic gameboard

We can distinguish new game strategies according to the following characteristics:

- New game strategies are more effective and successful the more competitors are taken by surprise.
- New game strategies aim at shaping competitive conditions in a way that favors the particular strengths of the company.
- New game strategies can lead to high profits, but also pose significant risks.

Focus on Marketing 4-6 illustrates an example of a new game strategy.

Focus on Marketing 4-6 The Starbucks customer experience

Fortune magazine describes Starbucks as 'possibly the most dynamic new brand and retailer to be conceived over the past two decades'. The company has a huge global reach, and as of 2008, has over 7,500 locations in more than 40 countries worldwide.

Customers stream into Starbucks to buy coffee at far higher prices than they used to before the advent of the chain. They go to their local Starbucks to read on plush sofas, or to use the wi-fi connections available in over 400 UK branches, to read e-mail on their laptops and hold meetings. In the US and Canada, customers can load money onto the company's stored-value cards. The cards can be personalized to a design of their choice, and they entitle the customer to special offers such as free refills. Since October 2006, Starbucks has fostered a partnership with Apple's iTunes to offer complimentary digital music downloads to their US customers.

'Starbucks has become what I call the third place,' says Howard Schultz, the man who built the coffee company that has become an American institution. 'The first place is home. The second place is work. We are the place in between. It's a place to feel comfort. A place to feel safe. A place to feel like you belong.' The Starbucks website describes the atmosphere as:

Focus on Marketing 4-6 (Continued)

'specifically designed to be cosy and intimate, while at the same time providing people with their own personal space to use as they wish. . . . Those looking for peace and quiet away from home or the office can relax and linger in an armchair and escape into a book, whilst those looking for an intimate place to meet friends can huddle on a sofa and chat over a mug of coffee, as they would in their own home.'

These features are now familiar in many city center coffee shops around the world, but it was Starbucks who pioneered this new and unusual customer experience from the company's origins in Seattle. Schultz's aim was to try to create something that never really existed in the US: cafe life, for centuries a hallmark of Continental society.

Sources: Bonamici 2004; company information from www.starbucks.com and www.starbucks.co.uk, 14 April 2008.

Quantitatively oriented concepts can also be applied for the design of the marketing strategy. The most prominent quantitative concept is the **portfolio technique**.

The portfolio method is intended to support the process of **resource allocation** in markets – in other words, the question addresses to what extent a company should invest resources into developing a particular market or market segment. The term 'portfolio' originated in finance to address the problem of spreading investments across a securities portfolio. The original concept emphasizes the idea of balancing investments according to specific criteria (e.g. risk). This problem is akin to one of the resource allocation decisions firms face, particularly when they are operating in multiple markets. The portfolio technique as applied in marketing may recommend that firms invest heavily in markets to strengthen their competitive position, to maintain their position, to limit investment or to even discontinue activities in certain markets.

The markets/market segments that are analyzed during the course of a portfolio analysis can be defined according to various criteria (see Section 3.3 on market segmentation). In international marketing, for example, portfolios can be used to analyze local and national markets, and to set appropriate priorities for these markets (for more information on this topic see Chapter 12). If a company is divided into strategic business units (SBUs), portfolio analysis is usually conducted at the SBU level.

Most portfolio models share the common objective to support decisions related to resource allocation in markets, and they also share a common logic: within the course of a portfolio analysis, markets are positioned in a two-dimensional matrix, with one axis referring to market attractiveness in the broadest sense and the other axis, generally speaking, indicating the strength of the company's position in the markets being analyzed. A subsequent evaluation of these two dimensions results in basic recommendations with regard to resource allocation. In the following, we will examine the most important portfolio models:

- the market growth/market share portfolio
- the life cycle portfolio.

The **market growth/market share portfolio** (also referred to as the BCG Model, as it was developed by Bruce Henderson at the Boston Consulting Group in 1970) is a well-known application of the portfolio technique and was the first to be discussed systematically (see Abell and Hammond 1979; Hedley 1977). With this technique, the company's SBUs are evaluated by the relative market share (defined as the ratio of the company's own market share as compared to the market share of the strongest competitor). Obviously, this approach is shaped by the results of the PIMS project (see Section 2.2.1) as well as the theory of the experience curve model (see Section 2.2.2). Furthermore, the market attractiveness of SBUs is assessed based on market growth, an approach that is rooted in the logic of the Life Cycle Model (see Section 2.2.3).

Figure 4-7 illustrates the formal structure of this portfolio. The horizontal axis refers to relative market share and the vertical axis captures the market growth. For each axis, a cut-off point is determined so that the resulting matrix consists of four cells. As a rule, the vertical cut-off point is located at a relative market share of 1, which is exceeded only by the market leader. An additional line highlights market shares between 1 and 1.5. When formulating a marketing strategy, special attention should be paid to SBUs that fall into this area since the comparatively weak market leadership of the company is especially at risk here. There are no general criteria for determining the cut-off point for the horizontal dimension. Determining the cut-off point has important implications as above this threshold point growth is deemed to be significant (the selected 5% value in Figure 4-7 is used for illustrative purposes). Possible criteria for determining this point include, for example:

- average industry growth (if all examined markets belong to the same industry)
- general macroeconomic growth data (if the examined markets belong to different industries), or
- company-internal growth targets.

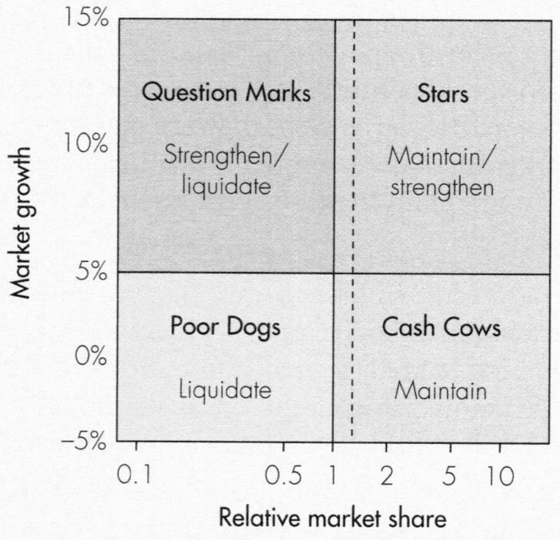

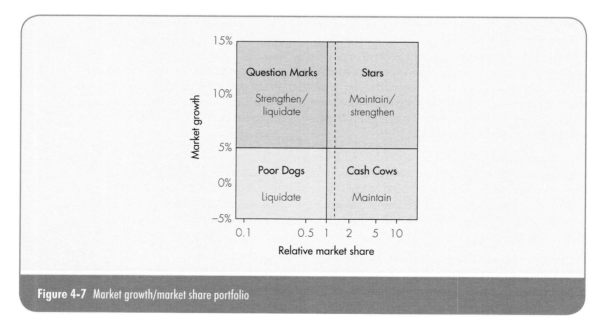

Figure 4-7 Market growth/market share portfolio

In general, the individual markets/SBUs are represented by circles whose size proportionally corresponds to the respective sales volume of the company. The affiliation of an SBU with one of the four cells in Figure 4-7 leads to basic recommendations (standard strategies) with regard to resource allocation, as described below.

- **Stars** (SBUs characterized by a high market share and a high market growth rate) often are highly profitable, however they require a significant allocation of resources if the objective is to maintain or strengthen the market position in a fast-growing market. The basic recommendation for these business units is to deploy extensive resources (e.g. with a view to developing new products/ acquiring new customers).

- **Question Marks** (SBUs characterized by a low market share and a high market growth rate) generally require the utilization of significant marketing resources relative to their sales in order to be able to sustain them in a fast-growing market. Accordingly, they are frequently unprofitable. The strategic key question here is whether major investments (e.g. for developing new products or establishing new sales channels) should be made in order to turn this SBU into a Star.
- **Poor Dogs** (SBUs characterized by a low market share and a weak or even negative market growth rate) should be managed in such a way that does not put any financial burden on the company. Options for action include a gradual retreat or limiting activities to individual market niches.
- **Cash Cows** (SBUs characterized by high market share and low market growth), with their strong position in a market that at best displays a weak growth performance, yield more cash flow than would be feasible to reinvest. Here, marketing resources (e.g. customer loyalty schemes) should be deployed only to the extent required to maintain the market position. In markets where SBUs are in such a position, the cash flow generated should be invested in growing markets (Stars or Question Marks).

A significant weakness of this basic portfolio lies in the very limited data basis: far-reaching recommendations for resource allocation are based on just three indicators (market growth, own market share, market share of the strongest competitor). Subsequently, other similar portfolio models have been conceptualized that are more comprehensive in nature (e.g. the GE product portfolio matrix).

Another model of the portfolio approach is the **life cycle portfolio**, which analyzes markets based on the life cycle phase that they are experiencing. This approach is therefore very strongly rooted in the logic of the Life Cycle Model (see Section 2.2.3).

The two dimensions applied in this model are the life cycle phase and the competitive position. With regard to the competitive position of the company, five positions can be distinguished (see Laukamm and Steinthal 1986):

1. dominant (quasi-monopoly)
2. strong (as a rule, large degree of independence from the strategies of the competition)
3. favorable (e.g. one of several market leaders in a fragmented market without any outstanding competitor)
4. tenable (e.g. specialization in a market niche)
5. weak (e.g. companies that are too small for the competitive dynamics in their sector, or companies that have made severe mistakes in the past).

This model displays a distinct conceptual similarity to the market growth/market share portfolio; however, the dimensions addressed here are more comprehensive than in the classic approach. From the evaluation of a market/SBU based on these two criteria, this portfolio derives recommendations for one of four strategic directions (see Figure 4-8):

1. progressive development (wide range of strategic options)
2. selective development (focus on particular segments or niches)
3. revitalization/proof of viability (significant improvement of competitive position or retreat to niches)
4. retreat (minimization of investments or exit).

At its core, the model states that the more advanced the life cycle, the fewer situations exist where a progressive development with a correspondingly high resource deployment would be feasible. Thus,

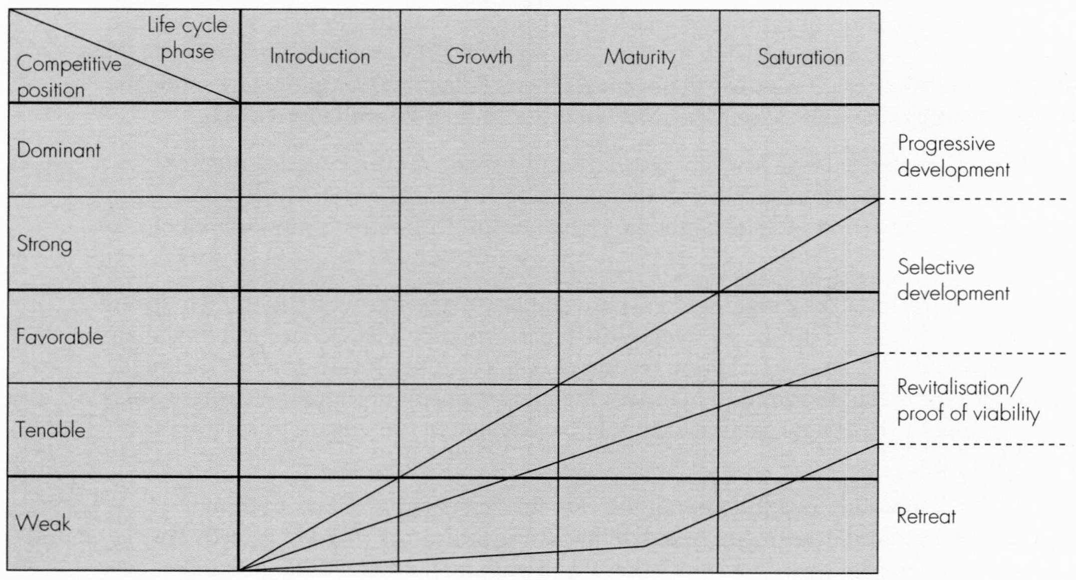

Figure 4-8 Strategic directions in the life cycle portfolio

such progressive development is considered to be more feasible in the introductory phase, virtually regardless of the competitive position, whereas in later life cycle phases, progressive development is recommended only in the case of a dominant or strong competitive position. In other words, this model discourages a costly rush to catch up in late life cycle phases. For more information on this portfolio, please refer to Jain (2004).

Despite the relevance of portfolio techniques for the design of the marketing strategy, a number of **weaknesses of portfolio analysis** have to be mentioned. When discussing the general deficits of portfolio analysis, a number of methodological problems should first be noted, including the dependency of the results on market definition, the issue of determining the cut-off points, and the sensitivity of the resultant strategy recommendations towards minor changes in data input. More severe than these methodological aspects, however, is the problem that the portfolio analysis neglects potential market, cost or technology-related synergies between the individual SBUs. For example, if synergies are significant, a market exit can be extremely problematic since other SBUs are likely to be affected by this.

In summary, the portfolio concept significantly contributes to systematic decision making pertaining to the central issue of resource allocation for markets. In view of this, it is not surprising that this method continues to play an important role in today's company practice for the design of corporate strategy and marketing strategy. In our opinion, an essential didactic benefit of the concept is that it clearly demonstrates to companies the importance of a well-balanced portfolio structure (especially when it concerns markets with different growth rates). The aforementioned problems do not pose a fundamental challenge to the portfolio approach, but rather illustrate that it should not be applied without reflection. In particular, portfolio analyzes should be accompanied by additional, and ideally complementary, analyzes (see, e.g., the methods described in Chapter 2).

4.3 Evaluating Marketing Strategy

Strategy formulation, as described here, frequently results in several alternative marketing strategies that can differ significantly or only gradually. It is therefore the company's task to evaluate the alternative strategies with regard to suitable criteria and select an alternative on the basis of this evaluation.

Marketing strategies can be evaluated based on both qualitative and quantitative aspects. During the course of a **qualitative evaluation** of the various alternative strategies, several aspects have to be considered. The **consistency** of the marketing strategy is the first issue in this consideration, which concerns maintaining consistency to the company objectives as well as to other strategies that are deployed by the company (e.g. business unit strategies). A second aspect when evaluating a marketing strategy is its **information basis**. The core question here is whether the marketing strategy has a sufficient information basis or if parts of the strategy were formulated based on managerial 'gut feeling'. An essential key aspect when evaluating a marketing strategy is an assessment of the **strategy content**. In this, the most important aspect is the extent to which the central strategic questions raised in Section 2.1 have been addressed adequately and to what degree those answers are feasible and useful. Furthermore, a marketing strategy should also be evaluated with regard to the feasibility of **strategy implementation** (see also Part 4 of this book).

Summary

In this chapter, we focused on the formulation, evaluation and selection of marketing strategies. First of all, a company has to define the strategic marketing objectives and the customer groups to be targeted in the marketing strategy. Then, a set of closely intertwined questions has to be addressed. Among them, the decision as to whether the company focuses mainly on providing core benefits to its customers or also offers additional benefits is of central importance as it influences the company's competitive strategy. Focusing solely on core benefits often goes hand in hand with a cost leadership strategy, whereas providing additional benefits can be the basis for a differentiation strategy. Another question concerns the innovation strategy to be pursued. The decision here is whether the company focuses on new products, new markets, or both. The Product-Market Growth Matrix has important strategic implications for this consideration. The next set of questions deals with aspects of customer relationship management (e.g. whether customer loyalty should be established with regard to the company or rather with regard to certain representatives of the company). Furthermore, it has to be decided what customer groups should be targeted and how customer loyalty should be ensured. As outlined in the previous chapters, strategy also has to consider the competitive environment. Key questions here are whether the company adopts a cooperative or hostile stance towards competitors. At the instrumental level, questions arise regarding product decisions, pricing, communication and sales. The key decision is to what extent the marketing mix should be standardized across different market segments or whether a customized development of different segments is more suitable. Finally, we presented two methods that can be used to support the process of strategy formulation. The strategic gameboard combines the market where competition takes place (entire market vs niche) and the business system (old rules vs new rules) in order to deduce appropriate strategies. The more quantitatively oriented portfolio technique helps to classify the attractiveness of different market segments or SBUs in order to derive optimal resource allocation decisions.

Case Study: The Rise of the Superbrands

Consumer-goods firms find it hard to boost growth by letting go of older, slower-growing brands. These older brands have become so established in the mind of shoppers that customers buy them without thinking – they almost sell themselves. That makes them a good source of profit. However, these brands also eat up scarce management time and marketing talent on lines of business that are unlikely ever to grow much.

At Proctor & Gamble (P&G), the CEO made some changes to address this. Mr A.G. Lafley is a beauty-products specialist and took over the CEO role in June 2000. He decided to shed Punica, a German juice brand and Sunny Delight, an American one, Jif (peanut butter) and Crisco (pastry shortening). He also disposed of P&G's BIZ, Milton, Sanso, Rei and Oxydol detergent brands.

Case Study (Continued)

Mr Lafley sharpened the focus of his portfolio of brands by concentrating on beauty and grooming products which he felt had more potential for growth. He has also reinvested cash from the sale of these product lines back into P&G's strongest brands, funnelling the firm's resources into a smaller number of top 'superbrands', which are making a growing contribution to the company's overall sales.

In 2000, P&G owned ten brands each with annual sales of more than $1 billion. By 2004, it had 16 brands with sales over $1 billion, which earned the firm $30 billion of its $51.4 billion of sales in 2004. The merger with Gillette in 2005 brought five more billion dollar brands such as Oral-B, Duracell and Braun under the P&G banner. The company reached net sales of $76.476 million in 2007, thanks to a total of 23 billion-dollar brands. Lafley also hopes that P&G is fostering the 'superbrands' of the future – in 2007 there were 18 brands contributing between $500 million and $1 billion in annual sales waiting in the wings.

Speaking in an article in *The Economist* in May 2005, Uta Werner of Marakon Associates stated that 'P&G has done really well consolidating its brands down to a strong core'. P&G is hoping that this growing stable of 'superbrands' will secure its future in the industry's tough environment.

Sources: The rise of the superbrands, *The Economist*, 02/05/2005, and company factsheet from http://www.pg.com/company/who_we_are/ourhistory_5.jhtml.

Discussion Questions

1. Discuss the most important portfolio models and their underlying assumptions and conceptual origins.
2. What are the advantages of P&G's superbrand strategy?
3. What could be the potential negative consequences of P&G's superbrand strategy?
4. What implications, if any, does the Product-Market Growth Matrix have for P&G's portfolio development strategy?

Key Terms

Acquisition of new customers *69*
Basic factors, performance factors and excitement factors *71*
Benefits *70*
Cash Cows *87*
Competitive advantages being pursued *72*
Competitive reactions *79*
Competitive strategy *72*
Competitors *79*
Contractual reasons for loyalty *79*
Cooperative conduct *80*
Core benefits *70*
Cost leadership *72*
Cost-related advantages *78*
Customer loyalty *78*
Customers/customer groups *78*
Defence mechanisms *80*
Development of existing customers *69*
Differentiation on the basis of superior customer relationships *73*
Differentiation on the basis of superior products *72*
Differentiation *72*
Diversification *76*
Economic benefits *71*
Economic reasons for loyalty *79*
Emotional benefits *71*
Functional benefits *71*
Horizontal cooperations *80*
Hybrid competitive strategies *73*
Innovate in markets *75*
Innovate in products *75*
Innovation orientation *75*
Lateral cooperations *80*
Life cycle portfolio *87*
Long-term business relationships *78*
Market development *76*
Market growth/market share portfolio *85*
Market penetration *76*
Marketing budget *82*
Mass customization *74*
Merger *80*
New game strategy *83*
Poor Dogs *87*
Portfolio technique *85*
Process-related benefits *71*
Product development *76*
Product–price positioning *81*
Psychological reasons for loyalty *79*
Quantitatively oriented concepts *85*
Question Marks *87*
Reasons for loyalty *78*
Recommendations for marketing management *83*
Resource allocation *85*
Sales-related advantages *78*
Social benefits *71*
Stars *86*
Strategic alliance *80*
Strategic gameboard *83*
Strategy formulation *68*
Strategy implementation *89*
Technical/functional reasons for loyalty *79*
Vertical cooperations *80*
Weaknesses of portfolio analysis *88*
What customer benefits the company should create *70*
Which market segments should be developed *69*

References

Abell, D. and Hammond, J. (1979) *Strategic Marketing Planning*. Englewood Cliffs, NJ.
Anderson, J. and Narus, J. (1998) Business marketing: understand what customers value, *Harvard Business Review*, 76 (November/December), 53–65.
Anderson, J. and Narus, J. (2003) *Business Market Management: Understanding, Creating, and Delivering Value* (2nd edn). Englewood Cliffs, NJ.
Anderson, J. and Thomas, J. (1997) *Combining Value and Price to Make Purchase Decisions in Business Models*, Working Paper 3–1997, Institute for the Study of Business Markets, Pennsylvania State University, University Park, PA.
Anderson, J., Jain, D. and Chintaguanta, P. (1993) Customer value assessment in business markets: a state-of-practice study, *Journal of Business-to-Business Marketing*, 1, 3–29.
Ansoff, H. (1965) *Corporate Strategy*. New York.
Bain, J. (1956) *Barriers to New Competition*. Cambridge.
Barney, J. (2001) *Gaining and Sustaining Competitive Advantage* (2nd edn). Reading.
Blattberg, R. and Deighton, J. (1996) Manage marketing by the customer equity test, *Harvard Business Review*, 74, 4, 136–144.
Bonamici, K. (2004) Hot Starbucks to go, *Fortune*, 149, 2, 60–74.
Bowman, D. and Gatignon, H. (1995) Determinants of competitor response time to a new product introduction, *Journal of Marketing Research*, 32, 1, 42–53.
Capon, N., Farley, J. and Hoenig, S. (1990) Determinants of financial performance: a meta-analysis, *Management Science*, 36, 10, 1143–1159.
Economist, The (2005) The rise of the superbrands, 2 May.
Einhorn, B., Lakshman, N., Kripalani, M. and Ewing, J. (2006) Nokia connects, *Business Week*, 3977, 44–45.
Fournier, S. (1998) Consumers and their brands: developing relationship theory in consumer research, *Journal of Consumer Research*, 24, 343–372.
Foust, D. and Grow, B. (2006) Making every gallon count, *Business Week*, 3983, 54–55.
Gatignon, H., Robertson, T. and Fein, A. (1997) Incumbent defense strategies against new product entry, *International Journal of Research in Marketing*, 14, 2, 163–176.
Gruca, T. and Sudharshan, D. (1995) A framework for entry deterrence strategy: the competitive environment, choices, and consequences, *Journal of Marketing*, 59, 3, 44–55.
Gulati, R. (1998) Alliances and networks, *Strategic Management Journal*, 19, 4, 293–317.
Hagel, J. and Singer, M. (1999) Unbundling the corporation, *Harvard Business Review*, 77, 2, 133–141.
Hart, C., Heskett, J. and Sasser, W. (1990) The profitable art of service recovery, *Harvard Business Review*, 68, 4, 148–156.
Hedley, B. (1977) Strategy and the business portfolio, *Long Range Planning*, 10, 1, 9–15.
Jain, S. (2004) *Marketing Planning and Strategy* (7th edn). Cincinnati.
Kerin, R., Mahajan, V. and Varadarajan, P. (1990) *Contemporary Perspectives on Strategic Market Planning*. Boston, Mass.
Kuester, S., Homburg, C. and Robertson, T. (1999) Retaliatory behavior to new product entry, *Journal of Marketing*, 63, 4, 90–106.
Kuester, S., Homburg, C., Robertson, T. and Schäfer, H. (2001) Verteidigungsstrategien gegen neue Wettbewerber – Bestandsaufnahme und empirische Untersuchung, *Zeitschrift für Betriebswirtschaft*, 71, 10, 1191–1215.
Laukamm, T. and Steinthal, N. (1986) Methoden der Strategieentwicklung und des strategischen Managements – von der Portfolio-Planung zum Führungssystem, in: Arthur D. Little (Hrsg.) *Management im Zeitalter der strategischen Führung* (2nd edn). Wiesbaden.
McGregor, J., Arndt, M., Berner, R., Rowley, I., Hall, K., Edmondson, G., Hamm, S., Moon I. and Reinhardt, A. (2006) The world's most innovative companies, *Business Week*, 3981, 63–74.
Meyer, A. and Oevermann, D. (1995) Kundenbindung, in: Tietz, B., Köhler, R. and Zentes, J. (eds) *Handwörterbuch des Marketing* (2nd edn). Stuttgart, 1340–1351.
Neff, J. (2003) P&G to launch SK-II in US, *Advertising Age*, 74, 14, 33–34.
Oliver, R. (1997) *Satisfaction: A Behavioral Perspective on the Consumer*. New York.
Porter, M. (1980) *Competitive Strategy*. New York.
Reichheld, F. and Sasser, W. (1990) Zero defections: quality comes to services, *Harvard Business Review*, 68, 5, 105–111.

Schonfeld, E. (1998) The customized, digitized, have-it-your-way economy, *Fortune*, 28 September, 138, 6, 114–124.

Sheth, J. and Sisodia, R. (1999) Revisiting marketing's lawlike generalizations, *Journal of the Academy of Marketing Science*, 27, 1, 71–87.

Simon, H. (1989) *Price Management*. North-Holland.

Simon, H. (1992) *Preismanagement: Analyze – Strategie – Umsetzung* (2nd edn). Wiesbaden.

Treacy, M. and Wiersema, F. (2003) *The Discipline of Market Leaders*. Boston, Mass.

Ulaga, W. (1999) Creating superior customer value in industrial markets, in: Johnson, W. and Weinstein, A. (eds) *Superior Customer Value: Service Concepts and Cases*. Saint Lucie, PR.

Varadarajan, P. and Cunningham, M. (1995) Strategic alliances: a synthesis of conceptual foundations, *Journal of the Academy of Marketing Science*, 23, 4, 282–296.

End of Part Case Study – Tata Motors Ltd: An Indian Elephant Makes a Foray into the Global Auto Market

This case deals with strategic marketing questions in the automobile industry, taking up major concepts discussed in Part 1. Its questions center on the marketing strategies Tata Motors Ltd should pursue in order to become a global player in the automobile industry, and how these strategies should be implemented. As a predominant issue, it incorporates questions and concepts regarding the competitive conduct, market entry into international markets and competitive advantage.

Tata's Inspiration: A First Stepping Stone to Strategic Change

'We must help these people,' Ratan Tata, chairman of the Tata Group and Tata Motors, thought to himself in August 2003. He was driving back home from his office on a rainy night looking outside the window of his Tata sedan in downtown Mumbai, India's rising financial and economic capital, formerly called Bombay (Aiyar 2008). Later that night he figured relaxedly, 'My ideas indeed have the potential to upset the global auto market!' plunging comfortably into a warm bath. What Tata found to be so inspiring yet worrying was the sight of entire families on motorcycles blazing a trail through the overcrowded streets of Mumbai, which were flooded by heavy monsoon rains. Tata observed: 'The father drives with one child standing just in front of him, and the mother sits behind with a baby on her arm. I have seen that so often . . . even during rainstorms or at night. And each time, I think: Oh God, can't we do something to help these families travel more safely?' By that night in late summer 2003, Tata knew they could. The Tata Group, India's oldest and largest conglomerate, has ever since been committed to social responsibility and in that tradition, Tata was convinced, the company should make its way into the twenty-first century: 'Our goal is to develop an inexpensive and safe vehicle!' he asserted (Rao and Tuma 2007). Just a few months later car experts around the world were wide-eyed when they read the news: Tata was announcing the launch of a people's car named Nano – its price was set no higher than Rs100,000 ($2,500), and was therefore referred to as the one-lakh car.[1]

The Global Automobile Market

The industry for automobile manufacturers consists of the market for automobiles and the market for motorcycles, together worth about $1,209 billion worldwide in 2006. Having suffered a slowdown between 2000 and 2002, since then the industry has grown at a compound annual growth rate (CAGR) of 4.7 per cent (up from approximately $1,007 billion in 2002; see Exhibit 1 for further information). In terms of volume, global automobile production totalled 92 million units in 2006 (up from 77.7 in 2002, CAGR of 4.3 per cent). From a geographic perspective, the USA represented the largest automobile market with a share of 38.1 per cent, followed by Europe and the Asia-Pacific region (see Exhibit 2).

1 Rs stands for Indian rupees. A 'lakh' is a unit in the Indian numbering system, representing the number 100,000.

Exhibit 1 Global automobile industry value: $ billion, 2002–2006

Year	$ billion	% growth
2002	1,006.9	
2003	1,039.9	3.30%
2004	1,090.7	4.90%
2005	1,149.5	5.40%
2006	1,209.0	5.20%
Growth rate (CAGR), 2002–2006		**4.70%**

Source: Datamonitor 2007a.

Exhibit 2 Global automobile industry segmentation II: % share, by value, 2006

Geography	% Share
United States	38.1%
Europe	29.3%
Asia-Pacific	23.7%
Rest of the world	8.9%
Total	**100.0%**

Source: Datamonitor 2007a.

Looking forward, improving customer confidence, favorable borrowing rates and increased demand in emerging markets such as China, India, Brazil, Russia and Latin America are expected to fuel future growth in the automobile industry (Datamonitor 2007a; PricewaterhouseCoopers 2007). Growing at an expected CAGR of 4.5 per cent, the industry is expected to reach a total value of about $1,505 billion in 2011 (109.8 million units, CAGR of 3.6 per cent; Datamonitor 2007a; see Exhibit 3). Nonetheless, the automobile industry is facing several challenges in the years ahead,

Exhibit 3 Global automobile industry value forecast: $ billion, 2006–2011

Year	$ billion	% Growth
2006	1,209.0	5.2
2007	1,264.3	4.6
2008	1,322.8	4.6
2009	1,385.5	4.7
2010	1,445.5	4.3
2011	1,505.4	4.1
Growth rate (CAGR) 2006–2011		**4.5%**

Source: Datamonitor 2007a.

including the further increase of raw material prices and the public debate regarding climate change (PricewaterhouseCoopers 2007). As a result, the innovative use of materials and fuel-efficient cars will become more attractive to end customers.

The revenues of automobile manufacturers account for 97.3 per cent of the automobile industry's revenues ($1,176.9 billion in 2006, CAGR of 4.7 per cent between 2002 and 2006). The sector is strongly competitive and concentrated. It is mostly in the hands of five major players: General Motors, Daimler, Toyota, Ford, and Volkswagen. These companies together hold roughly 75 per cent of the global market (see Exhibit 4). In terms of volume, production totalled 65.7 million units in 2006 (CAGR of 3.5 per cent between 2002 and 2006). The growth of the global market in the past has mostly been due to the improvement of the economic situation in developed markets. However, North American and European car manufacturers have suffered from decreased sales volumes. Margins were negatively affected by increased labor, energy and raw materials costs. Considering these issues, manufacturers strive intensely for competitive advantage. As an example, changing customer perceptions and demand have led car manufacturers to focus on innovation (e.g. the development of hybrid cars; Datamonitor 2007a).

According to a recent study conducted by the German automotive supplier Robert Bosch, the market for cars priced under $9,870 will make up 13 per cent of the world's car market by 2010 (equivalent to 10 million cars a year). Bosch estimates that, by then, revenues in the low-price car segment will grow twice as fast as the rest of the market. To satisfy this demand, a Bosch executive says, 'slimmed down versions of existing components and systems are not sufficient' (Timmons 2007), posing an additional pressure for automobile manufacturers to innovate.

Exhibit 4 Global automobile market share: % share, by value, 2006

Company	% share
General Motors	16.8%
DaimlerChrysler	15.5%
Toyota	15.5%
Ford	15.5%
Volkswagen	9.3%
Other	27.4%
Total	**100.0%**

Source: Datamonitor 2007a.

The Tata Group and its Affiliates

The Tata Group, headquartered in India, is described as 'one of the world's most diverse and unusual conglomerates' (Timmons 2008). It operates in seven business sectors through its 98 affiliated companies and 333,000 employees (26 per cent of them outside India; Kripalani 2008). The sectors comprise information systems and communications, engineering, materials, services, energy, consumer products and chemicals (Tata Group 2008a).

Being inspired by the idea of helping to bring back India's wealth, the cornerstone of the company was laid by Jamsetji Tata in 1868 (Rao and Tuma 2007). In the following decades the company developed into one of the country's biggest enterprises, with products and services ranging from tea, watches, automobiles, steel and food additives to energy, as well as hotel and consultancy services. Since Ratan Tata, a distant relative of Jamsetji Tata, took over the fortunes of the group, business activities have begun to expand globally: 'We were so dependent on one economy,' Ratan Tata said (Timmons 2008). Acquisitions of recent years include Tetley Tea, Daewoo Commercial Vehicles and the startling $11.3 billion takeover of British steelmaker Corus in 2007. Corus 'came on us, we didn't seek them out,' said Ratan Tata, 'that opportunity was going to happen once, and it was not going to happen again' (Timmons 2008). The latter deal granted Tata access to the European market and made the company the world's sixth biggest steelmaker. 'We have been thinking bigger than we have done in the past,' stated Chairman Ratan Tata, 'we have been bolder . . . and we have been more aggressive in the marketplace' (Mahapatra 2008). As a result, within five years through 2007 sales of the Tata Group doubled to $29 billion (CNN.com 2008). In fiscal year 2006/2007 international revenues were $10.8 billion (up 58.8 per cent year on year), making up 37.5 per cent of overall revenues (Tata Group 2008b). In fiscal year 2008/2009, it is expected that more than half the group's revenue will accrue from its international operations (Timmons 2008), and Tata is aiming for more: 'We are at an early stage,' he promised (CNN.com 2008).

Traditionally, the group has seen itself as a value-driven organization: 'The one thing I had always felt is that I wanted to go to bed at night saying I had not succumbed to the temptation of giving up the values and the ethics that the group had been built on, just for short-term gains,' Tata says (CNN.com 2008). The company introduced the eight-hour working day (1912), maternity leave (1928) and profit sharing for employees (1934) long before these issues spread worldwide (Rao and Tuma 2007). Today, Tata companies are still known for offering worker benefits that are rare in India, including pension and childcare allowances. Tata executives are known for refusing to pay bribes (not an uncommon business practice in India) and living a modest lifestyle, just as Ratan Tata himself does (CNN.com 2008).

Tata Motors: A Company on the Move

Tata Motors Ltd

Tata Motors was established in 1945 and today is India's largest automobile company, with 22,000 employees (among them 1,400 engineers) and revenues of $7.2 billion in fiscal year 2006/2007, up 36 per cent year-on-year. It was the first Indian industrial company to be listed on the New York Stock Exchange (NYSE: TTM). Its strategic business units (SBUs) are commercial vehicles, where it is market leader in each segment (i.e. buses, trucks and defence vehicles), and passenger vehicles (including utility vehicles).

The manufacturing of commercial vehicles began in 1954 through a 15-year collaboration with Daimler, known as Daimler-Benz at that time. Tata Motors entered the passenger car market in 1991. Its passenger car product range includes the Tata Safari (India's first sports utility vehicle, launched in 1998), the Tata Indica (India's first indigenously designed and manufactured car, launched in 1998) and the Tata Ace (a $5,000 low-cost mini-truck), which is yet to be launched. The company has announced that it will introduce numerous new products in 2008 and export several of these to South Africa, Thailand and Russia. Tata Motors is already present in South America, Asia and some European markets (*Economic Times* 2008a; Sangameshwaran 2008; sify.com 2008). In the past the company has been pushing its growth internationally through acquisitions and alliances. However, Ratan Tata states that this will not be the dominant strategy for growth in the future: 'We are not in an acquisitive mode' (Tata Group 2008c).

In 2005, the Tata Motors European Technical Center (TMETC) was established in the UK. TMETC operations include design engineering and the development of products as a support to Tata Motors' skill sets (Tata Motors 2008). Among the company's partnerships is a distribution agreement with Fiat for the Indian market (Tata Motors 2008). Fiat has become an important partner for the international expansion of the company's own products too, as it uses a Fiat plant in Córdoba/Argentina (sify.com 2008). Another partnership exists with Chrysler's Global Electric Motorcars (GEM), which aims to develop and market an electric version of the Ace in the USA (Kshirsagar 2008). Other strengths of Tata Motors are its strong market position and – outperforming the industry – its robust sales growth. Its overall market share in the Indian four-wheelers market increased to nearly 28 per cent in the fiscal year 2006/2007. The company is leading the commercial vehicles market with a share of 64 per cent and ranks second in the Indian passenger vehicles market with a share of 16.5 per cent. Furthermore, Tata Motors rates high in customer satisfaction. Overall sales grew by 28 per cent in the fiscal year 2006/2007 in terms of volume, achieving its highest ever sales of 580,280 units. In the same year exports grew by 6.5 per cent (53,474 units). Nevertheless, the company suffers from declining cash flows (down 26 per cent year-on-year). This may have a strong negative impact on the company's growth efforts. Additionally, Tata Motor's weak presence in the luxury market (6.4 per cent market share in the Indian market) keeps the company from exploiting further growth potential, with India being the fourth biggest luxury car market in Asia (estimated annual growth of 30 per cent; Datamonitor 2007b).

Just like its parent company, Tata Motors is committed to corporate social responsibility, focusing on health, education, water management and environmental issues. For example, the company has initiated several anti-pollution efforts in the Indian automobile industry and introduced emission control engines before they became obligatory (Tata Motors 2008).

The company demonstrates its ambitions in the global auto market and marks milestones in the company's history – and maybe in automobile history as well – with two major strategic events: the introduction of the Tata Nano and the planned Jaguar/Land Rover takeover (Joshi and Gosh 2008).

Exhibit 5 The Tata Nano

Introducing the People's Car: The New Tata Nano

The Tata Nano was first presented to the public at the Auto Expo in New Delhi on January 10, 2008 (see Exhibit 5). It is a four-seater with a 623cc two-cylinder motor that can propel the car up to 105km/h. The retail price will be Rs1 lakh ($2,500) at its planned launch in September 2008, roughly half as much as its closest competitor, the Maruti 800. Having gained much attention worldwide, the car has already been compared to the Ford Model T and the Volkswagen Beetle, both milestones in automobile history. German-based research firm CSM Worldwide expects the Nano to drive Tata to the lead position among India's light-vehicle manufacturers by 2013 (Platt 2008). In India, just eight out of a thousand people own a car, indicating a huge market potential. Additionally, there seems to be potential to upgrade motorcycle owners (*Hindustan Times* 2008). Thus, annual production will be 250,000 units but is expected to increase to 1 million in 2010.

Despite the euphoric reactions that the Nano has elicited, opponents and competitors have raised their voices too. Critics say that the car might 'encourage millions of Indians to give up their two-wheel motor scooters and three-wheel motorized rickshaws', that jam-packed roads might even get worse, and that it will increase India's dependence on imported oil (Friedman 2007). Environmental activists warn of its pollution and climate consequences (Prasad and Mishra 2008), yet its consumption will be only 5 litres/100km and it will be able to meet the Euro IV norm (Joshi and Gosh 2008), which limits pollutants to obligatory thresholds. Other worrying issues for Tata include the danger of a major price war among manufacturers (Chaze 2008). Already Renault and Nissan have announced that they will bring a no-frills version of an existing model to the market at $3,000 (*Economic Times* 2008b). Crude oil and steel prices might increase, as they have done in the past (Aiyar 2008). If this happens, the price of the car may not remain as sensationally low as proposed (Sangameshwaran 2008). And, even if Tata manages this issue, low cost might not necessarily be the only salient selling argument.

From a business perspective, the most interesting question in this regard is 'How was Tata able to build a car at a cost that auto experts have labeled as impossible to achieve?' To answer this question several factors have to be taken into account. One important aspect is the experience Tata gained from developing the Indica, and especially designing and building the Ace, since that was a cost-based project too (Tata Group 2008c). The second aspect is the design of the car itself. As Tata points out, 'the rear passenger seat is on the engine, so you save space; the engine is driving the wheels directly so you save engineering for the drive; you save the space in the bonnet and construction helps keep the costs down but yet meets safety standards' (Aiyar 2008). Many features are missing in the entry-level model, such as air-conditioning, power brakes and a radio. Tata has put an aluminium engine inside and reduced the amount of steel in the car (Hagel and Brown 2008), leading not only to reduced purchase costs but to low operating costs as well (Aiyar 2008). Along with all the other features of the Nano that are low cost and future oriented, Tata didn't put the dashboard in front of the driver but right in the middle, so it will be easier to produce a left-hand drive vehicle (Tata Group 2008c). Putting together existing wisdom in an innovative way, the car is cheaper and smaller, yet offers about 20 per cent more seating capacity than the Maruti 800 (Hagel and Brown 2008).

What has really made an impact is its modular design. Tata was not focusing on single breakthrough innovations. The 34 patents hardly seem frightening to Western auto executives compared to, for example, the roughly 280 patents awarded to General Motors every year (Hagel and Brown 2008). Instead, the Nano is 'constructed of components that can be built and shipped separately to be assembled in a variety of locations. In effect, the Nano is being sold in kits that are distributed, assembled, and serviced by local entrepreneurs.' (Hagel and Brown 2008). Ratan Tata explained the approach – fully in line with his and his company's values – as follows: 'A bunch of entrepreneurs could establish an assembly operation and Tata Motors would train their people, would oversee their quality assurance and they would become satellite assembly operations for us. So we would create entrepreneurs across the country that . . . produce the car. We would produce the mass items and ship it to them as kits. That is my idea of dispersing wealth' (Hagel and Brown 2008).

The basic version of the Nano, however, will never appear on Europe's streets due to the high security standards. It is not a secret, though, that besides the primarily targeted Indian market customers in Western countries are also attracted by the affordable car, maybe offering the chance to target these markets too (Mamgain and Athale 2008). Ratan Tata points out: 'I feel that there is probably a market, maybe outside India . . . for a fully loaded power steering, automatic transmission, power windows, air-conditioned kind of car with a bigger engine at a very affordable price, which is far lower than what is available elsewhere and we should be able to address that kind of market also' but, he goes on, 'the obvious markets overseas for us would be the African markets, the Latin American markets like Brazil, Argentina and some of the Far East countries like Malaysia, Indonesia, etc.' (Gupta and Sriram 2008).

However, the pending launch of a hybrid version of the Nano (Chaze 2008) may indeed offer a significant chance to make automobile history in the developed markets too. Either way, the Nano has done something that automobile manufacturers didn't achieve in decades: it created an all-new set of customers (Joshi and Gosh 2008) – a market that just didn't exist before.

The Elephant Arrives: The Jaguar/Land Rover Takeover

In early 2008, Tata Motors was in detailed talks to take over two of the world's most famous auto brands from Ford, namely Jaguar and Land Rover. In the past the two brands have had to deal with harmful exchange rates and high production costs in Britain. In 2007, sales of Jaguar were down 24 per cent while Land Rover increased sales by 3 per cent compared to 2006 (Staff 2007). The proposed deal is worth $2 billion (Dutt 2008). Another bidder still in the race is JPMorgan's private equity arm, One Equity Partners, whose senior partner and former Ford chief Jacques Nasser is running the bid (Clark 2008).

Ford had acquired Jaguar for $2.5 billion in 1989 and Land Rover for $2.7 billion in 2000. Together with British luxury sportscar manufacturer Aston Martin and Swedish Volvo, the two brands made up Ford's Premier Automotive Group. Ford has gone through some tough years and is still looking for fast cash, having lost $12.6 billion in 2006 alone. It expects to burn at least another $12 billion through 2009, when it plans to turn profitable again. In 2007, Ford sold its controlling stake in Aston Martin for $931 million in cash and preferred stock. In contrast, Ford plans to keep Volvo and make it more of a premium brand (Staff 2007).

Regarding the proposed deal, Ratan Tata says that 'our intention about Jaguar/Land Rover is not to take over the technology, not to outsource [production], but instead we are only interested in the brands and the cultures behind them. We plan to retain the image, touch and feel of these brands and not tinker with them in any way.' In saying this, he reacted to concerns that the takeover would mark the end of the automobile industry in Britain (Dutt 2008). But Tata – once again – is committed to social responsibility: 'We don't break companies up and, under normal circumstances, we don't just shut down factories' (Rao and Tuma 2007).

Problems Ahead for Tata

'If Tata Motors wants to be at the forefront of the global automobile scene, it has to take the fast-track route to progress,' says an automobile industry analyst (Sangameshwaran 2008). Low-cost cars could well be the next big thing in a row of low-cost goods and services that have come up in today's global economy – after low-cost carriers, retail stores and notebooks, to name just a few. But how to market these tiny red and yellow candy lookalikes, Tata was wondering. And, even more importantly, what markets to enter in the years ahead? Tata was convinced it was way in front of the competition and – maybe – just as far ahead of the times.

Today, shortly before the launch of the Nano finally takes place, the company is heading the news once again: not only does it launch a car uncompromisingly designed for mass markets, costing just as much as a premium car's hi-fi system, it is also reaching out for two of the world's most respected auto brands – Jaguar and Land Rover. Acquiring the two brands from US auto giant Ford would put Tata in a position to compete with two-wheeler manufacturers on the one hand and, on the other, to be at eye level with premium brands such as BMW, Mercedes and Audi (Sangameshwaran 2008).

The Nano introduction and the acquisition of the luxury brands Jaguar and Land Rover might have one desirable aspect: to 'instantly push Tata Motors onto global centerstage' (Sangameshwaran 2008). But, nonetheless, both ventures are associated with significant challenges and risks, Ratan Tata is well aware. He is pondering the future steps to be taken and the way towards Tata's strategic goals while he leans back in his chair overlooking the bay opening widely to the Arabian Sea.

This case was written by Thomas Rilling, Department of Marketing University of Mannheim.

Discussion Questions

1. What kind of strategy is Tata Motors pursuing with its Nano?
2. What is the competitive advantage of Tata Motors in the auto market? What are the company's core competencies?
3. Outline the possible strategic marketing objectives of Tata Motors. Consider the structure outlined in Part 1.
4. Discuss several marketing strategy alternatives for introducing the Tata Nano regarding:
   (a) strategic marketing objectives/target groups addressed by marketing strategy
   (b) customer benefits and positioning in relation to competition
   (c) innovation orientation
   (d) CRM
   (e) competitive and cooperative conduct
   (f) design and structure of the marketing mix.
5. Where do you see Tata Motors' future strategic challenges?

References

Aiyar, S. (2008) Ratan's revolution, *India Today*, 11 January.
Chaze, A. (2008) Tata fires first shot in auto price war, *Global Finance*, February, 22, 2, 12.
Clark, N. (2008) Tata grabs lead for Jaguar, Land Rover, *Business Week*, 4 January.
CNN.com (2008) Tata steps into global limelight, 25 February; URL: http://edition.cnn.com/2008/BUSINESS/02/24/india.tata.ap/index.html.
Datamonitor (2007a) Global automobiles – industry profile, March.
Datamonitor (2007b) Tata Motors Limited – company profile, August.
Dutt, V. (2008) Jag, Rover to retain marque status: Tata, *Hindustan Times*, 5 March.
Economic Times (2008a) Tata Motors plans 15–20 new CVs launches, *Economic Times*, 11 January.
Economic Times (2008b) Tata to ride Nano to Geneva Motor Show, *Economic Times*, 7 February.
Friedman, T.L. (2007) No, no, no, don't follow us, *New York Times*, 4 November.
Gupta, I. and Sriram, R. (2008) Interview with Ratan Tata, Making of Nano, *Economic Times*, 11 January.
Hagel, J. and Brown, J.S. (2008) Learning from Tata's Nano, *Business Week*, 27 February.
Hindustan Times (2008) Tata Motors's $2,500 car to put India on global autos map, 11 January.
Joshi, D. and Gosh, S. (2008) Small wonder, *Hindustan Times*, 11 January.
Kripalani, M. (2008) Tata: master of the gentle approach, *Business Week*, 14 February.

Kshirsagar, A. (2008) Tata Motors inks deal with Chrysler electric vehicle unit, *Hindu Business Line*, 22 January.
Mahapatra, R. (2008) Tata Motors of India keeps its growth plan on track, *USA Today*, February.
Mamgain, P. and Athale, G.A. (2008) Tata's one-lakh car Nano: Western media on overdrive, *Economic Times*, 11 January.
Platt, G. (2008) India's little car has big ambitions, *Global Finance*, February, 22, 2, 14.
Prasad, S. and Mishra, A.K. (2008) Breathe easy, people's car, Nano, not that polluting, *Economic Times*, 12 January.
PricewaterhouseCoopers (2007) *Global Automotive Financial Review: An Overview of Industry Data, Trends and Financial Reporting Practices* (2007 edition).
Rao, P. and Tuma, T. (2007) 'We Indians have to struggle to catch up': interview with Indian industry mogul Ratan Tata, *Spiegel Online*, 9 April; URL: http://www.spiegel.de/international/business/0,1518,476262,00.html.
Sangameshwaran, P. (2008) What drives Tata Motors? *Business Standard*, 22 January.
sify.com (2008) Tata plans to launch 'Xenon' in Argentina with Fiat, 12 January; URL: http://sify.com/finance/fullstory.php?id=14588402.
Staff, B.W. (2007) Report: Tata Wins Jaguar, Land Rover, *Business Week*, 20 December.
Tata Group (2008a) Tata Group profile, company website; URL: http://www.tata.com/0_about_us/group_profile.htm.
Tata Group (2008b) Tata Group Investor Center, group financials, company website; URL: http://www.tata.com/0_investor_desk/group_financials.htm.
Tata Group (2008c) The making of the Nano: interview with Ratan Tata, company website; URL: http://www.tata.com/0_media/features/interviews/20080110_one_lakh_car.htm.
Tata Motors (2008) Tata Motors profile, company website; URL: http://www.tatamotors.com/our_world/profile.php.
Timmons, H. (2007) In India, a $2,500 pace car, *New York Times*, 12 October.
Timmons, H. (2008) Tata pulls Ford units into its orbit, *New York Times*, 4 January.

PART 2

The Marketing Mix

arketing strategy – as discussed in Part 1 of this book – requires the systematic use marketing instruments. These marketing instruments are commonly referred to as e marketing mix. Part 2 will focus on the marketing mix, which comprises the five mponents listed below.

Starting Part 2, Chapter 5, on *product decisions*, is concerned with all decisions related to the current and future product range. Here we will discuss decisions regarding product innovations as well as products that are already established in the market, including branding.

Pricing decisions discussed in Chapter 6 deal with all decisions concerning the price that customers have to pay for a product. To facilitate understanding of the relevant decisions we will discuss classic pricing theory as well as behavioral pricing.

Chapter 7, on *sales decisions*, covers decisions about acquisition activities aimed at the marketplace and decisions related to distribution logistics. Acquisition activities are geared towards acquiring new customers and generating sales. Distribution logistics focuses on the structure and design of the physical distribution of goods.

Chapter 8 looks at *communication decisions*, which concern all decisions regarding the company's communication in the market. The company can use various tools to communicate, including, for example, media advertising or online marketing.

In Chapter 9, on *the role of customer relationship management in the marketing mix*, the focus is on the two most relevant issues in customer relationship management: customer satisfaction and customer loyalty. We propose a range of customer relationship management tools within the individual marketing instruments discussed in Part 2 that can help to establish customer satisfaction and loyalty.

Contents

The design of the individual components of the marketing mix needs to be derived from the marketing strategy that the company has formulated. Whereas the individual components of the marketing mix are basically geared towards the marketing objectives related to market success and economic marketing objectives (see Section 2.1, Figure 2-2), significant differences arise with regard to objectives related to potential. The individual components of the marketing mix aim to achieve similar objectives with regard to market and economic success, however they do so by addressing different objectives related to potential (see Figure P2-1).

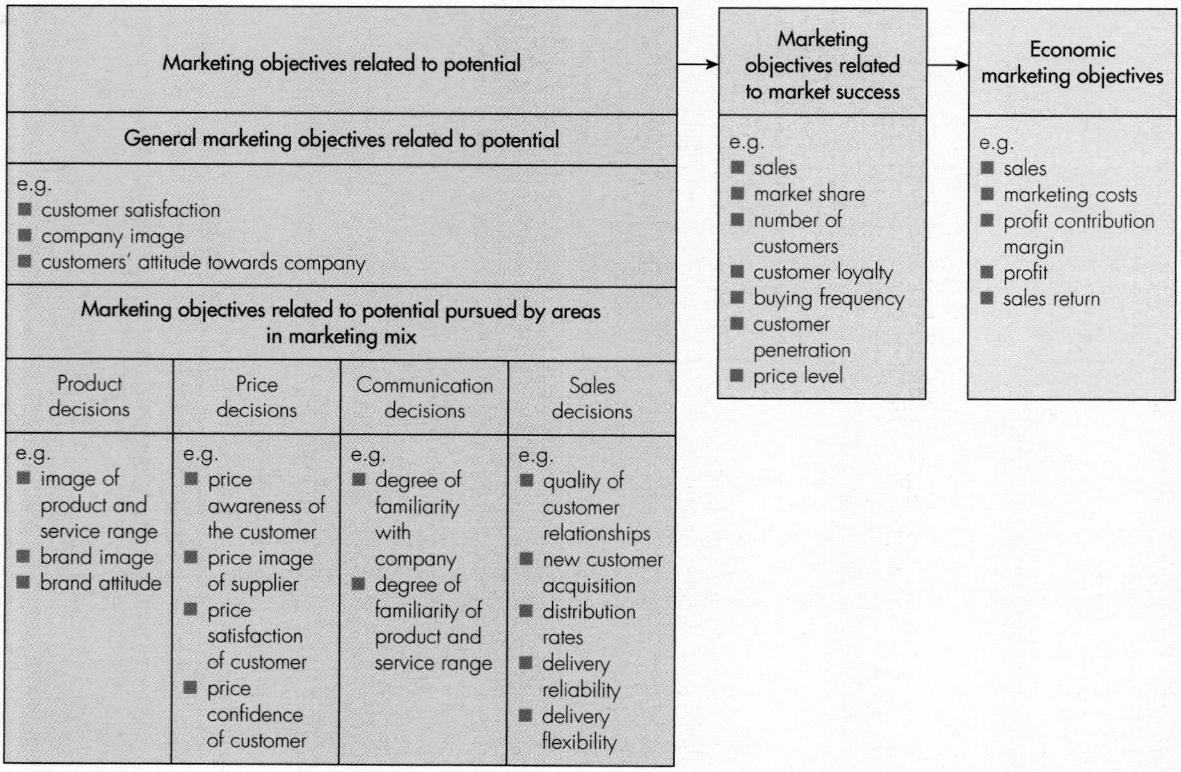

Figure P2-1 Definition of marketing objectives related to potential, with respect to the marketing mix

CHAPTER 5

Product Decisions

Contents

Learning Objectives

In this chapter you will become familiar with:

- the different definitions of 'product', basic product typologies and the main decision-making areas in the product mix
- the individual phases of the innovation process, from idea generation and product development to market introduction
- the fundamental tools that can be used in the individual phases of the innovation process or across all phases, and be able to assess their potential contribution to optimizing the innovation process
- the key decision-making areas and courses of action within the scope of managing established products
- the primary options with respect to brand strategy and branding
- the most important methods for evaluating brand success.

5.1 Areas of Product Decisions

A company's product decisions are the result of all decisions related to the design of existing and future products of the company. Product decisions play an especially important role within the marketing mix. The conceptual basis of the product decisions will be described in Section 5.2. Following that, we will examine decisions related to product innovations (see Section 5.3), which, in the face of ever shorter product life cycles (see Bayus 1994) are becoming increasingly more important to long-term company success. Once a product is successfully launched in the market, continuous efforts are required to secure its long-term market success. Accordingly, in Section 5.4, we will discuss the management of products that are already established in the market. Finally, in Section 5.5, we will discuss the important area of brand management.

5.2 Defining the Product

As a starting point for presenting the area of product decisions, it is important to understand what a product is. From the perspective of the customer, the product represents a means of satisfying a need and thus obtaining benefits. Based on this, Kotler (1972) distinguishes between three different concepts:

1. the substantial
2. the expanded, and
3. the generic definition of a product.

The **substantial product definition** views the core product as a package of physical-technical features. The focus of this definition is that the functional customer needs are satisfied by the physical features that the product offers. For example, the product 'sports car' is a combination of various features such as 'ability to transport persons' or 'fast acceleration'.

Within the scope of the **expanded product definition**, a product is considered to be a service package comprising physical products and/or intangible services that strive to meet comprehensively functional customer needs. According to this definition, a product can also be partially or wholly intangible and, consequently, a service can also be referred to as a product. In keeping with our example, the product 'sports car' comprises the core product as well as quality guarantees or free servicing (the intangible part of the product).

The **generic product definition** offers the broadest approach and, with this definition, a product consists of all the tangible and intangible product facets that can result in customer benefits. This definition is rather broad as it not only considers functional benefits but also other benefits, such as, say, emotional or social benefits. The product 'sports car' therefore comprises further features that represent additional benefits for the customer (e.g. a renowned brand offering the benefit of social prestige).

This book applies the generic product definition. In line with this approach, we consider a product to be a bundle of features that aim to create customer benefits. Accordingly, we differentiate between the different components of the product that can help to generate customer benefits (see Figure 5-1).

- The **product core** comprises the **core features** of the product, which substantially determine the functionality of the product. This level generates core benefits. For example, for a scheduled flight, core product features would be the departure and arrival time, duration of the flight and airline safety.

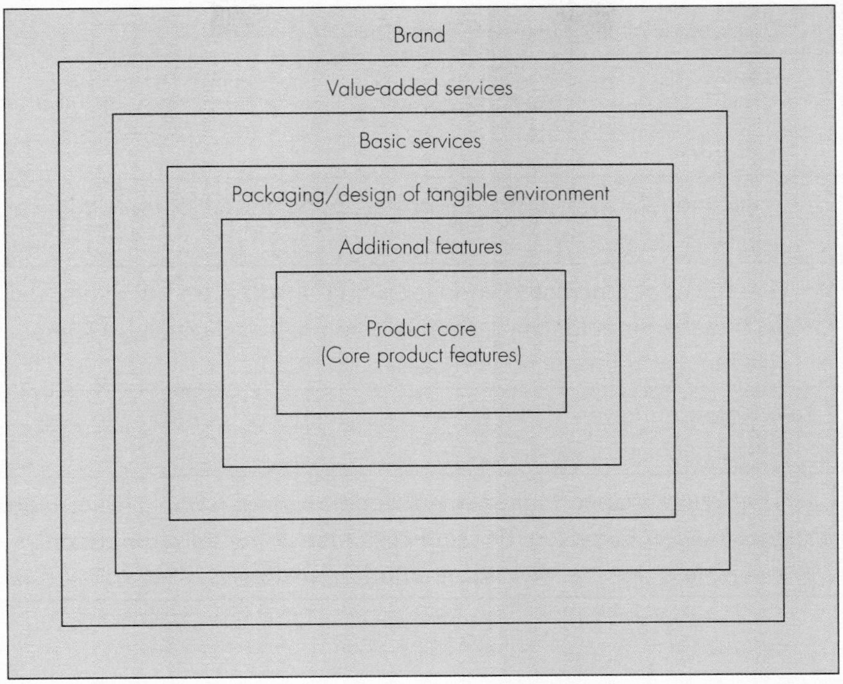

Figure 5-1 Components of a product

- **Additional features** contribute to generating a benefit that is not included in the core function of the product. For a scheduled flight, for example, onboard entertainment represents an additional feature.
- A further component of the product is the **packaging** and **design of the tangible environment**. The term 'packaging' refers primarily to physical products. Packaging serves various functions such as, for instance, protecting the product, handling properties, as well as ensuring that the product can be transported. Of special importance is the design of the tangible environment with regard to services (e.g. the design of the local branch of a bank or a doctor's office). The tangible environment is thus the 'packaging' of a service, so to speak.
- **Basic services** are those services that customers expect the company to provide when they purchase a product. These include, for example, engineering consulting services for technically sophisticated industrial facilities, or a company website providing basic information such as opening hours.
- In contrast, **value-added services** do not represent indispensable prerequisites for customers' purchase decisions, but offer additional benefits. By offering these additional services, companies strive to stand out from the competition and to generate customer loyalty. Value-added services can generate different types of benefit, such as functional, economic, process-related, emotional and social benefits (see Table 5-1 for examples).
- Finally, the **brand** has to be mentioned as a product component. Branding is a crucial issue and is discussed in detail in Section 5.5.

Table 5-1 Examples of value-added services with different target benefit categories

Type of benefit	Example of value-added services
Functional benefit	A bank offers individual financial consulting geared towards the special requirements and risk preferences of a private banking customer
Economic benefit	A car manufacturer offers car buyers loans at special rates to lower their financing costs
Process-related benefit	A supplier of machine components guarantees just-in-time delivery so that the manufacturing company can more efficiently structure its inventory and production processes
Emotional benefit	A restaurant gives a little gift to a guest having a birthday (e.g. a birthday cake for dessert)
Social benefit	The Private Wealth Management department of a bank invites high-profile, wealthy private banking customers to socially important events (e.g. private viewing of an art exhibition)

In addition to the general product definition, a key question concerns the classification of products on the basis of their characteristics. We propose a **typology of products** based on the following characteristics:

- degree of tangibility – physical products versus services
- type of customer – industrial goods (business customer) versus consumer goods (end customer)
- complexity/degree to which the services are customized – totally uncustomized products (mass products) versus totally customized products
- durability – non-durable products versus durable products
- frequency of use/consumption – products used/consumed on a daily basis versus infrequently used products
- branding – branded products versus non-branded products
- buying habits – convenience goods (products usually purchased frequently involving only limited time and a minimum of effort, e.g. snacks or newspapers), shopping goods (goods that are purchased infrequently and bought after a careful comparison of quality and prices, e.g. clothing), speciality goods (products with unique characteristics bought infrequently – these products often imply high involvement on the part of the customer, e.g. real estate, vintage cars) (for the issue of customer involvement, see the section on involvement in the Appendix)
- buying motivation – sought goods (goods generally purchased voluntarily and out of customer's own motivation) versus unsought goods (to some extent externally motivated purchases, e.g. legally required insurance)
- value-added stage that the product is allocated to in the production process – raw materials, intermediate or finished products.

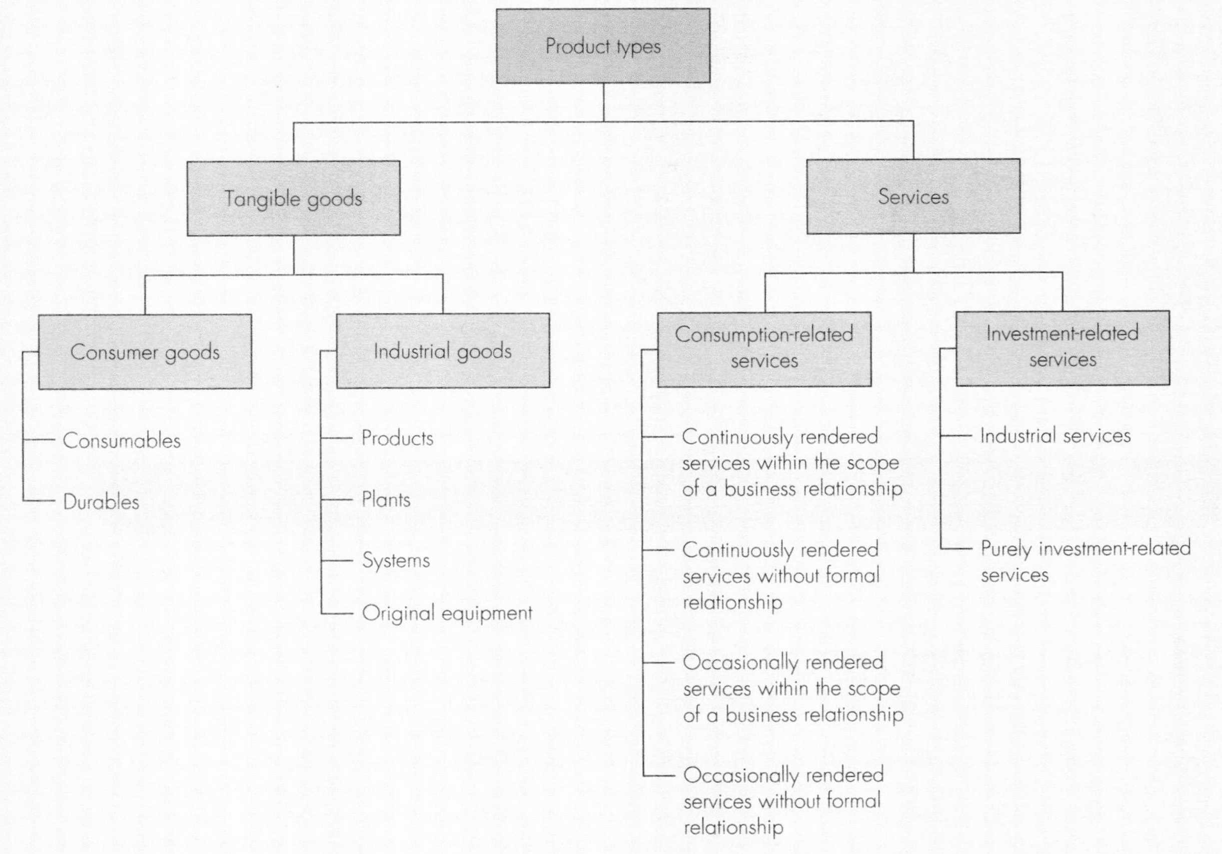

Figure 5-2 Basic typology of products

The different product characteristics introduced in this typology are important as customers' buying behavior often strongly depends on these characteristics. Figure 5-2 contains a product typology based on several of these characteristics. On the first level we distinguish products according to their degree of tangibility (tangible goods versus services). On the second level we further differentiate by type of customer (e.g. consumer goods versus industrial goods, and consumption-related services versus investment-related services). Other typologies can be found in Murphy and Enis (1986).

When making product decisions, management has to deal with several challenging **decision-making areas**. There are three important areas to consider:

1 innovation management

2 management of products already established in the market

3 brand management.

These decision-making areas relate to the various product life cycle phases (see also Section 2.2.3) and are reflected in the structure of this chapter (see also Figure 5-3).

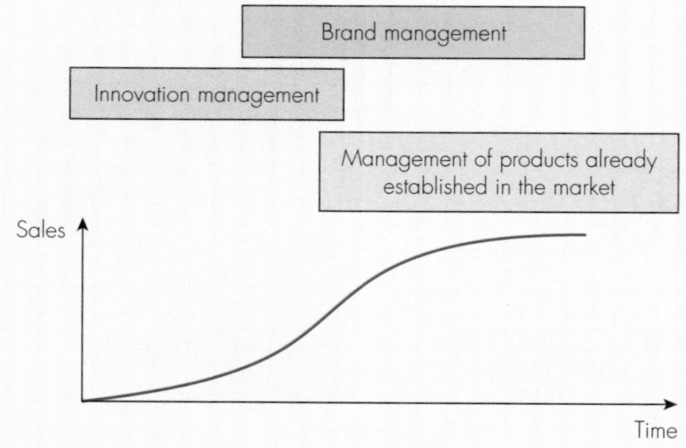

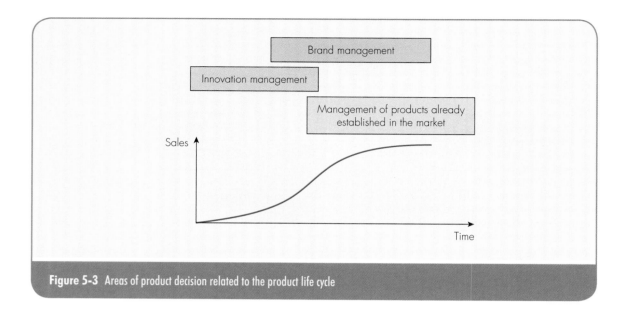

Figure 5-3 Areas of product decision related to the product life cycle

5.3 Innovation Management

5.3.1 Concepts and Challenges in Innovation Management

The development of new and successful products is of utmost importance for companies' long-term survival. Considerable challenges arise from innovation management where firms are concerned with the development of **product innovations**. Product innovations are considered to be products or product concepts that customers perceive as being new. Generally, two types of product innovation can be distinguished: market-driven product innovations and technology-driven product innovations. Innovations that are induced by the market usually address customer needs that were not catered for by existing products ('demand pull'). Technology-driven innovations come about due to technological developments on the supply side ('technology push'). R&D is usually the main driver of technology push innovations (see, e.g., Mohr *et al.* 2005).

The significance of product innovations for company success is illustrated by the fact that many products are subject to a life cycle (which in recent years has become increasingly shorter for a number of product categories – see Bayus 1994, 1998). This means, that at one point in time products usually experience declining sales (see the life cycle model described in Section 2.2.3). Against this background, and in view of the high failure rates for new products (for an overview, see Montoya-Weiss and Calantone 1994), systematic innovation management is becoming more and more important (see also Trott 2005). For an example of a company with a focus on innovation see Focus on Marketing 5-1.

An innovation refers to the development of a product that features a certain degree of newness. This degree of newness can be assessed from the perspective of the buyers in the market or from a company viewpoint. A classification of innovations emerges from combining these two perspectives, as is shown in Figure 5-4. For example, new-to-the-world products are perceived as new by both the company and the customer.

There are several empirical findings available with respect to the success factors of innovations (Astebro and Michela 2005; Balbontin and Yazdani 1999; Cooper and Kleinschmidt 1987, 1994,

Newness to company	Low (newness to market)		High (newness to market)
High	New product lines		New-to-world products
	Product improvements/revisions to existing products	Additions to existing product lines	
Low	Cost reductions	Repositionings of existing products	

Newness to market

Figure 5-4 Typology of innovations based on their newness for the company and the market (adapted from Booz *et al.* 1982)

1995, 1996; Cooper *et al.* 2004; Di Benedetto 1999; Mishra *et al.* 1996; Van Riel *et al.* 2004; and, for an overview, Henard and Szymanski 2001). Studies show that it is the design of the innovation process (from idea generation to market introduction) and the features of the new product (especially when they are aligned with customer needs) in particular that are relevant to success. In the following, we will therefore examine the different approaches to designing innovation processes that exist, and the different approaches that are used to take customer requirements on board in the process of developing innovations.

Focus on Marketing 5-1 The importance of innovation management

Innovation at Siemens Medical Solutions

Siemens Medical Solutions is one of the largest providers of medical devices and technologies in the world and a leading innovator in the field. Siemens is renowned for its innovative products, services and solution systems. These range from imaging systems for diagnosis and therapy equipment for treatment, to IT solutions which increase efficiency and optimize workflow in hospitals, clinics and doctors' offices.

The company traces its origins back to 1877, when Erwin Moritz Reiniger founded a workshop in Erlangen, Germany, to produce electro-medical devices. Siemens AG became the major shareholder in the company in 1925, and in 2002 the firm name was altered to its present designation. Throughout its history, Siemens Medical has been a major innovator. Innovations include: the first industrial manufacture of x-ray tubes in 1896, the first electrical hearing aid in 1913, manufacturing the first implantable cardiac pacemaker in 1958, the first ultra-sound device with real time display in 1966, installing the first Magnetic Resonance Imaging (MRI) system in North America in 1982, and several firsts in the development of networking and IT solutions for medical institutions.

Currently, the firm produces medical equipment in various branches, including nuclear medicine, patient monitoring, anesthesia, and medical imaging. Other offerings include advanced IT systems for clinical management, patient data management, and a wide variety of consulting services in the areas of strategic consulting, financial-administrative consulting, IT consulting, and clinical consulting.

Focus on Marketing 5.1 (Continued)

Innovation strategy is treated as a part of the overall business strategy. The Siemens website calls the excellence strategy 'P^3 – People, Processes and Products'. It is described in the statement, 'We bring together innovations and process optimization to help our customers provide higher-quality, patient-centered healthcare services more efficiently and at lower cost.' Siemens Medical has a clearly defined project management process and uses innovative financial models. Currently two-thirds of products are less than three years old.

The corporate culture allows for a degree of personal responsibility for employees in a challenging work environment and rewards creativity and initiative. Cross-functional teams are frequently used to develop new solutions and products. Team members come from a wide variety of technical, administrative and medical backgrounds and are able to bring different perspectives to the development teams. Researchers are given a high degree of latitude to pursue research and perform experiments of their own interest.

Sources: Riederer *et al.* 2005.

Figure 5-5 provides an overview of the different phases of the innovation process. For each phase we will discuss important tools that can be used to facilitate the tasks in these different phases. These will be described in more detail in the following sections.

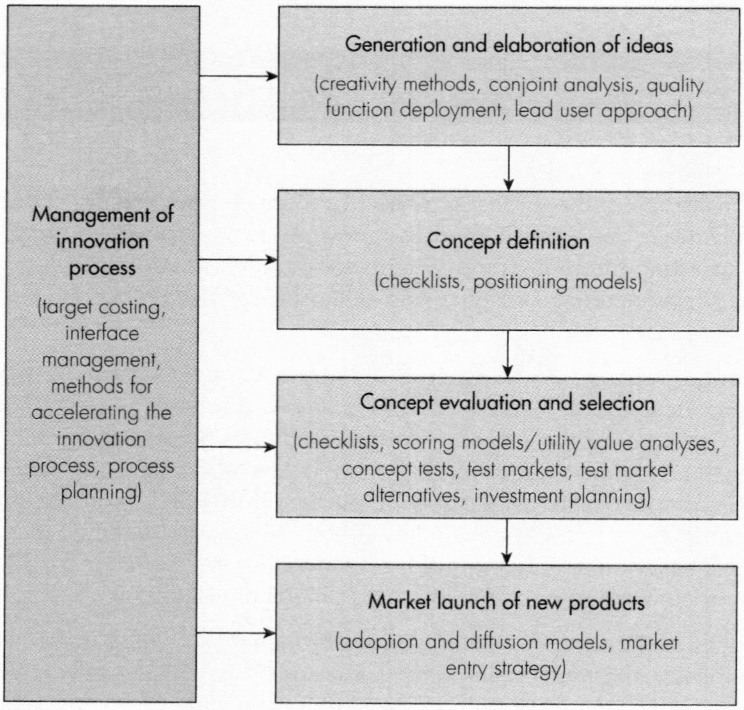

Figure 5-5 Phases and selected tools within innovation processes

Table 5-2 Important sources of new product ideas

Company-internal sources	Sources outside the company
■ R&D department employees (e.g. with respect to trends in technology) ■ Field salesforce employees ■ Customer service/service hotline employees ■ Complaint information ■ Suggestions from employees in general	■ Customers (direct interviews/surveying, focus groups with customers, observation of product usage by customers, customer suggestions/requests) ■ Competitors (e.g. analysis of exhibitions, trade fairs and new product announcements by competitors) ■ Market innovations in other markets ■ Technological developments ■ Experts (e.g. interviews with distributors and intermediaries or industry experts) ■ Findings from trend and market research institutes, business consultants and advertising agencies

5.3.2 Generation and Elaboration of Ideas

Methods for Generating Ideas

First and foremost, companies need to generate ideas for innovations. In general, ideas can come from company-internal sources or from external sources (see Table 5-2 for important sources of new product ideas). In some cases, company-internal sources are more directly available and less expensive, whereas company-external sources tend to lead to ideas that are more innovative – especially if there is a risk that people in the company are less able to 'think outside the box'. Many of these sources can be leveraged by using market research techniques. This is particularly important with regard to using customer sources for input. Here, qualitative approaches such as focus groups or in-depth interviews (for more on the focus group see the discussion on surveys in the Appendix) can play a key role. In the case of more complex products, observations of customers using the products can also be very useful and informative (for more on observations see the Appendix). For example, such observations are used by many manufacturers of technologies in order to identify any potential problems that may come up for customers in the early phases of the innovation process. These may arise because of particular product characteristics such as functionality or handling.

New product ideas can also be generated from using **creativity methods**. These methods can promote and encourage creative thinking by creating synergies, for example, on the part of the members of a cross-functional project team.

Creativity methods can be used by individuals or a group of people. The assumption is that groups of people with different backgrounds can often generate more innovative ideas than single individuals. When creativity techniques are applied in groups, the skill of the moderator plays a key role in ensuring the success of the method. The moderator has to supervise the process and manage the discussion, and the challenge is to ensure the moderator's objectivity throughout this process. While controlling this process the moderator also has to make sure that the flow of ideas is not restricted and creativity restrained.

Brainstorming and **brainwriting** are creativity methods that are usually applied in group situations. There are two principles underlying these methods for promoting and encouraging creativity. First, the objective is to generate as many new ideas as possible. In pursuing this goal the principle is that the quality of innovative ideas increases with the number of ideas expressed. This is due to the fact that human thinking is hierarchically structured and, consequently, conventional and easy ideas are expressed first. New ideas are therefore frequently generated only after the obvious, less innovative ideas have been voiced. As a second principle, the judgement of ideas is suspended (the phase of generating ideas is separated from the phase of judging the ideas). It is important here to create a positive atmosphere in which everybody is encouraged to express ideas – even the unconventional – without fear of being criticized.

A widely used brainwriting technique is the **6-3-5 method**. With this technique, six people are presented with a problem in writing and asked to suggest three written solutions within a five-minute period (which is why the method is termed 6-3-5) and then to hand these solutions to the person sitting next to them. That person then picks up on the ideas, develops them further or creates new ideas. The process continues until each person has worked with each of the six sets of solutions.

Another method is the **morphological box**. With this technique, a new product to be developed is described using several characteristics. Several variants are defined for each of these characteristics, and new product ideas can then be developed by combining the variants. The following example further illustrates this technique. The idea of a new coffee machine is examined with regard to the following characteristics:

- principle of operation
- raw coffee material
- water intake
- output quantity per operating cycle
- type of power supply.

Table 5-3 lists the various options for each of these characteristics, which can then be combined into new product ideas.

The following new product ideas could be developed from this.

- Principle of operation: filter machine.
- Raw coffee material: coffee capsules.
- Water intake: removable water tank.

Table 5-3 Morphological box using example of coffee machine

Principle of operation	Raw coffee material	Water intake	Output quantity per operating cycle	Power supply
■ Manual lever machine ■ Filter machine ■ Semi-automatic ■ Fully automatic household coffee maker ■ Fully automatic commercial coffee maker	■ Coffee beans ■ Ground coffee ■ Coffee capsules ■ Coffee tablets ■ Coffee bags	■ Integrated water tank ■ Removable water tank ■ Connection to water pipe	■ 1 × 1 cup ■ 1 × 2 cups ■ 2 × 2 cups ■ 3 × 2 cups ■ 4 × 2 cups	■ Power socket ■ Battery operated ■ Rechargeable battery ■ Hotplate

- Output quantity per operating cycle: 1 × 2 cups.
- Power supply: rechargeable battery.

Methods for Elaborating Ideas

In company practice, product ideas are usually not very concrete in the initial phase. In order to improve their feasibility they have to be further elaborated and, ultimately, substantiated. There are three methods that are particularly suited to the pursuit of this objective:

1. conjoint analysis
2. quality function deployment (QFD)
3. the lead user approach.

Conjoint analysis is a statistical technique that involves measuring preferences at the individual customer level. For the purpose of new product evaluation, customer preferences for different product ideas (concepts) can be measured. In order to do so, the product is decomposed into several features, each potentially offering utility for the customer. In particular, the overall customer utility associated with the product is decomposed into the utility contributions of the individual product attributes. The overall objective is to find the combination of attributes that customers prefer most. A conjoint analysis also provides information about how the customer utility changes when certain attributes are modified. This is feasible as customers are required to make a series of trade-off decisions and the analysis of these reveals the relative importance of the different attributes.

Due to the focus on customer utility, conjoint analysis is particularly useful in gearing the new product development process towards generating customer benefits. As this technique is applied in the early phase of elaborating new product ideas, the risk of new product failures can be substantially reduced.

Within the scope of elaborating ideas, conjoint analysis can facilitate knowledge in three important areas.

1. Conjoint analysis can be used to identify the attributes that are vitally important to customers. The design of these features should be given special consideration during the phase of idea elaboration.
2. With conjoint analysis it is feasible to examine for individual product attributes whether and how customer preferences vary depending on different levels of these attributes. This knowledge is especially crucial with respect to the identification of attributes that generate significant increases in benefit as compared to less favorable features. Moreover, this also allows identification of performance enhancements that offer only marginal increases in customer benefits (over-engineering).
3. Of special relevance is the option of considering the price as a product attribute in conjoint analysis. This way, for example, customers' willingness to pay a certain price can be assessed via explicit cost–benefit comparisons for product improvements.

(For a more detailed description of conjoint analysis refer to the Appendix.)

With the **quality function deployment (QFD)** method, customer requirements with regard to a product (which, e.g., were determined in the course of a conjoint analysis) are systematically translated into technical product characteristics. This method thus deals with the potential problem that customers usually base their requirements on the situation arising from product use and formulate them in their 'own' language. These formulations can be difficult to grasp for those involved in product development (e.g. engineers), who tend to describe the products by means of objective (technical) characteristics. The QFD method attempts to facilitate the translation of the 'voice of the customer' into the 'voice of the engineer' with as little loss of information or misinformation as possible.

The **lead user approach** is also relevant when discussing the phase of idea elaboration (see von Hippel 1988). The fundamental thought behind the lead user concept is that those customers whose current requirements set trends for the requirements of the other customers in the market should be identified, and possibly involved in the product conception and design. This condition can arise from the fact that, for instance, future customer requirements are characterized by certain trends that specific customers (called 'lead users') are already subjected to in the present. Another attribute of lead users is that they expect to gain a significant economic advantage from the new product development of the company and are therefore highly motivated to participate in solving problems.

An example taken from company practice is the inclusion of lead users in the development of surgical drapes – a material used to prevent the infections associated with surgical operations (see von Hippel *et al.* 1999). By involving lead users (e.g. top physicians) in the early phase of idea elaboration, a revolutionary form of infection protection was developed that facilitated a technologically innovative and substantially more cost-effective approach to infection control.

5.3.3 Concept Definition, Evaluation and Selection

Once a new product idea has been judged as potentially feasible during the phase of idea elaboration, it is then further investigated in the phase of concept definition. This more detailed version of the product idea is called a new **product concept**. It is a statement about the expected product features that will generate specific benefits relative to already existing offerings (see Crawford and Di Benedetto 2006). In particular, a product concept should include statements that relate to the following aspects.

- **Intended target group(s)**: when developing the product concept, the intended target group for the product(s) should be identified.
- **Unique selling proposition (USP)**: a unique selling proposition (i.e. the product's promise to deliver specific benefits in a unique way compared to other offerings) relevant to the target group should be defined. The USP will also help to differentiate the product from those of competitors.
- **Product features**: in addition to the functional features of the product (core product features) formal aesthetic product features and the intended product image are also defined.
- **Target positioning**: defining the target positioning for the new product in terms of relevant product features aims to distinguish the product from competitor products in customers' minds.

In the next step, those products that should be launched in the market are then selected from among the defined product concepts. A multi-stage process is recommended for the concept evaluation and selection phase (see Figure 5-6 and the following paragraphs). In this process a range of methods can be used. Often, from a large number of concepts, only a few are selected, which are then intended for implementation and market introduction.

Checklists, Scoring Models and Financial Analysis

Checklists are a method that is widely used for evaluating product concepts. Checklists can be used to check the extent to which alternative product concepts satisfy previously defined requirements – for example, regarding:

- the consistency of the product concept with the strategic corporate objectives and marketing objectives
- the technical feasibility of the product concept
- the availability of resources within the company for implementing the product concept.

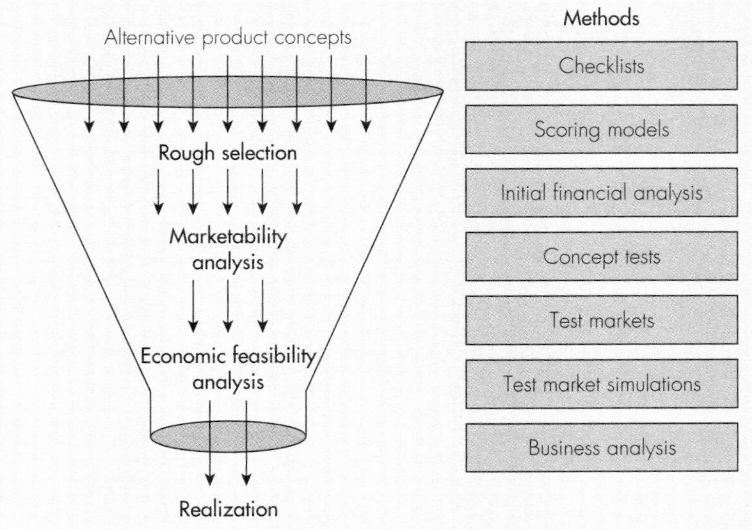

Figure 5-6 Phases and methods of concept evaluation and selection

Scoring models also serve to evaluate product concepts by means of previously defined criteria. In contrast to checklists, they consider the degree to which a product concept meets the different criteria. This method also allows the different criteria to be ranked according to their importance. Scoring models are created in several steps:

- evaluation criteria are defined that are relevant for the success of the new product
- the individual evaluation criteria are then prioritized by adding weights for the different criteria
- the product concept is then evaluated with respect to the evaluation criteria
- a total score is calculated as an evaluation of the overall product concept.

The use of such scoring models to evaluate new product concepts is also called **utility value analysis**. Table 5-4 illustrates the evaluation of a product concept by means of a scoring model. In this analysis criteria related to company, market, distribution, competition and environment are applied.

Due to their flexibility and simplicity, scoring models are frequently applied for evaluating and selecting concepts. However, it should be noted that scoring models are to a certain degree subjective in terms of both the selection and weighting of criteria as well as the evaluation of alternative product concepts.

Another important input in this phase is data gathered from an **initial financial analysis**. This analysis uses data from rough sales forecasts (sales projections over the planning period) and assessments of costs to project profits and key financial benchmarks (e.g. contribution margins).

Concept Tests

In the next step, product concepts that have withstood the initial selection phase based on checklists, scoring models and initial financial analysis can be evaluated with regard to their potential market acceptance, with a **concept test**. Along with identifying the product concepts that have the greatest sales opportunities, concept tests also strive to identify weaknesses and the potential for improvement of the individual product concepts.

Table 5-4 Sample scoring model for evaluating a product concept

Evaluation criterion	Score (1 to 10 points)	Relative weight of criterion	Overall score
1. Company-related criteria			
■ Technical feasibility	8	15%	1.20
■ Consistency with strategic objectives	2	15%	0.30
2. Market-related criteria			
■ Evidence of customer benefits	8	5%	0.40
■ Targeting of new groups of buyers	8	10%	0.80
■ Improvement of company's market position	7	5%	0.35
3. Distribution-related criteria			
■ Enhancement of image vis-à-vis distributors	3	5%	0.15
■ Degree of distributors' willingness to cooperate	3	10%	0.30
4. Competition-related criteria			
■ Attainment of competitive advantages	9	10%	0.90
■ Protection against imitation	9	5%	0.45
5. Environment-related criteria			
■ Legal protection of product concept	3	10%	0.30
■ Environmental compatibility	6	5%	0.30
■ Economic situation of industry sector	6	5%	0.30
Total points		100%	5.75
Rating scale: 0 – 3 = Poor, 4 – 7 = Fair, 8 – 10 = Good			

Concept tests are frequently conducted in focus groups (for more on this survey method see the discussion on surveys in the Appendix). In these groups, selected customers discuss the proposed new product concept under the supervision of a moderator. Concepts can also be presented to individual interviewees for evaluation. If a prototype of the concept is not yet available, it can either be described verbally, shown in the form of a picture or illustration, or visualized with the aid of new media (e.g. virtual reality imaging of the concept by means of computer graphics).

The objective of concept testing is to weed out ideas that are unlikely to make it in the market. Often this phase is used to gather data on the **purchase intentions** (**PIs**) of the respective target group. One reliable measure used to assess PI is the question 'How likely are you to buy this product if available in the market?' Five answer alternatives are then offered to respondents, as follows.

- ☐ I would definitely buy the product.
- ☐ I would probably buy the product.
- ☐ I am unsure (neutral position).
- ☐ I probably would not buy the product.
- ☐ I definitely would not buy the product.

Once a group of potential buyers has answered this question, a conservative way to look at this assessment is to check how many respondents have ticked the 'top box' (top box rule). For example, a large food manufacturer goes ahead with new yoghurt concepts only if more than 50 per cent of the respondents have ticked the top box.

During a concept test, the following specific questions can also be assessed.

- Is the product concept understandable and credible?
- From a customer standpoint, what advantages and disadvantages does the product concept have as compared to other products?
- What product features are particularly relevant for the customer?
- To which groups of buyers is the product concept most appealing and to what extent do these groups correspond to the target groups?
- Which products already established in the market represent the strongest potential competitors?
- Could the company's own products (already established in the market) be cannibalized or even replaced by the new product?

In company practice, such concept tests provide a broad spectrum of information concerning the potential customer acceptance of new products. Most of the data obtained is of a qualitative nature and is not suitable, for example, to obtain reliable sales estimates. To gather this type of data, test markets and test market simulations can be conducted.

Test Markets and Test Market Simulations

Test markets and test market simulations are used to assess the market acceptance of product concepts. In these tests either prototypes or already marketable products are tested so that the product idea is much more concrete than in the concept testing phase. This represents both a disadvantage, due to the high expense and effort involved in producing the prototype, and an advantage, since product concepts can be evaluated by customers on the basis of a tangible experience with the product, and not merely based on descriptions.

A **test market** can be a regional test market, a micro test market or an electronic test market. Within the scope of the concept evaluation and selection phase, the product being tested or alternative product concepts are introduced to the test market to allow customers to purchase and assess them. Of particular relevance here are the buying preferences for individual product concepts, which can be used in the course of the concept evaluation and selection to identify the most promising product concepts.

In a **test market simulation**, the adoption process of new products is simulated with a representative random sample of the target group selected for the product (see Urban and Hauser 1993). In a multi-stage experiment, the test subjects are interviewed about their current preferences and habits, and then exposed to videos of commercials or print advertisements promoting the test product. In a subsequent simulated shopping situation (shopping laboratory), they can choose between products. The test subjects then test the products. After using the products, they are questioned again about their attitudes and preferences. This process thus provides information about the first-time and repeat buying behavior of the target group. The information is used to **forecast the market share for the new product**. Such a forecast is the central objective of the simulation technique.

One of the best-known test market simulation models is the **ASSESSOR** (Silk and Urban 1978), which was further developed with DESIGNOR (see Choffray and Lilien 1982) and TESI (see Erichson 1981). The ASSESSOR model serves to evaluate new products for which the target groups and design of the marketing mix have already been largely defined. The model comprises two components: the trial-repeat model (including the estimation of the trial rate and repeat purchase rate) and the preference model (including the estimation of the purchase probability), which essentially supply two independent market share forecasts. The market share assessment by ASSESSOR is the average of the market share forecast by the two models (for more on the ASSESSOR model see the discussion on test markets in the Appendix).

Use of the model yields the following results:

- a forecast of the long-term market share for a new product
- an assessment as to which of the competitor products or the company's own products currently in the market could be driven out or substituted by the new product (if this occurs for the company's own products it is called 'cannibalization')
- information about the measures needed to improve the product, as well as the marketing activities necessary for the product (e.g. advertising).

ASSESSOR is an effective test market simulator whose forecast quality with regard to market share has been validated in numerous cases (see Urban and Katz 1983). However, the applicability of the model is limited to consumer goods with a high rate of buying frequency, since repeat buying plays a key role in terms of market share (which is not the case to the same extent for durables).

Analysis of Economic Feasibility (Investment Planning)

Innovations that have not been eliminated in the previous selection process (see Figure 5-6) should be evaluated with respect to their economic feasibility. Sales figures derived from market share forecasts (e.g. from ASSESSOR) and internal cost estimates form the basis for the analysis of economic feasibility. Since the introduction of new products invariably involves investments over a multi-period time frame, **dynamic investment planning** methods – such as, for example, the net present value (NPV) method – can be helpful tools.

As a first step, the costs and revenues associated with the development, launch and sale of a product have to be assessed for the entire life cycle of a product. In addition to information about market penetration and the life span of the product, this also includes previously obtained information concerning market growth, attainable market share and price. The net cash flow is then calculated as the differences derived from comparing the revenues (R_t) and costs (C_t) forecast for period t. This net cash flow (either positive or negative) is discounted to the present with a discount rate and summed over the respective time period. The following formula is used to calculate the net present value:

$$NPV = \sum_{t=0}^{T} (R_t - C_t) \times (1 + r)^{-t}$$

Here, NPV refers to the net present value, t to the period ($t = 0, \ldots, T$), R_t to the revenues in period t, C_t to the costs in period t, r to the interest rate and T to the time horizon of the investment (which can result from the estimated duration of the product life cycle). If the net present value is positive, the new product is evaluated as being profitable (given the assumptions in the analysis), and thus implementation of the product concept should be given serious consideration.

Table 5-5 shows an example of dynamic investment planning to evaluate a new product concept. In this example, the result is weakly positive. The net present value is indeed positive, however the last row of the table indicates that amortization of the initial investment occurs very late (i.e. only in the last period). In view of this, options for improving sales, accelerating the market penetration, extending the life cycle and, if necessary, cutting costs should be considered.

The results of a net present value method depend heavily on the set of assumptions applied by the decision maker. It can be helpful to develop different scenarios or conduct sensitivity analyses to assess the results' sensitivity with regard to specific variables in the analysis.

Table 5-5 Assessment of a new product concept in the industrial goods sector using the net present value method (in €)

Time period	t = 0	t = 1	t = 2	t = 3	t = 4	t = 5	t = 6
Quantity	48,600	54,600	72,300	75,360	95,000	110,000	120,000
Unit price	127.46	125.18	123.79	122.42	121.06	121.06	121.06
Variable unit costs	90.89	88.79	85.16	81.20	79.13	77.10	73.20
Unit contribution margin	36.57	36.39	38.63	41.22	41.93	43.96	47.86
Total contribution margin	1,777,302	1,986,894	2,792,949	3,106,339	3,983,350	4,835,600	5,743,200
Fixed costs							
Amortization	1,205,000	850,000	550,000	280,000	100,000	90,000	50,000
Personnel costs	650,000	550,000	450,000	450,000	420,000	400,000	380,000
Material costs	435,000	650,000	700,000	690,000	720,000	765,000	787,000
Marketing costs	3,500,000	2,420,000	500,000	250,000	120,000	100,000	80,000
Total of fixed costs	5,790,000	4,470,000	2,200,000	1,670,000	1,360,000	1,355,000	1,297,000
Difference between contribution margin and fixed costs	−4,012,698	−2,483,106	592,949	1,436,339	2,623,350	3,480,600	4,446,200
Discounted value of this difference (interest rate of 9%)	−4,012,698	−2,278,079	499,073	1,109,117	1,858,447	2,262,151	2,651,124
Cumulative discounted value of this difference	−4,012,698	−6,290,777	−5,791,704	−4,682,587	−2,824,140	−561,989	2,089,135 (net present value)

5.3.4 Market Launch of New Products

The next phase after technical realization of the product is the **planning and design of the market launch**. For this crucial stage it is essential to know how a new product will first be accepted by innovative buyers and then, potentially, penetrate the overall market. This process can be depicted by the adoption and diffusion processes. Based on this important input, the company can define the market entry strategy.

Adoption and Diffusion Processes: Basic Information and Models

Adoption is the decision of an individual to adopt an innovation (i.e. a new product). This process can be divided into various phases (see Figure 5-7 as well as Rogers 2003). In the first phase, buyers become aware of the innovation for the first time without having any detailed information about it (e.g. awareness of advertising for a new car). In the second phase, the buyer shows interest in the innovation and is encouraged to gather more information. In the third phase, the buyer evaluates the innovation and considers whether to try the product. In the next phase, the buyer tests the innovation in order to better evaluate its benefits (trial phase). In the adoption phase, the buyer decides to adopt the innovation to its full extent for regular use.

For companies offering an innovation, knowledge of the adoption process is essential to developing an effective market entry strategy and achieving fast market penetration. Companies should

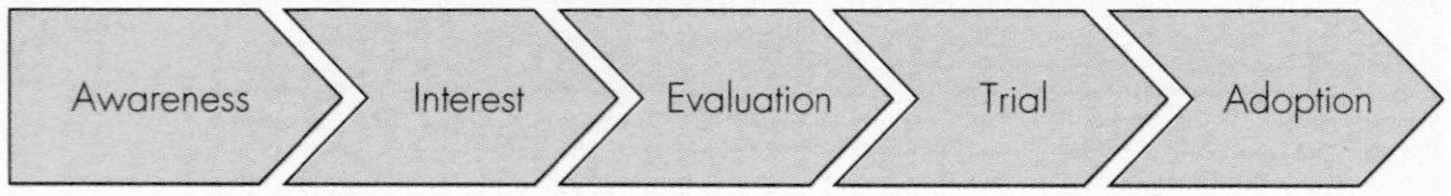

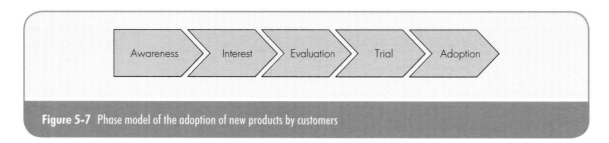

Figure 5-7 Phase model of the adoption of new products by customers

therefore support customers in the different stages of the adoption process in order to facilitate it. In particular, customers who show serious interest in the innovation should be provided with trial incentives. Companies in the consumer goods industry could, for example, distribute free samples of new products. Other examples are test drives (automobile) or trial applications (industrial pilot plants to test technical specifications or beta-sites for software).

Rogers (2003) defines **diffusion** as 'the spread of a new idea from its source of invention or creation to its ultimate users or adopters'. The concept is relevant in many areas (e.g. social science, epidemiology), and has also been applied in management and, specifically, in understanding the diffusion of new products. The diffusion process of a new product depends on a number of influencing factors, such as the product's relative advantage, product complexity, product compatibility, the adopters' willingness to take risks, effect of personal influence, as well as adopters' communication behavior (for example, information concerning new products is communicated by word of mouth between opinion leaders and followers).

It can be observed that some adopters are more innovative than others in that they adopt innovations earlier in a given market. Adopters can thus be characterized according to their different degree of innovativeness. The individuals that are first to adopt initiate the diffusion process. They are referred to as innovators and act as opinion leaders that buy the new product because they are particularly interested in innovations and are relatively risk-loving. Innovators are especially aware of advertising messages and buy regardless of whether or not other customers have already purchased the product. As imitators, followers buy the new product only if other customers have already purchased the new product and, consequently, the innovation has already achieved a certain degree of diffusion.

By summing up numerous individual purchases (on the part of innovators as well as followers), diffusion models can form a basis for deriving the diffusion rate of a new product in a market. Diffusion models can be categorized according to three basic types (see Mahajan *et al.* 1990):

1 models that consider innovative purchase behavior

2 models that consider imitative purchase behavior

3 models that include both aspects (integrative diffusion models).

The **Fourt/Woodlock model** (1960) is an example of a model of innovative purchase behavior. This model calculates the number of (first-time) buyers q_t in period t as follows:

$$q_t = \alpha \times (\bar{Q} - Q_{t-1})$$

In this formula, $\bar{Q}$ denotes the number of potential buyers (market potential) and Q_{t-1} the cumulative number of buyers who have adopted until period $t - 1$. Thus, the model assumes that in each period, a certain proportion of previous non-buyers $(\bar{Q} - Q_{t-1})$ purchases the new product. The value of parameter α specifies the size of this proportion, whereby α is also called the diffusion or penetration rate (the larger α, the quicker the diffusion). It is obvious that the number of first-time buyers q_t decreases over time, which is consistent with the model's focus on innovative purchase behavior (see also Lilien *et al.* 1992).

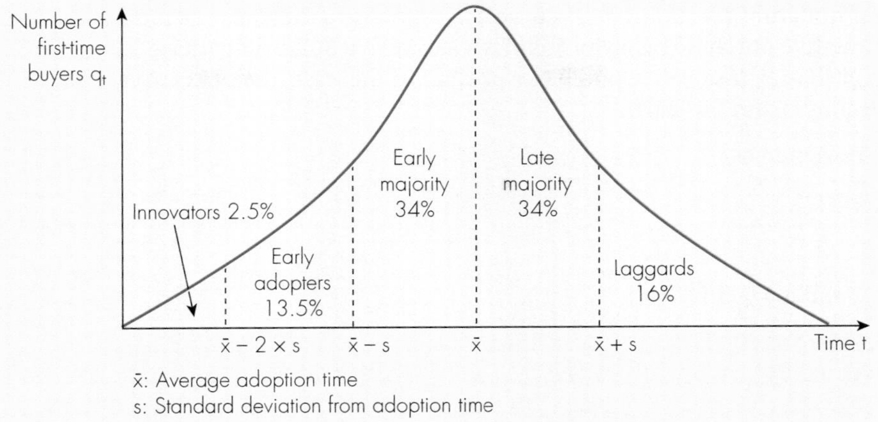

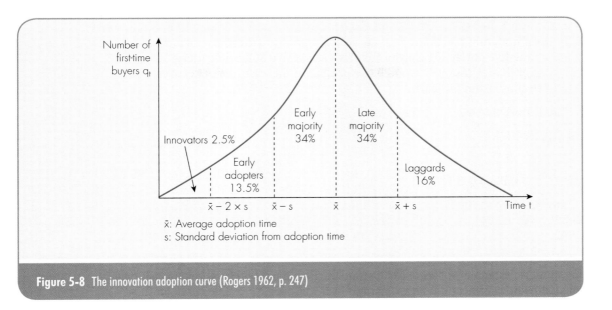

Figure 5-8 The innovation adoption curve (Rogers 1962, p. 247)

The classic **Mansfield model** (1961) is an example of a model of imitative purchase behavior (for a qualitative discussion of this model, see Rogers 1962). The formula

$$\frac{q_t}{\bar{Q} - Q_{t-1}} = \beta \times \frac{Q_{t-1}}{\bar{Q}}$$

is the core of this model, with q_t, $\bar{Q}$ and Q_{t-1} being equivalent to the Fourt/Woodlock model. The Mansfield model therefore assumes that the portion of previous non-buyers ($\bar{Q} - Q_{t-1}$) who purchase the product in period t is proportional to the previous market penetration ($Q_{t-1}/\bar{Q}$) and thus increases with a growing market penetration. This fact illustrates the imitative character of the purchase behavior: the larger the market penetration, the higher the probability that a previous non-buyer will make contact with a previous buyer, their encounter possibly leading to communication processes that can result in imitative behavior. Parameter β describes the intensity of imitative behavior. For the absolute number of buyers q_t in period t, this model results in a diffusion that can be modeled by a 'bell-shaped curve' (see Figure 5-8). Resolved for q_t, we get the following equation:

$$q_t = \beta \times \frac{Q_{t-1}}{\bar{Q}} (\bar{Q} - Q_{t-1})$$

Due to the similarity to the normal distribution, individual categories of buyers can be proportionally allocated with respect to the adoption rate of new products (also see Figure 5-8). Thus, for example, the approximately 34 per cent of persons whose adoption time exceeds the average adoption time by no more than the standard deviation is called the 'late majority'.

The best-known model of the third category (integrative diffusion models that include both innovative and imitative purchase behavior) is the **Bass model** (Bass 1969). The Bass model represents the sum of the two previously discussed diffusion models. Accordingly, the sales quantity of period t is

$$q_t = \alpha \times (\bar{Q} - Q_{t-1}) + \beta \times \frac{Q_{t-1}}{\bar{Q}} \times (\bar{Q} - Q_{t-1})$$

with all parameters in correspondence to the previous models. The first component of the model refers to innovative purchase behavior, while the second component models imitative purchase behavior. The sales curve implied by the Bass model depends on parameters α and β: If innovation rate α is smaller than imitation rate β, the sales curve corresponds to the life cycle model (see Section 2.1), since imitative purchase behavior follows a successive build-up pattern. If, on the other hand, α is larger than β, innovative purchases prevail. In this case, the sales curve according to the Bass model declines from the start.

The formula can be rewritten as

$$q_t = a_0 + a_1 \times Q_{t-1} + a_2 \times Q_{t-1}^2$$

with

$$a_0 = \alpha \times \bar{Q},\ a_1 = \beta - \alpha \text{ and } a_2 = -\beta/\bar{Q}$$

Thus, q_t can be expressed via Q_{t-1} by a quadratic function. This fact can be used for an estimation of parameters. Provided that a sufficiently long sales time series is available, a_0, a_1 and a_2 can be estimated with a regression analysis. The results can then be used to calculate α, β and Q using the above equations.

The following numeric example will serve to illustrate the Bass model. Regression analysis has resulted in the following specification of the Bass model:

$$q_t = 530 + 0.32 \times Q_{t-1} - 1/10^5 \times Q_{t-1}^2$$

Table 5-6 depicts how sales q_t develop, as well as cumulative sales Q_t for periods $t = 1$ to $t = 24$. As can be seen in Figure 5-9, the curve resembles a product life cycle with a peak at $t = 11$.

The following three equations are the basis for determining the parameters of the Bass model:

$$\alpha \times \bar{Q} = 530,\ \beta - \alpha = 0.32,\ \beta/\bar{Q} = 1/10^5$$

Resolving the first equation for α and the third equation for β and inserting these expressions into the second equation yields the following:

$$\frac{\bar{Q}}{10^5} - \frac{530}{\bar{Q}} = 0.32$$

Multiplying with $10^5 \times \bar{Q}$ yields the following quadratic equation:

$$\bar{Q}^2 - 32{,}000 \times \bar{Q} - 53{,}000{,}000 = 0$$

Table 5-6 The Bass model applied

t	q_t	Q_t	t	q_t	Q_t	t	q_t	Q_t
1	530	530	9	2,878	14,271	17	881	31,744
2	697	1,227	10	3,060	17,331	18	611	32,355
3	908	2,134	11	3,072	20,403	19	415	32,770
4	1,167	3,302	12	2,896	23,299	20	278	33,048
5	1,478	4,779	13	2,557	25,856	21	184	33,232
6	1,831	6,610	14	2,119	27,975	22	121	33,352
7	2,208	8,819	15	1,656	29,631	23	79	33,431
8	2,574	11,393	16	1,232	30,863	24	52	33,483

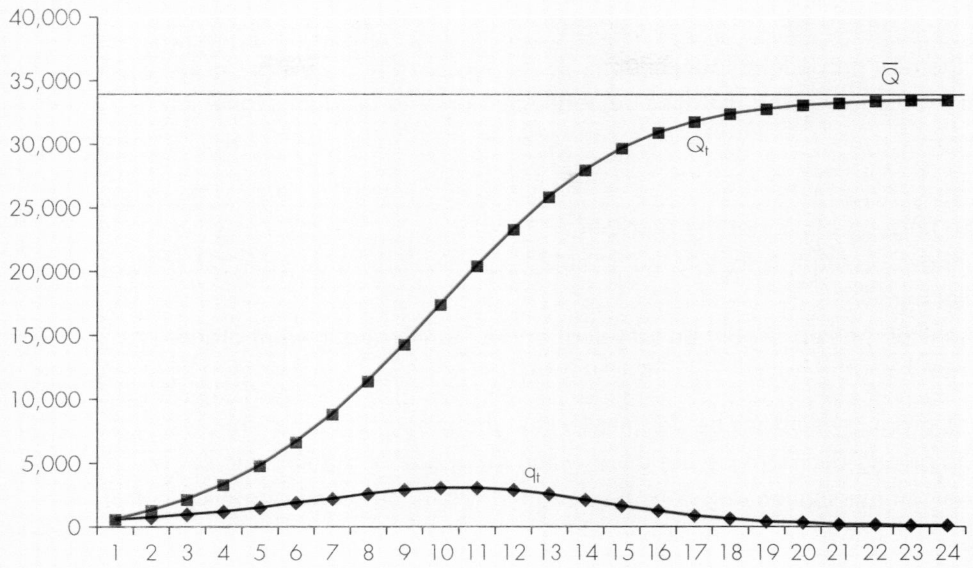

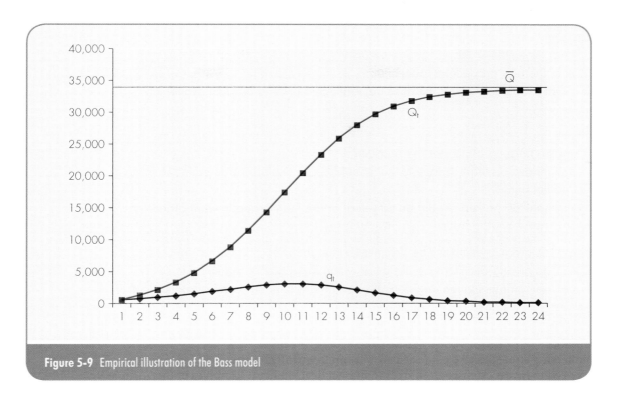

Figure 5-9 Empirical illustration of the Bass model

This equation has the positive solution $\bar{Q} = 33{,}578$. In addition, we have $\alpha = 0.01578$ and $\beta = 0.33578$.

It is thus shown that the market potential amounts to 33,578 units. After approximately 20 periods, this potential will essentially be saturated (see Table 5-6). Imitation rate β is significantly larger than innovation rate α, which explains the shape of the q_t curve. In the form of an S-shaped curve, the Q_t curve approaches its asymptote (see Figure 5-9).

The Bass model has been tested successfully in a number of practical applications (also see Lilien and Kotler 1983 and, for software issues and other practical examples, see Lilien *et al.* 2000 and Mahajan *et al.* 2000).

Development of the Market Entry Strategy

Introducing new products in a market is an inherently difficult task. After careful testing of the new product as described in the previous sections, it is necessary to devise a market entry strategy. Table 5-7 lists the central questions that should be addressed as part of the market entry strategy.

The first two questions in Table 5-7 relate to the timing of market entry. With respect to the **product launch time**, the basic question is whether the company strives to be first in introducing a product innovation to the market (pioneer strategy) or prefers to enter the market at a later date, after the competition has launched similar products (follower strategy).

Numerous studies have established the notion that pioneers achieve long-term competitive advantages. One of the fundamental advantages of the **pioneer strategy** lies in the opportunity to achieve high market share (see Golder and Tellis 1993). This effect can be based on several factors. For example, a pioneer can accumulate volume-related advantages, which in turn can result in cost advantages over followers. A pioneering company can also create buyer preferences for its product and can potentially establish superior customer loyalty. From a follower perspective, such factors represent entry barriers that might be expensive to overcome.

Table 5-7 Central questions for formulating a market entry strategy

When?
■ When should the new product be launched?
■ To what extent should marketing activities be conducted prior to product availability (pre-marketing)?
Where?
■ What is/are the target group(s) for the product?
■ Who are the innovators/early adopters that should be particularly targeted in the initial phase of market entry?
■ Which geographical markets should be targeted for the launch and in what order?
How?
■ How should the product decisions be designed within the scope of market entry?
■ How should the pricing decisions be designed within the scope of market entry?
■ How should the communication decisions be designed within the scope of market entry?
■ How should the sales decisions be designed within the scope of market entry?

However, pioneering strategies also come at a cost. It can frequently be observed, for instance, that pioneers need to invest extensive resources in market development. Examples of this include intensive marketing and/or sales activities to attract customers to the new product. Especially in the case of a highly innovative product, resources invested in these activities are allocated for preparing the market for the new product category (e.g. the first company to introduce digital photography needed to educate customers in how to use this new technology). Subsequently, **followers** can benefit from these pioneer activities ('free riding') and launch their products in the market at substantially lower costs. Table 5-8 compares the possible advantages and disadvantages of a pioneer strategy.

It is not possible to make a general statement with regard to the superiority of either pioneer strategies or follower strategies. Company practice provides numerous examples of both successful pioneer products as well as successful follower products (see, e.g. Robinson and Min 2002). Consequently, empirical success factor research does not provide conclusive results with respect

Table 5-8 Potential advantages/disadvantages of pioneer strategies

Potential pioneer advantages (disadvantages for followers)	Potential pioneer disadvantages (advantages for followers)
■ Temporary monopoly allowing premium price strategy ■ Cost advantages due to experience curve effects ■ Image/preference creation with buyers as well as development of customer loyalty ■ Establishment of barriers to switching on the part of customers (e.g. by setting industry standards) ■ Securing of key distribution channels	■ Extensive resources needed for market development ■ Uncertainty with respect to development of demand ■ Lack of experience with regard to the functionality of the product when used by the customer

to the superiority of pioneer strategies (for more information, see, e.g., Clement *et al.* 1998; Kalyanaram *et al.* 1995; Kerin *et al.* 1992; Makadok 1998; Robinson and Fornell 1985; Shankar *et al.* 1998; Urban *et al.* 1986; Vanderwerf and Mahon 1997). In their review article, Kerin *et al.* (1992) demonstrate that pioneer strategies are particularly promising in situations where the pioneering companies possess critical marketing capabilities as well as a solid marketing strategy. A distinction should also be made regarding **early and late followers**. This espouses the view that there is a window of opportunity for new products, and that opportunities that arise from this should be seized earlier rather than later.

Another important decision related to timing when designing a market entry strategy concerns the question of to what extent marketing activities should be conducted prior to the actual date when the product will be available on the market. Marketing activities prior to the actual market launch are referred to as **pre-marketing**. Pre-marketing is geared towards creating a more favorable environment for the new product prior to its launch. Information is provided for potential customers so that adoption and diffusion processes can be initiated as soon as the product is available in the market. Pre-marketing can, therefore, accelerate the diffusion of the new product.

The advantage of accelerated diffusion of the new product is balanced by two main potential disadvantages. First, there is a risk that, due to pre-marketing activities, the competition might become prematurely aware of the pending market launch of the company's product. This can trigger competitive activities that impede the subsequent market launch. There is also the potential risk that the pre-marketing activities lead to decreased demand for an old product that is offered by the company in the market (cannibalization). Customers may in fact wait for the new product to be launched and forego the purchase of the product already in the market (leapfrogging).

A second category of central questions concerning the formulation of a market entry strategy (see Table 5-7) deals with the target groups of the new product being launched in the market. A key question addresses **innovators/early adopters**, who should be particularly targeted within the scope of the market entry. Here, the aim is to identify buyers who are especially open-minded towards innovations and can thus influence other buyers (opinion leaders/multipliers). In this context, the issue of market entry with respect to **geographical factors** is of particular relevance for internationally operating companies. In addition to the question concerning the markets for the new product, the order of the market launch of the product has to be determined. A fundamental decision relates to two alternative strategies: sprinkler strategy (simultaneous product launch in several geographical markets) and waterfall strategy (successive product launch in various geographical markets). Please refer to Chapter 12, on international marketing, for a detailed discussion of this international marketing problem.

Subsequent to deciding on 'when' to enter the market and 'where' to enter it, a decision has to be made as to 'how' it should be entered (see Table 5-7). At its core, this question addresses the **design of the individual elements of the marketing mix**. Basically, most key decisions within the scope of the marketing mix, such as product decisions, pricing decisions, sales decisions, communication decisions and customer relationship management, also play an important role with respect to the design of a market entry strategy. Please refer to these decision areas, which are discussed in the individual chapters of Part 2 of this book.

Questions related to **product decisions** include the issue of how many and which product variants should be offered (see Section 5.4.2) and how the brand management should be designed (see Section 5.5). Within the scope of **pricing decisions**, the questions relate to the introductory price that should be charged for the product (see penetration and skimming pricing in Section 6.3). Also relevant are **communication decisions**, including the definition of communication objectives and target groups, allocation of budgets, selection of media and communication tools, and decisions concerning the form and presentation of the communication (see Chapter 8). Key challenges to be met by **sales management and customer relationship management** lie in particular in preparing

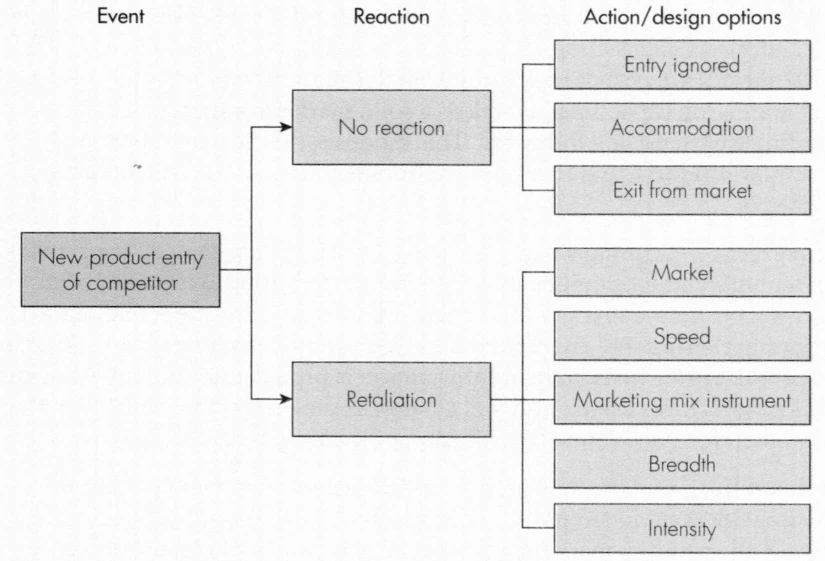

Figure 5-10 Behavioral patterns of established competitors in response to the launch of a new product by a competitor (adapted from Kuester *et al.* 1999, p. 91)

and motivating the company's sales department as well as intermediaries and distributors for the new product (see Chapters 7 and 9). When cooperating with intermediaries it is of particular importance to ensure channel support for the new product.

If a company launches a new product in a market, it can be assumed in most cases that the competitors that are already established in that market will respond to the new product introduction. These potential **competitive reactions** should be taken into account when formulating the market entry strategy: companies should try to anticipate the responses of the competition and decide how to react to the potential measures initiated by the competition.

Figure 5-10 provides a systematic overview of the possible responses of a firm when threatened by the new product of a competitor (see Kuester *et al.* 1999). A basic decision of the established company first addresses the question of whether to react at all. If the company decides to react, the **retaliatory move** has to be planned along several dimensions, as outlined below.

- First, it has to be decided in which market the response will be initiated. This can be either the market where the new product was launched or another market (e.g. a market that is key to the competitor that launched the new product).
- The second aspect concerns the timing of the response, including decisions regarding whether to delay the response until how the buyers are reacting to the product becomes evident.
- Then there is the question of which element of the marketing mix should be used to respond. Here, possible options include the entire marketing mix, such as reactions on the price mix (price cuts for established products), reactions on the communication mix (new advertising campaigns for established products) or on the product mix (improvement of established products).

- Another decision targets the number of marketing mix tools to be used for the response (breadth of response). Companies can limit their response to one single instrument (e.g. price) or deploy a combination of tools (e.g. price cuts in combination with an advertising campaign).
- Finally, the intensity of the response has to be decided (e.g. the scope of an advertising campaign or the extent of price cuts).

Potential responses by the competition are especially relevant to planning a market entry strategy. Research has provided a number of empirical findings in this connection.

- The more innovative the newly launched product, the more likely already established competitors will respond with the development of their own new products (see Kuester *et al.* 1999).
- The faster the relevant market grows, the more likely already established competitors will defend their own position in this (potentially profitable) market by quickly launching their own new products (see Bowman and Gatignon 1995; Kuester *et al.* 1999).
- If the switching costs on the part of customers are low (i.e. if switching to the newly launched product is not associated with high costs), established competitors will respond faster to the market entry of new products (see Bowman and Gatignon 1995).
- The larger the established competitor, the slower and weaker its response to the market entry of the new product (see Kuester *et al.* 1999).

After describing the individual phases of the innovation process, from the generation of ideas to market entry, aspects related to the management of the entire process across the different stages of innovation management need to be addressed as well. In the following, we will thus discuss tools that can contribute to **optimizing the overall innovation process** (as opposed to addressing issues relating to particular stages). These tools aim mainly to reduce the cost of innovation and accelerate the innovation process.

The goal of **accelerating the innovation process** is especially important in markets with short product life cycles. In principle, a faster innovation process can generate two advantages for the company (see Figure 5-11): a shorter innovation process facilitates earlier market entry relative to the competition and can thus lead to pioneer advantages (sales/cost lead for Company A, see pane (a) in Figure 5-11). In the case of a simultaneous market entry in our two-company example, a shorter innovation time makes it possible to initiate the innovation process at a later point in time, thus enabling the company to benefit from more recent information (information lead for Company A, see pane (b) in Figure 5-11).

Various methods for accelerating the innovation process are discussed in the literature. For example, the process can be accelerated by reducing the physical distance between the departments involved in the innovation process. In general, methods to accelerate the innovation process can be classified into four categories (see Mahajan and Wind 1997; Olson *et al.* 1995):

1. Within the scope of **technology-based approaches**, computer simulations and rapid prototyping have to be mentioned in particular. During the conceptual phase, the customer is presented with prototypes/simulations that illustrate the key features of the product and facilitate an evaluation of these features (e.g. with the help of computer-aided design (CAD)).
2. In addition to the relevant methods of interface management, concurrent engineering is an important **organizational approach**. It is based on the principle that tasks in the product development process are conducted in parallel, and aims for the simultaneous execution of the relevant activities. As compared to sequential processing, concurrent engineering should ensure effective and efficient development processes (see Seibert 1998).
3. **Controlling approaches** to be mentioned here particularly include planning, budgeting, controlling and monitoring systems (also see Chapter 15). The design of such systems can

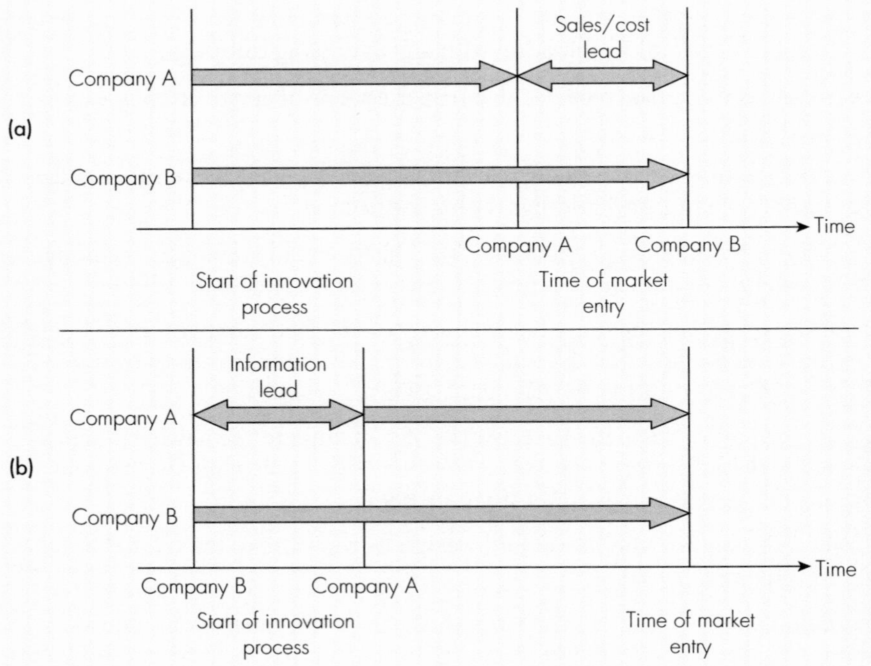

Figure 5-11 Principal advantages related to a fast innovation process

facilitate the acceleration of processes by, for example, incorporating both cost-related and time-related aspects into innovation controlling.

4 Approaches in human resource management to process acceleration largely correspond to the approaches in human resource management that are related to interface management (see Chapter 16).

5.4 Management of Established Products

Another set of important challenges arises in the area of product decisions regarding the management of products that are already established in the market (see the overview in Figure 5-3). In contrast to innovation management, where we are concerned with the creation of entirely new products, the focus in this decision area is on adapting established products to market requirements and conditions.

In this context, we will first address basic structural decisions concerning the product mix (see Section 5.4.1). We will then discuss the three essential decisions whose aim is to modify the product range:

1 decisions related to expanding the product mix (see Section 5.4.2)

2 decisions related to synergies within the product mix (see Section 5.4.3)

3 decisions related to reducing the product mix (see Section 5.4.4).

5.4.1 Deciding about the Structure of the Product Mix

The term **product mix** (sometimes also referred to as product assortment) refers to the entire range of products and items supplied by a company or a seller at a given point in time. In principle, the product mix of a company can be described by two essential structural characteristics, as follows.

1 **Width of product mix** describes the number of product lines that the company carries. A **product line** (also called **product group** or **product category**) refers to a group of interrelated products that share a certain level of similarity. On one hand, this similarity can concern external aspects such as, say, the customers to whom the products are marketed, as well as customer requirements that are addressed by the products. Similarities can also exist with regard to internal aspects (e.g. same production materials and processes).

2 Conversely, the **depth of product mix** describes the number of product variants and items within a product line, thus determining how many product alternatives are available to customers in a particular product line.

Table 5-9 provides an illustration of the structure of a product range offered by a consumer goods manufacturer.

There are a number of quantitative models for determining the optimal depth of a company's product range. For the most part these are based on conjoint analysis or multidimensional scaling (for more on this, see, e.g., Green and Krieger 1985, 1987; Nair *et al.* 1995). (Both methods are described in the Appendix.)

Table 5-9 Example of the product mix (depth and width) of a consumer goods manufacturer

	Width of product mix (= four product lines)			
	Laundry detergents	**Dental care**	**Paper products**	**Cleaning agents**
Depth of product mix (e.g. for the laundry detergent product line: depth = 8 variants)	All-purpose laundry detergent, Brand A: regular 10 kg (variant 1), compact 5 kg (variant 2), tabs (variant 3)	Toothpaste, Brand D: tooth decay and caries prevention (variant 1), tartar prevention (variant 2)	Paper tissues, Brand G: extra-soft (variant 1), summer scent (variant 2)	Surface cleaner, Brand J
	All-purpose laundry detergent, Brand B (3 variants)	Toothbrush, Brand E	Kitchen roll, Brand H	Glass cleaner, Brand K
	Fabric softener, Brand C (2 variants)	Mouthwash, Brand F	Sanitary paper, Brand I	Stain remover, Brand L

5.4.2 Expanding the Product Mix

In a dynamic market environment, companies need to continuously adapt their product offerings to changing customer needs and competitive situations. Decisions about the adaptation and modification of the existing product mix should be based on thorough market research (especially relevant here are methods to evaluate customer needs – see the section on surveys in the Appendix). Equally important is information provided by marketing control, especially information concerning the profitability of individual products (see Sections 15.3 and 15.4). Furthermore, analytical information garnered from a strategic evaluation of the company – as, for example, is possible with product life cycle analysis (see Section 2.2.3) or portfolio methods (see Section 4.2) – can yield useful insights for the adaptation of the product mix.

In particular, there are three options for expanding the product mix:

1 product variation

2 product differentiation

3 diversification.

Product variation refers to a modification of the characteristics and features of an already existing product without changing its core functions. In general, variations are made to a product's aesthetic properties (e.g. color, shape), physical-functional properties (e.g. material, quality) or symbolic properties (brand name, brand image). Examples of product variations include new packaging in the consumer goods industry or design 'facelifts' for automobiles. A product variation therefore does not create a new product, but rather alters an already existing product (see, e.g., Saunders and Khan 1986). Consequently, the number of products in a product range does not increase (the width and depth of the product range are not affected). In this context it has to be mentioned that the distinction between product variation and product innovation is not always straightforward. If modifications reach a certain level, we no longer speak of product variation, but rather of innovation. However, it is not always possible to make a clear distinction.

In the area of product variations we distinguish **product care** and **product relaunch**. The main difference between these types of product variation lies in the extent of the product modification: while product care tends to refer to smaller, continuous modifications (often not noticeable to the customer), the term 'relaunch' applies to modifications on a larger scale, as it usually involves the modification of the product positioning (see Focus on Marketing 5-2 for an example of a relaunch).

Focus on Marketing 5-2 Example of a product relaunch

Relaunch of the Mini

The original Mini Cooper was a pop-icon in England in the 1960s, sharing photo ops with the Beatles while making a name for itself on the rally circuit. BMW, which had acquired the marque in 1994, relaunched it in 2002 with a souped-up engine and a design that, while sleek and contemporary, was close enough to the original to be considered 'retro'. The company assigned the new unit a relatively paltry $40 million budget and staff just big enough to fill, well, a Mini.

The launch was a huge success, and in 2007 the Mk II Mini was launched, with new versions of the Mini Cooper models and also another relaunched brand – the Mini Clubman, which is a longer, estate version of the Mini with a distinctive larger shape and 'barn'-style rear doors, reminiscent of its 1960s predecessors, the Mini Traveler and Countryman.

Sources: Greenberg, K. (2002) Giving a small car Big 'tude, *Brandweek*, 12/9/2002, 43, 45, 31–33, and www.mini.co.uk, 18 April 2008.

Focus on Marketing 5-3 Example of product differentiation

MasterCard programs
MasterCard offers a range of payment solutions to enable its customers to design, package and implement programs targeted to the specific needs of their customers. The company's principal payment programs, which are facilitated through its brands, include consumer credit and debit programs, commercial payment solutions, and stored value programs. MasterCard's issuer customers determine the features for the cards issued under its programs, such as interest rates and fees. The company determines other aspects of the card programs, such as required services and marketing strategy.

MasterCard offers a number of consumer credit and charge (pay later) programs that are designed to meet the needs of its customers. The company offers customized programs to address specific consumer segments. Its consumer credit programs include Standard, Gold, Platinum, World, and World Elite MasterCard cards.

Standard MasterCard cards are general purpose credit cards targeted to consumers with basic needs for a credit card. Gold MasterCard cards are targeted to consumers typically requiring a higher line of credit or spending limit and one or more card enhancement services associated with a card. Platinum MasterCard cards are offered with still higher credit lines or spending limits, and also provide a range of card enhancement services, such as loyalty reward programs. World MasterCard cards, which are aimed at affluent consumers, have no pre-set spending limit and the option to revolve a designated portion of the charges made. In 2006, MasterCard launched the World Elite MasterCard card, a new card platform for high-income, high-net-worth consumers that offers a mix of travel benefits, rewards and global acceptance, including personalized travel agency benefits.

Source: www.investor.wallst.com/stocks/company-profile.asp?rpc=66&ticker=MA.

Usually, companies engage in product variations in order to resolve product defects, to adapt the product to changed customer preferences, to respond to new product launches by competitors or to reduce costs (see Lazer *et al.* 1984; Saunders and Khan 1986):

Potential indicators necessitating product variations include:

- decreasing absolute sales
- decreasing prices, or
- decreasing (relative) market share.

Product differentiation refers to the addition of new product variants to an already established product (see Dickson and Ginter 1987 as well as Focus on Marketing 5-3). With product variation the original product is modified and is thus no longer present in the market; the original product continues to exist in the case of product differentiation. Product differentiations thus result in an increased depth or, in some cases increased width, of the product mix.

Product differentiation can assume a vertical or horizontal form (Randall *et al.* 1998):

- **vertical product differentiation** exists if product variants of varying quality are offered at different prices (e.g. adding a 'gold version' to a standard credit card line)
- in the case of **horizontal product differentiation**, product variants featuring different functions are offered, which have comparable quality and price levels (e.g. addition of a station wagon model to a mid-sized sedan line).

Generally, companies have the following motives for employing product differentiation (see Connor 1981; Hoch *et al.* 1999; Karakaya and Stahl 1989; Quelch and Kenny 1994; Shaked and Sutton 1982):

- tapping into additional market segments
- allowing for changed customer preferences
- realizing higher prices
- creating market entry barriers for competitors by means of occupying vacant market niches
- using the positive image of an established brand for additional product variants (image transfer).

In the course of **diversification**, a company integrates products into its product mix that are not directly related to the products already available in the product portfolio. Diversification thus increases the width of the product mix. Such decisions frequently have significant strategic implications (diversification is also discussed within the scope of the strategic marketing perspective in Part 1 of this book). Diversification can be realized:

- by developing new products (see Section 5.3)
- by forming strategic alliances with partners (see Section 4.1.5), or
- by acquiring other companies (see Capron and Hulland 1999; Luo 2002).

There are three basic types of diversification (see Brockhoff 1999; Gebert 1983), as described below.

1. **Horizontal diversification** is characterized by an integration of products at the same market level with the aim of offering new services to previous customers or acquiring new customer groups. An example of this is the decision by a department store group to add travel agency services to its product mix and offer these in individual stores. The advantage of this type of diversification lies in the fact that a company can quite efficiently leverage its already existing knowledge regarding similar market conditions.
2. In the case of **vertical diversification**, a supplier conducts activities in the upstream or downstream stages of the value chain. For example, an ice cream manufacturer could decide to enter into the dairy business (upstream) or acquire an ice cream parlour chain (downstream). The company can benefit from this type of diversification if sales channels or raw materials need to be secured or if the potential for rationalization within the value chain can be secured. However, vertical diversification frequently implies that companies have to become familiar with completely new customer groups.
3. **Lateral diversification** is characterized by venturing into totally new markets that have no connection whatsoever with the previous operations of a company. A well-known example of such a diversification strategy is illustrated by the activities of the Daimler-Benz Group during the 1980s and 1990s, with the group expanding into sectors such as aeronautics and space technology, telecommunications and financial services, in addition to its traditional automotive business. This type of diversification aims at, for example, securing growth and diversifying risks.

Figure 5-12 depicts the different types of diversification by contrasting the different stages of the value chain (covered and not yet covered by the company) and the relationship of the new product to the products previously offered by the company. Figure 5-13 shows an example of a diversified luxury goods company.

5.4.3 Establishing Synergies within the Product Mix

A third central decision area in adapting the existing product mix is concerned with the establishment and design of synergies within the product mix. In this context, two options are particularly relevant:

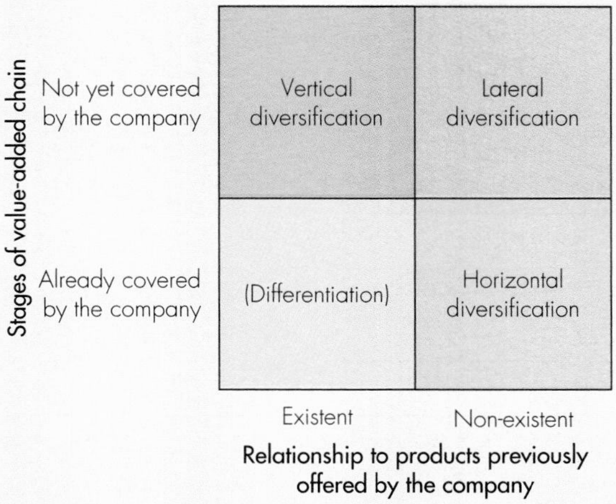

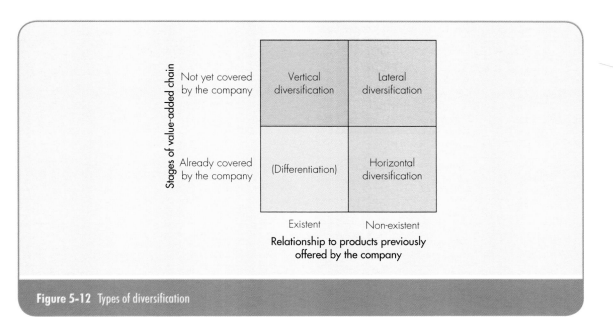

Figure 5-12 Types of diversification

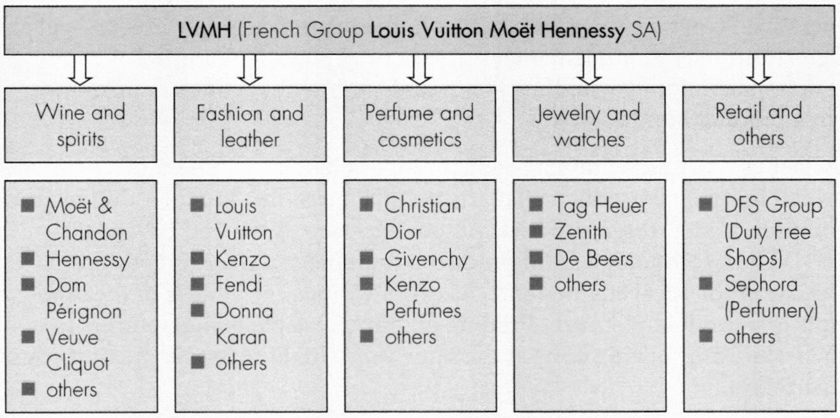

Figure 5-13 Example of a diversified luxury goods company

1 product bundling, and

2 product platforms.

Bundling is when a company sells two or more separate products in combination – that is, in a 'bundle' – and sells the bundle at a single price (see Stremersch and Tellis 2002). If pricing objectives are the predominant reason for the bundling decision, we speak of price bundling (for more information, see Chapter 6). If product objectives are at the forefront, as is the case with modifications to the product range, this is called **product bundling**. By combining products into a bundle, the company can leverage cross-selling potential with customers (see Section 9.5 on cross-selling) and reduce costs.

Table 5-10 Association matrix of a financial services provider (adapted from Schulz 1995, p. 272)

Complementary product (line) / Gateway product (line)	Life insurance	Savings and loan association contract	Mortgage	Home building insurance	Household contents insurance	Home construction financing
Life insurance		0.5	0.6	0.3	0.2	0.1
Savings and loan association contract	0.3		0.7	0.1	0.1	0.0
Mortgage	0.1	0.3		0.7	0.3	0.8
Home building insurance	0.3	0.4	0.2		0.9	0.1

An association matrix can facilitate the decision regarding what products should be included in a bundle. Such a matrix illustrates to what extent demand synergies exist for the various products of a company. The matrix provides statements regarding the probability with which customers who are already using a certain product as entry-level products will also use an additional product. In the example in Table 5-10, there is a 90 per cent probability that home insurance policy holders will also take out household contents insurance. Complementary products can then be bundled in a 'product package'. In this example, a home building insurance policy and a household contents insurance policy can be integrated in a product bundle.

A second option for establishing synergies within a product range is the development of a **product platform** consisting of several individual products that are manufactured in a modular design and can be produced using common standardized product components (see Putsis and Bayus 2001; Robertson and Ulrich 1999). Thus, technologies and product components are used repeatedly for different products. The use of identical engines and chassis in various car models of the same manufacturer is an example of a product platform. Product platforms enable manufacturers to offer a broad product range while minimizing costs at the same time (R&D costs, production costs) through technical standardization.

5.4.4 Reducing the Product Range

In the course of **product elimination**, a product or entire product line is removed from the market. In principle, product elimination should be considered if a product is unsuccessful in the market. The decision regarding product elimination should take into account several aspects. It is necessary to assess, for example, customers' preference for the product in question, current and future market share, and economic aspects (i.e. profitability).

In addition to evaluating the individual product, the synergies between the products have to be considered. In particular, attention must be paid to the question of the extent to which the decision to eliminate a product can have a positive or adverse effect on the market success of another product in the product mix. For example, it can be practical to continue a deficit-generating individual product if it is purchased in combination with successful products. Eliminating the product might then have a negative impact on the sales of the successful products. It is also possible that the elimination of products can have a positive impact on the performance of other products in the product mix.

5.5 Brand Management

In addition to innovation management and the management of products already established in the market, brand management is a third key area in product decision making. Systematic and professional brand management is particularly necessary in the face of the increasing variety of products and brands in the market, and the rising flood of communications. In such an environment, brands represent an important point of reference for customers when making their buying decisions. For companies, strong brands can be a significant asset. For example, in 2000, the brand equity of IBM was estimated at approximately US$53 billion (see *Financial Times* 2000 and Figure 5-21 for other brand equity figures). Consequently, brand management can substantially contribute to company success as well as the enhancement of company value.

The classic area of brand management is the consumer goods industry. Systematic brand management has a long-standing tradition in this sector. However, brand management is also of major importance in the service and industrial goods sectors. The fundamentals of brand management (see Section 5.5.1) and the different decisions involved in managing brands (see Section 5.5.2) will be presented in the following sections.

5.5.1 Introduction to Brand Management: Definition and the Relevance of Brands

The definition of the **brand concept** can be based on both a formal perspective and a perspective related to the effect of branding. According to the formal approach, a brand can be a name, an expression or phrase, a logo, symbol or design, or a combination of these elements that serves to make a supplier's products identifiable and sets them apart from competitor products (see Aaker 1991). The central idea of the approach related to the effect of branding is that a brand is ultimately created in the mind of the customer and thus cannot be defined exclusively by formal aspects. In line with this interpretation, which we will take as our basis for the following discussion, a brand is an image anchored in the mind of the customer that distinguishes the products or services of one company from those of a competitor (for a similar approach, see also Weinberg 1995).

The **functions of a brand** differ depending on the perspective of the observer (see Figure 5-14). From the standpoint of the buyer, a brand is an essential **reference point** that facilitates easier identification of the desired service or product. In particular, brands aid the buyer in obtaining and processing information about a product or service. Moreover, brands symbolize and indicate consistent product quality (representing a **quality promise** to the customer, so to speak) and can therefore reduce the perceived purchase risk on the part of the buyer. Along with the functional benefits, brands also convey an emotional experience (see, e.g., Aaker 1996; Ruth 2001, and for the role of emotions in marketing in general see Bagozzi *et al.*, 1999; Huang 2001). Finally, brands can be used by customers for image reasons, in order to express, say, an individual taste, an affiliation with a certain group or a particular social status (for example, by purchasing premium brands).

Our interest in this section focuses on the perspective of the brand owner. In many industries, products offered by different providers are relatively similar with regard to functionality, and thus a strong brand can be an important basis for **differentiating a company from the competition**. The brand's function as a **signal of quality** is especially crucial for service companies as the quality of services is difficult to assess for customers prior to the actual experience with the service (see Kim *et al.* 1998; Taylor 1987).

In this context, brands have the important core function to reduce the customer's uncertainty regarding quality. By differentiating the company's offer from those of competitors, and by communicating quality signals, companies use brands to create customer preferences for their products and ultimately establish **brand loyalty**. Loyal customers are often less price sensitive and enable companies to charge higher prices (and even price premiums). Furthermore, a successful brand helps the brand owner to

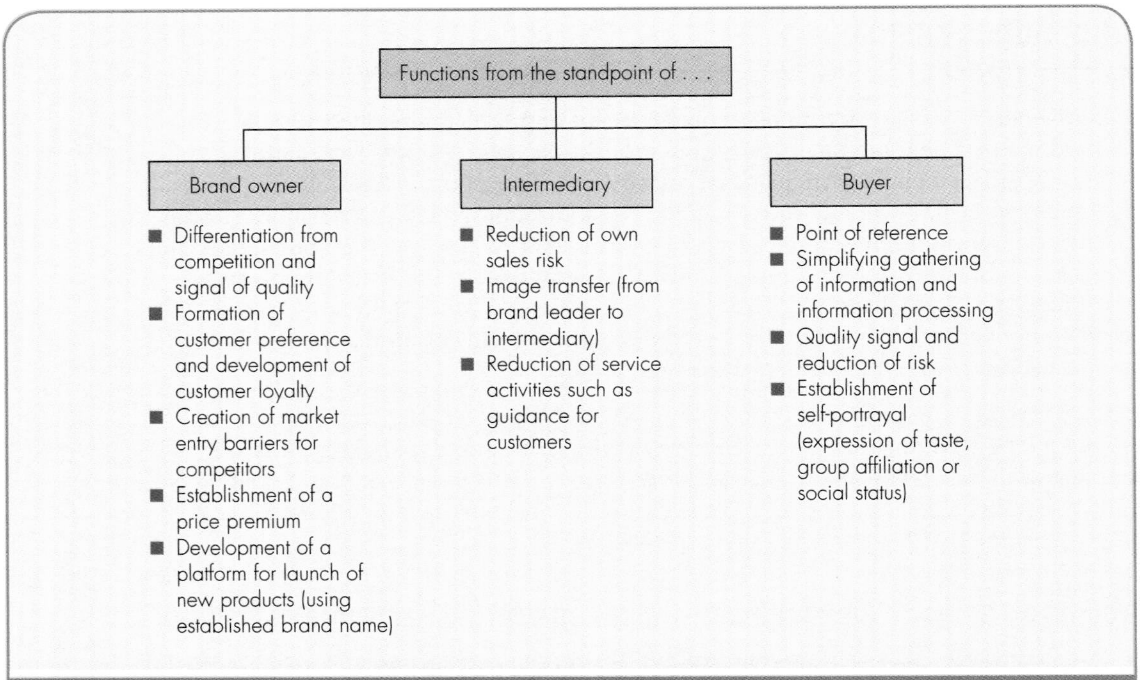

Figure 5-14 Central brand functions from various perspectives

establish a platform to launch new brands. Using the same brand name, positive associations can be leveraged to support the launch of a new brand and to enhance the probability of its success.

Intermediaries can also act as brand owners by marketing their own **private-label brands**. If this is the case, the brand will deliver the same functions for the intermediary as for the brand owner (see Figure 5-14). The importance of private-label brands has increased in the recent past in many product categories. (We will discuss this issue in detail in Section 11.5, on retailing.) For intermediaries, such as retailers, it is important to sell the established brands of other companies as well, because customer loyalty to these brands can decrease their own **sales risk**. Additionally, there can be a positive **image transfer** from the brand owner to the intermediary. A department store carrying a large range of luxury brands will benefit from this image transfer and will be perceived as upscale. This may even reduce the intermediary's own service activities such as providing guidance, advice and consulting to its customers.

Branding has been applied successfully in many different areas and in different forms. Therefore, brand typologies have been developed in the literature in order to provide a systematic overview of the different forms and types of branding. Table 5-11 provides an overview of these typologies.

5.5.2 Decisions in Brand Management

Brand management comprises three key decision-making areas:

1 formulation of the brand strategy (i.e. decisions about the brand reach, the brand positioning and brand architecture; see the following sections)

2 determination of the brand presentation (i.e. in particular, decisions about the brand name and the brand logo)

3 design of the brand monitoring system (see the last section of this chapter).

Table 5-11 Brand typologies (adapted from Bruhn 1995)

Typology characteristic	Brand types	Examples
Type of brand owner	Manufacturer brand	Pringles, iPod, Post-it
	Private-label brand	St Michael by Marks & Spencer (UK)
	Service brand	TUI, eBay, HSBC
Geographic reach of the brand	Local brand	Eichhof (beer in eastern Switzerland)
	National brand	Walkers Crisps (UK), Rivella (Switzerland)
	International brand	MasterCard, The North Face
	Global brand	Coca-Cola
Vertical penetration of brand in value chain	'Invisible' preliminary product brand	Styrodur (polystyrene foam)
	Ingredient brand	Gore-Tex, Intel, Nutrasweet
	Finished product brand	Suit by Hugo Boss
Number of brand owners	Individual brand	Red Bull (energy drink)
	Collective brand	Rioja (wine)
Number of branded goods	Single brand	Nespresso
	Umbrella brand (single)	Siemens
	Umbrella brand (multiple)	Nivea

Brand Strategy

There are three aspects within the scope of the brand strategy:

1 brand reach (coverage)
2 brand positioning
3 brand architecture.

Decisions about brand reach refer to issues of the geographical coverage of national and international markets, and the reach of the brand within the value chain. Brand positioning refers to defining how the brand should be differentiated in relation to other brands in the market. Brand architecture is the structure of all brands offered by a company, and defines the interrelationships between the individual brands of a company.

Brand Reach

Brand reach can be discussed from a geographical and vertical perspective, and with regard to aspects of cooperation with other companies. In terms of **geographical reach**, the following strategic options exist.

- With a **local brand strategy**, the brand development is intended for a specific country (e.g. England).
- Within the scope of an **international brand strategy**, the brand is targeted at several (at least two) national markets.
- A **regional brand strategy** targets multiple countries in geographic proximity (e.g. the Pacific Rim region).
- Finally, with a **global brand strategy**, the brand is aimed at the entire world (or at least a large portion of it).

The decision for or against one of these strategies is closely related to the international marketing strategy that the company pursues (see Chapter 12 for a more detailed discussion of strategic issues in international marketing). Accordingly, a company with a geocentric strategy will tend to pursue a global brand strategy, while a company with a polycentric strategy will develop and market mainly local brands in the individual countries (for a discussion of local vs global brands, see Kapferer 2001, 2005).

Vertical reach refers to utilizing the brand across several stages of the value chain, and is especially relevant to industrial goods companies. The core question concerns the extent to which the brand should also be visible for the customers of customers. There are two options with regard to the vertical reach of a brand.

1. With **ingredient branding** raw materials, components or parts that are used in producing other products are branded (e.g. the Intel or Gore-Tex brands) (see Desai and Keller 2002). Ingredient branding can create a pull effect on the part of customers in that a particular 'ingredient' of a product (such as the central processing unit of a computer) becomes a salient purchase attribute.
2. In contrast to the ingredient brand, a **processing brand** is not visible throughout the entire value chain. Rather, the brand is not perceived by the end customer but only by the manufacturers, end producers or intermediaries. For example, many **original equipment manufacturers** (**OEMs**), sell branded equipment that remains 'invisible' in the end product (car buyers usually do not know which company has supplied air-conditioning technology or the airbag).

The third aspect of brand reach concerns **cooperations** with other companies in the branding effort. The question here involves the extent to which and, if applicable, how, the brand should be developed in cooperation with other companies. In this context we should mention the concept of **co-branding** (dual branding), in which two brands are marketed in a combined fashion. The objective of co-branding is to strengthen both brands and to uncover new sales potential (see Freter and Baumgarth 2001; Shocker *et al.* 1994; and, for an example, see Figure 5-15). Co-branding can prove advantageous if, for economic reasons, the single brand cannot support the branding by itself. Another advantage arises if co-branding leads customers to perceive an additional functional or emotional benefit.

Figure 5-15 Example of co-branding by Philips and Nivea

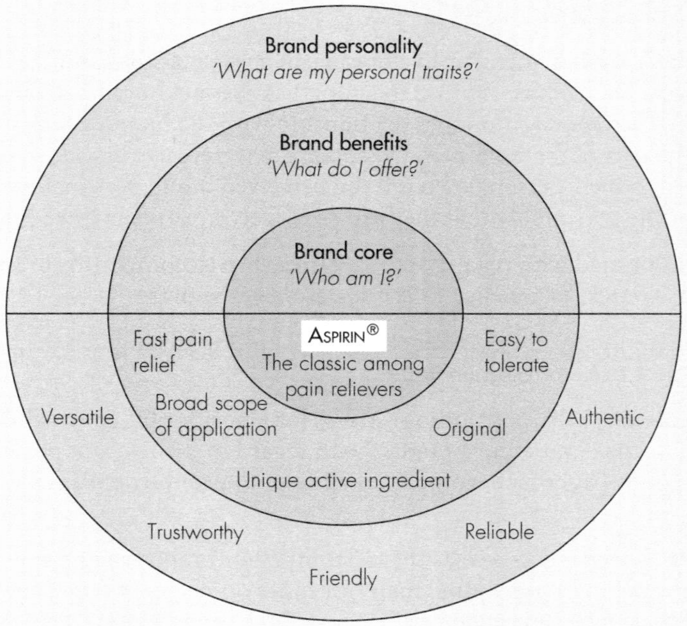

Figure 5-16 Dimensions related to brand positioning, illustrated with the example of the Aspirin pharmaceutical brand (see Homburg and Richter 2003, p. 15)

Brand Positioning

Another main decision-making area within the scope of the brand strategy relates to brand positioning, which predominantly deals with the design and definition of the following three dimensions of a brand (for more on these dimensions see Homburg and Richter 2003, as well as the illustration in Figure 5-16):

1 brand core

2 brand benefits

3 brand personality.

The **brand core** represents the identity of the brand. This can take the form of a concise expression or sentence (e.g. Esso – 'Put a tiger in your tank'; Visa – 'It's where you want to be').

Brand benefits relate to the main benefits that the brand should convey to buyers. For example, an industrial brand can stand for quality and precision, and a cosmetic brand for naturalness and purity. The key objective of brand positioning is to anchor a brand in the mind of the customer with certain benefit dimensions. We distinguish two aspects of positioning: the intended positioning (by the company) and the positioning that is actually realized (in the perception of the buyer).

Finally, considerations regarding the design of the **brand personality** have to be taken into account (for more on this concept, see Aaker 1997). This aspect of positioning relates to human characteristics that customers (should) associate with the brand. The concept lies in establishing an analogy between human personality profiles and the characterization of brands. Brands should thus convey their own 'personality', which can be described with attributes such as 'honest', 'cheerful', 'sporty', 'intelligent', 'reliable' and 'charming'. Such brand personality associations can aid in differentiating brands from the competition.

The assumption is that assigning a 'human identity' to a brand can augment the customer's identification with the brand (also see Ambler 1997 on this topic). A distinct brand personality therefore forms the basis for the customer's emotional relationship with the brand, which can lead to increased brand loyalty on the part of the customer. Customers may perceive brands as being especially important with regard to their personal needs if the perceived brand personality matches the personality of customers, or the personality that they aspire to (see, e.g., Aaker 1999; Sirgy 1982).

Brand positioning can also be examined with regard to the **relationship to competitor brands**. There are two basic approaches in this context (see Keller 1998), as described below.

1 **Differentiation positioning** (points-of-difference positioning) aims to distinguish the brand from competitor brands with respect to salient dimensions.

2 **Similarity positioning** (points-of-parity positioning) strives for a positioning in which the brand has the same characteristics as the competitor brand(s) with regard to the relevant positioning dimensions. With this positioning approach, companies attempt to profit from the halo effects of extremely strong brands.

The positioning of a company's own brand as well as that of competitor brands can be depicted in a two-dimensional (or multidimensional) **perceptual map** (for more on perceptual maps, see Baier and Gaul 1999; Bijmolt and Wedel 1999; Carpenter 1989; Hauser and Simmie 1981; MacKay and Dröge 1990; Schmalensee and Thisse 1988). Figure 5-17 shows a two-dimensional perceptual map. Such perceptual maps can be used to analyze the actual positioning of brands in the perception of buyers. Moreover, they can facilitate the definition of the target positioning. The distance between the company's own brand and the competitor brand(s) in this matrix provides information about the uniqueness of the company's own brand. The closer the brands are located to each other, the more interchangeable they are from a customer standpoint. In Figure 5-17, Brand 3 and Brand 4 are seen as rather similar, whereas Brand 5 and Brand 6 are judged to be dissimilar. Of particular interest with regard to marketing decisions are perceptual maps that also take into account the ideal positioning

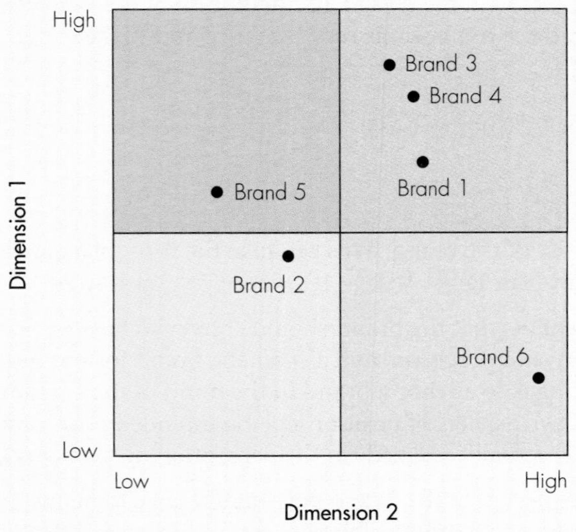

Figure 5-17 Two-dimensional perceptual map for analyzing the positioning of brands

as indicated by customers (see the section on perceptual maps in the Appendix). Ideal points of positioning help the company to better understand customer preferences.

Brand Architecture

The design of the **brand architecture** represents a further key area within the scope of the brand strategy. The brand architecture refers to the structure of all the brands of a company, and defines the roles of the brands and their interrelationships as well as the different product–market brand contexts (see Aaker and Joachimsthaler 2000). In contrast to brand reach and brand positioning, described above, brand architecture is not concerned with decisions relating to individual brands, but to structural decisions regarding a company's entire brand portfolio. In terms of brand architecture there are three basic strategic branding options to consider (for an illustration of these three options see Figure 5-18):

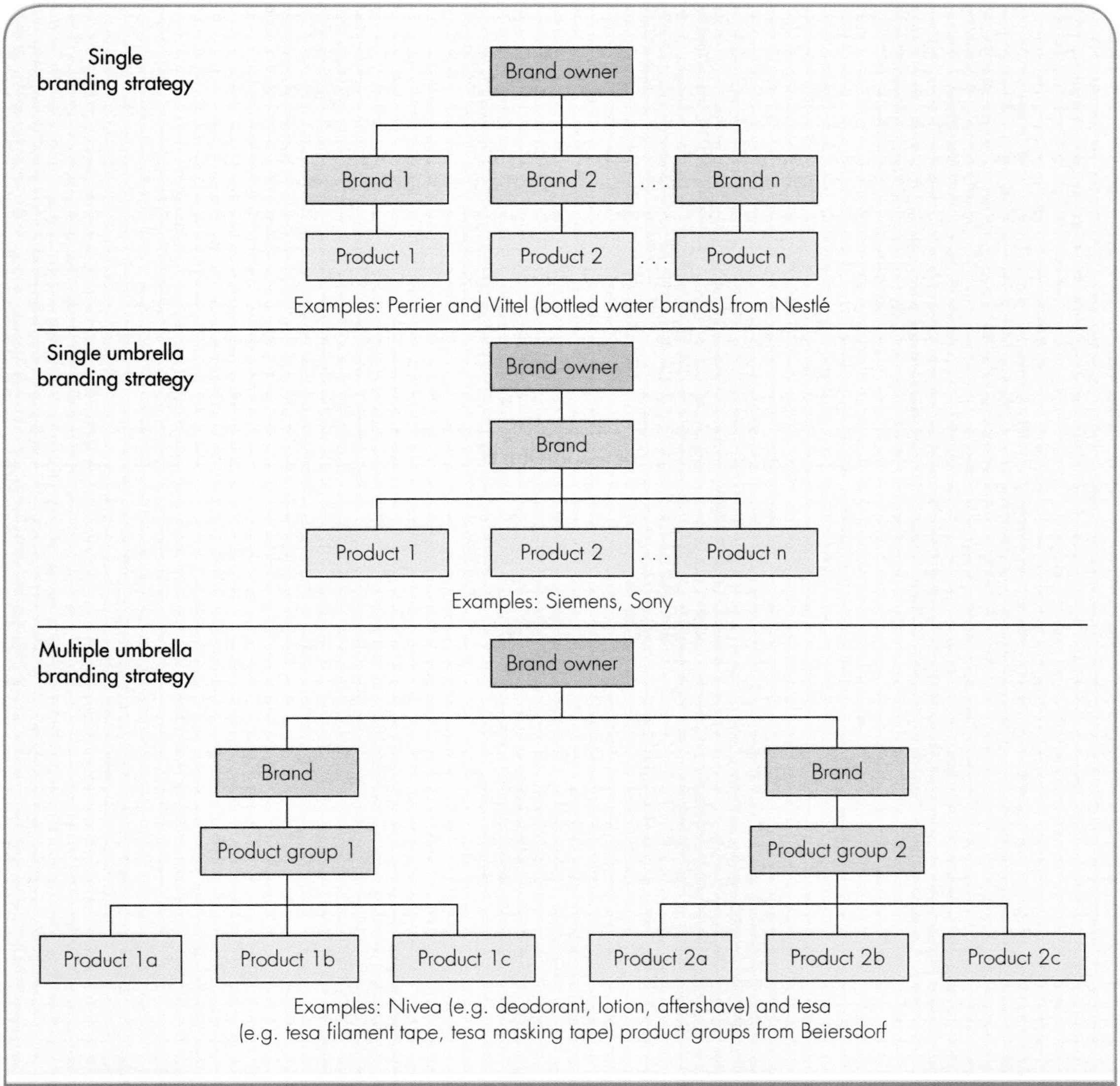

Figure 5-18 Illustration of different brand architectures (according to Homburg and Schäfer 2001, p. 161)

1 the single branding strategy

2 the single umbrella branding strategy

3 the multiple umbrella branding strategy.

With a **single branding strategy**, each service or product of a company is sold under its own separate brand and the company name takes a back seat. Important advantages of the single branding strategy include the option to precisely profile the individual brands and target a specific customer segment. In addition, it minimizes cannibalization effects or halo effects from impacting on other services or products offered by the company. A halo effect (which refers to a bias in the perception of a brand/ad/product/etc. – i.e. the transmission of the most prominent feature of an object on all its attributes) can occur when customers draw conclusions from one of a company's brands, and apply these to all its other brands. The main disadvantages of this are the costs and time involved in managing the brands. The single branding strategy is particularly recommended if a company has a heterogeneous product range and the individual products are intended to be positioned in different ways.

In the case of **single umbrella branding**, all the products of a company are marketed under one brand (for an in-depth discussion of umbrella branding, see Erdem 1998). A main benefit of umbrella branding is that the expense and effort (e.g., advertising costs) required for brand management form a joint investment for all products. Furthermore, an established umbrella brand can aid in the introduction of new products, since retailers and customers have already developed brand equity. A disadvantage to be mentioned here is that the number of and any differences between the different brands under the brand umbrella can dilute a clear brand positioning (see Pullig *et al.* 2006). Repositioning individual brands may prove problematic within a single umbrella branding strategy. Furthermore, there is also the risk that the negative halo effects caused by a failure of one of the products will impact the entire product range (brand portfolio contamination). In particular, a single umbrella strategy should be used if the product range is too large to feasibly pursue a single branding strategy or if the individual products are essentially equally positioned. An example of a single umbrella strategy is presented in Focus on Marketing 5-4. Figure 5-19 depicts a single branding strategy.

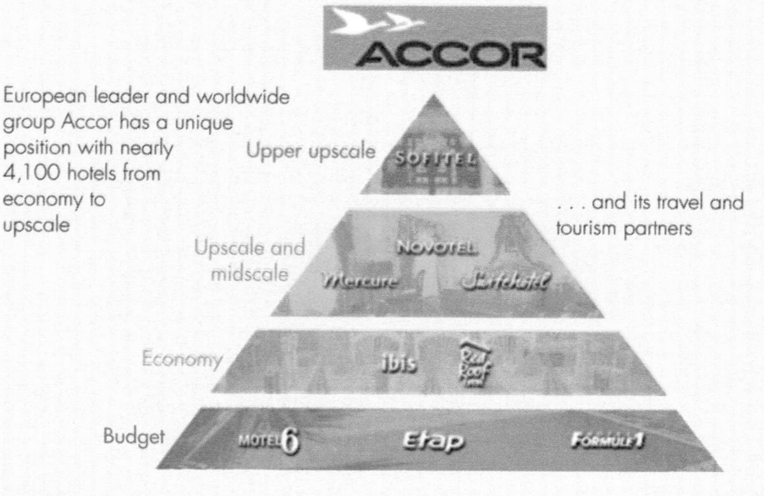

Figure 5-19 Brand architecture illustrated with the example of Accor (www.accor.fr)

Focus on Marketing 5-4 Example of Umbrella Branding

Virgin in redesign of umbrella brand logo

In 2006, Virgin made the first significant alterations to its branding in 21 years, with a refresh of its umbrella logo.

The changes, overseen by group brand marketing director Ashley Stockwell, were reported on www.brandrepublic.com as 'part of an effort to bring more cohesion to Virgin Group's marketing, which comprises more than 200 businesses'.

The Virgin logo had changed little since the launch of airline Virgin Atlantic in 1985. The new logo, designed by Start Creative, features a different script and is being rolled out steadily across the Virgin Mobile, Virgin Atlantic and Virgin Trains brands, as well as affiliates such as Virgin Holidays and Virgin Wines.

The site went on to explain that: 'Virgin claims the changes are being made because of the different ways in which the company now markets itself and communicates its breadth of products. It added that its old logo was not always clearly legible when used online, having originally been intended for use on a far bigger scale on the tailfins of Virgin Atlantic aircraft.'

The Virgin group has expanded into lifestyle products in recent years with Virgin Cosmetics and Virgin Active, but recently moved away from music retail industry, selling the Virgin Megastore chain to the Zavvi Entertainment group in September 2007.

Sources: Solley (2006); brandrepublic (http://www.brandrepublic.com/login/News/554338); Sarah Butler, 'Richard Branson turns to Zavvi to take Virgin Megastores off his hands', Times Online, 17 September 2007 (http://business.timesonline.co.uk/tol/business/industry_sectors/retailing/article2477452.ece).

With a **multiple umbrella branding strategy** (product line branding), a uniform brand is selected for a specific product group. This strategy thus represents an intermediate option between the single branding and single umbrella branding strategies. The goal is a combination of the targeting advantages of the single brand structure with the economic benefits of the single umbrella branding structure. Adopting a multiple umbrella branding strategy is, then, particularly suitable if several product lines with the same main benefits can be combined.

In addition to making the basic decision regarding one of the three design options, decisions pertaining to the further development of the brand architecture also have to be made by companies on a regular basis. In this context, a company can either further develop the existing brands (by extending the brand to new products in the existing product lines or via transfer to new product lines) or develop new brands (for existing or new product lines). Four strategic options result from this, as shown in Figure 5-20.

Line extension refers to expanding the existing brand by assigning it to a new product or product variant of a product line already established in the market. This strategy is frequently used for new product variants that differ only slightly from 'old' products. A line extension therefore generally corresponds to the product variant and product differentiation concepts discussed in Section 5.4.2. An example of a line extension would be supplementing a brewery's product lines by adding light or non-alcoholic versions to its beer brands.

The objective of a line extension strategy is to increase sales through more intensive product use by the current customers and by exploring new customer segments. However, if the product line is extended too far, this can have an adverse effect on the buying decision on the part of the customers (see Aaker 1998; Quelch and Kenny 1995).

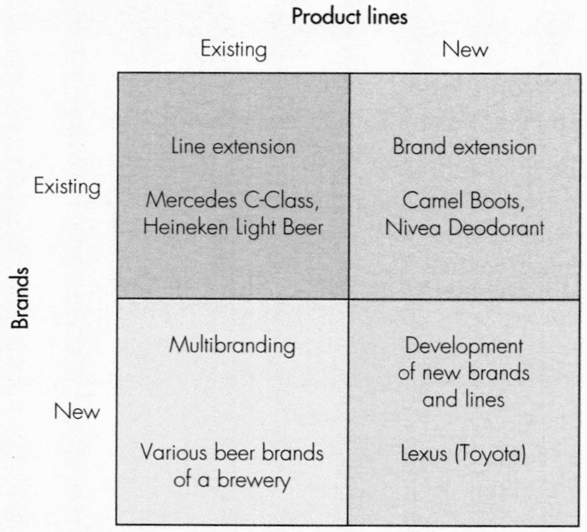

Figure 5-20 Strategic options for further developing the brand architecture

In view of this, the question regarding the **success factors of line extensions** becomes relevant. In an empirical study, Reddy *et al.* (1994) found that line extensions are particularly successful if they:

- start from a brand with a high degree of recognition
- build on a brand with a strong emotional or symbolic image
- are extensively supported by advertising and sales promotions
- are introduced in the market earlier than competitor products
- can facilitate the brand's entry into new markets
- can at least compensate for cannibalization effects by increasing sales.

Another option for developing the brand architecture is **brand extension**, in which an existing brand is extended to products of a different product line (see Aaker and Keller 1990; Broniarczyk and Alba 1994; Keller and Aaker 1992). In company practice, it is possible to extend brands to completely different products (e.g. from automobile brands to sunglasses).

The underlying logic of this approach lies in more intensively leveraging the buyer's existing positive perception of a brand by extending it to other product lines (the **spillover effect**; see Balachander and Ghose 2003). The positive assessment of the already-known brands on the part of the customer can thus facilitate entry into new product categories. From a cognitive perspective, customers can also simplify their buying decision processes by transferring their positive experiences with the brand's original product to the brand extension. However, the opportunities presented by brand extensions have to be weighed against considerable risks (see Martínez and Pina 2003). For example, the brand can lose its distinct image and profile if the main product and transfer product address very divergent target groups.

The most important **success factor associated with brand extension** is the degree of affinity of the images of the original brand and the extended brand. If the degree of affinity of the images is too low, negative spillover effects can be expected. Additional success factors include a positive quality perception of the brand with respect to the original brand as well as consistency with the history of previous brand extensions (see Aaker and Keller 1990; Keller and Aaker 1992).

A third option for modifying the brand architecture is **multibranding**. With this alternative, the company decides to introduce additional brands into an existing product line that already carries a brand. This can be useful if the objective is to, say, tap into new buyer groups that cannot be reached, or are hard to reach, with the current brand. Such approaches play a significant role if high-priced premium brands are being threatened in the market by less expensive competitor brands. A potential response on the part of the company could be to offer a less expensive brand as well. In this way, companies do not automatically lose customers that are not (or are no longer) willing to pay the price for the premium product. The greatest risk lies in cannibalization of the original brand – a risk that is particularly present if the brands are sold via the same sales channels.

Brand Monitoring

A third decision-making area of brand management is brand monitoring, which provides crucial information about **brand success**. With regard to the conceptualization of market success, a definite 'terminology jungle' exists in the literature: terms such as brand strength, brand equity and brand value are frequently used by a variety of authors to mean different things. There is no uniform opinion with respect to the relationships between these terms. Against this background, we will present an independent systematization of the various facets of brand success in the following, which is illustrated in Figure 5-21.

In Figure 5-21, we equate 'brand success' with 'brand equity' (for more on this, specifically, see Aaker 1991; Kapferer 2004; Keller 1993, 1998; Srivastava and Shocker 1991) and list the different facets of brand success. For a more detailed conceptualization of brand success, refer to the typology of marketing objectives in Section 2.1. Accordingly, brand success comprises the success of a brand with regard to success factors related to potential, to market and to economic success factors.

Brand success related to potential refers to the achievement of objectives that are located at a point in time before effects related to customer behavior come into play; it can particularly be measured by means of the following factors:

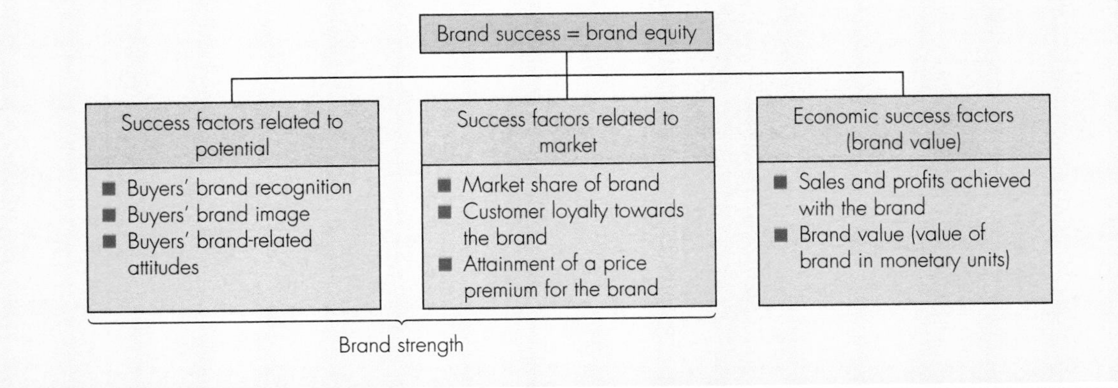

Figure 5-21 Systematization of brand success and categorization of the associated terms

- brand recognition on the part of the buyers
- brand image on the part of the buyers
- brand-related attitudes on the part of the buyers.

Success benchmarks related to market success refer to the achievement of objectives that map the success of a brand in the market on the basis of the actual behavioral patterns of customers. Success benchmarks here can be, for example, a brand's market share, the degree of customer loyalty towards the brand, or the attainment of a premium price for the brand.

Finally, **economic success benchmarks** are based on the achievement of objectives that represent conventional economic success. Along with the sales and profits made in association with a brand, **brand value** is another key economic success factor. Brand value refers to any monetary benefits a brand brings (for more on this concept, see, e.g., Duncan and Moriarty 1997). The estimates shown in Figure 5-22 illustrate the dimensions that the brand value can have. Often, the estimated brand value exceeds even the value of the real assets of a company. For example, in 1988, Philip Morris acquired Kraft Foods for US$12.9 billion, with an estimated US$11.6 billion of that attributed to brand value (see Aaker 1991).

Another term frequently associated with brand success (once again, with different meanings) is **brand strength**. We consider brand strength (also see Figure 5-21) to be the result of the evaluation of the market success in terms of all the relevant criteria related to potential and market success.

Following our discussion of the facets of brand success, the issue of the measurement of brand success arises (particularly with regard to non-economic factors). Potential-related and market success-related factors are analyzed using qualitative and quantitative market research methods.

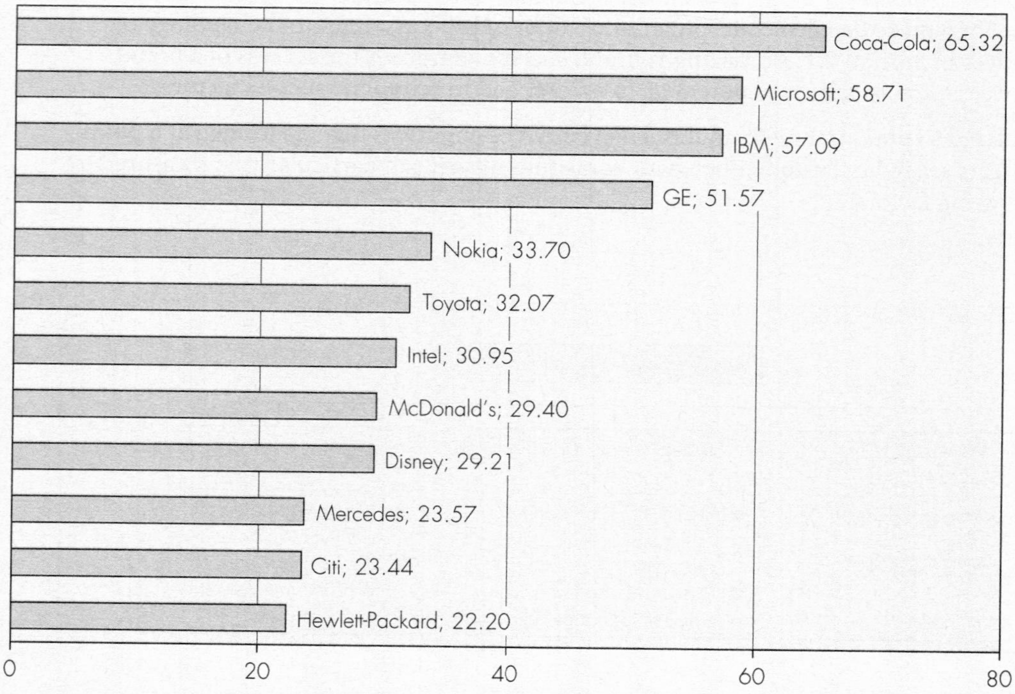

Figure 5-22 Estimated brand value (in billions €) of international leading brands in 2007 (Interbrand 2007)

For a detailed discussion of the application of such methods in connection with measuring brand success, please refer to Keller (1998).

A phenomenon that can greatly diminish the value of a brand is brand piracy (see also Focus on Marketing 5-5). As Focus on Marketing 5-5 shows, brand piracy is especially widespread in the Asian regions. However, a side note to be mentioned here is that this phenomenon can also have positive effects on suppliers of branded articles (e.g. accelerated product diffusion in the market and thus positive promotional and sales effects for the legal branded goods; see Givon *et al.* 1995; Haruvy *et al.* 2004; Prasad and Mahajan 2003).

Focus on Marketing 5-5 The problem of brand piracy

From knockoff bags to knockout brands

Paulo Zegna knows all about product counterfeiting in China, but he was still surprised to see his own name being stolen. He's co-chief of Ermenegildo Zegna Group, the Milan men's fashion house that also manufactures some of the world's best wool cloth, and earlier this year thousands of yards of fabric with the Zegna name woven onto the edge were discovered in southern China – but his company hadn't made it. Zegna cloth had joined the long list of products being faked in China.

A familiar tale but for one unexpected detail: Instead of the low-quality ripoff you'd expect, the cloth was pretty good. Zegna won't say it matched the real thing, but it was good. And why shouldn't it have been? As he noted last month at the *Fortune* Global Forum in Beijing, 'The Chinese now buy the same machines as everybody else, they hire the same consultants, they compete with us to buy the same raw wool in Australia.' Result: Somewhere in China a company is turning out high-quality woolens worthy of being marketed under its own name, which could presumably be built into a valuable brand, yet the firm chooses to steal someone else's name.

If that sounds crazy to you, you're not alone. It sounds crazy to many Chinese businesspeople too. Despite all we read about China's hundreds of thousands of engineering graduates, the next great phase of business development will center on a very different skill: brand building. And just as with China's earlier ascendancy to become the world leader in low-cost manufacturing, its development as a brand powerhouse may be far stronger and faster than many Western companies are ready for.

As the Chinese realize, brand owners typically collect most of the profit. A pair of Nike running shoes that leaves a factory in China at a cost of $5 may sell in the US for $100, and while Nike doesn't pocket all the difference, it makes way more than the factory owner. The situation is the same in consumer electronics, clothing, toys, and many other industries. Until recently, Chinese firms were happy to cash in on their labor-cost advantage and make more money than they'd ever seen. Now, led by companies like Lenovo (computers), Haier (appliances), TCL (consumer electronics), and others, they're going after the larger sums that flow to brand owners.

Chinese firms don't command any special brand-building talent. There is no analogue to their labor-cost advantage in manufacturing; on the contrary, they must overcome a business culture built in large part on brand piracy. Yet Western companies should fear the potential of Chinese brands. That's partly because Chinese marketers may understand their home turf better than anyone else, a significant edge when that market holds 22% of the world's people. And a Chinese company that builds a powerful brand at home may develop economies of scale and learning-curve advantages that will strengthen it globally. For decades those phenomena helped American companies stay on top. Now, in industries such as cellphones and PCs, where China is already the world's largest market or soon will be, the tables may be turning.

Source: *Fortune*,

Summary

In this chapter we discussed the main challenges that arise in making decisions about products. We defined the term 'product' and introduced product typologies before embarking on a discussion of innovation management. In this decision area the company needs to develop products that create value for customers. Therefore, the process of developing new products has to be carefully orchestrated involving the generation and elaboration of ideas, concept evaluation and selection, and – finally – the market launch. The chapter also looked at the issue of managing products that are already established in the market. Here we addressed decisions regarding the product mix and the expansion of the product mix, and how to create synergies in the product mix; we also discussed the need to reduce the product mix. In addition, we highlighted the importance of brands and brand management in today's competitive environment. With brands companies can differentiate their products from competitive products and reap important benefits for company success. We introduced the branding concept and elaborated on the main decisions in brand management, such as formulation of brand strategy and the design of a system to monitor brands.

Case Study: Nivea Revamps Deodorant Range

Nivea, the Beiersdorf-owned beauty brand, is overhauling its deodorant range in a bid to take on market leader, Unilever-owned Sure. The new strategy aims to reassure consumers that the range is as effective as other brands. The company is spending £5 million on a revamp of the packaging and a major new campaign. It is the first major focus on the brand since it was launched in 2002. The campaign will focus on Nivea's '24-hour protection' against sweat and odour after research showed consumers thought the deodorant range was less effective than its competitors. The range includes a male and female line of anti-perspirant sprays and roll-on deodorants. The German company will introduce new fragrances and formulations across its 'Dry and Fresh' variants with added minerals and ocean extracts that help to absorb sweat. Nivea plans to increase the distinction between its male and female ranges as it focuses on boosting sales of its men's products.

Source: excerpt from 'Nivea revamps deodorant range', by Noelle Waugh, *Marketing Week* (01419285), 1/4/2007, Vol. 30, Issue 1, 8.

Discussion Questions

1 In general there are three options for expanding the product mix: product variation, product differentiation and diversification. What are the main differences among these options?
2 Which option did Nivea choose for its deodorant range?
3 According to the example, what is probably the main reason for this choice? What are possible other reasons for such a product strategy?

Key Terms

6-3-5 method *116*
Accelerating the innovation process *131*
Additional features *109*
Adoption *123*
ASSESSOR *121*
Basic services *109*
Bass model *125*
Brainstorming *115*
Brainwriting *115*
Brand *109*
Brand architecture *145*
Brand benefits *143*
Brand concept *139*
Brand core *143*
Brand extension *148*
Brand loyalty *139*
Brand personality *143*
Brand strength *150*
Brand success *149*
Brand success related to potential *149*
Brand value *150*
Checklists *118*
Co-branding *142*
Communication decisions *129*
Competitive reactions *130*
Concept test *119*
Conjoint analysis *117*
Controlling approach *131*
Cooperations *142*
Core features *108*
Creativity methods *115*
Decision-making areas *111*
Depth of product mix *133*
Design of the individual elements of the marketing mix *129*
Design of the tangible environment *109*
Differentiating a company from the competition *139*
Differentiation positioning *144*
Diffusion *124*
Diversification *136*
Dynamic investment planning *122*
Early and late followers *129*
Economic success benchmarks *150*
Expanded product definition *108*
Followers *128*
Forecast the market share for the new product *121*
Fourt/Woodlock model *124*
Functions of a brand *139*
Generic product definition *108*
Geographical factors *129*
Geographical reach *141*
Global brand strategy *142*
Horizontal diversification *136*
Horizontal product differentiation *135*
Image transfer *140*
Ingredient branding *142*
Initial financial analysis *119*
Innovators/early adopters *129*
Intended target group(s) *118*
Intermediaries *140*
International brand strategy *142*
Lateral diversification *136*
Lead user approach *118*
Line extension *147*
Local brand strategy *142*
Mansfield model *125*
Morphological box *116*
Multibranding *149*
Multiple umbrella branding strategy *147*
Optimizing the overall innovation process *131*
Organizational approach *131*
Original equipment manufacturers (OEMs) *142*
Packaging *109*
Perceptual map *144*
Pioneer strategy *127*
Planning and design of the market launch *123*
Pre-marketing *129*
Pricing decisions *129*
Private-label brands *140*
Processing brand *142*
Product bundling *137*

References

Aaker, D. (1991) *Managing Brand Equity*. New York.
Aaker, D. (1996) *Building Strong Brands*. New York.
Aaker, D. (1998) Mit der Marke in einen neuen Markt, *Harvard Business Manager*, 20, 3, 43–52.
Aaker, D. and Joachimsthaler, E. (2000) *Brand Leadership*. New York.
Aaker, D. and Keller, K. (1990) Consumer evaluations of brand extensions, *Journal of Marketing*, 54, 1, 27–42.
Aaker, J. (1997) Dimensions of brand personality, *Journal of Marketing Research*, 34, 3, 347–356.
Aaker, J. (1999) The malleable self: the role of self-expression in persuasion, *Journal of Marketing Research*, 36, 1, 45–57.
Ambler, T. (1997) Do brands benefit consumers? *International Journal of Advertising*, 16, 3, 167–198.
Astebro, T. and Michela, J. (2005) Predictors of the survival of innovations, *Journal of Product Innovation Management*, 22, 4, 322–335.
Bagozzi, R., Gopinath, M. and Nyer, P. (1999) The role of emotions in marketing, *Journal of the Academy of Marketing Science*, 27, 2, 184–206.
Baier, D. and Gaul, W. (1999) Optimal product positioning based on paired comparison data, *Journal of Econometrics*, 89, 1/2, 365–392.
Balachander, S. and Ghose, S. (2003) Reciprocal spillover effects: a strategic benefit of brand extensions, *Journal of Marketing*, 67, 1, 4–13.
Balbontin, A. and Yazdani, B. (1999) New product development success factors in American and British firms, *International Journal of Technology Management*, 17, 3, 259–281.
Bass, F. (1969) A new product growth model for consumer durables, *Management Science*, 15, 5, 215–227.

Bayus, B. (1994) Are product life cycles really getting shorter? *Journal of Product Innovation Management*, 11, 4, 300–308.
Bayus, B. (1998) An analysis of product lifetimes in a technologically dynamic industry, *Management Science*, 44, 6, 763–775.
Bijmolt, T. and Wedel, M. (1999) A comparison of multidimensional scaling methods for perceptual mapping, *Journal of Marketing Research*, 36, 2, 277–285.
Booz, E., Allen, J. and Hamilton, C. (1982) *New Product Management for the 1980s*. New York.
Bowman, D. and Gatignon, H. (1995) Determinants of competitor response time to a new product introduction, *Journal of Marketing Research*, 32, 1, 42–53.
Brockhoff, K. (1999) *Produktpolitik* (4th edn). Stuttgart.
Broniarczyk, S. and Alba, J. (1994) The importance of the brand in brand extensions, *Journal of Marketing Research*, 31, 2, 214–229.
Bruhn, M. (1995) Markenstrategien, in: Tietz, B., Köhler, R. and Zentes, J. (eds) *Handwörterbuch des Marketing* (2nd edn). Stuttgart, 1445–1458.
Capron, L. and Hulland, J. (1999) Redeployment of brands, sales forces, and general marketing management expertise following horizontal acquisitions: a resource-based view, *Journal of Marketing*, 63, 2, 41–54.
Carpenter, G. (1989) Perceptual position and competitive brand strategy in a two-dimensional, two-brand market, *Management Science*, 35, 9, 1029–1044.
Choffray, J. and Lilien, G. (1982) DESIGNOR: a decision support procedure for industrial product design, *Journal of Business Research*, 10, 185–197.
Clement, M., Litfin, T. and Vanini, S. (1998) Ist die Pionierrolle ein Erfolgsfaktor? *Zeitschrift für Betriebswirtschaft*, 68, 2, 205–226.
Connor, J. (1981) Food product proliferation: a market structure analysis, *American Journal of Agricultural Economics*, 63, 4, 607–617.
Cooper, R. and Kleinschmidt, E. (1987) Success factors in product innovation, *Industrial Marketing Management*, 16, 3, 215–223.
Cooper, R. and Kleinschmidt, E. (1994) Determinants of timeliness in product development, *Journal of Product Innovation Management*, 11, 5, 381–396.
Cooper, R. and Kleinschmidt, E. (1995) Benchmarking the firm's critical success factors in new product development, *Journal of Product Innovation Management*, 12, 5, 374–391.
Cooper, R. and Kleinschmidt, E. (1996) Winning businesses in product development: the critical success factors, *Research Technology Management*, 39, 4, 18–30.
Cooper, R., Edgett, S. and Kleinschmidt, E. (2004) Benchmarking best NPD practices, *Research Technology Management*, 47, 1, 31–43.
Crawford, C. and Di Benedetto, A. (2006) *New Products Management* (8th edn). New York.
Desai, K.K. and Keller, K.L. (2002) The effects of ingredient branding strategies on host brand extendibility, *Journal of Marketing*, 66, 1, 73–93.
Di Benedetto, A. (1999) Identifying the key success factors in new product launch, *Journal of Product Innovation Management*, 16, 6, 530–544.
Dickson, P.R. and Ginter, J.L. (1987) Market segmentation, product differentiation, and marketing strategy, *Journal of Marketing*, 51, 2, 1–10.
Duncan, T. and Moriarty, S. (1997) *Driving Brand Value: Using Integrated Marketing to Manage Profitable Stakeholder Relationships*. New York.
Erdem, T. (1998) An empirical analysis of umbrella branding, *Journal of Marketing Research*, 35, 3, 339–351.
Erichson, B. (1981) TESI: Ein Test- und Prognoseverfahren für neue Produkte, *Marketing – Zeitschrift für Forschung und Praxis*, 3, 3, 201–207.
Financial Times (2000) Billion dollar brand, 17 July, 23.
Fortune (2005) http://money.cnn.com/magazines/fortune/fortune_archive/2005/06/27/8263409/index.htm, The problem of brand piracy (*Fortune*, ©2005 Time Inc. All rights reserved).
Fourt, L. and Woodlock, J. (1960) Early prediction of market success for new grocery products, *Journal of Marketing*, 25, 2, 31–38.
Freter, H. and Baumgarth, C. (2001) Ingredient Branding: Begriff und theoretische Fundierung, in: Esch, F. (ed.) *Moderne Markenführung: Grundlagen, Innovative Ansätze, Praktische Umsetzungen* (3rd edn). Wiesbaden, 317–344.
Gebert, F. (1983) *Diversifikation und Organisation*. Frankfurt.

Givon, M., Mahajan, V. and Muller, E. (1995) Software piracy: estimation of lost sales and the impact on software diffusion, *Journal of Marketing*, 59, 1, 29–37.

Golder, P. and Tellis, G. (1993) Pioneer advantage: marketing logic or marketing legend? *Journal of Marketing Research*, 30, 2, 158–171.

Green, P. and Krieger, A. (1985) Models and heuristics for product-line selection, *Marketing Science*, 4, 1, 1–19.

Green, P. and Krieger, A. (1987) A simple heuristic for selecting 'good' products in conjoint analysis, *Applications of Management Science*, 5, 131–153.

Greenberg, K. (2002) Giving a small car big 'tude, *Brandweek*, 45, 31–33.

Haruvy, E., Mahajan, V. and Prasad, A. (2004) The effect of piracy on the market penetration of subscription software, *Journal of Business*, 77, 2, 81–107.

Hauser, J. and Simmie, P. (1981) Profit maximizing perceptual positions: an integrated theory for the selection of product features and price, *Management Science*, 27, 1, 33–56.

Henard, D. and Szymanski, D. (2001) Why some new products are more successful than others, *Journal of Marketing Research*, 38, 362–375.

Hoch, St J., Bradlow, E.T. and Wansink, B. (1999) The variety of an assortment, *Marketing Science*, 18, 4, 527–546.

Homburg, C. and Richter, M. (2003) Branding Excellence – Wegweiser für professionelles Markenmanagement, Working Paper Series, Management Know-how, Institute of Market-Oriented Management, University of Mannheim, Mannheim.

Homburg, C. and Schäfer, H. (2001) Strategische Markenführung in dynamischer Umwelt, in: Köhler, R., Mayer, W. and Wiezorek, H. (eds) *Erfolgsfaktor Marke: Neue Strategien des Markenmanagements*. Munich, 157–173.

Huang, M.-H. (2001) The theory of emotions in marketing, *Journal of Business and Psychology*, 16, 2, 239–247.

Interbrand (2007) *The 100 Best Global Brands by Value*. London. http://www.interbrand.com/best_brands_2007.asp.

Kalyanaram, G., Robinson, W. and Urban, G. (1995) Order of market entry: established empirical generalizations, emerging empirical generalizations, and future research, *Marketing Science*, 14, 3, 212–222.

Kapferer, J. (2001) Is there really no hope for local brands? *Journal of Brand Management*, 9, 3, 163–170.

Kapferer, J. (2004) *The New Strategic Brand Management. Creating and Sustaining Brand Equity Long Term*. London.

Kapferer, J. (2005) The post-global brand, *Journal of Brand Management*, 12, 5, 319–324.

Karakaya, F. and Stahl, M.J. (1989) Barriers to entry and market entry decisions in consumer and industrial goods markets, *Journal of Marketing*, 53, 2, 80–91.

Keller, K. (1993) Conceptualizing, measuring, and managing customer-based brand equity, *Journal of Marketing*, 57, 1, 1–22.

Keller, K. (1998) *Strategic Brand Management: Building, Measuring, and Managing Brand Equity*. Englewood Cliffs, NJ.

Keller, K. and Aaker, D. (1992) The effects of sequential introduction of brand extensions, *Journal of Marketing Research*, 29, 1, 35–50.

Kerin, R., Varadarajan, P. and Peterson, R. (1992) First-mover-advantages: a synthesis, conceptual framework, and research propositions, *Journal of Marketing*, 56, 4, 33–52.

Kim, J., Reid, D., Plank, R. and Dahlstrom, R. (1998) Examining the role of brand equity in business markets: a model, research propositions, and managerial implications, *Journal of Business-to-Business Marketing*, 5, 3, 65–89.

Kotler, P. (1972) A generic concept of marketing, *Journal of Marketing*, 36, 2, 46–54.

Kuester, S., Homburg, C. and Robertson, T. (1999) Retaliatory behavior to new product entry, *Journal of Marketing*, 63, 10, 90–106.

Lazer, W., Luqmani, M. and Quraeshi, Z. (1984) Product rejuvenating strategies, *Business Horizons*, 27, 6, 21–28.

Lilien, G. and Kotler, P. (1983) *Marketing Decision Making: A Model-Building Approach*. New York.

Lilien, G., Kotler, P. and Moorthy, K. (1992) *Marketing Models*. Englewood Cliffs, NJ

Lilien, G., Rangaswamy, A. and van den Bulte, A. (2000) Diffusion models: managerial applications and software, in: Mahajan, V., Muller, E. and Wind, Y. (eds) *New Product Diffusion Models*. Boston, Mass., 295–311.

Luo, Y. (2002) Product diversification in international joint ventures: performance implications in an emerging market, *Strategic Management Journal*, 23, 1, 1–20.
MacKay, D. and Dröge, C. (1990) Extensions of probabilistic perceptual maps with implications for competitive positioning and choice, *International Journal of Research in Marketing*, 7, 4, 256–282.
Mahajan, V. and Wind, J. (1997) Issues and opportunities in new product development: an introduction to the special issue, *Journal of Marketing Research*, 34, 1, 1–12.
Mahajan, V., Muller, E. and Bass, F. (1990) New product diffusion models in marketing: a review and directions for research, *Journal of Marketing*, 54, 1, 1–26.
Mahajan, V., Muller, E. and Wind, Y. (eds) (2000) *New Product Diffusion Models*. Boston, Mass.
Makadok, R. (1998) Can first-mover and early-mover advantages be sustained in an industry with low barriers to entry/imitation? *Strategic Management Journal*, 19, 7, 683–696.
Mansfield, E. (1961) Technical change and the rate of imitation, *Econometrica*, 29, 4, 741–766.
Martínez, E. and Pina, J.M. (2003) The negative impact of brand extension on parent brand image, *Journal of Product and Brand Management*, 12, 7, 432–448.
Mishra, S., Kim, D. and Dae, H. (1996) Factors affecting new product success: cross-country comparisons, *Journal of Product Innovation Management*, 13, 6, 530–550.
Mohr, J., Sengupta, S. and Slater, S. (2005) *Marketing of High-Technology Products and Innovations* (2nd edn). New Jersey.
Montoya-Weiss, M. and Calantone, R. (1994) Determinants of new product performance: a review and meta-analysis, *Journal of Product Innovation Management*, 11, 5, 397–417.
Murphy, P. and Enis, B. (1986) Classifying products strategically, *Journal of Marketing*, 50, 3, 24–43.
Nair, S.K., Thakur, L.S. and Wen, K.-W. (1995) Near optimal solutions for product line design and selection: beam search heuristics, *Management Science*, 41, 5, 767–785.
Olson, E., Walker, O. and Ruekert, R. (1995) Organizing for effective new product development: the moderating role of product innovativeness, *Journal of Marketing*, 59, 1, 48–62.
Prasad, A. and Mahajan, V. (2003) How many pirates should a software firm tolerate? An analysis of piracy protection on the diffusion of software, *International Journal of Research in Marketing*, 20, 4, 337–353.
Pullig, C., Simmons, C.J. and Netemeyer, R.G. (2006) Brand dilution: when do new brands hurt existing brands? *Journal of Marketing*, 70, 2, 52–66.
Putsis, W.P. and Bayus, B.L. (2001) An empirical analysis of firms' product line decisions, *Journal of Marketing Research*, 38, 1, 110–118.
Quelch, J. and Kenny, D. (1994) Extend profits, not product lines, *Harvard Business Review*, 72, 5, 153–160.
Quelch, J. and Kenny, D. (1995) Markenpolitik I: Lieber den Gewinn steigern als die Anzahl der Varianten, *Harvard Business Manager*, 17, 1, 94–101.
Randall, T., Ulrich, K. and Reibstein, D. (1998) Brand equity and vertical product line extent, *Marketing Science*, 17, 4, 356–379.
Reddy, S., Holak, S. and Bhat, S. (1994) To extend or not to extend: success determinants of line extensions, *Journal of Marketing Research*, 31, 2, 243–262.
Riederer, J.P., Baier, M. and Graefe, G. (2005) Innovation management – an overview and some best practices, *C-Lab Report*, 4, 3, 46–47.
Robertson, D. and Ulrich, K. (1999) Produktplattformen: Was sie leisten, was sie erfordern, *Harvard Business Manager*, 21, 4, 75–85.
Robinson, W. and Fornell, C. (1985) Sources of market pioneer advantages in consumer goods industries, *Journal of Marketing Research*, 22, 3, 305–318.
Robinson, W. and Min, S. (2002) Is the first to market the first to fail? Empirical evidence for industrial goods businesses, *Journal of Marketing Research*, 39, 1, 120–128.
Rogers, E.M. (1962) *Diffusion of Innovations*. New York.
Rogers, E.M. (2003) *Diffusion of Innovations* (5th edn). New York.
Ruth, J. (2001) Promoting a brand's emotion benefits: the influence of emotion categorization processes on consumer evaluations, *Journal of Consumer Psychology*, 11, 2, 99–113.
Saunders, J. and Khan, S. (1986) Product phasing: the synchronous deletion and replacement of products, *Contemporary Research in Marketing, Proceedings of the 15th Annual Conference of the European Marketing Academy*, Helsinki, 1009–1023.
Schmalensee, R. and Thisse, J. (1988) Perceptual maps and the optimal location of new products: an integrative essay, *International Journal of Research in Marketing*, 5, 4, 225–249.

Schulz, B. (1995) *Kundenpotentialanalyze im Kundenstamm von Unternehmen*. Frankfurt am Main.
Seibert, S. (1998) *Technisches Management: Innovationsmanagement*. Stuttgart.
Shaked, A. and Sutton, J. (1982) Relaxing price competition through product differentiation, *Review of Economic Studies*, 49, 155, 3–13.
Shankar, V., Carpenter, G. and Krishnamurthi, L. (1998) Late mover advantage: how innovative late entrants outsell pioneers, *Journal of Marketing Research*, 35, 1, 54–70.
Shocker, A., Srivastava, R. and Ruekert, R. (1994) Challenges and opportunities facing brand management: an introduction to the special issue, *Journal of Marketing Research*, 31, 2, 149–158.
Silk, A. and Urban, G. (1978) Pre-test market evaluation of new packaged goods: a model and measurement methodology, *Journal of Marketing Research*, 15, 2, 171–191.
Sirgy, M. (1982) Self concept in consumer behavior: a critical review, *Journal of Consumer Research*, 9, 3, 287–300.
Solley, S. (2006) Virgin in redesign of umbrella brand logo, *Marketing*, 20 April, 6.
Srivastava, R. and Shocker, A. (1991) Brand equity: a perspective on its meaning and measurement, *MSI-Report 91*, 124, Cambridge.
Stremersch, S. and Tellis, G.J. (2002) Strategic bundling of products and prices: a new synthesis for marketing, *Journal of Marketing*, 66, 1, 55–72.
Taylor, R. (1987) The branding of services, in: Murphy, J. (ed.) *Branding: A Key Marketing Tool*. Houndmills, 1–30.
Trott, P. (2005) *Innovation Management and New Product Development*. Upper Saddle River, NJ.
Urban, G. and Hauser, J. (1993) *Design and Marketing of New Products* (2nd edn). Englewood Cliffs, NJ.
Urban, G. and Katz, G. (1983) Pretest market models: validation and managerial implications, *Journal of Marketing Research*, 20, 3, 221–234.
Urban, G., Carter, T., Gaskin, S. and Mucha, Z. (1986) Market share rewards to pioneering brands: an empirical analysis and strategic implications, *Management Science*, 32, 6, 645–660.
Van Riel, A., Lemmink, J. and Ouwersloot, H. (2004) High-technology service innovation success: a decision-making perspective, *Journal of Product Innovation Management*, 21, 5, 348–359.
Vanderwerf, P. and Mahon, J. (1997) Meta-analysis of the impact of research methods on findings of first-mover advantages, *Management Science*, 43, 11, 1510–1519.
von Hippel, E. (1988) *The Sources of Innovation*. New York.
von Hippel, E., Thomke, S. and Sonnack, M. (1999) Creating breakthroughs at 3M, *Harvard Business Review*, 77, 5, 47–55.
Waugh, N. (2007) Nivea revamps deodorant range, *Marketing Week*, 30, 1, 8.
Weinberg, P. (1995) Markenartikel und Markenpolitik, in: Tietz, B., Köhler, R. and Zentes, J. (eds) *Handwörterbuch des Marketing* (2nd edn). Stuttgart, 2679–2690.
www.accor.fr
www.interbrand.com
www.investor.wallst.com/stocks/company-profile.asp?rpc=66&ticker=MA

CHAPTER 6

Pricing: Making Profitable Decisions

Contents

Learning Objectives

In this chapter you will become familiar with:

- the key decision-making areas in pricing
- the problems related to establishing company-internal and external prices
- the basic forms of price-demand functions
- the concept of the price elasticity of demand
- the methods for determining demand functions
- the key concepts in behavioral pricing
- the primary approaches for demand-based pricing, price differentiation and price bundling
- the main approaches to cost-based pricing
- the primary methods related to competition-based pricing and price wars.

This chapter will first introduce the conceptual foundations of pricing decisions (see Section 6.1), with a focus on describing the various key decision-making areas. Following that, Section 6.2 will present the central theories underlying pricing decisions. Here, we will examine classical pricing theory and behavioral pricing. Subsequently, in Section 6.3, we will discuss pricing approaches (i.e. the ways in which companies can determine their prices). In this regard, we differentiate between demand-based, cost-based and competition-based pricing.

6.1 The Key Aspects of Determining Prices in a Complex Setting

As a component of the marketing mix, pricing comprises all decision-making aspects regarding the price to be paid by customers for a given product or service. In company practice, the importance of **pricing decisions** has risen greatly in recent years. Several developments have contributed to this, as outlined below.

- Many markets show signs of saturation and overcapacity. Pricing is used as an important weapon vis-à-vis competition.
- At the same time, growth markets (e.g. telecommunication) adopt price competition in the struggle for market share.
- Globalization of competition and the associated international market entry of a growing number of foreign companies (e.g. from low-wage countries) intensify the pricing pressure.
- In many industries, products being supplied by competitors become more similar in quality, which leads to price becoming an increasingly important decision-making criterion for buyers.
- Price transparency for buyers has increased considerably in many markets. This can be attributed partly to the growth of the internet, which has dramatically opened up the availability of price information for buyers. Monetary unions, such as the European Monetary Union, have also considerably simplified transnational price comparisons.

When comparing pricing to other marketing mix instruments, some **basic characteristics pertaining to pricing decisions** have to be mentioned here.

- Fast implementation: contrary to the majority of decisions concerning other elements of the marketing mix (e.g. the development and launch of a new product), pricing decisions can be implemented relatively quickly.
- Hardly reversible: once a price has been fixed, it functions as a point of reference that customers use to evaluate subsequent price changes.
- Major impact: pricing decisions have a major impact on customer behavior, since the price determines the 'negative' component of the purchase decision process.
- Fast impact: in many markets, customers and competitors respond quickly to price changes.

Pricing essentially compri ses six **decision-making areas** (see Figure 6-1). The main issues arising from these will be briefly described below. In this context, we will also discuss the way in which the theories, concepts and methods presented in Sections 6.2 and 6.3 can be used to facilitate decisions in the different decision-making areas.

In the case of **generic new product pricing** (i.e. when a new product is being launched in the market) there are two different basic approaches: the skimming strategy and the penetration strategy.

According to the **skimming strategy**, products are sold at comparably high prices during the market entry phase. The aim of this strategy is to take advantage of buyers' willingness to pay and

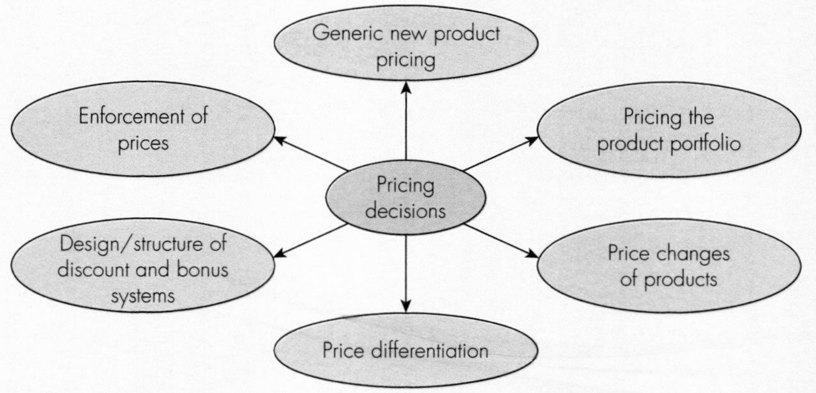

Figure 6-1 Key areas of pricing decision making

establish a positive quality image as a result of the high price positioning. Over the course of the product life cycle, and in the face of increased competitive pressure, the price is successively reduced. A skimming strategy helps to recoup investments in the new product (such as R&D costs) and thus substantially contributes to rapid amortization of these investments. For instance, skimming strategies are often applied in the pharmaceutical industry, where new drugs are generally positioned at high price levels (see Lu and Comanor 1998).

The objective of a **penetration strategy**, on the other hand, is to establish relatively low prices initially in order to achieve a rapid diffusion of the product and gain market share. The main advantage of a penetration strategy lies in the possibility of establishing a strong market position in a very short period of time and profiting from the benefits of volume-based cost advantages. Thus, this strategy has close ties with the experience curve concept (see Section 2.2.2). The price strategy used during the launch of the software for the Netscape Navigator internet browser exemplifies the penetration strategy. Because the software was available free of charge, Netscape was initially able to attain a top market leadership position and to establish a software standard, subsequently selling the software to corporate customers. This price strategy was so successful in winning market share that it was adopted by Microsoft when it introduced its rival product, Microsoft Internet Explorer (see Shapiro and Varian 1999).

The two approaches in generic new product pricing are depicted graphically in Figure 6-2.

The innovativeness of the new product plays an important role in deciding whether to adopt skimming or penetration pricing: if the new product is significantly differentiated from the products already established in the market, the skimming strategy can be the more favorable option. The company introducing the new product can thus benefit from an almost monopolistic situation until a competitor introduces a similar product.

Following this basic decision, the **actual pricing of the new product** has to be carried out. Here, an estimate based on the demand function can provide a crucial basis for making this decision. Section 6.2.1 provides an examination of the price-demand functions and how they can be measured empirically. A consideration of aspects from behavioral science can also be helpful in this context. During the pricing process, a company could, say, make a decision regarding what reference price should be specifically communicated to customers. The factors related to price assessment by customers are discussed in detail in Section 6.2.2.

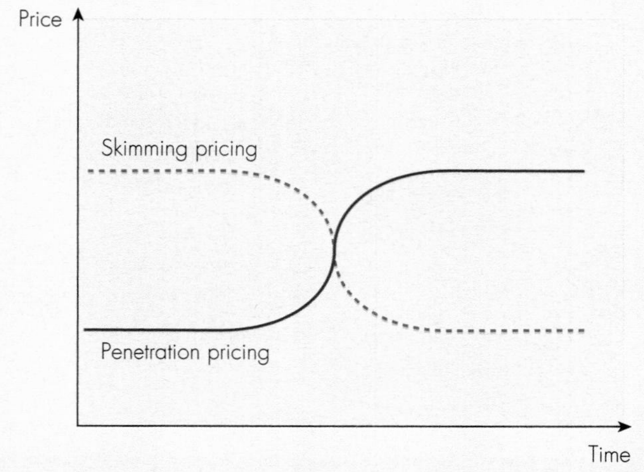

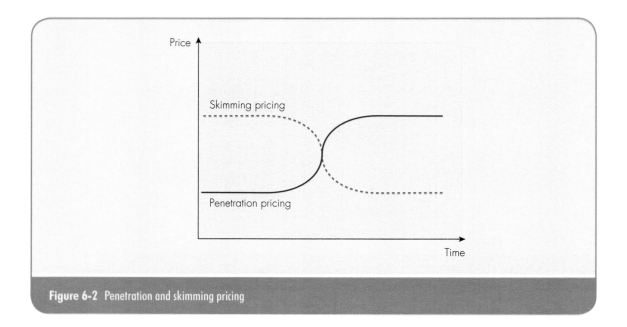

Figure 6-2 Penetration and skimming pricing

The **pricing of the product portfolio** represents a second decision-making area in pricing. Here, it is important to appreciate the fact that individual products are not viewed as separate entities, but rather in the context of the entire product portfolio. Due to synergies, the pricing of a product can have a positive or negative impact on the sales of other products within the company's overall portfolio.

As a first step, the **price positioning of individual product lines** needs to be defined on the basis of the company's product price positioning (for a detailed discussion, see Dobson and Kalish 1988) as specified in the marketing strategy (for more on this, see Chapter 1). Vital here is the question concerning what minimum price differentials between the product lines have to exist in order for the customer to be able to perceive price-related differences in positionings. Figure 6-3 shows an example of three product lines, comprising a total of ten different car models (models A–J), which illustrates the issue of price positioning within a product portfolio.

There are two general options here: a narrow or a broad price range for a particular product line. In the example shown in Figure 6-3, there is a relatively broad range in the product line for mid-sized cars, while the prices in the product line for compact cars are relatively close together. This is also the case for the range in the premium positioning.

A further basic decision with regard to determining the pricing of the product portfolio concerns which products should be offered together in a price bundle. We discuss **price bundling** in detail in Section 6.3.1.

As a third decision-making area, **price changes of products** concern either permanent or temporary price changes. Decisions related to **permanent price changes** can be of both an operative and a strategic nature. Operative decisions about price changes that are permanent include, for example, adjusting prices to monetary value trends, often leading to a nominal but not real price change. Strategic price changes that are permanent include, for instance, price repositionings of products or product lines. Price wars often result from particularly significant permanent price changes (see Section 6.3.1).

Temporary price changes are usually implemented by special price offers. Examples are special weekly prices in retail stores, and seasonal prices (e.g. in the tourism industry). In principle,

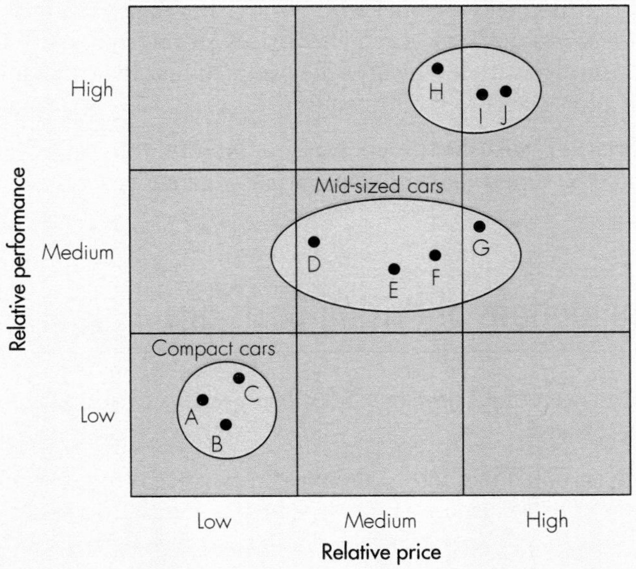

Figure 6-3 Example of the price positionings for the products and product lines of a car manufacturer

temporary price changes represent a form of temporal price differentiation, which we will discuss in Section 6.3.1.

Price differentiation is another main decision-making area in pricing. Price differentiation refers to the situation in which companies offer identical or similar products to different customers (or segments) at a different price. The underlying logic of this approach is tied to the fact that various customer groups differ in their willingness to pay (see Section 6.3.1).

A further decision-making area concerns the design and structure of the **discount and bonus system**. Discounts are price reductions granted to a customer at the time of invoicing and lower the price as compared to the regular price or list price (e.g. volume discounts, special promotional discounts or one-time discounts given by a sales representative). Bonuses are also price reductions, but are granted only after the purchase has been made (e.g. loyalty bonus if a customer buys a certain number of products or a bonus for a dealer in return for supporting a new product launch). The discount and bonus system of a company comprises all the guidelines concerning the granting of discounts or bonuses to customers and/or intermediaries.

The success of pricing decisions depends heavily on the extent to which defined pricing measures (especially the price itself) can actually be enforced in the marketplace. Accordingly, a further decision-making area is related to the **enforcement of prices**. Both company-internal and external aspects have to be considered in this context.

The **enforcement of company-internal pricing** refers to influencing the price-related behavior of the company's employees. Of particular relevance here is the employee's conduct in the course of direct customer contact (e.g. the behavior of sales employees). Company-internal pricing therefore has to ensure that employee behavior is in line with pricing objectives and decisions; it is also important to train sales employees to adhere to the discount and bonus system so that it is not undermined.

In contrast, the **enforcement of external pricing** refers to making customers accept the prices determined by the company. The following aspects are important here.

- Of primary relevance is the **communication of prices and pricing decisions**. For example, it is advisable to communicate price increases together with positive messages (e.g. improved delivery service) or to justify them in some way (e.g. higher prices for raw materials). This may help to positively influence consumer attitudes towards the products and the company (for more information on 'attitude' please refer to the Appendix).
- **Communication during negotiations with customers** is just as important in this context. Prices and price increases should be supported with appropriate arguments about the product's benefits.

6.2 The Theoretical Foundations of Pricing Decisions

With regard to the theoretical foundation of pricing, two basic perspectives exist that are relevant for company practice and research in this area.

1. **Classical pricing theory**, which is rooted in microeconomics: here, price is interpreted as an objective variable and customer price response is analyzed with quantitative models. The assumption of these models is that individuals are rational and maximize their utility (see Varian 2003).
2. **Concepts based on behavioral science**, which are rooted in psychology: these concentrate on how prices are perceived by individuals. The objective price and the way it is perceived by the customer are seen as quite different aspects.

In Section 6.2.1, we examine concepts based on microeconomics; Section 6.2.2 then discusses concepts based on behavioral science.

6.2.1 Pricing for a Rational Customer: Classical Pricing Theory

Price and Market Structure

A market is a commercial and social arrangement used for the exchange of products and services. The structure of the respective market largely determines the degree of flexibility the company has to make pricing decisions. When making decisions related to pricing, companies therefore have to consider the form of the relevant market.

Accordingly, the different market structures observed in practice – i.e. the monopoly (one company with many buyers), the oligopoly (a few companies and many buyers) and the polypoly (many companies and many buyers) – have different consequences concerning the degree of flexibility of pricing decisions. In the case of pricing in a **monopoly**, the company has only to take into account the reactions of customers, since competitors are either non-existent or their impact is negligible. In an **oligopoly**, firms have to consider both customer reactions and the actions of competitors. Differing from a monopoly or oligopoly, in a **polypoly**, companies tend to have less flexibility when it comes to pricing, especially if the larger number of competitors is associated with a higher degree of competitive intensity. Under these circumstances, a competition-based pricing approach (see Section 6.3.3) can be necessary or practical.

The Demand Function

The demand function is the basic concept for analyzing pricing with the aid of the classical pricing theory. This function describes that demand x depends on price p:

$$x = x(p)$$

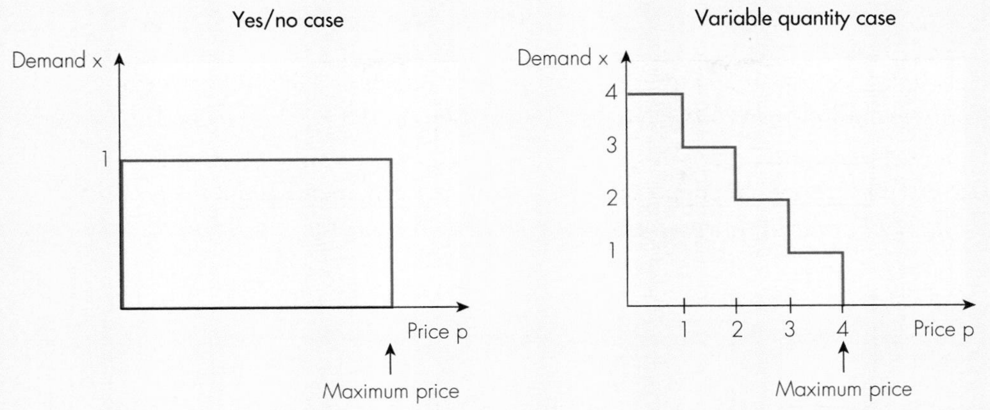

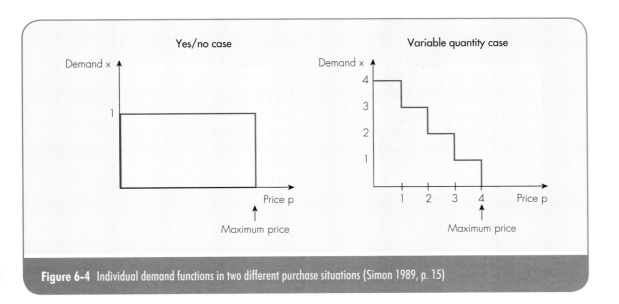

Figure 6-4 Individual demand functions in two different purchase situations (Simon 1989, p. 15)

Knowledge of the quantity of a product a customer will buy at what price is especially important when **pricing new products**. In the following, we will discuss the concept of the demand function as well as ways to measure it. Pricing based on demand functions is discussed in the section on demand-based pricing (Section 6.3.1).

Individual Demand Functions

Demand functions generally apply to an entire market or an individual customer segment. To better understand the demand function, however, it should be made clear that such a function always results from an aggregation of individual price-demand functions.

There are two different cases with regard to the individual demand function (see Simon 1989 and Figure 6-4).

1 Yes/no case: in this case, the customer buys the product as long as it does not exceed a certain threshold price. This threshold price (also referred to as the 'reservation price') is the maximum price that the customer is willing to pay for the product and depends on the perceived product benefits. The yes/no case is characteristic of purchases of durable goods (e.g. automobiles, freezers, machinery).

2 Variable quantity case: here, it is assumed that the customer will not only purchase just one unit of a product, but will buy a specific quantity of the product depending on the price; as a rule, the higher the price, the lower the quantity purchased. In the example shown in Figure 6-4, the customer would thus buy four units of the product at a price of one monetary unit, but buys only two units of the product at a price of three monetary units. The variable quantity case is typical of consumer goods (e.g. food, cosmetics).

Aggregating the individual functions results in the aggregated demand function, which shows what quantity of a product will be bought at what price by all customers. The aggregated demand function is usually negative: the higher the price, the fewer the purchases. Moreover, it becomes apparent that, with a sufficiently large number of customers, the 'kinks' of the aggregated price-demand function will smooth out; the functional curve becomes straight so that the function can be analyzed more easily (see Figure 6-5).

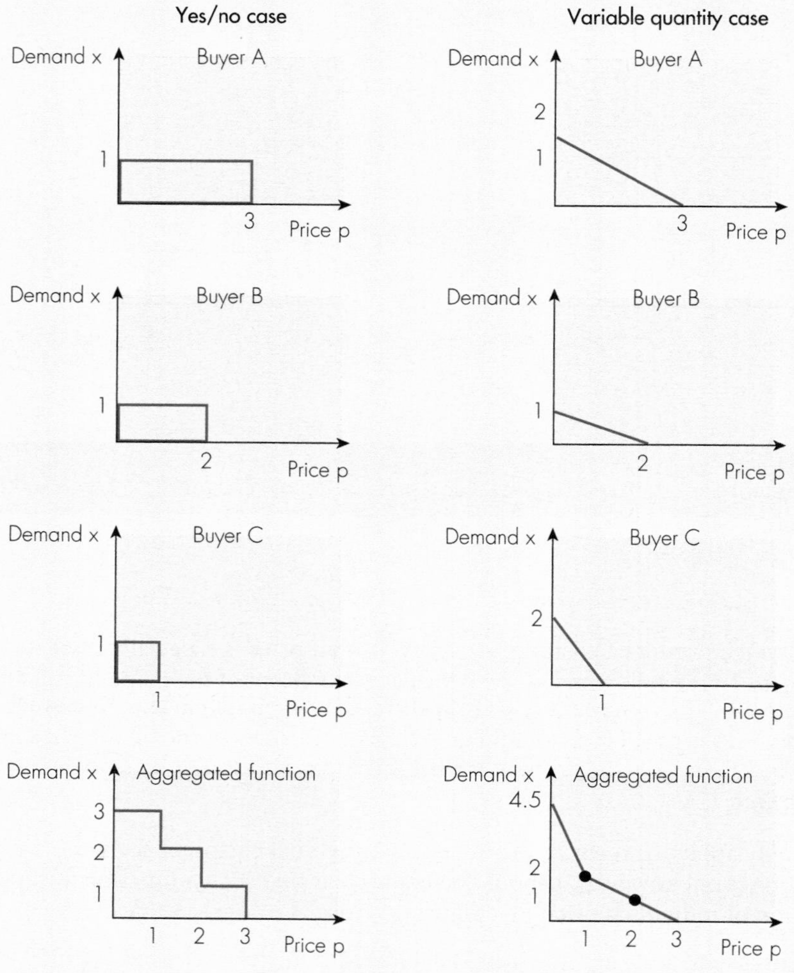

Figure 6-5 Aggregation of individual price-demand functions

Basic Forms of Demand Functions

Demand functions can have different functional forms:

- the linear demand function, and
- the multiplicative demand function.

The **linear demand function**, as shown in Figure 6-5, assumes a linear relationship between demand x with price p. It can be formally expressed as follows:

$x(p) = a - b \times p$

Parameter b describes the response of the demand to price changes. It is usually positive (decreasing demand with increasing price). The larger b is, the stronger the response of demand to price changes. More precisely formulated, b represents the **threshold demand**: with a price reduction of one unit, the demand rises by b units. Parameter a specifies the point where the demand axis is intersected.

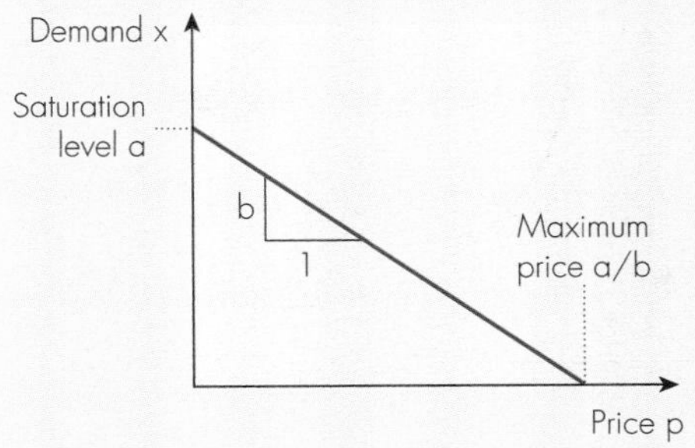

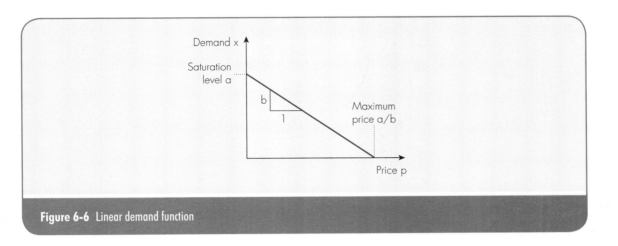

Figure 6-6 Linear demand function

This corresponds to the maximum demand (demand at a price of zero). Parameter a can also be interpreted as saturation level. Both parameters are components of the maximum price a/b, at which demand is zero (see Figure 6-6).

A major advantage of the linear demand function is its simplicity. If a number of price–quantity combinations are on hand, parameters a and b can be estimated without great effort by using bivariate regression analysis.

However, the basic assumption of the linear demand function, that a price change of one unit invariably results in demand changes of consistent quantity (b), regardless of the initial price level, is problematic. Findings in behavioral pricing research show that the threshold demand is not constant, as assumed in this concept. These findings show, for example, that customers generally assess price changes using an internal reference price (e.g. the initial price) and thus judge changes relative to this price point (see Kalyanaram and Winer 1995). Consequently, the threshold demand would not be constant, but would fluctuate depending on the initial price level. Nevertheless, in company practice, the linear function often shows satisfactory fit with the given data.

The **multiplicative demand function** takes the form:

$$x(p) = a \times p^{-b}$$

In this case, parameter b defines the dependency of demand on price. For a positive b, the resultant curve is shown in Figure 6-7. With this function, the absolute effect of the price change on the demand depends on the initial price p. The lower the initial price, the stronger the impact a price change has on demand. With a low initial price, a price increase of, say, 5 per cent leads to a considerably greater decline in demand than would be the case with a high initial price. Parameter a is a normalization parameter: a price of one monetary unit results in a demand of a units of quantity.

The multiplicative demand function can be illustrated with the following example. For a chemical product, the demand function for the South American market was determined as

$$x(p) = 15{,}800 \times p^{-2.1}$$

with demand x expressed in tons. Table 6-1 displays the resulting demand contingent on the price of product p.

Demand Functions and Price Elasticities

The **price elasticity of demand** ε is a measurement representing the impact of price p on demand x. Generally, it is used to consider what happens to the demand for a product when the price of the

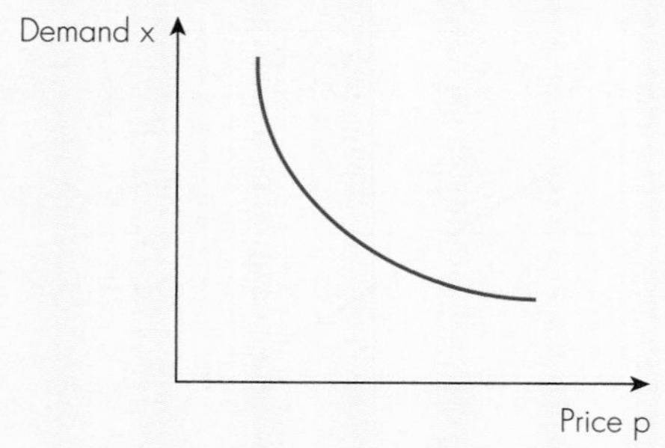

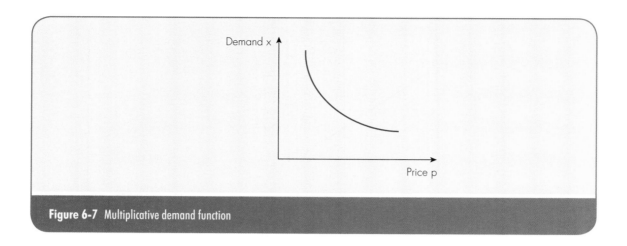

Figure 6-7 Multiplicative demand function

Table 6-1 Pricing example used to illustrate a multiplicative demand function

p	40	50	60	70	80
x	6.83	4.27	2.91	2.11	1.59

product changes. It defines the ratio of the relative change in demand with respect to the relative change in price that triggers it:

$$\varepsilon = \frac{\text{relative change in demand}}{\text{relative price change}}$$

The price elasticity usually has a negative value, since price increases are generally associated with decreasing demand, and price reductions with increasing demand. If, for example, demand decreases by 40 per cent with a price increase of 20 per cent, the price elasticity value is –2 (–40/20). In the context of this type of analysis, which determines elasticity based on comparing the demand at two price levels, we speak of **arc elasticity**.

Conversely, if the price elasticity of the demand for a certain price p is analyzed in connection with infinite small price changes, it is referred to as **point elasticity**, which forms the basis for the following discussion. This measure can be mathematically expressed as:

$$\varepsilon(p) = \frac{dx(p)/x}{dp/p} = \frac{dx(p)}{dp} \times \frac{p}{x}$$

This final equation is particularly useful for calculating elasticity, since the formula dx(p)/dp corresponds to the first derivative of the demand function.

If we assume that demand decreases as price increases, negative elasticity is the rule. With an elasticity of $\varepsilon = -1$, the relative change in quantity corresponds to the relative price change. If ε is smaller than –1, then the demand is price elastic. In this case, the demand responds disproportionately to price changes. However, if ε is between 0 and –1, demand is inelastic; here, the relative change in demand is smaller than the relative price change.

Many studies address the calculation of the price elasticity of demand (see, e.g., Bolton 1989; Hoch *et al.* 1995; Tellis 1988). One such study showed that the average price elasticity is –2.62 (see Bijmolt

Table 6-2 Price elasticities of various product categories (adapted from Danaher and Brodie 2000, p. 922)

Products	Number of brands analyzed	Average price elasticity
Jam	2	–4.34
Crackers	6	–4.33
Bathroom tissue	6	–4.16
Ice cream	4	–4.10
Butter	5	–3.75
Potato crisps	3	–3.48
Washing powder	5	–2.71
Mineral water	5	–2.40
Margarine	4	–2.13
Orange juice	6	–1.92
Dishwashing detergent	5	–1.87
Spaghetti	4	–1.80
Shampoo	8	–1.78
Band aids	3	–1.37
Disposable nappies	3	–0.86

et al. 2005), which basically indicates that – on average – demand reacts price elastically (ε is smaller than -1). Table 6-2 lists the empirical price elasticities of various product categories. Except for disposable nappies ($\varepsilon = -0.86$) the average price elasticities indicate elastic demand. In general, this means that demand for the brands analyzed responds disproportionately to price changes.

For company practice it is important to consider the question of under which conditions price elasticity tends to be high or low. It is difficult to provide universal recommendations, but general tendencies can be observed (see Monroe 2003; Nagle and Holden 1995; Simon 1989). It can be assumed that the price elasticity of demand tends to be lower if, for example:

- the product holds a distinctly unique position in the market
- customers have only limited knowledge of substitute products (i.e. alternatives to the company's products)
- it is difficult for customers to compare the quality of different substitute products
- the price of the product is low relative to the income of the customer
- the purchase price for the product is low in proportion to the overall costs of product usage over the product's life cycle
- customers associate the product with high quality, prestige and exclusivity
- customers have bought products from the same company before and there are certain barriers to switching to a competitor.

In company practice, the **impact of price changes on revenue** is also relevant. With a value of $-1 < \varepsilon < 0$, reactions of demand are disproportionately small. Therefore, in this case, a price increase can boost revenues. Conversely, with a value of $\varepsilon < -1$, however, reactions of demand to price changes are disproportionately large. Revenues can be increased in this situation as well, but as a result of price cuts. Thus, with an elasticity smaller than -1, sales can still be increased by implementing price-related measures.

This discussion shows that knowing the price elasticity of demand is vital when it comes to making pricing decisions in managerial practice. We will return to price elasticities when we discuss demand-based pricing in Section 6.3.1.

Empirical Estimation of the Demand Function

Up to now, we have focused on the conceptual foundations of the demand function. In order to use these functions for pricing decisions, their functional form has to be determined. The empirical calculation of demand functions therefore poses a major challenge. For the most part, the data basis needed for the calculation can be generated through:

- expert surveys
- price experiments
- analysis of actual market data
- customer surveys.

(See also Simon 1989.)

With **expert surveys**, persons with specialized knowledge of the market give their subjective assessments regarding what sales or market shares can be achieved at what price. Experts can include, for example, employees of the company (such as sales representatives) or external marketing experts.

A second method for empirically calculating the demand function is to conduct **price experiments** (for more on experiments see Gaur and Fisher 2005; Nevin 1974; see also the Appendix). In the course of price experiments, the price represents the primary variable that is manipulated in the experiment. Buyer responses to the price manipulations (e.g. purchase/no purchase, purchase quantity) are analyzed and translated into estimated demand functions.

A third method for calculating the demand function is the analysis of **actual market data**. This approach uses historical time series data. Thus its informational value has to be treated with caution with regard to future developments. This approach has limited applicability in company practice.

There are two types of **customer survey**: direct and indirect. In **direct customer surveys**, customers are asked explicit questions about their probable behavior at certain price levels. These include questions concerning price acceptance, price fairness, maximum price and purchase quantity. (For further information on 'surveys' please refer to the Appendix.)

The direct survey method is relatively simple and cost-efficient. However, its validity must be questioned since the respondent's attention is strongly focused on price due to the questions focusing mainly on price. This can raise price awareness to a level that is rather unrealistic, and therefore deviations between stated buying intentions and the actual purchasing behavior do occur. In particular, respondents frequently indicate very high willingness to pay, which is not in line with real willingness to pay (see Frykblom 2000; Johannesson 1997; Neill *et al.* 1994).

With **indirect customer surveys** aspects related to pricing are investigated, among other aspects of the product. Accordingly, price is not the main issue investigated in the survey, but rather one of several attributes of the product. Of particular importance in this context is **conjoint analysis** (see Green and Srinivasan 1990; Kalish and Nelson 1991, for a general overview; and Goldberg *et al.* 1984; Jedidi and Zhang 2002; Wertenbroch and Skiera 2002, for an overview on the measurement of customers' willingness to pay; for more information on 'conjoint analysis' see the Appendix). The indirect survey explicitly allows for an assessment of the relationship between the price and the perceived utility of a product. In this sense, the indirect method simulates a real purchase decision where customers not only focus on price, but also take into account other product attributes.

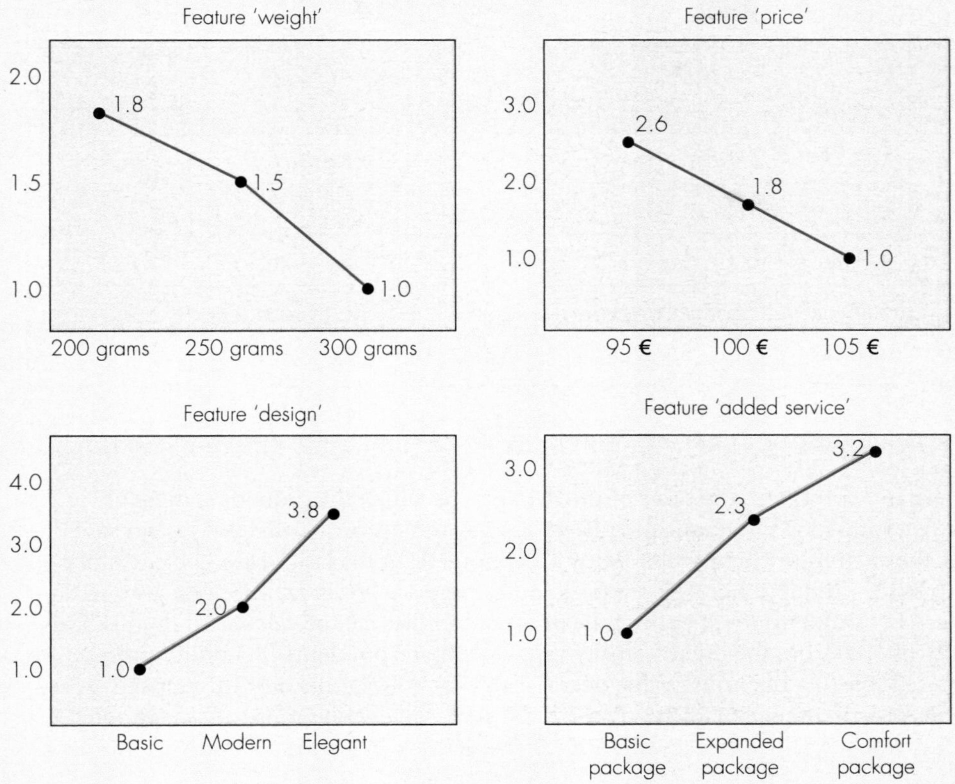

Figure 6-8 Part worths indicated by a customer for four attributes of a telephone

In the following, we will present an example to illustrate the use of conjoint analysis to empirically determine demand functions. Conjoint analysis assumes that a product is basically a bundle of attributes and that the utility of a product is a function of the utilities of these attributes (also called part worths or part worth utilities). The logic of conjoint analysis is that utility for a product predicts behavior, such as purchasing.

In the example (see also Simon 1989), a conjoint analysis is conducted for the telephone market. Figure 6-8 shows the results of the conjoint analysis with one respondent with regard to the part worths of four telephone attributes.

The part worths indicate how the overall utility of a telephone changes if product attributes are changed. The overall utility of a telephone can be determined by aggregating the part worths. Table 6-3 illustrates this for three different telephones for which the different attributes were 'bundled' in a particular way. Telephone A has the highest overall utility and is thus the telephone preferred among the three alternatives.

Based on this information, individual demand functions can be estimated for a particular product bundle within a set of alternative products. In the example, a company may calculate the individual demand functions for the various customers with regard to its Telephone A. The example assumes that the two competitor products, Telephone B and Telephone C, are also available in the relevant market.

Table 6-3 Part worths and overall utility for three telephones

Telephone A		Telephone B		Telephone C	
Feature	**Part worth**	**Feature**	**Part worth**	**Feature**	**Part worth**
300 grams	1.0	250 grams	1.5	200 grams	1.8
Price at €95	2.6	Price at €100	1.8	Price at €105	1.0
Elegant design	3.8	Basic design	1.0	Modern design	2.0
Basic package	1.0	Comfort package	3.2	Expanded package	2.3
Overall utility	8.4	Overall utility	7.5	Overall utility	7.1

For such a set of alternative products, the price of the product for which the individual demand functions are being determined is systematically varied. Similar to Figure 6-4, this is a yes/no case (i.e. at a given price, the customer will or will not buy Telephone A; in the latter case, the customer will purchase a competitor product). For Telephone A, different price levels are specified: €95, €100 and €105. The respective overall utility of each of the product bundles can be calculated on this basis. At a price of €95, Telephone A has the highest utility value for the respondents (8.4 utility units). When the price is raised to €100, the utility value decreases to 7.6 utility units. For the respective customer, Telephone A is still the first choice. At a price of €105, the overall utility of Telephone A reduces to 6.8 utility units. At this price level, the customer prefers Telephone B (with an overall utility of 7.5 utility units).

Therefore, at a price of €95 and €100 respectively, the individual demand function results in a value of 1 as compared to a value of 0 at the price of €105. If one assumes a linear part worth function (as indicated in Figure 6-8), a maximum price of €100.60 can be determined for this customer. At this price, Product B starts to appear more advantageous than Product A in terms of overall utility. The individual demand function is presented in Figure 6-9.

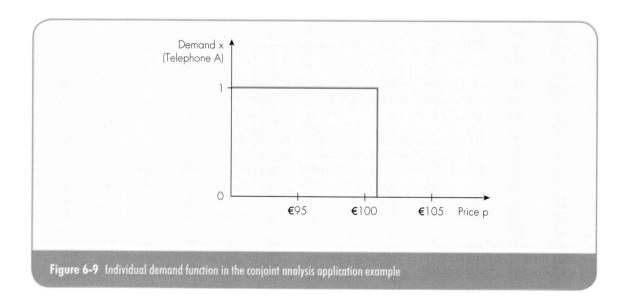

Figure 6-9 Individual demand function in the conjoint analysis application example

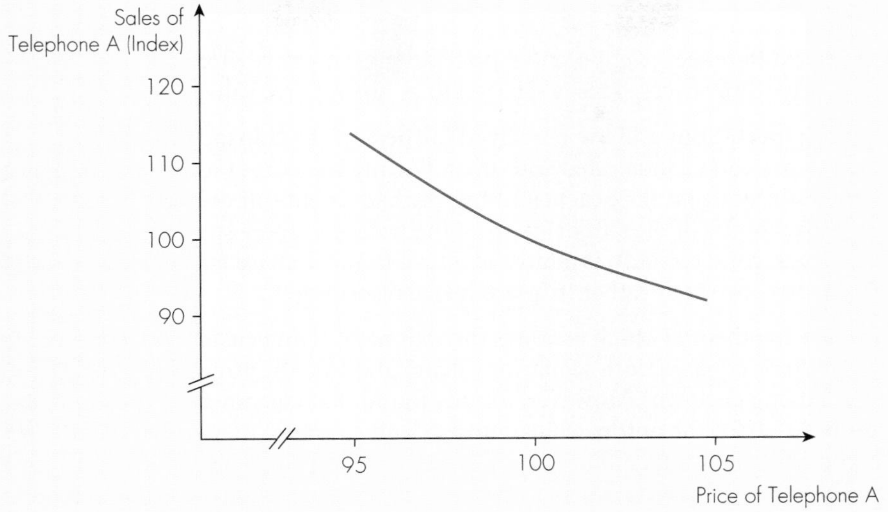

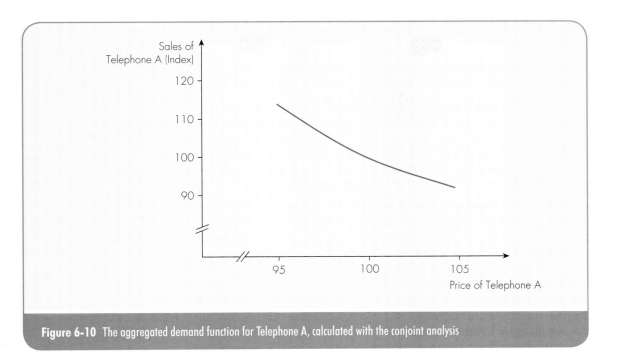

Figure 6-10 The aggregated demand function for Telephone A, calculated with the conjoint analysis

Using the same approach, the individual demand function was calculated for 300 representative customers and then consolidated into an aggregated demand function. Figure 6-10 shows this demand function for Telephone A.

Conjoint analysis is widely used in market research practice. There is no doubt that it represents a sophisticated and analytically challenging approach. It also has to be stated that the data collection process involved in conjoint analysis approximates the real decision-making situation of the buyer more precisely than other methods. This is because conjoint analysis takes into account the trade-off between price and the utility of particular attributes. Nevertheless, conjoint analysis is not necessarily superior to direct survey methods. For example, since it involves a high degree of cognitive involvement on the part of the respondents, conjoint analysis is better suited to high-involvement buying decisions and less to low-involvement purchases (for more on the issue of customer involvement please refer to the section on 'involvement' in the Appendix). With respect to the empirical determination of demand functions, it is recommended that conjoint analysis is supplemented with other methods (e.g. expert surveys, price experiments, direct customer surveys).

6.2.2 The Complexity of the Price Perceptions of a Real-Life Customer: Behavioral Pricing Theory

How Behavioral Pricing Theory Differs from Classical Pricing Theory

In classical price theory, rational cost–benefit considerations are central to the understanding of customer purchase decisions. However, empirical studies show that the behavior of individuals frequently deviates from this assumption.

This phenomenon is investigated in the field of **behavioral pricing theory**, in which psychological factors play an important role in customer decision-making. The significance of behavioral science with regard to pricing is illustrated by the following issues.

- Willingness to pay is influenced by price expectations and the perceived fairness of the transaction.
- When evaluating price differences (e.g. potential price savings), relative price differences are used more than absolute price differences. This is referred to as 'the relative value of money'.

The influence that **price expectations** and the **perceived fairness of the transaction** exert on a customer's willingness to pay can be illustrated with the following scenarios (according to Thaler 1985). In the first, a tourist is lying on the beach, wishing she had a cold soft drink in her hand. Her friend offers to bring back a bottle of the soft drink from the nearby grocery store and asks what she is willing to pay for it. The second scenario is almost identical to the first, except that the beverage is not being sold at the grocery store, but rather in an exclusive resort hotel.

According to classical pricing theory (which assumes the rationally acting customer), the tourist's willingness to pay ought to be equal in both scenarios (identical drink, the atmosphere of the point of sale does not affect the buying decision). However, a study found that customers in the first scenario would pay an average of $1.50 for the bottle, while in the second scenario, they would pay $2.65 (see Thaler 1985). Willingness to pay is thus influenced by the expectations customers have with regard to the prices they would normally have to pay in a grocery store versus a resort hotel. Moreover, the consideration that an exclusive resort hotel has higher personnel expenses than a grocery store, and therefore the higher price is considered as 'fair', also plays a role here. Accordingly, willingness to pay not only depends on the economic aspects of the transaction; price expectations and the perceived fairness of the transaction also have an impact on a customer's willingness to pay.

According to classical pricing theory, the value of money is absolute and thus always remains constant (e.g. €10 has the same value for the customer in any purchase transaction). This is not the case, however, with the concept of the relative value of money. The effect of the **relative value of money** on willingness to pay can be illustrated by the following example (according to Thaler 1980).

In the first scenario, a customer wants to buy a radio in a store that he considers offers the lowest prices. On entering the store, he is informed that the radio costs €29. He then finds out from another customer that the exact same radio is being sold for €19 at a different store located 10 minutes away. The second scenario is identical to the first, except that the price and type of product differ: in this case, the customer wants to buy a video camera at a price of €495, while the same product costs €485 at another store. In this case, it would also take the customer an extra 10 minutes to realize a savings of €10.

In classical pricing theory, the customer would have to ask himself whether he is willing to travel an extra 10 minutes to save €10. It is assumed that, in both scenarios, the customer will opt for the lower-priced product and the 'detour' associated with it.

Studies demonstrate that the same customers opt for the detour in the case of the product with the lower base price (see Thaler 1980). Given the scenarios above, the customer would make the extra trip for the radio, but not for the video camera. This phenomenon can be explained by the concept of the relative value of money. While the absolute monetary value of the price savings is €10 in both scenarios, the relative values differ. A €10 discount in relation to a radio priced at €29 represents a saving of 34 per cent, whereas €10 less for a video camera costing €495 corresponds to savings of only 2 per cent. In the first scenario, the customer perceives the €10 price advantage as being of a relatively greater value than in the second scenario. Saving €10 on the radio priced at €29 provides sufficient incentive to make the extra trip to the other store, while this does not apply to the same saving in the case of the video camera being sold for €495.

These examples nicely demonstrate that classical pricing theory may be too narrow in scope to explain all pricing-related behaviors that can be observed in the marketplace. Concepts in behavioral pricing can help to understand the described situations.

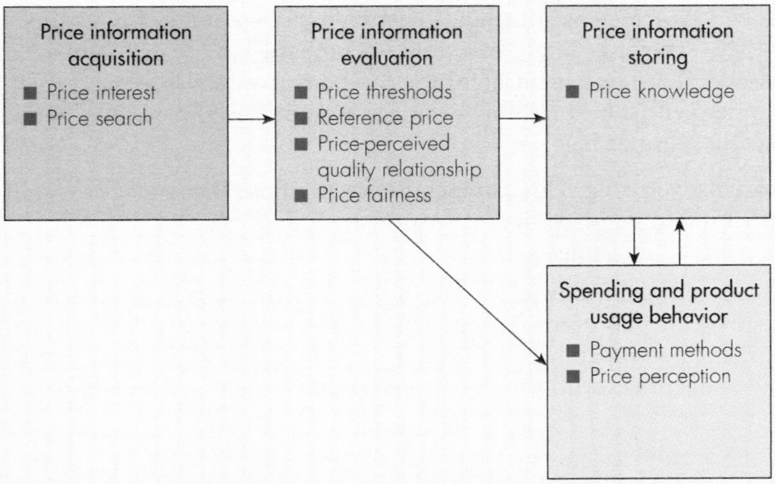

Figure 6-11 Key research fields and concepts of behavioral pricing research (see Homburg and Koschate 2005a, 2005b)

Key Concepts of Behavioral Pricing

The growing importance of concepts of behavioral science with regard to pricing research has become manifest in the emergence of an independent research area called 'behavioral pricing' (for an overview, see Homburg and Koschate 2005a, 2005b). In this section, we will describe the key concepts of behavioral pricing research. A simplified model provides four phases.

1. **Acquisition of price information** refers to the processes that lead to price information being stored in the short-term memory.
2. **Evaluation of price information** comprises the price assessment processes in short-term memory, including the decoding, mental processing and evaluation of the perceived price information.
3. **Storing of price information** describes the learning process. Price information is stored in long-term memory (i.e. learned) and can be retrieved by short-term memory and processed (in this connection, see also the discussion on the 'memory model' in the Appendix).
4. Finally, the **spending and product usage behavior** of customers deals with the impact of different payment methods on spending and product usage.

Figure 6-11 shows various behavioral pricing concepts that refer to these four phases. Consumer behavior also deals with the question of how individuals process information (for more information on 'consumer behavior' please refer to the Appendix). In the following sections, we will examine these concepts in more detail.

The Acquisition of Price Information

Two concepts are relevant in price information acquisition: price interest and price search. **Price interest** relates to the customer's desire to search for price information in order to take this information into account when making purchasing decisions (see Dickson and Sawyer 1990). In general, the more customers are interested in price, the less they are willing to pay (i.e. a high price interest corresponds to a low willingness to pay).

Price search refers to the actual efforts customers expend in obtaining and comparing price information (see Urbany *et al.* 1996). Here we distinguish between-store searches from within-store searches (see Grewal *et al.* 1996). The price image of a store or company has the main impact on price search (see Simester 1995). It can be beneficial for the company to establish a low price image as this helps to reduce customers' effort in searching for prices. Companies have various options for influencing their price image, as outlined below.

- A first option is price-based advertising. This can include, for example, the strategy of retail companies to create a corresponding price image by consistently emphasizing their low prices in advertising campaigns – in some cases regardless of the actual price positioning.
- Companies can also deliberately charge low prices for those products that are associated with extensive price knowledge on the part of the customers (known value items, or KVI). For example, some supermarket chains operate petrol stations on their sites, selling fuel (a typical known value item) at favorable prices with the objective of transferring this price image to the entire supermarket.
- Finally, companies can offer low-price guarantees to their customers. These can be offered in connection with a refund of the price difference if the customer can purchase the product at a lower price from another company (i.e. price matching). This also leads to a low price image, which reduces the level of price search intensity (see Srivastava and Lurie 2001).

In addition to the general intensity of price search on the part of customers, it is also crucial to identify which customers search for prices and how intensely they search for them (see Wakefield and Inman 1993). Some factors influence the intensity of price search (see Grewal and Marmorstein 1994; Urbany *et al.* 1996); price search is more intense, for example, when price information can be obtained with minimum effort. This point highlights the impact of the internet, which greatly facilitates price search.

Evaluation of Price Information

Price threshold is a key concept with regard to the evaluation of price information (see Gabor and Granger 1979; Gedenk and Sattler 1999). It is assumed that a customer assesses prices that range below a certain price (i.e. price threshold) as being significantly more favorable than prices that are equal to or exceed this price threshold. Accordingly, price thresholds refer to prices at which the customer's price evaluation changes significantly. With respect to this, we distinguish absolute and relative price thresholds.

Absolute price thresholds mark the upper and lower limits of the price range in which customers assess prices as being acceptable; products with prices beyond this range are not purchased. Thus, an analysis of a customer's absolute price thresholds usually leads to an absolute minimum price as well as a maximum price for which the customer is willing to purchase the product.

In contrast to absolute price thresholds, **relative price thresholds** do not relate to the customer's decision whether or not to purchase, but merely to the pre-evaluation of prices within an acceptable price range. Basically, it concerns the issue of what price differential needs to exist in order for customers to perceive prices as different.

Price thresholds are particularly relevant with regard to price increases: frequently, demand for a product rapidly decreases if a certain price threshold is reached or exceeded, mostly irrespective of whether the price threshold has been exceeded by a narrow or substantial margin. Therefore, it is usually advisable to clearly surpass the price threshold when raising prices that are located close to a price threshold (see Kaas and Hay 1984), since this can lead to significantly increased sales. However, the next price threshold must not be exceeded.

Many customers perceive 'even' prices (e.g. €1 or €100) to be price thresholds, making 'odd' prices (prices slightly below these price thresholds) widely used (see Gedenk and Sattler 1999; Schindler and Kirby 1997). Therefore, even prices ending in a zero (e.g. €4.00) are used less often than prices ending with a 9 (e.g. €3.99).

A number of arguments back the existence of price thresholds (see Simon 1989), as noted below.

- In many cases, customers use even numbers to determine their **maximum prices** (e.g. a price under €4, see Lange 1972).
- Customers evaluate prices below an even price as being disproportionately more favorable than the even price (see Müller and Hoenig 1983), since the first digit is key to price perception and thus price evaluation: often, €3.99 is perceived as '€3 plus x' and thus significantly less expensive than €4.00 (see Schmitz 1964). This **underestimation effect** is due to the left-to-right processing of numbers, where the last digits are usually cut off (see Schindler and Kirby 1997).

Reference price is another main concept when evaluating price information. Reference price refers to the price that is used by customers as a benchmark for evaluating other prices (see Briesch *et al.* 1997). There are both external and internal reference prices (see Rajendran and Tellis 1994). External reference prices are obtained in a certain purchase situation based on the observable prices in the purchase environment (e.g. prices for other products of the same category). In contrast to this, internal reference prices are stored in memory and based on the observed prices during previous purchase occasions (e.g. the last prices paid).

Three generalizable findings can be derived from reference price research (see Kalyanaram and Winer 1995):

1. reference prices do play a consistent and significant role in purchase decisions
2. the price previously paid is an important influencing factor in the formation of reference prices (see Rajendran and Tellis 1994)
3. customers respond differently to price increases vs price decreases relative to the reference price, with price increases having a stronger effect than price decreases.

These findings are particularly relevant for the assessment of special prices. Special prices pose the risk that customers quickly become accustomed to the reduced price, which might then be established as the new (lower) reference price.

Given the significance of reference prices with regard to customers' price evaluation, companies should consider options for communicating reference prices to their customers. 'Manufacturer recommended selling prices' (MRSPs) are a commonly used approach, often introduced by consumer goods manufacturers.

Another important concept in connection with the evaluation of price information is the **price–perceived quality relationship** (Zeithaml 1988). This refers to the issue that customers base their quality evaluation on price information obtained prior to purchase. This is especially the case when they are uncertain about a product's quality. In general, high prices are perceived as a signal of high quality, whereas low prices are viewed as indicating poor quality. Studies have demonstrated that, in many product categories, prices are indeed used as quality indicators (see e.g. Rao and Monroe 1989; Zeithaml 1988).

A last key concept to be mentioned in connection with price evaluation is **price fairness** (for more information, also see Bolton *et al.* 2003; Campbell 1999). Research in this area has focused in particular on the factors influencing perceived price fairness. For example, it has been found that, in the case of price increases, the presumed motives of the company have a significant impact on whether customers perceive prices as being fair (see Campbell 1999; Etzioni 1988). If customers assume that the price increase was driven by a positive or justified motive (e.g. if a company is forced to compensate for rising costs) (see Kalapurakal *et al.* 1991), they tend to evaluate a price increase as being fair. In contrast, customers perceive a price increase as being unfair if they presume that it was triggered by a negative motive (e.g. a company wants to exploit its strong market position).

Studies show that customers' intentions to purchase are negatively affected when they perceive prices as unfair (see Campbell 1999). Moreover, in conjunction with customer satisfaction, customer loyalty is moderated by the perceived fairness of a price increase after the price has been raised (see Homburg *et al.* 2005). For satisfied customers, loyalty after the price increase is significantly higher in the case of high perceived fairness as opposed to low perceived fairness. However, a similar effect has not been observed for dissatisfied customers.

Storing of Price Information

During the process of storing price information, price observations and price experiences are transferred to the long-term memory. This learning process is selective: not all price information is transmitted from short-term to long-term memory. Customers tend to learn price information more thoroughly (see Diller 2000) if:

- the products are relevant to them
- price information can be obtained with minimum effort (e.g. via the internet)
- the prices are particularly easy to memorize (e.g. even prices such as €200 or numbers with repeated digits, such as €222), or
- the prices remain stable for an extended period of time.

Price learning creates **price knowledge** (also called **price awareness**). Price knowledge refers to all price-related information stored in a customer's long-term memory, including, for example, reference prices for specific products, which can be used as a benchmark when evaluating prices.

Studies on price knowledge have shown that if customers have no or only limited price knowledge, there is a risk that they will possibly not even notice a price reduction for the respective product. In turn, demand would remain unaffected by the price change. These issues are therefore important as they may determine the success of pricing decisions.

Spending and Product Usage Behavior

Another area of behavioral pricing addresses the **spending and product usage behavior** of customers and thus examines how price-related factors influence the spending behavior of customers as well as their product usage.

An important area in this context deals with the effects of **different payment methods** (e.g. cash vs credit card payment) on the spending behavior of customers. It was found that willingness to spend (i.e. the maximum price that customers are willing to pay for a product) is higher with credit card payments than with cash payments, and that the credit line positively affects the spending behavior of customers (see Feinberg 1986; Prelec and Simester 2001; Soman and Cheema 2002).

The way the price is presented also affects the evaluation of a purchase (and thus the purchase probability). If the price is communicated to the customer as a series of small instalments rather than a large one-time payment, the continuous small payments become the benchmark for evaluating the purchase, resulting in a more positive evaluation of the transaction (see Gourville 1998). In practice, this strategy is primarily used in the automotive sector or for other high-priced durable consumer goods (see the example in Figure 6-12). For example, the customer is not presented with the total cost of €15,000, but with comparatively small monthly installments of, say, €299. Conversely, in the case of luxury products, offering monthly instalments can result in a negative quality perception and reduce demand on the part of quality-conscious customer segments (see Anderson and Simester 2001).

Figure 6-12 Example of communicating price as a series of small installments

6.3 Understanding Customers, Costs and Competition: Approaches to Pricing

Price determination plays a key role in several decision-making areas of pricing – in particular with respect to pricing new products, pricing the product portfolio and changing the price of products. Against this background, we will now examine the basic pricing approaches. An introduction to this topic can be facilitated by illustrating the main factors that influence pricing decisions. Figure 6-13 provides such an overview. In this context, we differentiate between the direct and indirect factors that influence pricing decisions.

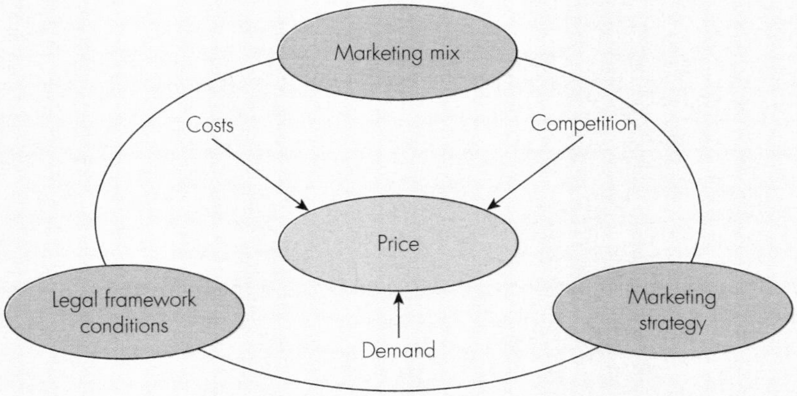

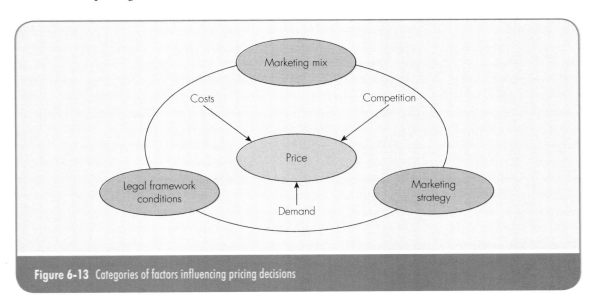

Figure 6-13 Categories of factors influencing pricing decisions

The product cost is the first direct factor of major importance since, in the end, the profitability of a product depends on its price–cost ratio. Another key point is associated with demand for the product (or demand for other products, respectively). Competitive aspects are also important (i.e. the pricing behavior of competitors).

In addition to direct factors, indirect factors also have an impact on pricing decisions. For one, strategic marketing objectives can significantly affect pricing decisions. As an example, a company aiming for fast market penetration for a product tends to set lower prices. Interaction with other instruments in the marketing mix also has to be taken into account. As a rule, pricing decisions are not isolated and independent from the design and structure of the other instruments. Finally, legal aspects frequently have to be considered when making pricing decisions. For example, regulatory laws apply, and international pricing options are limited by national taxes and tariffs.

Due to the great significance of factors that directly influence pricing decisions, we will discuss three related pricing approaches:

1 **demand-based pricing** (pricing based on customer analyses)
2 **cost-based pricing** (pricing based primarily on accounting and controlling information)
3 **competition-based pricing** (pricing based primarily on the pricing behavior of competitors).

6.3.1 Demand-based Pricing: Price Determination – Having the Customer in Mind

The primary source of demand-based pricing is the effective demand for a product in the market. Based on analytic evaluations, we will discuss pricing in connection with the demand function. Subsequently, we will turn to price differentiation, which tries to account for differences in customers' willingness to pay. Value-based pricing approaches place a special emphasis on integrating the customer benefit of a product into pricing. Finally, we will discuss a company's options for influencing customers' reference prices.

Pricing in Connection with Demand Functions

Based on the demand function and a corresponding cost function we illustrate how to calculate the profit-maximizing price. For this, profit P can be expressed as a function of price by applying the following formula:

$$P(p) = S(p) - C(x(p)) = p \times x(p) - C(x(p))$$

S denotes sales, C costs, p price and x demand. Sales is the product of price and demand. Costs depend on x and thus indirectly on price.

To determine the profit-maximizing price we calculate the first derivative of the profit equation:

$$\frac{dP(p)}{dp} = x(p) + p \times \frac{dx(p)}{dp} - \frac{dC(x(p))}{dx(p)} \times \frac{dx(p)}{dp} = 0$$

We multiply the individual terms in this equation with p/x(p) and obtain the following:

$$x(p) \times \frac{p}{x(p)} + p \times \frac{dx(p)}{dp} \times \frac{p}{x(p)} - \frac{dC(x(p))}{dx(p)} \times \frac{dx(p)}{dp} \times \frac{p}{x(p)} = 0$$

We include the elasticity of demand (see Section 6.2)

$$\varepsilon = \frac{dx(p)}{dp} \times \frac{p}{x(p)}$$

and solve for p*. Then we obtain:

$$p^* = \frac{\varepsilon}{1+\varepsilon} \times C'$$

This equation is called the Amoroso–Robinson Relation, and can be interpreted as follows. The revenue-maximizing price *p** is obtained as an elasticity-based mark-up on the marginal costs *C′*. The higher the price elasticity, the lower the mark-up will be. According to the Amoroso–Robinson Relation, firms can optimize revenues by pursuing a high-price strategy for a price elasticity close to −1 and a low-price, high-volume strategy for a higher price elasticity below −1.

If the demand function and the cost function are linear, optimal *p** is given by:

$$p^* = \frac{1}{2} \times \left(\frac{a}{b} + c\right)$$

where *a* and *b* represent the coefficients of the linear demand function ($x = a - b \times p$) and *c* the variable unit costs. This price *p** is also referred to as the **Cournot price**. The ratio *a/b* equals the maximum price, i.e. the price where demand equals zero. In the linear case, the optimal price *p** is situated in the range between variable unit costs *c* and the maximum price *a/b*.

Price Differentiation

Approaches to price differentiation are based on the fact that, for many markets, customers exhibit a different willingness to pay for the same product. Accordingly, the basic idea of price differentiation is to offer the same product to different target groups, but at varying prices.

Conceptual Basis

We speak of price differentiation if a company offers identical or slightly differing products at varying prices to different customer segments. The products do not have to be completely identical, since such a price differentiation concept would be too restrictive. For example, price differentiation also exists if the products offered to the various customer segments show minor differences in terms of their features.

The main purpose of price differentiation is to boost profits by means of leveraging the 'consumer surplus'. Consumer surplus is created if a manufacturer offers its customer a product at a price that is lower than the maximum price the customer is willing to pay for this product. Consumer surplus corresponds to the difference between the customer's willingness to pay and the actual price.

Figure 6-14 illustrates how companies can use price differentiation. The example is based on a monopolistic situation, no fixed costs and constant marginal costs c, no additional costs associated with price differentiation and a linear demand function. The extreme case is where all customer segments are offered the product at the same price. The optimal standard price corresponds to the Cournot price p_c that results as the mean value of the marginal costs and the maximum price. The maximum profit that can be achieved with this price corresponds to the area of FDBA. Triangle DEB represents the consumer surplus that is realized by the customers.

The other extreme case refers to the situation of completely individualized price differentiation (e.g. oriental bazaar). Each customer is offered the product at the respective individual maximum price, leading to profits in the amount as indicated by triangle FEC. In this case there is no consumer surplus.

In between these extreme cases, there lies a range of solutions. For example, Figure 6-14 shows a price differentiation with three prices, p_1, $p_2 = p_c$ and p_3. The additional profit that can be realized through price differentiation as compared to a unique price is indicated by the two highlighted squares.

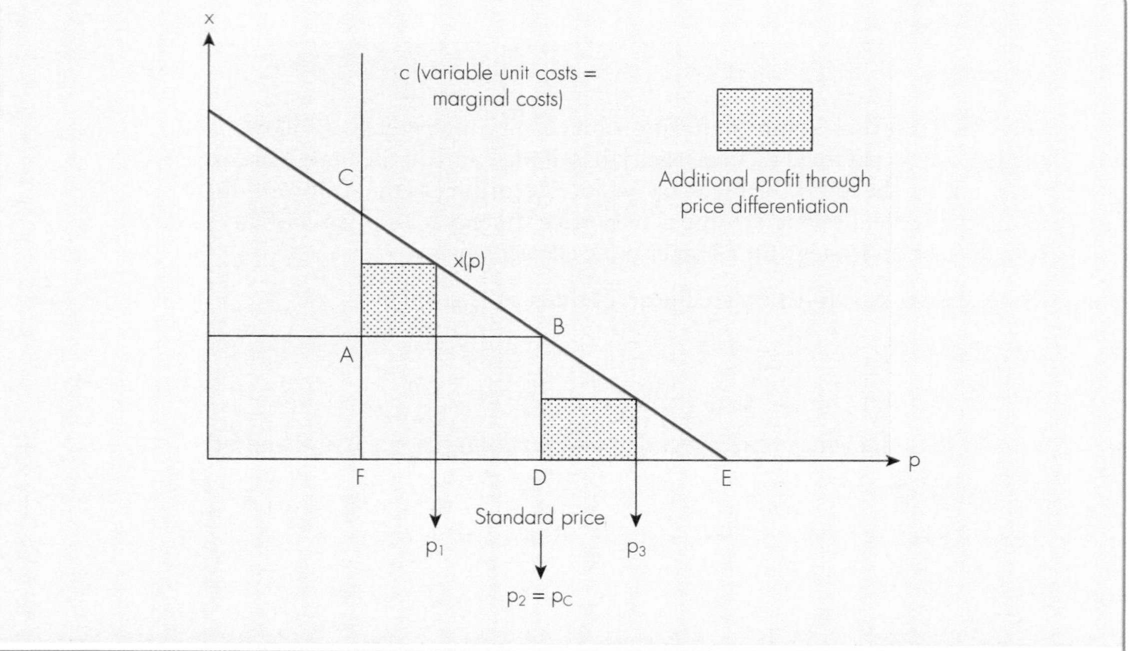

Figure 6-14 Illustration of price differentiation (adapted from Doyle 1995, p. 24)

The following example demonstrates how price differentiation can help to increase profits: a company offers its product to two customer segments that differ in their willingness to pay. For both segments, the company has determined the demand functions. For segment A, the function is

$$x_A(p_A) = 400 - 2 \times p_A$$

and for segment B, it is

$$x_B(p_B) = 150 - 0.5 \times p_B$$

Since the company sells the product only to these two customer segments, the total demand results from $x = x_A(p_A) + x_B(p_B)$. For the product under consideration, the cost function is:

$$C(x) = 10{,}000 + 20 \times x$$

$p_A = p_B = p$ applies to **standard pricing**. In this case, the aggregated demand function across the two customer segments is expressed by:

$$x(p) = 550 - 2.5 \times p$$

The profit-maximizing price corresponds to the Cournot price (see Section 6.2.1) – that is:

$$p^* = \frac{1}{2} \times \left(\frac{a}{b} + c\right) = \frac{1}{2} \times \left(\frac{550}{2.5} + 20\right) = 120$$

Thus, the profit-maximizing standard price is 120 monetary units and results in a demand of:

$$x(p^*) = 550 - 2.5 \times 120 = 250$$

Accordingly, the maximum profit in the case of standard pricing amounts to:

$$P(p^*) = S(p^*) - C(x(p^*)) = 120 \times 250 - (10{,}000 + 20 \times 250) = 15{,}000$$

Conversely, in the case of **price differentiation**, the optimal price is calculated separately for both segments. By determining the Cournot price, the resultant optimal prices are

$$p_A^* = \frac{1}{2} \times \left(\frac{400}{2} + 20\right) = 110$$

and

$$p_B^* = \frac{1}{2} \times \left(\frac{150}{0.5} + 20\right) = 160$$

The corresponding demand amounts to

$x(p_A^*) = 400 - 2 \times 110 = 180$ and

$x(p_B^*) = 150 - 0.5 \times 160 = 70$

Based on this information, the maximum profit for a price differentiation scenario is calculated as follows:

$$P(p_A^*, p_B^*) = S(p_A^*, p_B^*) - C(x(p_A^*, p_B^*))$$
$$= p_A^* \times x(p_A^*) + p_B^* \times x(p_B^*) - C(x(p_A^*) + x(p_B^*))$$
$$= 110 \times 180 + 160 \times 70 - (10{,}000 + 20 \times (180 + 70)) = 16{,}000$$

This example proves that the maximum profit is higher when using price differentiation than the maximum profit in the case of uniform pricing. Readers should also note that the total demand in both cases amounts to 250 units. Accordingly, the increased profit in this example does not result from increased sales, but from a better leverage of the willingness to pay in customer segment B.

It must be mentioned, however, that these simplified analyzes include only the benefits of price differentiation and not the associated costs. From this viewpoint, the derived message of 'the more differentiated the prices, the higher the profit' should be handled with care. In company practice, price differentiation is frequently associated with considerable costs. Therefore, the benefits and costs of price differentiation have to be considered in each individual case.

Price Differentiation: Forms of Implementation

In company practice, price differentiation can be based on various criteria. Accordingly, there are various **forms of price differentiation**:

- demographic price differentiation
- geographical price differentiation
- temporal price differentiation
- benefit-based price differentiation
- quantity-based price differentiation
- bundling.

With **demographic price differentiation** specific customer characteristics are used as differentiation criteria, including age (e.g. special prices for children), gender (e.g. different hair salon prices for women and men), income situation (e.g. discounted magazine subscription prices for students) or job-related factors (e.g. special prices for employees of a company).

Geographical price differentiation is based on geographic markets – represented by, for example, national markets, regions or even cities. A particularly important form of geographical price differentiation is that between countries, which is often used in many product categories (e.g. in the pharmaceuticals market). We will discuss this in more detail in Chapter 12, on international marketing.

In the case of **temporal price differentiation**, different prices apply depending on the purchase date/time; examples include prices differentiated according to time of day (e.g. phone and electricity charges, tennis court fees), weekday (e.g. hotel, air fares) or season (e.g. vacation trips). Service providers often make extensive use of temporal price differentiation in order to sufficiently utilize their capacities even during periods of weak demand (see Section 11.4.1).

In the case of **benefit-based price differentiation**, the company modifies service/comfort-related product benefits. An example of this is when airlines differentiate between economy, business and first class.

In **quantity-based price differentiation**, the average price per unit varies depending on the quantity purchased (i.e. customers benefit from volume discounts). This type of price differentiation can be used to increase customer loyalty: the greater a customer's loyalty, the better the price offered.

Bundling is a special form of price differentiation (for more information, see Stremersch and Tellis 2002). If a company combines several products in a bundle (package) and sells it at a package price, this is called bundling. Price bundling aims at better leveraging the customer's willingness to pay than would be possible with individual prices. Depending on whether product-related objectives or price-related objectives are the primary motives of bundling, the terms **product bundling** and **price bundling** are used as well (see Stremersch and Tellis 2002, and Section 5.4). Increasing the sales within a product line is the main objective of price bundling (see Monroe 2003).

With respect to **implementing price differentiation in company practice**, it has to be mentioned that the significant profit potentials of this approach, described above, can be counteracted by serious problems. Accordingly, companies should be cautious with price differentiation. For practical implementation, for example, it is crucial that segments are independent from each other. Furthermore, transparency between customer segments should be limited. In addition, the extent to which demand shifting (arbitrage) can occur between segments also has to be taken into account. If this occurs to a great extent, price differentiation can result in a shift in demand towards lower price segments.

Value-based Pricing

In value-based pricing, prices are based on the value of a product as perceived from the customer's perspective. The perceived value determines the customer's willingness to pay and thus the price a company can charge for its product.

In value-based pricing it is crucial to determine the **value for the customer**. Examples of value-based pricing include business consultants who determine their rates as a percentage of costs saved, software providers that receive a share in the savings associated with using the software, and the alignment of tuition fees for MBA programs with the expected salaries that graduates can expect to realize in the market.

An appropriate concept for determining the customer value associated with a product is the customer value model (see Anderson and Narus 1999), which evaluates the economic benefit a product offers to customers. For example, the individual customer value associated with a machine can be calculated via a cost comparison by comparing costs before and after the commissioning of the machine.

6.3.2 Profitability Analysis: Cost-based Pricing

Cost-based pricing approaches use cost accounting information and are widely applied in company practice. Cost-based pricing is particularly relevant for determining **price floors** (i.e. the lowest price that can be charged for a product). Depending on the period under consideration, there are long-term and short-term price floors.

Long-term price floors are calculated on the basis of total costs. A company will be able to supply a product in the long term only if the variable and fixed costs are covered. In the event that, for short periods of time, costs are only partially covered, this has to be compensated for in the long term by profits realized by other means or in another period.

Short-term price floors are derived from variable unit costs. In difficult market conditions, it can be practical for companies not to cover the total costs and accept prices located between the variable unit costs and total unit costs (including fixed unit costs). This can be especially feasible in cases of high price elasticity of demand (see Section 6.2.1). The underlying logic of such an approach lies in the fact that the fixed costs cannot be influenced in the short term and are thus not relevant to the decision. Therefore, the goal of this approach is to cover at least the variable unit costs (i.e. the portion of unit costs that depends on quantity), so that a unit sold achieves a positive contribution margin with regard to covering the fixed costs. However, this elementary logic is limited by the fact that customers grow accustomed to such low prices (i.e. low reference prices are established). In view of this, companies should be very cautious when using variable costs as a short-term price floor.

Cost-plus pricing represents cost-based pricing in its pure form. This method calculates prices by means of adding a mark-up to the unit costs:

$$\text{price} = \text{unit costs} \times (1 + \text{mark-up rate})$$

Frequently, the amount of the mark-up is in line with what is customary for a given industry or company. As a rule, mark-up rates can be based on either total unit costs or variable unit costs.

The fundamental problem of this approach is that demand-related and competition-related factors are not taken into account. Therefore, cost-based pricing should be included as one aspect in setting prices. It is in this context that the analysis of the relationship between unit costs, demand and unit price (see Figure 6-15) plays a role as well. It is obvious that demand depends on unit price. Furthermore, unit costs depend on demand: the higher demand, the lower the fixed costs per unit. If, within the scope of cost-plus pricing based on total costs, a company derives the price from the unit costs, this leads to the circular reasoning illustrated in Figure 6-15: in order to be able to calculate the price based on unit costs, the unit costs must be known, but these depend on demand. Demand, on the other hand, depends on price. The practical application of cost-plus pricing based on total costs therefore means that companies need to ignore one of the interdependencies shown in Figure 6-15. A possible approach is to specify a target demand as the basis for calculating the unit costs and, in turn, deriving the price.

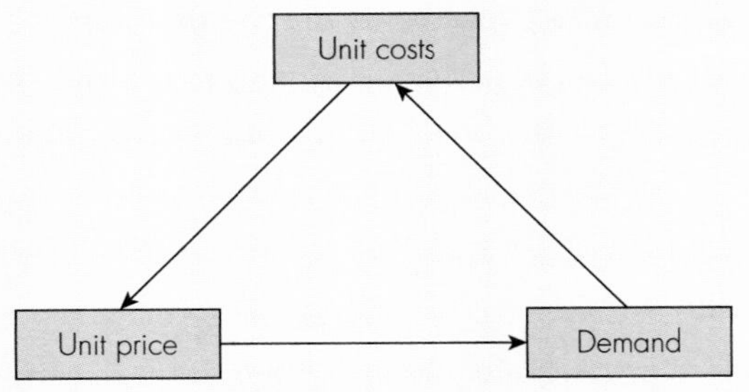

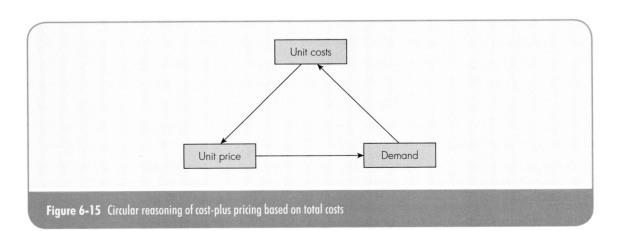

Figure 6-15 Circular reasoning of cost-plus pricing based on total costs

6.3.3 Don't Forget the Competitors: Competition-based Pricing

In competition-based pricing the prices and the pricing behavior of competitors are taken into account when setting prices. We will first discuss how classical pricing theory analyzes the influence that the competition has on pricing within the scope of oligopoly models. Following that, pricing based on guiding prices will be presented as a pragmatic approach to competition-based pricing.

In company practice, monopolies are comparatively rare, while oligopolies (few companies and many customers), and thus **pricing in oligopolies**, are more relevant. Oligopoly models in classical pricing theory usually limit their analysis to two firms (duopoly).

In contrast to monopolists, oligopolists have to include the pricing activities of the competition in their pricing decisions. In this connection, there are three basic types of behavior (see Gutenberg 1966), as described below.

1. **Peaceful economic behavior**: pricing decisions are not primarily intended to harm competitors, but rather to realize the company's own key objectives.
2. **Cooperative pricing behavior**: based on more or less explicit arrangements and agreements, companies avoid intensive price-based competition. Pricing is dominated by cooperation.
3. **Aggressive pricing behavior**: pricing aims to eliminate the competition from the market.

When competitors pursue aggressive pricing behavior price wars very often emerge. Such **price wars** are characterized by competitors undercutting their prices repeatedly and in quick succession, thus bringing prices down to an unprofitable level. Price wars can be observed in numerous industries. The following reasons for price wars are often quoted (see Garda and Marn 1993; Heil and Helsen 2001).

- Many companies exaggerate their focus on market share, which often leads to aggressive pricing behavior aimed at the elimination of competitors.
- Persistent **overcapacities** in a market represent another important cause of price wars. Several manufacturers try to use their capacities by reducing prices, which can also lead to price wars.
- In particular, price wars also arise due to a **lack of product differentiation** (e.g. in the case of commodity products). Such a scenario poses the risk that competition between manufacturers is based primarily on prices.

Price wars are frequently lose/lose scenarios (except in the case of customers) (see Focus on Marketing 6-1, on the negative consequences of price wars). Against this background, companies (especially in industries characterized by overcapacity) should thoroughly address the question of how to avoid price wars. In this context, the following precautionary measures should be mentioned (see Garda and Marn 1993; Rao *et al.* 2000):

- avoidance of overreactions to price reductions triggered by the competition
- 'tit-for-tat' strategy (i.e. launching carefully measured counterblows – e.g. price reductions in another market or for a different product group – in order to communicate to the competing company that aggressive behavior on its part will only backfire)
- thorough analysis of competitor responses to price changes made by the company
- systematic monitoring of the competition
- unambiguous communication prior to price changes in order to prevent misinterpretation on the part of competitors (e.g. notification that the intended price reduction is due to a planned inventory reduction)
- establishing complex price structures so that customers cannot easily compare prices

- product bundling in order to make direct price comparison more difficult
- creation of additional customer benefit(s) by means of product modifications
- product differentiation (e.g. launch of a lower-priced second brand on the part of a premium brand company).

The destructive nature of price wars can be illustrated by game theory (see Focus on Marketing 6-2) (for more information on 'game theory', see the Appendix).

Focus on Marketing 6-1 Negative consequences of price wars

Ford: repeated price wars cannot sustain growth

In an article in the *Automotive Business Review* of 21 November 2005, Ford's pricing policy was discussed in relation to its competitors, and the car industry as a whole.

The article described how Ford had joined the 'big three' carmakers in the 'discount game', following a similar move by its main competitor General Motors: 'Not only do the recurring price wars between the leading US players indicate the underlying seriousness of their current situation, the discounting strategy represents what is arguably an unsustainable "quick-fix" solution.'

Ford, the second-biggest US carmaker, had moved to intensify the climate of competition by introducing new discounts that combine reduced prices and rebates. As the author of the article stated, Ford clearly regarded 'incentive schemes as a way to guarantee a sales spike in the last quarter, obscure a disappointing full-year performance and limit its market share losses.'

The pricing tactics used by Ford reflected the wider issues in the automotive market. Slashing prices has become a familiar last resort for the US market leaders as they continue to suffer considerable market share attrition. The sales figures for Ford, General Motors and DaimlerChrysler from 1999 to 2004 show decreases by 36%, 28% and 9%, respectively. In comparison, their Asian and European competitors gained substantial ground: Nissan, BMW and Hyundai's sales rocketed by 33%, 47%, 85% respectively.

The article commented that 'as these declines become more deeply entrenched, the strategies adopted by US manufacturers have become symmetrically aligned and their resultant performance increasingly homogeneous.' This claim is borne out in the identical performance of Ford and GM in October 2005 as their US sales both fell 26%. They also adopted very similar strategies, as in November 2005, GM began a discount program (called 'Red Tag') on most 2005 and 2006 Buick, Pontiac, GMC and Chevrolet cars and trucks. Just a couple of days later, Ford started its 'Keep It Simple' program on most 2005 and 2006 models including the gasoline-electric hybrid vehicles.

Equally, as Ford's financial situation continues to deteriorate the manufacturer has come to rely on discounting to maintain its share price and drive sales. Although the incentives that Ford employs are likely to boost sales volumes, they will also erode margins. Given that the groups need to buy time for innovation and new model development – on average it takes five years for US manufacturers to develop a new model compared to just three years for their Japanese rivals – discount schemes are not a sustainable way to achieve this.

It is easy to understand why Art Spinella, president of CNW, described a price war as 'certainly not healthy for GM, Ford, or Chrysler'. *Automotive Business Review* took a similar view, concluding that although discounting at the end of a given year 'may provide a final-quarter sales boost, many would argue that the big three should be focusing on vehicle quality and brand image.

Focus on Marketing 6-1 (Continued)

Moreover, if price wars become a regular occurrence, as appears to be the case, the current negative trend is likely to continue.'

Was the article's prediction correct? Since this article was written, Ford Motor Company has continued to face similar issues in the US market. For example, it posted a 13% drop in US unit sales during April 2007.

Sources: 'Ford: repeated price wars cannot sustain growth', *Automotive Business Review*, 21 November 2005; Leah Vyse, 'Ford sales fall in April', *Automotive Business Review*, 2 May 2007.

Focus on Marketing 6-2 Prisoners' dilemmas

As an example, we will examine two companies, A and B, each of which have the option to 'maintain prices' or 'reduce prices'. We assume that both companies have previously opted to maintain prices and have thus realized average profits (see field 1 in Figure 6-16). If company A now decides to reduce prices, this leads to the scenario in field 3: in the case of high price sensitivity on the part of buyers, company A will realize significant additional sales, which might lead to high profits for company A in the short term, while company B will neither achieve satisfactory profits nor experience losses. Based on this situation, the optimal choice for company B is to reduce prices as well, which leads to the scenario in field 4: both companies achieve lower profits due to the reduced price level as compared to field 1.

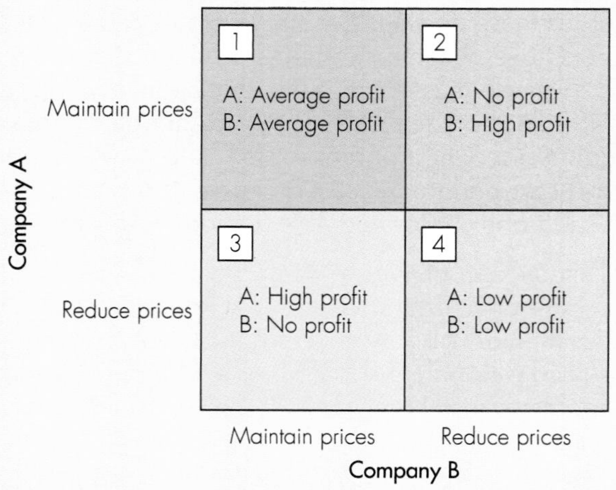

Figure 6-16 Example game theory scenarios – prisoners' dilemmas

Focus on Marketing 6-2 (Continued)

The key aspect of our analysis lies in the fact that it is the optimal choice for company B to reduce prices in response to a previous price reduction on the part of company A, which illustrates the momentum of emerging price wars. A similar momentum is created (field 2 in Figure 6-16) if B is the first to reduce prices.

It is therefore demonstrated that the initial situation is more favorable for both companies, but that the momentum of the process – as soon as one company reduces prices – leads to a state of equilibrium (also see Section 4.2) in which both companies are worse off than in the initial situation. In game theory, such scenarios are also called 'prisoners' dilemmas'.

Source: Varian, H.R. (2003) *Intermediate Microeconomics* (6th edn). Copyright © 2003, 1999, 1996, 1993, 1990, 1987 by Hal R. Varian. Used by permission of W.W. Norton & Company, Inc.

In company practice, some companies align their pricing decisions with the prices of their competitors, which thus function as **guiding prices** (also called pilot prices). Smaller firms, in particular, frequently use the market leader's price or the average market price as a guiding price.

In oligopolistic market structures with generic products (such as, say, raw materials, steel, paper or chemicals), the average market price is often used as a guiding price by all companies. Consequently, all companies usually have very similar prices. Price changes often occur in response to price changes effected by the price leader (the company, holding the price umbrella often has the highest market share) and less in response to demand or cost trends.

Summary

In this chapter we highlighted the importance of pricing decisions as these can be implemented quickly, and can have a major and speedy impact in markets. Pricing therefore is a potentially formidable instrument in the marketing mix. Decisions in pricing, however, are not easy and – once implemented – are difficult to reverse. A thorough understanding of key decision areas and their implications for the customer is therefore of utmost importance. Key areas to consider here are: generic new product pricing (skimming and penetration pricing), pricing the product portfolio, price changes, price differentiation, discount and bonus systems, and enforcement of prices.

We also discussed the theoretical foundations of pricing, which can be rooted either in classical pricing theory or in behavioral pricing concepts. The classical pricing theory – which assumes a rational customer – helps us to derive and study demand functions and price elasticities. We can also calculate demand functions with the help of expert surveys, price experiments, analysis of actual market data (e.g. via conjoint analysis), and with customer surveys. Psychological factors play an important role in behavioral pricing. Price expectations, perceived price fairness and relative value of money are concepts that impact price-related behavior. Key concepts discussed in behavioral pricing are the acquisition, evaluation and storing of price information, as well as the spending and usage behavior of customers related to different payment methods. These concepts illustrate that it is crucial for companies to understand the role of psychological factors and how these impact price-related customer behavior. The chapter concluded with a discussion of the most important approaches in pricing: demand-related pricing, cost-based pricing and competition-based pricing.

Case Study: Apple Reinvents the Phone with iPhone

Apple, a major manufacturer of computers and consumer electronics such as iMac and iPod, has developed a product which marks a breakthrough in mobile phone technology.

The iPhone was announced in January 2007, and went on sale in the US in June 2007 and in Germany, France, and the UK in November of that year. The iPhone combines three products – a mobile phone, a widescreen iPod with touch controls, and an internet communications device with desktop-class email, web browsing, searching and maps – into one small and lightweight handheld device. Apple describes the iPhone as introducing 'an entirely new user interface' which is based on a large multi-touch display. The display uses pioneering new software which lets users control the device's sophisticated features by touching the screen with their fingers. For example, users can scroll through their phone directory, or flick through their music collection by moving their fingers across the screen. The innovative new device and its software is certainly stylish and impressive, and Apple is confident that it offers a 'sophistication never before seen in a mobile device, which completely redefines what users can do on their mobile phones'.

Case Study (Continued)

'iPhone is a revolutionary and magical product that is literally five years ahead of any other mobile phone,' says Apple's CEO Steve Jobs. 'We are all born with the ultimate pointing device – our fingers – and iPhone uses them to create the most revolutionary user interface since the mouse.'

iPhone is available in a 4GB model and an 8GB model, and works with either PC or a Mac. For the market entry phase in 2007, Steve Jobs had to consider the pricing strategy for the new product very carefully.

Sources: Apple reinvents the phone with iPhone. Press release, Apple Inc.

Discussion Questions

1 What are the generic new product pricing approaches that Apple's CEO has to consider?

2 Discuss the various advantages and disadvantages that pertain to the different new product pricing strategies.

3 As the product is launched Apple can also differentiate the price for the different models of the iPhone. What would be the basis of this price differentiation strategy?

4 Discuss the advantages and disadvantages of price differentiation.

5 For the pricing of the 4GB model, two prices were discussed: the engineering department advocated a price of €500 whereas the marketing department proposed a price of €499. Which price would you recommend and why?

Key Terms

Absolute price thresholds *176*
Acquisition of price information *175*
Actual market data *170*
Actual pricing of the new product *161*
Aggressive pricing behavior *186*
Arc elasticity *168*
Basic characteristics pertaining to pricing decisions *160*
Behavioral pricing theory *173*
Benefit-based price differentiation *184*
Bundling *184*
Classical pricing theory *164*
Communication during negotiations with customers *164*
Communication of prices and pricing decisions *164*
Competition-based pricing *180*
Concepts based on behavioral science *164*
Conjoint analysis *170*
Cooperative pricing behavior *186*
Cost-based pricing *180*
Cost-plus pricing *185*
Cournot price *181*
Customer survey *170*
Decision-making areas *160*
Demand-based pricing *180*
Demographic price differentiation *183*
Different payment methods *178*
Direct customer survey *170*
Discount and bonus system *163*
Enforcement of company-internal pricing *163*
Enforcement of external pricing *163*
Enforcement of prices *163*
Evaluation of price information *175*
Expert surveys *170*
Forms of price differentiation *183*
Generic new product pricing *160*
Geographical price differentiation *183*
Guiding prices *189*
Impact of price changes on revenue *169*
Implementing price differentiation in company practice *184*
Indirect customer survey *170*
Individual demand functions *164*
Lack of product differentiation *186*
Linear demand function *166*
Long-term price floors *185*
Maximum prices *177*
Monopoly *164*
Multiplicative demand function *167*
Oligopoly *164*
Overcapacities *186*
Peaceful economic behavior *186*
Penetration strategy *161*
Perceived fairness of the transaction *174*
Permanent price changes *162*
Point elasticity *168*
Polypoly *164*
Price awareness *178*
Price bundling *162, 184*
Price changes of products *162*
Price differentiation *163, 183*
Price elasticity of demand *167*
Price expectations *174*
Price experiments *170*
Price fairness *177*
Price floors *184*
Price interest *175*
Price knowledge *178*
Price positioning of individual product lines *162*
Price search *176*
Price threshold *176*
Price wars *186*
Price–perceived quality relationship *177*
Pricing decisions *160*
Pricing in oligopolies *186*
Pricing new products *165*
Pricing of the product portfolio *162*
Product bundling *184*
Quantity-based price differentiation *184*
Reference price *177*
Relative price thresholds *176*
Relative value of money *174*
Short-term price floors *185*
Skimming strategy *160*
Spending and product usage behavior *175, 178*
Standard pricing *182*
Storing of price information *175*
Temporal price differentiation *184*
Temporary price changes *162*
Threshold demand *166*
Underestimation effect *177*
Value for the customer *184*

References

Anderson, J. and Narus, J. (1999) Welchen Wert hat ihr Angebot für den Kunden? *Harvard Business Manager*, 21, 4, 97–107.

Anderson, E.T. and Simester, D.I. (2001) Research note: price discrimination as an adverse signal: why an offer to spread payments may hurt demand, *Marketing Science*, 20, 3, 315–327.

Apple Inc. (2007) Apple reinvents the phone with iPhone, press release, www.apple.com/pr/library/2007/01/09iphone.html.

Automotive Business Review (2005) Ford: repeated price wars cannot sustain growth, www.automotive-business-review.com/article_feature.asp?guid=8B9BD5A1-163D-4A82-A701-B2A9D7EBB6B5.

Bijmolt, T., van Heerde, H. and Pieters, R. (2005) New empirical generalizations on the determinants of price elasticity, *Journal of Marketing Research*, 42, May, 141–156.

Bolton, L., Warlop, L. and Alba, J. (2003) Consumer perceptions of price (un)fairness, *Journal of Consumer Research*, 29, 4, 474–491.

Bolton, R.N. (1989) The relationship between market characteristics and promotional price elasticities, *Marketing Science*, 8, 2, 153–169.

Briesch, R., Krishnamurthi, L., Mazumdar, T. and Raj, S. (1997) A comparative analysis of reference price models, *Journal of Consumer Research*, 24, 2, 202–214.

Campbell, M. (1999) Perceptions of price unfairness: antecedents and consequences, *Journal of Marketing Research*, 36, 2, 187–199.

Danaher, P. and Brodie, R. (2000) Understanding the characteristics of price elasticities for frequently purchased packaged goods, *Journal of Marketing Management*, 16, 917–936.

Dickson, P.R. and Sawyer, A.G. (1990) The price knowledge and search of supermarket shopper, *Journal of Marketing*, 54, 3, 42–53.

Diller, H. (2000) *Preispolitik* (3rd edn). Stuttgart.

Dobson, G. and Kalish, S. (1988) Positioning and pricing a product line, *Marketing Science*, 7, 2, 107–125.

Doyle, P. (1995) Marketing in the new millennium, *European Journal of Marketing*, 29, 13, 23–41.

Etzioni, A. (1988) *The Moral Dimension: Toward a New Economics*. New York.

Feinberg, R. (1986) Credit cards as spending facilitating stimuli: a conditioning interpretation, *Journal of Consumer Research*, 13, 3, 348–356.

Frykblom, P. (2000) Willingness to pay and the choice of question format: experimental results, *Applied Economics Letters*, 7, 10, 665–667.

Gabor, A. and Granger, C.W. (1979) Price sensitivity of the consumer, *Management Decision*, 17, 8, 569–575.

Garda, R. and Marn, M. (1993) Price wars, *McKinsey Quarterly*, 3, 87–100.

Gaur, V. and Fisher, M.L. (2005) In-store experiments to determine the impact of price on sales, *Production and Operations Management*, 14, 4, 377–387.

Gedenk, K. and Sattler, H. (1999) The impact of price thresholds on profit contribution – should retailers set 9-ending prices? *Journal of Retailing*, 75, 1, 33–57.

Goldberg, S.M., Green, P.E. and Wind, Y. (1984) Conjoint analysis of price premiums for hotel amenities, *Journal of Business*, 57, 1, 111–132.

Gourville, J. (1998) Pennies-a-day: the effect of temporal reframing on transaction evaluation, *Journal of Consumer Research*, 24, 4, 395–408.

Green, P.E. and Srinivasan, V. (1990) Conjoint analysis in marketing: new developments with implications for research and practice, *Journal of Marketing*, 54, 4, 3–19.

Grewal, D. and Marmorstein, H. (1994) Market price variation, perceived price variation, and consumers' price search decisions for durable goods, *Journal of Consumer Research*, 21, 3, 453–460.

Grewal, D., Marmorstein, H. and Sharma, A. (1996) Communicating price information through semantic cues: the moderating effects of situation and discount size, *Journal of Consumer Research*, 23, 2, 148–155.

Gutenberg, E. (1966) *Grundlagen der Betriebswirtschaftslehre: Der Absatz* (9th edn). Berlin.

Heil, O. and Helsen, K. (2001) Toward an understanding of price wars: their nature and how they erupt, *International Journal of Research in Marketing*, 18, 1/2, 83–98.

Hoch, S.J., Kim, B.D., Montgomery, A.L. and Rossi, P.E. (1995) Determinants of store-level price elasticity, *Journal of Marketing Research*, 22, 1, 17–29.

Homburg, C. and Koschate, N. (2005a) Behavioral Pricing-Forschung im Überblick – Teil 1, *Zeitschrift für Betriebswirtschaft*, 75, 4, 383–423.

Homburg, C. and Koschate, N. (2005b) Behavioral Pricing-Forschung im Überblick – Teil 2, *Zeitschrift für Betriebswirtschaft*, 75, 5, 501–524.

Homburg, C., Hoyer, W. and Koschate, N. (2005) Customers' reactions to price increases: do customer satisfaction and the perceived motive fairness matter? *Journal of the Academy of Marketing Science*, 33, 1, 36–49.
Jedidi, K. and Zhang, Z.J. (2002) Augmenting conjoint analysis to estimate consumer reservation price, *Management Science*, 48, 10, 1350–1368.
Johannesson, M. (1997) Some further experimental results on hypothetical versus real willingness to pay, *Applied Economics Letters*, 4, 8, 535.
Kaas, K. and Hay, C. (1984) Preisschwellen bei Konsumgütern: Eine theoretische und empirische Analyze, *Zeitschrift für betriebswirtschaftliche Forschung*, 36, 5, 333–346.
Kalapurakal, R., Dickson, P. and Urbany, J. (1991) Perceived price fairness and dual entitlement, *Advances in Consumer Research*, 18, 1, 788–793.
Kalish, S. and Nelson, P. (1991) A comparison of ranking, rating and reservation price measurement in conjoint analysis, *Marketing Letters*, 2, 4, 327–335.
Kalyanaram, G. and Winer, R. (1995) Empirical generalizations from reference price research, *Marketing Science*, 14, 3, 161–169.
Lange, M. (1972) *Preisbildung bei neuen Produkten*. Berlin.
Lu, Z. and Comanor, W. (1998) Strategic pricing of new pharmaceuticals, *Review of Economics & Statistics*, 80, 1, 108–118.
Monroe, K.B. (2003) *Pricing – Making Profitable Decisions* (3rd edn). New York.
Müller, S. and Hoenig, J. (1983) Die Preisbeachtung in einer realen Kaufsituation, *Jahrbuch der Absatz- und Verbrauchsforschung*, 29, 321–343.
Nagle, T. and Holden, R. (1995) *The Strategy and Tactics of Pricing* (2nd edn). New York.
Neill, H.R., Cummings, R.G., Ganderton, P.T., Harrison, G.W. and McGuckin, T. (1994) Hypothetical surveys and real economic commitments, *Land Economics*, 70, 2, 145–154.
Nevin, J.R. (1974) Laboratory experiments for estimating consumer demand: a validation study, *Journal of Marketing Research*, 11, 3, 261–268.
Prelec, D. and Simester, D. (2001) Always leave home without it: a further investigation of the credit-card effect on willingness to pay, *Marketing Letters*, 12, 1, 5–12.
Rajendran, K. and Tellis, G. (1994) Contextual and temporal components of reference price, *Journal of Marketing*, 58, 1, 22–34.
Rao, A. and Monroe, K. (1989) The effect of price, brand name, and store name on buyers' perceptions of product quality: an integrative review, *Journal of Marketing Research*, 26, 3, 351–357.
Rao, A., Bergen, M. and Davis, D. (2000) How to fight a price war, *Harvard Business Review*, 78, 2, 107–116.
Schindler, R.M. and Kirby, P. (1997) Patterns of rightmost digits used in advertising prices: implications for nine-ending effects, *Journal of Consumer Research*, 24, 2, 192–201.
Schmitz, G. (1964) *Zwischenbetrieblicher Vergleich der Einzelhandelspreise sortengleicher Konsumwaren*. Köln.
Shapiro, C. and Varian, H. (1999) *Information Rules: A Strategic Guide for the Network Economy*. Boston, Mass.
Simester, D. (1995) Signaling price image using advertised prices, *Marketing Science*, 14, 2, 166–188.
Simon, H. (1989) *Price Management*. Elsevier.
Soman, D. and Cheema, A. (2002) The effect of credit on spending decisions: the role of credit limit and credibility, *Marketing Science*, 21, 1, 32–53.
Srivastava, J. and Lurie, N. (2001) A consumer perspective on price-matching refund policies: effect on price perceptions and search behavior, *Journal of Consumer Research*, 28, 2, 296–307.
Stremersch, S. and Tellis, G. (2002) Strategic bundling of products and prices: a new synthesis for marketing, *Journal of Marketing*, 66, 1, 55–72.
Tellis, G.J. (1988) The price elasticity of selective demand: a meta-analysis of econometric models of sales, *Journal of Marketing Research*, 25, 4, 331–341.
Thaler, R. (1980) Toward a positive theory of consumer choice, *Journal of Economic Behavior and Organization*, 1, 1, 39–60.
Thaler, R. (1985) Mental accounting and consumer choice, *Marketing Science*, 4, 3, 199–214.
Urbany, J., Dickson, P. and Kalapurakal, R. (1996) Price search in the retail grocery market, *Journal of Marketing*, 60, 2, 91–104.
Varian, H.R. (2003) *Intermediate Microeconomics* (6th edn). New York. Copyright © 2003, 1999, 1996, 1993, 1990, 1987 by Hal R. Varian. Used by permission of W.W. Norton & Company, Inc.
Wakefield, K. and Inman, J. (1993) Who are the price vigilantes? An investigation of differentiating characteristics influencing price information processing, *Journal of Retailing*, 69, 2, 216–233.
Wertenbroch, K. and Skiera, B. (2002) Measuring consumers' willingness to pay at the point of purchase, *Journal of Marketing Research*, 39, 2, 228–241.
Zeithaml, V. (1988) Consumer perceptions of price, quality, and value: a means–end model and synthesis of evidence, *Journal of Marketing*, 52, 3, 2–22.

CHAPTER 7

Sales Decisions

Contents

Learning Objectives

In this chapter you will become familiar with:

- the important internal and external sales entities of the company
- the general advantages and disadvantages of direct and indirect sales channels
- the concepts concerning the 'depth' and 'width' of a sales channel, and the options to design channels
- what is meant by the 'width' of a sales system, and problems connected with a multichannel system
- the options concerning the design of relationships with sales partners and key accounts
- the main phases of personal selling, and the important principles for successfully designing the individual phases
- the different types of sales negotiations used in personal selling, and the corresponding objectives
- the most important sales techniques (presentation techniques, rhetorical methods and closing techniques)
- the key decision-making areas and the design options of sales logistics.

7.1 Basic Terms, Concepts and Overview

The area of sales decisions is more difficult to define than the other areas of the marketing mix. Numerous marketing textbooks call this fourth component of the marketing mix **distribution.** This term has to be understood against the background of the historical development of marketing, and particularly the marketing mix concept. As noted in Chapter 1, the term 'marketing mix' originated in the USA in the 1950s, with consumer goods companies at the forefront of the concept. In this environment, the main marketing tasks were to develop, price and advertise products, as well as ensure their availability for customers.

The latter task was realized through cooperations with local 'distributors'. These distributors were primarily locally oriented retailers who undertook little or no marketing activities on their own behalf. Cooperations with these distributors were more operative in nature and had little in common with the relationships we can observe today between consumer goods manufacturers and large, self-reliant retail enterprises that hold considerable market power and have their own marketing approaches (see the discussion on retail marketing in Section 11.5.) Such retail establishments are essential partners within the scope of marketing activities. To reduce them to a distributor role would clash with today's reality.

The modern marketing concept gives appropriate consideration to the acquisitional aspect within the scope of the marketing mix. Therefore, we refer to **sales decisions** as the fourth component of the marketing mix. The distribution of physical goods is one issue to cover among others with regard to these acquisitional activities. However, the majority of this chapter will be devoted to market-oriented activities that are geared towards closing sales.

There are four main decision-making areas pertaining to sales decisions:

1 the design and structure of the sales system (for more information, see Section 7.2)

2 the design and structure of relationships with sales partners and key accounts (see Section 7.3)

3 the design of selling activities (see Section 7.4)

4 the development of the sales logistics system.

With regard to the **design of the sales system**, the questions relate to who should undertake the selling activities (selection of the sales entities) and how to combine the sales entities into sales channels (design of the sales channels). The **design and structuring of relationships with sales partners and key accounts** concerns the form and contents of these cooperations, aspects such as distribution of power and conflict management, as well as contractual arrangements. Finally, the type of contact with customers and the use of sales techniques are essential elements of the **design of sales activities.**

Sales logistics focuses on ensuring the physical availability of the product for customers. Key decision-making areas here include the location of finished goods warehouses, warehousing, consignment, packaging and packing, as well as transportation of products (see Section 7.5).

A key challenge inherent in all these decisions is to deliver the required value to the customer. In order to do this successfully companies need to build **value networks** that establish relationships with critical partners in this process, the customer included.

7.2 The Design and Structure of the Sales System

Most decisions in sales relate to a company's **sales system.** The individual components of the sales system are called sales entities (see Section 7.2.1), and these are combined into sales channels (see

Section 7.2.2). The sales system of a company comprises all the sales channels that a company establishes to deliver value to customers.

7.2.1 Selection of Sales Entities

Sales entities refer to any company-internal and company-external individuals, departments or institutions that directly carry out or support sales activities for a company's products. They include the company's internal sales departments as well as external sales partners (e.g. intermediaries).

When selecting sales entities, the company determines which sales entities should be used for which sales activities and to what extent (see Figure 7-1 for an overview of the sales entities that can be involved). We will differentiate between company-internal and company-external sales entities.

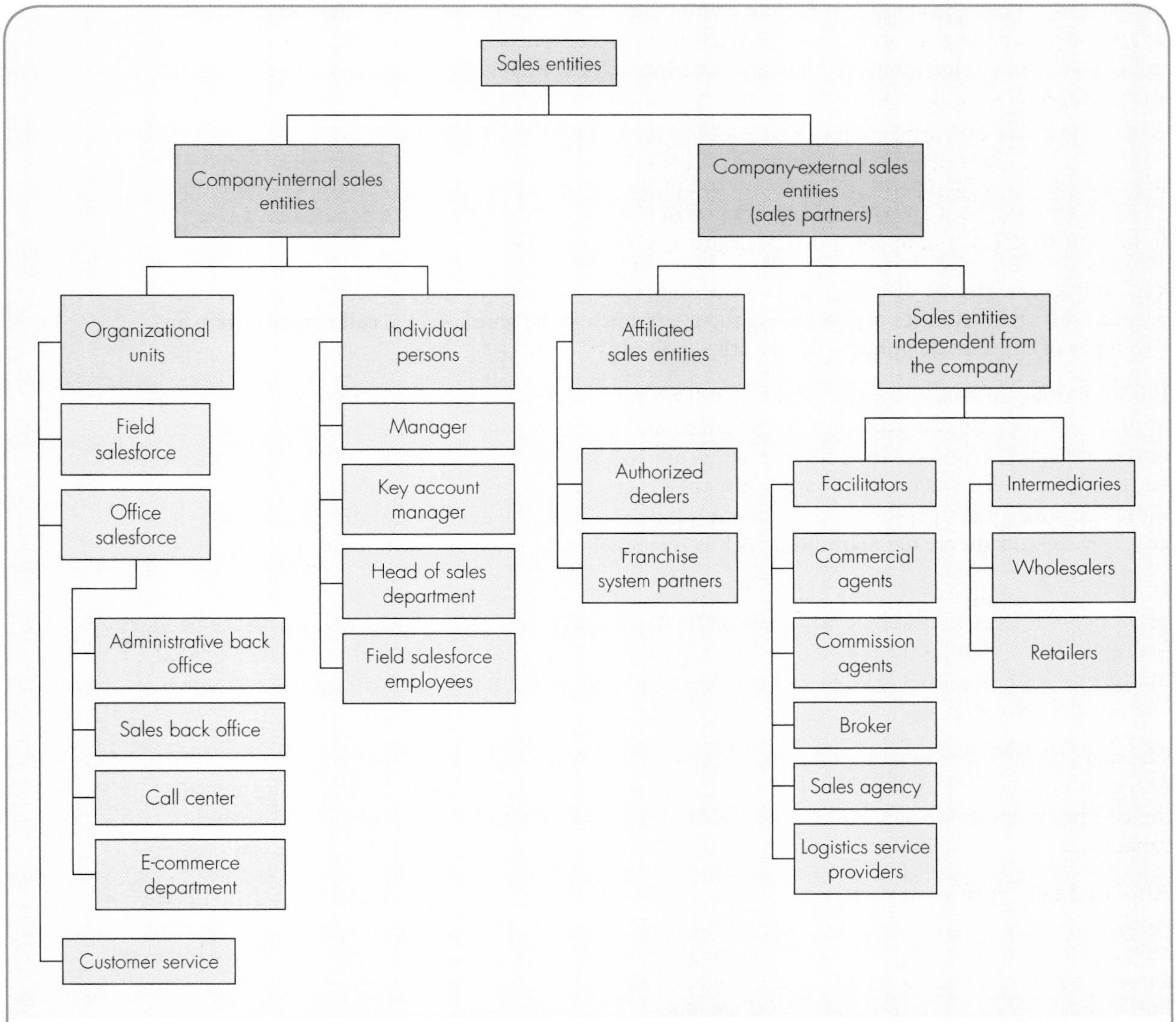

Figure 7-1 Overview of sales entities

There are two types of **internal sales entity**: organizational units and individual persons performing sales tasks. These individuals can – but do not have to – be assigned to organizational sales units. While the organizational units are responsible for the day-to-day business (routine sales), individual persons are delegated on a case-by-case basis with sales tasks that often involve important customers (for example, a manager who has a crucial meeting with key accounts or who attempts to acquire the first order for a major new product.)

The **field salesforce** of a company is usually organized on a regional basis, often centralized into regional sales offices. The field salesforce is responsible for managing and maintaining the existing customer base, supporting sales partners (e.g. dealers) and acquiring new customers. The primary activity of field salesforce employees is to visit customers on a regular basis.

The field salesforce is supported by the back office (also called back office support). In terms of regional organization, the back office often has a higher degree of centralization compared to the field salesforce. It is important to distinguish the administrative and acquisition-related tasks of the sales office (see also Figure 7-1). The primary duty of the **administrative back office** is order processing, which mainly involves coordination between the customer and internal departments, such as, say, sales logistics. In establishing an administrative back office, companies particularly strive to ensure that the field salesforce can concentrate on acquisition-related interaction with customers to the greatest extent possible. Conversely, the **sales back office** focuses on closing sales with the company's customers. This involves preparing bids and quotations, as well as conducting negotiations with customers (for more on bid proposals and quotations, see Hamper and Baugh 1995; Riley 2002; Sant 2004). In company practice, however, the back office departments will frequently undertake both administrative and acquisitional duties.

Back offices can also be distinguished by the media they use for interfacing with customers (see Figure 7-1): sales activities processed via the telephone can be handled by a **call center**. There are two types of call centers: inbound and outbound.

Inbound call centers are responsible for handling communication coming in from customers (such as order processing), for providing information and for receiving customer complaints. In contrast, outbound call centers take the initiative when approaching customers. Such call centers, for example, verify address information, make appointments or conduct phone sales. Outbound call centers therefore have a stronger focus on acquisition than inbound call centers. Another back office area is the **e-commerce department**, which is responsible for managing internet-based sales.

In the case of complex products (e.g. in the industrial goods sector), in particular, **customer service** plays a vital role as a sales-supporting department. Its spectrum of duties (depending on the product being marketed) ranges from providing information to customers with regard to product-related matters to rendering on-site services for customers (e.g. maintenance services) up to developing customized solutions.

The main differentiating factor of external sales entities is whether or not they are economically or legally dependent (see Figure 7-1). The advantage of affiliated sales entities lies in the fact that the company can implement its sales concepts in the market with limited investment in sales capacity.

Affiliated sales entities in particular include authorized dealers and franchise system partners (see Anderson and Coughlan 2002; Coughlan *et al.* 2001). Authorized dealers are legally independent, but represent a fixed component of the company's sales strategy since they are bound by contractual agreements. In company practice, authorized dealers are common – for example, in the automotive industry (car dealerships; for an example see Figure 7-2) or the petroleum industry (petrol stations). The company can link a dealer contract to certain sales conditions and service requirements. The

Figure 7-2 Example of a car dealership

authorized dealer can thus be obligated to sell the company's brand exclusively and follow its sales strategy closely (e.g. sales promotion campaigns). In return, the company can guarantee territorial protection for authorized dealers (i.e. only one authorized dealer exists in a defined regional sales territory).

In the case of cooperations with **franchise system partners**, the contractual relationship is, for the sales partner, even stronger than is the case with the authorized dealer system. Upon the conclusion of a contract, a franchisee acquires both the right and the obligation to participate in the market presence of a company (franchisor) and to use the company's associated sales concept (for an example, see Focus on Marketing 7-1). Along with a fixed franchise fee, the franchise system partner generally makes sales-based payments to the franchisor.

Sales entities that are independent from companies can be categorized into facilitators and intermediaries. The common characteristic shared by these two sales entities is that they are legally independent. The main difference is that, in contrast to intermediaries, facilitators do not acquire any ownership in the product that they market and sell.

Table 7-1 gives an overview of the most common types of **facilitator**. Due to the difficulty in transferring ownership in the case of services (because services are essentially intangible – see Section 11.1), facilitators play a particularly crucial role in service industries. They represent a cost-effective option for companies (e.g. sales costs are variable costs when using agents and brokers). This is one of the main reasons for companies to employ them. Facilitators also often have special expertise; this is particularly the case with sales agencies and logistics service providers.

Table 7-1 Types of facilitator

Type of facilitator	Description	Examples
Commercial agent	Trades as independent sales manager in the name of and on behalf of one or more companies	■ Cosmetics sales representative ■ Commercial agents for industrial kitchen equipment ■ Commercial agents for ophthalmology supplies and equipment
Commission agent	Trades in own name on behalf of the company (consigner). The company provides these agents special rights, e.g. to issue instructions (such as price guidelines)	■ Book distributors ■ Commission agent for antiques and works of art
Broker	Negotiates contracts between company and customers in the name of third parties and on behalf of third parties	■ Financial and insurance brokers ■ Travel agency ■ Internet broker/online auctions platforms
Sales agency	Supports the company in contacting potential customers and with order processing	■ Exporter ■ Sales agency for technical supplies and equipment
Logistics service provider	Undertakes packing, transportation and warehousing for the company	■ Warehouse company ■ Freight/transport company/ forwarding agents

Focus on Marketing 7-1 Example of franchising

> "Innovation power needs sales power. A professional and systematically managed worldwide sales network is key for future growth."
>
> *Uwe Raschke, President Power Tools*

Bosch Car Service program in the Philippines
The role of automobile electronics has become increasingly significant in modern vehicles. From 18% in 1990, the share of electronics in automobile production now stands at 25% and is expected to reach 35% in 2010.

As a result, vehicle servicing has become more complicated and technical due to the nature of the components and systems now fitted to most modern cars. Many car problems can no longer be solved simply by a neighborhood mechanic and his wrench.

In response to this growing necessity for vehicle diagnostics and repair service that would match increasingly complex vehicle systems, Robert Bosch Inc. is adopting the Bosch Car Service Concept in the Philippines. The concept is part of a global initiative to identify and accredit workshops and garages that could offer a one-stop shop for diagnostics and spare parts.

There are a total of 288 Bosch Service workshops in Southeast Asia (Malaysia, Thailand, Indonesia, Singapore and the Philippines). In the Philippines, Bosch has initially identified 29 workshops nationwide for accreditation as part of the Bosch Car Service program.

Focus on Marketing 7-1 (Continued)

Bosch Car Service brings together everything that is needed to carry out successful testing, diagnosis and repair – systems know-how, technical information, test devices, technical consulting and spare parts in original equipment quality.

Bosch test equipment technology optimizes the combination of hardware and software for rapid troubleshooting, qualified repair and high-time savings. Along with the testing equipment, the Esitronic software package allows mechanics to carry out diagnostic tests on passenger cars regardless of the make or model. One hundred and twenty specialists are working full time in making Esitronic even more effective by further increasing the size of the vehicle database. Bosch invests around 15 million Euros annually for the continuous development of this comprehensive software.

Another important part of Bosch Car Service is the service training. Bosch also offers immediate advice on repair to around 36,000 callers a year.

Source: *Business World*, September 15, 2004. p. 24.

Intermediaries are commercial enterprises that, in contrast to facilitators, trade in their own name and on their own behalf. Depending on the type of customers they cater to, intermediaries can be divided into wholesalers and retailers.

- Customers of **wholesalers** are commercial buyers such as retail companies or manufacturers. Wholesalers usually sell goods in larger quantities. In the industrial goods sector, industrial business-to-business trading companies play a key role. They procure raw materials, parts and machines, and resell these to a large extent as unmodified goods to manufacturing companies.
- On the other hand, **retailers** serve end customers. Chapter 11 presents a discussion of the various forms of retailer (e.g. department stores, bricks-and-mortar businesses, mail-order businesses).

7.2.2 The Design of Sales Channels

As already mentioned, **sales channels** emerge from the selection and combination of sales entities that are involved in delivering value to the customer. In terms of the design of sales channels, there are two basic alternatives: direct and indirect sales. In this section we will compare these two alternatives. Following that, we will discuss two special aspects of sales channel design: the width and depth of sales channels.

Direct and Indirect Sales Channels: What is the difference?

A decision that influences the design of the sales system in a fundamental way is the choice of direct or indirect sales. We speak of **indirect sales** if company-external sales partners assume responsibility for sales and acquisitions. If this is not the case, we refer to **direct sales**. A sale is thus indirect if it takes place via an intermediary (trading company). But indirect sales can also be sales that involve authorized dealers or franchise system partners, or if a facilitator takes over a significant acquisition-related function. Accordingly, customer acquisition via a broker represents a form of indirect sales, which, however, does not apply to the participation of sales agencies or logistics service providers (for more on the different types of facilitator, please refer to Section 7.2).

From a theoretical viewpoint, the choice between direct and indirect sales can be analyzed by means of **transaction cost theory** (for more on 'transaction cost theory', see Appendix). This theory provides the logic to identify the most favorable (i.e. transaction cost minimizing) way to conduct transactions. According to this theory, the decision to use either direct or indirect sales would be determined on the basis of **efficiency considerations**. The dominant issue here concerns the extent to which the inclusion of sales partners can save transaction costs as compared to the direct sales approach (see Anderson 1996; Anderson and Coughlan 2002; Rindfleisch and Heide 1997).

Significant influencing factors when deciding between direct and indirect sales include the following:

- The **level of customization and complexity of the product**: if a product is strongly aligned with the individual requirements of the customers (**specificity**), the direct sales method is usually the most cost-efficient alternative. The same also applies in the case of highly complex products (see also the empirical findings of Anderson 1985; Anderson and Gatignon 1986; John and Weitz 1988). This also clarifies why direct sales play such a major role in the industrial goods sector.
- The **number of customers/concentration of demand**: when demand is very concentrated on a relatively small number of customers, direct sales tend to be the more efficient option (Jackson and d'Amico 1989). On the other hand, indirect sales are usually the better alternative for a company with a large and diffuse customer base.
- The **monetary value of the product**: products with a low monetary value are more often sold indirectly (see Anderson and Schmittlein 1984; Rangan *et al.* 1992).

Apart from these considerations, issues of effectiveness can also affect the decision regarding mode of sales. Direct sales can help the company to establish close relationships to customers as well as customer loyalty. Additionally, sales activities can be more easily monitored by the company.

In many product categories, the internet has forced companies to re-evaluate direct sales in terms of transaction cost factors. This particularly applies to digitizable products that can be distributed and sold via computer networks (e.g. software, music products, movies). Internet sales lead to drastically reduced transaction costs that make direct sales a viable alternative to the indirect sales option that historically has had dominance in many markets. Therefore, markets exist today where even niche products can make up the bulk of the market. This phenomenon has been termed the **long tail economy** (see Anderson 2006; Focus on Marketing 7-2; Figure 7-4). Indeed, the internet has made various inroads into markets with considerable success (see Focus on Marketing 7-3).

In practice it can be observed that particular products and product categories tend to be sold either directly or indirectly. Figure 7-3 shows various products and the predominant sales method (direct

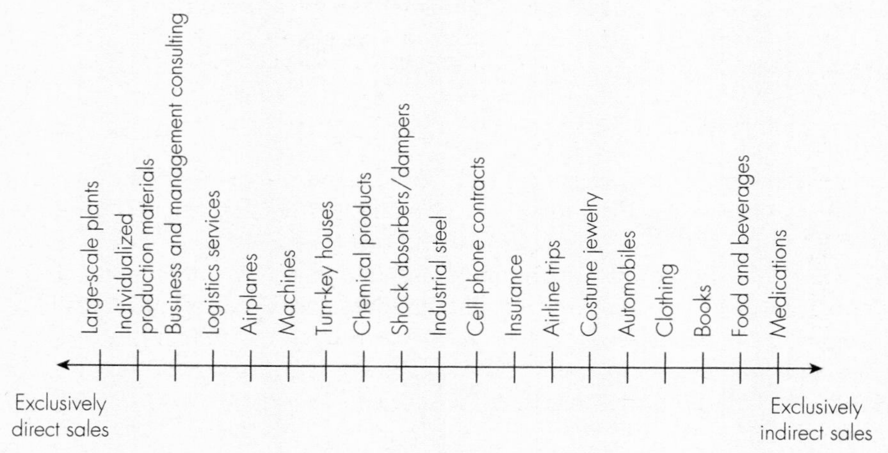

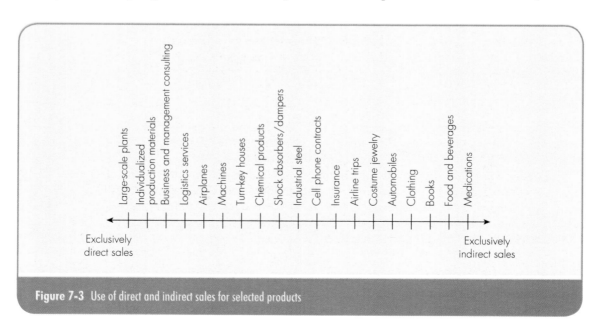

Figure 7-3 Use of direct and indirect sales for selected products

vs indirect) used in company practice for those products. In this context, it should be noted that a company (as indicated in Figure 7-3) does not necessarily have to choose between using only direct sales or only indirect sales. Instead, in many cases, direct *and* indirect sales channels can be combined, resulting in a **hybrid sales system**.

Focus on Marketing 7-2 The impact of the internet on sales

The long tail, in a nutshell

The theory of the Long Tail is that our culture and economy is increasingly shifting away from a focus on a relatively small number of 'hits' (mainstream products and markets) at the head of the demand curve and toward a huge number of niches in the tail. As the costs of production and distribution fall, especially online, there is now less need to lump products and consumers into one-size-fits-all containers. In an era without the constraints of physical shelf space and other bottlenecks of distribution, narrowly-targeted goods and services can be as economically attractive as mainstream fare.

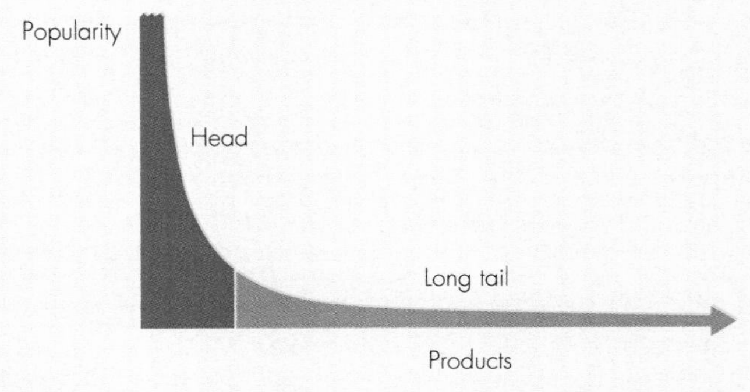

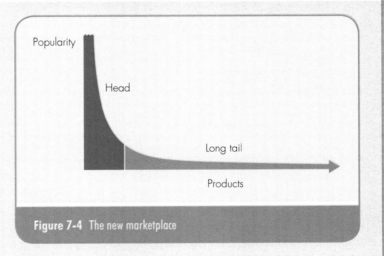

Figure 7-4 The new marketplace

One example of this is the theory's prediction that demand for products *not* available in traditional bricks and mortar stores is potentially as big as for those that are. But the same is true for video not available on broadcast TV on any given day, and songs not played on radio. In other words, the potential aggregate size of the many small markets in goods that don't individually sell well enough for traditional retail and broadcast distribution may someday rival that of the existing large market in goods that do cross that economic bar.

The term Long Tail refers specifically to the orange part of the sales chart above, which shows a standard demand curve that could apply to any industry, from entertainment to hard goods. The vertical axis is sales; the horizontal is products. The red part of the curve is the hits, which have dominated our markets and culture for most of the last century. The orange part is the non-hits, or niches, which is where the new growth is coming from now and in the future.

Traditional retail economics dictate that stores only stock the likely hits, because shelf space is expensive. But online retailers (from Amazon to iTunes) can stock virtually everything, and the number of available niche products outnumber the hits by several orders of magnitude. Those millions of niches are the Long Tail, which had been largely neglected until recently in favor of the Short Head of hits.

When consumers are offered infinite choice, the true shape of demand is revealed. And it turns out to be less hit-centric than we thought. People gravitate towards niches because they satisfy narrow interests better, and in one aspect of our life or another we all have some narrow interest (whether we think of it that way or not).

Source: http://www.thelongtail.com/about.htm.

Focus on Marketing 7-3 Development of direct sales over the internet

Online, offline – what's the difference?
Consumers clearly love to shop on the internet. So they should: leading websites, after early teething problems, now provide a superb service. Certain sites, such as Amazon, have won some of the highest customer-satisfaction scores ever seen in the retail industry. In fact, websites have had little choice but to raise service levels, often far above those of offline retailers. Competition on the web is fierce. Price transparency is the rule. With shopping-comparison services, it is possible to check the price offered by hundreds of merchants with a couple of mouse clicks. Consumers also have access to an unprecedented amount of product information, not just from manufacturers' websites but also from online reviews written by previous customers.

The growth of internet shopping is producing a profound change in consumer behavior. People are not just becoming more confident about buying goods and services online, they are also increasingly adept at using the internet to decide where and how to spend their money offline. As yet, very few new cars are sold online. But in America three out of four customers walking into a car showroom have already researched their choice online, down to what color and accessories they want.

And most will know exactly what they need to pay. Some will even have armed themselves with competing quotes from different dealers, often by using specialist websites. Much the same thing is happening with other goods and services, from domestic appliances to holidays.

No company can any longer afford to ignore the internet, even if it does not itself sell much or anything at all online. Consumers are behaving as if they see no great distinction between online and offline shopping. They do both. For most consumers, the internet is just another sales channel, and a convenient tool for browsing and research, and they make their purchase in whatever way happens to suit them best. To reach these customers, companies have had to look at new and different advertising and marketing strategies. This is why firms are finding that paying for sponsored links to appear on search sites like Google and Yahoo! has become one of the most effective marketing tools, especially for categories of consumers who spend as much time on the internet as they do watching television, such as teenagers.

Source: E-commerce takes off, *The Economist*, 5/12/2004, Vol. 371, Issue 8375, pp 8–9.

The Depth of a Sales Channel

In the case of an indirect sale, the question arises as to how many sales tiers a product should pass through from the company – in this case often the manufacturer – to the customer. This number of intermediate sales tiers is also referred to as the **'depth' of a sales channel**.

When only one sales tier (e.g. a retailer) is used, it is called a **single-tier sales channel**. Such sales channels are used, for example, for consumer goods, with only the retailer located between the manufacturer and the end customer in most cases.

A **two-tier sales channel** exists if, say, manufacturers do not supply retailers themselves, but rather via wholesalers. Wholesalers are mostly used in cases where the logistics or competencies of a retailer are not sufficient to serve the customer base. The two-tier sales channel is often preferred, for example, for the sale of pharmaceutical products: pharmacies, with their relatively small storage capacities and few transportation resources, cannot store the complete range of medications requested by customers. Therefore, a regional pharmaceutical wholesaler with the necessary capacity and skills in logistics can create added value for both manufacturer and customer.

Single-tier and two-tier sales channels are depicted in Figure 7-5.

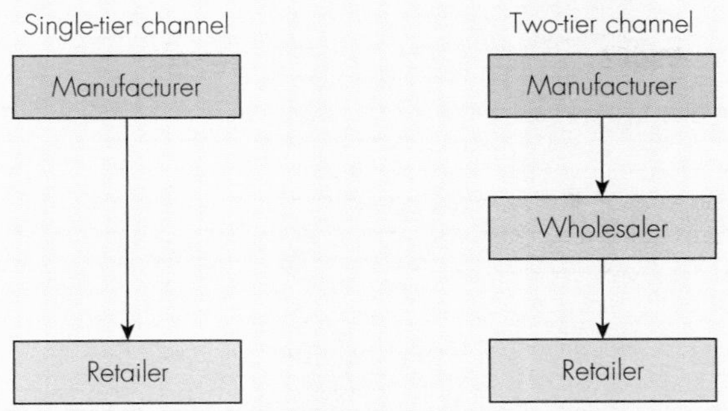

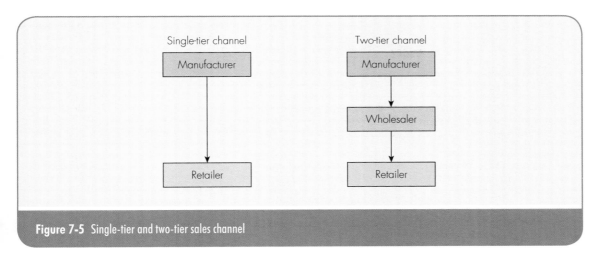

Figure 7-5 Single-tier and two-tier sales channel

The Width of a Sales Channel

Another question connected to designing an indirect sales channel is concerned with the **width of a sales channel**. The decision here relates to how many sales partners within a sales channel should be used simultaneously by the company in order to serve the market and its customers in an optimal way. There are three relevant design options:

1 exclusive selling

2 intensive selling

3 selective selling.

When the company uses the **exclusive selling method**, it relies on only a few selected sales partners. In company practice, such an approach can be observed in, for example, the case of luxury goods, and speciality goods or services. The other extreme is **intensive selling**. Here the company cooperates with a large number of sales partners (in some cases with all available sales partners). This type of selling is often selected for convenience products (such as everyday household products). **Selective selling** lies between these two extremes: the supplier selects some sales partners, but it is less restrictive than exclusive selling.

An advantage of exclusive selling is that this limited number of sales partners ensures a consistent market presence (e.g. with respect to advising customers and presenting the products in a uniform way). This is particularly relevant for products positioned in the high price range. A potential disadvantage of this approach is limited market coverage. Of course, when a company chooses intensive selling it pursues comprehensive coverage of the market. For mass products this is vital for market success. However, the large number of sales partners, which are often dissimilar in quality, makes it difficult for the company to control and monitor the marketing of its products. Intensive selling can also lead to intense competition between sales partners selling and marketing the same products.

7.2.3 The Width of the Sales System

When we speak of the width of a sales channel we refer to the number of sales entities and sales partners the company is using in parallel to serve a certain market. When speaking of the **width of a sales system** we refer to the number of sales channels a company decides to use at the same time to serve a certain market. The company can, in fact, decide to use one, two or more different types of channel for the same product. Here we distinguish single-channel systems and multichannel systems.

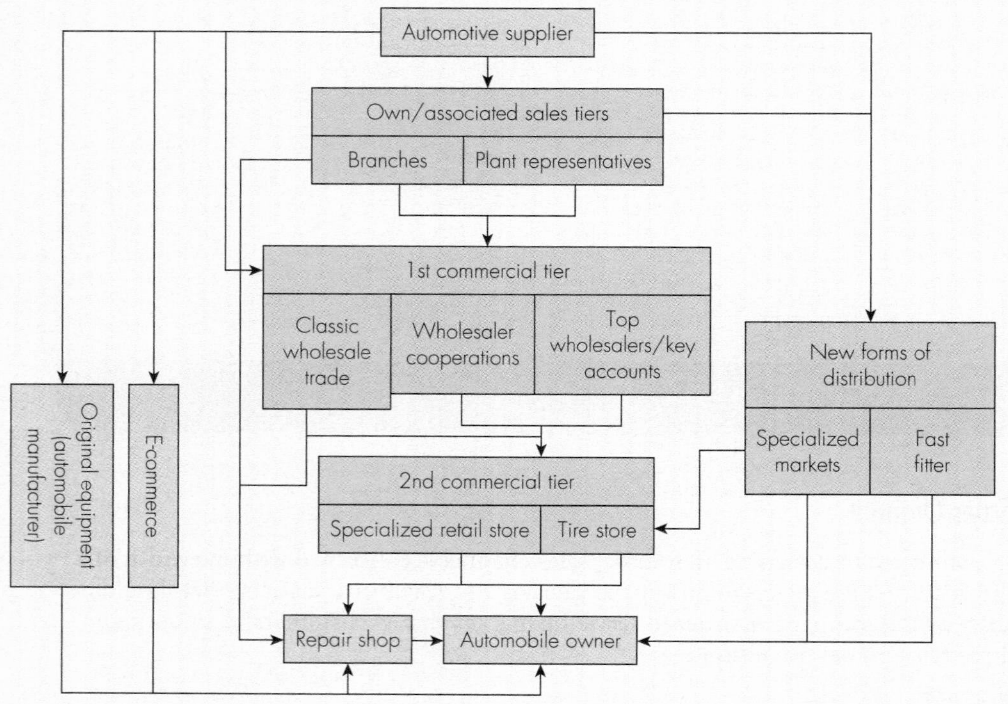

Figure 7-6 Multichannel system illustrated with the example of an automotive supplier (see Homburg *et al.* 2002a)

A **single channel** exists if the sales system comprises only one sales channel. Examples of this include an industrial goods company that only sells its products directly and a consumer goods company that sells its products exclusively via retailers.

On the contrary, if a company uses several sales channels for selling its products, this is called a **multichannel system** (see Cespedes and Corey 1990; Moriarty and Moran 1990). This is sometimes also referred to as a dual channel. For example, many airlines use their own sales offices, online shops, independent travel agencies, tour operators and brokers. Along with field salesforces, insurance companies commission independent brokers and sell insurance direct via the telephone and/or the internet.

Figure 7-6 illustrates a complex multichannel system, using the example of a car company that sells its products both indirectly (e.g. spare parts are sold to automobile owners via car repair shops) and directly (e.g. spare parts are sold to automobile owners over the internet).

There are several reasons for choosing a multichannel system. Often, such a system helps to cover the market more broadly and allows the company to address various customer segments with different requirements more cost-efficiently than is the case with a single-channel system. At the same time, a multichannel system can also prevent a company from becoming too dependent on individual sales partners.

However, significant problems can also arise in connection with multichannel selling. **Channel conflicts** between sales channels can crop up if different sales channels target similar or even identical customer groups. Focus on Marketing 7-4 illustrates these types of conflicts.

An important approach to minimize such conflicts lies in clearly **defining the target customer groups and tasks of the various sales channels.**

Focus on Marketing 7-4 Managing conflicts in multichannel selling

Living with channel conflict

The spread of new distribution channels, primarily via the Internet, is tempting for many manufacturers seeking the shortterm sales boost that often results from an expansion of distribution points. However, creating a situation in which too many channels are chasing too few consumers can have a deleterious impact on a brand's longterm sales as well as its image.

From the manufacturer's perspective, channel conflict becomes destructive rather than productive when existing channels react to the emergence of a new channel by reducing support or shelf space for the manufacturer's brand. When Estée Lauder set up a website to sell its Clinique and Bobbi Brown brands, Dayton Hudson reduced space in its department stores for Estée Lauder products. In extreme cases, an existing distributor may drop the brand entirely: When Levi Strauss began expanding its distribution into department stores, The Gap stopped stocking Levi's and began concentrating on its own Gap brands.

The brand owner should ensure that the number of distribution points within a particular channel category is balanced against the size of the customer segment that the channel reaches. Bang & Olufsen, for example, had far too many distribution points in the early 1990s to support sales of its highend electronics products, leading dealers to frequently discount the company's brands. Between 1994 and 1997, the company reduced the number of US dealers from 200 to 30. The remaining dealers upgraded their service and support to help the firm refocus from price to a luxury lifestyle brand.

A popular method of managing channel conflict is to dedicate parts of the product line to different channels of distribution. Many clothing designers that have expanded sales through outlet stores managed the potential conflict with existing retailers by developing special products for the outlet stores.

Similarly, many luxury brand companies, like Camus Cognac and Guylian chocolates, offer specialized packages for duty-free shops at airports in order to minimize the conflict with regular high street retailers. (These packaging decisions are also functional, as they are attractive to travelers.) On the Internet, manufacturers can offer SKUs that retailers usually are unwilling to carry.

At the extreme, some manufacturers create dedicated 'channel brands.' MyTravel, a tour operator in Sweden, formerly distributed its Ving brand directly while developing the similar Always brand for travel agents.

Source: Kumar, N. (2006) Living with channel conflict, *Managementletter*, 5, October.

7.3 The Design and Structure of Relationships with Sales Partners and Key Accounts

Along with the design and structure of the sales system discussed in Section 7.2, another main decision-making area in sales is the design and structure of the company's relationships with its top **sales partners** and key accounts. **Key accounts** are those customers (generally corporate customers) who are extremely important to a company due to their actual or potential purchasing volume. For reasons of clarification, it should be noted here that we do not refer to major sales partners as key accounts in this book; the term 'key accounts' refers to companies that purchase a company's product (for example, the situation refers to an industrial company purchasing from a manufacturing company).

The common characteristic shared by major sales partners and key accounts is that they are both relevant to the market success of the company to such a degree that it is very important to establish and maintain relationships. This section examines the relationship between a consumer goods manufacturer and its key sales partners (a large chain of stores), as well as the relationship between industrial goods manufacturers and their industrial key accounts.

The main issues regarding the structure of a company's relationships with sales partners and key accounts are:

- cooperation (see Section 7.3.1)
- influencing the distribution of power (see Section 7.3.2)
- managing conflicts (see Section 7.3.3)
- the design and structure of contractual relationships (see Section 7.3.4)

between the companies.

7.3.1 Cooperation in Sales Systems

In connection with the business relationships discussed here, **cooperation in sales systems** refers to companies working together with their sales partners or key accounts in certain areas that go beyond the scope of conducting mere business transactions (for more on cooperations between business partners, see Anderson and Narus 1990; Dwyer *et al.* 1987; Skinner *et al.* 1992). From the company standpoint, the **objectives of a cooperation** can be:

- qualitative improvement of the business relationship (e.g. establishes trust and reduces conflicts)
- reduction of costs (e.g. order processing costs)
- increase in the effectiveness of the cooperation (e.g. in terms of quality aspects or joint market success).

Achieving these objectives can considerably enhance the profitability of the business relationship and help to stabilize it.

Crucial here is the question concerning the areas in which the company will be cooperating with its sales partners and key accounts. Figure 7-7 contains an overview of the most significant **fields of cooperation** (see also Homburg *et al.* 2002b; Ingram *et al.* 2001).

Key account programs include activities for key accounts that would not normally be offered to standard customers. With regard to the design of products, there can be special product variants produced especially for key accounts or even developed in cooperation with these accounts.

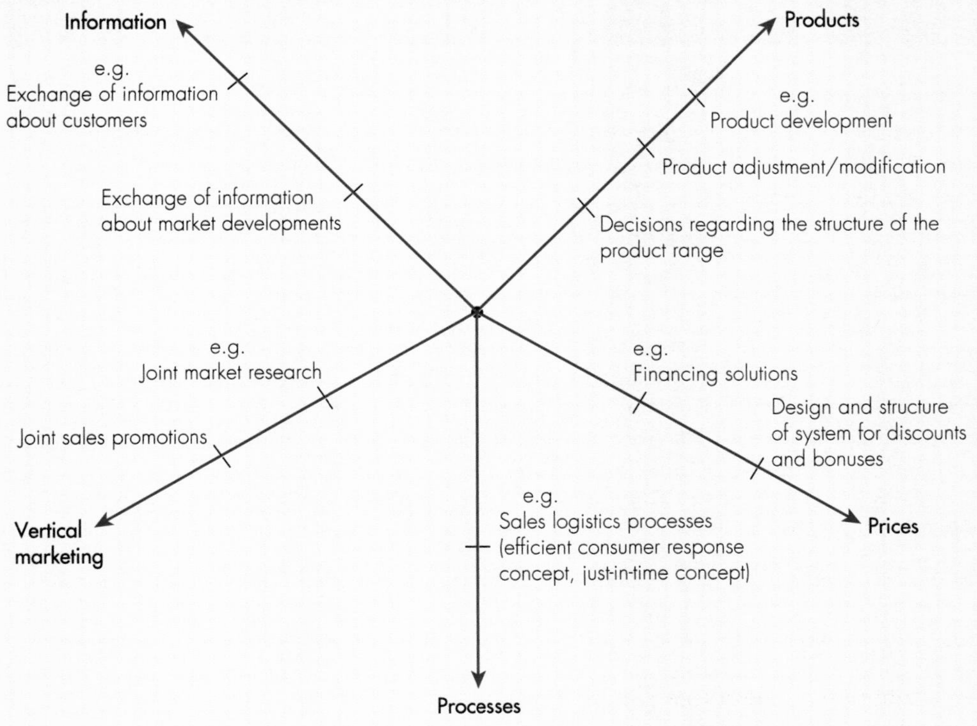

Figure 7-7 Fields of cooperation between companies and sales partners/key accounts

In addition to product decisions, key account programs can also include pricing activities, such as better prices for key accounts as compared to other customers, or offers of special financing solutions.

With regard to the design of processes between companies and their sales partners/key accounts, the process of sales logistics plays a key role. With respect to cooperation with sales partners, the concept of **efficient consumer response** (ECR) should be specifically mentioned here, as it is particularly suited to cooperations between consumer goods manufacturers and their sales partners. ECR is a strategic cooperation initiative between the trade (wholesale and retail) and manufacturers that aims to optimize the entire value chain, spanning from the manufacturer to the customer (see Corsten and Kumar 2005; ECR Europe 1997). The main goal of this approach is to reduce transaction costs on the basis of consistent and integrated monitoring and optimization of the goods and information flows between the manufacturer and sales partner (see Corsten and Kumar 2005; Heide and John 1992; Lusch and Brown 1996). Warehousing costs are also especially relevant in this context, since large inventories represent inefficiencies in the logistics chain that are in part caused by a lack of information between the manufacturer and the wholesale and/or retail sector. Consequently, eliminating such information deficits can decrease warehousing capacity and therefore costs.

Table 7-2 shows the four potential fields of cooperation in ECR. Here, it can be seen that, apart from logistics, such a cooperation can also involve acquisition-related aspects. This is especially the case with regard to designing the product mix – also called **category management**. Essential to understanding category management is that products are bundled into categories and grouped together in a way that addresses specific customer needs. The intention is to promote combined purchases (for more on category management, see the example in Focus on Marketing 7-5).

Focus on Marketing 7-5 An example of joint category management efforts

Categorical imperatives

The Economist examines how supermarkets and their suppliers hope to sell more by sharing what they know about customers. But can they trust each other with the information?

In an article from 1997, *The Economist* explains category-management projects that involve the brands of major manufacturers who are powerful enough to call the shots. The article explains how Procter & Gamble (P&G), which makes over half of the detergents sold in Britain, has worked with local retailers to restructure its portfolio of soaps:

> Detergent sales in Britain have been static partly because shoppers are confused by the clash of proliferating brands: 180 possible packets in all. P&G thinks it can reduce its range by 40% and still meet 95% of the needs of consumers it satisfies at the moment – and in the process raise the profitability of its detergents by 40%. So far it has cut its range by 20% in several store chains, a move that helped the stores' sales of all detergents (including P&G's) grow by 8%. In a similar experiment in America, P&G raised its sales by 6% and its profits by 22% after reducing the range on the shelf by 13%.

As P&G and similar manufacturing giants begin to experiment with joint category management, some supermarket chains have responded by appointing certain leading manufacturers 'category captains'. The status of 'category captain' grants companies such as P&G a formal say in how their goods are stocked on shelves. However, it also allows them to determine how other manufacturers' goods in the same category are stocked too. As *The Economist* notes, 'this brings up the notion, terrifying to smaller manufacturers, that category management will eventually create a world in which stores often use only one supplier for certain products, topping up with own-label'.

But would this single-supplier model ever happen? Martin George, the space-planning manager of Nestlé, argues that it would not, because big retailers and manufacturers both realize it would drive consumers away from the stores. George cites a recent example of a store which appointed Nestlé as its category manager for coffee. Nestlé has demanded just 60% of the shelf space for its jars, even though the firm's Nescafé brands account for 86% of sales. This is because they reasoned that a more varied category with a breadth of products from different manufacturers would be more attractive to the customer, and therefore, more likely to grow. Whether smaller manufacturers feel any happier with Nestlé's explanation is another matter. *The Economist* concludes that 'category management is as likely to be a source of friction as of trust'.

Source: The Economist, 17 May 1997, Vol. 343, Issue 8017, 75.

However, the ECR concept can be successful only if there is a certain basis of trust between the manufacturer and the sales partner. Often conflicts arise in company practice that can endanger the objectives, as outlined in Table 7-2.

As far as logistical processes are concerned, the concept of **just-in-time** (see Ansari and Modarress 1990; Dong *et al.* 2001; Fullerton and McWatters 2001; Giunipero *et al.* 2005) is relevant to cooperation with key accounts. With this concept, the sales logistics activities of the company are coordinated with the key account's production logistics, so that the key account receives the manufacturer's products on an as-needed basis (just in time). This allows the key account to significantly reduce its stock-keeping and warehousing costs.

Table 7-2 Overview of the ECR concept

Field of cooperation	Main activities	Primary objectives
Efficient reordering process	■ Direct (electronic) transmission of sales data from wholesalers and retailers (sales partners) to the manufacturer ■ Delivery triggered by manufacturer without explicit order from sales partners ■ Delivery to sales partners in line with demand	■ Reduce stock-keeping/ warehousing costs ■ Avoid non-availability of product on the part of sales partners
Efficient product range design (category management)	■ Optimization of shelf placement/ shelf impact of products/brands (several manufacturers) within one category ■ Individualization of the product range design for individual stores ■ Reduction of the brands marketed within one category	■ Increase the frequency of the turnover of merchandise and thus the profit per unit of area for sales partners ■ Promote combined customer purchases within one category
Efficient sales promotion	■ Coordination of joint sales promotion activities ■ Customization of sales promotion activities for individual stores ■ Reduction in the number of sales promotion activities	■ Prevent quantity fluctuations (stockpiling on the part of customers) and price fluctuations caused by sales promotion activities ■ Increase the effectiveness and efficiency of sales promotion activities
Efficient new product development/launch	■ Close cooperation during the development of new products ■ Joint product tests ■ Cooperative market entry	■ Reduce the flop rate of new products and the costs associated with new product failure

Another important field of cooperation between manufacturers and sales partners is **vertical marketing**. Here, the manufacturers and sales partners jointly plan and sometimes also perform marketing activities.

Figure 7-8 shows the structure of the vertical marketing concept very much involving standard marketing activities on the part of manufacturers and sales partners. Manufacturers can undertake both **push and pull activities**. Push activities are carried out by manufacturers within the scope of trade marketing. This means providing incentives for sales partners to place the manufacturer's products on their shelves and promote them so that they 'push' them into the market. In contrast, 'pull activities' are marketing measures oriented towards the end customer that are initiated by manufacturers. Pull activities stimulate demand for the products and, in this way, customers are 'pulled' into the market. In vertical marketing a combination of push and pull methods is usually used.

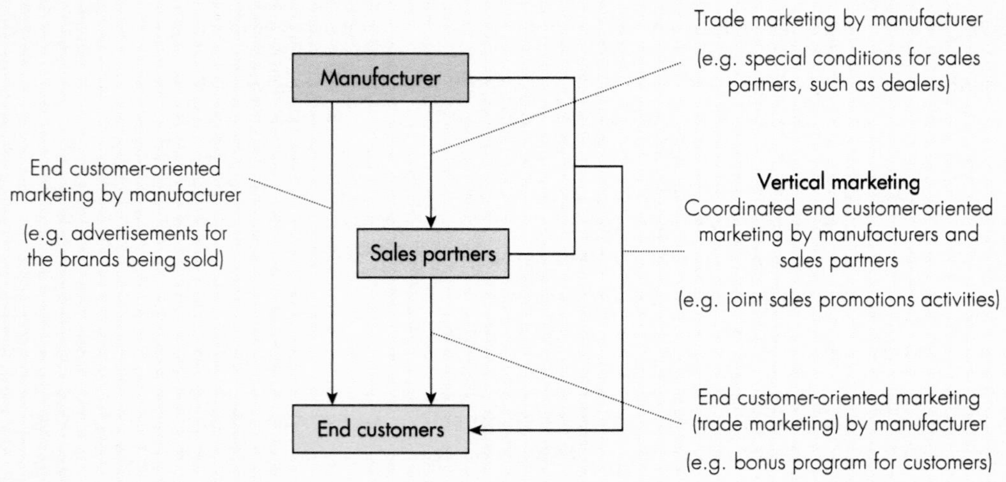

Figure 7-8 Structure of vertical marketing

7.3.2 Conflict Management

In practice, conflicts between a company and its sales partners and key accounts, and the need to manage these conflicts, pose a major challenge in the area of sales decisions. Such conflicts have also been the subject of numerous studies (see e.g. Bradford *et al.* 2004; Dant and Schul 1992; Katsikeas 1992; Weitz and Bradford 1999). For an example of channel conflict, see Focus on Marketing 7-6.

Focus on Marketing 7-6 Aspects of power distribution between suppliers and their sales partners

When big is big enough – the power of major retailers in the USA

The major retailers, known as 'big box stores' because their outlets often occupy most of a city block, include Wal-Mart, Target and Costco. According to industry officials, these chains command so much market share that they can exert near-dictatorial power over producers.

Ernie Rosenberg, president of the US Soap and Detergent Association, says that Wal-Mart alone can account for more than 20% of a given company's national sales, in particular product lines such as laundry detergents. These low-cost retailers have gained increasing market share over the past five years, expanding their power even more.

'If a producer wants to raise the prices of its brand, and Wal-Mart says "no", there's not much the producer can do about it,' Rosenberg adds. If the manufacturer insists on a price increase, Wal-Mart or Target can unilaterally reduce or even eliminate the brand's shelf space.

'Producers have to maintain market share, shelf space and brand identity,' Rosenberg notes. 'As a producer, you don't want consumer traffic flowing into these major retailers where there are shelves after shelves of detergent – and your product isn't there.'

Although the major retailers have relented somewhat of late and have accepted some price hikes, he said, their power over producers has begun to manifest itself in a new direction. 'Lately,' says

Focus on Marketing 7-6 (Continued)

Rosenberg, 'these retailers are trying to have an impact on products themselves.' One major retailer has demanded that a producer reformulate a well-known premium detergent to the retailer's specifications.

That development, adds Rosenberg, is not a question of better or worse. 'But when you start fooling with product formulations, and a retailer says it wants a bargain version of a well-established premium line, producers cannot help but worry about their brand identity.'

Source: Kamalick, J. (2006) Big stores monopoly of power, *ICIS Chemical Business*, 1, 33, 16–17.

In general, there are two different types of conflict that may occur in sales systems: vertical conflicts and horizontal ones (also see Palamountain 1969; Kotler and Keller 2006). **Vertical conflicts** occur between the company and its sales partners and key accounts. We will focus primarily on this form of conflict. Potential areas of conflict between a company and its sales partners are shown in Figure 7-9. It appears that, in particular, pricing and the margins of sales partners give rise to conflicts.

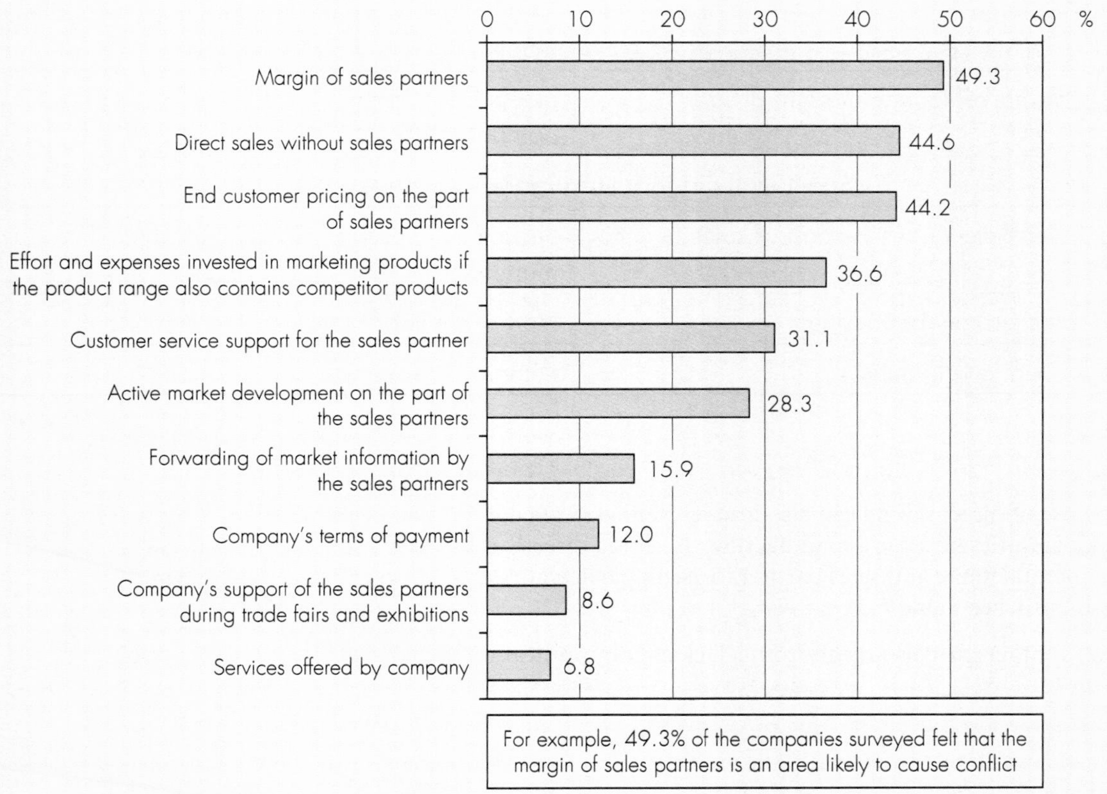

Figure 7-9 Areas of conflict between companies in the industrial goods sector and their sales partners (according to Homburg and Schneider 2000, p. 20)

Table 7-3 Typical conflicts of interest between manufacturers and sales partners (adapted from Winkelmann 2005a, p. 378)

Manufacturer's interests	⇔	Sales partner's interests
Inclusion of all new products in product range of sales partners	⇔	Preference for inclusion of top-selling products
Dominance of manufacturer's brand image	⇔	Dominance of trademark image
Distribution of entire product range	⇔	Product range oriented towards specific customer segment(s) targeted by sales partner
Stable quantity of sales	⇔	Flexibility of order quantity
Production capacity aligned with order volumes	⇔	Shelf-replenishing order volumes
Minimum order quantity	⇔	Flexible reordering options
Pricing problems that negatively affect the trade margin	⇔	Pricing problems that negatively affect the purchase price
Avoidance of returned goods	⇔	Right to return goods
Assumption of sales risks by the sales partner	⇔	Assumption of sales risks by the manufacturer
Prominent shelf placement for company's own products	⇔	Merchandise placement in line with requirements of product portfolio
Joint design of market launch at point of sale	⇔	Independent (own) market launch design at point of sale
Specifically in industrial goods markets		
High service competence on the part of sales partners	⇔	Service responsibility on the part of the manufacturer
Respect of sales territory boundaries	⇔	Non-existence of sales territory boundaries
Joint strategic market planning	⇔	Planning autonomy

A company's use of direct selling can also lead to conflict. Such conflict can occur when sales partners lose sales opportunities because a manufacturer is selling directly into the market. Vertical conflicts between the manufacturer and sales partners arise in particular from divergent interests (for typical conflicts of interest, see Table 7-3).

Furthermore, conflicts can also result from a lack of communication between the manufacturer and its sales partners.

Horizontal conflicts refer to conflicts between sales partners on the same sales tier. For example, two franchisees can come into conflict with one another if one franchisee 'violates' the other's territory, does not comply with specified pricing guidelines or causes quality problems that can be detrimental to the image of the franchise.

Conflict management strategies can generally be categorized by comparing the company's own interests and the interests of the sales partner/key account (see Figure 7-10). Cooperative forms of conflict management include joint problem solving and compromising. In both cases, a balanced

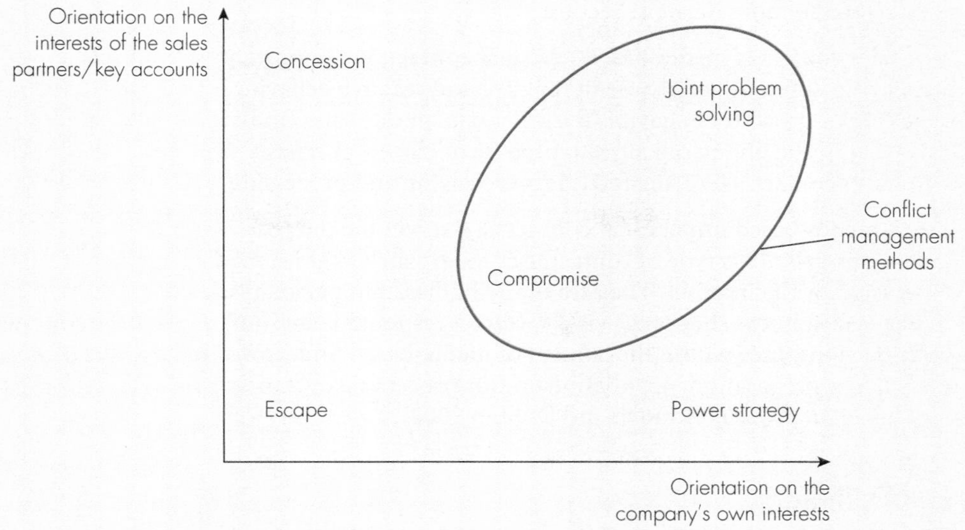

Figure 7-10 Strategies for resolving conflicts with sales partners and key accounts (adapted from Kollmannsperger 2000)

consideration both of the company's interests and the interests of the sales partner or key account takes place (see Figure 7-10). One-sided forms of conflict resolution include concession and the power strategy approach. These forms of dealing with conflict, however, address the conflict in the business relationship on only a rather superficial level; the actual conflict itself might continue to exist below the surface. Therefore, these forms do not represent true conflict management strategies. Escape is then the only way out of a cooperation when the interests of neither party are pursued.

7.4 The Design of Selling Activities

The design of selling activities is a key decision-making area in sales. In particular, this decision-making area is concerned with the mode of customer contact (for an in-depth discussion, see Section 7.4.1). Personal selling is the most important type of customer contact and will be discussed in detail in Section 7.4.2.

7.4.1 Mode of Customer Contact

There are three basic types of customer contact:

1 direct personal contact

2 media-based personal contact

3 media-based impersonal contact.

Direct contact via personal selling can be a powerful way to acquire customers and obtain orders from them. Certainly, it is important to appeal to the decision maker so that the buying decision is made in favor of the company's products. Sales conversations in department stores are an example of direct contact in personal selling (see Chapter 11). In the industrial goods sector, direct contact via personal selling is especially crucial. Direct personal contact is the basis of personal selling, which will be discussed in more detail in Section 7.4.2.

Another type of sales contact is **media-based personal contact**. An important form of this is telephone contact. We differentiate between proactive and reactive behavior on the part of the company. In the case of proactive behavior, the seller uses phone sales (individual sales employees or call centers) – that is, the phone call aims to prepare or close a purchase. With reactive behavior, the customer initiates contact. Here, the focus is on receiving and processing customer orders.

In a sales context, **media-based impersonal contact** also serves the purpose of initiating or establishing sales contracts. This type of contact uses media such as print media (e.g. mailings or catalogs), television or the internet. The area of media-based impersonal selling includes **teleshopping** (also called home shopping) via TV (direct response television). **Electronic commerce** also carries certain significance within the context of media-based impersonal selling. Electronic commerce refers to the preparation, negotiation and/or processing of transactions mainly using the internet (see Straub *et al.* 2002; Torkzadeh and Dhillon 2002).

7.4.2 Personal Selling

In many businesses, **personal selling** is the key to market success. This applies in particular to the marketing of complex products (i.e. products requiring explanation) – for example, in the business-to-business segment. Personal selling is also important when marketing more complex products to end customers (e.g. financial services products, automobiles, real estate).

In the case of personal selling, the **sales situation** is characterized by the following factors (see Dalrymple *et al.* 2004):

- the seller and customer have direct visual contact
- due to the personal contact, the seller can adjust particularly well to the customer as a discussion partner and to the customer's particular situation
- the seller can immediately detect and assess the customer's verbal and non-verbal responses
- the seller can repeat the sales arguments several times, if necessary.

In principle, we can distinguish between proactive and reactive personal selling. **Proactive personal selling** is initiated by the seller or company, as is the case when, say, a sales employee of a bank offers a consultation to a customer of the bank. **Reactive personal selling** is initiated by the customer – for example, when a bank customer seeks advice. In the retail segment, reactive personal selling is the usual approach, typically triggered by a customer entering a store.

The key objective of personal selling is **closing a sale**. Preliminary goals can include establishing initial contact with potential customers and informing them about the advantages of a product or a service during a personal sales conversation. The purpose is to achieve a positive assessment of the offer and to arouse purchase interest.

In line with these objectives, the selling process can be broken down into a sequence of individual phases that, in company practice, are described by selling process formulas. One example is the **AIDA formula** (Attention, Interest, Desire, Action). This defines the phases of drawing attention to an offer, establishing interest by providing relevant information, creating a desire to purchase, and finally leading up to the closing of the sale (action on the part of the customer).

In the following, we will differentiate between **four main phases of personal selling**:

1. preparatory phase
2. starting phase of sales conversation

3 core phase

4 ending phase of sales conversation.

Not every sales conversation has a **preparatory phase**. In a retail store, for example, a sales employee is directly addressed by a customer and does not really have the opportunity to prepare for the conversation. However, a meeting that is arranged in advance (which is frequently the case in the corporate customer segment and, for instance, with regard to meetings between a bank's investment consultants and its customers) usually involves a preparatory phase. Sales employees should use this phase to familiarize themselves with the following information (see Kurtz *et al.* 1999):

- participants in the discussion (e.g. objectives, expectations, competencies and influence on purchase decision)
- company's situation from the customer's perspective (e.g. customer satisfaction, schedule for pending deliveries, unresolved customer complaints)
- customer purchase history (e.g. frequency of purchases, compliance with contractual regulations and agreements, outstanding customer accounts)
- customer potential (e.g. untapped sales potential with respect to the customer, customer's own new products, relationship of customer to competitors, business development and economic situation of the customer).

Furthermore, sales employees should consider their own objectives regarding the conversation, which can have a different focus depending on the purpose of the meeting (see Table 7-4 for the typical objectives and purposes of such sales conversations).

The actual sales conversation begins with the **starting phase** of the conversation. During this phase, the sales employee aims to create an initial impression that conveys an image that is as favorable as possible. It has to be mentioned that, in general, the first contact has a significant impact on sales success, since it is in this stage that first impressions and expectations are established (see Evans 2000). Moreover, the sales employee should form a clear picture of the conversation situation (conversation atmosphere, characteristic traits of the conversation partners, and his/her own situation in the conversation such as, for example, position of power vis-à-vis the conversation partner).

The **core phase** of a sales conversation depends very strongly on the type of conversation. For example, the core phase in a customer care context has to be handled considerably differently from the core phase of a negotiation.

During negotiations, **tactical negotiation considerations** play an important part with regard to how the core phase is structured. Two important negotiation principles are:

1 the commonality principle (conversation centers on common interests such as, say, achieving high customer benefits, and avoiding a focus on areas of clashing interests, e.g. prices and conditions; see Sebenius 2001; Lewicki *et al.* 1999)

2 the quid pro quo principle (concessions on the part of the sales employee are made only in return for corresponding concessions on the part of the customer).

Selling techniques play a role in all sales conversations where acquisition is the main objective (e.g. presentations/initial contact, contract awarding meetings, negotiations; see Table 7-4). Selling techniques include:

- presentation techniques
- rhetorical methods
- closing techniques.

Table 7-4 Main conversation objectives of various types of sales conversation

Reason for sales conversation	Main conversation objectives
Presentation/initial contact	■ Establish trust ■ Communicate product offer and arouse customer interest ■ Obtain general customer information ■ Schedule follow-up visit
Contract awarding meeting	■ Identify customer requirements and central contract awarding criteria ■ Positive presentation of company's own offer ■ Well-founded explanation of company's own price level ■ Identify and eliminate problems that conflict with the contract being awarded to the company
Negotiations	■ Close the sale ■ Ensure a favorable price level ■ Realize additional purchases from the customer
General discussion	■ Identify and agree on measures for optimizing the business relationship ■ Obtain information from the customer about future plans
Order processing/ project discussion	■ Coordinate open issues related to the processing of a specific order ■ Eliminate coordination problems related to the processing of a specific order
Complaint discussion	■ Gain full understanding of the cause(s) for complaint ■ Determine and communicate compensation measures for 'making amends' ■ Restore customer satisfaction
Conversation in a customer care context	■ Establish relationships on a personal level ■ Further develop basis of trust ■ Obtain background information

Benefit selling is an important **presentation technique** (for further details, see Futrell 2001). Benefit selling tries to relate the features of the presented product to important customer benefits. During the process, the customer is first introduced to and familiarized with the product features. These features are then taken as the basis for deriving product advantages and the associated customer benefits. Benefit selling is the opposite of a presentation technique that primarily focuses more on product features and less on the transfer of these features to customer benefits. Such techniques are called **feature selling**, or **character selling**. The examples in Table 7-5 illustrate the fundamental difference between the two presentation techniques.

Rhetorical methods represent a second key category of selling techniques (for more information, see e.g. DelVecchio *et al.* 2002; Dubinsky 1980; Dwyer *et al.* 2000). The specific use of questions is an important rhetorical method. In company practice, sales departments sometimes cite the slogan 'the asker steers the conversation'. Depending on the sales conversation situation, different types of questions can be useful – for example:

Table 7-5 Comparison of character selling and benefit selling (see Homburg *et al.* 2005, p. 240)

Feature selling	Benefit selling
'This printer has an output of up to ten pages per minute.'	'This printer saves you a lot of time. It prints out your presentations almost twice as fast as your old printer.'
'This desk chair features an ergonomic design.'	'This desk chair is very comfortable. No more backache in the evening.'
'ABS and side airbags are standard features of this automobile.'	'This car provides a high degree of safety for you and your family.'
'This machine has a capacity of 1,000 packaging cycles per hour.'	'This machine reduces your production times by 20%.'
'Our hotel rooms are equipped with fax machines and internet access connections.'	'Our hotel provides you with everything you need for conducting your business.'

- introductory questions lead to the main topic
- factual questions concern the main topic of the conversation
- motivational questions bridge phases when concentration fades
- tag questions let conversation partners corroborate the status of the conversation or negotiations
- direct questions immediately address critical issues
- open-ended questions let the conversation partner respond freely, possibly leading to the uncovering of previously overlooked aspects.

Closing techniques are particularly important during negotiations. They aim to actually realize a purchase that seems close at hand. Table 7-6 provides an overview of the most relevant closing techniques and illustrates them.

During the **ending phase** of the conversation, the key issues of the discussion, as well as further steps and tasks, are summarized. Also, the conversation should end in a pleasant atmosphere. As already mentioned, the focus of the conversation during this phase should shift back to the relationship level.

To a large extent, personal selling success depends on the **behavior of the seller**. A crucial success factor for sales employees lies in their ability to adjust their behavior to the customer during an interaction. This flexible approach is called **adaptive selling** (for detailed information on this concept, see Weitz *et al.* 1986; Spiro and Weitz 1990). Several studies have already demonstrated the relevance of adaptive selling as a success factor (see e.g. Boorom *et al.* 1998; Pettijohn *et al.* 2000).

In adaptive selling, **customer typologies** can be an important orientation aid. Identification of the special behavioral patterns on the part of the various customer types is very important so that the different types can be addressed personally. A typology that has reached a certain level of importance in adaptive selling distinguishes customers based on two dimensions of their personality: determination (striving for control and exercise of power) and emotionality (willingness to express emotions and enter into relationships) (for more information on these dimensions, see Marks 1985; Merril and Reid 1981). Sales employees should apply different approaches to the different types of customers resulting from these typologies (see Figure 7-11).

Table 7-6 Illustration of closing techniques (adapted from Weis 2005; Winkelmann 2005b)

Closing technique	Description	Exemplary formulations
Impending event technique	Addresses the limited validity period of an offer	■ 'This special offer ends today.'
Now-or-never technique	Addresses the limited availability of the product	■ 'We only have two more of these in stock.'
Alternative technique	Formulation of two positive alternatives in order to avoid a fundamental decision ('yes' or 'no')	■ 'Do you like this better in red or blue?' ■ 'Do you need this delivered this week or next week?'
Summary technique	Summary of the most important arguments with the key argument mentioned last	■ 'Let me summarize . . .' ■ 'If I have understood you right, it is essential to you that . . .'
Recommendation technique	Making objective recommendations	■ 'We recommend . . .' ■ 'Taking your situation into account, we recommend . . .'
Reference technique	Citing positive experiences and statements of other customers	■ '75% of our customers have already purchased our new product.' ■ '65% of the companies in the printing sector already deploy these machines.'
Partial decision technique	Attempt to reach a decision with regard to certain aspects or less important issues of the negotiation	■ 'Do you need the machine right at the start of the season?' ■ 'Surely you would like to go ahead and trade in your car now?'
Wrong decision technique	Attempt to 'force' the negotiation partner into a decision by deliberately offering an alternative that is probably not the preferred one	■ 'So, would you like to buy the XY offroad vehicle with the diesel engine?' ■ 'I assume you want the complete package, including PC, printer and monitor?'
Advantage technique	Emphasis on the advantages of a certain purchase	■ 'If you decide to buy now, we'll give it to you at the old price.'

Amiables avoid conflicts and value a good personal relationship with the seller. They are relatively sensitive and generally tend to shy away from risks, and should therefore be gently steered towards decisions. Power-selling strategies are thus effective only if the sales employee can guarantee that there are no risks associated with the purchase decision. The sales argumentation should address personal feelings and emotions.

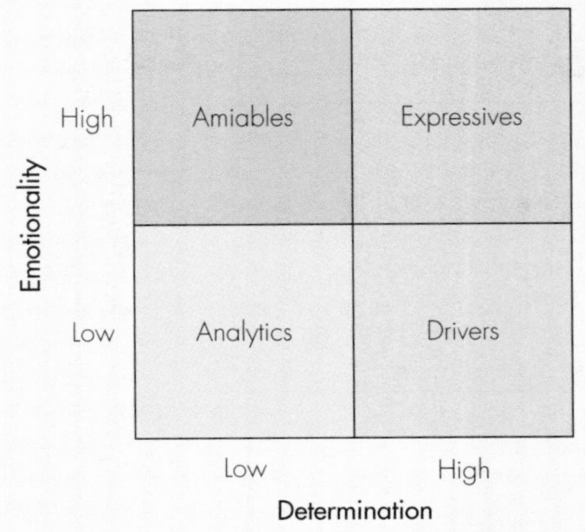

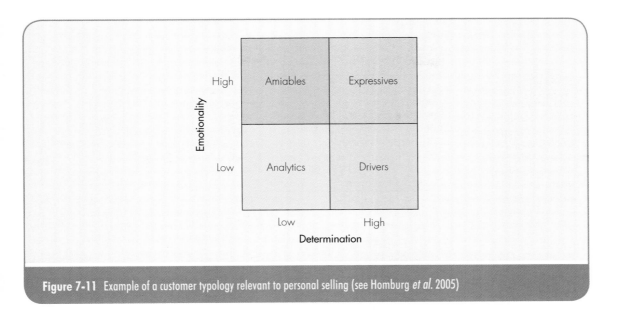

Figure 7-11 Example of a customer typology relevant to personal selling (see Homburg *et al.* 2005)

Expressives are friendly and prefer informal interactions. They also include status and image aspects in their product evaluation. Whether they like the sales employee or not plays a key role in their purchase decision. Expressives can best be addressed with creative sales presentations, since they tend to be bored by a mere list of product-related details. Citing the experiences of reference customers can also help in the selling process. With this personality type, 'gentle pressure' at the end of the sales conversation may prove successful in closing the sale.

Analytics focus on details and facts, and use a systematic problem-solving approach. They tend to act slowly, deliberately and with little aggression. This type can best be convinced with data and facts. Written offers that provide comprehensive information help 'analytics' make decisions. The sales employee should primarily center arguments on quality, product reliability and price–performance ratio. Comparing the company's own product to competitor products can also be effective. Power-selling strategies should be avoided here as well, since 'analytics' need considerable time to make their purchase decisions.

Drivers are dominant in personality; they are ambitious, active and independent. They frequently take the initiative and do not shy away from confrontation. As a rule, they make quick decisions. They primarily evaluate offers based on the benefits of the product or service. It is therefore advisable to focus arguments on the actual product benefits. Sales employees should keep their arguments clear, factual and concise, and should stick to formal interaction. This customer type should not be put under pressure, either.

7.5 Sales Logistics

7.5.1 Sales Logistics: Basic Information

Sales logistics (also called marketing logistics) include all activities related to the design, management and monitoring of warehouse and transport processes concerning the delivery of end products to customers (see Mollenkopf *et al.* 2000). Sales logistics also include decisions regarding the type, design and structure of logistics facilities and systems (e.g. computer systems, vehicle fleets,

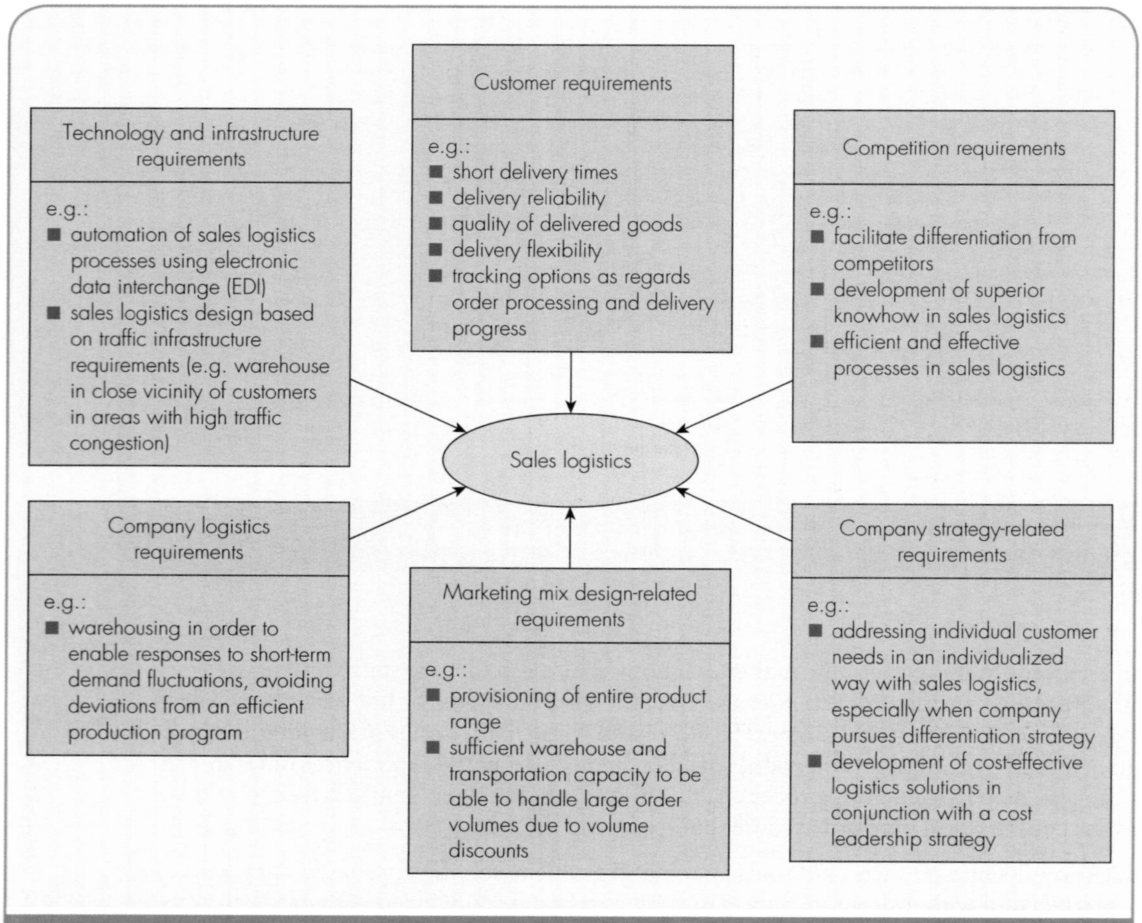

Figure 7-12 Sales logistics requirements

warehouses) needed to fulfill the required tasks. Sales logistics aim to supply the customer with the required quantity of the desired product at the right time and right place, as cost-effectively as possible.

The design and structure of the sales logistics system poses numerous challenges in company practice. Figure 7-12 provides an overview of the key requirements related to sales logistics.

In connection with logistics requirements, the **integration of sales logistics activities within the supply chain** has to be mentioned (for more on the concept of supply chain management, see Bowersox *et al.* 1999; Cooper *et al.* 1997). This refers especially to the comprehensive coordination of sales logistics activities with both the procurement and production logistics of the company, as well as logistics requirements on the part of sales partners and customers. The goal of such coordination is to avoid excess stock and prevent long throughput times, rising costs and sales losses. The **bullwhip, or whipsaw, effect** should be mentioned in this context (see, e.g., Lee *et al.* 1997 for further details). This effect refers to the phenomenon that the variance in demand is magnified along the stages of the supply chain (from customers to various sales partner stages to the company and suppliers). Since the stakeholders are only aware of the demand situation of their direct downstream follower, an increasing distance from the end customer poses the risk of underestimating customer demand and thus making the wrong decisions. For example, an increased order volume on the part of retailers due to special offers or anticipated supply bottlenecks might lead a manufacturer to misinterpret this as an increase in demand on the part of end customers, and thus result in excessive and costly overproduction (excess stock).

Key **decision-making areas of sales logistics** include:

- decisions related to **warehouse locations** for finished goods (see Section 7.5.2)
- decisions related to warehousing, consignment, packing and packaging (see Section 7.5.3)
- decisions related to transportation (see Section 7.5.4).

7.5.2 Decisions Related to Warehouse Locations for Finished Goods

An essential decision-making area in sales logistics concerns the geographical location of finished goods warehouses. These are the warehouses where the products manufactured by the company are stored. Important decisions are:

- the vertical sales and distribution structure (number of different warehouse levels)
- the horizontal sales and distribution structure (number of warehouses on each level, their location and assigned sales territories).

With respect to the **vertical sales and distribution structure**, we distinguish four warehouse levels: at the first level, the products a company manufactures can be stored in **factory warehouses** located in the vicinity of the respective production site (in general, only short-term storage). On the next level, products from the company's various factory warehouses can be concentrated in **central warehouses**, which can then supply downstream warehouses or customers. On the next level, **regional warehouses** can be established in the different sales territories, for storage of the products that are in demand in a given sales region. Finally, customers in the various sales districts are supplied direct via decentralized **outbound warehouses**.

Depending on how many of these warehouse levels are combined, the vertical sales and distribution structure can have one, two, three or four tiers (see Figure 7-13). Assuming that, as a rule, central warehouses exist, the vertical sales and distribution structure becomes increasingly decentralized with each additional warehouse level. The decision concerning the degree of centralization of the vertical sales and distribution structure depends on factors related to the customers, to the company itself and to the competition.

When designing the **horizontal sales and distribution structure**, the following questions need to be addressed:

- How many distribution warehouses should be established at each warehouse level (factory warehouses, central warehouses, regional warehouses, outbound warehouses)?
- At which locations should these warehouses be established?
- Which customers should be supplied by which warehouse?

As is the case when deciding on the vertical sales and distribution structure, the optimal answers to these questions depend on several criteria, including, for example:

- the number and geographical distribution of the production sites
- the geographical distribution of customers
- the order volumes and order patterns on the part of customers
- warehousing costs
- the cost of transportation between production sites, warehouses and customers.

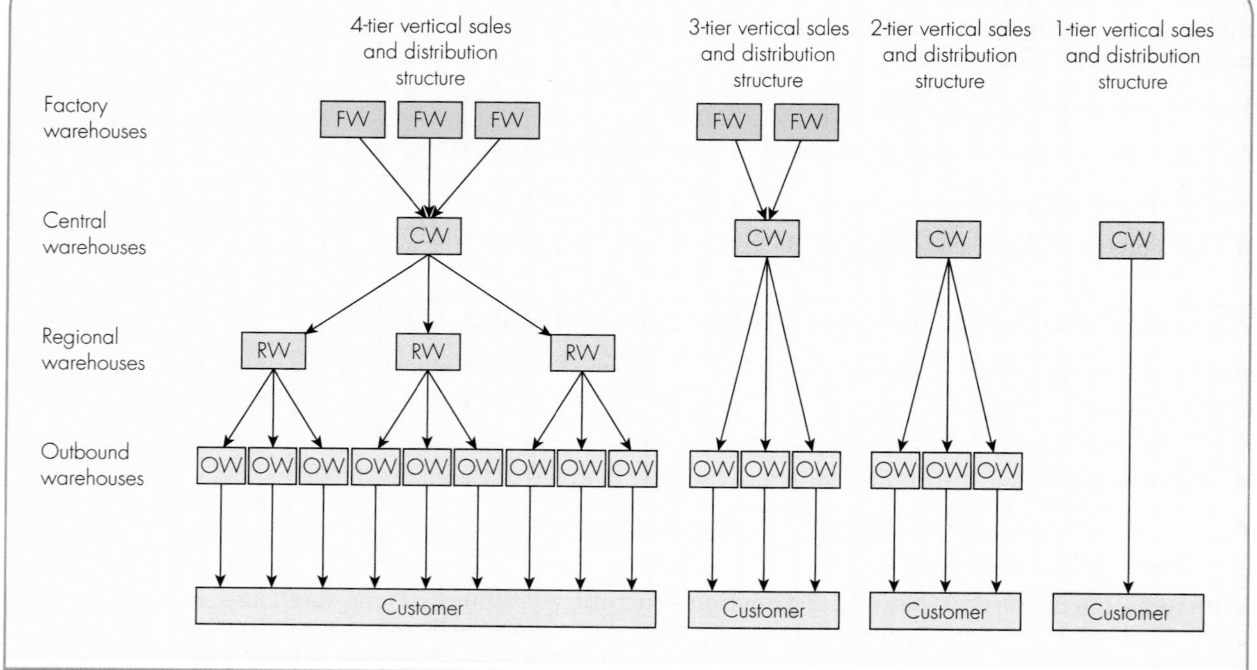

Figure 7-13 Alternative vertical sales and distribution structures (adapted from Schulte 2005, p. 279)

Figure 7-14 illustrates the factors related to the centralization of vertical sales and distribution structures.

7.5.3 Decisions Related to Warehousing, Consignment, Packing and Packaging

When companies consider **warehousing**, the **decision regarding the quantity of stock** of a product to be held takes center stage. In particular, the area of sales logistics is concerned with outbound warehouse stock-keeping. Therefore, the question of where the company should request which quantities (e.g. from a regional or central warehouse; see Section 7.5.1) becomes important. When making this decision the company has to ensure that supply is always guaranteed (high supply capability) and that warehousing costs are kept low. The degree of supply capability and warehousing costs are associated with conflicting goals: as a rule, high supply capability usually goes hand in hand with high warehousing expenditure.

Stock quantities are determined based on the **inventory policy**, which provides guidelines regarding when to request which quantities (for further information see Gupta 1994; Harris 1915; Lambert and Stock 1993). With respect to the order point ('when'), there are two main options (see Figure 7-15):

1. an order is initiated if the stock quantity has diminished to a value s or lower
2. orders are initiated at regular intervals of period t.

With regard to the order quantity ('how much'), the following procedures may be distinguished:

- the order quantity for each order is q units
- the order quantity is calculated for a stock quantity of S after receipt of the goods.

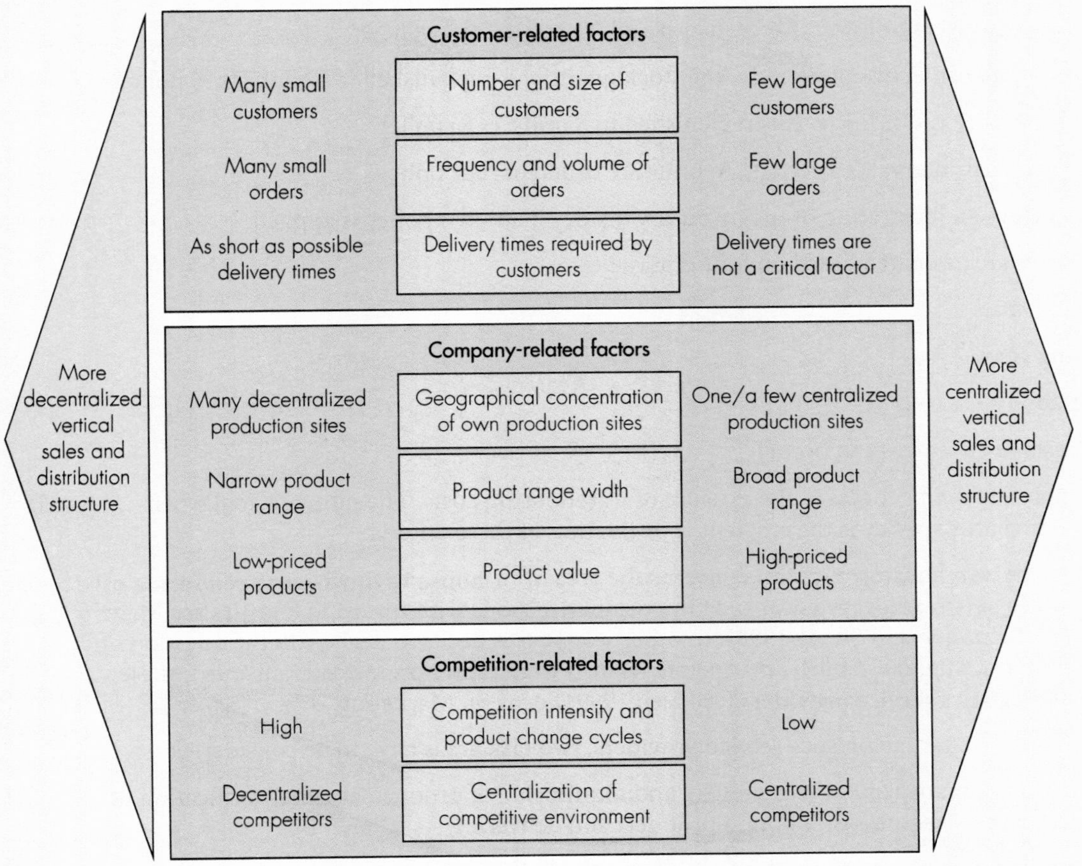

Figure 7-14 Factors influencing the decision to centralize the vertical sales and distribution structure

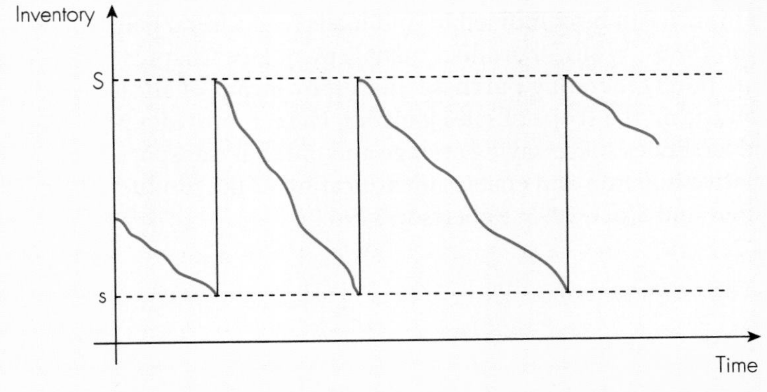

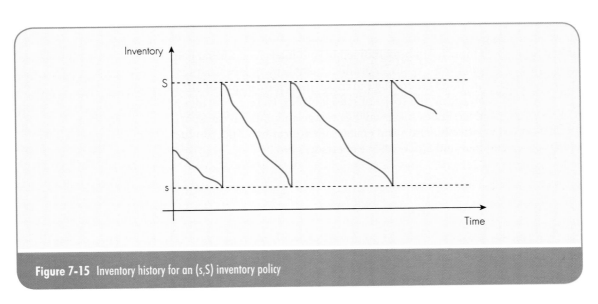

Figure 7-15 Inventory history for an (s,S) inventory policy

Combining these options results in four **inventory policy types:**

1 If the stock quantity is s or lower, fixed quantity q is ordered: (s,q) policy.

2 At constant regular intervals of period t, the stock quantity is replenished to S units: (t,S) policy.

3 If the stock quantity is s or lower, it is replenished to S units: (s,S) policy.

4 At constant regular intervals of period t, q units are ordered: (t,q) policy.

Figure 7-15 provides an illustration of the inventory history if an (s,S) policy is applied.

Inventory policies are evaluated based on four criteria:

1 procurement costs

2 warehousing costs

3 supply capability

4 shortage costs (if shortages can occur).

In general, supply capability comes at the expense of warehousing costs. The ultimate goal when formulating an inventory policy is the efficient coordination of these criteria.

Another important warehousing decision concerns the area of **in-house vs third-party rendering of warehousing services** (for an overview of such important decisions with regard to logistics see Maltz and Ellram 1997; Razzaque and Sheng 1998). In other words, this decision deals with the question of whether the company should establish and operate its own warehouses or, instead, outsource these tasks to external **logistics service providers** (see Lieb 1999; Focus on Marketing 7-7).

With respect to using external logistics service providers, two task areas have to be considered:

1 warehouse process management (e.g. control and monitoring of product labeling, verification of completeness and correctness of inbound products and deliveries)

2 inventory management (decision making with regard to goods to be stored, stock quantities, as well as order quantities and order points for stock replenishment).

In general, outsourcing warehouse process management tasks to external service providers is relatively unproblematic. When transferring inventory management tasks, the service provider should be given incentives to maintain a low inventory level or decrease it, and thus maintain or reduce costs for the commissioning company.

Within the scope of **packaging and packing**, the products are bundled in master cartons (e.g. products on a pallet), which in turn can be combined in unit loads (e.g. several pallets in a container) (see Bowersox *et al.* 1986). While in product management (see Chapter 5), packaging has an acquisition-related function (generating purchase interest by means of attractive packaging), it assumes a physical function within the scope of sales logistics. Here, it provides protection against dirt and damage, and facilitates space-saving storage and optimal transportation. Moreover, the packaging has an informative function and enables identification of the products – for example, by means of labels (see Lambert and Stock 1993; Robertson 1990).

Focus on Marketing 7-7 Example of outsourcing logistics

Outsourcing at Hard Rock Cafe

Collectors of Hard Rock Cafe paraphernalia may have better luck finding souvenirs in stock when they visit the music-themed restaurant chain's North American locations. Hard Rock Cafe International Inc. is outsourcing logistics for its signature souvenirs and apparel in an effort to improve service levels to its stores and cut costs.

The company has selected USCO Logistics, a subsidiary of Kuehne & Nagel, to take over distribution and replenishment of collectible and fashion merchandise for its cafes, hotels, and casinos in North America.

Naugatuck, Conn.-based USCO will manage distribution of items representing 85,000 stock-keeping units to more than 47 Hard Rock cafes, hotels, and casinos from its multi-customer distribution centers.

Previously, Hard Rock leased facilities at several locations in the U.S. and Canada, using third-party carriers to make weekly deliveries to its venues. According to Paladino [director of planning, distribution, and logistics at Hard Rock Cafe], the company wanted to reduce its transportation costs and in-transit times. The existing facilities also used very little automated material-handling equipment, although bar code tracking was in place.

'Upgrading those facilities would have involved a high cost, and the company was unwilling to make that sort of capital investment,' says Paladino.

Projected benefits from the outsourcing initiative include reducing North American warehouse space by 44%; reducing operating costs by 20%; improving service levels by 22%.

Source: Albright, B. (2004) Hard Rock Cafe turns to outsourced logistics, *Frontline Solutions*.

7.5.4 Decisions Related to Transportation

Transportation decisions address the following aspects:

- suitable means of transport
- in-house vs third-party transportation
- the appropriate tools for planning, managing and organizing transportation.

Suitable **means of transportation** include transport by road, rail, air and water. Frequently, different means of transportation are combined in transport chains in order to benefit from their respective advantages. A very common combination is road and rail, with trucks and freight trains taking turns to transport the containers. In the case of roll-on/roll-off transport, traffic, land and water transportation are combined. In addition to cost aspects, transportation time, frequency, quality and flexibility have to be taken into consideration when trying to identify suitable means of transportation.

Similar to warehousing decisions (see Section 7.5.3) transport decisions also have to be made with regard to the question of whether the task should be performed by the company itself or outsourced to logistics service providers. Many companies frequently apply an in-house approach to, for instance, company-internal transport (for example, between procurement warehouses and production sites). Within the scope of production logistics (**in-house transportation operations**) company-external transportation (e.g. from outbound warehouses to customers) is often outsourced to external logistics service providers (**third-party transportation**) (see Langley *et al.* 2004; Van Laarhoven *et al.* 2000). This is primarily due to the already existing infrastructure provided by logistics service providers.

Summary

In this chapter, we discussed the central decision-making areas pertaining to sales decisions. We introduced the important internal and external sales entities of the company, and discussed the main activities of each entity, as well as general conditions for their use. These entities can be combined to form sales channels. A basic decision here is the selection of direct or indirect sales. We identified transaction costs as a main driver of this decision. The inclusion of sales partners should, accordingly, reduce transaction costs and thus enhance the efficiency of the sales system.

Another important decision relates to the depth (number of sales tiers) and width (single-channel vs multi-channel) of the sales system. A central issue concerning multi-channel systems is the management of channel conflicts. Within the sales system, the relationship with top sales partners and key accounts is of high importance to sales decisions. Here, sales decisions include the degree and areas of cooperation, the management of power, conflict management and the design of selling activities. The latter issue includes the basic decision on the mode of customer contact. Here, personal selling is a key issue. We identified its main phases and introduced the main selling techniques.

To deliver products to customers, decisions have to be made concerning sales logistics. We introduced the main requirements for sales logistics and subsequently discussed the main decision areas, notably the structure and design of warehousing and transportation.

Case Study: Conflict Management with Sales Partners at HP

Hewlett-Packard President and CEO Mark Hurd last week in his first public message to partners made a clear distinction between those that sell a broad HP solution demonstrating a high attach rate and those that go to market in a spotty manner with HP.

'What we don't like are the partners that lead with the HP brand and then hollow out the HP product and replace it with other content,' said Hurd. 'That is not what we call a true partnership. So you are going to see us investing more energy in those partners that really line up behind HP and with HP, and within that respect, we are going to be highly energized.'

Clearly, Hurd's comments are a big win for the strong and loyal stable of HP partners who have been prospering through a PartnerOne program already ripe with incentives for partners that commit more sales time, energy and resources to HP. The big question now is, just how many partners HP will go broad and deep with as the vendor aligns those partners with HP's direct-sales force in both the enterprise and SMB segments?

Hurd says cutting partners is not the aim of the new channel drumbeat. 'Our real objective isn't to cut partners,' he said. 'That is not how we go at it. It is to really focus on the strategy by partner

Case Study (Continued)

and to make sure we have the right alignment of what the partner is doing and what HP is doing so that we maximize the HP content as we go to market. If we could get that right with every partner, we'd frankly keep the same number of partners.'

That said, the first sign of just how deep HP will go with this effort is a new initiative to improve the integration of valuable, value-oriented partners with the Technology Solutions Group's Value Sales Organization. That move, effective Nov. 1, will affect fewer than 100 partners in the United States. So how does this tightly focused strategy play out for the thousands of HP VARs in the SMB market? And when does the HP direct-sales force lead the charge vs the channel? Will there be new compensation models and rules of engagement?

Right now, partners feel plenty of angst and conflict in the sales trenches each and every day. Hurd has made his first channel stand. Now the channel awaits his next move. That action could determine the fate of thousands of solution providers that have built healthy businesses over the years partnering with HP.

Source: Burke, S. (2005) Hurd's first move, *Computer Reseller News*, p. 92

Discussion Questions

1. Focusing on the design and structure of HP's sales system, describe it in a few words, paying particular attention to the related complexity of its sales channels. What are potential benefits of HP's sales system, both for HP and its partners?
2. What are the main areas of conflict between HP and its sales partners? What are the main goals of HP in deploying sales partners? What are the specific interests of the sales partners?
3. How can the most valuable sales partners for HP be characterized? Which specific criteria can be used by HP to identify the sales partners 'that really line up behind HP and with HP'?
4. How can HP align the sales partners to deliver high benefits for HP? Which incentives should HP offer the sales partners to do so? What are potential areas of cooperation to enhance both HP's and the sales partners' benefits?
5. How can the direct salesforce and the sales partners be interlocked to avoid channel conflicts? Should HP avoid channel conflict for all sales partners? Which strategy for solving current conflicts with HP's partners would you suggest?

Key Terms

Adaptive selling *219*
Administrative back office *198*
Affiliated sales entities *198*
AIDA formula *216*
Behavior of the seller *219*
Benefit selling *218*
Bullwhip, or whipsaw, effect *222*
Call center *198*
Category management *209*
Central warehouses *223*
Channel conflicts *206*
Character selling *218*
Closing a sale *216*
Closing techniques *219*
Conflict management strategies *214*
Cooperation in sales systems *208*
Core phase *217*
Customer service *198*
Customer typologies *219*
Decision regarding the quantity of stock *224*
Decision-making areas of sales logistics *223*
Defining the target customer groups and tasks of the various sales channels *206*
Depth of sales channel *204*
Design and structuring of relationships with sales partners and key accounts *196*
Design of sales activities *196*
Design of the sales system *196*
Direct contact via personal selling *215*
Direct sales *201*
Distribution *196*
E-commerce department *198*
Efficiency considerations *201*
Efficient consumer response (ECR) *209*
Electronic commerce *216*
Ending phase *219*
Exclusive selling method *205*
Facilitator *199*
Factory warehouses *223*
Feature selling *218*
Field salesforce *198*
Fields of cooperation *208*
Four main phases of personal selling *216*
Franchise system partners *199*
Horizontal conflicts *214*
Horizontal sales and distribution structure *223*
Hybrid sales system *203*
Indirect sales *201*
In-house transportation operations *227*
In-house vs third-party rendering of warehousing services *226*
Integration of sales logistics activities within the supply chain *222*
Intensive selling *205*
Intermediaries *201*
Internal sales entity *198*
Inventory policy *224*
Inventory policy types *226*
Just-in-time *210*
Key accounts *208*
Level of customization and complexity of the product *202*
Logistics service providers *226*
Long tail economy *202*
Means of transportation *227*
Media-based impersonal contact *216*
Media-based personal contact *216*
Monetary value of the product *202*
Multichannel system *206*
Number of customers/concentration of demand *202*
Objectives of a cooperation *208*
Outbound warehouses *223*
Packaging and packing *226*
Personal selling *216*
Preparatory phase *217*
Presentation technique *218*
Proactive personal selling *216*
Push and pull activities *211*
Reactive personal selling *216*
Regional warehouses *223*
Retailers *201*
Rhetorical methods *218*

References

Albright, B. (2004) Hard Rock Cafe turns to outsourced logistics, *Frontline Solutions*, April.

Anderson, C. (2006) The long tail, http://www.thelongtail.com/about.html (26.03.2008).

Anderson, E. (1985) The salesperson as outside agent or employee: a transaction cost analysis, *Marketing Science*, 4, 2, 488–500.

Anderson, E. (1996) Transaction cost analysis, in: Groenewegen, J. (ed.) *Transaction Cost Economics and Beyond*. Norwell.

Anderson, E. and Coughlan, A.T. (2002) Channel management: structure, governance, and relationship management, in: Weitz, B. and Wensley, R. (eds) *Marketing Handbook*. London, 223–247.

Anderson, E. and Gatignon, H. (1986) Modes of foreign entry: a transaction cost analysis and propositions, *Journal of International Business Studies*, 17, 3, 1–26.

Anderson, J. and Narus, J. (1990) A model of distributor firm and manufacturer firm working partnerships, *Journal of Marketing*, 54, 1, 42–58.

Anderson, E. and Schmittlein, D.C. (1984) Integration of the sales force: an empirical investigation, *Rand Journal of Economics*, 15, 3, 385–395.

Ansari, A. and Modarress, B. (1990) *Just-in-Time Purchasing*. New York.

Boorom, M., Goolsby, J. and Ramsey, R. (1998) Relational communication traits and their effect on adaptiveness and sales performance, *Journal of the Academy of Marketing Science*, 26, 1, 16–30.

Bowersox, D., Closs, D. and Helferich, O. (1986) *Logistical Management* (3rd edn). New York.

Bowersox, D., Closs, D. and Stank, T. (1999) *21st Century Logistics: Making Supply Chain Integration a Reality*. Oak Brook.

Bradford, K.D., Stringfellow, A. and Weitz, B.A. (2004) Managing conflict to improve the effectiveness of retail networks, *Journal of Retailing*, 80, 3, 181–195.

Burke, S. (2005) Hurd's first move, *Computer Reseller News*, 1156, 92.

Business World (2004) Bosch Car Service program in 29 workshops nationwide, 24.

Cespedes, F. and Corey, R. (1990) Managing multiple channels, *Business Horizons*, 33, 4, 67–77.

Cooper, M., Lambert, D. and Pagh, J. (1997) Supply chain management: more than a new name for logistics, *International Journal of Logistics Management*, 9, 2, 1–19.

Corsten, D. and Kumar, N. (2005) Do suppliers benefit from collaborative relationships with large retailers? An empirical investigation of efficient consumer response adoption, *Journal of Marketing*, 69, 3, 80–94.

Coughlan, A.T., Anderson, E., Stern, L.W. and El-Ansary, A.I. (2001) *Marketing Channels* (6th edn). New Jersey.

Dalrymple, D.J., Cron, W.L. and DeCarlo, T.E. (2004) *Sales Management* (8th edn). Hoboken.

Dant, R.P. and Schul, P.L. (1992) Conflict resolution processes in contractual channels of distribution, *Journal of Marketing*, 56, 1, 38–54.

DelVecchio, S.K., Zemanke, J.E., McIntyre, R.P. and Claxton, R.P. (2002) Buyers' perceptions of salespersons' tactical approaches, *Journal of Personal Selling & Sales Management*, 23, 1, 39–49.
Dong, Y., Carter, C.R. and Dresner, M.E. (2001) JIT purchasing and performance, an exploratory analysis of buyer and supplier perspectives, *Journal of Operations Management*, 19, 471–483.
Dubinsky, A. (1980) A factor analytic study of the personal selling process, *Journal of Personal Selling & Sales Management*, 1, 1, 26–33.
Dwyer, F., Schurr, P. and Oh, J. (1987) Developing buyer–seller relationships, *Journal of Marketing*, 51, 2, 11–28.
Dwyer, S., Hill, J. and Martin, W. (2000) An empirical investigation of critical success factors in the personal selling process for homogenous goods, *Journal of Personal Selling & Sales Management*, 20, 3, 151–159.
Economist, The (1997) Categorical imperatives, 343, 8017, 75.
Economist, The (2004) E-commerce takes off, 371, 8375, 9.
ECR Europe (1997) *Value Chain Analysis*. Brussels.
Evans, K. (2000) How first impressions of a customer impact effectiveness in an initial sales encounter, *Journal of the Academy of Marketing Science*, 28, 4, 512–526.
Fullerton, R.R. and McWatters, C.S. (2001) The production performance benefits from JIT implementation, *Journal of Operations Management*, 19, 81–96.
Futrell, C. (2001) *Fundamentals of Selling* (7th edn). Burr Ridge.
Giunipero, L.C., Pillai, K.G., Chapman, S.N. and Clark, R.A. (2005) A longitudinal examination of JIT purchasing practices, *International Journal of Logistics*, 16, 1, 51–70.
Gupta, O. (1994) An inventory model with lot-size dependent ordering cost, *Production Planning and Control*, 5, 6, 585–587.
Hamper, R.J. and Baugh, L.S. (1995) *Handbook for Writing Proposals*. Lincolnwood.
Harris, F.W. (1915) What quantity to make at once, *Library of Factory Management*, 5, 47–52.
Heide, J.B. and John, G. (1992) Do norms matter in marketing relationships? *Journal of Marketing*, 56, 2, 32–44.
Homburg, C. and Schneider, J. (2000) Partnerschaft oder Konfrontation? Die Beziehung zwischen Industriegüterherstellern und Handel, Institut für Marktorientierte Unternehmensführung, Working Paper M 44, Mannheim.
Homburg, C., Schäfer, H. and Schneider, J. (2005) *Sales Excellence: Vertriebsmanagement mit System* (4th edn). Wiesbaden.
Homburg, C., Schäfer, H. and Scholl, M. (2002a) Wieviele Absatzkanäle kann sich ein Unternehmen leisten? *Absatzwirtschaft*, 44, 3, 38–41.
Homburg, C., Workman, J. and Jensen, O. (2002b) A configurational perspective on key account management, *Journal of Marketing*, 66, 2, 38–61.
Ingram, T., LaForge, R., Avila, R., Schwepker, C. and Williams, M. (2001) *Sales Management: Analysis and Decision Making* (4th edn). Fort Worth.
Jackson, D. and d'Amico, M. (1989) Products and markets served by distributors and agents, *Industrial Marketing Management*, 18, 1, 27–33.
John, G. and Weitz, B.A. (1988) Forward integration into distribution: an empirical test of transaction cost analysis, *Journal of Law, Economics and Organization*, 4, 3, 121–139.
Kamalick, J. (2006) Big stores monopoly of power, *ICIS Chemical Business*, 1, 33, 16–17.
Katsikeas, C. (1992) The process of conflict in buyer–seller relationships at domestic and international levels: a comparative analysis, *Journal of Marketing Management*, 8, 4, 365–381.
Kollmannsperger, M. (2000) *Erfolgskriterien des Konfliktmanagements: Eine empirische Untersuchung*. Frankfurt am Main.
Kotler, P. and Keller, K. (2006) *Marketing Management* (12th edn). New Jersey.
Kumar, N. (2006) Living with channel conflict, *Managementletter*, 5 October.
Kurtz, D., Dodge, H., Fullerton, S. and Braden, J. (1999) *Professional Selling* (7th edn). Cincinnati.
Lambert, D.M. and Stock, J.R. (1993) *Strategic Logistics Management* (3rd edn). Homewood.
Langley, C.J., Allen, G.R. and Dale, T.A. (2004) Third-Party Logistics Study: Results and Findings of the 2004 Ninth Annual Study. URL: http://www.tli.gatech.edu/downloads/TLIGT-2004_3PLStudy.pdf.
Lee, H., Padmanabhan, V. and Whang, S. (1997) Der Peitscheneffekt in der Absatzkette, *Harvard Business Manager*, 19, 4, 78–87.
Lewicki, R., Litterer, J., Minton, J. and Saunders, D. (1999) *Negotiation* (3rd edn). Boston, Mass.
Lieb, R. (1999) *Third Party Logistics: A Manager's Guide*. Houston.

Lusch, R. and Brown, J.R. (1996) Interdependency, contracting, and relational behavior in marketing channels, *Journal of Marketing*, 60, 3, 19–38.
Maltz, A.B. and Ellram, L.M. (1997) Total cost of ownership: an analytical framework for the logistics outsourcing decision, *Journal of Business Logistics*, 18, 1, 45–66.
Marks, R. (1985) *Personal Selling: An Interactive Approach* (2nd edn). Newton.
Merril, D. and Reid, R. (1981) *Personal Styles and Effective Performance*. Radner.
Mollenkopf, D., Gibson, A. and Ozanne, L. (2000) The integration of marketing and logistics functions: an empirical investigation of New Zealand firms, *Journal of Business Logistics*, 21, 2, 89–112.
Moriarty, R. and Moran, U. (1990) Managing hybrid marketing systems, *Harvard Business Review*, 68, 6, 146–155.
Palamountain Jr, J.C. (1969) *The Politics of Distribution*. New York.
Pettijohn, C., Pettijohn, L., Taylor, A. and Keillor, B. (2000) Adaptive selling and sales performance: an empirical examination, *Journal of Applied Business Research*, 16, 1, 91–111.
Rangan, V.K., Menezes, M.A.J. and Maier, E.P. (1992) Channel selection for new industrial products: a framework, method, and application, *Journal of Marketing*, 56, 3, 69–82.
Razzaque, M.A. and Sheng, C.C. (1998) Outsourcing of logistics functions: a literature survey, *International Journal of Physical Distribution & Logistics Management*, 28, 2, 89–107.
Riley, P.G. (2002) *The One Page Proposal: How to Get Your Business Pitch onto One Persuasive Page*. New York.
Rindfleisch, A. and Heide, J.B. (1997) Transaction cost analysis: past, present, and future applications, *Journal of Marketing*, 61, 4, 30–54.
Robertson, G.L. (1990) Good and bad packaging: who decides? *International Journal of Physical Distribution and Logistics Management*, 20, 8, 38–39.
Sant, T. (2004) *Persuasive Business Proposals: Writing to Win More Customers, Clients, and Contracts*. New York.
Schulte, C. (2005) *Logistik: Wege zur Optimierung des Material- und Informationsflusses* (4th edn). Munich.
Sebenius, J. (2001) Six habits of merely effective negotiators, *Harvard Business Review*, 79, 4, 87–95.
Skinner, S., Gassenheimer, J. and Kelley, S. (1992) Cooperation in supplier–dealer relations, *Journal of Retailing*, 68, 1, 174–193.
Spiro, R. and Weitz, B. (1990) Adaptive selling: conceptualization, measurement, and nomological validity, *Journal of Marketing Research*, 27, 1, 61–69.
Straub, D.W., Hoffman, D.L., Weber, B.W. and Steinfield, C. (2002) Measuring e-commerce in net-enabled organizations: an introduction to the special issue, *Information Systems Research*, 13, 2, 115–124.
Torkzadeh, G. and Dhillon, G. (2002) Measuring factors that influence the success of internet commerce, *Information Systems Research*, 13, 2, 187–204.
Van Laarhoven, P., Berglund, N. and Peters, M. (2000) Third-party logistics in Europe – five years later, *International Journal of Physical Distribution & Logistics*, 30, 5, 425–442.
Weis (2005) *Verkauf* (6th edn). Ludwigshafen.
Weitz, B. and Bradford, K. (1999) Personal selling and sales management: a relationship marketing perspective, *Journal of the Academy of Marketing Science*, 27, 2, 241–254.
Weitz, B., Sujan, H. and Sujan, M. (1986) Knowledge, motivation, and adaptive behavior: a framework for improving selling effectiveness, *Journal of Marketing*, 50, 4, 174–191.
Winkelmann, P. (2005a) *Marketing und Vertrieb: Fundamente für die marktorientierte Unternehmensführung* (5th edn). Munich.
Winkelmann (2005b) *Vertriebskonzeption und Vertriebssteuerung: Die Instrumente des integrierten Kundenmanagements (CRM)* (3rd edn). Munich.

CHAPTER 8

Communication Decisions

Contents

Learning Objectives

In this chapter you will become familiar with:

- the planning, implementation and monitoring of communication decisions
- the main objectives of the communication decisions, as well as approaches to defining target groups
- advertising response functions, as well as their potential application within the scope of advertising budgeting
- the key qualitative and quantitative criteria that can help in making decisions regarding media planning
- the most significant techniques for creative work and the various instruments of communication
- the main methods for monitoring the impact of communication (before and after implementing communication measures).

Focus on Marketing 8-1

"With the digital revolution of the media landscape, integrated marketing communication powered by digital media has become an imperative for marketing managers. Therefore, business students just as executives need a broad understanding of media and the impact of underlying technologies and how they work together in order to use resources efficiently and effectively.

More than ever before, integrated marketing communication in the digital age has to focus on the customer and the brand at the center of all communication activities and establish a personal relationship via continuous interactivity and emotional experiences.

Matthias Ehrlich, CEO United Internet Media AG"

Communication decisions are an important field in the marketing mix (see Focus on Marketing 8-1). With competition intensifying, there is an ever-increasing need for companies to differentiate their offerings by communication. In addition, communicating to the customers is a prerequisite for actual purchasing (e.g. by way of advertising). Table 8-1 underlines the increasing importance worldwide of communication, by comparing advertising spending (measured in the purchasing power of the G7 countries) over several years. Spending has risen for all countries in Table 8-1.

This chapter will provide the reader with an introduction to communication decisions. In Section 8.1, we present the foundations and theories as they pertain to communication decisions. A key prerequisite for effective communication is the careful and precise definition of the objectives and target groups of the company's communication (see Section 8.2). After discussing budgeting and budget allocation (see Section 8.3), we will elaborate on the design of the communication measures (see Section 8.4). Finally, we will discuss approaches for monitoring the impact of communication activities (see Section 8.5).

Table 8-1 Advertising expenditures in G7 countries (without direct mail) (World Advertising Research Center Ltd 2008)

Advertising spending	2006	2007*	2008*
USA	177.4	138.1	191.0
Japan	33.0	33.4	33.9
UK	24.6	25.5	26.4
Germany	21.2	21.9	22.5
France	13.0	13.3	13.8
Italy	11.7	11.9	12.2
Canada	10.5	11.2	11.8

in bn purchasing power parities (PPP) * forecast
(PPP are currency conversion rates that equalize the purchasing power of different currencies)

8.1 'Who Says What in Which Channel, to Whom and with What Effect?'

Communication can be defined as the exchange of information. This exchange can be illustrated by a communication process and is characterized by a sender sending a communication message to a receiver via a communication channel, which then causes a specific communication impact. This linear communication process was proposed by Lasswell (1948) and can help us to understand 'who says what in which channel to whom with what effect' (1948, p. 37). For example, a company (= sender) can communicate the technical advantages of its product (= communication message) to potential users of the product (= receivers) in an advertisement in a trade journal (= communication channel) in order to create interest in the product (= communication impact). Within this process, the message is formulated (encoded) by the sender, and decoded and interpreted by the receiver. The receiver can then give feedback to the sender, which can take the form of direct (personal) feedback. Likewise, the impact of the communication on the receiver can serve as important feedback for the communication sender.

The communication between sender and receiver can be one-step or two-step.

- With a one-step flow of communication, the sender gears the message directly to the receiver. In this case, the sender (i.e. the communicating company) has a relatively large degree of control over the content of the communication being conveyed.
- With a two-step flow of communication, the sender (i.e. the communicating company) initially addresses its message to 'opinion leaders', who act as 'multipliers' and forward the message to the less active receiver(s) (see Figure 8-1) (Katz 1957; Lazarsfeld *et al.* 1944). For example, a pharmaceutical company can direct its communication to physicians, who then pass on the message to their patients. In the course of forwarding the message, the original message can be changed, toned down or intensified. These indirect effects should be taken into account when planning communication decisions.

Furthermore, the communication can be personal or non-personal. Personal communication refers to the direct communication between the sender and the receiver as an immediate interpersonal contact. An example of personal communication is a conversation between company representatives and customers at a trade fair. In contrast, non-personal communication is indirect as sender and receiver do not establish personal contact during this exchange. An example is print advertising. Two-step communication is characterized by non-personal communication between sender and receiver(s).

When planning communication decisions the company conveys information with the intention of influencing the recipients of the communication message, in terms of their knowledge, attitudes, expectations and behavior, in favor of the communication objectives. The recipients of the communication primarily comprise (potential and existing) customers of the company, as well as any persons or organizations that can exert influence on the company's market success. To ensure that communication decisions are in line with the communication objectives, they should be systematically planned. This process is illustrated in Figure 8-2.

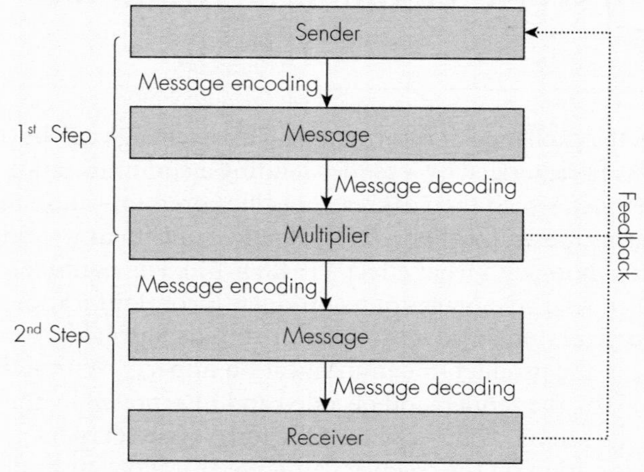

Figure 8-1 Structure of a multi-step communication process

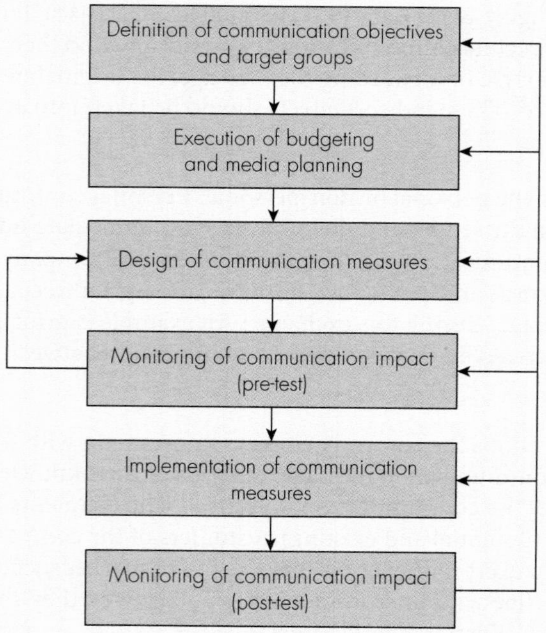

Figure 8-2 Process for planning, implementation and monitoring of communication decisions

In the first step of this process, both the communication objectives and the intended target groups have to be defined (see Section 8.2). Defining the objectives and target groups facilitates making decisions concerning the subsequent steps of the planning process. In a second step, the communication budget is determined and the media channels are selected (see Section 8.3). During the budgeting process, the amount of funds available for communication measures is specified. Appropriate media channels and media vehicles are then selected and the communication budget is allocated to each respective media and media vehicle. The next step consists of designing the communication measures (see Section 8.4), including the content of the communication message, and the linguistic, stylistic, visual and auditory implementation of that content. Theoretical considerations may be taken into account when implementing the communication design. In addition to the fundamental theories of consumer behavior (for more information on 'consumer behavior', see the Appendix), the theoretical foundations related to designing communication measures (discussed in Section 8.4.1) are also relevant in this regard. The design of the individual communication measures will also be discussed in Section 8.4. The communication impact should be evaluated prior to the actual implementation (pre-tests), especially in the case of cost-intensive communication activities. At this stage, approaches to improving communication activities often arise. It is also necessary to monitor the success of communication activities. This can be done in post-tests, where the company can assess whether communication objectives have been reached (see Section 8.5).

8.2 Understanding the Audience

In general, companies pursue marketing objectives related to potential, market success and financial marketing objectives (see Figure 2-2 in Chapter 2). These objectives also apply in communication. When communication decisions are particularly directed towards objectives related to potential, the following issues can be addressed:

- the degree of awareness, as well as the image of the company and its products in the eyes of customers
- the attitudes of customers with regard to the company and its products
- the customer's intention to buy the company's products.

The **attitude toward the advertisement** (A_{AD}) as a communication objective related to potential plays an important role in influencing advertising response. In this sense attitude is the tendency of a person to respond favorably or unfavorably to a particular ad (Lutz 1985). Important factors determining this attitude are advertising credibility, advertising perceptions, attitude towards advertiser, attitude toward advertising, and mood (see Figure 8-3). A_{AD} then, in turn, impacts attitude toward the brand and brand perceptions in a positive or negative way (MacKenzie and Lutz 1989; MacKenzie *et al.* 1986). It is therefore an important factor that receives considerable attention in company practice.

The **AIDA model** is a well-known model specifying communication objectives (see Figure 8-4; Lewis 1898). According to this model, customer Attention to the product has to be aroused as a first step. In phase 2, Interest has to be stimulated, which leads to Desire for the product. The desire then triggers a certain Action (e.g. purchase of the product).

In addition to defining the communication objectives (What should be achieved?), it is also essential to define the target group(s) (With whom should it be achieved?). The selection of the target group(s) can generally be based on the same criteria discussed in the section on market segmentation (Section 3.3.2):

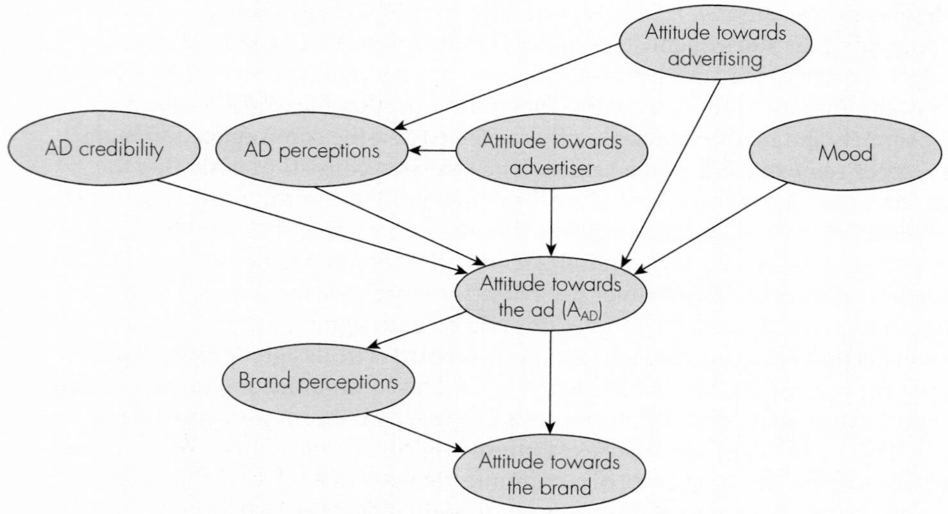

Figure 8-3 Determinants and consequences of attitude toward the ad (adapted from MacKenzie and Lutz 1989, p. 53)

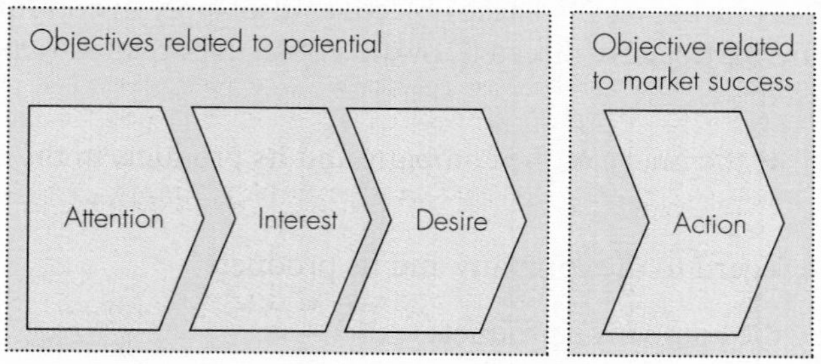

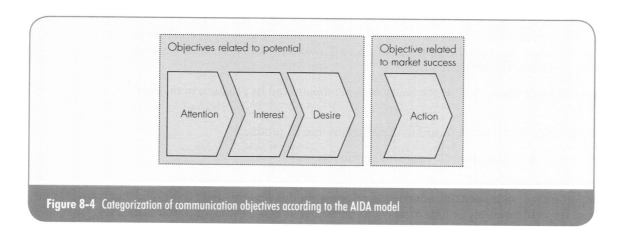

Figure 8-4 Categorization of communication objectives according to the AIDA model

- sociodemographic criteria
- geographic criteria
- psychographic criteria
- criteria related to benefits
- behavioral criteria.

In managerial practice, a combination of these criteria is often used when defining the target group(s) within the scope of the communication decision (see Table 8-2 for some examples).

Table 8-2 Examples of target groups for communication measures in various industries

	Example of target group A	Example of target group B	Example of target group C
Company	Cosmetics company	Insurance company	Manufacturer of printing machine
Product	High-quality moisturizing cream for treating dry skin	Life insurance	Digital laser printers in the mid-range performance class
Description of target groups			
Demographic criteria	Employed women between the ages of 25 and 35 with dry skin, strong interest in beauty care and with relatively low price sensitivity	Married male with young children, conservative, university graduate, first-time employee between the ages of 25 and 30, net household income of min. 2,000 euros and above	Existing customers of the company, medium-sized printing companies with 10–30 employees, with a high affinity towards digital printing technology

With communication activities that address private customers (as opposed to corporate customers), **target groups are commonly defined on the basis of typologies.** In these typologies customers are categorized into different types based on empirical data. Companies can either develop their own typologies or use already established ones.

An example of a well-established typology is a **lifestyle typology**. Lifestyle typologies classify customers into groups with different lifestyles, on the basis of values, attitudes, consumer behavior and socioeconomic characteristics (Lastovicka *et al.* 1990; Vyncke 2002).

One of the most popular lifestyle segmentations is the **Values and Lifestyles Survey VALS™ 2**, created by the consulting group SRI. Based on the two factors of consumers' resources (including income, education, self-confidence, health, eagerness to buy, intelligence and energy level) and their self-orientation (including activities and values) US customers were grouped into eight segments: Thinkers, Believers, Achievers, Strivers, Experiencers, Makers, Innovators and Survivors (Hoyer and MacInnis 2004; SRI 2007). Although VALS™ 2 was created to describe the lifestyle of US consumers, researchers also modified it to the Japanese context. In Japan, on the basis of two factors (life orientation and attitudes to social change) ten VALS™ segments were identified: Integrators, Self Innovators, Self Adapters, Ryoshiki ('social intelligence') Innovators, Ryoshiki Adapters, Tradition Innovators, Tradition Adapters, High Pragmatics, Low Pragmatics and Sustainers (Kotler and Keller 2006, p. 254; SRI 2007). Figure 8-5 shows a lifestyle typology for US and Japanese customers.

Lifestyle typologies are relevant to communication decisions because customers categorized by the various types use different communication media and respond to different communication content.

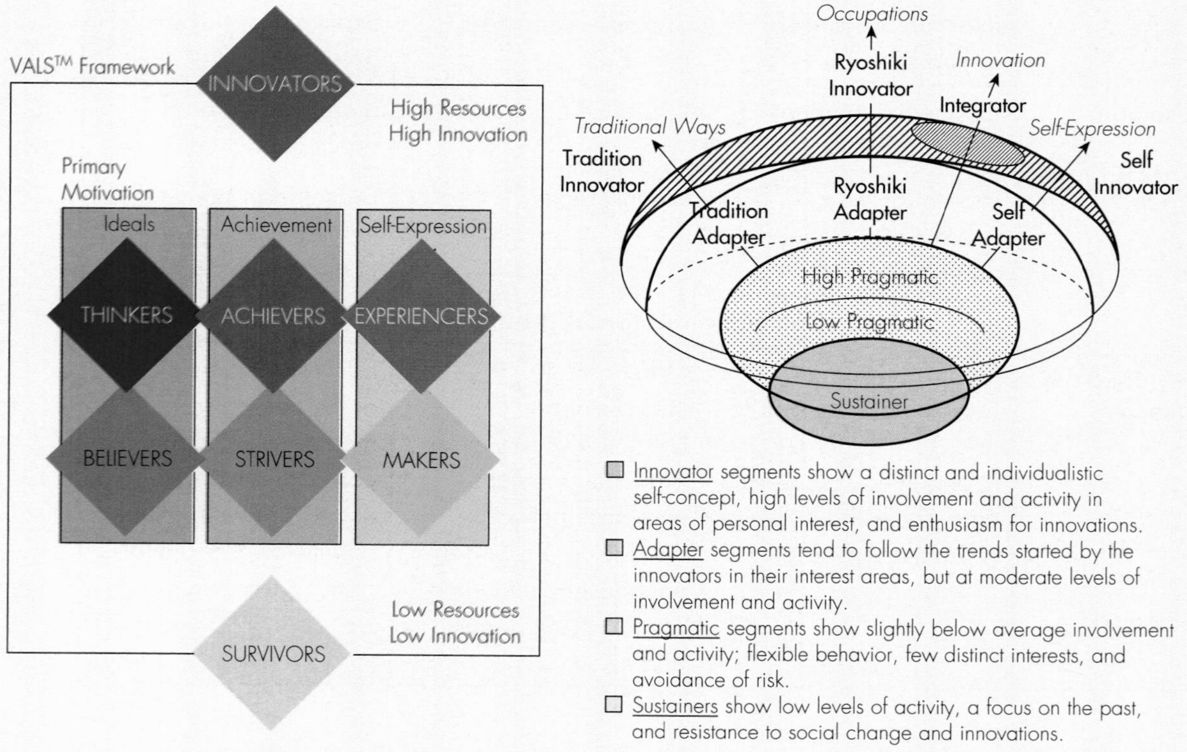

Figure 8-5 VALS™ Segments in the USA and Japan (SRI 2007)

Table 8-3 shows an example of a customer segmentation based on behavioral criteria. The various segments would require different communication media and content.

8.3 Another W: 'What Are We Going to Spend?'

In the **budgeting** phase, the company specifies the amount of the total investment in communication for a planned period (e.g. fiscal year) (see Section 8.3.1). In the next step, the budget is allocated to the various communication media and media vehicles. (We will discuss this topic in Section 8.3.2.)

8.3.1 How Are We Going to Spend the Money?

With regard to determining the communication budget, we will differentiate between heuristic and analytical approaches. Heuristic budgeting methods are characterized by using rules of thumb as a reference point. Analytic methods, on the other hand, evaluate the effectiveness of communication spending by looking at cause-and-effect relationships. They can be static or dynamic. In the next section, we will first examine the conceptual basis of heuristic techniques, followed by a discussion of analytical models.

Table 8-3 Segmentation of the Australian wine market (Bruwer *et al.* 2002)

Type	Characterization	Segment percentage
Enjoyment-oriented social wine drinkers	■ Focus on pleasure seeking and enjoyment ■ Drink wine in pubs/wine bars or at home while just relaxing ■ Purchase wine brands impulsively in specialist wine stores where there is a great variety and assortment of wines	14%
Fashion/image-oriented wine drinkers	■ Drink wine because it fits the image they like to portray to others, or for mood enhancement purposes ■ Low wine knowledge ■ Pre-plan their wine purchases while engaging in safe brand buying	19%
Ritual-oriented conspicuous wine enthusiasts	■ Drinking wine is an important aspect of their lifestyle (so-called wine 'connoisseur') ■ Drink wine often and in large quantities, whether relaxing privately at home or at a social occasion ■ Like to browse around in specialist wine stores with large assortments when shopping for wine	18%
Purposeful inconspicuous premium wine drinkers	■ Inconspicuous wine drinkers ■ Wine is regularly consumed in a social setting away from home ■ Pre-plan their wine purchases	25%
Basic wine drinkers	■ Low level of involvement in wine, and low wine knowledge ■ Drink wine when engaged in a celebration occasion ■ Purchase safe brands, mostly mainstream large commercial wine brands and also cask wines	24%

Heuristic Methods

As already mentioned, **heuristic budgeting methods** are based on rules of thumb or company experience. There are five main heuristic approaches to budgeting:

1. budgeting based on the previous period's budget (extrapolation method)
2. budgeting based on sales/profit (percentage-of-sales/profit method)
3. budgeting based on available monetary funds (affordable method)
4. budgeting based on competitive activities (competitive-parity method)
5. budgeting based on communication objectives (objectives-and-task method).

In the case of **budgeting based on the previous period's budget**, the budget for the previous period is applied without change, or is increased or reduced by a certain amount. This **extrapolation method** is very easy to use. However, it is problematic because the spending in the previous period may not be representative of the present period's financial requirement.

With the **percentage-of-sales method** or **percentage-of-profit method**, the budget amount is determined as a percentage of the sales or profits achieved in either the previous period or forecast for the current planning period. This procedure is relatively straightforward, since the data can easily be obtained. Problematic here, however, is that the actual value of the previous period (e.g. the sales volume achieved with a certain budget) cannot simply be transferred to the target values of the current period. For example, a tough market environment can call for a higher percentage share than allocated in the previous period. Similarly, budgeting on the basis of the previous period can lead to procyclical budgeting, the result being, for example, that the more sales a company has achieved in the previous period, the more money it spends on communication activities.

When applying the **all-you-can-afford (affordable) method**, the company first determines the target profit. The communication budget is then calculated on the basis of the available funds that remain after all costs to achieve the target profit have been covered. The problem with this method is obvious: it does not take into account the causal relationship between the communication budget and the targeted sales/profit. As with the approach based on sales, this technique is strongly characterized by a procyclical budgeting pattern.

With the **competitive-parity method**, the budget is based on the amount of the (current or previous) budget of the competitor(s). According to this method, the company has to spend the same amount for communication activities as the competitor in order to maintain its own market share. However, the problem here is that the company's own communication objectives can differ from those of the competitors.

Lastly, **budgeting based on the objectives-and-task method** derives the required communication budget from the communication objectives (e.g. increase the degree of awareness, improve the attitude that buyers have towards the company, boost the market share). If the necessary communication measures are not economically feasible, the communication objectives have to be revised. Figure 8-6 illustrates the basic process for budgeting based on the communication objectives. A problem with this method lies in the difficulty in knowing upfront whether the communication measures are really appropriate in achieving the communication objectives.

Despite their conceptual deficits, heuristic models find widespread use in managerial practice. The main reason is their simplicity. Apart from budgeting based on communication objectives, however, they are not based on sound rationales. In light of this, we now turn to the analytical methods.

Analytical Budgeting Methods

There are two types of **analytical approaches to budgeting** (according to Lilien and Rangaswamy 2003; Homburg 2000):

1. static analytical methods (i.e. measurement at one point in time)
2. dynamic analytical methods (i.e. measurement over a certain time period).

The vantage point for **static analytical methods** is the relationship between the communication budget (especially the advertising budget) and a communication objective. Frequently, this relationship is formally expressed by an **advertising response function** (Belch and Belch 1998; Rossiter and Percy 1987; Sethuraman and Tellis 1991; Stewart 1989; White 2000).

Advertising response functions are of rather a complex nature (Lilien *et al.* 1992; Stewart 1989). A primary reason for this is that advertising has a significantly weaker impact on demand than price

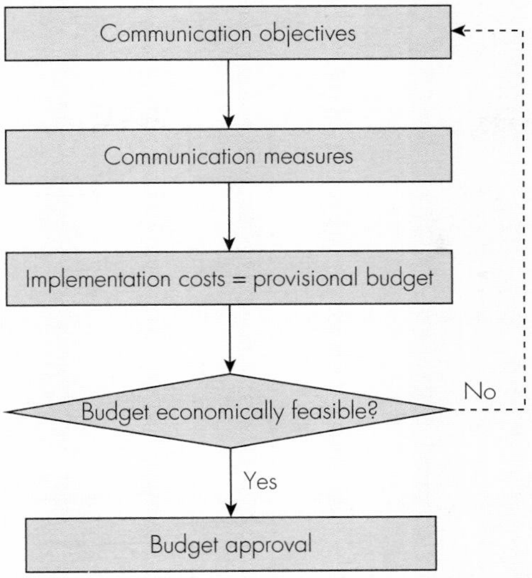

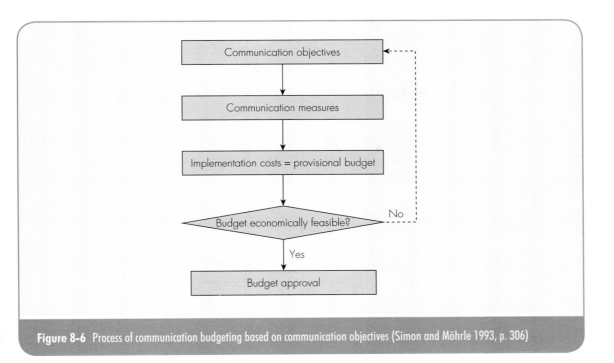

Figure 8-6 Process of communication budgeting based on communication objectives (Simon and Möhrle 1993, p. 306)

(Sethuraman and Tellis 1991). Accordingly, the basic challenge here is to separate the advertising response from other factors. In principle, this can be accomplished with historical data (Rossiter and Percy 1987; White 2000). As a rule, however, other marketing mix variables have to be controlled. Another problem associated with the empirical calculation of advertising response functions is that advertisements often have a delayed or carry-over effect on demand (Belch and Belch 1998) (see Figure 8-7 for advertising response functions with delayed effects).

Dynamic Analytical Methods

Dynamic analytical methods are especially relevant because advertising measures often impact sales with a **time delay**. These **carry-over effects** on demand are the result of the goodwill created by advertising activities in the past.

With respect to the impact on demand caused by changes in the communication budget, we differentiate several **dynamic response parameters** (see also Lilien *et al.* 1992; Simon 1982). Figure 8-7 shows the following different response patterns.

- First, we distinguish between immediate (see section (b) and (d)) or delayed response (see sections (a) and (c)).
- Second, we distinguish between responses that manifest themselves at one point in time (see section (a), where we can see one larger increase in demand due to an increase in advertising budget), or successively (see section (c), where the increase in demand occurs in smaller successive steps in response to the increase in budget).
- Third, we distinguish between persistent (see sections (a) and (c)) and decreasing advertising effectiveness (see sections (b) and (d)) and the extent of these **wear-out effects** as they can be observed partially (see section (d), where demand remains on a higher level even after wear-out has been considered), or totally (see section (b), where demand goes back to the previous level before the budget was allocated).

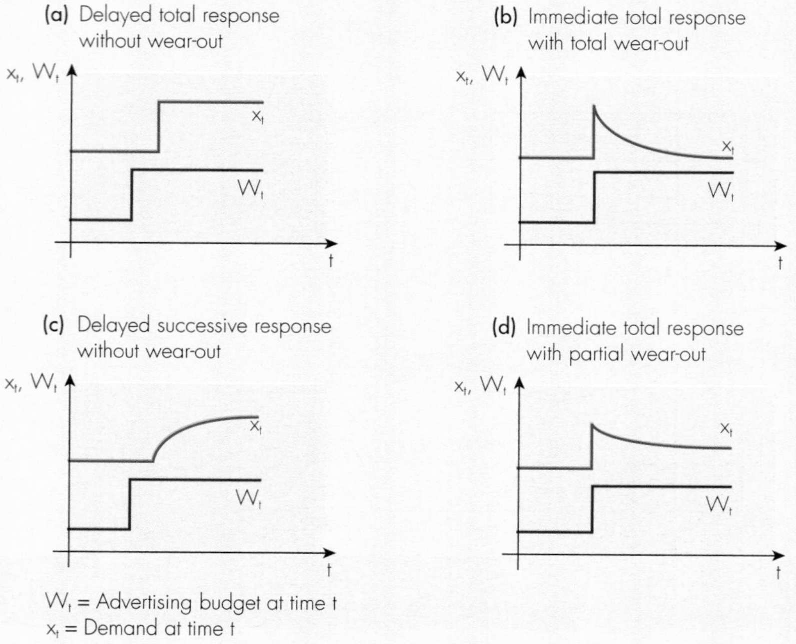

Figure 8-7 Response patterns in connection with dynamic advertising response analyzes (adapted from Simon 1982, p. 353)

8.3.2 Media Planning: How the Budget is Spent

Budget allocation (also called **media planning**) is concerned with the optimal distribution of the communication budget. In addition to allocating the budget to the different products of the company and the countries that the company serves, the

- allocation to various categories of communication media (**media allocation**),
- allocation to individual communication media (**media vehicle allocation**), and
- allocation of the budget over time

have to be specified (Belch and Belch 1998).

In this context, a **communication medium** is a delivery medium used to transmit the communication message to the receiver (Bruhn 2003a). Communication media include television, radio, newspapers, magazines, and the internet, among others. The term media allocation is also used to describe the allocation of the communication budget to the various categories of communication media. On the basis of this allocation, the budget is then allocated to the individual communication media within the respective categories (media vehicle allocation). For example, if a company has decided to allocate a certain portion of the budget for TV commercials (= media allocation), the question is how to distribute the budget share to the different television channels (= media vehicle allocation).

When making decisions about media allocation, it is important to examine the relative effectiveness of the different media. Table 8-4 provides an overview of criteria for evaluating media.

Table 8-4 Criteria for evaluating the various media in the process of media allocation (adapted from Althans 1993, p. 414; Bruhn 2003a, p. 236)

Medium / Evaluation criteria	Popular magazines	Daily newspapers	Television	Radio	Cinema	Outdoor	Internet	Mobile phones
Ability to precisely define target group	+ +	+	0	+	+ +	+	+ + +	+ + +
Possibility to provide more detailed information/appeal to cognitive aspects	+ +	+ +	0	0	0	0	0	0
Options for visual representation	+	+	+ + +	0	+ + +	+ +	+	0
Aural reinforcement	0	0	+ + +	+ + +	+ + +	0	+	0
Cost-effectiveness	+ +	+	0	+	0	+ +	+	+
+ + + Very positive assessment, + + Positive assessment, + Average assessment, 0 Below-average assessment								

With allocation to **media vehicles**, more specific criteria for evaluating the different individual media vehicles are then used, including aspects such as the question regarding which magazine is most appropriate for addressing a certain target group. In addition to qualitative aspects (e.g. the characteristics of the target group reached by the medium), quantitative criteria can also be used. A main quantitative criterion that can be used to compare media and media vehicles is the **reach** of a medium. The reach of a medium specifies the number of contacts/persons that can be reached with communication activities using the given medium. Other quantitative criteria for evaluating media are shown in Table 8-5.

Particularly relevant here is the question of the costs involved in reaching a specific number of persons, which applies to both media and media vehicle comparisons. The key evaluation criteria here is the **cost per thousand (CPM)** (see Table 8-5), which specifies the costs that are required to reach 1,000 contacts via a given medium. Accordingly, the CPM is calculated as

$$\text{CPM} = \frac{c}{C} \times 1{,}000$$

with c representing the costs for using the medium and C the number of contacts realized with each use of the medium (reach). The CPM is a widely applied evaluation criterion for communication media.

The following example illustrates how an advertising budget can be allocated on the basis of the CPMs: there are four magazines available, the advertising budget is €220,000. The goal is to reach the highest possible number of contacts. The media data for the four magazines are summarized in Table 8-6.

Based on the CPM, the following procedure can be selected when allocating the advertising budget to the four magazines (media allocation planning for the entire year). First, as many issues as possible of the magazine with the lowest CPM are booked. In the example in Table 8-6, this is Magazine 4. In this case, all 12 issues of the year are booked; 60,000 euros of the budget are thus allocated for Magazine 4, resulting in a remaining budget of:

$$€220{,}000 - 12 \times €5{,}000 = €160{,}000$$

Table 8-5 Quantitative criteria for evaluating media (in accordance with Batra *et al.* 1996; DePelsmacker *et al.* 2004; Kotler and Keller 2006)

Criterion	Parameter	Description
Circulation of medium	Circulation	Number of printed copies of an issue
	Issues sold	Number of issues sold (total number of copies sold minus number of complimentary issues and returns)
Reach of medium	Gross reach	Number of contacts that can be reached with the medium (one-time or repeated use of a medium or several media), often indicated in gross rating points (GRPs)
	Gross rating points (GRPs)	Reach × frequency (Reach = % of the target group exposed to the medium containing the advertisement) (Frequency = # of times an individual of the target audience is exposed to the medium containing the advertisement)
	Cumulative audience	Number of contacts that can be reached with repeated use of a medium (gross reach adjusted by internal overlapping, i.e. persons who are repeatedly reached via this medium)
	Unduplicated reach	Number of contacts that can be reached by the repeated usage of several media (gross reach adjusted by external and internal overlapping)
Cost of the media	CPM (cost per thousand)	Cost required to reach 1,000 contacts
	CTU (cost per thousand users)	Cost required to reach 1,000 contacts (without accounting for the number of contacts per person)

Table 8-6 Example of media data for four magazines

Media vehicle	Readers (C)	Cost per issue (c)	Issues/year	CPM (c/C × 1,000)
Magazine 1	2,500,000	€25,000	4	€10
Magazine 2	1,600,000	€40,000	6	€25
Magazine 3	3,000,000	€60,000	2	€20
Magazine 4	2,000,000	€5,000	12	€2.5

In a second step, as many issues as possible of Magazine 1 (second-lowest CPM) are covered with the remaining budget. With a maximum of four possible placements, the cost of this amounts to 4 × €25,000 = €100,000, resulting in a remaining budget of:

€160,000 – 4 × €25,000 = €60,000

This remaining budget of 60,000 euros is used to cover as many issues of Magazine 3 (next highest CPM) as possible. Here, it is apparent that only one advertisement can be placed in one issue of Magazine 3. The budget is then fully spent. Consequently, the number of contacts is maximized by using Magazine 4 twelve times, Magazine 1 four times, and Magazine 3 once.

A significant limitation of the CPM lies in the fact that it does not distinguish between a first contact or a repeat contact; only the absolute number of contacts is taken into consideration. Moreover, the method does not take into account the quality of contacts and whether they do indeed belong to the intended target group.

Along with budget allocation based on the selection of media and media vehicles, it has to be decided how the budget is spent over time. For this, ad placement dates have to be determined and a decision made in terms of **advertising scheduling**. In this regard, **advertising spending policies** (according to Lilien *et al.* 1992; Mahajan and Muller 1986) can be:

- concentrated
- even
- pulsing
- pulsing/maintenance.

With **concentrated advertising**, a very large share of the advertising budget is spent within a relatively short period of time. This type of communication budget allocation is particularly appropriate for advertisements for products that have been newly launched in the market. Sometimes it is also referred to as **blitz policy** (Lilien *et al.* 1992).

Pulsing advertising refers to the spending of a relatively large share of the advertising budget at regular intervals. In the interim between these advertising campaigns, the advertising expenditure and activities are scaled down to zero. This method of allocation is especially appropriate for products associated with seasonal demand (e.g. advertising expenditure for champagne regularly peaks prior to holiday periods).

In the case of **even advertising**, the communication budget is spent at a constant level over the planning period. This form of budget allocation is particularly appropriate for products that are already established in the market and of which target groups need to be continuously reminded (e.g. everyday necessities).

Finally, **pulsing/maintenance advertising** combines any of the above advertising policies with a low level of advertising during the 'off' period, usually a maintenance level. For example, a company can alternate between high and low levels of advertising (Lilien *et al.* 1992; Mahajan and Muller 1986). Figure 8-8 illustrates these advertising spending policies.

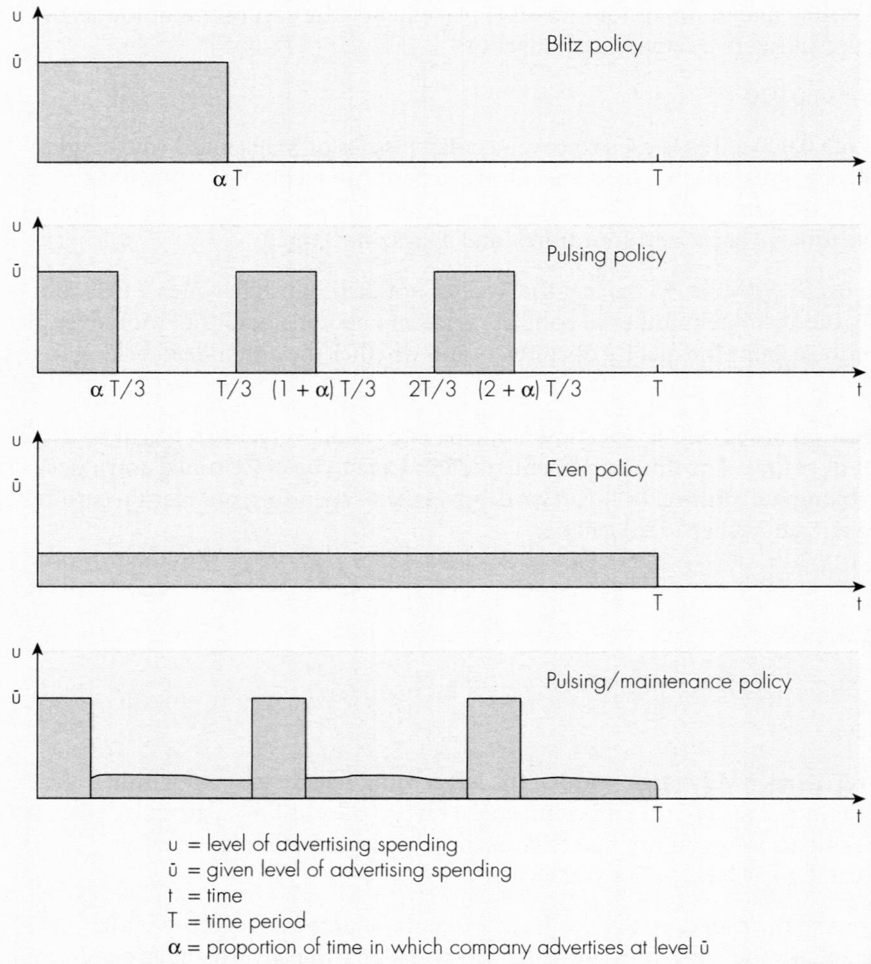

Figure 8-8 Advertising spending policies (Mahajan and Muller 1986, p. 92)

8.4 Making the Audience Receptive

Communication measures have to be designed once the media have been selected for the planned communication activities. This concerns the question of how to use a specific communication measure (e.g. an advertisement) to elicit a certain response from the target group (e.g. with regard to a product, brand or company). The design of the communication measures encompasses four aspects, as outlined below.

1 When designing **elements related to the content of the communication**, the linguistic component of the communication measure (e.g. slogan) has to be developed.

2 When designing **visual elements**, decisions have to be made regarding the main components of the picture, supplementary visual elements, typographies and colors, as well as font types, layouts

and sizes. With multimedia communication, animation elements (e.g. moving visuals such as video clips) also have to be taken into consideration.

3 **Auditory elements**, such as music, noises, sound and volume, are of particular importance when designing audio-verbal forms of communication.

4 Finally, other design elements have to be considered, such as smell (e.g. for product samples), taste or haptic impressions (i.e. impressions conveyed by touch, such as using a special type of paper).

In this section, we will examine the conceptualization and design of the communication in conjunction with the individual communication measures. Prior to that we will take a perspective that extends across the entire spectrum of communication measures and discuss the topic of **integrated marketing communications (IMC)** (Cornelissen 2003; Schultz *et al.* 1995). The major significance of IMC arises from the fact that at any moment in time the different departments and divisions of a company communicate with multiple audiences (such as customers, employees, competitors, intermediaries and the community) via several communication measures (see Figure 8-9). One consequence of this coincidence is the high cost associated with a lack of coordination between the communication measures. In addition, there is a possibility that messages may conflict. The result could be negative or dysfunctional effects on the part of customers and/or other stakeholders (Cornelissen 2003; Duncan and Moriarty 1998; Pickton and Hartley 1998).

In IMC, the communication activities have to be coordinated across all measures with regard to:

- formal aspects (e.g. consistent symbols and logos)
- timing
- content (e.g. consistent message, arguments and visuals).

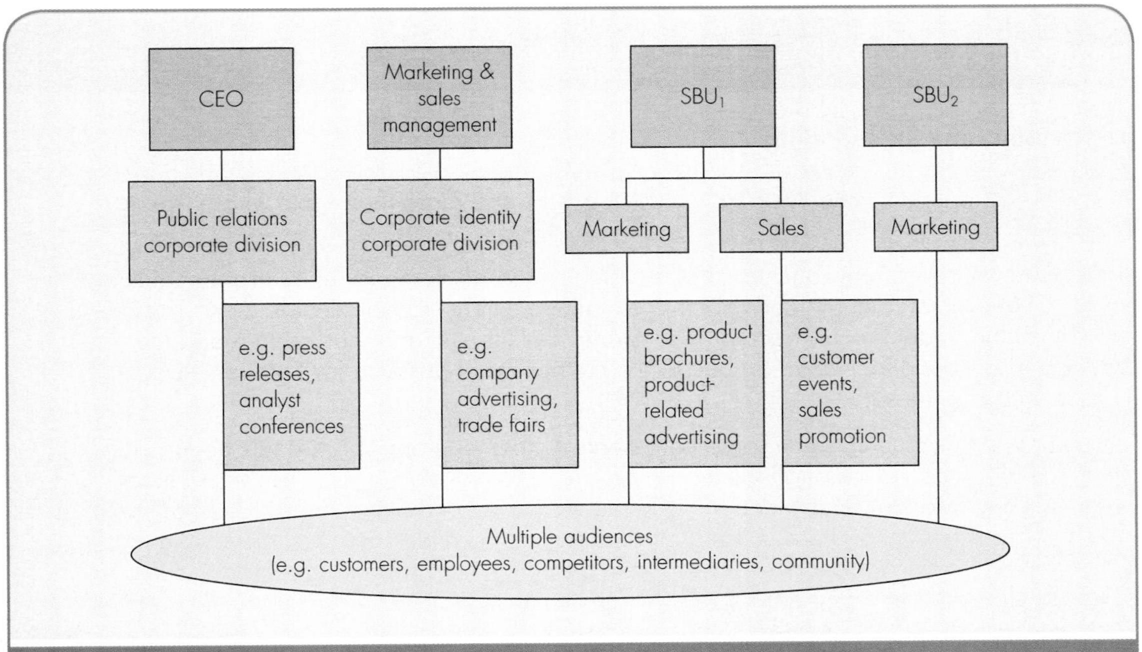

Figure 8-9 Illustration of the relevance of integrated communications using the example of a chemical company

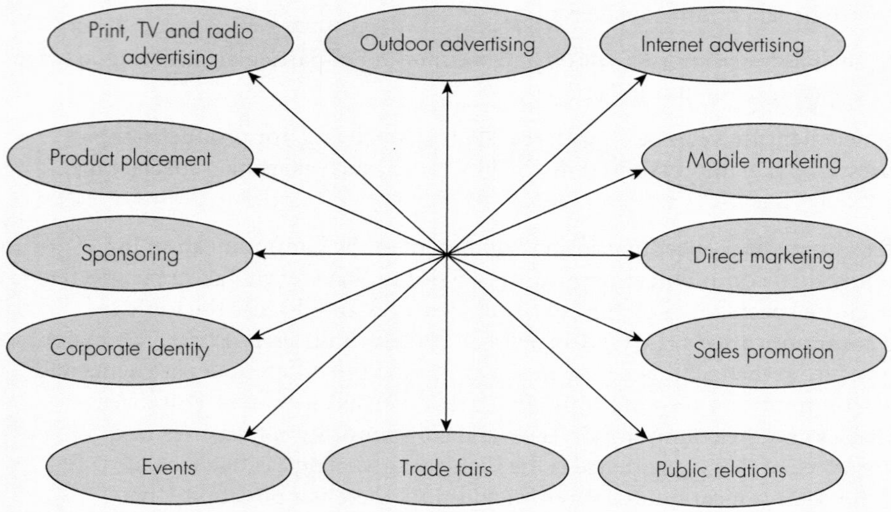

Figure 8-10 Communication measures

In the following, we will describe the design of the individual communication measures. The spectrum of the communication measures discussed in this section ranges from classic print advertisements to TV and internet marketing (Belch and Belch 1998; DePelsmacker *et al.* 2004; Kotler and Keller 2006; see also Figure 8-10). Internet marketing in particular has experienced a significant growth in importance in recent years (for an example see Focus on Marketing 8-2).

Focus on Marketing 8-2 Example of media spending

Ford ups 'targeted' media spending

FORD MOTOR CO.'S Ford Division will spend 30% of its estimated $1 billion-plus marketing budget this year on 'targeted' media, up from 20% last year and more than triple what it spent five years ago.

While Ford defines 'targeted' approaches as direct mail, video on demand, mobile-phone ads, sponsorships, CRM and Internet marketing, it is the digital element that will benefit most. The brand will spend 15% of the budget there, according to Martin Collins, general marketing manager. 'Our media spending in digital will go up because it creates more business for FordVehicles.com,' the marketer's Web site, he said.

The online component is crucial, since some Ford dealers close one out of five deals begun via online contracts. Still, about 40% of all the industry's Internet leads don't get a response within 24 hours, Mr. Collins said, the equivalent of not being waited on in a department store that can result in lost business. To fix that, Ford is using a proprietary tool called Lead Response Time that monitors how long it takes Ford dealers to respond to an online lead from its site. 'Leads acted on more quickly close at a rate four times higher' than slower responses, he said.

Source: Halliday, J. (2005), p. 8, reprinted with permission from *Advertising Age*, 22 August 2005. Copyright, Crain Communications, Inc. 2005.

Print Advertisements

Print advertising (advertisements in print media) is a classic communication measure. The most common types of print media are described below.

- **Newspapers** can be differentiated in terms of frequency of appearance (weekly or daily), sales channels (subscription or single purchase) and circulation area (local or national). For most newspapers, very detailed reader analyzes are available, but reaching a specific target group is often difficult. Companies placing advertisements frequently use newspapers as an additional medium to supplement other media. The main advantage of newspaper advertising lies primarily in the flexibility (short-term planning) and exact scheduling they offer. Furthermore, specific target groups can be addressed via advertisements placed in certain sections of the newspaper (e.g. ads for athletic goods in the sports section) and locally aligned advertisements can also be published (e.g. ads in a local newspaper).
- The range of **popular magazines** spans from magazines with a very broad readership up to magazines with a very specific readership (special interest magazines). When placing ads in magazines with a broad readership considerable **coverage waste** (i.e. communication messages reach people who are not part of the target group) may occur. Popular magazines appear less frequently and require longer-term planning than newspapers. However, at the same time, they offer more flexibility in design than newspapers (e.g. more color options).
- Likewise, **trade journals** generally appear periodically. They have a very specific readership and a stronger orientation on certain product groups. In contrast to popular magazines, trade journals focus more on conveying information and knowledge rather than providing entertainment. A positive factor with regard to media advertising is the **high involvement** on the part of the reader (for more on the concept of 'involvement' see the Appendix).
- Examples of other print media include supplements (e.g. TV guides enclosed with newspapers), advertising newspapers, customer magazines and telephone directories.

Scholars of marketing science and consumer behavior have identified several **techniques for creative work** (Kroeber-Riel and Esch 2004), also called creative tactics (Percy and Elliot 2005). Adopted from the social and behavioral sciences, these techniques focus on how to construct the social environment in order to influence people. These techniques are based on research of emotional and cognitive processes, which provides an understanding of the determinants of consumer behavior (for more information on 'consumer behavior' see the Appendix). With this knowledge the effect of communication messages on behavioral responses can also be assessed. The techniques are helpful when designing the visual elements of a print advertisement (e.g. shape or color of a brand logo) in such a way that the target audience perceives and memorizes them, and ultimately exhibits the desired behavioral response (Percy and Elliot 2005). At this point, it should be mentioned that such techniques for creative work were not developed exclusively for print advertisements, but are also relevant to other media.

The use of these techniques when designing print advertisements obviously cannot replace creativity, but rather should complement it to a certain extent by defining the framework of creativity. Even a very creative advertisement will not lead to the desired result if it disregards these basic techniques.

Techniques for creative work aim to (Kroeber-Riel and Weinberg 2003; Kroeber-Riel and Esch 2004):

- establish contact
- ensure that the communication message is absorbed
- convey emotional aspects

- promote understanding
- embed the message into memory.

There are two types of methods for establishing contact: **activation techniques** and **frequency techniques**.

Activation refers to the stimulation ('mental activity') of receivers so that they assimilate impressions or information (for more on the concept of 'activation' refer to the Appendix). Activation can be achieved through:

- physically intensive stimuli
- emotional stimuli
- cognitive stimuli.

Physically intensive stimuli refer to large, loud and colorful stimulation (Percy and Elliot 2005; White 2000). Examples here include advertisements that use striking, bold colors in extra-large-format ads (see the example in Figure 8-11).

Figure 8-11 Example of activation through physically intensive stimuli

Emotional stimuli are key stimuli that, to a great extent, trigger pre-programed biological responses. For example, advertisements featuring cute babies (Kotler and Keller 2006) can arouse 'protective instincts' in adults, and may be used in, say, product ads for insurance, or car commercials that strongly emphasize safety attributes. The use of erotic stimuli (Fill 2005), such as those frequently used in perfume advertisements, as well as arousing fear as an emotional state can also be included in this category (see the examples in Focus on Marketing 8-3 and in Figure 8-12).

Focus on Marketing 8-3 Example of arousing fear as an emotional state

AMV 'Don't Drive Tired' ad uses shock tactics

Government commercials are increasingly turning to shock tactics in order to hammer home safety messages to British drivers. In March 2008, the Department of Transport's THINK! group launched a new driver tiredness campaign targeting all drivers, with a particular focus on those who drive for work.

This initiative has been launched in the wake of figures showing that driver tiredness accounts for around one fifth of accidents on major roads. Around 300 people are killed and 3,000 injured every year in accidents caused by drivers falling asleep.

The new campaign is based on research into people who drive for work, such as company car and heavy goods vehicle drivers. This research confirmed that these people are an at risk group, demonstrating key risk behaviors such as talking on mobile phones whilst driving, speeding and driving whilst tired. Although an at risk group, they do not recognize themselves as being at risk, nor do they recognize themselves as a group. THINK! therefore decided to address the at risk behaviors, targeting the communications at drivers for work through the way they are placed. As the THINK! website states:

> The campaign focuses on radio advertising as this enables us to target drivers in-situ, at a point when the driver tiredness message will have most relevance to them. The advertising is supported with ambient advertising in Motorway and A-road service stations, online advertising, partnership marketing activity, PR activity and publicity materials that are reinforced with the key message – *Tiredness kills. Take a 15 minute break every two hours.*

The new campaign is one in a long line of shocking images used to target tired drivers. An earlier commercial launched in 2002, created by Abbott Mead Vickers BBDO, shows a family's death in a spectacular and horrific motorway crash, which underlines the fatal consequences of driving while tired.

The ad opens with a peaceful image of a man with his eyes closed. A voiceover says: 'Tonight John will die in his sleep. He is comfortable and has his family by his side.'

The camera pans back to show the same man, asleep at the wheel, as he drives home at night from a family holiday. The car is seen drifting across the road before hitting a barrier and turning over. The endline is: 'Think. Don't drive tired.'

The strategy was for a heavy-weight short burst of activity to shock people out of their complacency so the advert ran on national TV for two weeks with an accompanying radio campaign. The film was one of a series of commercials by AMV – from anti-drink-driving to the encouragement of rear seat belt wearing – which have relied on shock tactics to deliver the safety message.

Source: Tylee, J. (2002) AMV 'Don't Drive Tired' ad uses shock tactics, *Campaign*, 12, 10–11, and the Department of Transport website (http://www.thinkroadsafety.gov.uk/campaigns/drivertiredness/drivertiredness.htm).

Figure 8-12 Example of activation through erotic stimuli

Finally, **cognitive stimuli** can be used to activate customers. Particularly relevant here are surprise effects and contradictions (White 2000). However, there is a risk of '**vampire effects**', i.e. a distraction from the intended statement of the communication message (Catanescu and Tom 2001; Rossiter and Bellman 2005), also known as '**overshadowing**' (Belch and Belch 1998; Charbonneau and Gerlan 2005; Erdogan *et al.* 2001; Pornpitakpan 2003). Apart from this, '**boomerang effects**' (i.e. the message leads to a negative or opposite response; Arias-Bolzmann *et al.* 2000; Clee and Wicklund 1980; Mann and Hill 1984) or '**irritation effects**' (i.e. the communication makes the receiver feel uncertain or unsettled; Aaker and Bruzzone 1985; Chakrabarty *et al.* 2004) may occur (see the example in Focus on Marketing 8-4).

Focus on Marketing 8-4 Example of irritation effect

Crazy Frog named most irritating ad of the year

Jamster's Crazy Frog ringtone ad was named the most irritating TV execution of 2005 by the British public. The survey of 1000 adults, which was carried out exclusively for *Marketing* by TNS, revealed that 60% of the public thought the ad, showing the creature riding an invisible motorcycle to the backing of a version of Beverly Hills Cop theme Axel F, was the most irritating of the year. Much of their irritation was undoubtedly caused by Jamster's media buying strategy, which saw it spend £10m in May 2005 alone. The ad, created by Jamster's in-house team, was aired 83 times an hour.

Source: Barrand 2006, p. 1.

Besides these effects, the communication impact depends on the number of repetitions (frequency) as another form of cognitive stimuli. An example of a frequency technique is the **reminder method**. With this technique, the communication message is repeated, for example in several print ads in

Figure 8-13 Example of ensuring absorption of the communication message by means of a large picture with a relatively large amount of text

a magazine. The goal of this method is to use several contacts to increase the opportunity for the receiver to encode the information the communicator wishes to convey. Thus, repetition is required to get the message across (Shimp 2007).

In this context it is important to consider the level of **activation**, which refers to the process whereby a person is prepared for a subsequent reaction (for more information on 'activation' refer to the Appendix). A person can exhibit states from high activation (state of panic) to low activation (state of sleep), and a host of states in between these two extremes. Activation has an impact on the performance of a person (such as information processing). According to the **Lambda hypothesis** (Malmo 1959), the relationship between activation and cognitive or behavioral performance is described by an inverted U-curve. This means that, from a low activation level up to an optimum, the behavioral performance rises with increasing activation. Beyond this optimal point, further increases in activation produce a fall in performance level. According to this hypothesis it is important that the audience for an ad is neither very low activated nor extremely activated as this can result in low cognitive performance, such as low ad recall (for more on ad recall see Section 8.5).

A second objective of the techniques for creative work relates to **ensuring absorption of the communication message**. Communication receivers generally pay attention to the communication message for only a relatively short time – for example, the average time spent looking at a magazine advertisement is about 1.65 seconds (Percy and Elliot 2005). Often, the contact with the communication message is discontinued before the viewer/reader has reached the end (e.g. **zapping** – switching TV channels during commercials, see Batra *et al.* 1996), so that complete absorption of the information is not always guaranteed. This fact should be considered when designing the communication message.

In this context, it is important to note that **pictures** are perceived and processed more quickly than text (White 2000). Consequently, placing the product benefits or technical information directly in a picture can be helpful.

Techniques for creative work also provide information about how picture and text information is absorbed by the recipients of the communication. For example, large ads are usually looked at longer than smaller ones (White 2000), and color advertisements draw more attention than black-and-white ones (Percy and Elliot 2005). An example of creating associations between picture and text information is shown in Figure 8-13.

Conveying **emotional aspects** is another objective of techniques for creative work (see the Appendix for more on the concept of 'emotion'). Emotional stimuli are used to build awareness and brand strength (Fill 2005). Classical and emotional conditioning methods (for more on conditioning methods see the discussion of 'learning theory' in the Appendix) are employed to transfer emotional experience to the product/company through the repeated combined presentation of emotional stimuli and the product/company (Belch and Belch 1998; Hoyer and MacInnis 2004). An example of this is provided in Figure 8-14.

The fourth objective of the techniques for creative work relates to promoting a **cognitive understanding**. From the advertiser's viewpoint, the communication measure has to be designed so that the receiver processes and interprets the information contained in the communication message in the way it was intended by the company.

From the outset, the communication message should be designed so that it promotes understanding. In this connection, when developing print advertisements, it should be borne in mind that readers usually notice pictures first and often remain focused on them (Percy and Elliot 2005). Another important element in print ads is the headline. Only about 20 per cent of readers go beyond the headline and read the body copy (Belch and Belch 1998).

This **picture superiority effect** demonstrates that it is not sufficient to try to promote understanding primarily by means of text. Instead, understanding is best supported when the picture, headline and text complement each other so well that the reader can easily understand the message (Batra *et al.* 1996).

The fifth objective of the techniques for creative work concerns the **enhancement of learning and creation of knowledge** about the product/company being promoted. The activation and frequency techniques already discussed in this section help in embedding the communication message in the receiver's memory (i.e. the communication presentation has to be designed in such a way that it

Figure 8-14 Example of conveying emotion (sensuality) in an advertisement

facilitates the receiver in memorizing the communication message to the greatest extent possible). A catchy text and the use of memorable **key visuals** can also help in this process (Shimp 2007). Figure 8-15 shows an example of a print ad using key visuals.

As already mentioned, the techniques for creative work do not apply exclusively to print advertisements, but are also pertinent to other media. In this context, let us now turn to the design of television and cinema commercials.

Television and Cinema Commercials

With **TV commercials**, voice, sound and pictures can be combined, offering a particularly wide range of design options. Another advantage of television commercials lies in the fact that the availability of the medium for advertising purposes has increased significantly in recent years due to the burgeoning number of private channels. The CPMs for TV commercials are relatively low.

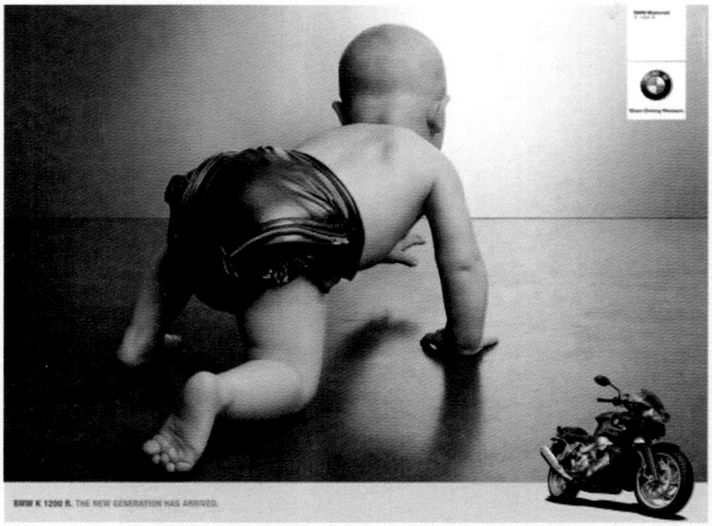

Figure 8-15 Example of embedding the communication message into memory by using key visuals

Table 8-7 TV advertising spending as a % of total advertising expenditure, G7 countries (World Advertising Research Center Ltd 2008)

TV advertising spending	2005	2006	2007 (forecast)
USA	36%	35%	35%
Japan	44%	43%	43%
UK	28%	26%	26%
Germany	24%	24%	25%
France	30%	29%	29%
Italy	48%	46%	46%
Canada	31%	29%	29%
in % of total advertising expenditure			

However, the absolute costs for a TV advertising campaign are generally relatively high, since most television channels broadcast nationwide (making local television commercials problematic) and the production costs are comparatively high (considerably higher than, say, for print ads). Table 8-7 lists TV advertising spending as percentage of total advertising expenditure in the G7 countries.

A disadvantage of TV commercials is that it is difficult to address a specific target group (particularly in programs seen by a broad public). This leads to coverage waste. If the objective is to address a special target group, it is recommended to place TV commercials on special interest channels (e.g. sports, music or news channels).

Another disadvantage is that, for a growing number of customers, TV commercials have become less and less acceptable. In a recent study on acceptance of TV ads in Europe, large percentages of TV watchers indicated that 'advertising is too much' (indicated by 74 per cent of TV viewers in Sweden, 80 per cent in France, 85 per cent in Italy and Russia, and 92 per cent in Spain; see GfK 2006). In this context, the phenomena of **zapping** (switching channels), **zipping** (fast-forwarding through recorded shows) and **muting** (switching off the sound) have to be mentioned. Special forms of advertising offer a response to these 'dodging' tactics on the part of the audience; for example, zapping can be prevented by a 'skyscraper' that is visible on the screen while the TV show is running. With 'single spots', a remark is inserted to say that the show will be interrupted briefly by a single TV spot and then continued immediately afterwards.

Some recommendations can be made as follows, with regard to designing TV commercials.

- The content of the TV spot's **storyline** should correspond to the product being advertised, otherwise the audience could become irritated (Young 2004).
- **Humor** can increase attention, especially if competitors do not use humor in their advertisements (Young 2004).
- The individual scenes should not be too short, otherwise there will be insufficient memory impact. To promote an effective memory impact, individual scenes should last a minimum of 1.5 seconds.
- An advertising spot is more positively received in a cheerful environment. The greatest impact of a humorous TV commercial can be achieved when presented in a cheerful **program environment** (DePelsmacker *et al.* 2002; Goldberg and Gorn 1987).
- While **music** is emotionally processed, text and voice messages are processed on a higher cognitive level. Therefore, music and jingles (i.e. short music sequences that play in conjunction with the product being advertised) from TV spots are usually remembered more easily than pure text or voice commercials (Reid 2001; Stewart *et al.* 1990).

Celebrity endorsers are widely used in television commercials to increase the effectiveness of advertising campaigns. Indeed, figures show that, worldwide, one in six commercials features a celebrity (Shimp 2007). According to the **Match-up hypothesis** (Kamins 1990; Till and Busler 1998, 2000) it is of crucial importance that the **spokesperson** is congruent with the product and/or brand being promoted. This fit has a positive impact on advertising outcomes, such as recall, attitude towards the brand and purchase intention (Kamins and Gupta 1994; Misra and Beatty 1994). See Figure 8-16 for an example of celebrity endorsement.

Cinema/screen advertising is characterized by a high probability of exposure and intensity (Kroeber-Riel and Weinberg 2003). On the other hand, the forced exposure can trigger adverse responses on the part of viewers, which can have a negative impact. In principle, the same recommendations for TV commercials apply to the design of cinema/screen ads.

Radio Spots

In many countries, the radio market is fragmented and local, which generally allows for effective segmentation. Other advantages of radio spots include low costs, relatively high reach and opportunities for integration with other communication measures (Bruhn 2005). Obviously, radio does not offer visual design options; however, it is known as the 'everywhere medium' because it can be heard in both an inside and outside environment (for example, in the car) (Klingler and Müller 2004).

The following design recommendations apply to **radio spots**.

- As with TV commercials, music and jingles should also be used in radio ads. Since there are no visual elements, music should play an even larger role than in television commercials. **Musical**

Figure 8-16 Supermodel Heidi Klum as celebrity endorser for McDonald's

elements increase attention and promote recognition of (i.e. the ability to remember) the radio spot and the product being advertised (Rossiter and Bellman 2005; Stewart *et al.* 1990) (for more on recognition, see Section 8.5).

- Studies show that listeners only follow radio programs with concentration for eight per cent of the time. They are most attentive to radio in the afternoon or evening while listening alone, during breakfast, when they first wake up and when they drive to work. Accordingly, these times offer the best opportunities to broadcast informative radio spots.

Outdoor Advertising

Outdoor advertising refers to advertisements that are placed in public areas. Most common are **poster advertisements** (e.g. large-format posters, illuminated 'city light' posters, electronic videoboards) and **transit advertisements** (e.g. ads on taxis, buses or trams) (for examples, see Figure 8-17).

Posters can be very precisely placed – for example, at a specific location – making them particularly effective for regional or local advertising. Moreover, customers perceive posters on the way to the **point of sale** or even at the point of sale. Poster advertisements therefore represent an advertising measure that is aimed at customers just before they make their purchase decision.

The following recommendations can be applied when designing outdoor advertisements.

- The effectiveness of outdoor advertising depends on the quality of the location, especially with regard to traffic frequency and visibility (Pasquier 1997). High traffic frequency and good visibility increase the OTS (**opportunities to see**) associated with a location.
- The **readability** of outdoor advertisements has the greatest impact on memory. Accordingly, outdoor ads should have large letters in an easy-to-read font. The colors used in the ad should also facilitate readability.

Figure 8-17 Examples of outdoor advertising (Agora 2007; Marketing Ad Ventures 2003; Van Wagner 2004)

- Furthermore, due to the short viewing period, outdoor advertisements should convey only limited information content.

Internet Advertising

Internet advertising comprises all advertising activities realized via websites on the World Wide Web (www). Since the internet has established itself as a mass medium, the majority of target groups can also be reached online (DePelsmacker *et al.* 2004). Table 8-8 underlines the commercial relevance of the web advertising market in Western Europe.

Important advantages of online advertising include excellent opportunities to customize ads on the basis of specific user profiles, as well as precise measurement of advertising effectiveness (e.g. through click-through rates). The interactive nature of online advertising is also beneficial: an appropriate advertisement design can provide customers with the option to directly interact with the advertising company (DePelsmacker 2005; DePelsmacker *et al.* 2004).

The following types of ads can be used within the scope of internet advertising (Fritz 2004).

- **Banners** are graphic images that can be integrated into a website (DePelsmacker *et al.* 2004; Rossiter and Bellman 2005). The user can click on the banner to switch to the website of the advertising company.

Table 8-8 The web advertising market in Western Europe (Forrester Research 2003)

Europe's web advertising market	Web advertising spend as % of traditional ad spend	Web advertising spend (in €m)	Adult web users (in thousands)	Web penetration of total population
Austria	0.6%	12	4,089	61%
Belgium	0.9%	17	4,383	53%
Denmark	1.3%	20	3,227	61%
Finland	1.1%	11	2,756	66%
France	1.0%	97	18,635	39%
Germany	0.8%	147	37,897	55%
Greece	0.0%	1	0,720	7%
Ireland	0.5%	3	1,180	41%
Italy	0.4%	34	23,180	48%
Luxembourg	1.9%	3	0,258	67%
Netherlands	1.2%	37	7,796	61%
Norway	2.5%	41	2,357	66%
Portugal	0.4%	9	3,245	40%
Spain	1.0%	37	10,622	32%
Sweden	5.0%	86	4,930	68%
Switzerland	1.1%	32	3,888	66%
UK	1.2%	198	29,315	61%

- **Pop-ups and interstitials** are online ads that open automatically in a separate browser window (DePelsmacker *et al.* 2004). With pop-ups, a new, small window appears over the website currently being visited. Pop-ups can be closed with a click. Interstitials are ads that function in the same way as commercial breaks and interrupt the user process; in extreme cases, they can take up the entire computer screen.
- **Hover ads** are layered over the content page and do not open in a separate window. They include floating ads, mouse-over banners and sticky ads. Floating ads give the impression that the advertisement is floating over the website being viewed. With mouse-over banners, the ad enlarges as soon as the mouse cursor is positioned over the banner. Sticky ads refer to advertisements that remain continuously in the visual range of the users, even when they scroll down the page.
- In the case of **search engine advertising** (also called search engine marketing or keyword advertising), the advertising company purchases advertising space from search engine providers

such as, say, Google; the ads are then linked to specific search terms. If a customer enters one of these search terms into the search engine, the ads of the advertising company are displayed, along with the search results obtained (DDV 2004).

- A **corporate blog** ('blog' is short for 'web log') is a 'website where an organization publishes and manages content to attain its goals' (Lee *et al.* 2006, p. 317). In 2007, 32% of the respondents to a global executive survey stated that they are currently using or planning to use blogs (McKinsey 2007). Mostly, companies employ blogs for the purposes of promotion, thought leadership, product development and customer service. Based on the characteristics of authors and content, corporate blogs are categorized as employee blogs, group blogs, executive blogs, promotional blogs and newsletter blogs (Lee *et al.* 2006).

The following design recommendations apply to internet advertising.

- In the consumer goods industry, rich media advertising (i.e. interactive elements, animations) yields significantly higher click-through rates than non-rich media advertising (Doubleclick 2004). In the business-to-business sector, however, animation usually does not lead to higher click-through rates (Lohtia *et al.* 2003).
- The quality of the website used as the advertising environment (e.g. user friendliness/accessibility, attractive design, easy navigation) has a positive impact on banner effectiveness (Danaher and Mullarkey 2003).
- Adverse responses towards internet advertising correlate directly with how often the surfing activities of the internet user are interrupted by the advertising. Accordingly, pop-ups should be used sparingly.
- The success of corporate blogs depends on their authenticity rather than the number of bloggers. A genuine executive blogger can provide significant benefits to the company in terms of thought leadership (Lee *et al.* 2006).

Mobile Marketing

Mobile marketing refers to marketing activities via mobile terminal devices (in particular cell phones) (Kavassalis *et al.* 2003). As with the internet, cell phones have evolved into a mass communication medium in many countries and are widely used in many population and age segments. In this section, we will focus on the use of mobile terminal devices for communication purposes. However, it should be noted that mobile marketing also comprises other marketing aspects (e.g. payments or product distribution via mobile terminal devices).

There are two basic mobile marketing approaches.

1. When applying the **push principle**, a company contacts the target persons via messages to their cell phones. Popular forms of messages are SMS (short message service, also called text messaging), MMS (multimedia messaging service), mobile coupons or mobile discount tickets. The target persons then respond with a cell phone message (e.g. via SMS).
2. The **pull principle** is based on making individuals aware of the mobile marketing presence of the advertising company by means of messages in other communication media (e.g. TV commercials, product packaging). In this case too, responses are submitted via cell phone messages (e.g. SMS), for example in order to participate in a contest, download an advertising ringtone or request a mobile coupon (see Focus on Marketing 8-5 for an example).

Key advantages of mobile marketing include location independence, interactivity and the option to address customers using a customized approach.

Focus on Marketing 8-5 Example of a mobile marketing pull campaign

Promotion goes digital at McDonald's
In the past McDonald's has always reinvented the way that it used within-store promotions. Such promotions often revolved around the launch of new films such as blockbuster cartoon films like *The Little Mermaid*, *Shrek*, *The Incredibles*, *Finding Nemo* and *Bee Movie*. For the launch of *Finding Nemo*, McDonald's launched a mobile marketing campaign in 2003. This campaign targeted 16–22 year olds, young families and mums, inviting customers to text a code that appeared on soft drink cups. With these codes, over 70 different Nemo-related mobile specials were offered, such as postcard greetings, movies, ringtones and voicemail messages. For the launch of the movie *The Incredibles* in 2004, McDonald's offered a Java game and movie soundbites.

McDonald's has run similar campaigns since then throughout Europe in markets including France, the UK, Germany and Scandinavia. During the World Cup in 2006, McDonald's also used mobile marketing to support its sponsorship of this event. The promotion revolved around a text-and-win campaign giving away tickets to the World Cup. In addition to the prize, each entrant could receive free mobile content such as ringtones, wallpapers and SMS tones. These campaigns can be very effective especially if supported by TV advertising, radio and PR.

Source: Brand Strategy 2005.

In addition to their key advantages, mobile marketing campaigns can also be implemented quickly. Only a short lead time is required and due to the interactive nature of the medium, responses from the target group come in quickly after the message has been sent. Another advantage lies in **viral effects**, which arise from receivers forwarding the advertising message (e.g. an advertising SMS) to friends and peers. Such viral effects increase the range of advertising and reduce costs, while also lending the advertising message more credibility with the secondary receivers, since they receive the message from their friends or peers (Bauer *et al.* 2005).

With regard to disadvantages, mobile marketing can trigger adverse responses on the part of customers (Bauer *et al.* 2005). Moreover, mobile marketing push campaigns are associated with comparatively high CPMs (Boyce 1998; Cuneo 2006).

The following recommendations can be made for mobile marketing.

- In order to avoid adverse responses on the part of the receivers of push campaigns, it is advisable to request their permission prior to sending messages (e.g. via registration on a website) (**permission marketing**; see Kavassalis *et al.* 2003).
- In conjunction with permission, data concerning the personal preferences and interests of the target persons can be collected, which in turn can be used to achieve a customized approach.
- Mobile marketing should be associated with benefits for the receivers. Possible benefits include entertainment value, information, incentives (e.g. free ringtones) or price discounts (e.g. mobile coupons; see Bauer *et al.* 2005).
- Mobile campaigns should be designed in such a way that the company can benefit from viral effects. For example, receivers can be directly informed of the option to forward the advertising message; the forwarding concept can be an integrated component of the campaign itself (e.g. 'Send an MMS love message to your girlfriend!') (see Focus on Marketing 8-6 for an example of mobile marketing).

Focus on Marketing 8-6 Example of mobile couponing campaigns

European brands support use of mobile campaigns
Cosmetic brand Yves Rocher and Club Nokia have thrown their weight behind mobile marketing with new campaigns in France and Turkey. In France it launches a mobile couponing campaign for cosmetic brand Yves Rocher. Supported by point-of-sale, poster and flyer advertising, the campaign enables consumers to redeem coupons either online or in store. The campaign, to win rugby tickets, captured the date of birth of participants to ensure no under-18s were entering, thereby revealing the average age of the respondents.

In Turkey, [the mobile marketing company] Aerodeon was behind the launch of three campaigns for Nokia. [E.g.] an MMS greeting card campaign went out to Club Nokia members, and a mobile couponing campaign gave winners free entry to a Nokia sponsored music festival.

Source: Aerodeon 2004, p. 9.

Direct Marketing

Direct marketing comprises all market-related activities that use the one-step flow of (i.e. direct) communication (see also Section 8.1) to specifically address individual target groups. Means of communication include media such as advertising letters, advertising postcards, postal mail, faxes and emails. This individualized approach establishes direct contact with the receiver. Direct marketing overlaps with other communication measures (e.g. direct marketing activities can also be implemented with internet marketing and mobile marketing measures). This section will concentrate on direct marketing using the above-mentioned 'offline' media.

In recent years, direct marketing has gained in importance. To obtain an overview of the full range of direct marketing activities, it is useful to examine their **degree of customization**. As illustrated in Figure 8-18, direct marketing activities range from completely standardized measures to completely customized measures, impacting costs, response, precision of targeting, focusing, but also target group size.

An advantage of direct marketing as compared to other communication measures is that it allows customers to be addressed in a personalized way. Additional advantages include easy measurability of the impact and effectiveness of direct marketing (e.g. response rates to a mailing) and the ability to control the process. A major disadvantage is associated with the increasing number of direct marketing activities and possible adverse responses from customers. For example, in connection with the internet, unsolicited and mostly unwanted **junk mail** and **spam** have become widely used (Keaney and Remenyi 2004). Moreover, acceptance of direct marketing activities is decreasing on the part of many individuals, who feel that their private space is being invaded (Sheehan and Hoy 1999).

The following general design recommendations apply to direct marketing.

- In general, **addressed mailings** arouse more interest.
- With addressed mailings, the **address quality** is particularly important (i.e. complete and correct addresses) (Del Polito 2005). The mailing list can therefore be an important success factor of direct mailings (Belch and Belch 2004). To reduce coverage waste in mailing campaigns, microgeographic segmentation can be used, with which lifestyle and purchasing behavior can be identified based on housing and residential conditions (Holland 2004; Kothe 2002; Meinert 1997).

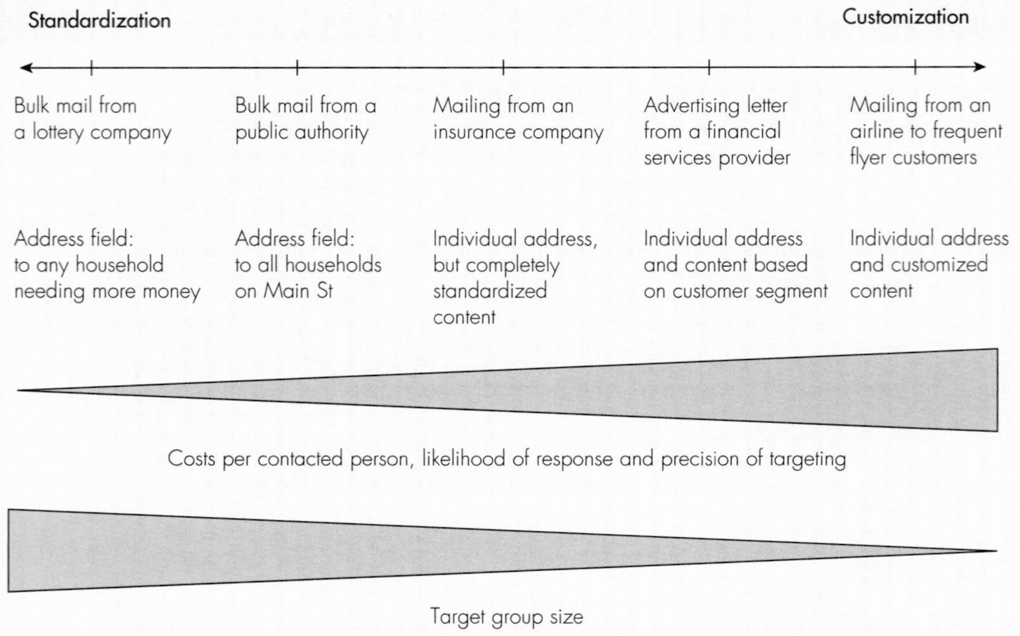

Figure 8-18 Characterization of direct marketing measures based on various dimensions

- If direct marketing activities are based on customer data, the addressing of customers in the target groups within the scope of these activities should be as *specific* as possible. By using customer data from the customer database, communication content can be developed that matches the specific preferences and interests of customers (e.g. an airline offering special destinations to customers based on data from its frequent flyer program).
- With respect to the adverse responses that customers have had to direct marketing activities, and in line with the permission marketing approach, those who have opted out of direct marketing contact (e.g. by placing themselves on opt-out lists) should not be contacted.

Sales Promotion

Sales promotion is 'action communication', which aims to increase sales in the short run from both existing and new customers on the basis of a temporary incentive or deal (DePelsmacker *et al.* 2004). There are two basic categories: **price-based sales promotions** and **non-price-based sales promotions**. In this chapter we focus on non-price sales promotions.

Sales promotions can target either end customers or dealers/sales organizations. **Sales promotions targeted at end customers** can be undertaken by both manufacturers and retailers (Neslin 2002, p. 33; for more information, also see Ailawadi *et al.* 2001). Sales promotions intended for end customers have the following functions:

- provide information (e.g. brochures, consumer exhibitions, training events)
- trigger motivation (e.g. contests, product samples, special promotions)
- promote sales (e.g. bonuses, giveaways, coupons, retail displays).

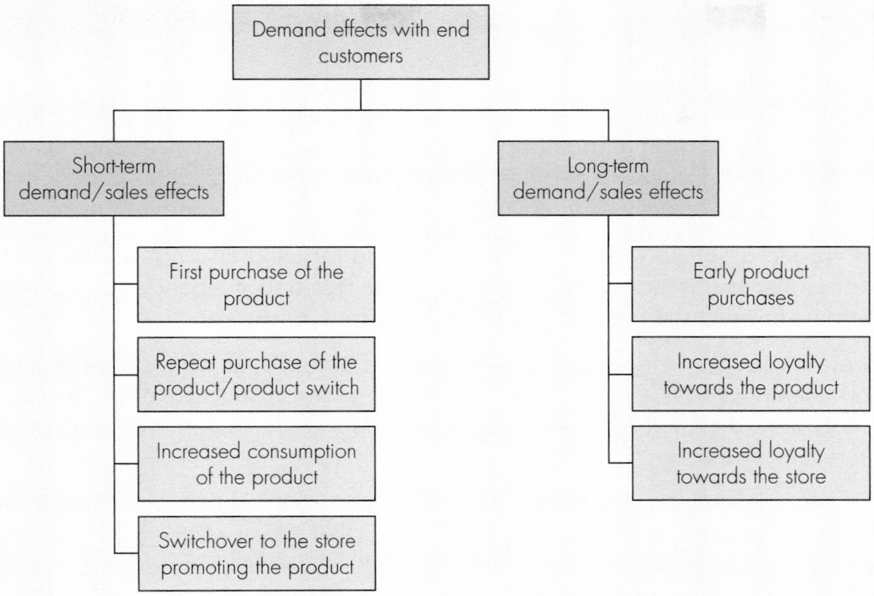

Figure 8-19 Effects of end customer-related sales promotion on the demand for the promoted product at the store conducting the promotional activities (adapted from Gedenk 2002, p. 104)

The resulting effects on end customers' demand are depicted in Figure 8-19 (Gedenk 2002). Objectives include both short-term and long-term increases in demand and sales.

Sales promotions can also be directed at dealers and sales organizations. Basically, these promotional efforts pursue the same objectives as if they were directed at end customers (i.e. an increase in sales using temporary incentives). The specific incentives for intermediaries are aimed at:

- providing information (e.g. dealer mailings, seminars, training courses)
- triggering motivation (e.g. bonus systems, free gifts)
- promoting sales (e.g. manuals, argumentation aids, test results).

The following recommendations apply to the design of these measures of sales promotion.

- An important aspect of sales promotion concerns its integration with other communication measures. For example, to boost the impact of sales promotion measures, it is recommended that they are integrated with media advertising and direct marketing activities.
- The **bonus** or prospective advantage(s) offered to the customer plays an essential role in the success of the sales promotion measure (D'Astous and Jacob 2002).

Public Relations

Public relations (commonly referred to as PR) helps to identify, establish and maintain relationships between the company and various public target groups that may have an impact on the company's success (Cutlip *et al.* 2006). **Target groups** can be categorized into **social groups** and **stakeholders**,

Focus on Marketing 8-7 Example of a public relations campaign

UNICEF's media relations in Nigeria

High mortality rates, illness and nutritional deficiencies threaten the survival of Nigerian children. Child labor, child trafficking and harmful traditional cultural and religious practices such as female genital mutilation and sharia endanger their freedom and rights. In 2000, advocacy and communication efforts on behalf of protecting children's rights were at a low ebb in the country.

In response, UNICEF forged an effective partnership with media for children's rights. The goal of the Media Alliance for Children campaign was to create awareness and advocacy, and to stimulate action of the stakeholders to meet the needs and rights of children in Nigeria.

Foreign journalists were invited for field visits and dialogs. Media packages were developed for the media houses. In partnership with NGOs, media programs were organized. Children Special Day programs and materials were distributed. The federal government's information policy makers/ managers were invited to workshops.

The media campaign was successful in bringing children's rights to the public's attention because of the response of both the Nigerian and foreign journalists to UNICEF's program. The result was positive reports in the media locally and internationally on UNICEF's activities, advocacy and support for the protection of children's rights. The support of the federal government for children also increased.

Source: Odedele and Faith 2004, p. 126.

with each group having different information requirements. In addition to the population in general, social groups include, for example, the public media and their representatives, public authorities and politicians, as well as political organizations. Among stakeholders, there are customers, shareholders, suppliers, employees, consumer organizations, public community groups and environmental protection organizations, all of which can have a significant impact on public opinion. For example, a consumer protection organization can initiate a campaign against the genetically modified products of food manufacturers (i.e. those with GM ingredients).

With respect to **content**, public relations addresses an organization or person, and not usually an individual product. Topics communicated within the scope of public relations particularly include staff changes, new products launches, annual reports, initiatives in corporate social responsibility, important visits, etc. For an example see Focus on Marketing 8-7.

Public relations aims to develop public trust, designing and sustaining relationships with the public, establishing and maintaining a positive company/product image, as well as keeping employees up to date and motivated (Fill 2001; Grunig and Huang 2000; Kotler and Keller 2006; Pieczka 2000). These **objectives** can be categorized into corporate goals with an internal focus (e.g. building corporate identity), corporate goals with an external focus (e.g. building goodwill) and marketing goals (e.g. support for marketing activities) (see Table 8-9).

The following primary public relation measures need to be mentioned.

- Press releases and publications, websites and interviews are key **media relations** measures (Herbst 1997).

Table 8-9 Various categories of public relations objectives (DePelsmacker *et al.* 2004, p. 281)

Corporate goals				Marketing goals
Internal focus	External focus			
	Public affairs	Financial	Media	
■ Information ■ Training ■ Motivation ■ Building corporate identity	■ Impact of trends ■ Public visibility ■ Information ■ Opinions ■ Attitudes ■ Corporate image ■ Build goodwill ■ Influence decision	■ Information ■ Credibility ■ Trust	■ Information ■ Opinions ■ Corporate image ■ Goodwill	■ Support marketing agenda ■ New products ■ Sponsorship ■ Events

- **Events** include press conferences, lectures, seminars, congresses, conferences and open house days.
- The objective of **relationship management** is to establish and maintain contacts, including contact with opinion leaders and multipliers with media presence for the dissemination of public relations messages, industry meetings, lobbying, journalism and donations.
- **Crisis management** aims at protecting and enhancing the corporate reputation and identity during a crisis (Lukaszewski 2001), with a focus on maintaining the credibility of the company by means of open communication (Ihlen 2002; also see Focus on Marketing 8-8 for more information).

Focus on Marketing 8-8 Example of crisis management

Odwalla and the E. coli outbreak

Odwalla (pronounced 'odewalla') is [a] health-conscious juice company. [In the 1990s] the company was growing strongly with annual sales rising 30% per year and approaching $90m. The company had established a strong brand with enormous customer loyalty.

On October 30, 1996, everything changed. Health officials in Washington state informed the company that they had discovered a link between several cases of E. coli 0157:H7 and Odwalla fresh apple juice. The link was confirmed on November 5. As the crisis played itself out, one child died and more than 60 people in the Western United States and Canada became sick after drinking the juice. Sales plummeted by 90%, Odwalla's stock price fell 34%. Customers filed more than 20 personal-injury lawsuits and the company looked as though it could well be destroyed.

Focus on Marketing 8-8 (Continued)

Odwalla acted immediately. Although at the point where they were first notified the link was uncertain, Odwalla's CEO Stephen Williamson ordered a complete recall of all products containing apple or carrot juice. This recall covered around 4,600 retail outlets in seven states. Internal task teams were formed and mobilized, and the recall – costing around $6.5m – was completed within 48 hours.

Internal communications were key: Williamson conducted regular company-wide conference calls on a daily basis, giving employees the chance to ask questions and get the latest information. This approach proved so popular that the practice of quarterly calls survived the crisis.

External communications were just as vital. Within 24 hours, the company had an explanatory web site (its first) that received 20,000 hits in 48 hours. The company spoke to the press, appeared on TV and carried out direct advertising with the website address. All possible attempts were made to provide up to the minute, accurate information.

The next step was to tackle the problem of contamination. The company moved quickly to introduce a process called 'flash pasteurisation' which would guarantee that E. coli had been destroyed whilst leaving the best flavored juice possible.

The year after the crisis, Odwalla was voted 'Best Brand Name in the Bay Area' by *San Francisco Magazine*. This was the first indication amongst many that Odwalla's reputation had survived.

Source: Baker 2007.

In terms of the design of public relations, the following recommendations can be made.

- With regard to content, public relations should be integrated with other communication tools in order to create synergies. For example, a company can communicate its sponsoring activities via press releases or interviews, and thus increase the impact and credibility of these activities.
- It is recommended that the tasks and responsibilities of the **PR department** are clearly defined and managed separately from other marketing communication departments (Cornelissen and Lock 2000; Ehling *et al.* 1992; Grunig and Grunig 1998; Kitchen and Moss 1995).

Trade Fairs

Trade fairs are measures of **personal communication** and are closely related to personal selling. To some extent, there are no clear-cut differences: for example, companies often use trade fairs not only to achieve communication objectives, but also to realize sales objectives.

A trade fair is an event that takes place at a certain time at a certain location, during which several companies present themselves to their target groups. In most cases, trade fairs are regular events with a clearly defined focus (often geared towards specific industry sectors). Many trade fairs are attended by international suppliers and visitors.

Trade fairs have several functions: they offer companies the opportunity to establish customer contact, present the company, provide customers with information, support the launch of new products, generate sales, tap into export opportunities, directly compare their own products and services to those offered by the competition, and identify trends (Bello and Barksdale 1986; Bonoma 1983; Smith *et al.* 2004).

Table 8-10 Objectives associated with participating in trade fairs (Kerin and Cron 1987)

Selling objectives	Non-selling objectives
Examples: ■ introducing new products ■ selling at the trade show ■ stimulating add-on sales ■ testing new products	Examples: ■ widening exposure ■ identifying new prospects ■ servicing current customers ■ gathering competitive information ■ enhancing corporate image ■ enhancing corporate morale

The objectives associated with participating in trade fairs can be categorized into **selling and non-selling objectives** (Bonoma 1983; see also Table 8-10). When pursuing selling goals, companies focus mainly on maintaining relationships with current customers or acquiring new customers. Non-selling goals focus on providing information to customers, and gathering information about potential customers and competitors. Another purpose is to communicate the 'event experience' in order to trigger certain emotions with the visitors and enhance the corporate image.

The interpersonal communication with (potential) customers at trade fairs is especially important in business-to-business marketing. Since complex products are frequently sold in this particular segment face-to-face communication during trade fairs can help customers to assess product features more easily and adequately than communication through conventional media channels. For many companies in the industrial goods sector, funding allocated to trade fairs is a key factor in the communication budget. A particularly widespread practice is the use of trade fairs to present new products. In some industries, it is customary to present new products for the first time to industry specialists and expert audiences at certain trade fairs (see Focus on Marketing 8-9).

Focus on Marketing 8-9 Example of an international trade fair

Frankfurt Motor Show

The Frankfurt Motor Show is one of the largest and most important international auto shows in Europe. Although it occurs on an annual basis, it alternates between passenger vehicles one year and commercial vehicles the next. Because of this, the Frankfurt auto show swaps positions with the biannual Paris International Motor Show as Europe's most important auto show.

As you might expect, the Frankfurt Motor Show is dominated by German manufacturers. Companies like Audi, BMW, Mercedes-Benz and Porsche typically use the Frankfurt Motor Show as their launching pad for new models.

It's still an international show, however, so there's an occasional US or Japanese debut thrown in for good measure. If there's one thing that distinguishes the Frankfurt Motor Show from the other international auto shows, it's the sheer size of its displays. Spread out over roughly 10 halls, walking the show floor means putting in at least a few good miles. It takes 10 minutes just to get from one hall to another, and once you're in them they have so many cars on display you can spend hours in each one.

Source: Edmunds' *Inside Line* 2007.

Figure 8-20 Example of an event concept: 'Red Bull Flugtag'

Events

Events offer customers opportunities to interact with the company and its products. Events help to establish **personal contact** with customers in an informal and pleasant setting. The aim is to create a **memorable experience** for the event participants and make them feel that they are taking part in something special, or even unique. Therefore, events are associated with a high degree of **emotionality** (Sneath *et al.* 2005). Figure 8-20 shows an example of event marketing.

With respect to designing events, the following recommendations can be made.

- The content and activities offered during the event should have an emotional character in order to attract the interest of the target group (Nufer 2002).
- To create synergies, events should be integrated into the marketing mix (Gupta 2003). Depending on the company's objectives and target groups, a combination of classic advertising in mass media (e.g. promoting an event within the scope of advertising activities), public relations (e.g. promoting an event in press releases) and direct marketing (e.g. personalized invitations for important customers) is particularly effective (Sneath *et al.* 2005).
- The theme of the event should correspond with the company or product being promoted (Gupta 2003), both for credibility purposes and to facilitate the desired **image transfer** from the event to the product or company. An example in this context is a winter sports event organized by a fashionable wristwatch company that addresses a young, stylish, and hip target group.

Corporate Identity

Corporate identity (CI) is a holistic concept that comprises various aspects of a company (Melewar 2003). As a comprehensive communication measure, corporate identity represents the orientation of all the internal and external communication processes of a company. The aim of CI is the standardization and consistency of communication activities in order to establish a distinct corporate 'personality'.

Such standardization is growing in importance in view of the increasing information overload for customers, and against the background of numerous company mergers, which require merging enterprises to integrate their communication activities (for more information, also see Melewar and Harrold 2000).

A strong CI has many effects, ranging from employee motivation (through identification with the company) to the development of a strong brand, up to differentiation from the competition.

Corporate identity comprises three areas (Berndt 2005):

1 corporate design

2 corporate communications

3 corporate behavior.

The **corporate design** includes all visual cues by which a target group recognizes the company and distinguishes it from other companies. It can be understood as the visual implementation of the CI (Melewar 2003). The following design elements can be standardized on a company-wide basis using very specific guidelines: company name, slogan, logo, symbol, typeface and color palette (Melewar and Saunders 1998, 1999).

Corporate communications comprise the application of the corporate identity principles as well as, in particular, corporate design with regard to the use of communication measures (e.g. within the scope of advertising in mass media and direct marketing).

Corporate behavior refers to the attitude and behavior of the company's employees, particularly towards customers. Examples here include standardized employee attire and codes of conduct (see Focus on Marketing 8-10 for an example from company practice).

Focus on Marketing 8-10 Example of standardized employee conduct

Corporate identity at the Ritz-Carlton

Our Motto is: 'We are Ladies and Gentlemen serving Ladies and Gentlemen.' As service professionals, we treat our guests and each other with respect and dignity.

'Smile – We are on stage'. Always maintain positive eye contact. Use the proper vocabulary with our guests and each other. (Use words like – 'Good Morning,' 'Certainly,' 'I'll be happy to' and 'My pleasure.')

Use Ritz-Carlton telephone etiquette. Answer within three rings with a 'smile.'

The Three Steps of Service:

1. A warm and sincere greeting. Use the guest name, if and when possible.
2. Anticipation and compliance with guest needs.
3. Fond farewell. Give them a warm good-bye and use their names, if and when possible.

Source: © 1992–2007 The Ritz-Carlton Hotel Company, LLC. All rights reserved. Reprinted with permission of The Ritz-Carlton Hotel Company, LLC.

Sponsoring

Sponsoring (specific activities are called **sponsorships**) includes all activities aimed at promoting and supporting individuals or organizations in the area of sports, culture, social services, environmental protection or the media (Crimmins and Horn 1996; Dolphin 2003; Meenaghan 1998). In contrast to patronage or donations, sponsoring functions on a quid pro quo basis and expects compensation in the form of a contribution to achieving the communication objectives (Bruhn 1998). Sponsors are entitled to associate their companies with the promoted and supported activities, and to use these associations in their marketing activities (Cornwell and Maignan 1998). In the recent past, sponsoring has become increasingly important in company practice. This is due to its high acceptance on the part of customers, and the strong credibility of this communication tool.

In principle, companies can use four different **forms of sponsoring** (Bruhn 2003a, 2003b), as described below.

1. **Sports sponsoring** (promotion and support of individual athletes, teams or sports events) has the greatest economic significance among the forms of sponsorship described here, which is primarily attributed to the intensive media coverage of sports events (Levin *et al.* 2001). Focus on Marketing 8-11 offers an example of sports sponsorship.
2. In the case of **program sponsoring** (promotion and support of program content, broadcasts, movies, series or talk shows in electronic media such as TV, radio or the internet), the sponsor's name or a spot featuring the sponsor are shown before, during or after a TV or radio broadcast.
3. **Cultural sponsoring** (promotion and support of cultural activities, including, say, music, visual arts, performing arts, media art, literature, architecture, design or leisure culture, as well as individual artists, cultural events or foundations; see Focus on Marketing 8-12 for an example) strives to positively influence the image of a sponsor by demonstrating its social responsibility.
4. The goal of **social and environmental sponsoring** is to improve the image of the sponsor (Meenaghan and Shipley 1999) by promoting and supporting activities related to healthcare and social systems, science and education, as well as the protection of nature and endangered species. This form of sponsorship is also known as **public sponsoring**.

Focus on Marketing 8-11 Example of the continual alignment of a sponsorship concept

Sponsorship occupies an important position in the firm's overall marketing and communications strategies. UBS is the first main partner of the Alinghi Challenge to the America's Cup as a result of the perfect symbiosis between its brand values and attributes and those of sailing and the America's Cup in particular. Sailing represents an ideal business metaphor with the interplay between strategy, tactics, stamina, speed and mastery of state-of-the-art technology reflecting UBS's approach in the global finance business.

Source: Alinghi 2006.

Focus on Marketing 8-12 Example of cultural sponsorship

Airline Emirates sponsors Melbourne, Sydney, and Western Australian Symphony Orchestras

'Music touches the hearts of people worldwide, bringing pleasure, creating memorable experiences and allowing people from a variety of cultures and communities to come together. It is this ability to bring people together and provide a memorable and lasting experience that makes the Melbourne Symphony, Sydney Symphony, and Western Australian Symphony ideal partners for Emirates.'

'Emirates' involvement as Principal Partner in 2003 is an expansion of Emirates' existing relationships with the Melbourne and Sydney Symphony Orchestras. The Principal Partner sponsorship in 2003 is the first major sponsorship arrangement Emirates has entered into in Western Australia, following the launch of services between Perth and Dubai in August 2002.'

'Both the Melbourne and Sydney deals include exclusive sponsorship of the Chief Conductor and Artistic Directors Designate – Gianluigi Gelmetti and Oleg Caetani respectively. In addition, the sponsorship provides various opportunities, including the potential for the Symphonies to travel to Dubai to perform, and the Concertmasters to visit Dubai to undertake a training program or masterclass for young musicians' (Emirates 2007).

[For Emirates] 'the sponsorships provide opportunities to treat top customers and valued partners to the "Emirates experience". The airline hosted several hospitality nights every year with each symphony, inviting guests to enjoy magnificent concerts and exclusive cocktail receptions. Emirates hosted a range of events with each orchestra, ranging from intimate pre-concert dinners for 20 to post-concert parties for 200' (Pando Publications 2005).

Source: Emirates 2007; Pando Publications 2005.

With regard to the design of sponsorships, the following steps are recommended.

- When selecting the objects and activities to be sponsored, their affinity to the target groups should be considered (**target group affinity**) (Gwinner and Eaton 1999).
- The selection should also ensure that the image of the sponsored object or activity is in line with the desired image of the company (sponsor) or, at a minimum, that the images do not conflict (**image affinity**) (Gwinner 1997; Gwinner and Eaton 1999).
- Sponsoring has a particularly strong positive impact on individuals who have personally attended or participated in the event (Bennett 1999; D'Astous and Bitz 1995; Heuer and Reisberg 1990). Consequently, the sponsor should specifically encourage addressees to get involved in the sponsored event (e.g. by providing free tickets).
- The sponsor should aim at high visibility of the company's own name and brands during the event (Stipp and Schiavone 1996).
- Since failures and personal scandals involving sponsored individuals (e.g. athletes) can lead to negative image transfer, the promotion and support of individuals (e.g. individual athletes) should be carefully evaluated in advance (Walliser 2003).
- Sponsoring activities should be integrated with the other communication mix components (Stipp and Schiavone 1996) and should have a long-term focus.

Product Placement

Product placement refers to the integration of products into the plot of various media programs (e.g. movies, TV series, entertainment programs). While product placement takes a back seat compared to other communication measures, its overall importance is increasing (in part due to negative reactions towards advertising) (for more on the acceptance of product placement, see Gupta *et al.* 2000; McKechnie and Zhou 2003).

A significant advantage of product placement over other communication measures is that the product is not perceived within an advertising context, but as part of the plot. Moreover, many more customers are reached, since, in contrast to TV commercials, viewers do not usually zap through the program. Product placements are mainly used in order to increase awareness and sales. Table 8-11 provides an overview of the various types of product placement (see Figure 8-21 for an example and Focus on Marketing 8-13 for the importance of product placement in Korea).

Table 8-11 Types of product placement (according to Tolle 1995, column 2096; Vergossen 2004, p. 294)

Distinctive characteristic	Types of product placement	Description
Product type	Product placement in the strictest sense	Placement of branded products
	Corporate placement	Placement of companies
	Generic placement	Placement of generic (non-branded) products
	Innovation placement	Placement of new products
	Location placement	Placement of locations
	City placement	Placement of cities
Degree of integration	On-set placement	Placement not directly connected to the plot
	Creative placement	Placement directly connected to the plot
	Image/drama placement	Theme of the movie is aligned to the product
Type of information transmission	Visual placement	Transmission of visual information
	Verbal placement	Transmission of verbal information
	Combined placement	Combination of visual and verbal information transmission
Degree of association with leading actor	Placement with endorser	Placement endorsed by leading actor
	Placement without endorser	No direct connection between leading actor and product

Figure 8-21 Example of product placement: BMW's Z8 launch in the James Bond movie *The World is not Enough*

Focus on Marketing 8-13 The significance of product placements for the film industry

Paying off the stars through advertising

When actor Yeon Jeong-Hoon drove a new Audi A6 equipped with KTF's global positioning system to the Hotel Shilla during a scene in the drama 'Sad Love Story', none of the brand-name posturing was unplanned.

Such advertisements in dramas as a marketing tool have existed for a long time, but product placement has become an indispensable part of Korean TV dramas due to increasing advertising costs. Independent production companies produce most TV dramas while television stations finance the shows and retain the copyright.

'It is impossible to cast top stars without product placement,' said Lim Hoi-Joung, the president of Olive Communication & Production, a product placement marketing agency. And the top stars are a decisive factor in a drama's success. Product placement is taken into consideration at the initial stages when a script is created, Ms. Lim said. First, the producers of the drama ponder what kinds of products would be suitable. Proposals go to prospective advertisers, and they compete for an advertising slot before they go into negotiations. Producers talk to scenario writers about what the advertisers want from the drama and where they want their products placed.

Although scripts are modified in consideration of product placement, 'the outline of the scenarios remains unchanged,' said Lee Mee-Jee of Kimjonghak Production, the producer of the drama 'Sad Love Story'.

'Television commercials are too expensive and product placement as an indirect advertisement is relatively effective in terms of cost,' Ms. Lim said. 'It is a win-win condition for both advertisers and producers.'

Source: Jae-Un 2005.

The following recommendations apply when designing product placement.

- Similar to sponsorships, ensuring **affinity** is an important aspect of product placement. To this end, the product and program target groups should match (target group affinity), and the themes and actors should reflect the product image (image affinity).
- The advertised product should be integrated into the plot/environment in a way that does not irritate viewers (Brennan *et al.* 1999). Associating the product placement with the leading actor is especially effective (D'Astous and Chartier 2000). However, placing the product in very suspenseful scenes poses the risk of viewers being overactivated, leading to a reduction in cognitive performance and thus possibly to the product not being perceived (for more on the concept of 'activation' see the Appendix and refer to the discussion in Section 8.4).

8.5 Making a Splash? Monitoring the Impact of Communication

In Section 8.1 we have already discussed that monitoring the impact and effectiveness of communication becomes relevant during two phases of the planning process: before and after the implementation phase (see Figure 8-2). Before the implementation phase, the impact of the communication measures has to be evaluated, particularly in the case of cost-intensive communication activities (via pre-test). After the implementation phase, the actual market success of these communication measures has to be analyzed (via post-test).

It is important to determine which variables need to be measured in order to assess whether the communication objectives (see Section 8.2) have been met. The main measurement variables considered here are as follows (Bauer *et al.* 1998; Vakratsas and Ambler 1999):

- **activation effects** (e.g. the creation of attention)
- **cognitive effects** (e.g. short-term assimilation and understanding of the communicated message, evaluation of the credibility of the communicated message, storage of the communicated content in long-term memory)
- **emotional effects** (e.g. attractiveness and acceptance of the communicated content, storage of emotional triggers in long-term memory)
- **attitude-related effects** (e.g. attitude towards advertised brand)
- **behavioral effects** (e.g. intention to purchase the advertised product).

Further, it has to be considered whether measurements are taken under laboratory conditions or in the field (see the Appendix for a discussion of 'experiments'). When measurements are taken under (artificial) laboratory conditions, interfering variables are easier to control than when measurements are taken under real-life conditions. Frequently, field measurements are conducted within the scope of panels or test markets (for a discussion of methods of 'market research' see the Appendix).

As already mentioned, there are pre-tests and post-tests. **Pre-tests** are conducted before implementing communication measures, even before these measures are finally conceptualized, designed and executed. The objective here is to select the communication alternative that shows the best results with respect to the desired outcome, taking into account the required effort and expense. Another goal of pre-tests is to adjust communication activities to the intended target audience. For example, preliminary versions of the communication measures are presented to the respondents for evaluation within the course of **copy tests** (Fenwick and Rice 1991; Haley *et al.* 1994).

Table 8-12 Example questions assessing attitudes with regard to the communication activities of a German newspaper introducing a small-format paper

	Possible questions
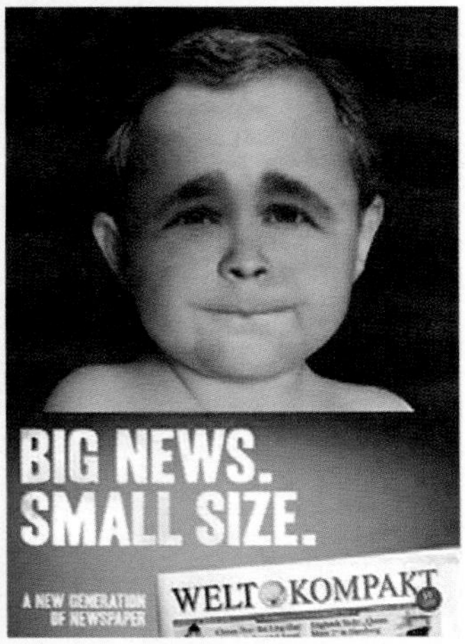	'What connotations do you associate with this advertisement?' 'Do you think this advertisement is funny?' 'In your opinion, does the picture match the advertising message?'

Post-tests are conducted after implementing communication measures, and can be categorized into test types that refer to either a specific point in time or a certain period of time (see Esch 2000 as well as Bauer *et al.* 2001 for an overview). In the first case, the advertising effect is analyzed for a specific point in time, an example being **day-after recall** on the day after a commercial was aired. Tests that refer to a certain period of time are called **tracking studies**; they periodically measure, for instance, the degree of awareness of a product over an extended period of time.

Two **measurement methods** are discussed here:

1 surveys, and

2 observations.

In **surveys**, questions assessing **attitudes** and **recall questions** play a key role. Measuring the communication impact and effectiveness by assessing attitudes aims to identify and record the attitudes of the target persons with regard to the advertised product or the advertising activity itself. Table 8-12 provides an example of assessing attitudes in a survey (for more information on 'surveys' and 'attitudes' refer to the Appendix).

In contrast, **recall questions** aim to determine to what extent a person recalls certain aspects of an advertisement. Recall questions can refer to, for example, the content of a commercial, advertised brand, background music or specific pictures. Of particular relevance here is the differentiation between **aided recall** and **unaided recall**. With aided recall, people are shown a list of brand names and asked to indicate which brand they remember from a recent ad. With unaided recall, no such list is provided and test subjects have to name the brand that comes to mind. Whereas recall refers to the retrieval of information about the advertisement from memory, **recognition** is the ability to remember having seen the advertisement before (Hoyer and MacInnis 2004). The validity of methods for recall and recognition measurement is limited by **spill-over effects**. For example, familiar, well-established brands always have higher recognition rates than less established brands, regardless of the advertisement motif. Table 8-13 provides examples of recall questions.

Table 8-13 Examples of questions used in survey-based post-tests

Influencing factor and example	Possible questions
Recognition 	'Do you recognize this automobile advertisement?'
Unaided recall	'Which automobile advertisements are you familiar with?'
Aided recall Ford advertisement Opel advertisement	'Are you familiar with ads from the following automobile companies?'

In addition to surveys, communications' impact can also be evaluated by means of **observation**. In this context, a fundamental difference concerns whether behavioral processes or behavioral outcomes are observed. **Behavioral processes** can be observed by means of, say, videotaping customer responses to advertisements in retail stores. Audience ratings for TV and radio broadcasts represent another example. With respect to internet-based communication, observations can provide data about visits (number of visitors to a website), page impressions (number of hits on a website) and click-through rates for banner ads (clicks on banners that link to the website of the company placing the ad). On this basis, for example, the 'conversion rate' (number of orders divided by number of visitors who clicked on the banner) can be calculated. Observations of **behavioral outcomes** are primarily concerned with observing purchase behavior and can be based on, say, scanner terminals or panels.

There are various **special instrumental measurement methods** that facilitate the analysis of the communication impact and effectiveness by using **observation techniques** (see the Appendix for more on 'observations'). These methods include non-verbal, psychobiological test procedures for measuring perceptions and attitudes in the form of physical reactions. Figure 8-22 provides an overview of such methods.

Activation measurement methods serve to identify the activation potential of communication. There are three categories of methods, as outlined below.

1 **Cardic pulse measurement** detects emotional responses to communication activities and thus identifies their activation potential (Wiles and Cornwell 1990).

2 **Galvanic skin response (GSR)**, frequently also called **electrodermal response (EDR)**, measures electrical conductance in the skin by means of two electrodes attached to the palm of the hand (Belch and Belch 1998; Klebba 1985). Emotion and agitation increase the conductance of the skin due to increased perspiration.

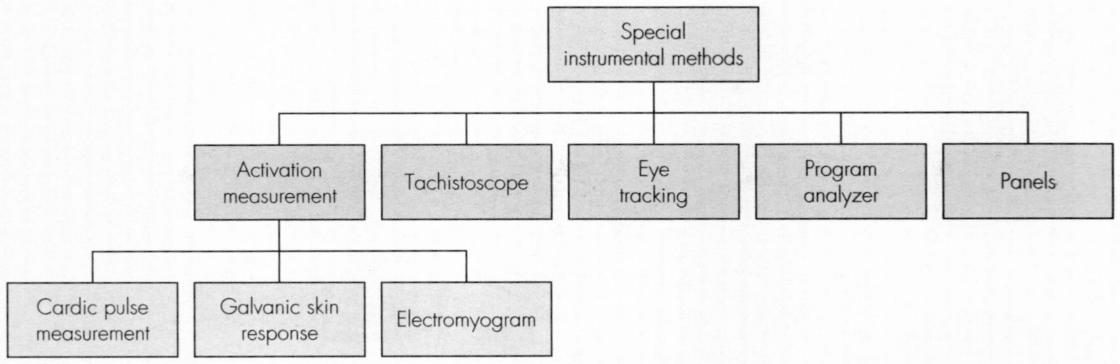

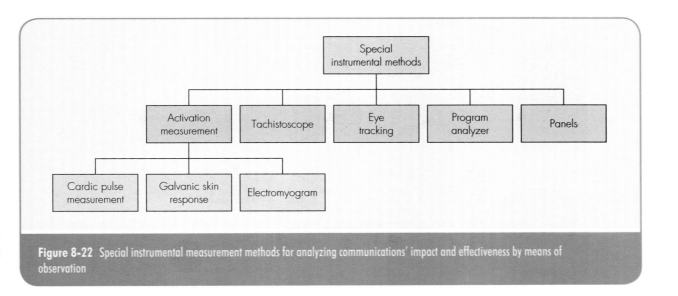

Figure 8-22 Special instrumental measurement methods for analyzing communications' impact and effectiveness by means of observation

3 An **electromyogram (EMG)** is used to measure tension in the individual facial muscles (Wiles and Cornwell 1990). To this end, small disk electrodes capable of detecting muscle tension are attached to the skin, covering the muscles of the receiver of the communicated message. This permits analysis of whether the communicated message is synchronized or conflicts with the attitudes of the recipient.

A **tachistoscope** is a slide projector with a control unit that enables an extremely short display of communication content (thousandths of a second), thus simulating the fleeting and selective perception of communicated messages under laboratory conditions (DePelsmacker *et al.* 2004; Klebba 1985). After the message has been displayed via the tachistoscope, test subjects are interviewed about what they were able to perceive or identify during this short time span.

Eye tracking can be used to analyze the degree of attention caught by the content of the communication (Batra *et al.* 1996; Belch and Belch 1998; DePelsmacker *et al.* 2004). For example, special eye tracking devices can record the test subject's field of vision, and thus provide information about which graphic and text elements of an advertising medium are viewed in what order. Both fixations (gaze is maintained on an element, the eye is focused) and saccades are recorded (see the example in Figure 8-23).

The **Program Analyzer** was invented in the 1930s by Lazarsfeld and Stanton to measure the 'quality' of the audience experience with a 'machine' (Levy 1982). Test subjects exposed to a radio or TV spot are given a green button to indicate pleasure and a red button to express dislike with respect to single sequences of an advertisement. The buttons activate a black or red record line, respectively, on a continuously moving tape. Additionally, one extra pen is connected to an electric second-timer and marks a time line on one edge of this tape (Peterman 1940). Thus, the measurement is simply based on the respondent's reactions; it may help in fine-tuning the advertisement, but is not adequate for making evaluative decisions (Biel 1996).

Panels can also be utilized to assess communication impact (see the Appendix for more information on this market research tool). This method is observation-based, mostly using scanner data. It can be complemented by surveys if the need arises. A particularly informative analysis of the impact and effectiveness of the communication is provided by panels that combine retail and household data ('single-source panels').

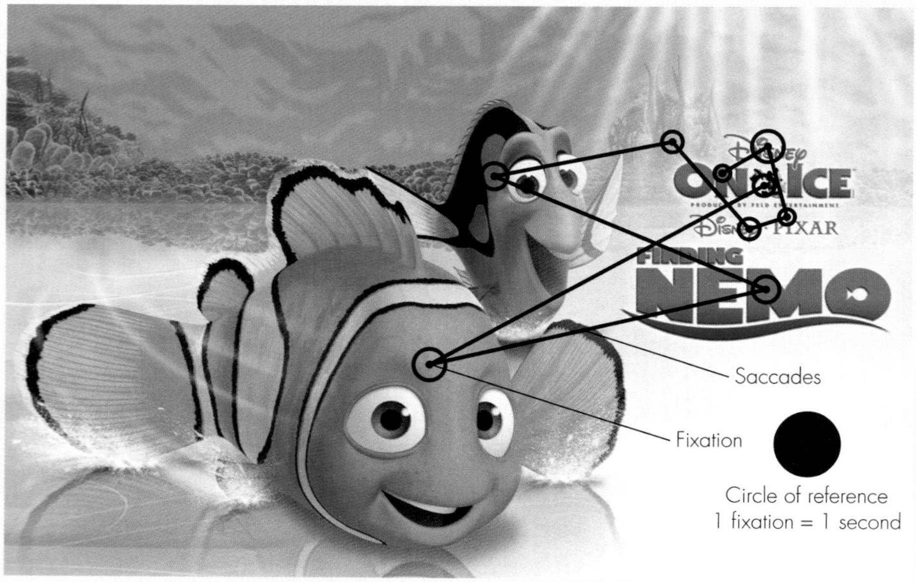

Figure 8-23 Example of eye tracking (SVI 2005)

Summary

Communication means exchanging information from the sender to a receiver via a communication channel. In a corporate context, marketing communications can be seen as a process encompassing the definition of communication objects and target groups, budgeting and media planning, design of the communication measures, monitoring the communication impact (pre-test), implementation of communication measures and, finally, monitoring the communication impact (post-test). The definition of the target group can be based on certain criteria (e.g. sociodemographics) or on specific typologies. When deciding on budgeting, it is important to be aware of different budgeting methods, such as heuristic and analytical methods. The latter require an understanding of advertising response functions, which describe the relationship between advertising budget and communication objective.

In the next step, the budget will be distributed to various categories of communication media (media allocation) and individual media vehicles (media vehicle allocation). Certain quantitative criteria should be used to evaluate media. Within the design of communication measures, this is used to define the elements related to the content of the message, and to define visual and auditory elements. These elements can then be integrated into various communication measures, such as print, TV and radio advertising, outdoor and internet advertising, mobile and direct marketing, sales promotion, public relations, trade fairs, events, corporate identity, sponsoring, and product placements. When using various communication measures simultaneously – which is usually the case in company practice – it is important that these measures are integrated in order to create a concise and consistent image (integrated marketing communications). The final step in the communication process consists of monitoring the communication's impact, which can be considered before or after the implementation of the communication measure. Here, a company can use different types of instruments, such as surveys, eye tracking systems or panels.

Case Study: Gillette to Axe Beckham for a Team of Global Sports Icons

Gillette dropped David Beckham as its sole brand ambassador in favor of a team of global sporting superstars. Beckham, whose deal with Gillette came up for renewal in 2007, had been the face of the brand since 2004, when he signed a three-year, £40 million agreement. However, because of the disappointing World Cup, followed by his resignation of the England captaincy and subsequent loss of a place in the international squad, his star was considered to have dimmed somewhat. Gillette drew up a shortlist of fresher-faced global sports icons to represent the brand, and decided upon Roger Federer, Tiger Woods and Thierry Henry. Beckham is a brand ambassador for several other global brands, including Motorola, Adidas and Pepsi. In July 2005, Beckham was dropped by Vodafone, although, according to exclusive research commissioned by *Marketing*, he remains the world's most sponsored footballer.

Source: adapted from Kemp 2006.

Case Study (Continued)

Discussion Questions

1. What are possible reasons that Gillette has dropped David Beckham from its endorsement strategy?
2. What are possible challenges or problems involved when engaging celebrity endorsers in a marketing campaign?
3. David Beckham had signed a three-year contract with Gillette. What were the possible advantages for Gillette in engaging Beckham for such a long time?
4. Which communications measures would be most suitable when using celebrity endorsers? What role is played by integrated marketing communications?

Key Terms

References

Aaker, D.A. and Bruzzone, D.E. (1985) Causes of irritation in advertising, *Journal of Marketing*, 49, 2, 47–57.
Aerodeon (2004) European brands support use of mobile campaigns, *New Media Age*, 3 June, 9.
Agora (2007) Our Media – Outdoor. Art Marketing Syndicate SA (AMS), http://www.agora.pl/aliasy/mod/zoomn.jsp?xx=3513142.
Ailawadi, K., Neslin, S. and Gedenk, K. (2001) Pursuing the value-conscious consumer: store brands versus national brand promotions, *Journal of Marketing*, 65, 1, 71–89.
Alinghi (2006) Partners – UBS, http://www.alinghi.com/en/alinghi/partners/index.php?idIndex=8&idContent=12.
Althans, J. (1993) Klassische Werbeträger, in: Berndt, R. and Herrmanns, A. (eds) *Handbuch Marketing-Kommunikation – Strategien, Instrumente, Perspektiven*. Wiesbaden, 393–418.
Arias-Bolzmann, L., Chakrabarty, G. and Mowen, J.C. (2000) Effects of absurdity in advertising: the moderating role of product category attitude and the mediating role of cognitive responses, *Journal of Advertising*, 29, 1, 35–41.
Baker, M. (2007) Companies in crisis – what to do when it all goes wrong. Odwalla and the E-coli outbreak, http://www.mallenbaker.net/csr/CSRfiles/crisis05.html.
Barrand, D. (2006) Crazy Frog named most irritating ad of the year, *Marketing* (UK), 4 January, 1–2.
Batra, R., Myers, J.G. and Aaker, D.A. (1996) *Advertising Management* (5th edn). Englewood Cliffs, NJ.

Bauer, H., Huber, F. and Hägele, M. (1998) Zur präferenzorientierten Messung der Werbewirkung – Ergebnisse einer empirischen Studie, *Marketing – Zeitschrift für Forschung und Praxis*, 20, 3, 180–194.
Bauer, H., Meeder, U. and Jordan, J. (2001) Ausgewählte Instrumente des Werbecontrolling, Institut für Marktorientierte Unternehmensführung, Working Paper M 59, Mannheim.
Bauer, H., Lippert, I., Reichardt, T. and Neumann, M.M. (2005) Effective Mobile Marketing – Eine empirische Untersuchung, Institut für Marktorientierte Unternehmensführung, Working Paper M96, Mannheim.
Belch, G.E. and Belch, M.A. (1998) *Advertising and Promotion – An Integrated Marketing Communications Perspective* (4th edn). Boston.
Belch, G.E. and Belch, M.A. (2004) *Advertising and Promotion – An Integrated Marketing Communications Perspective* (6th edn). Boston.
Bello, D. and Barksdale, H. (1986) Exporting at industrial trade shows, *Industrial Marketing Management*, 15, 3, 197–206.
Bennett, R. (1999) Sports sponsorship, spectator recall and false consensus, *European Journal of Marketing*, 33, 3/4, 291–313.
Berndt, R. (2005) *Marketingstrategie und Marketingpolitik* (4th edn). Berlin.
Biel, A.L. (1996) Do you really want to know, *Journal of Advertising Research*, 36, 2, RC-2–RC-7.
Bonoma, T. (1983) Get more out of your trade shows, *Harvard Business Review*, 61, 1, 75–83.
Boyce, R. (1998) Exploding the web CPM myth, *Advertising Age*, 69, 5, 16–18.
Brand Strategy (2005) Case studies: mobile marketing – McDonald's, *Brand Strategy*, 190, 28.
Brennan, I., Dubas, K.M. and Babin, L.A. (1999) The influence of product-placement type and exposure time on product-placement recognition, *International Journal of Advertising*, 18, 3, 323–337.
Bruhn, M. (1998) *Sponsoring, Systematische Planung und integrativer Einsatz* (3rd edn). Wiesbaden.
Bruhn, M. (2003a) *Kommunikationspolitik* (2nd edn). Munich.
Bruhn, M. (2003b) *Sponsoring: Systematische Planung und integrativer Einsatz* (4th edn). Wiesbaden.
Bruhn, M. (2005) *Unternehmens- und Marketingkommunikation – Handbuch für ein integriertes Kommunikationsmanagement*. Munich.
Bruwer, J., Li, E. and Reid, M. (2002) Segmentation of the Australian wine market using a wine-related lifestyle approach, *Journal of Wine Research*, 13, 3, 217–242.
Catanescu, C. and Tom, G. (2001) Types of humor in television and magazine advertising, *Review of Business*, 22, 1/2, 92–96.
Chakrabarty, S., Yelkur, R. and Brown, G. (2004) Gender differences in ad irritation: implications for market segmentation, *Marketing Management Journal*, 14, 2, 67–76.
Charbonneau, J. and Gerlan, R. (2005) Talent, looks or brains? New Zealand advertising practitioners' views on celebrity and athlete endorsers, *Marketing Bulletin*, 16, 1, 1–10.
Clee, M.E. and Wicklund, R.A. (1980) Consumer behavior and psychological reactance, *Journal of Consumer Research*, 6, 4, 389–405.
Cornelissen, J.P. (2003) Change, continuity and progress: the concept of integrated marketing communications and marketing communications practice, *Journal of Strategic Marketing*, 11, 4, 217–234.
Cornelissen, J.P. and Lock, A.R. (2000) The organizational relationship between marketing and public relations: exploring paradigmatic viewpoints, *Journal of Marketing Communications*, 6, 4, 231–245.
Cornwell, T.B. and Maignan, I. (1998) An international review of sponsorship research, *Journal of Advertising*, 27, 1, 1–21.
Crimmins, J. and Horn, M. (1996) Sponsorship: from management ego trip to marketing success, *Journal of Advertising Research*, 36, 4, 11–21.
Cuneo, A.Z. (2006) Mobile-media chiefs' pitch falls on deaf ears, *Advertising Age*, 77, 15, 2–5.
Cutlip, S.M., Center, A.H. and Broom, G.M. (2006) *Effective Public Relations* (9th edn). Upper Saddle River, NJ.
D'Astous, A. and Bitz, P. (1995) Consumer evaluations of sponsorship programs, *European Journal of Marketing*, 29, 12, 6–22.
D'Astous, A. and Chartier, F. (2000) A study of factors affecting consumer evaluations and memory of product placements in movies, *Journal of Current Issues and Research in Advertising*, 22, 2, 31–40.
D'Astous, A. and Jacob, I. (2002) Understanding consumer reactions to premium-based promotional offers, *European Journal of Marketing*, 36, 11, 1270–1286.
Danaher, P.J. and Mullarkey, G.W. (2003) Factors affecting online advertising recall: a study of students, *Journal of Advertising Research*, 43, 3, 252–266.
DDV Deutscher Direktmarketingverband eV (2004) *Suchmaschinenmarketing*. Wiesbaden.
Del Polito, G.A. (2005) Address it right, *Direct*, 17, 14, 80.

DePelsmacker, P. (2005) The internet and the World Wide Web, in: Kitchen, P.J., DePelsmacker, P., Eagle, L. and Schultz, D.E. (eds) *A Reader in Marketing Communication.* London and New York, 199–200.

DePelsmacker, P., Geuens, M. and Anckaert, P. (2002) Media context and advertising effectiveness: the role of context appreciation and context/ad similarity, *Journal of Advertising*, 31, 2, 49–61.

DePelsmacker, P., Geuens, M. and Van den Berg, J. (2004) *Marketing Communications. A European Perspective* (2nd edn). London.

Dolphin, R.R. (2003) Sponsorship: perspectives on its strategic role, *Corporate Communications: An International Journal*, 8, 3, 173–186.

Doubleclick 2004 (2004) AdServing Trend Report, BVDW-Präsentation: Online-Werbung.

Duncan, T. and Moriarty, S.E. (1998) A communication-based marketing model for managing relationships, *Journal of Marketing*, 62, 2, 1–13.

Edmunds' *Inside Line* (2007) Frankfurt Auto Show, www.edmunds.com/insideline/do/Features/articleId=106037.

Ehling, W.P., White, J. and Grunig, J.E. (1992) Public relations and marketing practices, in: Grunig, J.E. (ed.) *Excellence in Public Relations and Communication Management.* Hillsdale, 357–393.

Emirates (2007) Australian Sponsorships. Melbourne, Sydney and Western Australian Symphony Orchestras, http://www.emirates.com/au/AboutEmirates/AustralianSponsorships/Events_22184_1.asp.

Erdogan, B.Z., Baker, M.J. and Tagg, S. (2001) Selecting celebrity endorsers: the practitioner's perspective, *Journal of Advertising Research*, 41, 3, 39–49.

Esch, F. (2000) Werbewirkungsforschung, in: Herrmann, A. and Homburg, C. (ed.) *Marktforschung* (2nd edn). Stuttgart, 861–910.

Fenwick, I. and Rice, M.D. (1991) Reliability of continuous measurement copy-testing methods, *Journal of Advertising Research*, 31, 1, 23–29.

Fill, C. (2001) *Marketing-Kommunikation. Konzepte und Strategien* (2nd edn). Munich.

Fill, C. (2005) *Marketing Communications: Engagements, Strategies and Practice* (3rd edn). Harlow.

Forrester Research (2003) Data from Interactive Advertising Bureaus in Europe, http://www.forrester.com/rb/.

Fritz, W. (2004) *Internet-Marketing und Electronic Commerce: Grundlagen – Rahmenbedingungen – Instrumente* (3rd edn). Wiesbaden.

Gedenk, K. (2002) *Verkaufsförderung.* Munich.

GfK (2006) Einstellung zur Werbung in Europa, http://www.ihagfk.ch/gfk/UploadsUser/Doc119.pdf.

Goldberg, M.E. and Gorn, G.J. (1987) Happy and sad TV-programs: how they affect reactions to TV commercials, *Journal of Consumer Research*, 14, 3, 387–403.

Grunig, J.E. and Grunig, L.A. (1998) The relationship between public relations and marketing in excellent organizations: evidence from the IABC Study, *Journal of Marketing Communications*, 4, 3, 141–162.

Grunig, J.E. and Huang, Y.-H. (2000) From organizational effectiveness to relationship indicators: antecedents of relationship, public relations strategies, and relationship outcomes, in: Ledingham, J.A. and Bruning, S.D. (eds) *Public Relations as Relationship Management.* Mahawa, 23–53.

Gupta, P.B., Balasubramanian, S.K. and Klassen, M.L. (2000) Viewers' evaluations of product placement in movies: public policy issues and managerial implications, *Journal of Current Issues and Research in Advertising*, 22, 2, 41–52.

Gupta, S. (2003) Event marketing: issues and challenges, *IIMB Management Review*, 15, 2, 87–96.

Gwinner, K.P. (1997) A model of image creation and image transfer in event sponsorship, *International Marketing Review*, 14, 3, 145–158.

Gwinner, K.P. and Eaton, J. (1999) Building brand image through event sponsorship: the role of image transfer, *Journal of Advertising*, 28, 4, 47–57.

Haley, R.I., Staffaroni, J. and Fox, A. (1994) The missing measures of copy testing, *Journal of Advertising Research*, 34, 3, 46–60.

Halliday, J. (2005) Ford ups 'targeted' media spending. Reprinted with permission from the 8.22.05 issue of *Advertising Age*. Copyright, Crain Communications, Inc. 2005, 76, 34, 8.

Herbst, D. (1997) *Public Relations.* Berlin.

Heuer, F. and Reisberg, D. (1990) Vivid memories of emotional events: the accuracy of remembered minutiae, *Memory&Cognition*, 18, 5, 496–506.

Holland, H. (2004) *Direktmarketing* (2nd edn). Munich.

Homburg, C. (2000) *Quantitative Betriebswirtschaftlehre: Entscheidungsunterstützung durch Modelle* (3rd edn). Wiesbaden.

Hoyer, W.D. and MacInnis, D.J. (2004) *Consumer Behavior* (3rd edn). Boston.

Ihlen, O. (2002) Defending the Mercedes A-Class: combining and changing crisis-response strategies, *Journal of Public Relations Research*, 14, 3, 185–206.

Jae-un, L. (2005) Paying off the stars through advertising, http://ww.hancinema.net/korean-movie-news_2868.php.

Kamins, M.A. (1990) An investigation into the 'Match-up' hypothesis in celebrity advertising: when beauty may be only skin deep, *Journal of Advertising*, 19, 1, 4–13.

Kamins, M.A. and Gupta, K. (1994) Congruence between spokespersons and product type: a Matchup hypothesis perspective, *Psychology & Marketing*, 11, 6, 569–586.

Katz, E. (1957) The two-step flow of communication: an up-to-date report on a hypothesis, *Public Opinion Research*, Spring, 61–78.

Kavassalis, P., Spyropoulou, N., Drossos, D., Mitrokostas, E., Gikas, G. and Hatzistamatiou, A. (2003) Mobile permission marketing: framing the market inquiry, *International Journal of Electronic Commerce*, 8, 1, 55–79.

Keaney, A. and Remenyi, D. (2004) Spamming and scamming: the real picture! *Irish Journal of Management*, 25, 1, 23–40.

Kemp, E. (2006) Gillette to axe Beckham for global sports icons, *Marketing*, 20 September, 1.

Kerin, R.A. and Cron, W.L. (1987) Assessing trade show functions and performance: an exploratory study, *Journal of Marketing*, 51, 3, 87–94.

Kitchen, P.J. and Moss, D. (1995) Marketing and public relations: the relationship revisited, *Journal of Marketing Communications*, 1, 2, 105–119.

Klebba, J.M. (1985) Physiological measures of research: a review of brain activity, electrodermal response, pupil dilation, and voice analysis methods and studies, *Current Issues & Research in Advertising*, 8, 2, 53–77.

Klingler, W. and Müller, D.K. (2004) ma 2004 Radio II: Hörfunk behauptet Stärke, *Media Perspektiven*, 9.

Kothe, P. (2002) Von der mikrogeografischen Marktsegmentierung zum Mikromarketing, in: Dallmer, H. (ed.) *Das Handbuch Direct Marketing & More* (8th edn). Wiesbaden, 737–754.

Kotler, P. and Keller, K.L. (2006) *Marketing Management* (12th edn). Upper Saddle River, NJ.

Kroeber-Riel, W. and Esch, F.-R. (2004) *Strategie und Technik der Werbung: Verhaltenswissenschaftliche Ansätze* (6th edn). Stuttgart.

Kroeber-Riel, W. and Weinberg, P. (2003) *Konsumentenverhalten* (8th edn). Munich.

Lasswell, H. (1948) The structure and function of communication in society, in: Bryson, L. (ed.) *The Communication of Ideas*. New York, 37–51.

Lastovicka, J.L., Murry, J.P. and Joachimsthaler, E.A. (1990) Evaluating the measurement validity of lifestyle typologies with qualitative measures and multiplicative factoring, *Journal of Marketing Research*, 27, 1, 11–23.

Lazarsfeld, P., Berelson, B. and Gaudet, H. (1944) *The People's Choice: How the Voter Makes up his Mind in a Presidential Campaign*. New York.

Lee, S., Hwang, T. and Lee, H.-H. (2006) Corporate blogging strategies of the *Fortune* 500 companies, *Management Decision*, 44, 6, 316–334.

Levin, A.M., Joiner, C., Cameron, G. (2001) The impact of sports sponsorship on consumers' brand attitudes and recall: the case of NASCAR fans, *Journal of Current Issues and Research in Advertising*, 23, 2, 23–31.

Levy, M.R. (1982) The Lazarsfeld–Stanton Program Analyzer: an historical note, *Journal of Communication*, 32, 4, 30–38.

Lewis, E. St Elmo (1898) AIDA, in: Strong, E.K. (1925, ed.) *The Psychology of Selling*. New York.

Lilien, G. and Rangaswamy, A. (2003) *Marketing Engineering: Computer-Assisted Marketing Analysis and Planning*. NJ.

Lilien, G., Kotler, P. and Moorthy, K. (1992) *Marketing Models*. Englewood Cliffs, NJ.

Lohtia, R., Donthu, N. and Hershberger, E.K. (2003) The impact of content and design elements on banner advertising click-through rates, *Journal of Advertising*, 43, 4, 410–418.

Lukaszewski, J.E. (2001) Crisis communication management: protecting and enhancing corporate reputation and identity, in: Kitchen, P.J. and Schultz, D.E. (eds) *Raising the Corporate Umbrella. Corporate Communications in the 21st Century*. New York, 199–243.

Lutz, R.J. (1985) Affective and cognitive antecedents of attitude toward the ad: a conceptual framework, in: Alwitt, L.F. and Mitchell, A.A. (eds) *Psychological Processes and Advertising Effects: Theory, Research, and Application*. Hillsdale, NJ, 45–63.

MacKenzie, S.B. and Lutz, R.J. (1989) An empirical examination of the structural antecedents of attitude toward the ad in an advertising pretesting context, *Journal of Marketing*, 53, 2, 48–65.

MacKenzie, S.B., Lutz, R.J. and Belch, G.E. (1986) The role of attitude toward the ad as a mediator of advertising effectiveness: a test of competing explanations, *Journal of Marketing Research*, 23, 2, 130–143.
Mahajan, V. and Muller, E. (1986) Advertising pulsing policies for generating awareness for new products, *Marketing Science*, 5, 2, 89–106.
Malmo, R.B. (1959) Activation: a neuropsychological dimension, *Psychological Review*, 66, 6, 367–386.
Mann, M.F. and Hill, T. (1984) Persuasive communications and the boomerang effect: some limiting conditions to the effectiveness of positive influence attempts, *Advances in Consumer Research*, 11, 1, 66–70.
Marketing Ad Ventures (2003) Out of home formats, http://www.adsoutdoor.com/formats.asp.
McKechnie, S.A. and Zhou, J. (2003) Product placement in movies: a comparison of Chinese and American consumers' attitudes, *International Journal of Advertising*, 22, 3, 349–374.
McKinsey (2007) How businesses are using Web 2.0: a McKinsey Global Survey, *McKinsey Quarterly*, 4.
Meenaghan, T. (1998) Current developments and future directions in sponsorship, *International Journal of Advertising*, 17, 1, 3–28.
Meenaghan, T. and Shipley, D. (1999) Media effect in commercial sponsorship, *European Journal of Marketing*, 33, 3/4, 328–347.
Meinert M. (1997) Mikrogeographische Marktsegmentierung – Theorie und Praxis, in: Dallmer, H. (ed.) *Handbuch Direct-Marketing* (7th edn). Wiesbaden, 451–466.
Melewar, T.C. (2003) Determinants of the corporate identity construct: a review of the literature, *Journal of Marketing Communications*, 9, 4, 195–220.
Melewar, T.C. and Harrold, J. (2000) The role of corporate identity in merger and acquisition activity, *Journal of General Management*, 26, 2, 17–31.
Melewar, T.C. and Saunders, J. (1998) Global corporate visual identity systems: standardization, control and benefits, *International Marketing Review*, 15, 4, 291–308.
Melewar, T.C. and Saunders, J. (1999) International corporate visual identity: standardization or localization? *Journal of International Business Studies*, 30, 3, 583–598.
Misra, S. and Beatty, S.E. (1994) Celebrity spokesperson and brand congruence: an assessment of recall and affect, *Journal of Business Research*, 21, 2, 159–173.
Neslin, S.A. (2002) *Sales Promotion*. Relevant Knowledge Series, Marketing Science Institute, Cambridge.
Nufer, G. (2002) *Wirkungen von Event-Marketing: Theoretische Fundierung und empirische Analyze*. Wiesbaden.
Odedele, S. and Faith, P. (2004) Maximizing media relations for effective program execution: UNICEF in Nigeria, in: VanSlyke Turk, J. and Scanlan, L.H. (eds) *The Evolution of Public Relations: Case Studies from Countries in Transition* (2nd edn), published by the Institute for Public Relations at www.instituteforpr.org, Gainesville, Florida, 126–134.
Pando Publications (2005) Hospitality and sponsorships. Emirates ties its hospitality to large sponsorships, http://www.ami.org.au/amimu/0504April/0504_hospitality_emirates.htm.
Pasquier, M. (1997) *Plakatwirkungsforschung: Theoretische Grundlagen und praktische Ansätze*. Freiburg.
Percy, L. and Elliot, R. (2005) *Strategic Advertising Management* (2nd edn). Oxford.
Peterman, J.N. (1940) The 'Program Analyzer'. A new technique in studying liked and disliked items in radio programs, *Journal of Applied Psychology*, 24, 728–741.
Pickton, D. and Hartley, B. (1998) Measuring integration: an assessment of the quality of integrated marketing communications, *International Journal of Advertising*, 17, 4, 447–465.
Pieczka, M. (2000) Objectives and evaluation in public relations work: what do they tell us about expertise and professionalism? *Journal of Public Relations Research*, 12, 3, 211–233.
Pornpitakpan, C. (2003) Validation of the celebrity endorsers' credibility scale: evidence from Asians, *Journal of Marketing Management*, 19, 1/2, 179–196.
Reid, A. (2001) Variation in the ways that instrumental and vocal students experience learning in music, *Music Education Research*, 3, 25–40.
Ritz Carlton Hotel Company, LLC (2000) Application Summary, © 1992–2007 The Ritz-Carlton Hotel Company, LLC. All rights reserved. Reprinted with permission of The Ritz-Carlton Hotel Company, LLC, http://www.ritzcarlton.com/resources/rcappsum.pdf.
Rossiter, J.R. and Bellman, S. (2005) *Marketing Communications: Theory and Applications*. Frenchs Forest, NSW.
Rossiter, J.R. and Percy, L. (1987) *Advertising and Promotion Management*. New York.
Schultz, D.E., Tannenbaum, S.I. and Lauterborn, R.F. (1995) *The Marketing Paradigm: Integrated Marketing Communications*. Lincolnwood.

Sethuraman, R. and Tellis, G. (1991) An analysis of the tradeoff between advertising and price discounting, *Journal of Marketing Research*, 28, 2, 160–174.
Sheehan, K. and Hoy, M. (1999) Flaming, complaining, abstaining: how online users respond to privacy concerns, *Journal of Advertising*, 28, 3, 37–51.
Shimp, T.A. (2007) *Integrated Marketing Communications in Advertising and Promotion* (7th edn). Mason.
Simon, H. (1982) ADPULS: an advertising model with wearout and pulsation, *Journal of Marketing Research*, 19, 3, 352–363.
Simon, H. and Möhrle, M. (1993) Werbebudgetierung, in: Berndt, R. and Hermanns, A. (eds) *Handbuch Marketing-Kommunikation*. Wiesbaden, 301–316.
Smith, T., Gopalakrishna, S. and Smith, P. (2004) The complementary effect of trade shows on personal selling, *International Journal of Research in Marketing*, 21, 1, 61–76.
Sneath, J.Z., Finney, R.Z. and Close, A.G. (2005) An IMC approach to event marketing: the effect of sponsorship and experience on customer attitudes, *Journal of Advertising Research*, 45, 4, 373–381.
SRI Consulting Business Intelligence (2007) VALS^{TM}-Values and Lifestyle Survey, http://www.sric-bi.com/VALS.
Stewart, D. (1989) Measures, methods, and models in advertising research, *Journal of Advertising Research*, 29, 3, 54–60.
Stewart, D., Farmer, K. and Stannard C. (1990) Music as a recognition cue in advertising-tracking studies, *Journal of Advertising Research*, 30, 4, 39–48.
Stipp, H. and Schiavone, N.P. (1996) Modeling the impact of Olympic sponsorship on corporate image, *Journal of Advertising Research*, 36, 4, 22–28.
SVI (2005) Insight eye tracking, http://www.sv-institut.de/publikationen.php?PHPSESSID=0a843f455ff909873 51a1ce193377152.
Till, B.D. and Busler, M. (1998) Matching products with endorsers: attractiveness versus expertise, *Journal of Consumer Marketing*, 15, 6, 576–584.
Till, B.D. and Busler, M. (2000) The Match-up hypothesis: physical attractiveness, expertise, and the role of fit on brand attitude, purchase intention and brand beliefs, *Journal of Advertising*, 29, 3, 1–13.
Tolle, E. (1995) Product placement, in: Tietz, B., Köhler, R. and Zentes, J. (eds) *Handwörterbuch des Marketing* (2nd edn). Stuttgart, 2095–2101.
Tylee, J. (2002) AMV 'Don't Drive Tired' ad uses shock tactics, *Campaign*, 12, 10–11.
Vakratsas, D. and Ambler, T. (1999) How advertising works: what do we really know? *Journal of Marketing*, 63, 1, 26–43.
Van Wagner (2004) Outdoor advertising – New York, http://www.vanwagner.com/images/NY_pix/pic_1246thavenue.jpg.
Vergossen, H. (2004) *Marketing-Kommunikation*. Ludwigshafen.
Vyncke, P. (2002) Lifestyle segmentation, *European Journal of Communication*, 17, 4, 445–463.
Walliser, B. (2003) An international review of sponsorship research: extension and update, *International Journal of Advertising*, 22, 1, 5–40.
White, R. (2000) *Advertising* (4th edn). London.
Wiles, J.A. and Cornwell, T.B. (1990) A review of methods utilized in measuring affect, feelings, and emotions in advertising, *Current Issues & Research in Advertising*, 13, 2, 241–276.
World Advertising Research Center Ltd (2008) European Advertising and Media Forecast 2007, http://www.warc.com/EAMF.
Young, C.E. (2004) Capturing the flow of emotion in television commercials: a new approach, *Journal of Advertising Research*, 44, 2, 202–209.

CHAPTER 9

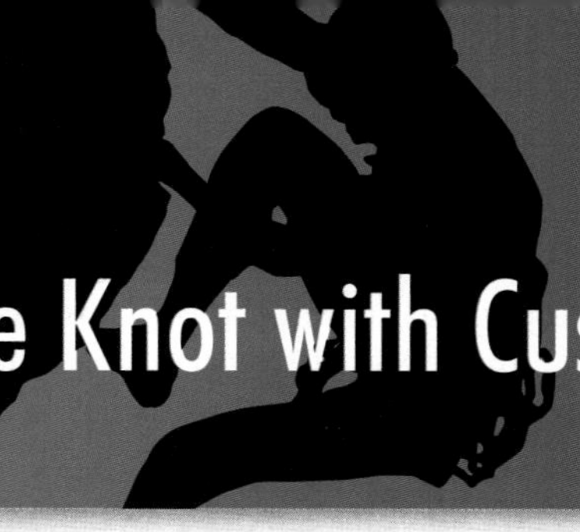

Tying the Knot with Customers

Contents

Learning Objectives

In this chapter you will become familiar with:

- the concepts of customer satisfaction and customer loyalty
- the most important tools in customer relationship management
- customer clubs and customer cards, and how they are used in the management of customer relationships
- an overview of the various methods and main success factors of cross-selling
- complaint management within customer relationship management
- the processes involved in systematic customer recovery, and the key success factors associated with it.

Customers are the focus of all marketing activities and managing customer relationships has gained great relevance for most companies operating in competitive markets. This trend is also evident in the growing importance of relationship marketing (see Chapter 1; see also Grönroos 1994; Homburg and Werner 1998; Mithas *et al.* 2005; Payne and Frow 2006; Reinartz *et al.* 2004; Zablah *et al.* 2004). Because customer relationship management is so central to marketing we have already examined how it can be aligned strategically within the company (Section 3.1.4). This chapter will now address the fundamental logic that guides customer relationship management and the implementation issues that arise in this context.

Section 9.1 takes an in-depth look at the most relevant issues concerning customer relationship management: customer satisfaction and customer loyalty. Section 9.2 describes the various instruments of customer relationship management within the individual components of the marketing mix. Sections 9.3 to 9.7 then examine the range of tools used in customer relationship management. Common to all these is the effort to secure customer loyalty, which is the primary objective of customer relationship management (see Section 3.1.4).

9.1 From Customer Satisfaction to Customer Loyalty

Studies show that both customer satisfaction and customer loyalty are essential to company success. For example, it could be shown that customer loyalty and customer satisfaction are positively related (see Grønholdt *et al.* 2000; Gustafsson *et al.* 2005; Homburg *et al.* 2003; Mittal and Kamakura 2001; Olsen 2002). This, in turn, has a positive impact on a number of factors related to company success, such as cost and revenue (see Anderson and Mittal 2000; Rust *et al.* 2002; Smith and Wright 2004). As customer satisfaction by itself does not represent an economic benefit for the company we will discuss in the following how satisfaction and loyalty are interrelated. This is necessary as customer satisfaction is a prerequisite for customer loyalty, which impacts company success.

The confirmation/disconfirmation (C/D) paradigm serves as a framework that helps to understand the **formation of customer satisfaction** (see Bolton and Drew 1991; Fournier and Mick 1999; Oliver 1997). This concept states that customers compare the actual experience with a company or product to the expected experience. Confirmation means that the actual experience equals the expected experience. Disconfirmation, on the other hand, occurs if there is a discrepancy. If this is negative (i.e. expectation exceeds actual experience), dissatisfaction occurs and, vice versa, if it is positive (actual experience exceeds expectation), satisfaction is the result (for more on the concept of 'customer satisfaction', see the Appendix).

To find out the level of customer satisfaction, it is common practice to **measure it**. Customers can be asked directly about their level of satisfaction with a company, or with a company's offerings. Examples include the customer's level of satisfaction with the product's functionality, reliability of delivery and the friendliness of employees when interacting with the customer. Multi-item Likert scales are commonly used in these types of measurement (for a description of 'Likert scales', see the Appendix).

Of particular relevance to company practice is the effect of customer satisfaction on customer behavior (e.g. its effect on repeat buying). Striving for greater customer satisfaction makes economic sense for a company only if **customer satisfaction positively affects customer behavior**. Here it is crucial to understand not only the impact of satisfaction on customer loyalty but also on customers' price sensitivity.

Behavioral science offers many theories for explaining **customer loyalty**. In particular, risk theory, dissonance theory and learning theory play a key role in this context (for an examination of 'risk theory', 'dissonance theory' and 'learning theory', see the Appendix).

From a historical perspective, customer loyalty research initially concentrated only on repeat buying behavior. More recent research also incorporates other aspects, such as word-of-mouth recommendations or cross-selling, to assess whether the customer has a positive attitude towards the company (for an explanation of 'attitude', see the Appendix). Thus, customer loyalty comprises (see, e.g., Homburg and Bruhn 2005; Szymanski and Henard 2001):

- the repeat buying pattern
- the customer's willingness to purchase other products sold by the company (cross-selling)
- the customer's willingness to recommend the company and its products to other buyers (word-of-mouth).

Today, it is generally considered proven knowledge that customer satisfaction has a positive correlation with all three of these customer loyalty dimensions.

Studies indicate that the connection between customer satisfaction and customer loyalty is frequently linear (for more on this topic, see Grønholdt *et al.* 2000; Gustafsson *et al.* 2005; Mittal *et al.* 1998; Homburg *et al.* 1999). However, it is still not entirely clear how these two variables are related. Research has proposed two different functional forms: an exponential curve and an S-shaped curve (see Figure 9-1).

In Figure 9-1 (a) shows that the effect of satisfaction on loyalty increases exponentially as the level of satisfaction grows. Such a correlation has been empirically proven in several studies (see, e.g., Johnson and Auh 1998). By contrast, other studies also conceptualize an S-shaped correlation, as shown in Figure 9-1 (b). The S-shaped correlation includes a zone of indifference where customer satisfaction is at a medium level. In this range, a change in customer satisfaction has only a slight effect on customer loyalty. Outside the zone of indifference (above and below), however, the intensity with which a customer reacts to changes in satisfaction increases strongly.

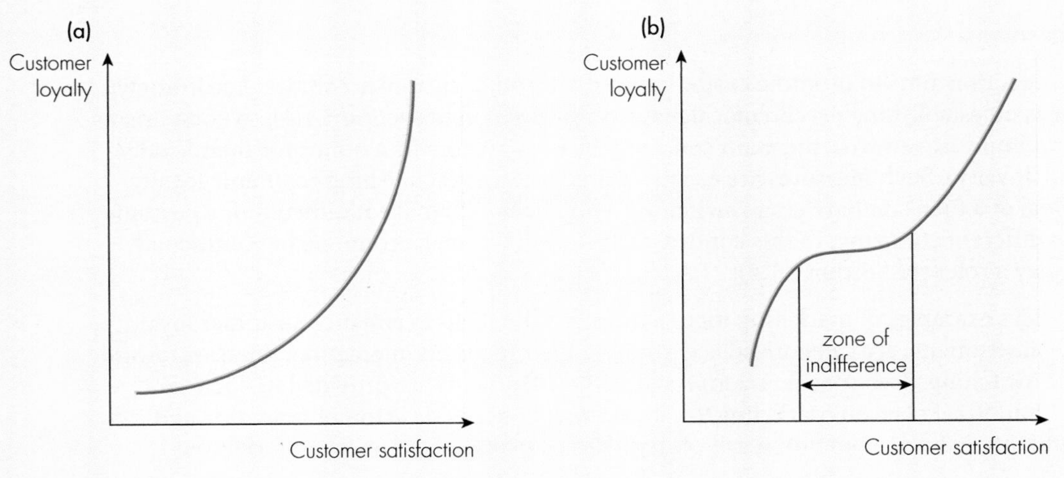

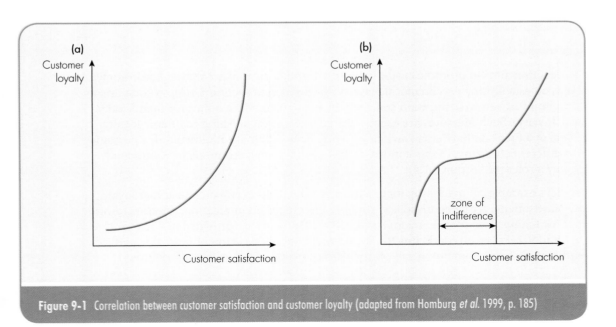

Figure 9-1 Correlation between customer satisfaction and customer loyalty (adapted from Homburg *et al.* 1999, p. 185)

So far, there is no empirical evidence of either form. Nevertheless, the positive relationship between customer satisfaction and customer loyalty is not questioned. Thus, to build loyal customers, a company first and foremost needs to satisfy its customers. The points below illustrate how companies can achieve this objective:

- First, a company can enhance the quality of its product(s) and service(s). This can be achieved, for example, by enhancing product functionality, increasing the product's reliability or improving the product design. An example is the launch of a new and improved version of software.
- Second, the company can influence customers' quality perceptions by effective communication. Numerous approaches apply such as, for instance, emphasizing product quality in advertisements, communicating positive test results and using customer testimonials.
- Third, a company can also impact customers' expectations. Here the company should avoid creating expectations that are difficult or impossible to fulfill. For example, sales personnel should communicate realistic promises and avoid over-optimistic statements.

9.2 Creating the Customer Relationship

In this section we discuss approaches that aim to promote customer loyalty (see also Bhote 1996; Homburg and Bruhn 2005; Johnson and Gustafsson 2000; Lowenstein 1997; Uncles *et al.* 2003). However, companies need to focus primarily on valuable customers. There are tools to measure the value of customers (e.g. ABC analysis, see Section 15.4.1, or customer lifetime value analysis, see Section 15.4.4). Especially the valuable customers need to be turned into loyal customers. We differentiate between the various approaches according to the 'levers' they primarily use to create customer loyalty:

- focus on interaction
- focus on bonuses/rewards
- focus on barriers to switching companies.

A focus on interaction aims to promote customer loyalty through customer contact. Accordingly, the focus here is on establishing psychological reasons for loyalty (see Section 3.1.4). In comparison, with a focus on bonuses/rewards, the main concept is to offer customers a bonus for their loyalty (i.e. to 'reward' loyalty). Such measures are usually geared towards establishing economic loyalty factors. The goal of a focus on barriers to switching companies is to make it difficult for a customer to change to a different company. In this context, technical/functional, economic or contractual reasons may play a role (see Section 3.1.4).

Table 9-1 provides examples of marketing mix instruments that help to enhance customer loyalty. The respective instruments are categorized according to their focus on interaction, bonuses/rewards and barriers to switching. Two specific examples of such instruments are provided in Focus on Marketing 9-1 and 9-2. Focus on Marketing 9-1 illustrates the use of a customer magazine and Focus on Marketing 9-2 describes how a call center helps to manage customer relationships.

Table 9-1 Examples of instruments of customer relationship management in the marketing mix

Primary orientation / Marketing mix area	Focus: interaction	Focus: bonuses/ rewards	Focus: barriers to switching
Product decisions	■ Integration of customer in product development	■ Customized product modifications ■ Additional services at no charge	■ Incompatibility of the company's own product with competitor products ■ Service warranties
Price decisions	■ Price concessions in price negotiations	■ Volume discounts ■ Loyalty discounts ■ Bonus programs	■ Price guarantees ■ Price escalation clauses
Communication decisions	■ Call center/service numbers ■ Customer forums	■ Customer magazines ■ Invitations to special events	■ Joint advertising agreements (co-branding)
Sales decisions	■ Visit by salesperson	■ 24-hour service ■ Express delivery	■ Long-term supply contracts ■ Locations in the vicinity of the customer

Focus on Marketing 9-1 Example of the use of customer magazines in customer relationship management

Keeping in touch with customers at Nikon

With ever-improving technology at their disposal, European photographers are today faced with steep learning curves and accelerating product turnover. Consequently, they need a guiding hand and constant reassurance that they are backing the right brand and products. *NikonPro* provides for this by showcasing the best images from some of the world's leading photographers taken with the latest Nikon equipment in its award-winning *NikonPro* magazine. *NikonPro*'s goal is to demonstrate Nikon in action and to highlight its potential, supplying information and advice to users, which goes to the heart of the image.

NikonPro has a circulation of approximately 70,000 copies and is read by professional photographers and enthusiasts across Europe. Published three times a year in six languages (English, German, French, Spanish, Italian and Swedish), the magazine is distributed to

Focus on Marketing 9-1 (Continued)

27 countries. Andy Robinson, *NikonPro*'s consulting editor at the publishing house Cedar Communications, said: '*NikonPro* has the enviable task of finding the best Nikon photographers in Europe and showcasing their work. With such a pool of talent to draw on, we will never be short of great images.

'But throughout its long and illustrious life, *NikonPro* has always been more than just a gallery. It is a community of peers in which the very best photographic images, techniques and equipment are examined, explained and celebrated. We're looking forward to the next decade of serving and celebrating its readership and membership.'

Research by Nikon supports the publication's appeal and integrity amongst its influential and discerning readership: 95 per cent of *NikonPro* readers said they would recommend the magazine to other professionals, and 90 per cent rated it good or excellent. This research was reinforced when the Association of Publishing Agencies (APA) gave *NikonPro* the Customer Magazine of the Year and International Magazine of the Year awards in 2004. The APA judges especially pointed out that *NikonPro* is, besides being an excellent example of international publishing, a skilful customer loyalty tool. This is underlined by Martina Beckmann, Manager Marketing Communications & Services, at Nikon Europe: 'Throughout its existence, *NikonPro* has become established as a highly regarded, top-quality communication tool for professional photographers and others involved in the world of imaging.'

Source: Hissink 2005.

Focus on Marketing 9-2 Example of the use of a call center

Proactive call center at a major Hong Kong insurer

Dao Heng Insurance (DHI) was established in Hong Kong in 1973. It offers a wide range of general insurance products, including personal and group insurance and group medical insurance, to meet the needs of individual, commercial and industrial clients.

'DHI's mission is to become the leading provider of personal insurance, delivering first-class services to the customers,' Ms. Lim said.

Key to the company's success is a proactive approach at its call center:

'I think we have been very successful in transforming our call center from a reactive passive service-handling center to a proactive customer loyalty and cross-selling-driven center over a short period of two years,' Ms. Lim said. 'The past two years was a period of change management. We have to change our people's mindset and skills set, and the call center's way of doing things.'

Four strategies were adopted for the transformation: standards were established, human resources were developed, business processes were revamped and quality assurance was implemented.

'We have established standard operating procedures for all call types to provide clear performance guidelines and best practices to our frontline staff,' she said.

'The benefit, of course, is consistent high-level performance that will lead to a delightful customer experience.'

Focus on Marketing 9-2 (Continued)

In terms of human resources, staff development has been strongly emphasized.

'In a nutshell, we provide our staff with good training, motivation and incentive program and development opportunities,' Ms. Lim said. 'We provide our people with high-impact training, equipping them with professional service skills and effective telemarketing skills. Our training approach is unique in that we train people by skills set and help them to progress to a higher skills set, step by step.'

The company has revamped its business processes by integrating its three core functions of marketing, sales and customer service into a single system.

'This enables our frontline staff to handle inquiries and transactions in these areas without referring back and forth to internal departments,' Ms. Lim said. 'This greatly improves our service quality and enables effective cross-selling. Of course, the results are more happy customers and higher revenue for the company.'

Source: Taylor 2005.

9.3 The Power of Belonging to Customer Clubs

A **customer club** is a program organized by one or more companies with the objective of establishing customer loyalty (see Butscher 2002). Often customer clubs come along with other customer loyalty tools (e.g. customer magazines or customer cards, see Section 9.4). Most customer clubs offer a package of exclusive services, such as invitations to special shopping occasions, or price advantages. This illustrates that, in general, customer clubs comprise several elements of the marketing mix. An example of such a customer club is described in Focus on Marketing 9-3.

Focus on Marketing 9-3 Example of the use of a customer club within the scope of customer relationship management

Microsoft's customer club establishes relationships in Africa

In a bid to partner and support local IT companies, Microsoft Nigeria has launched a System Builders Club (SBC) in the country. The club would afford members the advantage of being exposed to online and hands-on technical and sales training facilities and receive latest information on product development.

Microsoft System Builders Partner Account Manager for Nigeria and Ghana, who addressed the audience at the launch in Lagos last week, said members would also become part of a worldwide network of Microsoft partner organisations. By joining, members, also gain access to key resources. Microsoft conceived the club as a way to help strengthen local brands in the market and give them a competitive base with other global brands.

System Builders are primarily small, local businesses with local customers. The club is a relationship management scheme that aims at establishing a firm bond with the breadth channel, driven by a continuous, rolling reward mechanic.

Focus on Marketing 9-3 (Continued)

It enables members to receive training and resources that help them differentiate their businesses, create new sales and growth opportunities, and strengthen their customer relationships.

The club is designed to function as a framework to assist system builders grow their business, and grow in their commitment to selling genuine Microsoft software and training that help strengthen customer relationships, extend market reach and reduce operational cost.

Microsoft further explained that the club would ensure that system builders maximize their potential, adding that the club has been functioning in places like Kenya, South Africa and other African countries. The club helps members strengthen their relationship with Microsoft which will affect their bottom line and expand their influence beyond Nigeria, he said.

Source: *Africa News* 2006.

As already discussed, the main objective of customer clubs is to increase and maintain customer loyalty towards the company (including aspects such as boosting purchase frequency and product usage, and promotion of word-of-mouth communication as well as cross-selling). Furthermore, customer clubs can be beneficial to companies by:

- facilitating communication (e.g. communication can be intensified, more dialog-oriented and can specifically address customers)
- supporting market research (e.g. by addressing members of the customer club for market research activities)
- helping in the acquisition of new customers.

A key issue is deciding between **limited or open customer clubs** (see Butscher 2002; Murphy 1997). Limited customer clubs are not accessible to everyone. Customers have to meet certain requirements in order to become members of the club. Limited clubs frequently offer their members special advantages, such as bonus systems, exclusive services or regular communication (e.g. via a club magazine). Conversely, open customer clubs are generally accessible to all customers.

Another differentiation concerns whether membership in the customer club is associated with a **membership fee**. If membership fees are required, they can cover the cost of operating the club. If fees are not required, the costs of running the club have to be covered by the marketing budget.

To further illustrate the concept of customer clubs, the typology in Figure 9-2 can be useful to distinguish different types of club. The various types of club can be classified according to the basic benefits associated with club membership. Here we contrast the economic and emotional benefits offered to customers. Table 9-2 provides further information regarding the seven types of club. For example, membership in a VIP club is typically connected with emotional rather than economic benefits.

In summary, it can be stated that a well-designed and effectively implemented customer club is an important customer relationship management tool, which can also contribute to optimizing marketing activities. In company practice, however, it can be observed that customer clubs are often too enthusiastically implemented, while it is not always evident what the benefits for the company are (see also Diller 1997). In view of this, the objectives of the customer club need to be clearly defined and periodically reviewed.

Table 9-2 Description of the basic types of customer club (adapted from Butscher 2002)

Club	Typical marketing objectives	Typical target groups	Typical services/benefits/ characteristics
VIP club	■ Retention and loyalty of attractive customer segments	■ Attractive customers with high sales/profitability	■ Exclusivity (particularly with additional/service features) ■ Financial/intangible benefits
Fan club	■ Support/improvement of brand image	■ All customers ■ Regular customers (customer base)	■ Meetings/group events for fans ■ Gifts/surprises ■ Fan club mail ■ Attractively priced special products
Product interest club	■ Retention/acquisition of heavy users	■ All customers ■ Non-customers	■ Dialog-based communication ■ Telephone hotline ■ Club magazine and letters ■ Attractively priced special products ■ Exclusive advance information
Customer advantage club	■ More effective customer retention/acquisition ■ Improved dialog with customers ■ Increase in visit/ purchase frequency	■ All customers	■ Delivery/order service ■ Premiums ■ Exclusive offers for club members
Lifestyle club	■ Customer loyalty and retention of customers, with a strong focus on lifestyle	■ Customer segments with specific (often premium) lifestyles	■ Special services ■ Offers for prestigious products
Refer-a-friend club	■ Retention/acquisition of new and existing refer-a-friend club members ■ Increase in number of friends recommending friends	■ Existing refer-a-friend group ■ All customers	■ Offers for premiums (attractive, high-quality premiums) ■ Additional/service features ■ Contests
On-top club	■ Retention/loyalty of particularly active members (defined by intensive use of club services and extremely high purchase frequency)	■ All club members	■ Exclusive additional services ■ Cash, tangible (non-monetary) and intangible additional benefits

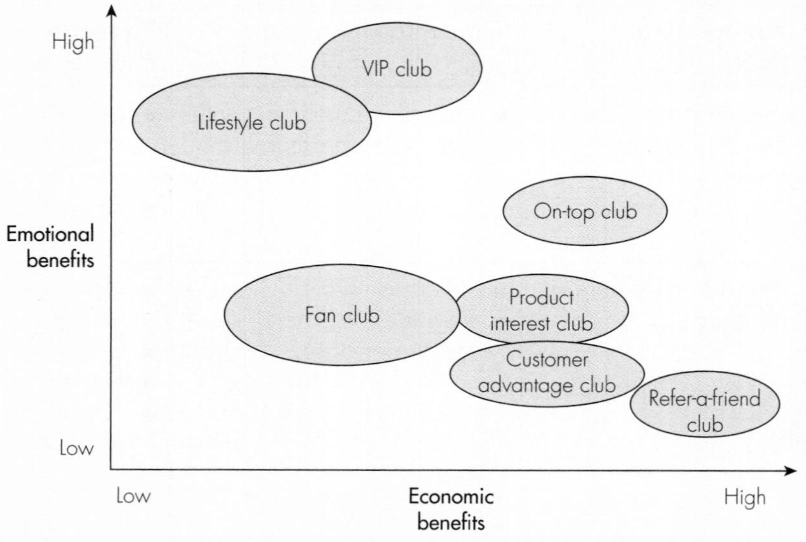

Figure 9-2 Positioning of customer club types categorized by club membership benefits (adapted from Butscher 2002)

9.4 Retaining Customers via Customer Cards

In recent years, **customer cards** (also known as loyalty cards) have become increasingly important in many industries as a customer relationship management tool. For example, department stores, airlines, petrol stations and car rental companies use customer cards intensively. Customer cards originated during the 1980s in the US airline industry (see Focus on Marketing 9-4 for a historical perspective on customer cards). Focus on Marketing 9-5 illustrates an example of the use of customer cards.

Focus on Marketing 9-4 The historical development of customer cards in the US airline industry

Frequent-flyer miles

The mania began in 1981, when American Airlines launched Advantage, the world's first mileage-based frequent-flyer program, to encourage customer loyalty. Today more than 130 airlines issue miles, and according to Randy Petersen, the founder of *Inside Flyer* magazine, 163m people around the globe collect miles of some sort. Indeed, calculations by *The Economist* in January 2005 suggested that the total stock of unredeemed miles was worth more than all the dollar bills in circulation. The record for the biggest individual account is 25m miles (enough to fly from London to Sydney and back 250 times), reputedly belonging to a publishing executive who charged his firm's postage bill to his own credit card.

Focus on Marketing 9-4 (Continued)

The biggest collectors of miles today are not frequent flyers but frequent buyers. More than half of all miles are earned on the ground, notably on credit cards linked to airlines' programs or on telephone calls. Miles are doled out by hotels, car-rental firms, retailers, real-estate agents and mortgage brokers. In America, if you pay by credit card you can earn miles for hospital surgery, income-tax payments and funerals. Some airlines even award miles to pets that fly with their owner. Frequent-flyer programs are no longer just a marketing gimmick; they have become a lucrative earner for airlines, through their sale of miles to partners, such as credit-card companies.

When United Airlines filed for bankruptcy in 2002, it said that its frequent-flyer program was the only part of its business that was making money. The economics is certainly attractive. Charging partners for each mile earned on a credit card, say, by a member of a frequent-flyer program, brings in estimated annual revenue of more than $10 billion for the industry worldwide. Better still, the airlines get this revenue upfront, while the miles are not redeemed until well into the future – if ever.

If current losses persist, might some airlines try to raise money by selling off their frequent-flyer programs? In 2005, Air Canada sold 12.5% of its loyalty scheme, Aeroplan, into a separate income trust. This raised C$250m, putting a total valuation of C$2 billion ($1.6 billion) on the scheme. United's Mileage Plus has eight times as many members as Aeroplan. On the other hand, United's estimated revenue from sales of miles to partner companies is perhaps only three to four times larger. This suggests a valuation of United's mileage scheme of $5 billion–$10 billion.

That would come in handy, but in the long run, airlines that flogged off their loyalty programs would risk killing the goose that lays the golden (or perhaps platinum?) eggs.

Source: *The Economist* 2005.

Focus on Marketing 9-5 Example of the use of customer cards within the scope of customer relationship management

A customer card success story at Tesco

Tesco, the UK supermarket chain, is helping packaged-goods marketers and hurting Wal-Mart with 'a data-driven strategy' that puts it 'at the vanguard in retailing as traditional advertising loses effectiveness', reports Cecilie Rohwedder in *The Wall Street Journal*. A loyalty card program – Tesco Clubcard – is at the heart of Tesco's success, having attracted some 12 million shoppers (about 80% of the total) and boosted its 'market share in groceries to 31%, nearly double the 16% held by Wal-Mart's Asda chain' according to Taylor Nelson Sofres. Basically, Tesco is using 'its knowledge of shoppers to fight Wal-Mart's core appeal: low prices'. For example, Tesco's Clubcard data 'showed that new fathers tend to buy more beer because they are home with the baby and can't go to the pub'.

So, now, shoppers buying 'diapers for the first time at a Tesco store can expect to receive coupons by mail for baby wipes, toys – and beer'. In another data-driven twist, Tesco rolled out 'Asian herbs, cooking oil and other ethnic foods to 25 stores in mostly white parts of the country' after the data showed the items were popular not only with the Indians and Pakistanis for whom they were intended, but also 'upscale white shoppers with an interest in non-European foods'.

Focus on Marketing 9-5 (Continued)

Clubcard data also showed Kimberly-Clark that buyers of its Aloe-infused Andrex toilet paper were 'also big buyers of skin-care products. Kimberly-Clark then sent direct mail to 500,000 customers, offering them free beauty treatments if they could show that they bought the toilet paper twice.' Redemption rates on such promotions are pretty amazing, too.

'While the industry adage says that only one percent or two percent of all coupons ever get redeemed, about 15 percent to 20 percent of all Tesco coupons are redeemed.' In part, this is simply because the coupons are so well targeted. 'They definitely know your shopping habits,' says Karen Masek, a Tesco Clubcard holder. 'They've never sent me anything totally off the mark.' It's also because points earned can be redeemed not only for groceries but also things like frequent flier miles. 'I always open the mail from Tesco,' says Adele Fiala of London, who recently flew to Spain using Tesco points. Asda/Wal-Mart 'executives believe Tesco's databases have little to do with its success.' Asda's Jon Owen says their problems are because 'we took our eye off the customer.' Hm. He also notes that the Tesco program is very expensive. 'Tesco doesn't disclose its investment in Clubcard but spokesman Jonathan Church says "it is worth every penny".'

Source: Manners 2006.

From a **customer's point of view**, customer cards can have various functions. For example:

- holders of customer cards can be entitled to discounts and bonus features as well as exclusive special offers
- holders of customer cards are offered special services
- holders of customer cards can be permitted exclusive access to certain events
- in addition, holders of customer cards can use their cards to pay for products directly; the payment function is often linked to financing as well – in this case, the customer card acts as a credit card; to enable this function, the company offering the card frequently cooperates with financial service providers.

From a **company's point of view**, customer cards fulfill two functions: a customer retention function and an informational function. The **customer retention function** (see Bolton *et al.* 2000; Noordhoff *et al.* 2004; Uncles *et al.* 2003) is essentially based on economic and psychological reasons for loyalty (in this connection, see the typology of customer loyalty factors in Section 3.1.4). Since customers present their customer cards at the time of purchase, extensive information can be recorded about customer buying patterns. This is the **informational function** of customer cards. It can then be linked with the demographic and socioeconomic data of the customer (see Uncles *et al.* 2003). This information can be used for marketing purposes; for example, for direct marketing activities geared towards very specific target groups (see also Focus on Marketing 9-5). In particular, the information can also be used to identify cross-selling potentials (see Section 9.5 for more on cross-selling).

Customer cards are primarily suited to companies with a large number of end customers. Nevertheless, it should be noted that this tool has been overused. In several Western countries, customers often have so many customer cards that it is difficult to keep an overview of the specific features and benefits of each one. In light of this fact, companies that offer customer cards should conduct regular acceptance and effectiveness analyses (see also Reinartz and Kumar 2002). The image on the next page shows some examples of Customer Cards.

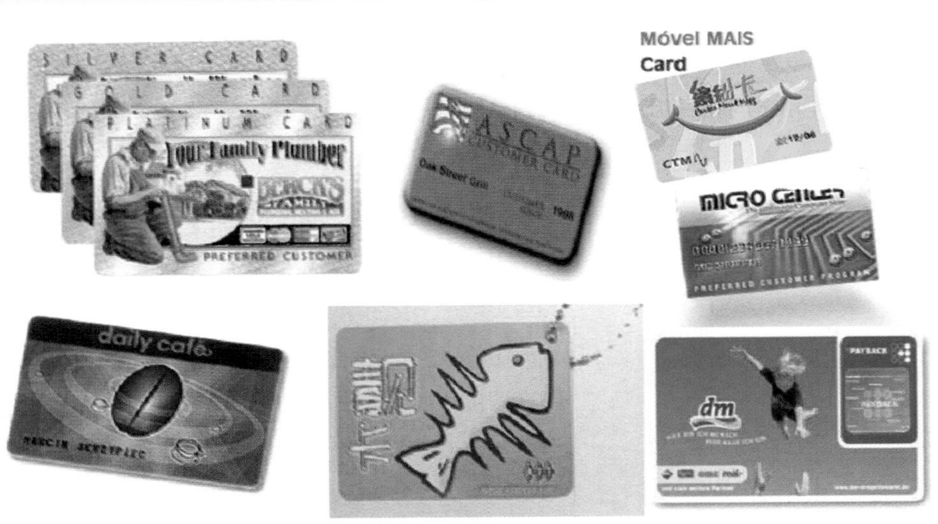

Figure 9-3 Examples of customer cards

9.5 Cross-selling: a Tool for Relationship Building

Cross-selling aims to encourage the customer to purchase several products sold by a company. It is based on an existing business relationship in which the customer already buys a certain product of the company. In the course of cross-selling, the company strives to sell additional products to the customer (see Nash and Sterna-Karwat 1996; Schmiedeberg 1995). Whereas the term 'upselling' refers to selling more upmarket and more expensive products of the same category, the concept of cross-selling also includes selling products from a different product category at the same price level. For example, a cheque account at a bank can represent the baseline product, while a mortgage or insurance policies can be sold to the same customer as additional products. Table 9-3 provides examples of core and additional products in various industries.

Success in cross-selling can significantly help companies in realizing the potential **sales-related benefits** that come with long-term customer relationships. Sales-related benefits are achieved if cross-selling results in the acquisition of products a customer did not previously buy from the company. Moreover, cross-selling success can also aid the company in realizing the **cost-related and stability-related benefits** of long-term customer relationships (for more on these two advantages of long-term customer relationships, see Section 3.1.4). Cost-related benefits can be realized through cross-selling – for example, if the achieved increases in sales are not compensated by a corresponding increase in the costs of customer relationship management (see e.g. Schmiedeberg 1995). Stability-related benefits can be attained if cross-selling results in a business relationship based on a larger number of products. This can lead, for example, to a more stable business relationship in situations where customer requirements frequently change for a single product (see Kalwani and Narayandas 1995; Kumar 1999).

A number of studies regarding the **success factors of cross-selling** have been conducted (see, e.g., Crosby *et al.* 1990; Evans *et al.* 1999; Homburg and Schäfer 2000, 2002; Kamakura *et al.* 1991, 2004;

Table 9-3 Core and additional products associated with cross-selling activities in various industries (adapted from Homburg and Schäfer 2001, p. 4)

Industry	Core products	Additional products
Bank (corporate customer segment)	Overdraft credit	Project financing, management consulting services
Bank (private customer segment)	Checking account	Savings account, credit card, construction financing, investment consulting services, insurance
Credit card company	Credit cards	Insurance packages, travel services, investment services
Insurance provider (corporate customer segment)	Building/ equipment/plant insurance	Asset management, investment banking services
Postal service/ telecommunications provider	Delivery service, telephone systems	Direct marketing services, IT/hardware solutions, e-commerce services
IT service provider	Hardware/software solutions	Business consulting services, e-commerce services, process re-engineering services
Advertising agency	Advertising concepts	Business consulting services
Tour operator	Train trips, flights, accommodation	Package tours, club vacations
Chemical company	Chemical substances	Storage, safety engineering, special-purpose chemicals
Life science/ pharmaceutical company	Therapeutic agents, diagnostic products	Vitamin preparations, skincare products, nutritional advice
Automobile manufacturer	Automobiles	Financial services, tour operator services, cultural programs
Mechanical engineering company	Machinery	Product-related services (e.g. training), other machines deployed at preceding or subsequent stages of the value chain
Energy provider (corporate customer segment)	Energy	Extended technical customer service, energy controlling, general consulting services, project financing (contracting), facility management, facility planning and development

Li *et al.* 2005; Reichheld and Sasser 1990). Obviously, an essential prerequisite for successful cross-selling is a sufficiently broad product range on the part of the company (see Sections 5.4.1 and 5.4.2 for issues related to product range). In addition, cross-selling can work in business relationships only when there is customer trust and satisfaction. Moreover, studies have shown that cross-selling success depends to a large extent on **company-internal factors**, such as:

- the company's strategy (e.g. the company strategy should also focus on existing customers)
- the organizational structure of the company (e.g. customer-oriented organizational forms such as key account management, customer segment manager and multifunctional customer care teams; see Chapter 13)
- the company's information systems (e.g. the company should incorporate information suitable for identifying cross-selling potential in its information system; see Chapter 14)
- the incentive system of the company (e.g. rewards and bonuses for cross-selling activities should be part of the company's incentive system)
- the company culture (e.g. the culture should also be customer-oriented and not purely product-oriented).

9.6 Dealing with Customer Complaints

Customers often voice their dissatisfaction towards a company by means of customer complaints. When customers complain they may have the following objectives (see also Estelami 2000):

- they want to make the company aware that they were dissatisfied with an aspect of the product or service offering
- they seek compensation for a damage incurred or service failure
- they hope that the company will consider changing the behavior or conduct with which they felt dissatisfied.

Studies have shown that customers whose complaints are adequately addressed often show greater loyalty to the company than before (see Davidow 2003; Hart *et al.* 1990; Homburg and Fürst 2005; Nyer 2000; Smith and Bolton 1998). Therefore, complaint management is particularly important in relationship management.

Figure 9-4 provides an overview of the **decision-making areas of complaint management** (see Homburg *et al.* 2005; Johnston and Mehra 2002). An important issue here is the **definition of complaint**. A company needs to establish a company-wide, standardized and as comprehensive as possible understanding of what constitutes a complaint. In particular, the definition relates to the following questions:

- Who submitted the complaint (customer, potential customer, sales partner)?
- In what way was the complaint submitted (written form, phone, email)?
- What does the complaint refer to (products, processes, employee conduct)?
- Is the complaint 'justified' or not?
- Who caused the complaint: the company itself or a third party (e.g. sales or service partners)?
- Does the customer attach a financial claim to the complaint or not?

The decision regarding the **organizational embedding** of the complaint management system concerns the assignment of responsibilities within the company. A key question here pertains

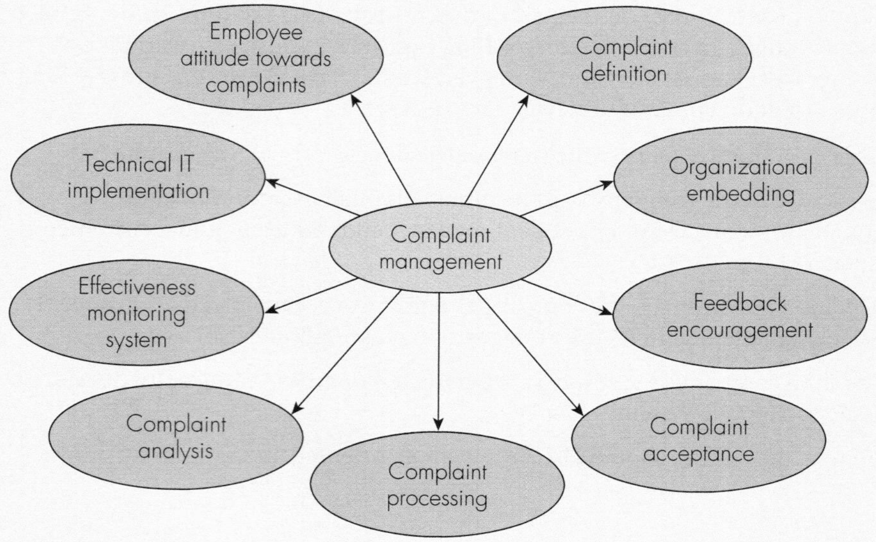

Figure 9-4 Decision-making areas of complaint management (adapted from Homburg *et al.* 2005, p. 289)

to whether complaint management tasks should be centralized in the company. It seems to be important that companies refrain from implementing an exclusively centralized or exclusively decentralized complaint management system, but rather strike the right balance between centralization and decentralization.

As far as **encouraging feedback** is concerned, dissatisfied customers should be motivated to express their complaints. The importance of this is demonstrated by numerous study findings, which show that a significant portion of dissatisfied customers do not voice their complaints to the company (see Table 9-4). These customers are troublesome as they are unlikely to become loyal but are likely to speak about their dissatisfaction to other individuals.

The numbers in Table 9-4 illustrate that the percentage of customers who have not expressed a complaint to the company displays a strong correlation to the customer's financial loss associated with the reason for the complaint (for more information, see also Estelami 1999; Singh and Wilkes 1996; Stephens and Gwinner 1998). Accordingly, a customer's tendency to complain increases when a substantial financial loss is anticipated. In principle, it can be assumed, however, that the 'hidden dissatisfaction' phenomenon (dissatisfied customers who do not voice a complaint to the company) exists in virtually any situation. The approach of encouraging feedback therefore aims at minimizing this hidden dissatisfaction. The significance of feedback encouragement has also been emphasized by empirical findings which show that dissatisfied customers frequently communicate their dissatisfaction to third parties. For example, Blodgett *et al.* (1995) have shown that 77 per cent of dissatisfied customers intensively communicated their negative experiences to third parties, whereas only 48 per cent of the customers who had expressed a complaint to the company did the same. These findings illustrate the risk posed by hidden dissatisfaction. Feedback encouragement (see Davidow 2003) can be implemented with a wide variety of tools, including, for instance, complaint hotlines, suggestion boxes and customer surveys (e.g. after a purchase or subsequent to the use of certain services) (for a description of different forms of 'survey', see the Appendix).

Table 9-4 Complaint behavior of dissatisfied customers correlated with potential financial loss (adapted from TARP 1979, p. 10)

Potential financial loss	$0	$1–5	$6–10	$11–25	$26–50	$51–100	$101–500	$501–999	> $1,000
Portion of dissatisfied customers who expressed a complaint	52.9%	58.7%	73.8%	71.0%	81.7%	89.4%	84.2%	94.4%	90.5%
Portion of dissatisfied customers who did not express a complaint	47.1%	41.3%	26.2%	29.0%	18.3%	10.6%	15.8%	5.6%	9.5%

When making decisions about **complaint acceptance** the company establishes guidelines for employees who receive complaints. For example, it can be specified that employees should not blame the customer, and what type of information should be collected at the first point of contact with a complaining customer (see Berry 1995; Goodwin and Ross 1990; Homburg *et al.* 2005; Johnston 2001).

Complaint processing requires the development of guidelines with respect to the timeframe and quality of complaint processing (see Homburg and Fürst 2005). Rules can be established to determine how fast complaints should be processed. For example, online companies often send an automatic confirmation that a complaint has been received, indicating how long it will take until the complaint has been dealt with and a response can be expected.

With **complaint analysis**, the focus lies on evaluating the information that complaints can provide to the company. The company can use such information to identify and remedy systematic problems. In this context, it is assumed that a frequently occurring reason for complaints can indicate systematic problems in a company (for more on complaint analysis, see Berry 1995; Lapidus and Schribrowsky 1994).

When developing an **effectiveness monitoring system**, the core issue is how a company rates the effectiveness of its complaint management system on the following aspects:

- quality (e.g. degree of customer satisfaction with complaint handling, duration of complaint processing)
- costs (e.g. personnel costs, costs for making amends)
- economic benefit(s) (e.g. repeat purchase behavior of customers who expressed a complaint)
- learning effects (e.g. measures of improvement developed on the basis of information provided by complaints).

Another decision-making area is concerned with the **technical IT implementation** of the complaint management system. The complaint management system can integrate the complaint into the information technology systems (see Chapter 14). On the one hand, the complaint management system generates a vast amount of information that is made available to the various departments within the company. On the other hand, information from other areas of the company is also required for the effective processing of complaints (for a more detailed discussion, see Homburg and Fürst 2005).

Finally, successful complaint management requires the company to foster a positive attitude on the part of its employees in terms of complaints and complaint processing (see, e.g., Maxham and Netemeyer 2003; for an explanation of the concept of 'attitude', see the Appendix). The objective of managing **employee attitude towards complaints** should be that employees do not perceive complaints as personal criticism; they should rather view complaints as an opportunity to establish and maintain good customer relationships. Influencing the attitude of employees can be facilitated by, for example, establishing a company culture that promotes this (see Chapter 13) as well as an appropriate human resources management system (see Chapter 16).

In summary, it can be stated that the significance of complaint management as a customer relationship management tool can hardly be overestimated. This major importance arises from the fact that an effective complaint management system not only helps to reinstate customer loyalty to the previous level, but can also raise it to a higher level (see Fornell and Wernerfelt 1988; Homburg and Fürst 2005; Rust *et al.* 1992). Furthermore, it can be observed in company practice that companies with a well-established and efficient complaint management system tend to have a stronger customer focus (see Davidow 2003; Johnston and Mehra 2002). Effective complaint management means nothing less than applying a customer-focused approach in one of the most difficult situations for a business, i.e. when a customer specifically expresses dissatisfaction.

9.7 Winning back Customers: on the Road to Customer Recovery

In contrast to the other instruments discussed in this chapter, customer recovery focuses on those customers who have terminated their business relationship with the company or are planning to do so (also see Griffin and Lowenstein 2001; Reichheld 1996; Stauss and Friege 1999; Thomas *et al.* 2004). In company practice, systematic customer recovery is still rarely used as a tool in customer relationship management.

The underlying logic of customer recovery is based on the fact that many of the lost customers had their share of positive experiences with the company and probably have been loyal, satisfied customers of the company at some point in time. Against this background, it can be assumed that these customers, despite their possible irritation, have still retained some amount of goodwill towards the company (also see Thomas *et al.* 2004; Vavra 1995). Systematic customer recovery thus aims to leverage this goodwill in order to revitalize the business relationship. Figure 9-5 illustrates the process of customer recovery. In the following text, we will briefly examine the individual steps in this process.

The **identification of lost customers** should target former customers who still have a demand for the company's products. Customers who have discontinued use of a product due to reasons outside the company's sphere of influence are not suitable targets (an example is a subscriber to a local daily newspaper who has moved to another city).

The question of when a customer should be considered 'lost' is not trivial at all. Companies should not consider a customer to be 'lost' only when there has been a formal termination of the business relationship, since, frequently, such a formal termination does not occur. In general, the movement of customers from company to company in search of better and less expensive products and services is referred to as **customer churn**. Moreover, many business relationships exist without any contractual agreement (e.g. in B2C markets), so that a formal termination of the business relationship is not possible. Therefore, companies should consider customers to be 'lost' when they exhibit very different purchasing behavior than they used to, especially if these customers buy significantly less than before.

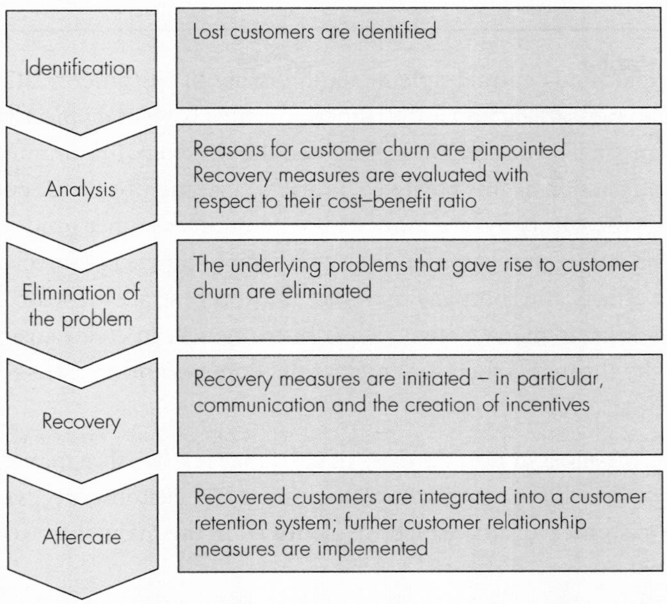

Figure 9-5 Systematic customer recovery process (Homburg and Schäfer 1999, p. 5)

In the concluding **analysis phase**, two questions take center stage:

1 What are the main reasons for customer churn?

2 For which customers does the initiation of certain recovery measures appear profitable?

The first question can primarily be answered through qualitative market research (for more information on 'market research', see the Appendix), for example, with in-depth interviews.

With respect to the second question, strategies can be devised that specify how to deal with individual customers in the next stages of the recovery process. When developing these strategies, the attractiveness of the customers and the probability of recovery are taken into account. Particular efforts should focus more on those customers that are especially attractive to the company (e.g. customers with high demand) and for whom recovery is highly probable (see Section 15.4 for methods that can be used to assess the attractiveness of customers).

After the analysis phase, the **problem elimination phase** follows. Although this phase can also be used to address individual problems with key customers, the focus is on those reasons for the customer churn that have been identified as being inherent to the system. Typical problems include inadequate customer communication, interpersonal problems and barriers to customer-oriented behavior that are rooted in the organizational structure (see Homburg and Schäfer 1999).

In the actual customer **recovery phase**, a wide variety of measures can be used. Customers can, for example, be provided with tangible or intangible incentives to re-enter into a business relationship (see Homburg and Schäfer 1999; Thomas *et al.* 2004).

Finally, during the **aftercare phase**, the aim is to secure and stabilize the revitalized business relationship. In this connection, special customer retention measures can be used for the recovered customers. The company could, for example, issue special VIP club cards to such customers.

Summary

In this chapter, we discussed the logic and central implementation issues of customer relationship management. We introduced customer satisfaction and customer loyalty as pivotal objectives of customer relationship management. The discussion highlighted that it is very important for a company to establish customer satisfaction as this positively impacts customer loyalty. If customers are loyal, they repeatedly buy from the company, are more willing to purchase other products offered by the company (cross-selling) and will even recommend the company to others (positive word of mouth). In order to achieve these effects, the company must carefully orchestrate the instruments that are available in customer relationship management. These instruments can create customer satisfaction and/or customer loyalty through a focus on interaction, bonuses and rewards or barriers to switching to a competitor.

In this chapter we also focused on the most important tools of customer relationship management: customer clubs, customer cards, cross-selling, complaint management and customer recovery. These tools aim mainly to create customer loyalty, which we identified as the main objective of customer relationship management.

Case Study: Cult Lifestyle at Harley-Davidson: the Mythical HOG Club

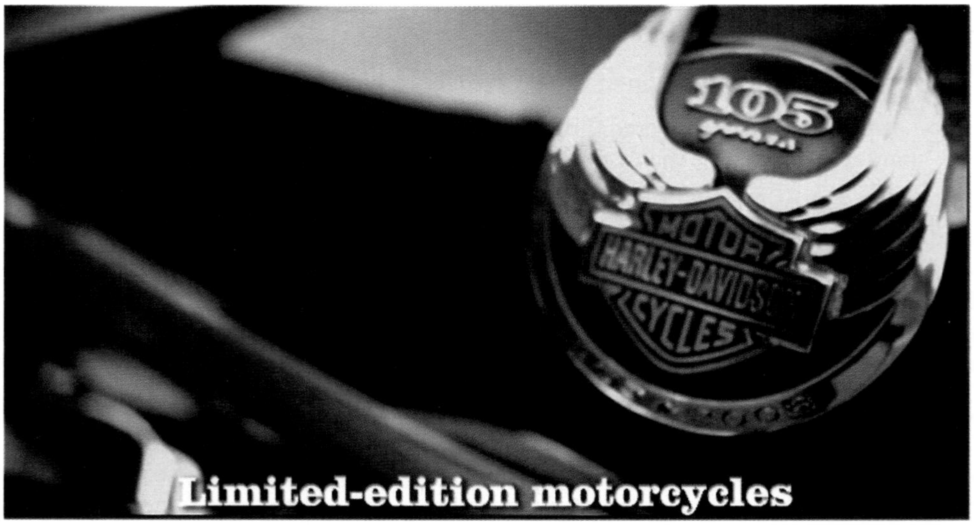

It was in June 1981 that the employees of Harley-Davidson (HD) wrestled the business away from a faltering AMF. With this change in ownership came a whole new philosophy of marketing. Prior to '81, you bought a motorcycle. After '81 you bought a lifestyle – often for upwards of $30,000.

Case Study (Continued)

How can that be, I thought, comfortable in my HD rainwear over my HD vest over my HD jacket over my HD chaps over my HD jeans? All of which cost me twice the commodity price. What is it about the HD brand that suspends price as a discriminator?

The answer is continuity, consistency, a discreet image and a reinforcement of the core equity and individualism at every point of customer contact. Last, but perhaps most important, is the Harley Owner's Group best customer program, affectionately known as HOG.

All HOG members wear their colors proudly at the many annual Harley events. HOG members have access to special rates on insurance. They can fly and rent a Harley at any participating dealer for $700 per week. They have their own magazine.

The HOG concept has solidified relationships among people who share the common values of freedom and individualism regardless of their socioeconomic status. The brand has become an icon for these values. Ironically, no one needs to ride a Harley or buy HD badged products. The entire strategy is want-based, ideally suited for the Next Economy, where we will be segmenting psychographically not demographically.

In HD, we have a brand successfully operating as a premium product in every single commodity it licenses. Not because the quality is best in class ('Harleys don't leak . . . they just mark their spot'). Not because it's the least expensive (the machines are premium priced out of the box but you can run them up $40,000 to $50,000 for a truly unique pig). Not because it operates in a niche marketplace (almost all its product offerings are premium priced in a commodity business). But because at HD, they view the sale of a Harley as the beginning, not the end of the relationship. They understand that bonding between products and people is a by-product of people bonding with people who share values. The product is a means to the end.

Source: Ettenberg, E. (2003) The church of Harley-Davidson, *Marketing magazine*, 11964650, 28 July 2003–4 August, 108, 27.

Discussion Questions

1. Which levers to create customer loyalty does HOG use?
2. Which marketing instruments does HOG use for customer relationship management? How are they used?
3. Which club type with respect to Figure 9-2 in this chapter does HOG represent? Is it appropriate for Harley-Davidson? What are the specific advantages and disadvantages of each type of customer club for Harley-Davidson?
4. What other tools of customer relationship management are used by HOG? Which of them would be appropriate for Harley-Davidson to effectively enhance customer loyalty?

Key Terms

Aftercare phase *313*
Analysis phase *313*
Company's point of view *306*
Company-internal factors *309*
Complaint acceptance *311*
Complaint analysis *311*
Complaint processing *311*
Cost-related benefits *307*
Cross-selling *307*
Customer cards *304*
Customer churn *312*
Customer club *301*
Customer loyalty *297*
Customer retention function *306*
Customer satisfaction *296*
Customer's point of view *306*
Decision-making areas of complaint management *309*
Definition of complaint *309*
Effectiveness monitoring system *311*
Employee attitude towards complaints *312*
Focus on barriers to switching *298*
Focus on bonuses/rewards *298*
Focus on interaction *298*
Formation of customer satisfaction *296*
Identification of lost customers *312*
Informational function *306*
Limited or open customer clubs *302*
Membership fee *302*
Problem elimination phase *313*
Recovery phase *313*
Sales-related benefits *307*
Stability-related benefits *307*
Success factors of cross-selling *307*
Technical IT implementation *311*

References

Africa News (2006) Nigeria; Microsoft to support local IT companies, 15 February.
Anderson, E.W. and Mittal, V. (2000) Strengthening the satisfaction–profit chain, *Journal of Service Research*, 3, 2, 107–120.
Berry, L.L. (1995) *On Great Service: A Framework for Action*. New York.
Bhote, K.R. (1996) *Beyond Customer Satisfaction to Customer Loyalty – The Key to Greater Profitability*. New York.
Blodgett, J., Wakefield, K. and Barnes, J. (1995) The effects of customer service on consumer complaining behavior, *Journal of Services Marketing*, 9, 4, 31–42.
Bolton, R.N. and Drew, J. (1991) A longitudinal analysis of the impact of service changes on customer attitudes, *Journal of Marketing*, 55, 1, 1–9.
Bolton, R.N., Kannan, P.K. and Bramlet, M.D. (2000) Implications of loyalty program membership and service experience for customer retention and value, *Journal of the Academy of Marketing Science*, 28, 1, 95–108.
Butscher, S. (2002) *Customer Loyalty Programs and Clubs* (2nd edn). Aldershot.
Crosby, L.A., Evans, K.R. and Cowles, D. (1990) Relationship quality in service selling: an interpersonal influence perspective, *Journal of Marketing*, 54, 3, 68–81.
Davidow, M. (2003) Organizational responses to customer complaints: what works and what doesn't, *Journal of Service Research*, 5, 3, 225–250.
Diller, H. (1997) Was leisten Kundenclubs? *Marketing – Zeitschrift für Forschung und Praxis*, 19, 1, 33–45.
Economist, The (2005) Funny money, 377, 8458, 24 December.
Estelami, H. (1999) The profit impact of consumer complaint solicitation across market conditions, *Journal of Professional Services Marketing*, 20, 1, 165–195.
Estelami, H. (2000) Competitive and procedural determinants of delight and disappointment in consumer complaint outcomes, *Journal of Service Research*, 2, 3, 285–300.
Ettenberg, E. (2003) The church of Harley-Davidson, *Marketing* magazine, 108, 27, 9.
Evans, K.R., Arnold, T.J. and Grant, J.A. (1999) Combining service and sales at the point of customer contact: a retail banking example, *Journal of Service Research*, 2, 1, 34–49.
Fornell, C. and Wernerfelt, B. (1988) A model for customer complaint management, *Marketing Science*, 7, 3, 287–298.
Fournier, S. and Mick, D. (1999) Rediscovering satisfaction, *Journal of Marketing*, 63, 4, 5–23.

Goodwin, C. and Ross, I. (1990) Consumer evaluations of responses to complaints: what's fair and why, *Journal of Services Marketing*, 4, 3, 53–61.
Griffin, J. and Lowenstein, M.W. (2001) *Customer Winback: How to Recapture Lost Customers – And Keep Them Loyal*. San-Francisco.
Grønholdt, L., Martensen, A. and Kristensen, K. (2000) The relationship between customer satisfaction and loyalty: cross-industry differences, *Total Quality Management*, 11, 4/5/6, 509–514.
Grönroos, C. (1994) From marketing mix to relationship marketing: towards a paradigm shift in marketing, *Management Decision*, 32, 2, 4–20.
Gustafsson, A., Johnson, M.D. and Roos, I. (2005) Effects of customer satisfaction, relationship commitment dimensions, and triggers on customer retention, *Journal of Marketing*, 69, 4, 210–218.
Hart, C., Heskett, J. and Sasser, W. (1990) The profitable art of service recovery, *Harvard Business Review*, 68, 4, 148–156.
Hissink, D. (2005) *NikonPro magazine celebrates 10th anniversary*, http://www.letsgodigital.org/en/News/Articles/Story_3774.html.
Homburg, C. and Bruhn, M. (2005) Kundenbindungsmanagement – Eine Einführung in die theoretischen und praktischen Problemstellungen, in: Bruhn, M. and Homburg, C. (eds) *Handbuch Kundenbindungsmanagement: Grundlagen – Konzepte – Erfahrungen* (5th edn). Wiesbaden, 3–37.
Homburg, C. and Fürst, A. (2005) How organizational complaint handling drives customer loyalty: an analysis of the mechanistic and the organic approach, *Journal of Marketing*, 69, 3, 95–114.
Homburg, C. and Schäfer, H. (1999) Customer Recovery: Profitabilität durch systematische Rückgewinnung von Kunden, Institut für Marktorientierte Unternehmensführung, Working Paper, Management Know-How, Nr. 39, Mannheim.
Homburg, C. and Schäfer, H. (2000) Cross-selling – Aus der Kundenbeziehung mehr herausholen, *Harvard Business Manager*, 22, 6, 35–44.
Homburg, C. and Schäfer, H. (2001) Profitabilität durch Cross-Selling: Kundenpotentiale professionell erschließen, Institut für Marktorientierte Unternehmensführung, Working Paper, Management Know-How, Nr. 60, Mannheim.
Homburg, C. and Schäfer, H. (2002) Die Erschließung von Kundenpotenzialen durch Cross-Selling: Konzeptionelle Grundlagen und empirische Forschung, *Marketing – Zeitschrift für Forschung und Praxis*, 24, 1, 7–26.
Homburg, C. and Werner, H. (1998) *Kundenorientierung mit System: mit Customer-Orientation-Management zu profitablem Wachstum*. Frankfurt am Main.
Homburg, C., Giering, A. and Menon, A. (2003) Relationship characteristics as moderators of the satisfaction–loyalty link: findings in a business-to-business context, *Journal of Business-to-Business Marketing*, 10, 3, 35–62.
Homburg, C., Giering, A. and Hentschel, F. (1999) Der Zusammenhang zwischen Kundenzufriedenheit und Kundenbindung, *DBW – Die Betriebswirtschaft*, 59, 2, 173–195.
Homburg, C., Schäfer, H. and Schneider, J. (2005) *Sales Excellence: Vertriebsmanagement mit System* (4th edn). Wiesbaden.
Johnson, M. and Auh, S. (1998) Customer satisfaction, loyalty and the trust environment, *Advances in Customer Research*, 25, 1, 15–20.
Johnson, M.D. and Gustafsson, A. (2000) *Improving Customer Satisfaction, Loyalty, and Profit: An Integrated Measurement and Management System*. San Francisco.
Johnston, R. (2001) Linking complaint management to profit, *International Journal of Service Industry Management*, 12, 1, 60–69.
Johnston, R. and Mehra, S. (2002) Best-practice complaint management, *Academy of Management Executive*, 16, 4, 145–154.
Kalwani, M.U. and Narayandas, N. (1995) Long-term manufacturer–supplier relationships: do they pay off for supplier firms? *Journal of Marketing*, 59, 1, 1–16.
Kamakura, W.A., Kossar, B.S. and Wedel, M. (2004) Identifying innovators for the cross-selling of new products, *Management Science*, 50, 8, 1120–1133.
Kamakura, W.A., Ramaswami, S. and Srivastava, R. (1991) Applying latent trait analysis in the evaluation of prospects for cross-selling of financial services, *International Journal of Research in Marketing*, 8, 4, 329–349.
Kumar, P. (1999) The impact of long-term client relationships on the performance of business service firms, *Journal of Service Research*, 2, 1, 4–18.
Lapidus, R.S. and Schibrowsky, J.A. (1994) Aggregate complaint analysis: a procedure for developing customer service satisfaction, *Journal of Services Marketing*, 8, 4, 50–60.
Li, S., Sun, B. and Wilcox, R.T. (2005) Cross-selling sequentially ordered products: an application to consumer banking, *Journal of Marketing Research*, 42, 2, 233–239.
Lowenstein, M.W. (1997) *The Customer Loyalty Pyramid*. Westport.

Manners, T. (2006) Tesco Clubcard, http://www.reveries.com.
Maxham, J.G. and Netemeyer, R.G. (2003) A longitudinal study of complaining customers' evaluations of multiple service failures and recovery efforts, *Journal of Marketing*, 66, 4, 57–71.
Mithas, S., Krishnan, M.S. and Fornell, C. (2005) Why do customer relationship management applications affect customer satisfaction? *Journal of Marketing*, 69, 4, 201–209.
Mittal, V. and Kamakura, W.A. (2001) Satisfaction, repurchase intent and repurchase behavior: investigating the moderating effect of customer characteristics, *Journal of Marketing Research*, 38, 1, 131–142.
Mittal, V., Ross, W. Jr and Baldasare, P. (1998) The asymmetric impact of negative and positive attribute-level performance on overall satisfaction and repurchase intentions, *Journal of Marketing*, 62, 1, 33–47.
Murphy, I.P. (1997) Customers can join the club – but at a price, *Retention Marketing*, April 28, 8.
Nash, D. and Sterna-Karwat, A. (1996) An application of DEA to measure branch cross selling efficiency, *Computers & Operations Research*, 23, 4, 385–393.
Noordhoff, C., Pauwels, P. and Odekerken-Schroeder, G. (2004) The effect of customer card programs: a comparative study in Singapore and the Netherlands, *International Journal of Service Industry Management*, 15, 4, 351–364.
Nyer, P.U. (2000) An investigation into whether complaining can cause increased consumer satisfaction, *Journal of Consumer Marketing*, 17, 1, 9–19.
Oliver, R.L. (1997) *Satisfaction: A Behavioral Perspective on the Consumer*. Boston.
Olsen, S.O. (2002) Comparative evaluation and the relationship between quality, satisfaction, and repurchase loyalty, *Journal of the Academy of Marketing Science*, 30, 3, 240–249.
Payne, A. and Frow, P. (2006) Customer relationship management: from strategy to implementation, *Journal of Marketing Management*, 22, 1/2, 135–169.
Reichheld, F. (1996) Learning from customer defections, *Harvard Business Review*, 74, 2, 56–69.
Reichheld, F. and Sasser, E.W. (1990) Zero defections – quality comes to service, *Harvard Business Review*, 68, 5, 105–111.
Reinartz, W.J. and Kumar, V. (2002) The mismanagement of customer loyalty, *Harvard Business Review*, 7, 86–94.
Reinartz, W.J., Krafft, M. and Hoyer, W.D. (2004) The customer relationship management process: its measurement and impact on performance, *Journal of Marketing Research*, 41, 3, 293–305.
Rust, R.T., Moorman, C. and Dickson, P.R. (2002) Getting return on quality: revenue expansion, cost reduction, or both? *Journal of Marketing*, 66, 4, 7–24.
Rust, R.T., Subramanian, V. and Wells, M. (1992) Making complaints a management tool, *Marketing Management*, 1, 3, 40–45.
Schmiedeberg, A. (1995) Seeking synergy – the role of organizational learning in corporate diversification strategies. Dissertation, Bonn University.
Singh, J. and Wilkes, R. (1996) When consumers complain: a path analysis of the key antecedents of consumer complaint response estimates, *Journal of the Academy of Marketing Science*, 24, 4, 350–365.
Smith, A. and Bolton, R. (1998) An experimental investigation of customer reactions to service failure and recovery encounters, paradox or peril? *Journal of Services Research*, 1, 1, 65–81.
Smith, R.E. and Wright, W.F. (2004) Determinants of customer loyalty and financial performance, *Journal of Management Accounting Research*, 16, 183–205.
Stauss, B. and Friege, C. (1999) Regaining service customers: cost and benefits of regain management, *Journal of Service Research*, 1, 4, 347–361.
Stephens, N. and Gwinner, K. (1998) Why don't some people complain? A cognitive-emotive process model of consumer complaint behavior, *Journal of the Academy of Marketing Science*, 26, 3, 172–189.
Szymanski, D. and Henard, D. (2001) Customer satisfaction: a meta-analysis of the empirical evidence, *Journal of the Academy of Marketing Science*, 29, 1, 16–35.
TARP – Technical Assistance Research Program, Inc. (1979) *Consumer Complaint Handling in America*, Final Report, US Department of Commerce, Washington.
Taylor, M. (2005) High-impact training ensures big success, *South China Morning Post*, 14 June, 4.
Thomas, J., Blattberg, R. and Fox, E. (2004) Recapturing lost customers, *Journal of Marketing Research*, 41, 2, 31–45.
Uncles, M.D., Dowling, G.R. and Hammond, K. (2003) Customer loyalty and customer loyalty programs, *Journal of Consumer Marketing*, 20, 4, 294–316.
Vavra, T. (1995) *After-Marketing – How to Keep Customers for Life Through Relationship Marketing*. Homewood.
Zablah, A.R., Bellenger, D.N. and Johnston, W.T. (2004) An evaluation of divergent perspectives on customer relationship management: towards a common understanding of an emerging phenomenon, *Industrial Marketing Management*, 33, 6, 475–489.

End of Part Case Study – Magnum Ice Cream: A Unilever Success Story

People are passionate about ice cream around the globe. And a clear worldwide favorite among the many ice cream products available to the fans of frozen popsicles is Magnum, a Unilever brand – the most popular ice cream brand in the world. Its success builds on innovative ideas that are brought to market in a carefully crafted mix. Take a glimpse into the many details that marketing managers at Unilever thought about when creating 'Origin selection', one of Magnum's latest success stories.

Unilever and the Ice Cream Business

Unilever offers its ice cream products in almost every country in the world, covering the three segments, impulse (single pieces in one-portion sizes, sold mainly at outdoor and convenience stores), multipack (a bundle of several singles, sold in grocery stores) and take home (tubs for scooping or ice cream logs that can be cut into slices, also available at grocery stores). The portfolio differs from region to region, and even from country to country – each nation has its favorites. In many cases, these products have been around for decades and often reflect the countries' particularities regarding ice cream flavors and textures. Almost as diverse is the number of umbrella brand names in the different countries: while Eskimo is every child's dream in Austria, the US equivalent's name is Good Humor; in South Africa, Ola refreshes consumers and Langnese is an all-time favorite in Germany. In an attempt to unify these diverse brands, in 2002 Unilever globally switched to a heart-shaped logo while sticking to the local brand names. The so-called 'Heartbrand' logo has been well accepted by consumers, and has successfully been established as a link between most Unilever ice cream brands.

In light of Unilever's portfolio diversity, Magnum's global success story is even more remarkable – it is part of Unilever's ice cream portfolio in every market in which the consumer goods manufacturer is active. Among all Unilever's sub-brands, Magnum is by far the most important, both in terms of sales as well as consumer awareness.

Magnum's Brand Image

The secret of Magnum's success lies in the simplicity of the product, in combination with a comparably large size: 120 ml of creamy vanilla ice cream covered with a thick layer of cracking chocolate. When Magnum had its debut in 1988, it seemed to be what ice cream fans had been waiting for all along – a truly grown-up ice cream product, large, without any childish attribute and presented in a very adult, sensual manner, suggesting pure indulgence. Its premium positioning supported this impression: Magnum was the first ice cream lolly covered in real chocolate instead of chocolate-flavored fat coating. The metallic wrapper gave it a shiny and very precious look, and it was priced at the upper level of the price range.

Over time, Magnum's brand image has continuously been strengthened by advertising campaigns and innovations. Consumers associate it with sensuality and indulgence. It is perceived as a brand that offers small, yet intense, breaks for oneself. It is mystic and represents style, and it has itself become an icon. Magnum's image has been brought about by ever recurring communicative elements. For example, there is the use of that very distinct sound of cracking chocolate, which has become a true retrieval cue for Magnum. Advertising for Magnum always includes scenes of intense relaxation. The brand is consistently advertised by a certain type of exotic woman indulging in a Magnum and truly forgetting everything around her. Innovations such as the Seven Deadly Sins and the Five Senses editions have sharpened the image of Magnum as the perfect treat that's always worth sinning for – it's just too good to miss out on.

Marketing for Magnum

At Unilever, marketing is a shared task between development centers in charge of innovations, communication and overall brand strategy, and the local marketing teams that take care of building the brand in the respective national market. These local teams roll out the ideas generated by brand development and adapt them to their home market and consumers' particular needs in that country.

In 2006, preparing next year's ice cream program, the global brand development team in charge of Magnum innovations and communication worked on ways to underpin Magnum's chocolate competence with a forceful new product. While recent years' innovations had focused on interesting new flavors, and had often been inspired by an overall idea such as the Seven Deadly Sins edition, in 2007 Magnum had been 'relaunched' in an effort to strengthen its premium positioning and, alongside that, the superior quality of the brand. The development team intended to take that story further by coming up with a product that was perceived as being innovative and, at the same time, of selected quality. Brand development therefore decided to develop a new variant using an especially fine kind of chocolate for the coating, sourced exclusively from Ecuador, a country famous for its superb cocoa beans. The variant was supposed to feature a dark chocolate that Ecuador cocoa is especially well suited for and, even more important, a kind of chocolate that was perceived as exquisite by customers, as market research had shown.

Another important driver for this idea was the very interesting development in a parallel segment to ice cream: the chocolate market. The development here not only supported the decision to launch a speciality chocolate variant under the Magnum brand, but also influenced the choice of important features of the local marketing mix in a number of countries. For illustration, we will look at the situation in Germany and how Unilever dealt with it there.

Finding the Perfect Mix for a Local Market

In many European countries, the chocolate market had been stagnating for years. In particular, the German market had been characterized by discounters gaining market share constantly, deteriorating the price level of food in general. Additionally, private labels had been flooding the market with chocolate bars at price entry points. Chocolate had become something of a commodity, with a steadily declining price level. However, this trend has recently been brought to a halt by a couple of innovative products that some chocolate manufacturers had launched: shelves started to fill with semi-dark and dark chocolate of selected countries of origin, such as Ecuador, Java, Trinidad and Venezuela. Apart from the provenance of the cocoa beans used in the chocolate, the percentage of cocoa content was printed very prominently on these new products. Interestingly, they were priced with a significant premium compared to existing offers. By lucky coincidence for the manufacturers of this chocolate, a lot of lifestyle and cooking magazines around the time of the launch picked up on the fact that dark chocolate might be 'healthier' than other chocolate due to its higher percentage of cocoa and, by consequence, lower percentage of sugar. This very positive and, in some countries such as Germany, rather massive PR for dark chocolate certainly helped the success of the products, especially since market growth was driven mainly by an increase in frequency of consumption, as opposed to growth by an increase in the number of buyers. Soon, all major chocolate manufacturers had a variety of dark and semi-dark variants with cocoa of diverse origin in their portfolio. Also, the practice of indicating the origin and percentage of cocoa in the chocolate was extended to milk chocolate variants, allowing for price premiums there too. The development also brought about the launch of new formats such as pure chocolate bars, a variety of packaging sizes, as well as more exotic flavors such as chili and ginger.

Given this favorable market development, hopes were high that the trend could also be exploited in ice cream. Market research confirmed once again the strong relevance of specially selected dark chocolates of different origins, but also that German customers were thrilled about the idea of extending the concept to ice cream. Moreover, it became clear that Magnum was the perfect brand to convey the story in a convincing and credible way due to its strong link to chocolate. Magnum's mystic and sensual image fitted the exotic origin of the ingredient too.

The same research offered important insights about the requirements for the German marketing mix. First of all, consumers expected to find not only one, but a whole range of products, covering different cocoa percentages, chocolate types and cocoa origins. This can be explained by a number of reasons. First of all, consumers had got used to being offered a wide selection in the chocolate department. Second, although dark chocolate had started the chocolate hype, the German chocolate market was still dominated by milk chocolate bars: about 70 per cent of the total market was made up of milk chocolate variants that remained the German favorite and had benefited well from the favorable development of the dark variants. Third, German customers had come to love the 'edition' approach (a range of products under the umbrella of one connecting idea) that Magnum had been taking in previous years. They were eager to be presented with an exciting new edition idea. Also, from a budget point of view, the idea to launch more than just the one variant was attractive: Magnum being a Unilever focus brand, each year's innovations were supported by advertising in a multitude of channels. By communicating two or three variants, the sales uplift would work for all of them instead of just one, making spending much more efficient.

In response to these requirements, which were similarly detected in other countries, Unilever's development department created an additional variant: a milk chocolate with chocolate from Java. In addition, a coffee variant with coffee beans sourced from Colombia could be offered. In order to satisfy customers' desire for a new edition, as well as for a range of interesting products, the German team developed a collection, calling the set of three new products Origin Selection, as the element connecting them was the provenance of ingredients from particular selected countries.

To make full use of the edition, the new products would be on offer both in impulse format as well as multipack format, allowing for availability in all sales channels. This distribution strategy affected not only volume planning, but also the pricing of the new products. Obviously, the Origin Selection gave grounds for considering premium pricing, as the chocolate example had demonstrated. However, both from a customer perspective as well as from a promotional point of view, there was strong reason to price the new Magnum products at the same level as the existing portfolio. First of all, higher prices for the new variants made customers suspicious of the chocolate quality of the regular variants that, so far, had been evaluated as being of acceptable quality. In general, the price level of Magnum products was already judged as being rather high (i.e. 'premium' in comparison to other products of a similar type). Regarding impulse, Magnum was priced at €1.50 per piece, making it the most expensive product in the Unilever German impulse portfolio. Research offered strong evidence that this price represented an important price point in the perception of customers. To cross it would have incorporated the serious risk of missing out on a large number of trial purchases. Similarly, there was an important constraint regarding the multipack price: for the German grocery retailing industry, money-off promotions play an important role in attracting customers on the one hand and reaching critical sales volumes on the other. These promotions in most cases last one week and are always advertised in the respective retailer's weekly information brochure. Space in these brochures is limited, and only one or two products of the range on sale are usually featured. Therefore, products from the same product range are offered at an identical price so that they can then be promoted in a money-off promotion together as well. Pricing the multipack differently from the existing Magnum multipack range would inadvertently have meant taking it out of money-off promotions, consequently limiting its market potential substantially.

In terms of packaging, research demonstrated the importance of accentuating the unique benefits of the product (i.e. chocolate percentage, for the two chocolate variants, and the provenance of the ingredients). These two aspects were identified as the key reasons-to-believe for high quality and authenticity for customers. In fact, the majority of customers participating in the market research considered them as highly relevant, yet had no clear idea either of what percentage of cocoa equaled which type of chocolate (dark or milk), or of the countries of origin of the ingredients and their specific impact on their quality.

For them to easily understand the concept of selected ingredients, research showed that customers needed a well-established stamp-like graphic containing information about percentage and country of origin used by the chocolate industry. The challenge for the design agency now clearly consisted of integrating the new products in the existing Magnum packaging design while differentiating them in a way that would allow customers to be aware of their newness as well as the conceptual idea. Exhibit 1 shows how the challenge was mastered.

Regarding promotion, the same issue needed to be addressed, especially regarding impulse ice cream. In Germany, Unilever's complete impulse portfolio is presented to the customer on the so-called price board. It is on prominent display at every point of sale and offers consumers a chance to look at pictures of the different products before making a choice. German shoppers have got used to

Exhibit 1

choosing an impulse ice cream based on the selection and prices presented on the board. This makes the price board an important element in the promotional mix. For the presentation of the new Origin Selection, it was a prerequisite to integrate the range in the part of the board where all other Magnum variants were shown. However, it should clearly stand out and highlight the fact that these variants were not only new, but also exotic. The final design incorporated a picture of a dancing native woman, who is supposed to represent the 'origin' idea. At the same time, the picture was used to separate the new variants from the rest of the portfolio while still keeping them embedded in the regular Magnum design. Exhibit 2 depicts the German price board of 2007.

Exhibit 2

As for the above-the-line communication (i.e. TV, print and poster advertising), the challenge was even bigger: it would need to serve the local roll-out plans of many different countries that had all created a slightly different marketing plan, tailored to the needs of each country individually. However, as the significant benefit of the products – the exotic origin of the ingredients – was essentially the same in all countries, the communication would focus on these. At the same time, the recurring communicative elements mentioned above needed of course to feature in the new advertising. As a result, all communication was set in a jungle with exotic elements appearing together with the usual Magnum cues. Print advertising and TV spots were adapted to local language requirements. An example of a print advertisement can be seen in Exhibit 3. The impact of the communication measures that had been predicted by pre-tests in several countries proved to hold true with the German audience in terms of sales, but also for communication scores such as awareness of the spot, for example.

As an example of below-the-line activity, the German team picked up on the idea of 'jungle' and presented their yearly loyalty award program with the theme of a treasure hunt. An example of an execution can be found at the top of the price board in Exhibit 2.

Succeeding with a Well-Crafted Mix

Apparently, the marketing team's attention to detail was well worth the effort. In 2007, Magnum grew substantially. The brand's market share has been extended by about a quarter. Of even greater value to Unilever, however, are certainly the longer-term effects: as panel data reveals, more than a third of the consumers who bought one of the 'Origin Selection' impulse products were new to the brand, thereby growing the group of brand users significantly. From a brand point of view, the Origin Selection was also a success. Consumers' image of Magnum as being of superior quality

NEW JAVA MILK CHOCOLATE, 36% COCOA
OUR SEARCH FOR PERFECTION ENDED IN JAVA
JAVA SELECTED COCOA
MAGNUM

Exhibit 3

could be strengthened further due to 2007's innovation – a comfortable position for other exciting Magnum ideas in the years to come!

This case was written by Sophie Nietfeld, Department of Marketing, University of Mannheim. The authors wish to thank Unilever Deutschland GmbH for the generous support in compiling this case.

Discussion Questions

1. Why is Magnum such a strong brand for Unilever? How does the Origin Selection further strengthen Magnum's brand image?
2. How was the Magnum product mix affected by the launch of the Origin Selection range? What risks might be connected with this launch, especially with regard to the existing portfolio?
3. Explain the decision against premium pricing – what external as well as internal reasons exist?
4. Using arguments from behavioral pricing, discuss why premium pricing was apparently possible in the chocolate market, but not for Magnum.
5. Unilever develops some elements of the Magnum marketing mix with respect to the local market, in this case Germany only. In particular, communication measures, however, are used uniformly in many countries. What may be the reasoning behind this strategy?
6. For all elements of the marketing mix, show how consumers' needs and perceptions are reflected in the chosen execution.

PART 3

Marketing in Specific Contexts

This part of the book deals with the specific characteristics of marketing under certain institutional framework conditions. These conditions can arise when a company is active in a particular economic sector or due to the internationality of the company's marketing activities. With regard to specific economic sectors, we will discuss business-to-business marketing in Chapter 10 and services marketing in Chapter 11. Chapter 12 will then focus on international marketing.

Our discussion so far in this book has generally been relevant for many different types of industry, and thus also applies, for instance, to the marketing of services and industrial goods. Part 3 focuses exclusively on the specific challenges that arise for marketing in these different areas. The information provided in this part of the book is intended to supplement the discussion in the other parts of the book.

Contents

CHAPTER 10

Business-to-Business Marketing

Contents

Learning Objectives

In this chapter you will become familiar with:

- the different types of organizational customer
- the main typologies for categorizing the purchasing and selling processes in business-to-business marketing
- the primary specific characteristics of business-to-business marketing on both the buyer and seller side
- the essential characteristics of product decisions, pricing decisions, communication decisions and sales decisions in business-to-business marketing
- industrial services and their most important characteristics
- the key aspects of customer relationship management in business-to-business marketing.

Many transactions take place between companies and organizational customers. Organizational customers can be manufacturers, service companies, intermediaries, governments and other public institutions. This chapter deals with the marketing activities related to such business situations. We will also discuss the special characteristics of organizational buying behavior.

In Section 10.1, we will discuss the basic concepts in business-to-business marketing and the characteristics of organizational buying behavior, and we will distinguish the different patterns of organizational buying and typologies of buying situations. Following a discussion of the strategic characteristics of business-to-business marketing in Section 10.2, in Section 10.3 we will examine the specific marketing mix instruments used in business-to-business marketing; here, we will focus on the areas of product, price, communication, sales decisions and customer relationship management. In particular, sales management and customer relationship management are vitally important in business-to-business marketing (see also Focus on Marketing 10-1).

Focus on Marketing 10-1

> “In order to provide top quality products and solutions in today's competitive business-to-business environment, it is essential that the company works very closely with its clients. Sales management and customer relationship management (CRM) are key competencies with increasing importance for the future.
>
> *Christoph Wigger, Vice President Sales & Marketing, John Deere, Western Europe.*”

10.1 Business-to-Business Marketing: Setting the Scene

At the center of business-to-business marketing are transactions between companies and organizational customers. Companies are buyers and make purchases – and not individual end customers. But business-to-business marketing also refers to the marketing of consumer goods to intermediaries such as retailers (see Backhaus and Voeth 2004), as well as the marketing of services to organizational customers (for a literature review see, e.g., Reid and Plank 2000).

We start by introducing a **typology of organizational customers**, as shown in Figure 10-1.

Private-sector companies comprise users, original equipment manufacturers (OEMs) and retailers. **Users** purchase products to support their own production processes, for the purpose of creating new products. For example, an automobile manufacturer buys machinery that is used in the production of cars. **Original equipment manufacturers (OEMs)** integrate the product procured as a component of the newly produced product. For instance, a computer manufacturer buys computer chips and then integrates them into its own computers. **Retailers** sell the purchased products in virtually unmodified forms to other organizational customers (users and OEMs). An example: a computer chip reseller buys the chips from various chip manufacturers for the purpose of reselling them to computer manufacturers. **Public and non-profit institutions** include churches, hospitals, schools, universities and charities. With many institutions, there is a similarity to governmental customers, since the purchasing process is regulated by political considerations and laws. **Governmental organizations** (e.g. military, police) demand goods and services in order to provide the public with services.

This differentiation between the various types of organizational customers is relevant to business-to-business marketing for several reasons. For one, the buying behavior and buying patterns of

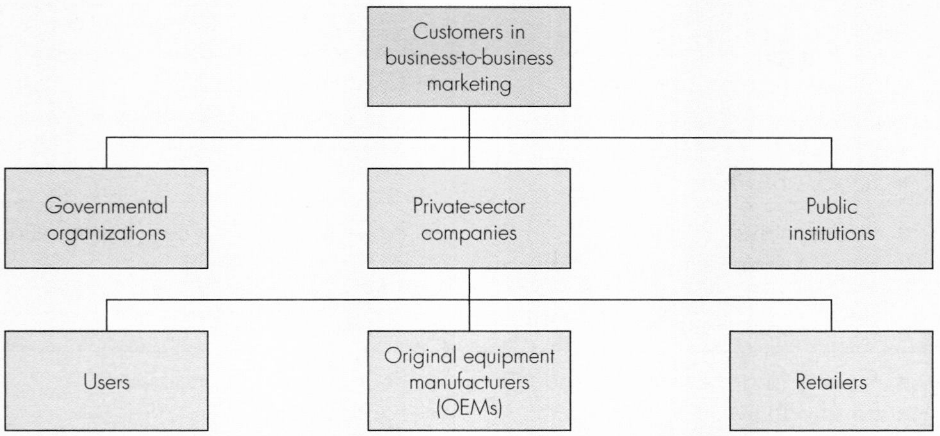

Figure 10-1 Typology of organizational customers

the various types of customers differ significantly in some areas, with governmental organizations and public institutions applying a more strongly formalized approach than many public-sector companies. Governmental organizations and public institutions are also less profit-oriented in their purchase decision process compared to private-sector companies. The particularly high importance that OEM customers put on trust and on the company's quality image should be mentioned since, in the OEM sector, the quality of the company's products has a direct impact on the quality of the OEM products (see Doney and Cannon 1997; Ganesan 1994).

In business-to-business marketing, numerous companies offer a wide range of products and services to the various customer types. This broad scope of business-to-business marketing is illustrated in Table 10-1.

In the text that follows, we will address the **basic characteristics of business-to-business marketing**. These include:

- the derivative character of the demand
- the multiple buying influences
- the high degree of formalization
- the high degree of individualization
- the particular relevance of services
- multi-organizational participation
- the long-term nature of business relationships
- the high degree of interaction.

We will now discuss some of these characteristics in more detail.

The **derivative character of organizational demand** relates to the fact that organizational demand is derived from the requirements of the customers of the respective organizations. The derivative character of organizational demand can be illustrated with the following example:

A manufacturer of synthetic materials sells its products to plastics manufacturers, whose demand for synthetic materials depends on demand from manufacturers of plastic components for automobile

Table 10-1 Examples of company–customer relationships and products/services offered in business-to-business marketing

Company	Products/services	Customers
Automotive suppliers	■ Vehicle seats ■ Tires ■ Brakes ■ Shock absorbers	■ OEMs (automobile manufacturers) ■ Spare parts dealers and wholesalers ■ Garages, service stations
Manufacturer of building/ construction materials	■ Roof systems ■ Facade systems/facade cladding ■ Fittings ■ Cement	■ Processing companies (e.g. construction company/installers) ■ Architects ■ Hardware/DIY stores
Chemicals companies	■ Primary pharmaceutical products ■ Food additives ■ Paints/lacquers ■ Adhesives ■ Dyes and colorings ■ Plastic granulates ■ Textile fibers ■ Fuel additives	■ Pharmaceuticals industry ■ Food industry ■ Automotive industry (suppliers and OEMs) ■ Textile manufacturers ■ Plastic parts manufacturers ■ Petroleum companies
Engineering firms	■ Product development ■ Project planning ■ Technical consulting ■ Surveying	■ Automotive industry (suppliers and OEMs) ■ Mechanical engineering and plant construction companies ■ Railroad companies ■ Construction companies (building and road construction) ■ Public institutions (e.g. road construction authorities)
Manufacturer of technical glass	■ Precision glass ■ Lenses ■ Special packaging (test tubes)	■ Automotive industry (suppliers and OEMs) ■ Manufacturers of home entertainment products ■ Medical technology companies ■ Pharmaceuticals industry
Microelectronics companies	■ Airplane electronics/avionics ■ Discrete components (transistors, resistors) ■ Microcontrollers	■ Automotive industry ■ Computer manufacturers ■ Motherboard manufacturers ■ Mechanical engineering and plant construction companies
Pharmaceutical and medical technology companies	■ Prescription medications ■ Medical technology equipment ■ Reagents	■ Physicians/medical offices ■ Hospitals ■ Health insurance companies ■ Laboratories
Business consultants	■ Strategy/management consulting ■ Implementation support ■ IT consulting	■ Private-sector companies in all sectors and industries ■ Public institutions (e.g. government departments, government agencies)

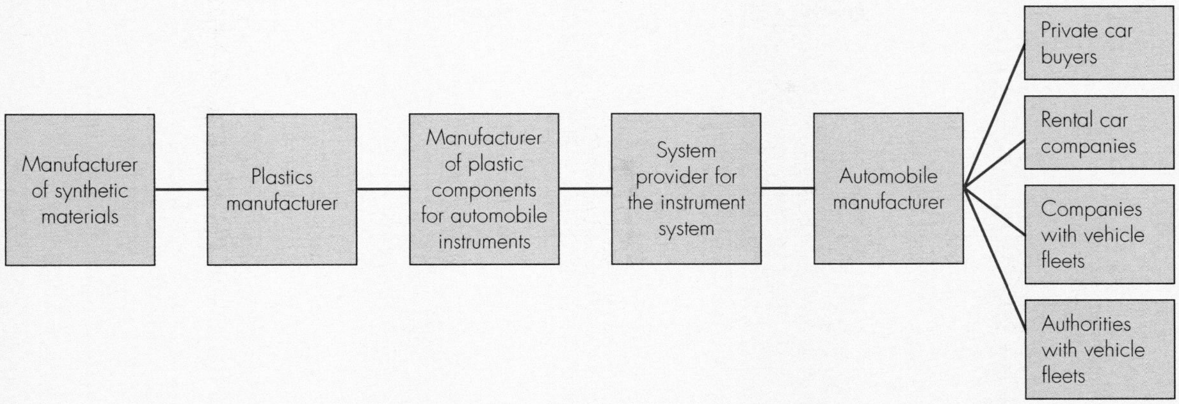

Figure 10-2 Illustration of derived demand using the example of a plastic chemicals manufacturer

instruments, as well as on the demand arising from a number of downstream tiers (e.g. the demand for cars; see Figure 10-2).

A primary implication of the derivative character of demand is that, when conducting market research, a company has to consider not only direct customers, but also the customers located downstream in this process (i.e. the customer's customer). Demand from the company's customers depends on the market success of those customers. Consequently, in the long term, the company should also promote the preferences of downstream customer tiers when planning activities (e.g. in communications). This way it can offer its direct customers competitive advantages in their markets. This idea is illustrated, for example, by the following advertising slogan, from a company in business-to-business marketing: 'We keep your promises.'

Another characteristic of organizational buying behavior refers to the involvement of several members of an organization in the purchase decision, which leads to **multiple buying influences**. In this context the term **buying center** has been coined, which refers to a group of individuals or groups who participate in an organizational purchase decision (Bonoma 2006; Johnston and Bonoma 1981; Lilien and Wong 1984; Spekman and Stern 1979; Webster and Wind 1972) (see Figure 10-3 for an illustration of a buying center). In order to sell effectively to the buying center it is necessary to consider the way that this decision-making unit makes decisions and the various needs of the individuals within this unit. Accordingly, it is of vital importance that the company identifies the members of the buying center and their degree of influence on the purchase decision. It is also useful to find out which decision-making behavior is exhibited by them (see Bonoma 2006). Table 10-2 presents a list of questions that help to evaluate a customer or buying center.

Furthermore, it can be useful to establish a selling center as a counterpart to the buying center (see Hutt *et al.* 1985; Moon and Gupta 1997). The selling center is a multi-person team that can help to meet the different requirements of the various parties in the buying center. It also helps to ensure cross-functional coordination within the organization of the supplier.

Another characteristic of organizational buying behavior is **multi-organizational participation** (i.e. the involvement of additional organizations in the procurement process, in addition to the supplier and buyer organizations). The example in Figure 10-4 illustrates such multi-organizational participation: in the course of making a purchase decision on a large-scale plant, an industrial customer includes banks in decisions related to financing the plant, and commissions an engineering

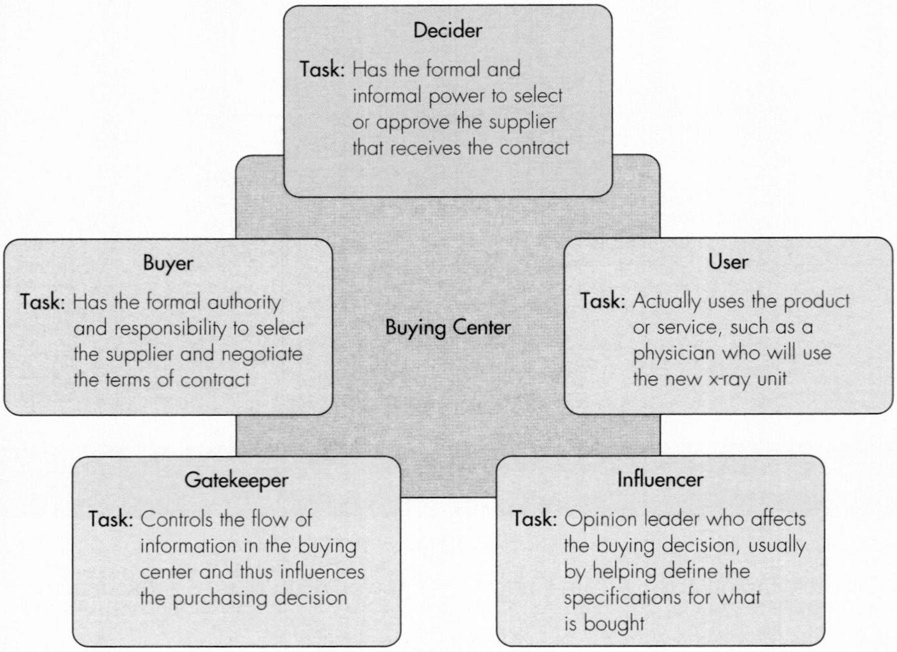

Figure 10-3 The buying center

Table 10-2 Some key questions for analyzing a buying center

- Which formal buying processes are in place?
- Is there a systematic evaluation checklist for suppliers? If yes, what are the criteria?
- Do we need central approval in order to get through to local decision makers?
- Who are the key influencers of the buying decision?
- Is the decision made on a local level or on a central international level?
- Who has the formal budget authority? Who makes the buying decision?
- Who makes the technical decision?
- Who is his/her boss?
- What is important to the key influencers?
- What is his/her career background?
- Is he/she more open to technical or to commercial arguments?
- Which personal benefits would arise for the decision maker when selecting a specific supplier?
- How can he/she justify the decision to select a specific supplier?
- How do the key influencers perceive a specific supplier?
- Which supplier capabilities are perceived?
- What is the perception of the competition?

firm for the technical planning. Moreover, the customer seeks out advice from external technology consultants and applies for the legal permissions required for plant operation. The supplier should systematically take into account these external partners of the industrial customer, for example within the scope of communication decisions.

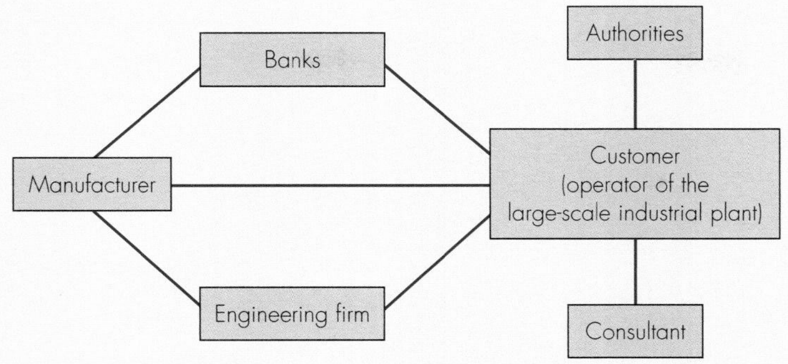

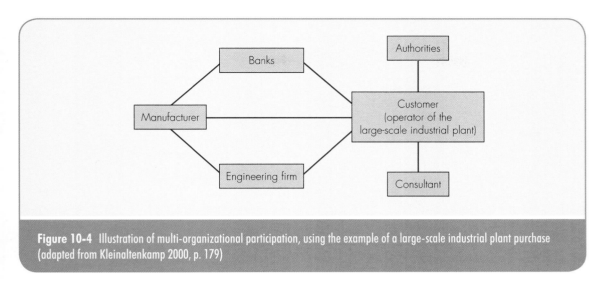

Figure 10-4 Illustration of multi-organizational participation, using the example of a large-scale industrial plant purchase (adapted from Kleinaltenkamp 2000, p. 179)

A further characteristic associated with organizational buying behavior is the **long-term nature of the business relationship**. This is partly due to the longevity of the products and the importance of ongoing service. To promote such long-term business relationships, the supplier needs to implement measures that help to establish an excellent reputation with its customers.

Finally, the **high degree of personal interaction between the company and the organizational buyer** should be mentioned as a characteristic of organizational buying behavior. When marketing industrial goods, personal contacts play a key role in the success of the business relationship. These personal relationships have to be developed and maintained actively and, thus, both personal selling (see Chapter 7) and systematic customer relationship management (see Chapter 9) play a particularly important role in the marketing of industrial goods (Doney and Cannon 1997).

The differentiation of **business types** helps to gain an overview of the broad field of business-to-business marketing. For instance, marketing a standardized digital printer requires far fewer transactions than marketing a customized newspaper printing machine. The typology usually comprises two dimensions, with one dimension reflecting the products and services being marketed, and the other referring to the customer relationship.

Figure 10-5 shows a classification of business types. The horizontal axis represents the activity-related dimension with the individuality of the services rendered, as well as the degree of integration of the customer into the service/product development process. The vertical axis describes the relationship dimension: here, both the continuity of the business relationship and the intensity of repeat purchases are depicted.

Four business types can be derived from combining these two dimensions, as outlined below.

1. In **product business/spot transactions**, the individuality of the service and products, the continuity of the business relationship and the intensity of repeat purchases are rather less distinct. Here, as a rule, mass-produced products are marketed. Since organizational customers request these products on a case-by-case basis, the establishment of long-term business relationships between the company and the organizational customers is not of greatest importance. Examples of these products include screws, motors and paint.
2. In the **investment business/project business**, the products and services are highly individualized and there is a high degree of customer integration. However, the business relationship is not characterized by intense repeat purchases. In this case, complex products or systems are marketed, which are sold to the customer according to the customer's requirements. Due to the customized

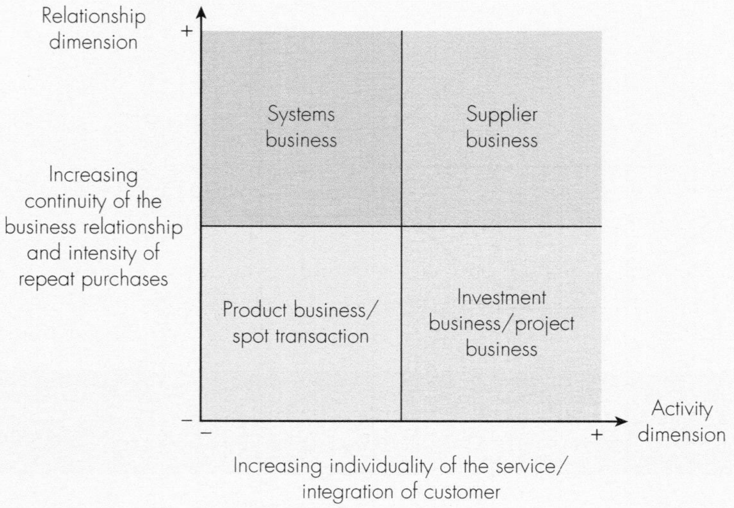

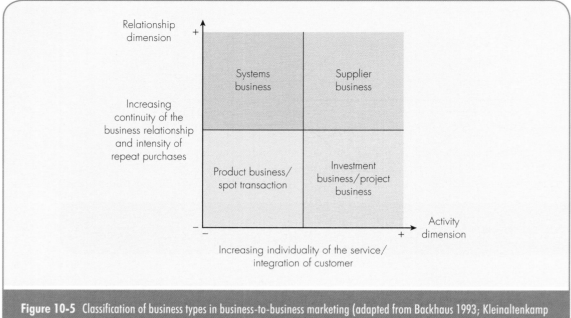

Figure 10-5 Classification of business types in business-to-business marketing (adapted from Backhaus 1993; Kleinaltenkamp 1997; Plinke 2000)

manufacturing involved, products and services in the investment business exhibit a relatively high degree of specificity as compared to the product business. For example, for a plant that has been customized for a specific customer it will generally be difficult to find other buyers. Examples include beverage bottling plants, rolling mills and solar power plants.

3 The **systems business** is characterized by long-term relationships associated with intense repeat purchases and a low degree of product and service individuality with regard to customer integration. This means that the customer decides to purchase a company's system technology and buys a product as a first system component. During subsequent purchases, the buyer acquires additional system components from this company. Examples are telecommunication systems that consist of modular component and information technologies.

4 Similar to the system business, the **supplier business** is characterized by repeat purchase relationships. In this category, the supplier develops customized services and products for a long-standing organizational customer, who then purchases them successively. If suppliers and customers jointly develop new product technologies, they most often enter into a steady relationship for the duration of the product life cycle and beyond. An example of this is the individualized service and product range that suppliers offer to automobile manufacturers.

According to the transaction cost theory of specific investments (see the Appendix for more on 'transaction cost theory'), the two axes of the business type matrix in Figure 10-5 differ with respect to the respective interdependencies: with increasing individuality in the services and products and customer integration (horizontal axis), the company becomes dependent on the buyer due to the increasingly specific investments (see investment/project business). In the case of more intense repeat purchase relationships (vertical axis), the customer becomes dependent on the company (this applies to the system business). If both dimensions are equally pronounced (i.e. in the supplier business), there tends to be a reciprocal dependency.

The respective types pose different fundamental challenges for marketing strategy, which we will discuss in Section 10.2.

10.2 Marketing Strategy: Specific Characteristics in Business-to-Business Marketing

In general, the discussion of marketing strategy presented in Part 1 of this book also applies to business-to-business markets. Therefore, here we will examine only the key strategic aspects associated with business-to-business marketing. Particularly interesting in this regard is the **influence that a business type has on the marketing strategy** and on the relevant challenges.

With product business/spot transactions, the company markets standardized products to a relatively large customer segment, thus there is a certain similarity to classic consumer goods marketing. In light of this standardization, a key challenge of **mass customization** strategy lies in providing individualized products in large quantities (for more information on mass customization strategy, see 4.1.2).

In the case of investment business/project business, the products and services of the company are tailored to the customer's individual needs. These requirements are specified prior to the development of the actual product. A primary strategic challenge is **business development** (new business development, stimulation of demand for industrial plants), which calls for effective and efficient **acquisition of order**. The overall objective is to prevail over competitors in calls for bids (e.g. for large-scale industrial plants). Moreover, the often high costs of preparing a bid (e.g. travel costs, engineering costs, costs of documentation) have to be limited by selectively responding to invitations to bid or requests. Another issue that often arises in this context is that customers change performance specifications already agreed upon after the order has been placed. This leads to the strategic challenge of ensuring **flexibility in the production process and the range of goods and services**, in order to realize these adjustments in a cost-effective way. Finally, a special characteristic of investment business/project business (especially in the case of large-scale plants) is that a single company usually cannot perform all the related tasks by itself. Therefore, another main challenge lies in establishing successful and effective **strategic cooperations** with other companies (see Focus on Marketing 10-2 for an example of such a cooperation).

In the systems business, customers commit themselves to repeat purchases from the same company. From the customer's perspective, this initial purchase represents a relatively risky decision, since

Focus on Marketing 10-2 A strategic cooperation of Vodafone and Oracle

Vodafone calls on Oracle

With the enterprise market becoming increasingly reliant on the need for workers to stay productive while away from the office, Vodafone has teamed with Oracle Corp. to develop integrated mobility software and commercial links to enable mobile access to business systems.

The companies plan to co-develop, market and launch the enterprise data service based on Oracle 10g and Vodafone Network Services. Specifically, Oracle is providing the mobile-enabling middleware, as well as access to its Oracle Collaboration Suite, which consists of tools to e-mail, calendar, voicemail, faxes and files.

'Increasing productivity through mobilizing software applications is one of the key growth opportunities for Vodafone,' Vodafone Group Marketing Officer Peter Bamford said in a statement.

The partnership also will enable developers to create and extend current and future Oracle-based applications so they are easily accessible by mobile devices, the companies said.

Source: Rush 2003.

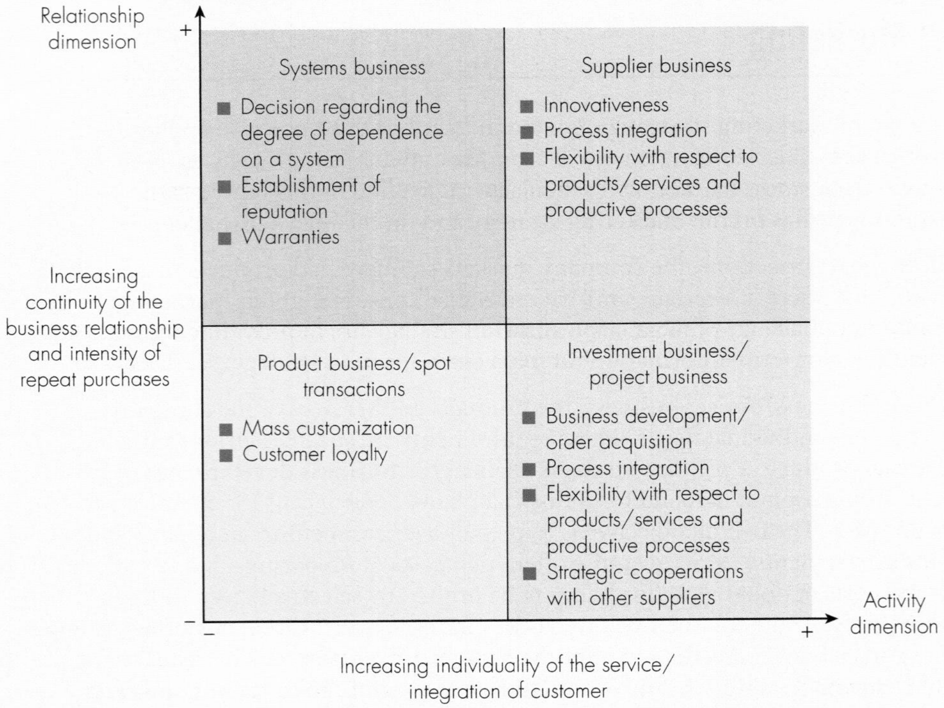

Figure 10-6 Central strategic challenges of various business types in business-to-business marketing

the customer is 'automatically' bound to the company after the first purchase. Therefore, there is a risk of opportunistic behavior on the part of the seller (e.g. subsequent price increases for system components). The term **lock-in effect** is often used in this context. From a seller's perspective, the key challenge thus lies in positioning the company in a way that supports the customer's decision to initially buy the company's system (see Anderson and Narus 1998).

Finally, the supplier business poses specific strategic challenges, such as convincing customers (mostly OEMs, see Section 10.1) of the benefits of a long-term business relationship. In this regard, pivotal strategic challenges on the supplier side include ensuring **innovativeness** (especially in the case of new products developed jointly with the customer), **ability to integrate processes** (e.g. in terms of logistics and/or electronic data processing), and **flexibility** of the production process and the range of goods and services offered (e.g. ability to make changes to the product range at short notice).

Figure 10-6 shows an overview of the strategic challenges described here according to the various business types in business-to-business marketing.

10.3 Specific Characteristics of Marketing Mix Instruments in Business-to-Business Marketing

In the following, we will discuss the features of the marketing mix specific to business-to-business markets.

10.3.1 Product Decisions: Specific Characteristics

As the starting point of our discussion, we will examine the three central decision areas with regard to product decisions (see Chapter 5): innovation management, management of established products, and brand management. In the area of **innovation management**, the **integration of customers into the innovation process** is particularly relevant to companies manufacturing industrial goods (especially in the investment business/project business, as well as the supplier business). The integration of customers can help to launch new products successfully. It is also important since, in business-to-business marketing, commercial test markets are not available as is the case with consumer goods marketing. Instead, market acceptance of new products can be tested by including lead customers in the innovation process (see Focus on Marketing 10-3 for an example).

When making decisions about customer integration, a main question concerns which customers should be integrated into which phases of the innovation process (for a more in-depth discussion of this topic, see Gruner and Homburg 2000). The customers integrated into the innovation process

Focus on Marketing 10-3 An example of innovation management in medical-surgical markets

Creating breakthroughs at 3M

Given the imperative to grow, why can't product developers come up with breakthroughs more regularly? They fail primarily for two reasons. First, companies face strong incentives to focus on the short term. Second, developers simply don't know how to achieve breakthroughs, because there is usually no effective system in place to guide them and support their efforts.

The latter is a problem even for a company like 3M, long known for its successful innovations. In September 1996, a product development team in 3M's Medical-Surgical Markets Division became one of the first groups in 3M to test the merits of the lead user process. The team was charged with creating a breakthrough in the area of surgical drapes – the material that prevents infections from spreading during surgery. By November 1997, the team had come up with a proposal for two new line extensions, one breakthrough product, and a breakthrough strategy that would take a revolutionary approach to treating infection. And the team may have done even more for 3M's long-term health: it persuaded senior managers that the lead user process could indeed systematize the company's development of breakthroughs.

The group spent the first month and a half of the project learning more about the cause and prevention of infections by researching the literature and by interviewing experts in the field. For the next six weeks or so, team members focused on getting a better understanding of important trends in infection control. Much of the team's research at this early stage was directed at understanding what doctors in developed countries might need. But as the group's members asked more and more questions and talked to more and more experts, they realized they didn't know enough about the needs of surgeons and hospitals in developing countries, where infectious diseases are still major killers. The team broke up into pairs and traveled to hospitals in Malaysia, Indonesia, Korea, and India.

They learned how people in less than ideal environments attempt to keep infections from spreading in the operating room. They especially noted how some surgeons combat infection by using cheap antibiotics as a substitute for disposable drapes and other, more expensive measures. Those insights led the team to redefine its goal: find a much cheaper and much more effective way to prevent infections from starting or spreading that does not depend on antibiotics – or even on surgical drapes.

Source: von Hippel *et al.* 2000.

can participate in new product development, test initial prototypes and contribute their experiences in using the product (see Enkel *et al.* 2005; Nambisan 2002). The benefits associated with such an integration of selected customers include time and cost savings, quality improvements due to an increased customer orientation, image enhancement and gaining information on competitors. At the same time, there is the risk that the company's knowhow can leak to customers and thus possibly also to competitors.

Another specific characteristic related to innovation management is that the process of **market launch** is considerably more complex than in consumer goods marketing. This is particularly the case since in business-to-business marketing many different people usually have to be convinced of the advantages offered by the new product (i.e. all members of the buying center, see Section 10.1).

The second area of product decisions, the **management of established products** is also relevant to industrial goods companies. Regarding the decision about the depth of the product range, the question arises as to how many customer-specific product variants should be developed. The issue of individualization is especially relevant in the industrial goods sector, since customers in that area often insist on customized products. As a result, a main challenge here is to determine the optimal degree of customization. International (e.g. technical) standards provide an important framework for defining the depth of the product range (e.g. standards developed by ISO – the International Standardization Organization).

In the context of deciding on the depth of the product range of established products, decisions need to be made both about tangible products, and particularly about industrial services (for more on their relevance, see Anderson and Narus 1995; Bowen *et al.* 1989; Boyt and Harvey 1997; Homburg and Garbe 1999; Hutt and Speh 2004). On the one hand, industrial services are actively demanded by customers as a result of their own outsourcing activities. On the other hand, industrial services offer advantages for companies, such as product differentiation (see Matthyssens and Vandenbempt 1998; Parasuraman 1998), a reduction of the price pressure, establishment of market entry barriers for competitors, increased profitability through direct allocation of services, stabilization of demand due to the ongoing provision of services (as opposed to one-time product sales), and potential diversification into the service sector. Advantages particularly result for customer relationship management, such as better knowledge of customer needs and an improvement in interpersonal customer relationships due to the more intense customer interaction in the context of service provision.

Industrial services can be differentiated into basic services and value-added services (see Chapter 11). **Basic services** are those services that have to be provided to the customer in order to purchase the basic product. In contrast, **value-added services** are services that are not necessary prerequisites for the acceptance of the product on the part of the customer, but whose availability can substantially increase the value of the product for the customer.

The differentiation between basic services and value-added services depends on both customer perception and industry conventions (see Kleinaltenkamp *et al.* 2004). For example, the commissioning of a large-scale technical plant is usually categorized as a basic service, while plant financing provided by the company would be considered a value-added service. On the other hand, when, say, a firm purchases PC workstations, the on-site installation is often classified as a value-added service (see Focus on Marketing 10-4 for an example of value-added services in the chemical industry).

In terms of **brand management**, a vast and important area in consumer goods marketing remains relatively unexplored in business-to-business marketing (see Reid and Plank 2000). The fact that business-to-business brands are less important is partly due to the relevance of objective product features such as quality or specifications. In the past, product names in business-to-business

Focus on Marketing 10-4 Value-added services in the chemicals industry

Chemical management services gain traction

Major consumers of chemicals are paying chemical management service (CMS) providers to reduce their overall spending on chemical purchases and handling. A growing army of CMS providers, including major chemical suppliers, are targeting the business to capture margins that are typically higher than those for materials supply alone particularly as many big suppliers such as auto makers are demanding continuous year-over-year price reductions.

CMS was spearheaded by General Motors and its key suppliers in the late 1980s, and is now widely used by large manufacturers in the automotive, aerospace and microelectronics sector.

The CMS provider lineup consists primarily of chemical makers, including Henkel – the largest with sales of nearly $200 million – as well as Ashland Specialty Chemicals, BP's Castrol unit and PPG Industries. 'For every dollar spent on chemical purchases, an additional $1–$10 is spent on handling them,' says Scott Follett, global director/PPG Total Services Solutions. A typical CMS program will reduce chemical handling costs by 10%–25%. 'That gives you an idea of the kind of savings that can be generated.' Chemical suppliers say they welcome the opportunity to supply value-added services. 'Chemical makers have had a tough few years,' says Kent Bonney, director of Henkel's Chemical Management Services (Nashville) subsidiary. 'Customers realize that you can only wring out so much from the physical cost of chemicals and procurement alone. CMS greatly expands the potential savings for customers, and provides an additional revenue source for the supplier.'

CMS contracts average 3–5 years and include several compensation methods, say providers. The key components include the cost of purchased chemicals; management fees, including the cost for employees a CMS provider may place at customer locations; and a portion of cost savings generated. A CMS Forum survey reported profit margins of 5%–30% for CMS providers in 2000. No CMS provider reports results separately, but most say their current profit margins exceed 10%.

Chemical makers that operate CMS units say they have set them up as stand-alone units, partly in response to customer demands that they remain neutral on product sourcing. 'There's a preference to get our material into those plants,' says one CMS provider. 'But there are many cases where we are managing materials made by our competitors.'

CMS offerings are becoming more sophisticated as they implement process improvements designed to improve efficiency and reduce overall chemical usage, as well as taking responsibility for related information technology, inventory management, training and safety programs, and environmental compliance reporting.

Source: Westervelt 2003.

marketing used to be more technical. Names, for the most part, comprised technical labels or item numbers. Today, a rise in the relevance of industrial brands can be observed.

Business-to-business brands can be divided into two types (see Figure 10-7; Baumgarth 2004; Born 2003; Kleinaltenkamp 2003): while a processing brand is typically not visible to the end customer, the **ingredient brand** is normally noticed (in connection with ingredient brands, see also the text on the concept of ingredient branding in Section 5.5).

10.3.2 Pricing Decisions: Specific Characteristics

Pricing new products is an important initial pricing decision in business-to-business marketing (see Hutt and Speh 2004; Noble and Gruca 1999). In this context, 'new' does not necessarily have

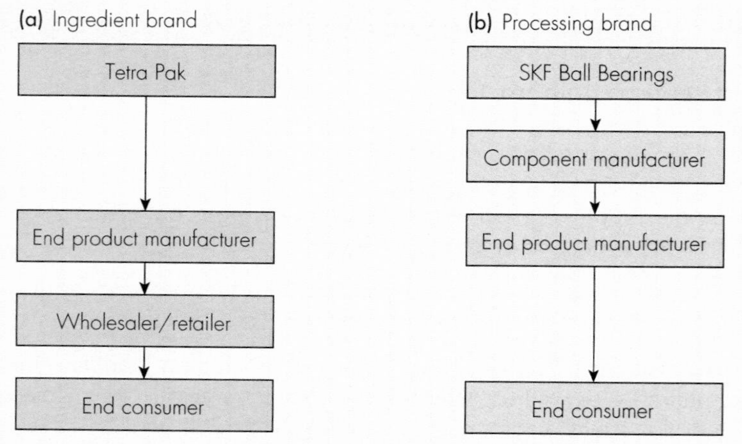

Figure 10-7 Ingredient brands and processing brands in business-to-business marketing (Homburg and Richter 2003)

to refer to a fundamental product innovation, but can also be a way to express that the product is being specially configured for a new customer order. Here, **individual pricing** is often applied (see Hutt and Speh 2004; Shapiro and Jackson 1978). This is especially the case in investment business, where customized quotations are calculated, in which the costs for customer-specific or project-specific services (e.g. travel and transportation costs, costs for bank guarantees, installation and assembly costs) are added to the price for a rough technical concept (for more detailed information, see Backhaus 2003).

Another special aspect of pricing is **competitive bidding**, which is used by organizational customers when issuing invitations to bid. The objective of competitive bidding is to obtain the lowest possible price (see Slatter 1990). Competitive bidding is initiated by organizational customers who invite the various suppliers to name their asking price for a specific project and/or service. From a supplier perspective, the goal is to have the bid accepted while at the same time obtaining the highest possible price. Competitive bidding plays a significant role in the bidding process by government organizations and institutions, which use competitive bidding for the majority of their procurement activities.

Auctions are becoming increasingly important as a pricing technique used in the business-to-business marketing sector (see Mester 1988; Skiera and Spann 2004). As an example, it has become common practice to auction off used capital goods (e.g. machines) via the internet. In addition to traditional auctions, **reversed auctions** are sometimes used in business-to-business marketing for organizational procurement activities. Reversed auctions are auctions in which the customer articulates a demand to several potential suppliers, who then enter into a software-supported process of successively underbidding each other. The order then goes to the supplier who wins the auction (i.e. the company that bids the lowest price for its services from among all the other suppliers).

The capacity to deliberately manipulate customer behavior by means of temporary and permanent price changes in order to promote the company's interests, taking into account a certain amount of 'irrational' aspects to customer behavior, is relatively limited in business-to-business marketing. This results from industrial customers tracking price trends more thoroughly and continuously than private customers (and therefore having more accurate historical price information at their disposal). Moreover, price changes are not an issue in most bidding situations – especially in the case of one-of-a-kind products (e.g. in the investment business). Instead, price changes can become inevitable during the productive processes, since the production, installation and assembly of a plant can span several years. In this case, the supplier has to implement price protection measures in order to be able to compensate for future price fluctuations on the cost side (e.g. by issuing escalation clauses).

Focus on Marketing 10-5 Example of an escalation clause from the building industry

'Where the price of material, equipment, or energy increases significantly during the term of the contract through no fault of the contractor, the contract sum shall be equitably adjusted by change order as provided for in paragraph ___ of this Agreement. A significant price increase means a change in price from the date of the contract execution to the date of performance by an amount exceeding ___ per cent. Such price increases shall be documented by vendor quotes, invoices, catalogs, receipts or other documents of commercial use.'

Source: ABC Copper 2006.

In business-to-business marketing the use of **price differentiation** as well as **discounts/allowances** and **bonuses/rebates** is generally applied. This is because products are often customized and prices derived by means of **price negotiations**. Here, prices are often differentiated on the basis of purchased quantities and customer segments, while price differentiation based on the time of purchase (as is common in the consumer goods sector) is rarely used in the business-to-business sector (see also Figure 10-8). It should be noted that the information exchange between customers often poses a problem when differentiating prices because of the small number of customers and a relatively high market transparency.

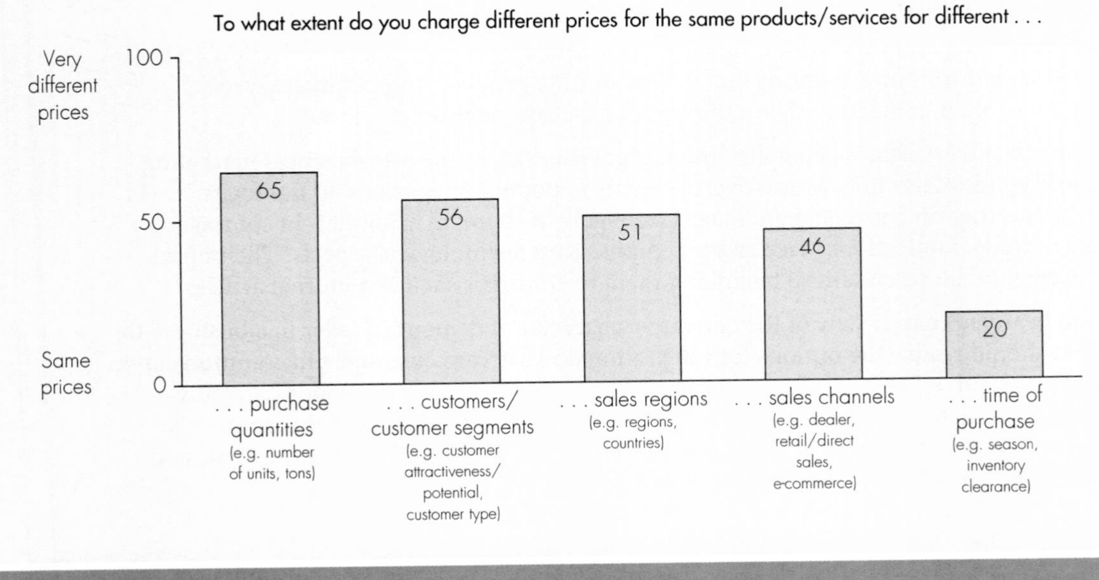

Figure 10-8 Intensity of price differentiation measures in business-to-business marketing (see Schuppar 2006)

In addition to the price, the terms of payment and financing services (e.g. leasing offers made by the company, the provision of loans) are also negotiated.

Finally, another decision-making area deals with the **enforcement of prices. Purchase decisions** in business-to-business-marketing generally tend to be more rational than those by end customers (Rese and Herter 2004). Business-to-business customers search for information (especially price-related information) more intensively, and assess alternatives more thoroughly. This is especially the case when a relatively large, formal buying center (see Section 10.1) is involved in the purchase decision. In particular, product/service-related benefits, which are relatively easy to measure in industrial goods marketing (also see Proscharsky 1998) and which are sometimes evaluated differently among the members of the buying center, play a key role in the purchase decision. Therefore, companies often make it difficult for customers to directly compare their products with competitive offerings (e.g. by offering additional services in competitive bidding situations). Additionally, the company should also put more emphasis on the benefit arguments (for more on this, see also the discussion on benefit selling in Section 7.4.2). For the company, it is therefore necessary to obtain as much information as possible about the customer's requirements (e.g. which benefits are especially important) when communicating the price to the individual members of the buying center (see Anderson and Narus 1998).

10.3.3 Communication Decisions: Specific Characteristics

Among the aspects discussed in the context of communication decisions, **technical information** plays a vital role in business-to-business marketing: organizational customers usually require more information and frequently possess a better understanding than private end customers in the consumer goods marketing sector.

One specific feature refers to the different **information requirements** of the various stakeholders in the buying center. Whereas the user requires information about application options, the buyer is interested in prices. The supplier needs to adapt to these needs and provide different information packages.

Moreover, business-to-business marketing communication is generally characterized by its pronounced **personal character**. This can be explained by the often limited number of customers and the key role of direct sales.

In view of this, **trade fairs** and **exhibitions** are important communication tools (see Section 8.4). Such events offer a platform for presenting and demonstrating products to potential buyers, establishing new customer contacts and keeping track of the competition.

Conventional **media advertising** is generally far less significant in business-to-business marketing than in consumer goods marketing. Most advertisements in popular magazines do not focus on technology, but rather on conveying an image (see Figure 10-9 for an example). In contrast, advertisements in trade publications place greater emphasis on technological aspects. The impact of such advertisements can be enhanced by linking them to editorials such as a journal article.

Finally, it has to be noted that in view of the derivative character of demand, a seller in a business-to-business context should review the options for integrating downstream customers in communication decisions. Here media advertisements (image advertisements for the industrial goods company itself, as well as its products) are a particularly suitable tool. A relevant concept in this context is ingredient branding, where the components contained in the finished product are communicated to the customers (e.g. 'Intel Inside') (see also Section 10.3.1).

10.3.4 Placing Sales in Business-to-Business: the Key Challenges

For many companies in the business-to-business sector, sales decisions are an essential tool in the marketing mix. Sales and distribution costs in business-to-business frequently amount to more than

Figure 10-9 Example of an advertisement from a business-to-business company (www.basf.com)

ten per cent of sales revenues; the advertising expenses of many companies amount to less than two per cent of sales revenues (see Krafft and Frentzen 2001 for the German business-to-business market).

The design and structure of the distribution system forms one aspect of the sales decisions of business-to-business companies. As a general rule, a strong **focus on direct sales** can be observed. This can be attributed to an often limited number of customers, as well as a high degree of product customization and complexity (particularly in the investment business/project business and the supplier business, see Figure 10-6). It necessitates close proximity to the customer (or a local presence) and a high competence level related to the company's product. Sales engineers and technical field salesforce employees are usually more competent than sales partners.

Despite the sometimes negative evaluation of intermediaries by industrial goods companies, due to insufficient competence and unsatisfactory product/service quality, intermediaries are nevertheless deployed in company practice. This is especially the case in the product business, where products are often highly standardized.

Hybrid systems of direct and indirect sales can be observed in cases where companies use direct sales for key accounts while opting for indirect sales via retailers for less important customers.

Another characteristic of sales decisions in business-to-business marketing is the design and structure of the relationship to sales partners and key accounts (see Section 7.3). Here, cooperations with sales partners and key accounts play a vital role (see Guenzi *et al.* 2007; Homburg *et al.* 2002; Sharma 2006), particularly cooperations in the technical sector. In the context of sales cooperations, the establishment of supplier alliances (cooperations of several suppliers) in the investment and systems business is an essential characteristic of business-to-business marketing (see Johnston *et al.* 1999). Such supplier alliances are necessary if individual suppliers are not in the position to submit a bid on their own due to the size of order or the required knowhow, or if the high risk of the overall project calls for a distribution of risk.

As a result of the great significance of direct sales, as well as customized consultation and on-site services, personal sales is a pivotal area when designing sales activities in the business-to-business sector. Sales employees therefore represent a key factor and an essential reference for customer loyalty. Due to the increasing pressure for efficiency, the importance of sales via call centers is growing.

Finally, there are also specific characteristics in **sales logistics**. A main aspect here (particularly in the supplier business, see Figure 10-5) is the crucial importance of **supply guarantees** (on-schedule, reliable and damage-free product shipments). A failure of supply can lead to a halt in production at the customer's facility, which may be associated with significant costs and loss of sales. Supply guarantees can be ensured by warehousing services on the part of the supplier or by using 'no-storage' manufacturing approaches (e.g. just-in-time production/just-in-time purchasing; see, e.g., Erdem and Swift 1998; Frazier *et al.* 1988).

Yet another characteristic is constituted by the **integration of the sales logistics** of the supplier into the procurement logistics and production processes of the customer (see Günter and Kuhl 2000), which enables faster procurement and production processes for the customer. These integrative approaches can be supported by implementing concepts such as electronic data interchange (EDI) (see also Section 14.2.1).

10.3.5 Customer Relationship Management: Specific Characteristics

It should first be stated that **customer loyalty** is extremely important in business-to-business marketing (see Gierl and Gehrke 2004). For suppliers, the loyalty of their organizational customers is essential if they supply them with highly individualized products and services. In most cases, this requires customer-specific investment (e.g. developing a certain technology for a specific customer), while amortization depends on the respective business relationship. For organizational customers, too, loyalty to suppliers is an important factor since specific investments can also become necessary on their part (see Dahlstrom *et al.* 1996; Mohr *et al.* 1996; Sengupta *et al.* 1997). Costs associated with evaluating suppliers, as well as the adaptation of production, represent examples of such specific investments.

A main characteristic of customer relationship management is related to its objective, namely customer loyalty. Due to the fact that **organizational purchase decisions** always involve several individuals we distinguish between **customer loyalty on an individual level** and **customer loyalty on an organizational level** (see also Doney and Cannon 1997). For example, if a certain person in the buying center is loyal to a supplier by repeatedly recommending that particular supplier is called for bids, then this represents customer loyalty on an individual level. In contrast, if a company enters into a long-term supply contract with a supplier and implements extensive IT integration measures with this supplier, we speak of customer loyalty on an organizational level.

On both individual and organizational levels, customer loyalty in business-to-business marketing can be analyzed according to the following criteria (Homburg and Jensen 2004):

- quantity-related aspects
- price-related aspects
- resource-related aspects
- time-related aspects.

The classic conceptualization of customer loyalty that typically differentiates between the dimensions of repeat purchase, additional purchase and recommendation is less applicable (see Homburg and

Table 10-3 Aspects of customer loyalty in business-to-business marketing (adapted from Homburg and Jensen 2004, p. 496)

Quantity-related aspects	Price-related aspects	Resource-related aspects	Time-related aspects
Expansion of the business relationship via additional purchases ('share-of-customer'); e.g. ■ a buyer of glass does not only purchase speciality glass, but also standard glass ■ buyer covers 80% of its demand for speciality glass with one supplier	The customer displays a disproportionately high willingness to pay compared to the competition; e.g. ■ buyer is willing to pay a higher price if the supplier's products and services are superior ■ preference for the supplier given an equal price level to the competition	Making relationship-specific additional investments; e.g. ■ adapting the production equipment to the customer's products ■ EDI-based networking of the transaction processes with the supplier ■ coordination of logistics	The customer decision remains stable over time; e.g. ■ obligation to the supplier due to a long-term framework contract ■ buyer decides to renew the contract without prior re-evaluation ■ buyer decides to renew the contract after re-evaluation

Bruhn 2005; Homburg and Jensen 2004; Szymanski and Henard 2001). For instance, customers in business-to-business marketing display a rather weak tendency to recommend products and services; purchasers in competing companies are less likely to recommend highly efficient suppliers to each other. Moreover, prices are subject to more intensive negotiation in business-to-business marketing than in business-to-consumer marketing. Organizational customers that offer a reasonable price level to their suppliers tend to be characterized as being more loyal to a supplier than customers who continuously and very aggressively negotiate prices with a supplier.

Table 10-3 illustrates this concept of customer loyalty in business-to-business marketing, and also provides examples of the four facets of loyalty.

Furthermore, three categories of **customer loyalty activities in business-to-business marketing** can be distinguished (see Homburg and Jensen 2004), as described below.

1. **Reinforcement tools** aim to 'reward' customers for their loyalty. Among these are added services of the supplier that the customer can continue to use even after the termination of the business relationship (e.g. consultancy for the optimization of the customer's production).
2. **Tools that create barriers** to 'punish' customers for poor loyalty: the lock in effect of a proprietary system standard is an example; here, the purchase of additional system components does not result in a significant added benefit, but switching to a different incompatible system causes considerable costs.
3. **Mixed tools** include, for example, the mutual coordination of logistics and production processes; these generate efficiency benefits for the customer, which are lost if the supplier is changed.

In general, each of the three categories applies to both the individual and organizational level of customer loyalty. Accordingly, Table 10-4 lists customer loyalty tools in business-to-business marketing.

Table 10-4 Customer relationship management tools in business-to-business marketing (adapted from Homburg and Jensen 2004, p. 506)

Type of incentive	Reinforcing tools	Tools that create barriers	Balanced tools	Loyalty tools that create barriers
Individual level	■ Visits by field sales employees ■ Customer events with a distinct social component ■ Customer magazines ■ Gifts ■ Invitations to theme trips	■ Development of a sense of social responsibility ■ Demonstration of personal disadvantages in case of switching suppliers	■ Development of good personal relationships ■ Supply of material for image promotion in the company (e.g. presentations) ■ Provision of a platform for image promotion in the industry (e.g. providing possibilities to participate in conferences, placement of magazine articles) ■ Full awareness of the expectations of a manager as regards process flows	■ Development of a sense of social responsibility ■ Demonstration of personal disadvantages in case of switching suppliers
Organizational level	■ Credits and other price concessions ■ Transfer of knowhow (e.g. one-time consulting) ■ Training ■ Financing of additional equipment	■ Incompatibility of the company's products with competitor products ■ Long-term supply contracts ■ Threat of not supplying other products	■ Individualized product variants, individualized packaging ■ System offers, product alliances, category management ■ Vendor-managed inventory (VMI), just-in-time delivery, fleet management, shipment optimization ■ Maintenance and repairs, coordination of production processes, operator models and facility management ■ Marketing and sales support, credit lines, cross-buying bonuses ■ Quality signal to the customer's customers ■ Reliability, availability, simplicity ■ Clearly defined responsibilities, primary contact partner	■ Incompatibility of the company's products with competitor products ■ Long-term supply contracts ■ Threat of not supplying other products

Summary

In this chapter we discussed the challenges that companies face when operating in business-to-business markets. We distinguished different types of organizational customers and discussed the concept of the buying center. The buying center is essential to understanding the multiple buying influences that arise when a group of individuals participate in an organizational purchase decision – a situation that often occurs in business-to-business marketing. Other challenges in organizational buying were also described, such as the derivative character of organizational demand, multi-organizational participation, the high degree of personal interaction between supplier and buyer, and the usually long-term focus that business partners in an organizational context pursue. Several types of business were distinguished, depending on the continuity of the business relationship, the individuality of the service and the integration of the customer.

We also discussed the specific characteristics of the marketing strategy in business-to-business marketing. The ability to integrate processes, flexibility in production and the range of the products and services offered, as well as the need to cooperate on a strategic level, have been emphasized. For product decisions, pricing decisions, communication decisions and sales decisions, we discussed the specific characteristics of business-to-business marketing and, finally, concluded the chapter with the issue of customer relationship management in an organizational context.

Case Study: Boeing Lets Airlines Browse 'Dreamliner' Showroom

Boeing Co., taking a leaf from the automobile industry's book, is now offering customers of its new 787 'Dreamliner' something that most car buyers take for granted: a showroom. Airline representatives who visit the new Dreamliner Gallery can't actually kick the tyres here – the four-wheeled main landing gear of a 787 is about the size of a Mini Cooper – but they can try out a variety of seats and even conduct 'bakeoffs' to test how well different flight ovens warm up chocolate chip cookies.

'Just like with a car, even though you can configure the 787 online, you still want to go down to the showroom to see if you like the seats and other options,' says Patty Rhodes, the Boeing executive in charge of the Dreamliner Gallery. The decisions these executives make add up quickly: outfitting an average interior costs around \$8 million, with first-class seats selling for \$25,000 on up to \$100,000.

Until recently, putting together the interior of an airplane was an 18-month shopping marathon that required airline officials to visit dozens of individual suppliers to pick out everything from seats and carpeting to crash axes and emergency lighting.

Both Boeing and Airbus in recent years have put considerable effort into making their customers' plane-buying experiences easier. Airbus, a unit of the European Aeronautic Defense & Space Co.,

Case Study (Continued)

scored points beginning in the late 1970s by building a mock-up center at its headquarters in Toulouse, France. Airbus now has mock-ups of each of its major new planes, including the giant double-decker A380.

Boeing is promoting its 'showroom' as the next step in designing and building jetliners, but it's also a tool to discourage airlines from going crazy with options. 'It got to the point that all of the customizations was getting out of control,' says Randy Atkins, senior manager of customer integration for the 787 program. Over-customization frequently adds costs to production and has led to problems, most recently for Airbus. Deliveries of the first A380s have been delayed as much as two years, in large part because of wiring problems associated with special interiors. Unlike automobile showrooms, the Dreamliner Gallery has an element of Fort Knox to it. Most airlines jealously guard their new interiors, so Boeing set up each room so that buying teams from only one airline at a time can be inside. Because most airline visits to the Dreamliner Gallery are expected to take from two days to two weeks, Boeing has also built two private office suites.

Source: Lunsford 2007.

Discussion Questions

1. Characterize the type of business that Boeing is catering to.
2. How does the Dreamliner Gallery help Boeing to connect with its customers? Which specific challenges that arise in organizational buying are addressed with this showroom?
3. The Dreamliner Gallery offers Boeing the opportunity to integrate customers in the innovation process. Why can this be important?

Key Terms

Ability to integrate processes *336*
Acquisition of order *335*
Auctions *340*
Basic characteristics of business-to-business marketing *329*
Basic services *338*
Bonuses/rebates *341*
Brand management *338*
Business development *335*
Business types *333*
Buying center *331*
Competitive bidding *340*
Customer loyalty activities in business-to-business marketing *345*
Customer loyalty *344*
Derivative character of organizational demand *329*
Discounts/allowances *341*
Enforcement of prices *342*
Exhibitions *342*
Flexibility *336*
Flexibility in the production process and the range of goods and services *335*
Focus on direct sales *343*
Governmental organizations *328*
High degree of personal interaction between the company and the organizational buyer *333*
Hybrid systems of direct and indirect sales *343*
Individual pricing *340*
Information requirements *342*
Ingredient brand *339*
Innovation management *337*
Innovativeness *336*
Integration of customers into the innovation process *337*
Integration of the sales logistics *344*
Investment business/project business *333*
Lock-in effect *336*
Long-term nature of the business relationship *333*
Management of established products *338*
Market launch *338*
Mass customization *335*
Media advertising *342*
Mixed tools *345*
Multi-organizational participation *331*
Multiple buying influences *331*
Organizational purchase decisions *344*
Original equipment manufacturers (OEMs) *328*
Personal character *342*
Price differentiation *341*
Price negotiations *341*
Pricing *339*
Private-sector companies *328*
Product business/spot transactions *333*
Public and non-profit institutions *328*
Purchase decisions *342*
Reinforcement tools *345*
Retailers *328*
Reversed auctions *340*
Sales logistics *344*
Strategic cooperations *335*
Supplier business *334*
Supply guarantees *344*
Systems business *334*
Technical information *342*
Tools that create barriers *345*
Trade fairs *342*
Typology of organizational customers 328
Users *328*
Value-added services *338*

References

ABC Copper Advisory (2006) May.

Anderson, J. and Narus, J. (1995) Capturing the value of supplementary services, *Harvard Business Review*, 73, 1, 75–83.

Anderson, J. and Narus, J. (1998) Business marketing: understand what customers value, *Harvard Business Review*, 76, 6, 53–63.

Backhaus, K. (1993) Geschäftstypenspezifisches Investitionsgütermarketing, in: Droege, W., Backhaus, K. and Weiber, R. (eds) *Strategien für Investitionsgütermärkte: Antworten auf neue Herausforderungen*. Landsberg, 100–109.

Backhaus, K. (2003) *Industriegütermarketing* (7th edn). München.

Backhaus, K. and Voeth, M. (2004) Industriegütermarketing – eine vernachlässigte Disziplin? in: Backhaus, K. and Voeth, M. (eds) *Handbuch Industriegütermarketing: Strategien, Instrumente, Anwendungen*. Wiesbaden, 5–21.

Baumgarth, C. (2004) Markenführung von BtoB-Marken, in: Bruhn, M. (ed.) *Handbuch Markenführung*. Wiesbaden.

Bonoma, T.V. (2006) Major sales: who really does the buying? *Harvard Business Review*, July–August, 172–181.

Born, C. (2003) *Investitionsgüter erfolgreich vermarkten: so steigern Sie kontinuierlich Ihre Marktanteile*. München.

Bowen, D., Siehl, C. and Schneider, B. (1989) A framework for analyzing customer service orientations in manufacturing, *Academy of Management Review*, 14, 1, 75–95.

Boyt, T. and Harvey, M. (1997) Classification of industrial services: a model with strategic implications, *Industrial Marketing Management*, 26, 4, 291–300.

Dahlstrom, R., McNeilly, K.M. and Speh, T.W. (1996) Buyer–seller relationships in the procurement of logistical services, *Journal of the Academy of Marketing Science*, 24, 2, 110–124.

Doney, P. and Cannon, J. (1997) An examination of the nature of trust in buyer–seller relationships, *Journal of Marketing*, 61, 2, 35–51.

Enkel, E., Perez-Freije, J. and Gassmann, O. (2005) Minimizing market risks through customer integration in new product development: learning from bad practice, *Creativity & Innovation Management*, 14, 4, 425–437.

Erdem, S.A. and Swift, C.O. (1998) Items to consider for just-in-time use in marketing channels, *Industrial Marketing Management*, 27, 21–29.

Frazier, G.L., Spekman, R.E. and O'Neal, C.R. (1988) Just-in-time exchange relationships in industrial markets, *Journal of Marketing*, 5, 3, 52–67.

Ganesan, S. (1994) Determinants of long-term orientation in buyer–seller relationship, *Journal of Marketing*, 58 (April), 1–19.

Gierl, H. and Gehrke, G. (2004) Kundenbindung in industriellen ZulieferAbnehmer-Beziehungen, *Zeitschrift für betriebswirtschaftliche Forschung*, 56 (May), 203–236.

Gruner, K. and Homburg, C. (2000) Does customer interaction enhance new product performance? *Journal of Business Research*, 49, 1, 1–14.

Guenzi, P., Pardo, C. and Georges, L. (2007) Relational selling strategy and key account managers relational behaviors: an exploratory study, *Industrial Marketing Management*, 36, 121–133.

Günter, B. and Kuhl, M. (2000) Industrielles Beschaffungsmanagement, in: Kleinaltenkamp, M. and Plinke, W. (eds) *Technischer Vertrieb: Grundlagen des Business-to-Business Marketing* (2nd edn). Berlin, 371–450.

Homburg, C. and Bruhn, M. (2005) Kundenbindungsmanagement – Eine Einführung in die theoretischen und praktischen Probelmstellungen, in: Bruhn, M. and Homburg, C. (eds), *Handbuch Kundenbindungsmanagement* (5th edn). Wiesbaden, 3–37.

Homburg, C. and Garbe, B. (1999) Towards an improved understanding of industrial services: quality dimensions and their impact on buyer–seller relationships, *Journal of Business-to-Business Marketing*, 6, 2, 39–71.

Homburg, C. and Jensen, O. (2004) Kundenbindung, in: Backhaus, K. and Voeth, M. (eds) *Handbuch Industriegütermarketing*. Wiesbaden, 481–521.

Homburg, C. and Richter, M. (2003) Branding Excellence – Wegweiser für professionelles Markenmanagement, Working Paper Series, Management Know-how, Institute of Market-Oriented Management, University of Mannheim, Mannheim.

Homburg, C., Workman, J.P. and Jensen, O. (2002) A configurational perspective on key account management, *Journal of Marketing*, 66, 2, 38–60.
Hutt, M. and Speh, T. (2004) *Business Marketing Management: A Strategic View of Industrial and Organizational Markets* (8th edn). Fort Worth.
Hutt, M., Johnston, W. and Ronchetto Jr, J.R. (1985) Selling centers and buying centers: formulating strategic exchange patterns, *Journal of Personal Selling and Sales Management*, 5, May, 33–40.
Johnston, W. and Bonoma, T. (1981) The buying center: structure and interaction patterns, *Journal of Marketing*, 45, 2, 143–156.
Johnston, W., Lewin, J. and Spekman, R. (1999) International industrial marketing interactions: dyadic and network perspectives, *Journal of Business Research*, 46, 259–271.
Kleinaltenkamp, M. (1997) Business-to-business marketing, *Gabler Wirtschafts-Lexikon* (14th edn), Volume 1, A–E. Wiesbaden, 753–762.
Kleinaltenkamp, M. (2000) Einführung in das Business-to-Business Marketing, in: Kleinaltenkamp, M. and Plinke, W. (eds), *Technischer Vertrieb: Grundlagen des Business-to-Business Marketing* (2nd edn). Berlin, 171–247.
Kleinaltenkamp, M. (2003) Ingredient Branding: Markenpolitik im Business-to-Business-Geschäft, in: Köhler, R. (ed.), *Erfolgsfaktor Marke: Neue Strategien des Markenmanagements*. Wiesbaden, 261–270.
Kleinaltenkamp, M., Plötner, O., Zedler, C. (2004) Industrielles Servicemanagement, in: Backhaus, K., Voeth, M. (eds), *Handbuch Industriegütermarketing: Strategien, Instrumente, Anwendungen*. Wiesbaden, 627–648.
Krafft, M., Frenzen, H. (2001) *Erfolgsfaktoren für Vertriebsteams, Studie des Zentrums für Marktorientierte Unternehmensführung (ZMU)*. Vallendar.
Lilien, G., Wong, M. (1984) An exploratory investigation of the structure of the buying center in the metal-working industry, *Journal of Marketing Research*, 21, 1, 1–11.
Lunsford, L.J. (2007) Boeing lets airlines browse 'Dreamliner' showroom, *Wall Street Journal*, www.lexisnexis.com.
Matthyssens, P. and Vandenbempt, K. (1998) Creating competitive advantage in industrial services, *Journal of Business & Industrial Marketing*, 13, 4/5, 339–355.
Mester, L. (1988) Going, going, gone: setting prices with auctions, *Federal Reserve Bank of Philadelphia Business Review*, 3/4, 3–13.
Mohr, J., Fisher, R. and Nevin, J. (1996) Collaborative communication in interfirm relationships: moderating effects of integration and control, *Journal of Marketing*, 60 (July), 103–115.
Moon, M. and Gupta, S. (1997) Examining the formation of selling centers: a conceptual framework, *Journal of Personal Selling and Sales Management*, 2, Spring, 31–41.
Nambisan, S. (2002) Designing virtual customer environments for new product development: toward a theory, *Academy of Management Review*, 27, 3, 392–413.
Noble, P.M. and Gruca, T.S. (1999) Industrial pricing: theory and managerial practice, *Marketing Science*, 18, 3, 435–454.
Parasuraman, A. (1998) Customer service in business-to-business markets: an agenda for research, *Journal of Business & Industrial Marketing*, 13, 4/5, 309–321.
Plinke, W. (2000) Grundkonzeptionen des industriellen Marketing-Managements, in: Kleinaltenkamp, M. and Plinke, W. (eds) *Technischer Vertrieb: Grundlagen des Business-to-Business Marketing* (2nd edn). Berlin, 101–168.
Proscharsky, N. (1998) *Preismanagement im Investitionsgütermarketing: Modelle für reife Märkte*. Wiesbaden.
Reid, D. and Plank, R. (2000) Business marketing comes of age: a comprehensive review of the literature, *Journal of Business-to-Business Marketing*, 7, 2 & 3, 9–185.
Rese, M. and Herter, V. (2004) Preise und Kosten – Preisbeurteilung im Industriegüterbereich, in: Backhaus, K. and Voeth, M. (eds), *Handbuch Industriegütermarketing: Strategien, Instrumente, Anwendungen*. Wiesbaden, 969–988.
Rush, S. (2003) Vodafone calls on Oracle, 22 October, http://www.wirelessweek.com/toc-newsat2/2003/20031022.html.
Schuppar, B. (2006) *Preismanagement: Konzeption, Umsetzung und Erfolgsauswirkungen im Business-to-Business-Bereich*. Wiesbaden.
Sengupta, S., Krapfel, R. and Pusateri, M. (1997) The strategic sales force, *Marketing Management*, Summer, 29–34.
Shapiro, B.P. and Jackson, B.B. (1978) Industrial pricing to meet customer needs, *Harvard Business Review*, 56, 6, 119–127.

Sharma, A.C. (2006) Success factors in key accounts, *Journal of Business & Industrial Marketing*, 21, 3, 141–150.
Skiera, B. and Spann, M. (2004) Gestaltung von Auktionen, in: Backhaus, K. and Voeth, M. (eds) *Handbuch Industriegütermarketing*. Wiesbaden, 1041–1056.
Slatter, S. (1990) Strategic marketing variables under conditions of competitive bidding, *Strategic Management Journal*, 11, 4, 309–317.
Spekman, R. and Stern, L. (1979) Environmental uncertainty and buying group structure: an empirical investigation, *Journal of Marketing*, 43, 1, 54–64.
Szymanski, D. and Henard, D. (2001) Customer satisfaction: a meta-analysis of the empirical evidence, *Journal of the Academy of Marketing Science*, 29, 1, 16–35.
von Hippel, E., Thomke, S. and Sonnack, M. (2000) Creating breakthroughs at 3M, *Health Forum Journal*, 7/8, 20–27.
Webster, F. and Wind, Y. (1972) *Organizational Buying Behavior*. Englewood Cliffs, NJ.
Westervelt, R. (2003) Chemical management services gains traction; new industries, offerings expand initiative, *Chemical Week*, June, 1–3.
www.basf.com

CHAPTER 11

Marketing of Services

Contents

Learning Objectives

In this chapter you will become familiar with:

- the fundamental characteristics that distinguish services from products
- the main approaches for defining a typology of services
- the key issues in conceptualizing service quality
- the different techniques used for measuring service quality on the basis of various data sources as well as methods for conducting more detailed analyzes of service quality
- the central approaches for influencing the quality of service
- the relationship between the characteristics of service and the strategic marketing decisions made by service companies
- the most important effects that the characteristics of service have on the design of the classic components of the marketing mix
- the necessity to expand the classic marketing mix with regard to services, and the key objectives of the expanded marketing mix
- the different functions of retailers
- the business forms used in the retail sector
- the specific characteristics of the marketing mix in retail marketing.

Over the past few decades, the service sector has become increasingly important to the overall economy in many countries worldwide. An indication of this is the percentage of value added from the service sector that contributes to the GDP. All service activities account for around 70% of total gross value added for the OECD countries as a whole, with higher and lower shares in particular countries (e.g. Norway 56.2, Korea 56.3, Czech Republic 58.8, Australia 68.9, Germany 69.7, France 76.9, Switzerland 72.3, UK 75.9, Luxembourg 83.4; see *OECD Factbook* 2007). Additionally, the share of total employment in services has increased in all regions in the world with one exception – the Middle East and North Africa (ILO 2006). At the same time, services marketing has also become well established as an academic discipline (see Berry and Parasuraman 1993; Bruhn and Georgi 2006; Fisk *et al.* 1995; Grönroos 1994, 2002). While marketing theories and concepts have been dominated by the manufactured goods sector, a clear understanding has emerged for the very specific challenges that service companies face (Grönroos 2002; Palmer 2000). As a result, a more relationship-oriented marketing approach has been advocated, where the customer becomes a more integral part of the overall value creation process (see also Bruhn and Georgi 2006; Grönroos 2002).

In the first section of this chapter, we will introduce services marketing. We define the concept of 'service' and outline the basic characteristics of services. Section 11.1 will also examine the typologies used to classify services, while Section 11.2 will deal with service quality. The separate discussion of service quality is justified by the extremely important role that quality aspects play in the marketing of services (for more on this particular significance, see also Section 11.2). In Section 11.3, we will take a closer look at the strategic aspects of services marketing. Section 11.4 examines the specific characteristics of the marketing mix in services marketing. We will first describe the specific characteristics in the classical areas of the marketing mix (product decisions, pricing decisions, communication decisions, sales decisions) and then present a discussion of the other areas of the marketing mix that are relevant to the marketing of services in particular.

11.1 Marketing of Services: What are Services?

We will first provide a definition of **service**. Service is defined as the 'production of an essentially intangible benefit, either in its own right or as a significant element of a tangible product, which through some form of exchange, satisfies an identified need' (Palmer 2001, p. 3). Services are also referred to as economic exchange activities that create a non-physical output for which production and consumption usually occur simultaneously (Zeithaml *et al.* 2006). Although services satisfy an identified need (e.g. for health, well-being, security, comfort, convenience) service customers normally do not acquire ownership of the physical elements that may well be involved in this exchange relationship (e.g. facilities in a hotel) (Lovelock and Wirtz 2007).

Frequently, services are defined by these fundamental characteristics, especially when contrasted to tangible goods. Although tangible goods and services have common features, they are different and distinct in a few important ways. The discussion of these distinctive characteristics of services is widespread in the literature on services marketing (see, e.g., Fitzsimmons and Fitzsimmons 1999; Grönroos 1994, 2002; Palmer 2001; Zeithaml *et al.* 2006). Five fundamental and distinctive characteristics can be differentiated when characterizing services:

1. intangibility
2. perceived purchase risk
3. inseparability
4. perishability
5. variability.

Intangibility refers to the fact that the result of a service activity is not concrete (i.e. it has no tangible properties). In contrast to the production of tangible goods, the process of providing a service does not lead to a physical product and, therefore, services cannot be experienced (seen, felt, tasted, heard, smelled) before they are purchased. Any claims regarding the service, especially to do with service quality, can therefore be verified only once the service has been rendered.

Due to the fact that it is very difficult for service customers to assess the service prior to purchase, the customer's **perceived purchase risk** is usually greater for services than for tangible goods. This arises, in particular, because services are usually associated with a higher level of uncertainty regarding the quality of the service. For more information on this, please refer to the discussion on 'information economics' presented in the Appendix, which provides a description of search, credence and experience characteristics with regard to the assessment of product and service quality. Generally, services tend to exhibit more credence and experience qualities, and fewer search qualities as compared to tangible goods (see Zeithaml 1981).

Inseparability refers to the fact that the production and consumption of services occur at the same time. In practical terms this implies that the producer of the service and the service customer must interact so that the exchange can occur. This means, for service companies, that the production process becomes a crucial element in the company–customer interaction.

The **perishability** of services reflects the fact that, due to the large degree of inseparability between service creation and service provision, services cannot be stored. Accordingly, service providers cannot produce their services in advance and cannot carry forward stock of services for later moments in time. Additionally, there can be daily (transportation during daily peak hours), weekly (weekend demand for leisure time activities) and seasonal (demand for winter vacation) demand variations that further intensify the challenges that arise from the issue of perishability.

Variability describes the fact that customers introduce an **external factor** into the process of service delivery because they are usually present during service production and consumption. The external factor can be a person (e.g. the customer during a visit to the doctor) or a tangible good (e.g. a car when using a repair service), a nominal good (e.g. money when using a service in investment banking) or information (e.g. information about the company when using a consulting service). Another issue that arises in this context is personnel variability. Different members of the service staff render services in different ways, and such variability in standards of production poses difficult challenges for service companies. Although variability can be bothersome for companies, this aspect of services also helps to ensure **individuality**. Individuality refers to the fact that, in contrast to tangible goods, services can generally be more easily tailored to individual customer needs (also referred to as **customization**).

These five characteristics differentiate between services and tangible goods. Nevertheless, we should point out that a clear-cut differentiation between services and products cannot be made on this basis. For example, a great number of products (e.g. food) are also perishable. In the industrial goods industry, it is common practice to market completely customized products by integrating the customer into the development process. Furthermore, a number of tangible goods (e.g. high-tech products) are associated with a greater purchase risk for the customer. There are also highly standardized services that show only a low degree of customization (e.g. information services). We should, thus, note that tangible goods can also demonstrate the distinct characteristics to varying degrees, and that services do not necessarily have to exhibit all these characteristics to a large extent. However, services tend to demonstrate the distinctive characteristics to a greater degree than tangible goods.

In view of the problem inherent in distinguishing services from tangible goods, the question arises as to whether such a differentiation even makes sense (Figure 11-1 illustrates this). Using service characteristics will not always help to clearly differentiate services from tangible goods. Often, company's offerings are predominantly intangible or have more intangible than tangible

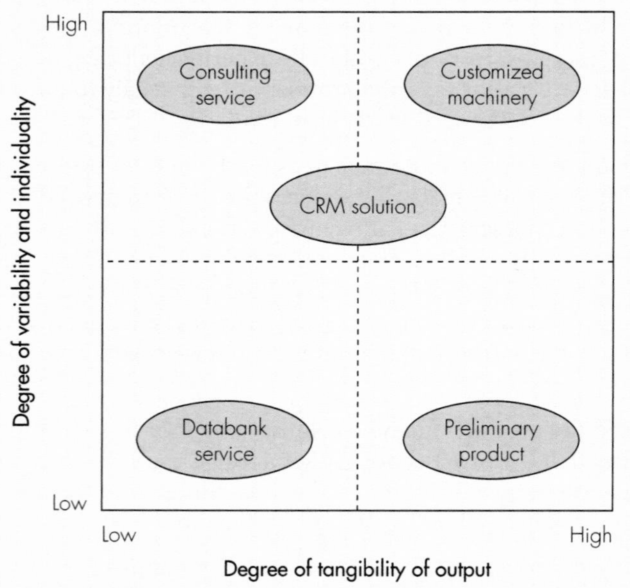

Figure 11-1 Typology of tangible and intangible output based on distinctive service characteristics

components and, in such cases, it is important to identify the distinct characteristics as they pose specific marketing challenges. This is especially the case when the service itself is the 'core product' (Lovelock and Wirtz 2007).

Service typologies can aid considerably in defining services. A one-dimensional or multidimensional typology can be used in this context. The majority of typologies found in the literature are one-dimensional (e.g. they differentiate services according to a time dimension – which services save time, which require time). Another relatively widespread approach is differentiation by means of criteria related to the purchase phase: distinguishing between services provided prior to the purchase, during the purchase and after the purchase.

Multidimensional typologies are more complex; such a technique is shown in Figure 11-2. One dimension of this typology is the degree of formalization of the relationship between the service provider and the customer. The second dimension is the continuity of the service delivery. This typology results in the four categories of services presented in Figure 11-2. Accordingly, a service organization can enter a membership relationship or can have no formal relationship with its customers. The advantage of a membership relationship is that the service organization knows the identities and consumption habits of its current customers, which can be valuable for marketing tasks such as segmentation, targeting and pricing. Furthermore, membership relationships often result in customer loyalty and repeat business and/or ongoing financial support (see Lovelock 1983, p. 14).

Figure 11-3 illustrates another typology, which categorizes services based on dimensions describing the degree of customer interaction/customization and personnel costs in relation to the value of the infrastructure. Customer interaction refers to the opportunity that the customer has to actively intervene in the service process, while customization comprises the consideration of customer preferences. The second dimension takes into account the amount of personnel costs in relation to the value of the infrastructure and thus refers to the labor intensity. A service that

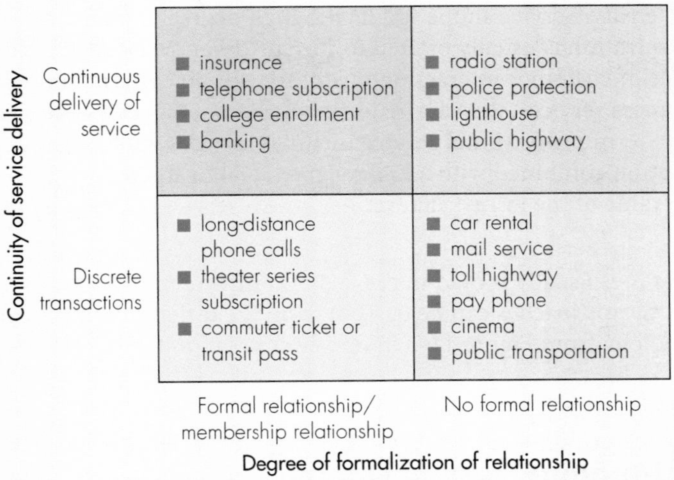

Figure 11-2 Service typology based on the degree of formalization of the relationship and continuity of the service delivery (adapted from Lovelock 1983)

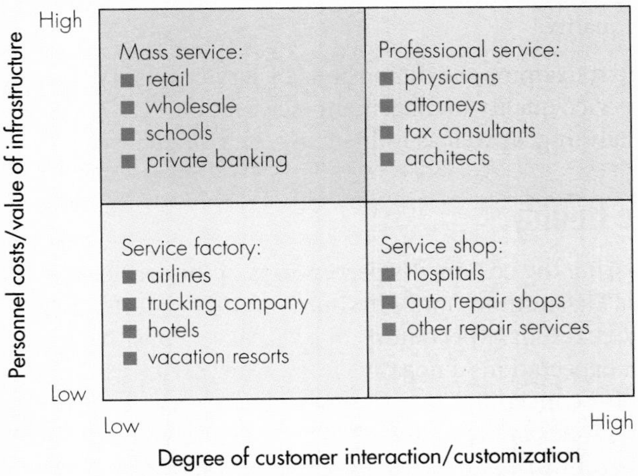

Figure 11-3 Service typology based on dimensions describing the degree of customer interaction/customization in relation to the value of the infrastructure (adapted from Schmenner 1992)

is very labor-intensive requires relatively little investment in the infrastructure, but necessitates high personnel costs.

The term **service factory** summarizes services that manifest a low degree of customer interaction/customization and relatively low labor intensity. Similar to highly technical production processes in high technologies that require intensive deployment of computers and automation, high investments are needed to maintain the infrastructure required for providing the service.

The **service shop** category characterizes services with a high degree of customer interaction/customization and low labor intensity. Service shops still have a high degree of plant and equipment, but more interaction and customization is usually offered to the customer. **Mass services** are those services that exhibit a low degree of customer interaction/customization in conjunction with a high degree of labor intensity. With mass services, the vast majority of customers receive the same or very similar services. Finally, the term **professional service** includes services with a high degree of customer interaction/customization combined with a high degree of labor intensity. The personnel costs are high in relation to the value of the infrastructure, since such services have to be provided by well-paid experts.

The relevance of such typologies is especially rooted in the fact that information about useful strategic marketing and marketing approaches can be derived from the different service categories. We will be using the service typology from Figure 11-3 in our discussion on the strategic issues of services marketing (see Section 11.3).

11.2 Designing and Managing Service Quality

In the previous section, we showed that many services pose a **high purchase risk** for the customer. This risk particularly results from the fact that numerous services tend to have more credence and experience qualities and are less easily characterized as search goods (see the section on 'information economics' in the Appendix). In services marketing quality is paramount. Furthermore, the special relevance of service quality arises from service variability (see Section 11.1) and the need to integrate external factors: the fact that the customer is involved and interacts in the service process makes it difficult to ensure consistent high quality.

In the following sections, we will first examine the dimensions of service quality (see Section 11.2.1). In the subsequent discussion on service quality management (see Section 11.2.2), we will delve into issues regarding measuring and analyzing, as well as influencing, service quality.

11.2.1 Dimensions of Service Quality

Service quality is defined by comparing the customer's perceptions of the service and the customer's desired expectations of the service (Fitzsimmons and Fitzsimmons 1999; Palmer 2001). When the customer's perception of the service exceeds expectations this will have a positive impact on service quality. If perceptions do not meet expectations a negative impact on service quality results. In the literature a number of approaches for conceptualizing the construct of service quality can be found. We will describe the most important ones in the following. The best-known is the **SERVQUAL approach**, which is based on empirical work (see Parasuraman *et al.* 1988; Zeithaml *et al.* 1990). It differentiates between five dimensions of service quality, as listed below.

1. **Tangibles**: the material environment in which the service is produced (e.g. physical facilities, equipment and appearance of personnel).
2. **Reliability**: the ability of the service provider to perform the promised service dependably and accurately (e.g. adherence to schedules and agreed-upon deadline).
3. **Responsiveness**: capability and willingness on the part of the service provider to help customers, and promptly respond to customer requests and requirements.
4. **Assurance**: the knowledge and courtesy of the service provider's employees, and their ability to inspire trust and confidence.
5. **Empathy**: in particular, the willingness and ability on the part of service employees to provide caring and individual attention to customers.

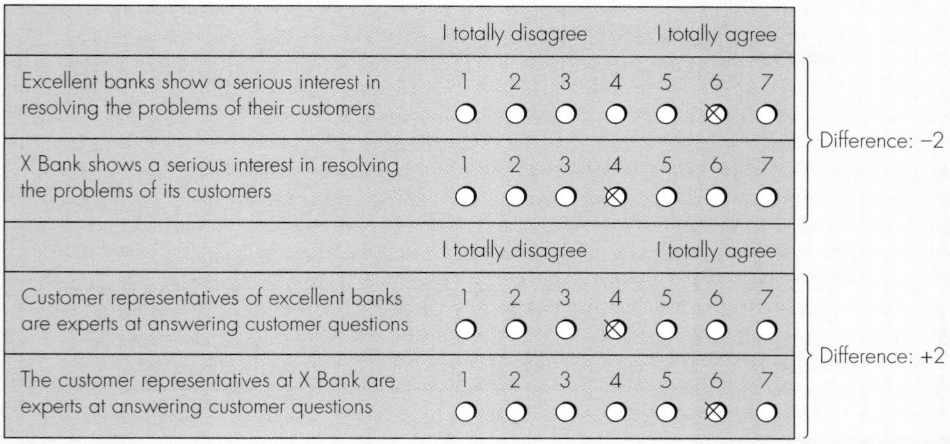

Figure 11-4 Illustration of a quality assessment based on the dual scale used in the SERVQUAL approach

In addition to this conceptualization of service quality, and based on this concept, the SERVQUAL approach provides a method to operationalize service quality. Using this approach, service quality is measured using 22 items in order to assess the service attributes that reflect the five quality dimensions (for a complete list of these indicators, please refer to Parasuraman *et al.* 1988, 1991; Zeithaml and Bitner 2003). These items are rated using a dual scale: the first scale measures customer expectations with regard to each of the service aspects.

The second scale measures perceived quality with respect to a specific service provider (see Figure 11-4 for an illustration of the application of this dual scale, with two indicators for the reliability and responsiveness dimensions). For each item, a positive or negative quantitative assessment of service quality is derived from the difference between the perceived service and the expected service (see Figure 11-4). For each of the five SERVQUAL dimensions, an average difference is then calculated across all items. Finally, overall service quality can be measured by the average scores across all five dimensions.

In principle, conceptualizing service quality using the SERVQUAL approach is helpful in terms of establishing a sound understanding of service quality. It must be assumed that the five dimensions have a certain relevance for the type of service being analyzed. Then SERVQUAL offers a framework for a comparative assessment of service quality across different service categories. Because of the general formulation of the items employed in the measurement, the assessment of the quality of very specific services is somewhat limited.

Finally, the difference between **routine and non-routine dimensions of service quality** should be mentioned (see Berry 1987; Brandt 1988). The focus here is the question of the extent to which the customer has specific expectations prior to using a service. In the case of routine dimensions, the customer almost always has such an expectation. These dimensions concern quality attributes that the customer takes for granted. Accordingly, a high level of quality in these dimensions rarely leads to a positive response on the part of the customer, while a low level of quality in these dimensions can lead to a strong negative customer response. In contrast, in the case of the non-routine dimensions, customers usually do not have strong expectations. Thus, a low level of quality in these dimensions does not usually lead to a strong negative customer response, but a high level of quality in these dimensions can lead to an extremely positive customer response.

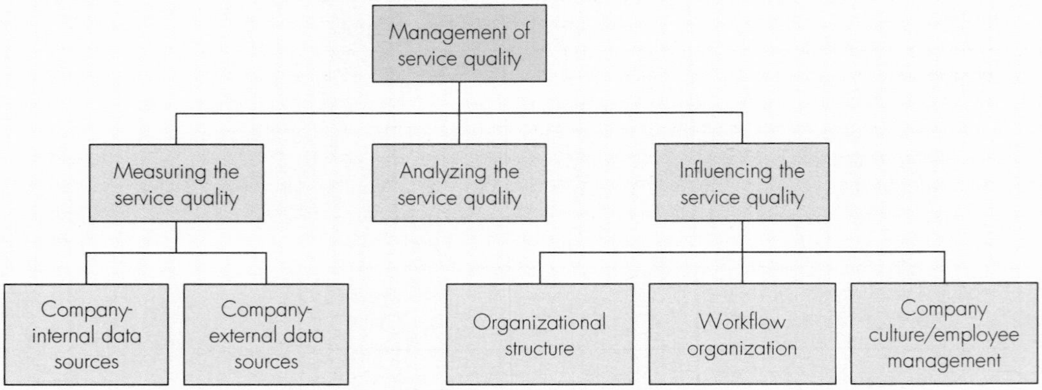

Figure 11-5 Overview of methods for managing services

11.2.2 Managing Service Quality

There are three different techniques for managing service quality (see Bruhn and Stauss 1999):

1 methods for measuring service quality

2 methods for conducting an in-depth analysis of service quality

3 methods for influencing (maintaining/improving) service quality.

Figure 11-5 provides a corresponding overview.

Before taking a look at the most important methods in each of the three areas, let us first examine the GAP model of service quality, an approach that fosters a basic understanding of the development of service quality. Therefore, it can also aid in analyzing and influencing service quality. The model distinguishes five 'GAPs' (gaps, or key discrepancies). The model is shown in Figure 11-6.

The starting point of the model is GAP 5, which refers to the discrepancy between the perceived and expected service (remember that this was the basis of defining service quality, see Section 11.1). From a customer-oriented perspective (in contrast to, say, a technical quality standpoint), service quality is equivalent to the degree to which customer expectations are fulfilled. The size of GAP 5 thus provides direct information about the service quality achieved. The following methods for measuring service quality are geared in part towards the measurement of GAP 5.

The other four GAPs refer to various discrepancies that are significant with regard to the resultant service quality. The size of GAP 5 therefore depends on the sizes of the other GAPs (also see Parasuraman *et al.* 1985).

- GAP 1 describes the discrepancies between actual customer expectations and customer expectations as perceived by the management. If the management has an incorrect perception of customer expectations this is mainly due to a lack of good market research (for more on methods of 'market research', see the Appendix).
- GAP 2 focuses on the discrepancies between customer expectations as perceived by management and the company's specifications of service quality. This discrepancy is caused by a lack of awareness of the problem and, more generally, an insufficient market orientation on the part of the management.

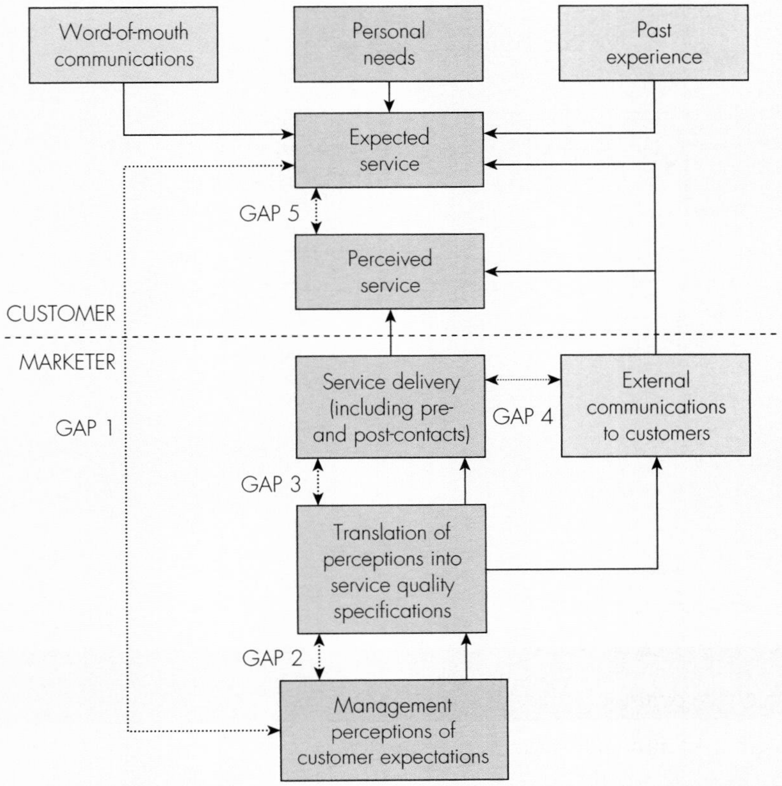

Figure 11-6 Illustration of the development of service quality using the GAP model (reprinted with permission from *Journal of Marketing*, published by the American Marketing Association, Parasuraman *et al.* (1985), 49, 3, 44)

- GAP 3 is derived from the discrepancy between the company's internal specifications for service quality and the actual service delivery. This gap can result, for example, from insufficient personnel qualifications (e.g. lack of competence) or unsound personnel management.
- Finally, GAP 4 concentrates on the disparities between the actual service delivery and the external communication to the customer. The GAP model illustrates that both the customer's perception of the service and their expectations are influenced by the way that the service provider communicates the service. For instance, excessive promises lead to unrealistically high customer expectations.

After discussing this model, which fosters a basic understanding of the issues involved in the quality management of services, we will turn to the most important approaches in the three areas of measuring, analyzing and influencing service quality.

Measuring Service Quality

A crucial question regarding the measurement of service quality concerns the **data sources** that can be used for the measurement (see Figure 11-7). A first differentiation relates to whether company-internal or company-external data sources will be used (for a discussion of these two data collection methods, see the discussion of 'data collection methods' in the Appendix). In both areas, further

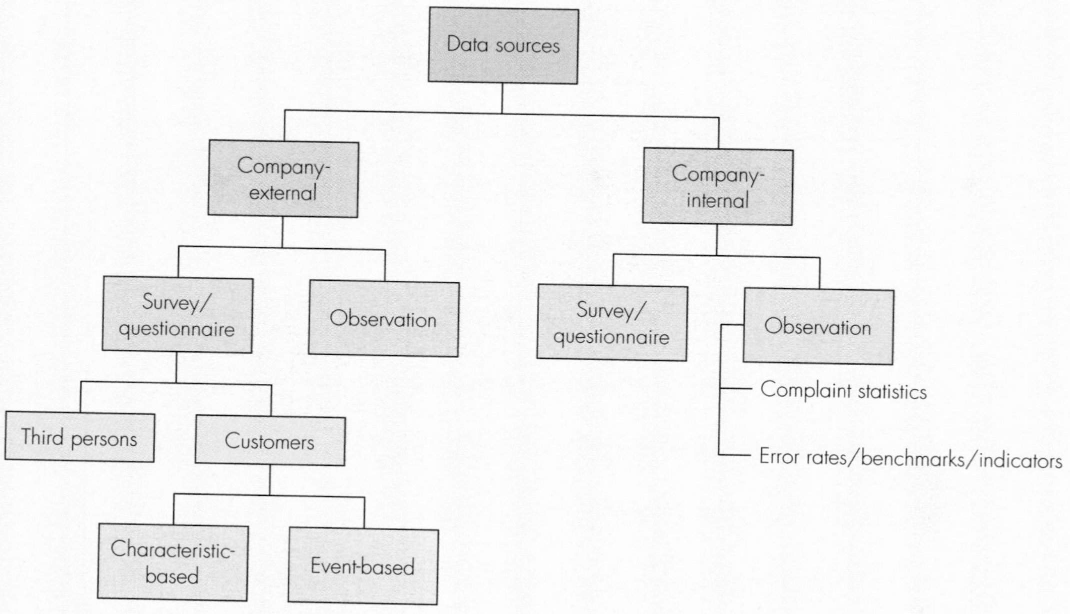

Figure 11-7 Data sources for measuring service quality

discrimination can then be made between data taken from observations and data collected from surveys (for a discussion of 'observations' and 'surveys', see the Appendix). Within the scope of **company-internal observations**, the analysis of quality indicators (e.g. the occurrence of errors in service delivery) and quality costs (e.g. the cost of resolving errors in service delivery) should be mentioned. In this context, **internal surveys/questionnaires** can be used (e.g. employee surveys on perceived service quality).

Company-external data sources are of greater relevance when measuring service quality. Together with **external observations** that can provide information about service quality, the following data sources can be useful:

- data on the frequency of complaints and reasons for complaints
- information from test shopper analyzes (also called silent shopper analyzes or mystery shopper analyzes)
- information from expert observations.

External surveys/questionnaires can be classified on the basis of whether third persons (e.g. experts) or the customers themselves are questioned in a survey. In company practice, customer surveys are by far the most useful tool. There are approaches that aim at measuring customers' perceptions of service quality over time. SERVQUAL is such an approach (see Section 11.2.1). The **vignette method** (for more on this, see Rossi and Anderson 1982; Sniderman and Grob 1996) represents a commonly used analysis. With this method, customers evaluate vignettes describing various combinations of primary service characteristics (e.g. the furnishings of the business premises, employee competence and the reliability of the service process). The vignettes are essentially very similar to the product profiles that are assessed by customers in the course of a conjoint analysis (refer to the Appendix for more information on 'conjoint analysis').

In contrast, there are methods that measure the customer's perception of quality in relation to a specific service event (e.g. a visit to a restaurant).

In general, it should be noted in this context that various data sources can complement each other. For example, the analysis of company-internal quality indicators can supplement data from customer surveys. Among the data sources described here, customer surveys are of particular significance since, ultimately, it is not the objective quality, but rather a customer's perceived quality that influences her/his attitude and behavior. Moreover, customer surveys are the only reliable source of information for service companies with regard to the extent to which they meet their customers' expectations. Thus, customer surveys are, for example, the only sound basis for evaluating GAP 5 within the scope of the GAP model (see Figure 11-6).

Analyzing Service Quality

The basic difference between methods for measuring and analyzing service quality is that analytical methods are usually more detailed than measurement techniques. Measurement techniques aim to record service quality as accurately as possible. Analytical methods also try to determine the *reasons for low/high service quality*. For example, with analytical methods, company-internal processes are also analyzed.

In the following, we will be presenting a number of techniques for **analyzing service quality**, specifically:

- the critical incident technique
- frequency-relevance analysis of quality problems
- the sequential incident method (also called blueprinting)
- fishbone analysis
- the benchmarking method.

The aim of the **critical incident technique** is to determine and analyze critical incidents (i.e. incidents between the customer and service company in a contact situation that the customer perceives as especially satisfying or especially dissatisfying – the so-called 'moments of truth') (see, primarily, Bitner *et al.* 1990 or Bäckström and Johansson 2006; Bruhn and Georgi 2006, p. 78). While the basic definition of critical incidents focuses on the role of service personnel, critical incidents can also arise in connection with the service provider's equipment (see Palmer 2001, p. 63). At its core, this method is a systematic customer survey, however one that is geared less to measuring service quality and more to analyzing the backgrounds on an aggregate level by combining quantitative and qualitative analyzes (and is thus classified as an analytical tool and not as a measuring method). The survey asks customers to recall situations when they had contact with the service provider that they found particularly satisfying or particularly dissatisfying (see Bruhn and Georgi 2006, p. 80). The procedure for the analysis can be illustrated by the following sample questions (here using the example of quality analysis for a restaurant, see Bitner *et al.* 1990):

- Do you remember having an especially satisfying (dissatisfying) interaction with an employee at Restaurant X?
- When did the incident take place?
- What were the specific circumstances leading to the situation?
- What exactly did the employee say or do?
- What made this interaction particularly satisfying (dissatisfying)?

The critical incident technique is a valuable tool for analyzing service quality, since the findings provide a depth that most traditional customer surveys measuring perceived service quality (e.g. using the SERVQUAL concept or similar approaches) cannot achieve. The primary significance of critical incidents arises from the fact that customers tend to have a strong recall of those incidents, and thus such incidents can have a major impact on the customer's long-term quality perception. Nonetheless, it should be pointed out that, due to its emphasis on very positive and very negative incidents, this method cannot provide a comprehensive picture of the overall quality perception of customers.

Frequency-relevance analyzes (FRA) (or frequency-relevance analyzes of complaints, in short FRAC) can be used to classify quality problems based on their frequency and their significance for the customer (for a more in-depth discussion of this method, see Stauss and Seidel 2004; Stauss and Weinlich 1997). FRA is a very simple analytical method that facilitates prioritization of services management: the more important the quality problem is to the customer, and the more frequently it occurs, the more urgently a service provider should attend to the problem. Being aware of the frequency of occurrence is crucial, since the frequency of a problem can indicate that it is rooted in the system.

A more sophisticated method for analyzing service quality is called **blueprinting**. This analytical method concentrates on the **service delivery process**, which is described in individual steps. Blueprinting helps to specify how the process *should* be designed (see Lovelock and Wirtz 2007; Palmer 2001). The result of the detailed description of the service delivery process is a graphic process flowchart that describes the ideal process of service delivery along all key activities (at the front end – visible to the customer – and the back end – not visible to the customer). An example of such a blueprint is shown in Figure 11-8. In this blueprint, three important lines are plotted: the line of external interaction; the line of visibility; the line of internal interaction (see Chase and Stewart 1994, p. 40; Lovelock and Wirtz 2007; Zeithaml *et al.* 2006). The line of external interaction separates the activities of the customers from those of the service provider. The line of visibility separates all activities that are visible from those that are not visible to the customer. The line of internal interaction separates the activities of the contact persons from activities taking place in the course of supporting processes (e.g. back-office processes).

A blueprint can be used to analyze service quality in several ways. On the basis of such a blueprint, a service provider can, for instance, conduct a systematic analysis of the service process and identify any potential quality problems (so-called **fail points**) in the process steps. The blueprinting approach also helps to identify internal interfaces, which are vital for service quality (see Bruhn and Georgi 2006; Lovelock and Wirtz 2007). Furthermore, blueprints can also be used in customer surveys. For example, the blueprint can be used to guide the customer step-by-step through the service process, with customers being asked to recap their interaction with the service provider (**storytelling**). Conclusions regarding service quality can then be drawn from customers' subjective impressions and assessments.

Another method for analyzing service quality is **fishbone analysis** (also known as a root-cause diagram, cause-and-effect diagram or Ishikawa diagram after its originator, who developed the diagram in 1943 and officially published it in 1968). This method provides a technique for conducting an analysis of the **causes of quality problems**. The fishbone analysis is not only used in the service sector, but is a general technique used in quality management (see Munro-Faure and Munro-Faure 1993). The method uses creativity techniques to identify the potential causes of quality problems, which are then entered into a fishbone diagram. The 'head' of the fishbone represents the quality problem that needs to be resolved, while the 'bones' represent the main causal dimensions (see Figure 11-9). The visualization of the problem structure serves as a basis for the discussion of quality problems in the company. However, this analysis does not offer any specific solution(s) to these problems: it helps to identify the most probable causes of a specific problem and can thus be used to specify what additional data are needed to further explore the problem.

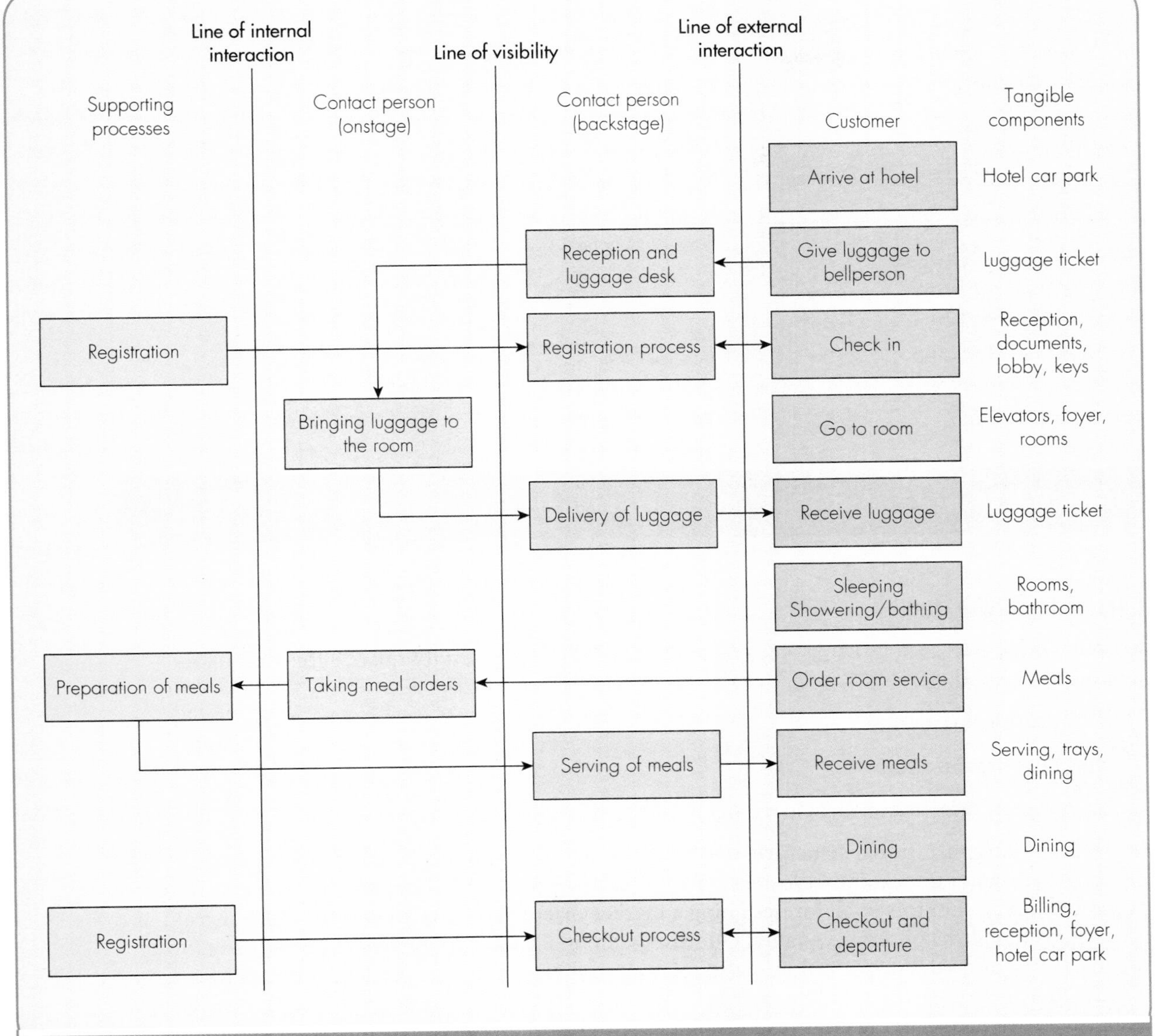

Figure 11-8 Blueprint using the example of an overnight stay at a hotel (adapted from Zeithaml *et al.* 2006, p. 271)

Finally, the **benchmarking** approach can be used to analyze service quality. The basic concept of benchmarking lies in systematically comparing certain company processes and activities with those of other companies by using standardized indicators and benchmarks (see also Section 3.4.2). The result of the comparison can identify ways to improve the company's own performance and service. Consequently, indicators and benchmarks that are related to service quality can also be used when analyzing service quality. For example, quality indicators (e.g. the punctuality of an airline company) or service process indices (e.g. customer satisfaction with the courtesy of the flight attendants) can be assessed.

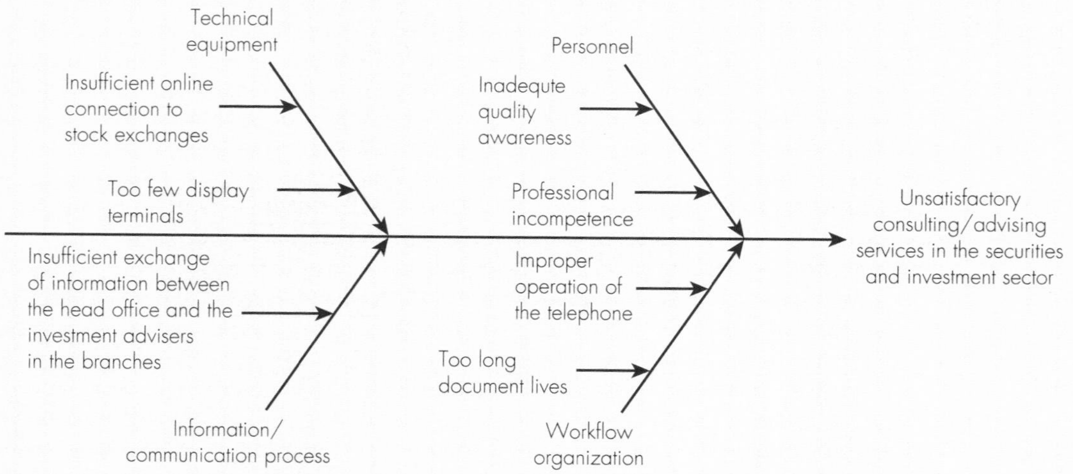

Figure 11-9 Example of a fishbone analysis of service quality in the financial services sector (see Bruhn 2004, p. 152)

Improving Service Quality

As we have already seen, in Figure 11-5, methods for influencing service quality are particularly relevant in three areas:

1 organizational structure
2 workflow organization
3 company culture/employee management.

In the area of **organizational structure**, the management of service quality concerns the creation of an organizational framework that fosters a high level of service quality. In principle, the approaches presented in Part 4 of this book for designing a market-oriented organizational structure also aid in achieving a high level of service quality. Our discussion in Chapter 13 on designing and structuring the marketing and sales organization is also relevant in this regard. Service quality can thus be promoted, for example, by avoiding over-specialization in the company and the interface problems associated with it. Specifying clear responsibilities with respect to service quality is yet another important organizational requirement.

The concept of **quality circles** is an organizational tool that can be used to influence service quality. Quality circles are discussion groups comprising several employees from various functional departments at the lower hierarchy levels of a company's business unit. These groups meet on a regular basis for the purpose of discussing service-related (mostly self-selected) quality problems within their own areas of responsibility (see Palmer 2001, p. 236; Schubert 1994). In quality circles, which are usually moderated by a supervisor or group leader, proposed solutions for resolving the problems are discussed. The quality circles are then responsible for implementing and monitoring the corrective measures. For this reason, it is essential that their members are trained to investigate problems and implement effective solutions (see Munro-Faure and Munro-Faure 1992, p. 188). To help improve the quality of service (and thus not only function as a 'debate club'), it is necessary to define precise objectives for the quality circles, continuously evaluate their contribution to success and provide them with support from higher management levels (see Palmer 2001, pp. 236/369; for a general discussion of quality circles, see Sherwood and Guerrier 1993; Silince and Sykes 1996).

Finally, the **Poka-Yoke method** (or fail-safe method) aims to systematically eliminate error sources in the service process (see, primarily, Shingo 1986, 1991, or Chase and Stewart 1994). This method is closely connected to the blueprinting method: approaches for avoiding errors in a service process are identified within the scope of the blueprinting method (see Bruhn and Georgi 2006, p. 90; Fitzsimmons and Fitzsimmons 1999, p. 87). A Poka-Yoke represents a simple, cost-effective service process design principle, such as a digital checklist, a printed guideline or an automatic reminder, whose objective is to immediately detect and prevent (generally unavoidable) human mistakes (e.g. confusion, forgetting, mix-ups, misreadings, misinterpretations) so that they don't lead to poor service (see Fitzsimmons and Fitzsimmons 1999, pp. 283f.; Lovelock and Wirtz 2007, p. 242; Zeithaml and Bitner 2000, p. 176). An example of how the Poka-Yoke method is applied is shown in Figure 11-10.

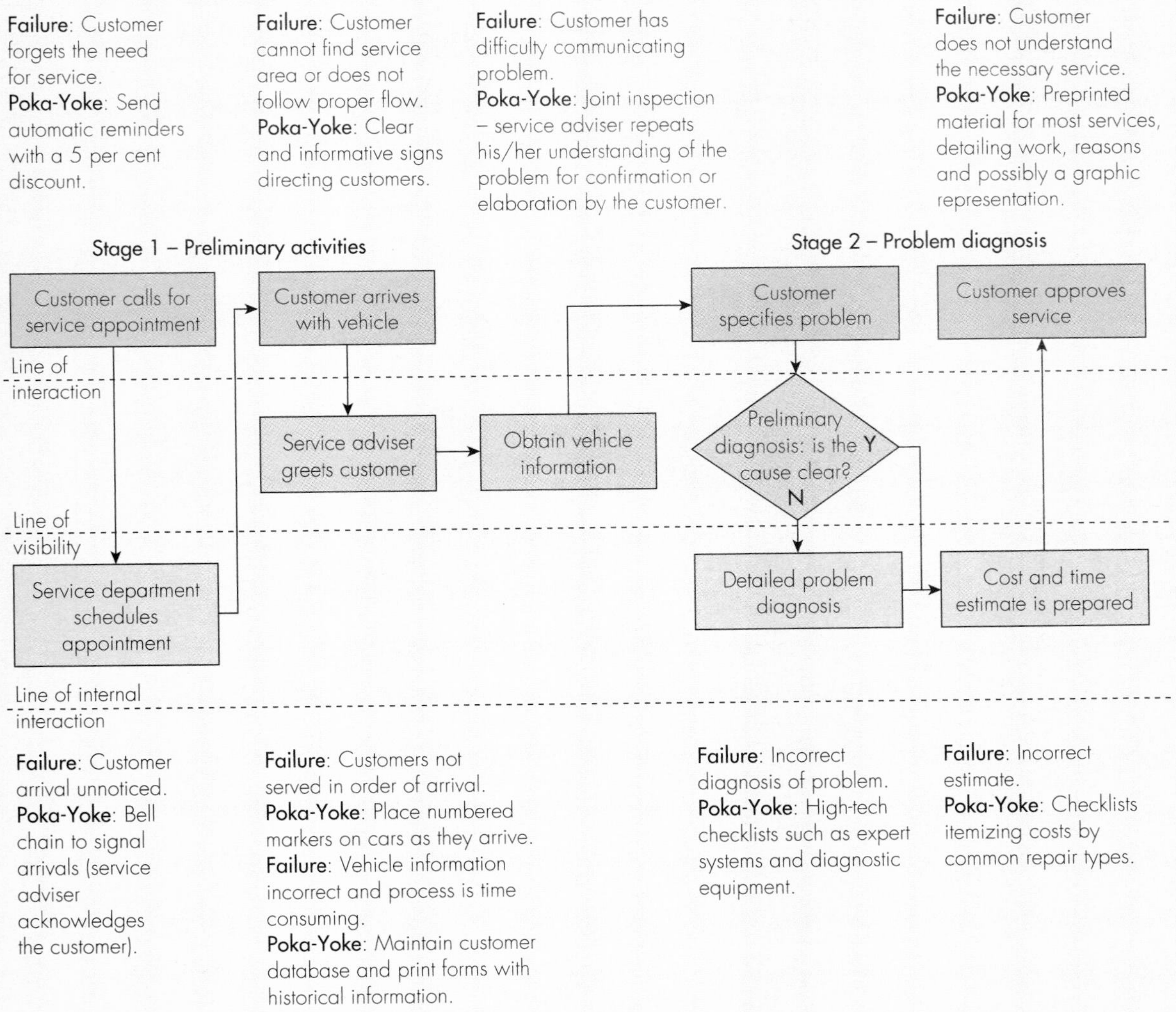

Figure 11-10 Illustration of the Poka-Yoke method using the example of a car repair shop (Chase and Stewart 1994, pp. 40f.)

Finally, there are numerous approaches that can be used to influence service quality in the area of employee management and company culture.

Employees of the company play a key role as customer contact personnel during the service delivery (see, e.g., Bitner *et al.* 1990). Therefore, **employee management** is an important area with regard to improving service quality with **personnel management** and **personnel supervision** (see also Chapter 16). In terms of personnel management, objectives related to service quality have to be adequately taken into consideration (for more on the associated tasks, please refer to Section 16.1). For example, hiring service-oriented employees is a key task. In the area of personnel supervision, which refers to the direct management of employees by their superiors, it is important to assess which management style promotes the development of service quality. In the scope of personnel supervision, it can generally be assumed that intensive communication between supervisors and employees about service quality can help to increase service quality. Furthermore, high service quality requires managers who demonstrate quality concepts and standards to the employees through their own decisions and activities.

With respect to the **company culture** (see also the discussion on market-oriented company culture in Chapters 17 and 18), a certain service and quality orientation has to be part of the company culture. Guidelines for ensuring service quality can be defined for this purpose.

In conclusion, we should point out that most of the approaches described here for influencing service quality can also be used for ensuring and maintaining the quality of tangible goods.

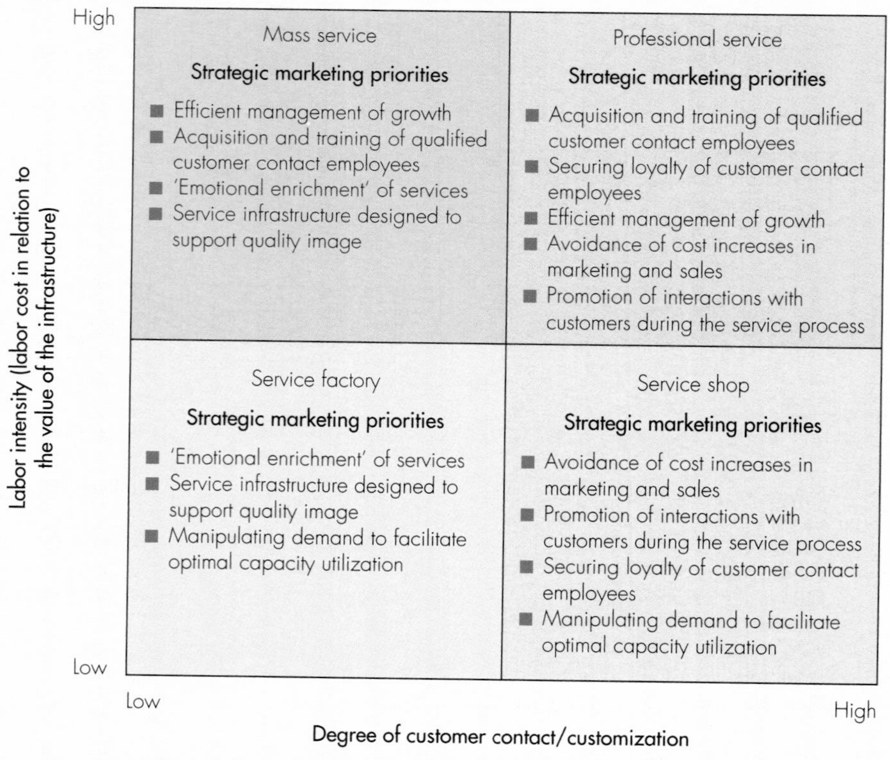

Figure 11-11 Strategic marketing priorities for various types of services (adapted from Verma 2000, p. 20)

11.3 Specific Characteristics of Services Marketing

In principle, the discussion of the strategic perspective of marketing (see Part 1 of this book) also applies to service providers. For example, the analysis of the initial situation (as presented in Chapter 3) generally does not depend on the type of product or service being marketed. The guiding questions related to the formulation of the strategy (see Chapter 4) are relevant for any company, regardless of whether it offers products or services. For this reason, the issues discussed in Part 1 of this book will not be repeated in this section with regard to service companies. Rather, we will discuss the specific characteristics pertaining to the strategic marketing of services.

In this connection, it is especially useful to address the distinctive service characteristics: intangibility, perceived purchase risk, inseparability, perishability and variability (for more information, see Section 11.1). The effect of service characteristics on strategic options can also be analyzed on the basis of a service typology, as illustrated in Figure 11-3. In the diagram, services are classified using the criteria of the degree of customer interaction/customization and personnel costs in relation to the value of the infrastructure. The different service types necessitate different strategic marketing priorities (see Verma 2000; Figure 11-11).

Service characteristics can also be affected by strategic decisions on the part of the service provider. Taking banks as an example, Figure 11-12 demonstrates that various processes inherent in the provision of services can be positioned in different ways. Thus, for example, back-of-house

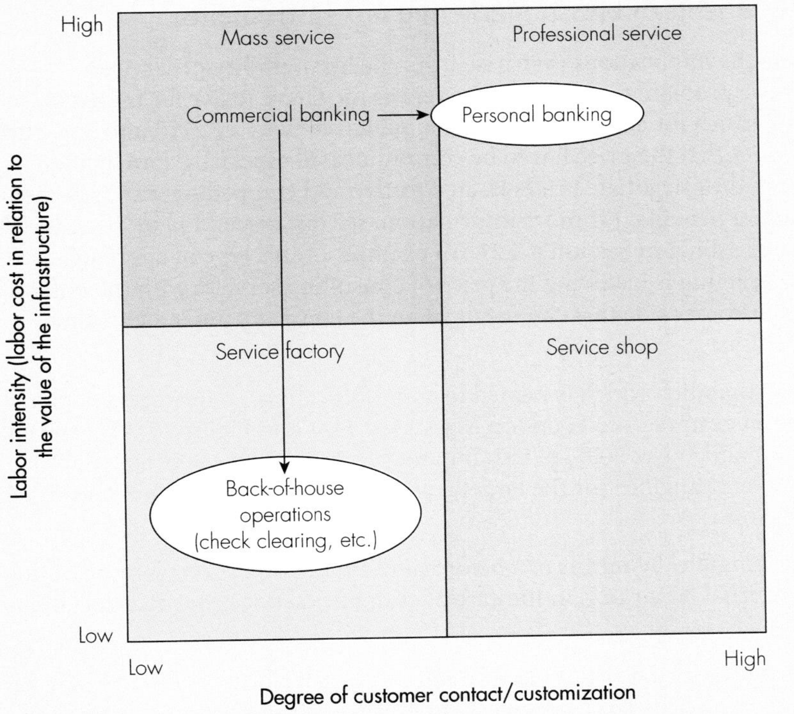

Figure 11-12 Different strategic positioning of processes inherent in the provision of services, taking banks as an example (adapted from Schmenner 1992)

operations can be conceived as a service factory, whereas the consulting-intensive processes, such as personal banking, that take place during customer interactions can be characterized as professional service.

In summary, service characteristics can be both influencing variables and design objects of the marketing strategy. Accordingly, there are interdependencies between service characteristics and the strategic orientation of service companies.

11.4 An Expanded Marketing Mix in Services Marketing

In Part 2 of this book we discussed the different instruments of the marketing mix. These instruments are relevant for the marketing of tangible goods as well as services. In view of this, this section will address only those issues connected with the marketing mix that are specific to the marketing of services. Our discussion will mainly address the question of which implications for designing the marketing mix arise from distinctive service characteristics (intangibility, perceived purchase risk, inseparability, perishability and variability; see Section 11.1 for more information). In Section 11.4.1, we will deal with the implications of these service characteristics with respect to the classic components of the marketing mix (product decisions, price decisions, communication decisions and sales decisions). Finally, Section 11.4.2 will examine the specific characteristics that are important when additional components are included in the marketing mix for services (personnel decisions, physical evidence and process decisions).

11.4.1 Specific Characteristics of Classic Marketing Mix Instruments

We will start by discussing the implications that arise from the **intangibility** of services. Intangibility presents a basic problem for service providers as they have to ask for monetary compensation (a price) in return for a non-physical (intangible) service (see Zeithaml and Bitner 2000, p. 13). This necessitates that the price has to be communicated especially convincingly. In order to communicate and/or negotiate prices in an effective and compelling way, arguments have to be based on customer benefits (for more information, see our discussion of 'benefit selling' within the scope of personal selling in Section 6.4.2). An example of this type of approach used in business-to-business marketing is justifying the price of consulting services with the potential reduction of costs on the customer side that can result when the company implements the consultant's recommendations.

Another implication of intangibility, which is related to communication, is the necessity to make the service more tangible (for an example, see Focus on Marketing 11-1 and Figure 11-13), particularly in advertising (see Lovelock and Wirtz 2007, p. 157, for an overview; Palmer 2001, p. 16). The aim here is to make the service 'tangible' for the target segments of the advertising. Some possible approaches are outlined below.

- A service can be made 'tangible' by means of a before-and-after comparison, demonstrating a visible change to the external factor (e.g. in the case of cosmetics services or modernization of buildings).
- Tangibility in advertising can also be achieved through the visualization of concrete service results; examples include depicting a relaxed guest (when advertising vacations or spas) or people who appear to be financially independent (when advertising financial services).
- Finally, services can also be made tangible in advertisements to some extent by attractively staging the tangible environment of service delivery; examples here are the presentation of high-quality and tastefully furnished hotel rooms.

Focus on Marketing 11-1 Example of the individualization of services in the financial services industry

Deutsche Bank goes personal in India

Mumbai, July 26, 2006: Deutsche Bank announced today that it has launched a full suite of credit cards in India. The launch marks the second pillar of Deutsche Bank's consumer banking strategy in India – following the roll-out of retail banking last year. Deutsche Bank's suite of products consisting of Classic, Gold, Platinum and Corporate Credit Cards comes packed with a host of innovative features. The customer can personalize his card by choosing from over 40 credit card designs which have been selected across categories as diverse as music, wildlife, zodiac signs, sports and child art. This feature has been introduced for the first time in India. The Deutsche Bank Gold Card offers the additional option to customize the card providing the choice from several 'Savings Plans' structured around different key lifestyle and spend patterns. These different options called 'Home Plan', 'Party Plan', 'Shop Plan' and 'Travel Plan' enable customers to maximize savings based on their personal usage habits. In addition to this feature the customer also has the option of choosing his billing cycle to better manage and control his finances.

With these innovative features, Indian customers will now have a unique opportunity to own credit cards that truly reflect their personality and interests. Cricketing legend Mr. Sunil Gavaskar, who is Deutsche Bank's product ambassador in India, was presented with the Bank's first Platinum credit card by Mr. Colin Grassie, Chief Executive Officer – Asia-Pacific for Deutsche Bank. Speaking at the occasion Mr. Gavaskar said, 'The Deutsche Bank Credit Cards draw from the power and financial strength of a leading global bank. I am looking forward to enjoying a premium offering with a comprehensive range of lifestyle benefits.' Mr. Shameek Bhargava, Head of Cards – Asia-Pacific for Deutsche Bank said, 'Our credit cards offering has been designed in line with Deutsche Bank's customer-centric approach. We have introduced several unique features that enhance customization and convenience. We believe that this will bring back the customer involvement in a category, which has become increasingly commoditized.'

Figure 11-13 Examples of individualized credit cards (see http://deutschebank.co.in/CC_Classic_Card.html)

Source: http://deutschebank.co.in/Press_Releases.html.

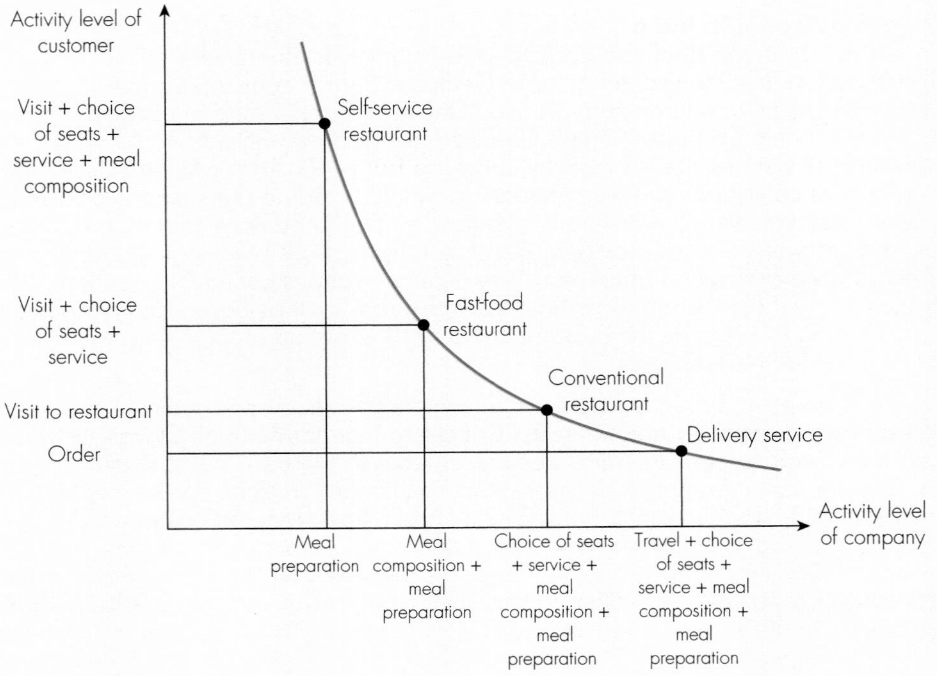

Figure 11-14 Design variants of customer integration into the service process, using the example of a restaurant (adapted from Meffert and Bruhn 2006, p. 56)

Due to their intangibility, services usually cannot be patented. The risk of successful services being rapidly copied by competitors is thus greater with services than with tangible goods (see Fitzsimmons and Fitzsimmons 1999, p. 33). Against this background, **product decisions** tend to be less important in terms of creating competitive advantage in the case of services as compared to tangible goods, which are characterized by a certain degree of protection against imitation. Therefore, additional components of the marketing mix are important in services marketing. These are personnel management and physical evidence, which are also referred to collectively as the **physical environment** (for more information, see Section 11.4.2).

For example, the use of **branding** is more complicated when it comes to services. With tangible goods, trademarks are usually displayed on the product or on its packaging. This is impossible in the case of services because they are essentially intangible (see Berry 2000). In view of this, it can be observed that many service companies use the infrastructure that is required for performing the service (e.g. the design of the service location, buildings, vehicles) or employees (e.g. on their working clothes) for advertising and branding purposes (also see Bruhn and Georgi 2006, p. 276; Webb Pressler 2005).

Finally, with respect to sales decisions, the intangibility of services results in the fact that indirect sales tend to be less important: there is no physical product that can be marketed by sales partners. Only service promises (e.g. admission tickets or flight tickets) can be marketed indirectly. Accordingly, facilitators (see Section 7.2.1 for more information) such as agents (e.g. travel agencies) or sales agencies (e.g. brokerage agencies for industrial services) play a certain role here, whereas intermediaries such as wholesalers or retailers (see Section 7.2.1) do not play such an important role.

The next service characteristic to be addressed is the **perceived purchase risk**, which arises in particular from the customer's level of uncertainty regarding quality. When marketing services it is important that the company aims for a reduction of the perceived purchase risk. Here are some approaches that will enable this to be achieved.

- From a customer perspective, an essential function of a brand is to reduce risk. Customers perceive brands as a quality promise made by the company. At this point, the **dilemma of branding** for service providers becomes obvious: on the one hand, due to the customer's quality uncertainty, brands are highly relevant to services marketing. However, as already described above, the intangibility of services impedes the use of branding concepts for services. Against this background, an umbrella branding strategy that places all service offerings of a company under one brand, is very widespread throughout the services sector. This strategy quite frequently uses the company's corporate name as the brand name. As compared to individual services, the company is more tangible to the customer.
- **Quality guarantees** represent another approach to reducing purchase risk (see Soberman 2003; Wirtz and Kum 2004). These guarantees are especially far-reaching and effective if they offer customers a full refund of the price paid if they are not satisfied with the product or service, regardless of the reason. Such guarantees are granted, for example, by certain hotel chains in the USA (see Zeithaml and Bitner 2003).
- **Promotional offers** (trial offers) at reduced prices can also contribute to reducing the customer's purchase risk. With these offers, customers are entitled to use lower-priced or even free services for a certain period of time in order to assess the quality of the service. For example, fitness clubs use these promotional offers.
- **Communication decisions** also offer approaches for reducing purchase risk. For example, service providers can advertise their services using opinion leaders and spokespersons, quality certificates, reference lists of existing customers or independent test results. With respect to reducing purchase risk, promoting communication between customers (word-of-mouth advertising) plays a special role, since many customers perceive peers to be more credible than advertising messages from companies (see Murray 1991). An example of this is the practice of arranging meetings between existing and potential customers during marketing events. This is frequently used by consulting firms.

Another implication of perceived purchase risk results from the fact that, in many cases, customers select high-priced products to compensate for uncertainty regarding quality. In such cases, the price functions as an indicator of product quality. This may lead to **image-based premium pricing** on the part of the service provider. Finally, the perceived purchase risk emphasizes the importance of selecting the right sales partners. As a rule, if customers have a negative perception of the sales partner, this will have a negative halo effect on the service or the service company itself. The halo effect is a bias in the perception of a brand, an ad, a product, etc. The halo effect occurs when the perception of a particular trait is influenced by the perception of other traits. In marketing, it refers to a situation where the most prominent feature of an object (e.g. a product, brand or company) carries over to all other attributes.

As pointed out earlier, **inseparability** refers to the fact that production and consumption of services occur at the same time. The most important consequence for service companies is that the production process becomes a crucial element in the company–customer interaction (Zeithaml *et al.* 2006). A key element in this interaction is that service employees can considerably influence the relationship with the service customer. The role of service employees is further pronounced as the simultaneous production and consumption involved in some services does not provide ample opportunity for quality control. The introduction of quality standards can be effective in exerting control over service delivery in order to ensure customer satisfaction.

We will now turn to the service characteristic of **perishability**. As already explained, this characteristic reflects the fact that services cannot be stored. The available service capacities of a provider (e.g. hotel, airline, freight forwarder) remain unutilized if they are not sold before a certain deadline. Considering this, the perishable nature of services necessitates the **harmonization of service capacities and service demand** (see Palmer 2001). There are two options for achieving this: making capacities more variable and flexible (e.g. an airline chartering additional planes to satisfy increased demand) and manipulating the demand. With regard to the latter aspect, marketing can help to bring capacity and demand more in line. For example, **temporal price differentiation** plays a key role here: during low demand periods, many providers offer their services at significantly lower prices than during high demand periods. Relevant examples include tour operators, telecommunications providers and energy suppliers. Last-minute offers are a particularly intensive form of temporal price differentiation.

In this context, **yield management** can also be an effective management tool (see McGill and Ryzin 1999). Yield management specifically aims to allocate service capacity to available demand so that profits or revenues are maximized (see Kimes 1992). For example, an airline can use yield management to allocate seats in an aircraft to several classes of service (e.g. first class, business class and economy class) so that revenues are maximized for a given demand situation. Sales promotion activities can support the yield management initiative.

We will now turn to the service characteristic of the **variability**, which is due to the customer being personally present during the provision of many services (**integration of external factors**) (see Bruhn and Georgi 2006, pp. 14f.; Corsten and Gössinger 2006; Meyer and Tostmann 1980). For the service provider, this gives rise to the question of to what extent the customer should assume an active role in the service delivery process. Based on a certain activity level on part of the customer, differentiation can be made between an **externalization strategy** and an **internalization strategy** (see Bruhn and Georgi 2006, pp. 179f.; Corsten 2000). With an externalization strategy, the service provider assigns a portion of the service to be rendered to the customer (e.g. partial self-service in restaurants by using self-service buffets or offering cash-and-carry self-assembly furniture). In contrast, with internalization strategies, service providers overtake activities that are normally conducted by the customer, thus reducing the customer activity level (e.g. special pick-up and delivery service provided by laundries and dry cleaners). Figure 11-14 illustrates various designs with respect to different customer activity levels in the service delivery process.

There are also consequences arising from the **integration of external factors** as this often implies the personal presence of the customer during the service delivery process. The presence of the customer during service delivery provides the service company with the opportunity to use the service delivery process to generate sales. Examples include financial services offered at automated teller machines, art being displayed at exclusive restaurants, and sales events during vacation trips. In principle, services thus provide excellent cross-selling opportunities (for more on cross-selling, see Section 7.5).

Moreover, the integration of external factors offers numerous opportunities for communicating with the customer in the course of the service delivery process. This increases the importance of personal communication with the customer. In particular, this implies that service providers need to systematically design the personal communication between the customer contact personnel and the customers. This is especially relevant when communicating critical information (e.g. justifying price increases).

With regard to pricing, the integration of external factors facilitates **price differentiation** (see Section 6.3.1) in two ways: first, direct customer contact makes it possible for the company to explain the reasons for varying prices to its customers, which can increase their acceptance of price differentiation. Second, the integration of external factors allows service providers to better evaluate the prerequisites for price differentiation measures (e.g. entitlement of the customer to a certain pricing scheme).

Finally, the integration of external factors makes the **close proximity** of the service providers to their customers a key issue. This aspect is particularly relevant to sales. In many service sectors, such as hotels and fast-food restaurants, many service providers maintain closeness to their customers via franchise systems (see Section 7.2.1). Experiences in numerous service sectors demonstrate that the use of online communication does not usually adequately compensate for insufficient proximity to the customer. Sometimes online security concerns can also be an impediment (for more information, see Focus on Marketing 11-2 on the challenges of online banking).

Focus on Marketing 11-2 Challenges of online banking

Online banking: increasing satisfaction but facing hurdles

A recent survey by Forbes.com and ForeSee Results found that customers who pay bills online are more satisfied than those who do not, providing banks an opportunity to increase satisfaction and loyalty by converting online bankers to online bill payers.

However, banks face significant challenges to achieving widespread adoption of the Web channel and to maintaining ownership of the online bill payment relationship. The survey found that 75 percent of online banking respondents pay bills directly at vendor web sites and other third party payment services instead of at their own bank.

The survey found that there is a wide discrepancy in perception of privacy issues between current online banking users and prospective users. Specifically, 34 percent of prospective online banking respondents cited privacy concern as a barrier to adoption.

'For banks the key message is that there is tremendous payoff for encouraging their customers to pay bills at the bank site. The more bills customers pay on their bank's Web site, the more satisfied they are and the more likely they are to purchase more products and services from their bank – online or in a branch,' said Larry Freed, an online satisfaction expert and head of ForeSee Results.

'Privacy concerns used to be a main impediment among online banking customers and prospects alike. Now, those who are banking online find they're comfortable with what they're asked to divulge,' said Freed. 'However, among prospects, banks will clearly benefit from doing a better job of addressing privacy and security concerns.'

Source: tellervision 2005.

11.4.2 The Additional Marketing Mix Components Required by Services

In the literature on services marketing, it has increasingly been acknowledged that the traditional breakdown of the marketing mix into the areas of product, pricing, communication and sales decisions needs to be supplemented with regard to services. In the service sector, the following three components are generally added to the four 'classic' components of the marketing mix (the 'four Ps'):

1 personnel decisions

2 physical evidence decisions

3 process decisions.

These additional 'three Ps' (personnel, physical evidence – also known as the 'physical environment' – and process) complement the classic market mix components and form the basis of the **expanded services marketing mix** shown in Figure 11-15.

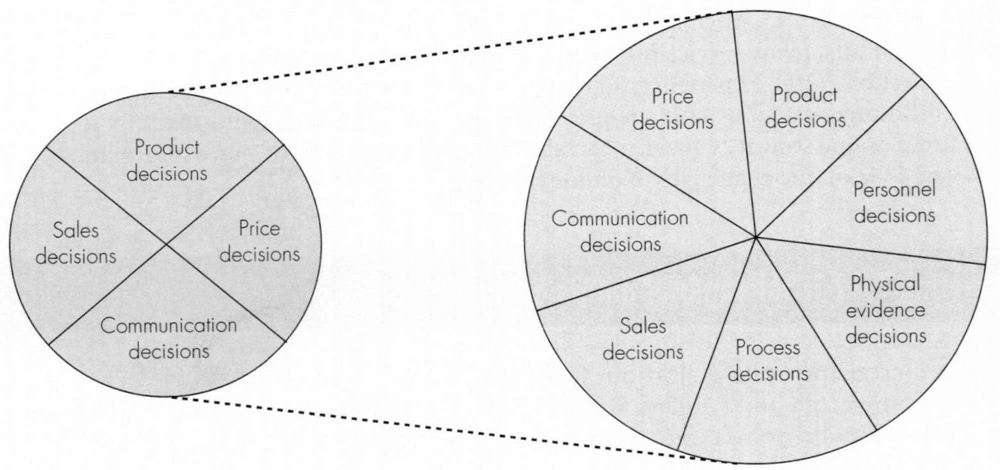

Figure 11-15 The expanded marketing mix in the service sector (adapted from Magrath 1986, p. 45)

The relevance of these additional marketing mix components can in turn be derived from the key service characteristics, as follows.

- Due to their **intangibility**, services usually cannot be patented. The risk of successful services being copied rapidly by competitors is thus greater with services than with tangible goods. Against this background, product decisions tend to be less important in terms of creating competitive advantage in the case of services as compared to tangible goods, which are characterized by a certain degree of protection against imitation. Personnel, physical evidence and pricing play a certain key role in creating competitive advantage.
- Measures implemented in the area of personnel, physical evidence and pricing can act as quality indicators for customers, thus reducing their **perceived purchase risk**. This applies, for example, to highly competent personnel as well as having an attractive service environment. For instance, the building and premises of a financial services provider could express respectability, financial solvency and high service quality.
- Obviously, the **variability and integration of external factors** also underlines the great relevance of all three areas (particularly personnel).

In the following, we will briefly outline the primary objectives related to these three additional marketing mix components. Figure 11-16 provides a corresponding overview.

Within the scope of **personnel decisions**, a key objective is to ensure that the service employees are highly competent. In addition to professional and social competence (which can aid in reducing service-related quality uncertainty on the part of customers), employees should also exhibit decision-making proficiency when interacting directly with customers. These service employees can be instructed and can support the customization of the service process to meet individual needs as they emerge during service delivery. Critical in this regard is the concept of employee **empowerment**, which offers customer contact employees a relatively high degree of independence and decision-making flexibility when dealing with customers (for more on this concept, see Bowen and Lawler 1992, 1995, 1999).

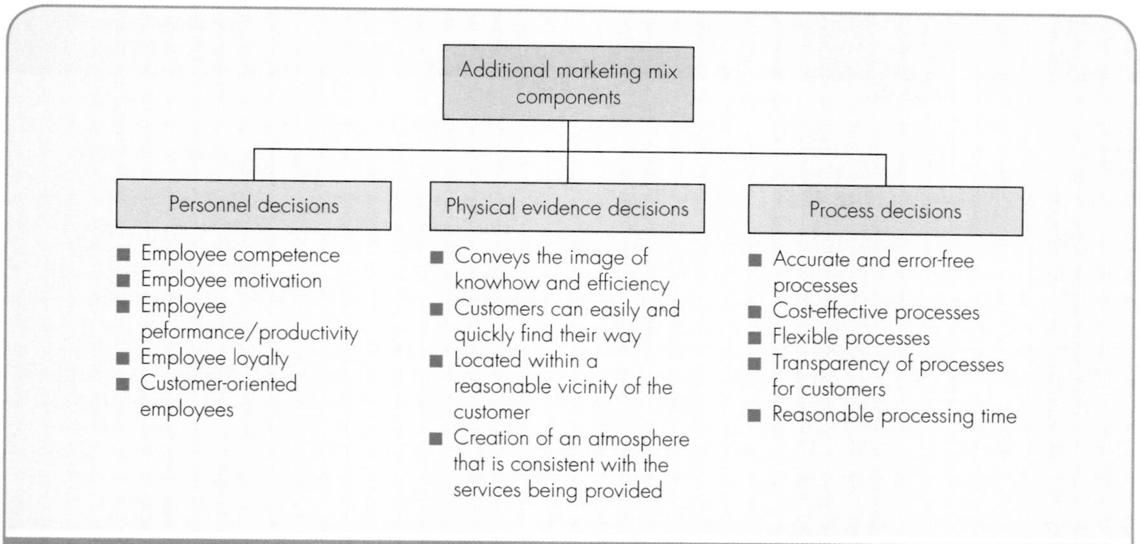

Figure 11-16 Basic objectives related to the three additional marketing mix components in services

Another important objective of personnel management is ensuring **high motivation on the part of employees**: only motivated employees use their full potential and incorporate it into the service process. Motivation and incentive systems play a central role in realizing this goal (for a discussion of these types of system in a service context, see Hentze and Lindert 1998). For example, employees can be offered monetary compensation for customer satisfaction in order to encourage employee motivation and thus foster a stronger service orientation (for more information on service orientation, see Berry and Seiders 2002; Homburg *et al.* 2002).

Maintaining **employee performance and productivity** represents another top-priority management task. In particular, overwork and, in the long term, burnout of employees who have direct contact with customers have to be avoided in order to maintain the desired quality of customer interaction. Sales counters and call centers are two examples of areas in which this management task is especially important (see, e.g., Deery *et al.* 2002). In conjunction with this objective, employees who are well suited to customer contact positions should already have been selected during the hiring process. Furthermore, within the scope of personnel training and further education courses, service employees should be taught strategies for handling frequent customer contact (for an in-depth examination of this concept, see Homburg and Stock 2000). Finally, timely measures should be taken to ease the workload of employees who have intense direct contact with customers or to make sure they are relieved by co-workers.

Employee loyalty is yet another objective of personnel management. Here it is particularly important for a service company to establish low employee turnover. This objective is particularly relevant in light of the fact that, in many companies, customers display a certain loyalty towards employees, which can be even greater than their loyalty to the company. In the worst-case scenario, customers switch companies if the respective employee leaves the company (as can be observed in, for example, the investment banking sector, advertising agencies, engineering firms and architects' offices).

With decisions regarding **physical evidence**, the visible factors of the service infrastructure (also called 'physical environment', such as the buildings, vehicles, decor and interior furnishings of sales, reception or meeting rooms, and employee uniforms) come into play. On account of the intangibility of services, such visible factors are used by customers as indicators of service quality. Consequently,

Focus on Marketing 11-3 Example of employee uniforms as physical evidence of the service

McDonald's have hired celebrity designer Bruce Oldfield to create the uniforms for its 67,000 UK staff. Oldfield is renowned for his glamorous gowns worn by the late Diana, Princess of Wales and counts Catherine Zeta Jones and Jerry Hall as his clients.

The new uniforms which were unveiled in April 2008 consist of black and mocha polo shirts, black cargo style trousers, a black and mocha baseball cap, black belt and apron for the employees, whilst managers will wear black suits with white or biscuit colored shirts and a choice of three ties.

In an effort to update the fast food giant's image and connect with young employees and customers McDonald's wanted to create a retro look that would capture the 'spirit of being young forever' and that heralded back to the 1960s when the company was first expanding. Experts believe that the new look clothes could help its mass market image and make its entry level jobs more attractive.

McDonald's spokesman David Fairhurst said: 'It's a mark of respect for our staff that an internationally renowned designer has created the uniform especially for them. Our people do a challenging job serving two million customers a day and we want them to feel good doing it. We believe the new designer uniforms will help achieve this, and better reflect the opportunities and aspirations that jobs and careers at McDonald's can offer.'

Just over two thirds of staff who trialed the new uniform preferred it to the old one, with almost half saying it made them feel more confident when dealing with customers.

In recent years McDonald's has attempted a major rebranding in a bid to shed its unhealthy and environmentally unfriendly image to attract more customers. Restaurants have been made over – with soft lights, wooden tables and sofas among other new designs – and salads have become best-selling items. Not content with that, the chain's latest green initiative is to turn its spent cooking oil into biodiesel fuel to power its vans in the UK.

Source: adapted from Burger and chic, *Daily Mail*, 23 April 2008.

these factors should be designed in a way that conveys to customers a positive image of the knowhow and efficiency of the service provider (see Focus on Marketing 11-3 for an example of employee uniforms).

Furthermore, the customer's purchase decision process can be manipulated to the benefit of the company if the service infrastructure is designed to be customer-friendly, so that customers can quickly find their way and relatively easily attain an overview of the range of services offered by the company.

Another chief objective is to establish locations within a reasonable vicinity of the customer. Companies should set up as many branch offices as possible for selling and/or providing services. Franchising is a key concept in this respect, since it enables the setting up of branches that are conveniently located for customers, but does not require a major investment on the part of the service company. Another option for meeting this goal is to have service company employees render the services directly on-site at the customer's premises (e.g. catering services, house calls by doctors).

The customer's purchase decision can also be influenced to the company's benefit if it uses its infrastructure to create an atmosphere that is consistent with the services being provided (for a detailed study, see Lovelock *et al.* 1999). Interior design, music selection, lighting and scents can be used to create an atmosphere that is in line with the services offered by the company (refer to the section on retail marketing in Section 11.5 for an in-depth discussion of this topic).

With regard to **process decisions**, the individual steps of the service process need to be defined. Equally, the tasks of the stakeholders involved in the service process – both functional departments within the company as well as customers – have to be specified when designing and structuring organization of the workflow. In addition, the time frame of the service process has to be planned. The objectives of process decisions basically relate to **process quality** and are thus closely related to the management of service quality. The key issues with regard to process quality are listed below.

- A first aspect of process quality relates to **maintaining an error-free service process** (for more information on this topic, also see Bougie *et al.* 2003; Hess *et al.* 2003).
- It is of course obvious that **cost-effective processes** represent a main objective for service providers (as well as for customers). Such cost-effective processes can help to increase profitability and establish lower price levels.
- Another objective is to attain **flexibility of processes**. To be able to respond promptly to changes in customer preferences and thus realize a high level of service quality, the service process should be flexible enough so that limited deviations from the process routine do not interfere with the successful execution of the process.
- The customer's quality assessment of the service process is positively influenced by the degree of **transparency of processes**. The higher the transparency, the more understanding the customer will have when quality problems occur.
- Finally, we need to mention the goal of **reasonable processing times**, which is greatly relevant to customers when assessing process quality. Here, the issue is whether customers use the service to save time (e.g. express delivery service) or for amusement (e.g. a leisure time activity) (see Stauss 1991). The duration tends to be more important in the former case.

11.5 Retailing

Retailing is 'the set of business activities that adds value to the products and services sold to consumers for their personal or family use' (Levy and Weitz 2007, p. 7; Gilbert 2003, p. 6; Berman and Evans 2007, p. 4). Retail marketing refers to those marketing activities that commercial enterprises use to target their customers (see Levy and Weitz 2003). Retail marketing has to be differentiated from trade marketing by companies that cater to commercial businesses.

In Section 11.5.1, we will address basic concepts in retail marketing. This is followed in Section 11.5.2 by a discussion of the specific characteristics of the marketing mix that arise in retail marketing.

11.5.1 The Importance of Retailing

Wholesalers and retailers play an important role in a distribution channel. A distribution channel is defined as a set of businesses that facilitates the movement of goods and services from the point of production to the point of sale to the customer (see Levy and Weitz 2007, p. 7; Berman and Evans 2007, p. 8). In Section 7.2.1 we characterized external sales entities (see Figure 7-1); two important sales partners (sales entities that are independent of the company) are wholesalers and retailers. These intermediaries aim to realize profits by acquiring and subsequently selling, on their own account, unmodified or only slightly modified products (for a similar definition, see Berekoven 1995). 'Slightly modified' refers to the fact that these intermediaries frequently offer services in conjunction with the tangible goods they sell, which might include minor product modifications (e.g. adjustments or alterations made specifically for the customer). Wholesaler and retailer can be categorized depending on the customer segment they target. **Wholesalers** target business customers (e.g. retailers or manufacturers that further process the goods acquired), while **retailers** focus on end customers. In this chapter, we will concentrate on retailers.

The functions that retailers fulfill in sales channels between product manufacturers and customers have already been described in Chapter 7 when we compared direct and indirect sales channels (Section 7.2.2). The retailer has the following **retailer functions** to fulfill: transport function, temporal buffer function, quantitative product assortment function (breaking bulk), qualitative product assortment function, credit/financing function and advertising/market impact function. In addition, in Chapter 7 we provided the rationale for the existence of intermediaries in sales channels (reduction of transaction costs through the use of retailers). The dominant issue here concerns the extent to which the inclusion of intermediaries can reduce transaction costs as compared to the direct sales approach. Although direct selling by a manufacturer can be a cost-effective way to serve customers, retail businesses often supersede this value-creating function in a cost-effective way (see Levy and Weitz 2007). They represent crucial sales partners for many manufacturing firms (see Table 11-1 for a list of the largest retailers in the world).

There are various categories of retailer. Because of the large number of **alternative forms of retailing**, retail institutions can be classified in several ways – by:

- retail location
- internationality
- product range
- price level
- sales area
- service principle.

In general, store and non-store retailing can be distinguished with regard to retail location. Store retailers are retailers that offer their goods at a fixed location such as markets and physical store facilities. Non-store retailing is not restricted to a fixed location (i.e. sales are not limited to stores). Non-store retailing includes automatic and street vending, direct mail and catalogs, television home shopping, online retailing and direct selling (i.e. representatives of the retailer visit customers in their own homes).

In recent years, there has been a decrease in the importance of conventional mail-order selling (e.g. catalog mail order) and a corresponding increase in the importance of another form of mail-order selling, namely online selling (also called e-commerce or internet-based mail-order selling) (see EHI 2005, p. 206). With this type of mail-order selling, products are offered, ordered and, in most cases, paid for online (see Siegel 2004, p. 6, for a more general discussion of the significance of the internet for the commercial sector; see also Hoffman *et al.* 1995; Siegel 2004, p. 17).

While e-commerce still uses conventional transportation channels (e.g. mail or parcel delivery services) for shipping the physical products, a specific characteristic of internet-based mail-order selling lies in the fact that digital products (e.g. software, music, movies) can be transmitted directly via the data network. Key advantages of internet-based mail-order systems include the ability to update the product range and price structure in a relatively quick and cost-efficient manner, as well as tailor them to individual customers and customer segments. Moreover, such systems offer the interesting option of generating real-time and computer-aided special product recommendations to specific customers based on their preferences or customer profile (see Levy and Weitz 2007, pp. 74ff.; Siegel 2004, pp. 4, 15). Online retailing could gain even more influence in the future,

Table 11-1 The world's top 25 retailers (Deloitte 2008)

Rank	Company (headquarters)	2006 retail sales (US$m)	2001–2006 retail sales CAGR*
1	Wal-Mart (US)	344,992	11.1%
2	Carrefour (FR)	97,861	2.3%
3	The Home Depot (US)	90,837	11.1%
4	Tesco (UK)	79,976	12.5%
5	Metro (DE)	74,857	4.0%
6	Kroger (US)	66,111	5.7%
7	Target (US)	59,490	8.3%
8	Costco (US)	58,963	11.6%
9	Sears (US)	53,012	8.0%
10	Schwarz-Group (DE)[e]	52,422	12.0%
11	Aldi (DE)[e]	50,010	4.4%
12	Walgreen (US)	47,409	14.0%
13	Lowe's (US)	46,927	16.2%
14	Rewe (DE)[e]	45,850	2.2%
15	Seven & I (JP)[e]	43,835	–
16	Auchan (FR)	43,154	5.6%
17	Edeka (DE)[e]	40,749	5.0%
18	CVS (US)	40,286	13.6%
19	Safeway (US)	40,185	3.2%
20	E. Leclerc (FR)[e]	38,692	3.9%
21	Aeon (JP)	38,058	8.9%
22	Koninklijke Ahold (NL)	37,149	–6.5%
23	Best Buy (US)	35,934	12.9%
24	Intermarché (FR)[e]	33,678	–3.8%
25	Woolworths (AUS)	32,456	11.8%

Ranking based on retail sales 2006; *CAGR = compound annual growth rate; [e] estimate.

especially for digital products. The long-tail phenomenon (Anderson 2006) postulates that demand for niche products distributed via the internet can outstrip demand for seemingly blockbuster products distributed via physical stores (see Focus on Marketing 11-4 for an example and Section 7.2.2 for a discussion of the long tail).

Focus on Marketing 11-4 Example of a long-tail economy

The long-tail effect of digital film archives

The BBC's Future Media & Technology Director Ashley Highfield launched iPlayer in the summer of 2007. iPlayer is a treasure trove of 1.2 million hours of film, where and when we want, and for free. The service will also be available via links from YouTube and could also appear on other websites such as MSN, Bebo and Facebook.

The key weapon in this transition, he believes, was the BBC's film archive. 'We've got one of the world's largest archives, if not the largest archive. And yet, because we've got so few channels – routes to our audience – inevitably 99.9 per cent of that content stays on the shelves. We ought to liberate it and make it available, how, when and where our audience would like to consume it.'

Opening up the archive offers a wealth of possibilities, Highfield says. 'My dad when he heard about it really got excited because he knew we had shot some footage from the Hendon air show before the Second World War. Every person's interest will be different. My interest is that I would love to be able to go into the archive and pick out clips of Ferraris. Not just the obvious things like *Top Gear* but all the little clips that maybe the BBC [doesn't know about]. Someone will know that there's just a fantastic little clip of a Dino on a 1969 episode of *Nationwide*.'

The BBC's iPlayer allows internet users to view the corporation's television shows for a week after they are broadcast. A similar audio service, bbc.co.uk/radio, already attracts 13 million listeners every month. Over time other features will be added to the iPlayer including live streaming of

Focus on Marketing 11-4 (Continued)

programs, the BBC Radio Player and 'series stacking', which will allow users to download episodes from series retrospectively.

Trials of iPlayer suggested that users are far more likely to try out shows from digital channels that have been largely ignored on television. Highfield believes that the introduction to the internet of television archives will create the same 'long-tail effect' as that seen elsewhere online, where the interest in vast numbers of niche products actually outweighs the demand for the small number of high-profile offerings. 'I think the long-tail effect is going to be just as seismic for the television industry as it has been for the book industry and the record industry.'

Director General Mark Thompson said: 'Forty years ago, in July 1967, BBC Television launched color TV. In our view, the iPlayer is at least as big a redefinition of what TV can be, what radio can be, what broadcasting can be, as what color television was 40 years ago.'

Source: Burrell 2006.

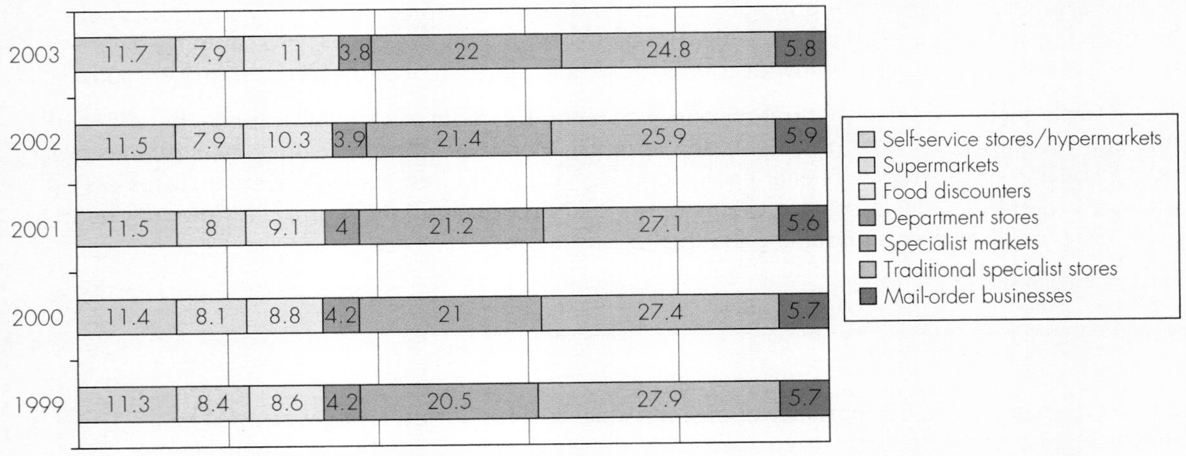

Figure 11-17 Business forms in the German retail sector: market share development (author unknown 2005, p. 12)

Figure 11-17 illustrates the development of the different forms of retailing in Germany. While the market situation of hypermarkets essentially remains stable, specialized markets are becoming increasingly important, which can in particular be attributed to the relatively low price level and, frequently, to convenient locations in suburban areas or on greenfield sites (see Zentes and Swoboda 1999). Discounters are also recording growth (see Focus on Marketing 11-5). Conversely, market share is diminishing for the traditional, small and medium-sized (independent) specialist stores that are mostly located in downtown areas and are often not able to keep up with the low price level of the specialist markets due to their lower level of competitiveness (see Liebmann and Zentes 2001). This trend towards a reduction in the number of traditional specialized stores is also associated with the depopulation of downtown areas. In conjunction with this decline, an increasing number of small and medium-sized specialist stores have been turned into chain stores: larger specialist retailers acquire smaller specialist stores that are unable to maintain competitive pace with the market development.

Focus on Marketing 11-5 Growing importance of discounters

Europeans warm to bargain groceries

European retailers have often dismissed Germany's hard-discount grocers as a local anomaly. But the country's two most successful discount chains are bringing their tactics to other parts of Europe and altering the rules of the grocery business. And hard-discount stores don't appeal just to low-income bargain hunters, a McKinsey survey indicates. They enjoy strong acceptance among a majority of Germans and are attracting loyal customers elsewhere.

The German chains – Aldi (Albrecht Discounts, which operates as two separate companies, Aldi Nord and Aldi Süd) and Lidl (Lidl & Schwarz) – eschew frills in a single-minded quest for rock-bottom prices. At 300 to 1,100 square meters (about 3,230 to 11,840 square feet), their stores are smaller than traditional supermarkets, which average 1,000 to 1,200 square meters. Both chains also offer their customers fewer choices (just 600 to 2,000 products, compared with about 7,000 to 9,000 at a typical supermarket), and private-label products predominate.

German respondents who shop at Aldi and Lidl said that they have much better prices than Edeka and REWE, competing traditional supermarket chains. Moreover, these customers rated the two hard-discounters highly in areas such as service and product assortment, where the broader selection and larger staffs of the traditional competitors should have given them an advantage. Market share trends reflect the popularity of the hard-discount stores: from 1999 to 2003, Aldi's increased by 2.5 percentage points, while Lidl gained 4.3. They are driving growth in the entire hard-discount segment, which now accounts for almost 40 percent of all German grocery sales.

Tough rivals such as France's Carrefour and the United Kingdom's Tesco will impede the efforts of Aldi and Lidl to make similar gains outside Germany. Moreover, consumers in some countries are used to paying a premium for better choice and higher quality. In our survey, French customers acknowledged Lidl's low prices, for example, but said that Auchan and Carrefour were far ahead in product assortment and in gaining the trust of customers.

Source: Hansen and Kliger 2004.

In addition to changes in the importance of the individual business forms, changes can also be observed with respect to the competitive structure in the retail sector: in particular, a growing trend towards the formation of oligopolies in the retail sector has been observed in recent years (see Peterson and Balasubramanian 2002; Rudolph and Einhorn 2001).

11.5.2 Specific Characteristics of Retail Marketing

In this section we will examine the specific issues that arise with regard to the marketing mix when considering retailing. We will discuss product decisions, pricing decisions, communication decisions and sales decisions, and furthermore, highlight additional components of the marketing mix: point-of-sale and human resources.

Specific Characteristics Related to Classic Marketing Mix Components: Product Decisions

We will base our discussion on the three main decision-making areas of product decisions (see also Chapter 5): innovation management, management of established products, and brand management. With respect to retailers, it must first be stated that innovation management is rather secondary in importance here: as a rule, retailers tend not to develop new physical products. If at all, innovation activities are undertaken for new services.

In contrast, the decisions we will address within the scope of managing established products (see Section 5.3) are crucial for retailers. This is especially the case for decisions concerning the width and depth of the product mix (in the retail sector, the term 'assortment' is frequently used instead of product mix). Principally, retailers have to make the same decisions regarding assortment as companies in other industry sectors. However, due to the enormous scope of the product range in retailing, product assortment decisions in the retail sector take on a special quality. Therefore, this section will briefly discuss the challenges in making product assortment decisions.

A question that is closely connected to product assortment decisions concerns the extent to which retailers should integrate services into their product portfolio. In recent years in particular, there has been a trend among intermediaries in numerous Western countries to increasingly emphasize services as a tool for both creating customer loyalty as well as to set themselves apart from competitors (for more information, see Homburg *et al.* 2002 and the literature cited therein).

The third area of product decisions – brand management – is also relevant to retailers, concerning both the role of retailers within the scope of the brand management of manufacturers, and with regard to private-label brands.

In summary, we will discuss three main specific characteristics of retail marketing with regard to product decisions:

1 product assortment design
2 design of services
3 brand management design.

Product Assortment Design

A first decision with regard to the assortment concerns the basic assortment structure (static design of assortment). This corresponds to a large extent to the decision concerning the basic structure of the product mix as it relates to the width and depth of the product line a retailer carries.

The **product assortment width** is characterized by the number of different product lines or types of goods. Consequently, a broad product assortment is characterized by a large number of different product lines. A comparatively large range of products is available at department stores, since they offer a broad variety of different product lines, whereas specialized stores offer a more narrow product assortment.

Product assortment depth (variety) refers to the number of different items that are offered within each product line. A product assortment is considered deep if, say, a wide variety of different articles is being offered within a product line.

Table 11-2 provides an overview of the number of different items included in three product lines, broken down by four types of retailer: self-service department store, hypermarket, supermarket and discounter. The differences are very marked, especially between the self-service department store and discounter.

Studies on the depth of product assortments demonstrate that not only the actual variety of an assortment can increase the quantity consumed but also the perceived variety can influence consumption (see Kahn and Wansink 2004). However, a product assortment that is too deep poses the risk of information overload on the part of the customer. This, in turn, can adversely affect their buying behavior (see Huffman and Kahn 1998; Iyengar and Lepper 2000).

Service Design

Service design represents a second area in product decisions in retail marketing. Augmenting products with services is an important way for retailers to gain differentiation. When retailers design the services offered, decisions have to be made concerning (see Homburg *et al.* 2002):

Table 11-2 Product assortment depth for different product lines and retailer types (Eurohandelsinstitut eV 2002, p. 242)

Product line	Type of retailer	Average number of items sold
Beer	Self-service department store	187
	Hypermarket	171
	Supermarket	101
	Discounter	9
Baby food	Self-service department store	506
	Hypermarket	338
	Supermarket	141
	Discounter	0
Ice cream	Self-service department store	161
	Hypermarket	149
	Supermarket	102
	Discounter	22

- the number of different services to be offered
- the number of customers to whom these services should be offered
- how strongly these services are actively offered to customers.

The service orientation of retailers can have a positive influence on company performance (see Homburg *et al.* 2002). However, the service strategy of competitors also has to be considered in this regard. As a rule, additional services are associated with higher costs, so that a retailer with a strong focus on services runs the risk of losing extremely price-conscious customers to competitors that offer no or only a few additional services. One problem in this context is the 'theft' of consulting services on the part of customers, which refers, for example, to the situation where a customer seeks advice in a store location but purchases the product in another retail outlet or online.

Brand Management

A third area in the context of the specific characteristics of retail marketing related to product decisions is brand management. Brand management of retailers can be divided into:

- the role of retailers within the scope of the brand management of the manufacturers
- the role of private-label brands.

An important characteristic here concerns the **role of retailers within the scope of the brand management of the manufacturer.** A central aspect of this is the consideration that the manufacturer brands selected in line with the product assortment should complement the image of the retailer. If the image of the retailer is consistent with the brand promise of the manufacturer, it can help boost the success of the retailer (for information on the consistency of manufacturer brand image and retailer image, see also Jacoby and Mazursky 1984).

A second area of brand management is the **design of private-label brands** (for an in-depth discussion, see Ailawadi *et al.* 2001; Dhar and Hoch 1997; Mills 1995; Raju *et al.* 1995; Richardson

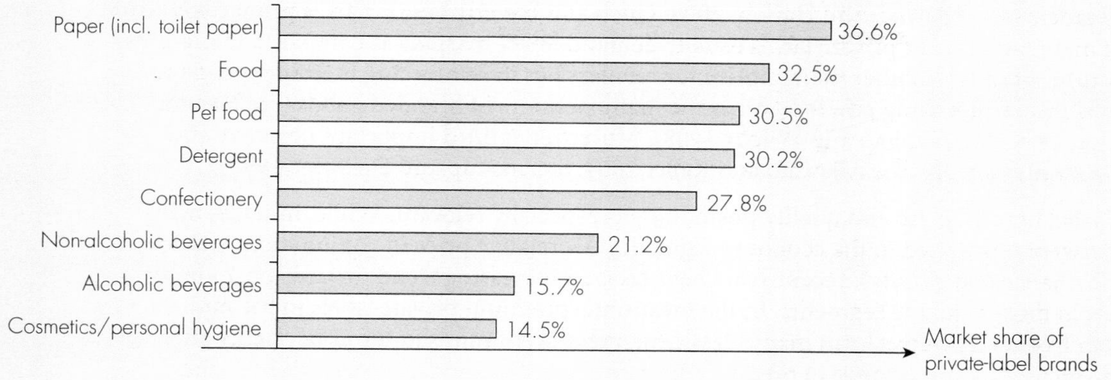

Figure 11-18 Private labels: share in retail sales classified by product category (adapted from GfK 2003)

1997). Private labels, which are also called store brands or own-label brands, are defined as 'consumer products which are produced by or on behalf of, distributors and sold under the distributor's own name or trademark through the distributor's own outlet' (Morris 1979). Meanwhile, this type of brand has become a real threat to manufacturer brands (Halstead and Ward 1995, p. 38). As illustrated in Figure 11-18, private labels have established strong market share in a number of product categories.

This trend can generally be observed globally. In 2005, value sales of private labels in 38 countries across 80 categories accounted for 17% overall, an increase of 5% on the year before. Europe was the most developed private-label region, with a share of value sales of 23% (ACNielsen 2005).

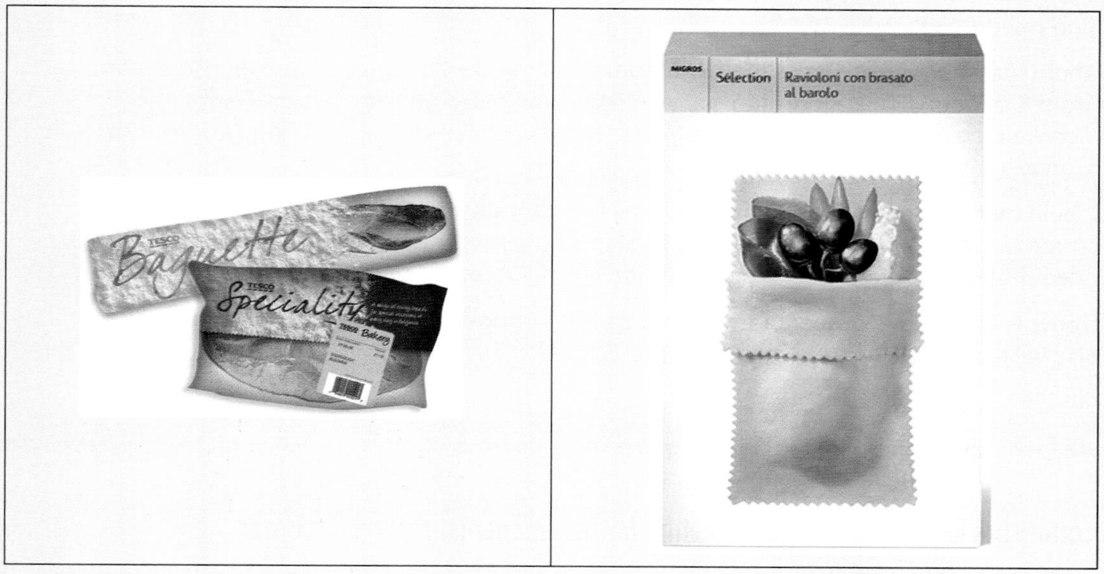

Figure 11-19 Examples of private labels in the UK and Switzerland

A key motive for retailers to introduce private-label brands is that they are an important source of profits for retailers (see Ailawadi and Harlam 2004; Hoch and Banerji 1993). This is primarily due to the fact that manufacturers of private labels usually demand lower margins as compared to margins for manufacturer brands. Another main motive for retailers lies in reinforcing their independence from and thus their negotiating power towards the manufacturers of branded goods (see Nandan and Dickinson 1994; Narasimhan and Wilcox 1998). Moreover, a third important objective aims to increase customer loyalty (see Ailawadi and Keller 2004; Steenkamp and Dekimpe 1997).

For private-label brands, price and quality positioning is especially relevant. While, initially, many private labels were positioned in the economy segment (low relative price in conjunction with low relative performance and quality), recent years have seen an increasing trend towards positioning private labels in higher-quality segments. In the meantime, premium private labels in the mid-price segment frequently outperform many classic manufacturer brands in terms of quality and price (on the increasing importance of premium private labels, see also Sayman *et al.* 2002 and Focus on Marketing 11-6). Figure 11-20 illustrates the price differences between private-label and manufacturer brands.

Focus on Marketing 11-6 Example of a private-label success based on quality

A private-label success story

Private label has been a tough go for many retailers in the United States, but Costco has turned Kirkland Signature into one of the most successful own-brands in the country. Target may come out with a new private label every week and IKEA may have made the retail and product brand one, but no other retailer has come as close to developing a successful private label across categories.

To be able to successfully sell national brands and private labels together hasn't been easy for US retailers. Some notable successes have been in general merchandise, particularly at Sears. But no US retailer of real size has been able to build a private label that commanded enough trust from shoppers to make it a hit throughout the store, both in durable goods and consumables, above the opening price point.

The fact that Loblaw sat right across the US border with President's Choice, taunting American retailers from Canada with its storewide success, was even more galling. Yet, even when US retailers licensed the President's Choice program, they couldn't make it work nearly as well as it did in Canada.

Kirkland, built methodically over many years, now is widely accepted throughout the store by Costco customers. From Seattle to Sarasota, Kirkland hamburger patties are a barbecue staple in the United States today, just one example of the line's successful products.

Costco's private-label development rested on a quality proposition, one in contrast to usual store-brand versus national-brand relationship.

Source: Duff 2005.

Specific Characteristics Related to Classic Marketing Mix Components: Pricing Decisions

The pricing of individual items is the first decision area in pricing (see Chapter 6 for general information). In this context, the purchase price of an item represents the base price, to which a margin is added. The amount of the mark-up (which is also called a trade margin) is influenced by both the costs for the retailer (see Section 6.3.2 for information on cost-plus pricing), as well as

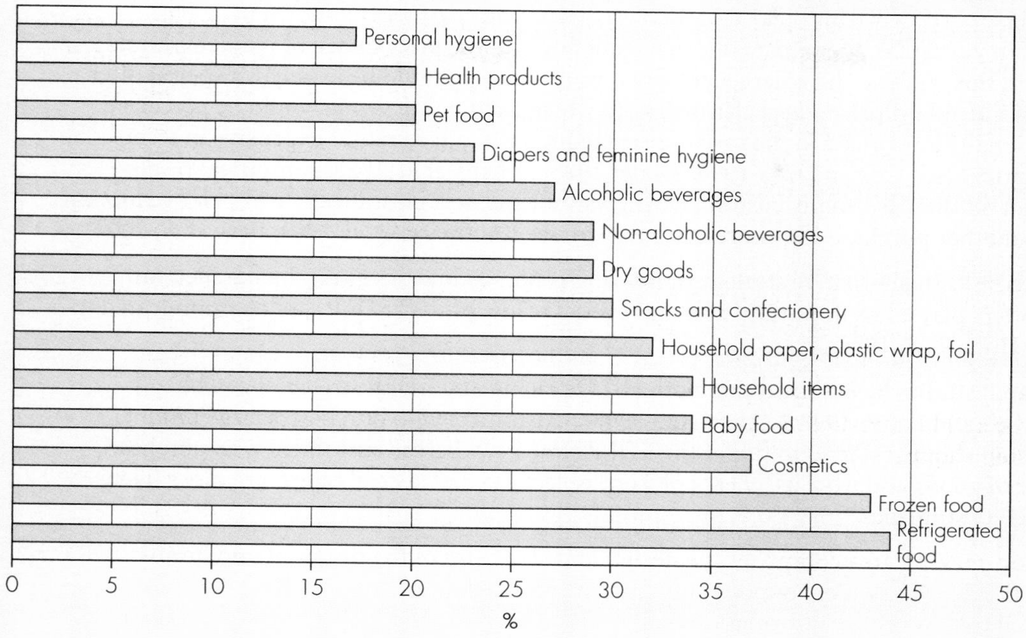

Figure 11-20 Price difference between private-label and manufacturer brands (adapted from KPMG 2004, p. 55)

customer-related and competition-related aspects. In particular, the following recommendations can be made with respect to the extent of the margin (see Simon 2004):

- The margin should be aligned with the competition.
- The lower the absolute price, the higher the margin.
- The higher the turnover rate, the lower the margin.
- For goods that are subject to a strong price perception on the part of customers (e.g. butter, milk, bread), the margin should be on the lower side (these articles are even often priced with a negative mark-up), since the pricing of these articles has a great impact on the image of the retailer.
- The amount of the mark-up should be lower for mass products than for speciality goods.

A second decision-making area concerns **price bundling** (see Stremersch and Tellis 2002). Here, a retailer offers two or more products for sale at one price. This approach offers customers a discount over unbundled prices. Price bundling reflects a hybrid costing approach. It aims to increase overall sales and units by increasing the amount of merchandise bought instead of maximizing the respective contribution margins of the individual articles (see Berman and Evans 2007; Levy and Weitz 2007, p. 416).

The low prices of some items play an especially central role in the retailer's price image (overall store price image, or OSPI): many customers base the formation of their price image on the prices of a few (frequently purchased) articles ('focal products' such as butter and milk; see Desai and Talukdar 2003). To evoke a low-price image for these customers, a cross-subsidizing strategy of using selected low prices can be practical.

In connection with **price changes**, special offers (temporary price reductions – also called high-low pricing, or HILO pricing) play a particularly important part (see Bolton *et al.* 2006; Ho *et al.* 1998). In particular, the impact of price reductions on the price image of retailers should be considered. In this context, the emergence of two price images should be avoided: a special offer price image and a standard price image, according to which a shopping venue would be perceived as being exceptionally low priced in the case of price reductions, but as rather expensive in terms of its standard prices (see Cox and Cox 1990; Thaler 1985; Urbany *et al.* 1988). Empirical results demonstrate that, in this case, many customers will wait for the next clearance sale or price reduction before making another purchase (for more information, see Kaufmann *et al.* 1994; Levy *et al.* 2004).

Considering this risk, an alternative strategy of offering generally low prices can be pursued, in which special offers play a less important role and everyday low prices (EDLP) are communicated to customers (see Hoch *et al.* 1994).

Empirical research studies have shown that both HILO pricing and EDLP strategies can be successful (see Bell and Lattin 1998; Lal and Rao 1997). Customers who purchase a large number of goods (one-stop shoppers) tend to prefer the EDLP strategy, whereas customers who purchase a small number of goods and who, as 'cherry pickers', select the best special offers, are more likely to appreciate HILO strategies.

Another decision-making area comprises the **design and structure of the discount and bonus systems**. Here, the distribution of coupons and customer cards that offer discounts for customers plays an essential role (for more information on customer cards in the retail sector, see East *et al.* 1995; Mauri 2003; Passingham 1998; Wright and Sparks 1999; Ziliani and Bellini 2004). A main goal here is to increase customer loyalty. In this context, please refer to the discussion in Section 9.3 on customer cards within the scope of customer relationship management.

Specific Characteristics Related to Classic Marketing Mix Components: Communication Decisions

Conventional media advertising, sales promotion and direct marketing are the main communication tools in retail marketing (see Liebmann and Zentes 2001). These tools are used to advertise:

- individual products and their prices
- individual shopping venues
- the retail business as a whole.

When **advertising individual products and prices**, a special focus can be placed on newly launched products, special offers, deviations from the manufacturer's recommended price, product price guarantees or special product bundles. The media of choice for such advertising content are advertisements in daily newspapers or point-of-sale activity within the scope of sales promotions. Since it facilitates easy updating, the internet is another obvious choice (see Figure 11-21).

When **advertising individual shopping venues**, communication frequently centers on regional special offers, the convenient location of the shopping venue, or additional services (such as delivery and installation of products, the quality of the information, and consulting services or price guarantees).

In most cases, **advertisements for the retailer** emphasize its (low) price image, price guarantees and special services. In this area, suitable media particularly include conventional media advertising (e.g. TV commercials, radio spots, and advertisements in daily newspapers and popular magazines), but also newer communication tools such as sponsoring or events.

In addition to the significance of the individual communication tools and special communication content, the great relevance of **personal communication** has to be mentioned as a specific characteristic of retail marketing. Personal communication plays an important role in closing sales in the course of sales negotiations, and is especially important for leveraging cross-selling potential (for more information, see Section 7.5).

Figure 11-21 Example of retailer communication via the internet (www.ikea.com)

Another significant specific characteristic lies in the fact that the communications of retailers are influenced by the communications of manufacturers (see Kumar and Pereira 1997; Sethuraman and Tellis 2002, for more information): customers are aware of both the manufacturer's and the retailer's communication, so that the content communicated by the manufacturer will have an impact on the actions of the retailer.

Specific Characteristics Related to Classic Marketing Mix Components: Sales Decisions

A key area in sales decisions in retailing is **personal selling**. As with personal communication, personal selling is highly relevant to retail marketing. The key objective here is to close a sale during a direct conversation between the salesperson and the customer. In this context, important success factors include the expertise and competence of the customer contact employees. It is the task of these employees to close sales using adequate conversation and negotiation techniques. (Please refer to the information on personal selling provided in Section 7.4.2.)

Another important area is **multichannel management**, which deals with the combined use of directly competing sales channels. Combining store retailing with non-store retailing (e.g. online sales) is a particularly relevant approach (for e-commerce, see also Berman and Thelen 2004). Here, a central question concerns the extent to which the product assortment and price structures should be harmonized between these two sales channels.

Specific Characteristics Related to Additional Components of the Marketing Mix

With regard to the additional components of the marketing mix related to retailing, the following issues have to be mentioned in particular:

- the design of the point of sale (salesrooms, store layout)
- human resources management (see Lamb *et al.* 2002).

The design of the point of sale, or 'in-store-management', comprises:

- the design of the salesrooms/store layout
- space utilization
- the design of the store atmosphere
- the design of the store environment
- the determination of store opening hours.

There is a certain similarity to services marketing here, in which the design of the physical environment represents a special marketing tool (see Section 10.4.2). In retail marketing, however, this tool has far greater scope and significance. In particular, the fundamental importance of salesroom design arises from the opportunity to use emotions as a means of differentiation from competitors (for more information, see also Lamb *et al.* 2002; Levy and Weitz 2003, as well as the example in Figure 11-22).

Figure 11-22 Example of using emotions in the design of salesrooms (see Ziehe 2005, p. 13)

The **design of the store layout** is concerned with dividing the salesrooms into several functional areas (floorspace allocation) and then arranging these (floorspace arrangement). Within the scope of **floorspace allocation**, the salesroom is divided into the following functional areas: goods area (space for presenting the products, e.g. using shelving/fixtures/displays), customer area (e.g. aisles for customer) and other sales areas (e.g. checkout stations, fitting rooms) (see Berekoven 1995).

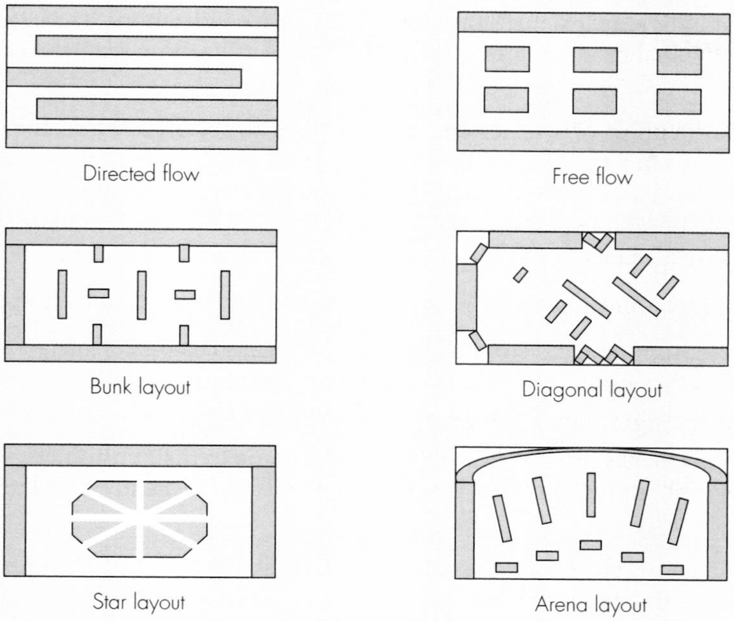

Figure 11-23 Basic principles of floorspace arrangement (store layouts) (see Liebmann and Zentes 2001, p. 549)

Within the scope of **floorspace arrangement** (also called shelving layout), the established functional areas are then arranged in a way that creates aisles for the customers between the various shelving and display areas. The key objectives are the formation of as many contact points as possible between the customers and the entire product assortment (see Berekoven 1995) and a smooth flow of customer traffic in which customers can easily navigate (see Liebmann and Zentes 2001). In general, there is a trade-off between the positive effects on the increased volume of purchased goods resulting from the customers staying longer in the store and the negative effects arising from loss of time and annoyance on the part of customers.

Basically, customers can be guided along a fixed path in a directed-flow layout, or can be given the option to choose alternative paths of various lengths in a free-flow layout (for detailed information on design options for floorspace arrangements, see Figure 11-23 and Berman and Evans 2007, p. 552). In addition to these two forms, there are alternative forms with varying degrees of freedom with regard to the flow of customer traffic:

- The bunk layout offers many contact points between customers and goods, while facilitating a relatively flexible customer flow.
- The star layout facilitates a relatively flexible customer flow and short paths while providing for clear separation between the various shelving and display areas. This makes this layout especially suitable for retail stores with extremely heterogeneous product categories.
- The diagonal layout allows high contact frequency, since the customers run directly into a new shelving area (a 'buffer stop', so to speak) on reaching the end of an aisle.
- The arena layout is extremely well structured and customer friendly, but distances are greater in comparison with the star layout.

Another decision-making area in point-of-sale design concerns **space utilization**, which is to do with the in-store placement of individual product lines (qualitative space utilization), as well as the allocation of sales space to individual product lines (quantitative space utilization; see Berekoven 1995).

An additional issue to consider in point-of-sale design concerns **store atmosphere**. Here, the main objective is to influence customers in a way that makes them feel good, stay longer in the store and ultimately purchase more goods, which can be achieved by using the right lighting, interior colors and decor, playing background music and using appealing scents, as well as maintaining a comfortable room temperature (see Liebmann and Zentes 2001 for more information).

With respect to the design of store atmosphere, the following research findings specifically apply.

- First and foremost, store environment and store atmosphere influence customers' behavior and evaluations. This means they can have a positive impact on store image, and they can elicit emotions and enjoyment (see Baker *et al.* 1994; Turley and Milliman 2000).
- The selective use of emotions makes retailers appear more interesting to their customers, which in turn can result in a longer shopping duration and willingness to buy or spend (see Baker *et al.* 1992; Donovan *et al.* 1994).
- As a rule, additional lighting leads customers to spend more time at displays, and in comparison to softer lighting, brighter lighting tends to make customers take a look at a significantly larger number of products (see Areni and Kim 1994; Summers and Hebert 2001).
- Playing music increases customers' desire to affiliate (see Dube *et al.* 1995).
- The atmospheric design elements should correspond to the intended retail strategy (for more information, see Turley and Chebat 2002) and should also be consistent with each other (see Mattila and Wirtz 2001).
- Using scents in sales areas can have a positive effect on perception of products (see Bone and Ellen 1999; Hirsch 1995; Knoblich 1994; Knoblich *et al.* 2003). For instance, it has been empirically proven that citrus fragrances have a positive effect on customer perception and that scents that do not complement the offered products adversely affect customers' decision-making processes (see Chebat and Michon 2003; Mitchell *et al.* 1995).

Human resource decisions are a second additional component of the marketing mix related to retail marketing (for a detailed discussion, see Sharma 2001). As is the case with services, retail marketing is based on the extensive integration of an external factor, namely the customers (for retailers that offer a broad range of services, the boundaries to service providers are blurred).

The integration of the human external factor is especially manifest in store retailing, where customers personally visit the stores. This makes personal selling particularly important (see Section 7.4.2) and, accordingly, this area has to be supported by appropriate human resource management.

The objectives of human resource management in retail marketing essentially correspond to those of services marketing (employee competence, employee motivation, employee performance and employee loyalty; see Section 14.4.2). Due to the major importance of personal selling, a special focus should be placed both on hiring sales employees that have the required qualifications (i.e. have excellent professional and social competence skills) and on developing their sales expertise.

With respect to designing the human resource strategy in retail marketing, the following recommendations can be made:

- **Staff availability** is a major success factor. Augmenting the number of sales employees can increase customers' willingness to buy (see Sharma and Stafford 2000; Williams and Seminerio 1985).
- Sales employees in a good **mood** provide better customer service and achieve better sales results (see Swinyard 2003; Westbrook 1980). Mood is especially influenced by the retail environment, and by interactions with sales personnel (see Gardner 1985; Gardner and Vandersteel 1984).
- Findings with regard to the **quality of customer interactions** demonstrate that sales employees provide unpleasant and aggressive customers with more and better information and services than they provide to pleasant customers. Therefore, sales employees should be trained to provide equivalent levels of good service to all customers, not just the assertive ones (see Swinyard 2003).
- The **credibility of sales personnel** has a positive effect on the buying behavior and loyalty of customers (see Ganesan 1994; Sharma 1990; Sharma and Stafford 2000), a fact that should be addressed during sales training courses by developing the professional expertise and rhetoric skills of sales employees (see Williams and Seminerio 1985).
- Many customers are willing to enter into a **loyal relationship with salespeople** (see, e.g., Beatty *et al.* 1996; Gwinner *et al.* 1998). To promote this, the main emphasis should be placed on hiring salespeople that excel at social and selling competence (see Reynolds and Beatty 1999; Sharma and Levy 2003).

Summary

Five characteristics distinguish services from tangible goods: intangibility, a higher perceived purchase risk, inseparability, perishability and variability. However, there is no clear-cut differentiation possible on this basis as some service characteristics can also apply to tangible goods. Service typologies can help to additionally define service. While commonly used one-dimensional typologies differentiate by single criteria, multidimensional typologies are more complex and integrate several dimensions. One important typology leads to the identification of four different services types: service factory, service shop, mass service and professional service.

In order to conceptualize the concept of service quality, the SERVQUAL approach uses the dimensions tangibles, reliability, responsiveness, assurance and empathy. Other approaches differentiate routine and non-routine dimensions of service quality. The measurement of service quality can be based on company-internal or company-external data sources. For more detailed analyzes, the critical incident technique, frequency-relevance analyzes, the sequential incident method (blueprinting), fishbone analysis and the benchmarking method can be used. To influence service quality, organizational structure, workflow organization and employee management/ company culture should be designed in order to favor a high level of service quality. Tools for this include quality circles and the Poka-Yoke method.

There is a reciprocal relationship between the service characteristics and strategic decisions of a service provider: while service characteristics influence the provider's strategic options, they are in turn affected by strategic decisions. Service characteristics also have an impact on the design of the marketing mix and account for three additional 'Ps' (personnel decisions, physical evidence decisions and process decisions), which together with the classic components of the marketing mix (the 'four Ps') form the expanded services marketing mix. Key objectives include high employee quality, a positive image of the service provider and optimized service processes.

A final focus in this chapter was placed on the retail sector, as this is where services are provided to end customers. Retailers provide a transport function, temporal buffer function, quantitative product assortment function, qualitative product assortment function, credit/financing function and advertising/market impact function. Retail business forms can be classified according to retail location, internationality, product range, price level, sales area or service principle. As with service marketing, retail marketing requires a specific design of the marketing mix and, in addition to the classical decisions regarding the marketing mix, the design of point-of-sale and human resource decisions is an additional component of the retail marketing mix.

Case Study: Low-Cost Carriers Drop Prices to Fill Seats

Stiff competition, weaker market conditions and increased capacity are taking their toll on budget carriers, long viewed as the darlings of the European aviation industry. On 9 May 2007, Britain's easyJet, Europe's second-largest discounter, conceded its load factor, or percentage of seats filled, had fallen to 83.1% in April from 86.4% a year earlier. The news followed similar revelations from British Airways, Dublin-based Ryanair and Germany's Air Berlin. easyJet CEO Andy Harrison said in a statement that, to reverse the trend, the company would lower prices on summer flights 'to sustain high load factors in weaker market conditions'. Rival Ryanair also announced its biggest fare sale ever, offering ten million seats from $20, including taxes. The move was expected to drive down prices across Europe and boost demand, said Ryanair CEO Michael O'Leary.

Years of strong profits have encouraged discounters to buy more planes and fly more routes, flooding the market with capacity and putting fares under pressure. easyJet alone has taken delivery of one new Airbus A319 every 12 days since September, 2003. With 104 Airbus planes on order, the carrier was expected to increase capacity by 15 per cent in the fiscal year ending 30 September 2007. Meanwhile, Ryanair has seen 21 per cent growth in capacity, taking delivery of 27 Boeing 737–800s for a fleet total of 138. By the first half of 2008, Ryanair plans to increase its fleet to 170. 'This increased capacity will make it even more difficult for low-cost carriers to navigate the increasingly competitive pricing environment,' says Yan Derocles, aviation analyst at Oddo Securities in Paris.

The discounters' ability to find ever more creative ways to get passengers to spend money is one reason why many analysts reckon the current turmoil won't dent full-year profits. 'Stronger growth in ancillary revenues and better cost management' is likely to offset the current pricing weakness, says Oddo's Derocles. Indeed, the gloomy summer forecast hasn't curbed the budget carriers' ambitious growth plans. Ryanair's O'Leary told an industry conference that he plans to double his number of passengers to 100 million and the number of bases he serves to 40 within five years. This summer may be choppy, but the long-term flight path still looks clear.

Source: adapted from Capell, K. (2007) *Business Week Online*, 14 May, p. 24.

Discussion Questions

1. What specific characteristic of services forces airline companies to lower prices in the situation described above?
2. What problems and downsides can occur due to the low prices of flights? In your opinion, has customer perception of low-cost carriers changed within the last ten years? What are the consequences for the airlines?
3. Besides pricing, what elements of the (additional) marketing mix can be used to fill capacities? What measures could be taken?
4. Considering the necessity for better cost management and for generating new kinds of revenue, what opportunities does the integration of external factors offer? What strategy should be embarked upon and what measures could be taken?

Key Terms

References

Ailawadi, K. and Harlam, B. (2004) An empirical analysis of the determinants of retail margins: the role of store-brand share, *Journal of Marketing*, 68, 1, 147–165.

Ailawadi, K. and Keller, K. (2004) Understanding retail branding: conceptual insights and research priorities, *Journal of Retailing*, 80, 4, 331–342.

Ailawadi, K.L., Neslin, S.A. and Gedenk, K. (2001) Pursuing the value-conscious consumer: store brands versus national brand promotions, *Journal of Marketing*, 65, 1, 71–89.

ACNielsen (2005) The Power of Private Label: A Review of Growth Trends Around the World, Executive News Report from ACNielsen Global Services, www2.acnielsen.com/reports/index_global.shtml.

Anderson, C. (2006) *The Long Tail: Why the Future of Business is Selling Less of More*. New York.

Areni, C.S. and Kim, D. (1994) The influence of in-store lighting on consumers' examination of merchandise in a wine store, *International Journal of Research in Marketing*, 11, 2, 117–125.

Bäckström, K. and Johansson, U. (2006) Creating and consuming experiences in retail store environments: comparing retailer and consumer perspectives, *Journal of Retailing & Consumer Services*, 13, 6, 417–430.

Baker, J., Grewal, D. and Parasuraman, A. (1994) The influence of store environment on quality inferences and store image, *Journal of the Academy of Marketing Science*, 22, 328–339.

Baker, J., Levy, M. and Grewal, D. (1992) An experimental approach to making retail store environmental decisions, *Journal of Retailing*, 68, 4, 445–460.

Beatty, S.E., Mayer, M.L., Coleman, J.E., Reynolds, K.E. and Lee, J. (1996) Customer–sales associate retail relationships, *Journal of Retailing*, 72, 223–247.

Bell, D.R. and Lattin, J.M. (1998) Shopping behavior and consumer preferences for store price format: why 'large basket' shoppers prefer EDLP, *Marketing Science*, 17, 1, 66–89.

Berekoven, L. (1995) *Erfolgreiches Einzelhandelsmarketing: Grundlagen und Entscheidungshilfen* (2nd edn). Munich.

Berman, B. and Evans, J. (2007) *Retail Management: A Strategic Approach* (10th edn). Upper Saddle River, NJ.

Berman, B. and Thelen, S. (2004) Special issue: Retail insights: Emerging technologies and the retail environment guide to developing and managing a well-integrated multi-channel retail strategy, *International Journal of Retailing and Distribution*, 32, 3, 147–156.

Berry, L. (1987) Big ideas in services marketing, *Journal of Services Marketing*, 1, 1, 5–9.

Berry, L.L. (2000) Cultivating service brand equity, *Journal of the Academy of Marketing Sciences*, 28, 1, 128–138.

Berry, L. and Parasuraman, A. (1993) Building a new academic field – the case of services marketing, *Journal of Retailing*, 69, 1, 13–60.

Berry, L. and Seiders, K. (2002) Understanding service convenience, *Journal of Marketing*, 66, 3, 1–18.

Bitner, M., Booms, B. and Tetreault, M. (1990) The service encounter: diagnosing favorable and unfavorable incidents, *Journal of Marketing*, 54, 1, 71–84.

Bolton, R., Montoya, D. and Shankar, V. (2006) Beyond EDLP and HiLo: a new customised approach to retail pricing, *European Retail Digest*, Spring, 49, 7–10.

Bone, P.F. and Ellen, P.S. (1999) Scents in the marketplace explaining a fraction of olfaction, *Journal of Retailing*, 75, 2, 243–262.

Bougie, R., Pieters, R. and Zeelenberg, M. (2003) Angry customers don't come back, they get back: the experience and behavioral implications of anger and dissatisfaction in services, *Journal of the Academy of Marketing Science*, 31, 4, 377–393.

Bowen, D. and Lawler, E. (1992) The empowerment of service workers: what, why, how, and when, *Sloan Management Review*, 33, 3, 31–39.

Bowen, D. and Lawler, E. (1995) Empowering service employees, *Sloan Management Review*, 36, 4, 73–84.

Bowen, D. and Lawler, E. (1999) Empowerment von Mitarbeitern in Dienstleistungsunternehmen, in: Payne, A. and Rapp, R. (eds) *Handbuch Relationship Marketing: Konzeption und erfolgreiche Umsetzung*. Munich, 207–225.

Brandt, D. (1988) How service marketers can identify value-enhancing service elements, *Journal of Services Marketing*, 2, 3, 35–41.

Bruhn, M. (2004) *Qualitätsmanagement für Dienstleistungen: Grundlagen, Konzepte, Methoden*. Berlin.

Bruhn, M. and Georgi, D. (2006) *Service Marketing: Managing the Service Value Chain*. Harlow.

Bruhn, M. and Stauss, B. (eds) (1999) *Dienstleistungsqualität: Konzepte, Methoden, Erfahrungen* (3rd edn). Wiesbaden.

Burrell, I. (2006) Ashley Highfield: '99 per cent of the BBC archives is on the shelves. We ought to liberate it', *Independent*, 14 August.

Capell, K. (2007) European travelers stand to enjoy fares as low as $20 this summer as several low-cost carriers drop prices to fill seats, *Business Week* Online, 14 May, p. 24, http://search.ebscohost.com/login.aspx?direct=true&db=buh&AN=25074075&site=ehos t-live.

Chase, R.B. and Stewart, D.M. (1994) Make your service fail-safe, *Sloan Management Review*, 35, 3, 35–44.

Chebat, J-C. and Michon, R. (2003) Impact of ambient odors on mall shoppers' emotions, cognition, and spending: a test of competitive causal theories, *Journal of Business Research*, 56, 7, 529–540.

Corsten, H. (2000) Der Integrationsgrad des externen Faktors als Gestaltungsparameter von Dienstleistungsunternehmungen – Voraussetzungen und Möglichkeiten der Externalisierung und Internalisierung, in: Bruhn, M. and Stauss, B. (eds) *Dienstleistungsqualität: Konzepte, Methoden, Erfahrungen* (3rd edn). Wiesbaden, 145–168.

Corsten, H. and Gössinger, R. (2006) Output flexibility of service enterprises – an analysis based on production theory, *International Journal of Production Economics*, 104, 296–307.

Cox, A. and Cox, D. (1990) Competing on price: the role of retail price advertisements in shaping store-price image, *Journal of Retailing*, 66, 4, 428–445.

Deery, S., Iverson, R. and Walsh, J. (2002) Work relationships in telephone call centers: understanding emotional exhaustion and employee withdrawal, *Journal of Management Studies*, 39, 4, 471–496.

Deloitte (2008) 2008 Global Powers of Retailing, Deloitte Development LLC, pp. 8–10. Persistent link: http://www.deloitte.com/dtt/cda/doc/content/de_CB_R_GPofRetailing08_140108(1).pdf.

Desai, K. and Talukdar, D. (2003) Relationship between product groups' price perceptions, shopper's basket size, and grocery store's overall store price image, *Psychology & Marketing*, 20, 10, 903–933.

Deutsche Bank, http://deutschebank.co.in/Press_Releases.html.

Dhar, S.K. and Hoch, S.J. (1997) Why store brand penetration varies by retailer, *Marketing Science*, 16, 3, 208–228.

Donovan, R., Rossiter, J., Marcoolynn, G. and Nesdale, A. (1994) Store atmosphere and purchasing behavior, *Journal of Retailing*, 70, 3, 283–294.

Dube, L., Chebat, J-C. and Morin, S. (1995) The effects of background music on consumers' desire to affiliate in buyer–seller interactions, *Psychology and Marketing*, 12, 4, 305–315.

Duff, M. (2005) Hard discounters raising the retail bar in Europe, *DSN Retailing Today*, 44, 12, 7–47.

East, R., Harris, P., Wittson, G. and Lomax, W. (1995) Loyalty to supermarkets, *International Review of Retail, Distribution, and Consumer Research*, 5, 1, 99–109.

Eurohandelsinsitut eV (2002) *Handel aktuell: Sortimentsbreitenerhebung 2000/2001*. Köln.

EHI (2005) *Retailing Factbook*.

Fisk, R., Brown, S. and Bitner, M. (1995) Services management literature overview: a rationale for interdisciplinary study, in: Glynn, W. and Barnes, J. (eds) *Understanding Services Management*. Chichester, 1–32.

Fitzsimmons, J.A. and Fitzsimmons, M.J. (1999) *Service Management: Operations, Strategy and Information Technology* (2nd edn). Boston, Mass.

Ganesan, S. (1994) Determinants of long-term orientation in buyer–seller relationships, *Journal of Marketing*, 58, 2, 1–20.
Gardner, M.P. (1985) Mood states and consumer behavior, a critical review, *Journal of Consumer Research*, 12, 281–300.
Gardner, M.P. and Vandersteel, M. (1984) The consumer's mood: an important situational variable, *Advances in Consumer Research*, 11, 525–529.
GfK (2003) *Anteil der Handelsmarken am Einzelhandelsumsatz nach Produktkategorien, zitiert nach COP Consulting Partners*. Bad Homburg.
Gilbert, D. (2003) *Retail Marketing Management* (2nd edn). Essex.
Grönroos, C. (1994) Quo vadis, marketing? Toward a relationship marketing paradigm, *Journal of Marketing Management*, 10, 347–360.
Grönroos, C. (2002) Marketing classic, *Marketing Review*, 3, 129–146.
Gwinner, K.P., Gremler, D.D. and Bitner, M.J. (1998) Relational benefits in services industries: the customer's perspective, *Journal of the Academy of Marketing Science*, 26, 101–114.
Halstead, D. and Ward, C. (1995) Assessing the vulnerability of private label brands, *Journal of Product & Brand Management*, 4, 3, 38–48.
Hansen, J.T. and Kliger, M. (2004) European warm to bargain groceries, *McKinsey Quarterly*, 4, 15–17.
Hentze, J. and Lindert, K. (1998) Motivations- und Anreizsysteme in Dienstleistungs-Unternehmen, in: Meyer, A. (ed.) *Handbuch Dienstleistungs-Marketing, Band 1*. Stuttgart, 1011–1030.
Hess, R., Ganesan, S. and Klein, N. (2003) Service failure and recovery, *Journal of the Academy of Marketing Science*, 31, 2, 127–145.
Hirsch, A.R. (1995) Effects of ambient odors on slot-machine usage in a Las Vegas casino, *Psychology and Marketing*, 12, 10, 585–595.
Ho, T.-H., Tang, C.S. and Bell, D.R. (1998) Rational shopping behavior and the option value of variable pricing, *Management Science*, 44, 12, 145–160.
Hoch, S. and Banerji, S. (1993) When do private labels succeed? *Sloan Management Review*, 34, 4, 57–67.
Hoch, S., Dreze, X. and Purk, M. (1994) EDLP, Hi-Lo, and margin arithmetic, *Journal of Marketing*, 58, 4, 16–27.
Hoffman, D.L., Novak, T.P. and Chatterjee, P. (1995) Commercial scenarios for the web: opportunities and challenges, Working Paper, Owen Graduate School of Management Vanderbilt University.
Homburg, C. and Stock, R. (2000) *Der kundenorientierte Mitarbeiter: Bewerten, begeistern, bewegen*. Wiesbaden.
Homburg, C., Hoyer, W. and Faßnacht, M. (2002) Service orientation of a retailer's business strategy: dimensions, antecedents, and performance outcomes, *Journal of Marketing*, 66, 4, 86–102.
Huffman, C. and Kahn, B. (1998) Variety for sale: mass customization or mass confusion? *Journal of Retailing*, 74, 4, 491–513.
ILO, International Labor Office (2006) *Global Employment Brief*, January.
Iyengar, S. and Lepper, M. (2000) When choice is demotivating: can one desire too much of a good thing? *Journal of Personality and Social Psychology*, 79, 6, 995–1006.
Jacoby, J. and Mazursky, D. (1984) Linking brand name and retailer images: do the potential risks outweigh the potential benefits? *Journal of Retailing*, 60, 2, 105–122.
Kahn, B. and Wansink, B. (2004) The influence of assortment structure on perceived variety and consumption quantities, *Journal of Consumer Research*, 30, 4, 519–533.
Kaufmann, P., Smith, N.C. and Ortmeyer, G. (1994) Deception in retailer high-low pricing: a 'rule of reason' approach, *Journal of Retailing*, 70, 2, 115–138.
Kimes, S. (1992) Yield management: a tool for capacity-constrained service firms, in: Lovelock, C. (ed.) *Managing Services: Marketing, Operations, and Human Resources* (2nd edn). Englewood Cliffs, NJ, 188–201.
Knoblich, H. (1994) Markengestaltung mit Duftstoffen, in: Bruhn, M. (ed.) *Handbuch Markenartikel, Bd. 2*. Stuttgart, 849–869.
Knoblich, H., Scharf, A. and Schubert, B. (2003) *Marketing mit Duft* (4th edn). Munich/Vienna.
KPMG (2004) Lebensmitteleinzelhandel, *Absatzwirtschaft*, 5, 55–56.
Kumar, V. and Pereira, A. (1997) Assessing the competitive impact of type, timing, frequency, and magnitude of retail promotions, *Journal of Business Research*, 40, 1, 1–13.
Lal, R. and Rao, R. (1997) Supermarket competition: the case of every day low pricing, *Marketing Science*, 16, 1, 60–80.
Lamb, C.W., Hair, J.F. and McDaniel, C. (2002) *Marketing* (6th edn). Cincinnati.

Levy, M. and Weitz, B. (2003) *Retailing Management* (5th edn). Boston, Mass.
Levy, M. and Weitz, B. (2007) *Retailing Management* (6th edn). New York.
Levy, M., Grewal, D., Kopalle, P. and Hess, J. (2004) Emerging trends in retail pricing practice: implications for research, *Journal of Retailing*, 80, 3, xii–xxi.
Liebmann, H. and Zentes, J. (2001) *Handelsmanagement*. Munich.
Lovelock, C. (1983) Classifying services to gain strategic marketing insights, *Journal of Marketing*, 47, 3, 9–20.
Lovelock, C., Vandermerwe, S. and Lewis, B. (1999) *Services Marketing: A European Perspective*. Harlow.
Lovelock, C. and Wirtz, J. (2007) *Services Marketing: People, Technology, Strategy* (6th edn). New Jersey.
Magrath, A. (1986) When marketing services, 4 Ps are not enough, *Business Horizons*, 29, 3, 44–50.
Mattila, A.S. and Wirtz, J. (2001) Congruency of scent and music as a driver of in-store evaluations and behavior, *Journal of Retailing*, 77, 2, 273–289.
Mauri, C. (2003) Card loyalty. A new emerging issue in grocery retailing, *Journal of Retailing and Consumer Services*, 10, 1, 13–25.
McGill, J.I. and Ryzin, G.J. (1999) Revenue management: research overview and prospects, *Transportation Science*, 33, 2, 233–256.
Meffert, H. and Bruhn, M. (2006) *Dienstleistungsmarketing* (5th edn). Wiesbaden.
Meyer, P. and Tostmann, T. (1980) The marketing of services, *European Journal of Marketing*, 14, 9, 16.
Mills, D. (1995) Why do retailers sell private label? *Journal of Economics and Management Strategy*, 4, 3, 509–528.
Mitchell, D.J., Kahn, B.E. and Knasko, S.C. (1995) There's something in the air: effects of ambient odor on consumer decision making, *Journal of Consumer Research*, 22, 229–238.
Morris, D. (1979) The strategy of own brands, *European Journal of Marketing*, 13, 2, 59–78.
Munro-Faure, L. and Munro-Faure, M. (1992) *Implementing Total Quality Management*. London.
Munro-Faure, L. and Munro-Faure, M. (1993) *Implementing Total Quality Management* (7th edn). London.
Murray, K. (1991) A test of services marketing theory: consumer information acquisition activities, *Journal of Marketing*, 55, 1, 10–25.
Nandan, S. and Dickinson, R. (1994) Private brands: major brand perspective, *Journal of Consumer Marketing*, 11, 4, 18–28.
Narasimhan, C. and Wilcox, R. (1998) Private labels and the channel relationship: a cross-category analysis, *Journal of Business*, 71, 4, 573–600.
OECD Factbook (2007) Persistent link: http://puck.sourceoecd.org/vl=349102/cl=14/nw=1/rpsv/factbook/02-04-01.htm http://puck.sourceoecd.org/pdf//fact2007pdf//02-04-01.pdf.
Palmer, A. (2000) The marketing of services, *Principles of Marketing*, 574–600 (see http://search.ebscohost.com/login.aspx?direct=true&db=buh&AN=7500362&site=ehost-live).
Palmer, A. (2001) *Principles of Services Marketing* (3rd edn). London.
Parasuraman, A., Berry, L. and Zeithaml, V. (1991) Refinement and reassessment of the SERVQUAL scale, *Journal of Retailing*, 67, 4, 420–450.
Parasuraman, A., Zeithaml, V. and Berry, L. (1985) A conceptual model of service quality and its implications for future research, *Journal of Marketing*, 49, 3, 41–50. Reprinted with permission from *Journal of Marketing*, published by the American Marketing Association.
Parasuraman, A., Zeithaml, V. and Berry, L. (1988) SERVQUAL: a multiple-item scale for measuring consumer perceptions of service quality, *Journal of Retailing*, 64, 1, 12–40.
Passingham, J. (1998) Grocery retailing and the loyalty card, *Journal of the Market Research Society*, 40, 1, 55–63.
Peterson, R.A. and Balasubramanian, S. (2002) Retailing in the 21st century: reflections and prologue to research, *Journal of Retailing*, 78, 1, 9–16.
Raju, J., Raj, K. and Dhar, S. (1995) The introduction and performance of store brands, *Management Science*, 41, 6, 957–978.
Reynolds, K.E. and Beatty, S.E. (1999) Customer benefits and company consequences of customer–salesperson relationships in retailing, *Journal of Retailing*, 75, 1, 11–32.
Richardson, P. (1997) Are store brands perceived to be just another brand? *Journal of Product and Brand Management*, 6, 6, 388–404.
Rossi, P. and Anderson, A. (1982) The factorial survey approach: an introduction, in: Rossi, P. and Nock, S. (eds) *Measuring Social Judgments: The Factorial Survey Approach*. Beverly Hills, 15–67.
Rudolph, T. and Einhorn, M. (2001) Herausforderungen im europäischen Einzelhandel, *Thexis*, 3, 2–7.

Sayman, S., Hoch, S. and Raju, J. (2002) Positioning of store brands, *Marketing Science*, 21, 4, 129–141.

Schmenner, R. (1992) How can service businesses survive and prosper, in: Lovelock, C. (ed.) *Managing Services*, Englewood Cliffs, NJ, 31–42.

Schubert, M. (1994) Qualitätszirkel, in: Masing, W. (ed.) *Handbuch Qualitätsmanagement* (3rd edn). Munich, 1075–1100.

Sethuraman, R. and Tellis, G. (2002) Does manufacturer advertising suppress or stimulate retail price promotions? Analytical model and empirical analysis, *Journal of Retailing*, 78, 4, 253–263.

Sharma, A. (1990) The persuasive effect of salesperson credibility: conceptual and empirical examination, *Journal of Personal Selling and Sales Management*, 10, 4, 71–80.

Sharma, A. (2001) Consumer decision-making, salespeople's adaptive selling and retail performance, *Journal of Business Research*, 54, 125–129.

Sharma, A. and Levy, M. (2003) Salespeople's affect toward customers. Why should it be important for retailers? *Journal of Business Research*, 56, 523–528.

Sharma, A. and Stafford, T.F. (2000) The effect of retail atmospherics on customers' perceptions of salespeople and customer persuasion: an empirical investigation, *Journal of Business Research*, 49, 183–191.

Sherwood, K. and Guerrier, Y. (1993) Quality circle program evaluation: a study in British manufacturing industry, *International Journal of Technology Management*, 8, 3, 396–410.

Shingo, S. (1986) *A Study of the Toyota Production System, from an Industrial Engineering Viewpoint* (9th edn). Tokyo.

Shingo, S. (1991) *POKA-YOKE, Prinzip und Technik für eine Null-Fehler-Produktion*. St Gallen.

Siegel, C. (2004) *Internet Marketing: Foundations and Applications*. Boston, Mass.

Silince, J. and Sykes, G. (1996) Implementation, problems, success and longevity of quality circle programs, *International Journal of Operations & Production Management*, 16, 4, 88–111.

Simon, H. (2004) *Price Management*. North Holland.

Sniderman, P. and Grob, D. (1996) Innovations in experimental design in attitude surveys, *Annual Review of Sociology*, 22, 1, 377–399.

Soberman, D. (2003) Simultaneous signaling and screening with warranties, *Journal of Marketing Research*, 40, 1, 176–192.

Stauss, B. (1991) Dienstleister und die vierte Dimension, *Harvard Manager*, 13, 2, 81–89.

Stauss, B. and Seidel, W. (2004) *Complaint Management: The Heart of CRM*. Mason.

Stauss, B. and Weinlich, B. (1997) Process-oriented measurement of service quality, *European Journal of Marketing*, 31, 1/2, 33–55.

Steenkamp, J.-B. and Dekimpe, M. (1997) The increasing power of store brands: building loyalty and market share, *Long Range Planning*, 30, 6, 917–930.

Stremersch, S. and Tellis, G. (2002) Strategic bundling of products and prices: a new synthesis for marketing, *Journal of Marketing*, 66, 1, 55–72.

Summers, T.A. and Hebert, P.R. (2001) Shedding some light on store atmospherics. Influence of illumination on consumer behavior, *Journal of Business Research*, 54, 145–150.

Swinyard, W.R. (2003) The effects of salesperson mood, shopper behavior, and store type on customer service, *Journal of Retailing and Consumer Services*, 10, 323–333.

*teller*vision (2005) Online banking: increasing satisfaction but facing hurdles.

Thaler, R. (1985) Mental accounting and consumer choice, *Marketing Science*, 4, 3, 199–214.

Turley, L.W. and Chebat, J.-C. (2002) Linking retail strategy, atmospheric design and shopping behavior, *Journal of Marketing Management*, 18, 125–144.

Turley, L.W. and Milliman, R.E. (2000) Atmospheric effects on shopping behavior: a review of the experimental evidence, *Journal of Business Research*, 49, 2, 193–211.

Urbany, J., Bearden, W. and Wellbaker, D. (1988) The effect of plausible and exaggerated reference prices on consumer perceptions and price search, *Journal of Consumer Research*, 15, 1, 95–110.

Verma, R. (2000) An empirical analysis of management challenges in service factories, service shops, mass services and professional services, *International Journal of Service Industry Management*, 11, 1, 8–25.

Webb Pressler, M. (2005) Uniform adjustment: McDonald's workers to get trendy duds, washingtonpost.com, 7 July, © 2005, *Washington Post*, reprinted with permission.

Westbrook, R. (1980) Intrapersonal affective influences on consumer satisfaction with products, *Journal of Consumer Research*, 7, 1, 49–54.

Williams, A.J. and Seminerio, J. (1985) What buyers like from salesmen, *Industrial Marketing Management*, 14, 2, 75–79.

Wirtz, J. and Kum, D. (2004) Consumer cheating on service guarantees, *Journal of the Academy of Marketing Science*, 32, 2, 159–175.
Wright, C. and Sparks, L. (1999) Loyalty saturation in retailing: exploring the end of retail loyalty cards? *International Journal of Retail & Distribution Management*, 27, 10, 429–439.
www.ikea.com
Zeithaml, V. (1981) How consumer evaluation processes differ between goods and services, in: Donnelly, J. and George, W. (eds) *Marketing of Services*. Chicago, 186–190.
Zeithaml, V. and Bitner, M. (2000) *Services Marketing: Integrating Customer Focus Across the Firm* (2nd edn). Boston, Mass.
Zeithaml, V. and Bitner, M. (2003) *Services Marketing: Integrating Customer Focus Across the Firm* (3rd edn). New York.
Zeithaml, V., Bitner, M. and Gremler, D. (2006) *Services Marketing: Integrating Customer Focus Across the Firm* (4th edn). Boston, Mass.
Zeithaml, V., Parasuraman, A. and Berry, L. (1990) *Delivering Quality Service: Balancing Customer Perceptions and Expectations*. New York.
Zentes, J. and Swoboda, B. (1999) Standort und Ladengestaltung, in: Dichtl, E. and Lingenfelder, M. (eds) *Meilensteine im deutschen Handel*. Frankfurt, 89–121.
Ziehe, N. (2005) real,- SB-Warenhaus GmbH, Vortrag an der Universität Mannheim, April.
Ziliani, C. and Bellini, S. (2004) From loyalty card to micro-marketing strategies: where is Europe's retail industry heading? *Journal of Targeting, Measurement and Analysis for Marketing*, 12, 3, 281–289.

CHAPTER 12

International Marketing

Contents

Learning Objectives

In this chapter you will become familiar with:

- the economic, political-legal and sociocultural international marketing environment
- the important theories of internationalization
- the relevance of cross-national coordination in international marketing
- the specific characteristics of international market research
- the main decisions specific to an international marketing strategy such as specification of the degree of internationalization, selection and prioritization of markets, design of the international market development strategy, decisions concerning cross-national standardization of marketing activities, decisions with respect to the relationship between headquarters and regional operations
- the most important specific characteristics of the international marketing mix as it relates to product, pricing, communication and sales decisions
- the main considerations of cross-national standardization and differentiation of product, pricing, communication and sales decisions.

This chapter differs from the other chapters in Part 3 of this book because the specific institutional context is not defined by a certain economic sector (such as services or business-to-business), but rather through the internationality of the business operations.

In Section 12.1, we will discuss the basic foundations of international marketing. In this context, we will examine the environmental conditions of international marketing as well as the theoretical approaches that are relevant in the context of international marketing. Following that, we will delve into the specific characteristics of international marketing research in Section 12.2. Section 12.3 then focuses on the formulation of the international marketing strategy of a company. In Section 12.4, we will examine the design of the marketing mix in an international context.

12.1 International Marketing: An Introduction

International marketing refers to the marketing activities a company undertakes when it conducts business operations in more than one country. In line with our definition of marketing (see Section 1.2), **international marketing** refers to design and realization activities on the part of a company, directed at its customers and potential customers located in more than one country. The objective of international marketing is to optimize the design of customer relationship management across countries. Therefore, a major task in international marketing is to establish favorable conditions within the company which ensure that these market-related activities can be implemented effectively across countries. International marketing also implies the application of a marketing orientation and marketing capabilities in an international context (Mühlbacher *et al.* 2006).

The importance of international marketing can be illustrated by looking at the economic interdependencies between the major economic regions of the world (see Figure 12-1).

Furthermore, international exports have risen much more sharply than global economic output in recent decades (see Figure 12-2). This highlights the worldwide growth in **international business operations**. This trend is due to companies pursuing internationalization strategies in order to make their products and services available to customers in different countries. Many companies start with a focus on their domestic market, and catering to other countries – and therefore cultures – often poses considerable challenges. In this chapter we will lay the groundwork for a better understanding of these challenges so that firms can reap the opportunities and benefits of international endeavors.

12.1.1 The International Market Environment

When a company is serving multiple markets in different countries it is crucial to understand and assess the **international marketing environment**. This comprises:

- technological
- political-legal, and
- sociocultural

market conditions.

In terms of **technological market conditions**, advances in communication and transportation technologies, along with the rise in the international division of labor, have been observed in recent years. Since 2002, spending on information and communication technology (ICT) has been growing continuously. In 2007, more than $3 trillion was spent worldwide on ICT (see WITSA 2006). This development is not surprising, considering that a country's investment in ICT is an important prerequisite for economic growth. The internet, for example, reduces transaction costs considerably, and therefore enables small firms to cooperate in order to develop global reach. ICT thus facilitates

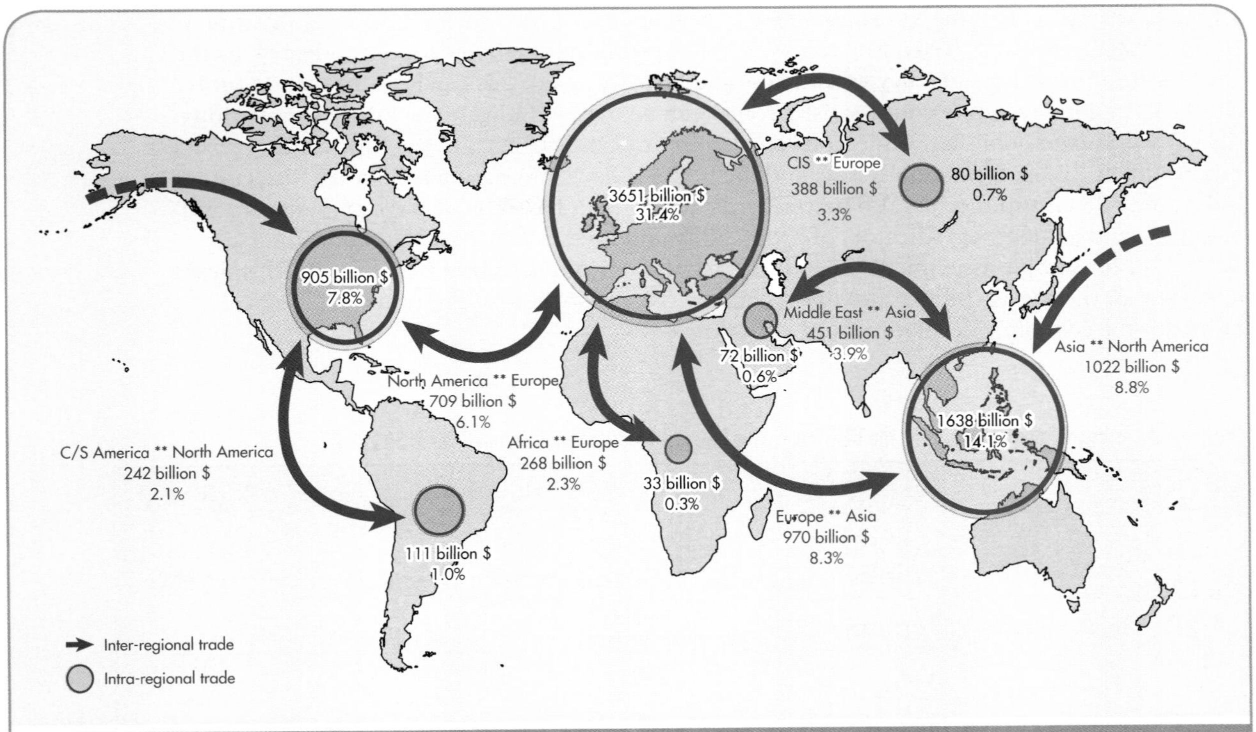

Figure 12-1 Quantification of the international flows of trade (figures for 2007, in billions of US dollars) (WTO 2008)

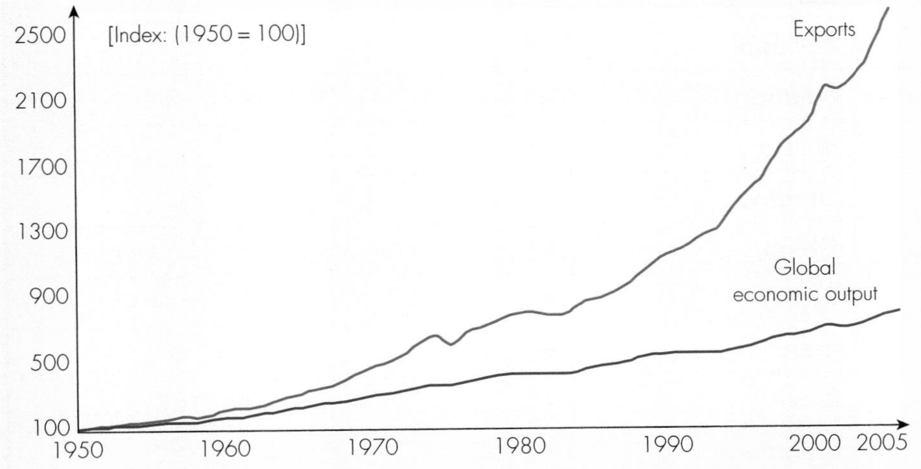

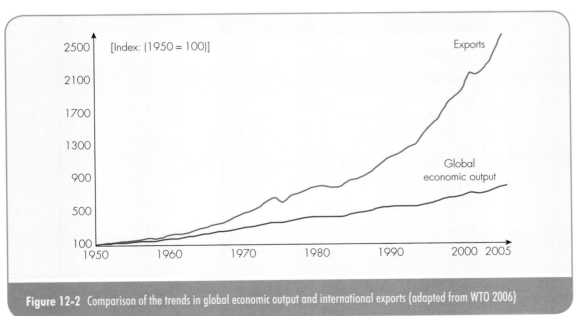

Figure 12-2 Comparison of the trends in global economic output and international exports (adapted from WTO 2006)

rapid diffusion of new technologies to emerging markets, often accompanied by an acceleration in economic growth (see Cateora and Graham 2006).

Political-legal market conditions refer to the political situation and stability in the countries under examination, as well as the legal system, including international statutory regulations. Concepts for qualitative and quantitative assessment can be used to evaluate the political-legal situation of a country (see Berndt *et al.* 1999; Meyer 1987). With qualitative methods, for example, risk factors can be determined (e.g. currency risks, safety and security risks); this can be done using country checklists and the resulting country risk profiles can be used to indicate the intensity of various risks. Well-known quantitative methods are country risk indices such as the BERI Index (Business Environment Risk Information Index) and the ICRG Index (International Country Risk Guide Index, see PRS Group Inc. 2001). These record country risks based on surveys of managers and scientists, and are used as indicators of profitability and investment in various countries (see Table 12-1 for sample assessments of country risks for various countries using the BERI Index). Focus on Marketing 12-1 illustrates that a country risk constitutes an important and critical factor for the economic development of a country.

Table 12-1 Assessing country risks using the BERI Index (see Business Environment Risk Intelligence SA 2006)

	Risk	Overall risk (2006)	Overall risk (5-year forecast)
	Country	Maximum risk = 0, Minimum risk = 100	
Highly industrialized nations	Germany	71	73
	USA	65	68
	France	62	65
	United Kingdom	61	62
Industrialized nations	Spain	59	61
	Italy	49	51
	Portugal	55	56
Newly industrializing nations	Poland	45	48
	Russia	45	47
	Ukraine	43	45
Developing nations	China	61	62
	Turkey	40	42
	India	46	49
	Brazil	42	44
	Indonesia	40	42

Interpretation of ratings

70–100: Stable environment typical of an advanced industrialized economy. Problems for foreign businesses are offset by the country's efficiency, market opportunities, financial system and advanced infrastructure.

55–69: Moderate-risk countries with complications in day-to-day operations. Usually the political structure is sufficiently stable to permit consistent operations without serious disruption. Dynamic economic expansion often has the potential for attractive profits.

40–54: High risk for foreign-owned businesses. Selection of management is critical to success in this risk range.

0–39: Unacceptable business conditions for foreign-owned businesses.

Focus on Marketing 12-1 Extracts from an interview with economist and Nobel Laureate, Professor Paul A. Samuelson, on globalization and the impact of politics on the economic development of a country

Spiegel: So politicians still have the power to shape globalization?

Samuelson: Yes, of course. Politics is extremely important. Had somebody asked me [author's note: in 1945] which part of the world would develop fastest in the next 30 years, I would probably have said Latin America: Argentina or maybe Chile. These countries have a temperate climate, a population primarily of European heritage.

Spiegel: You were wrong.

Samuelson: I was completely wrong. Not because I misjudged the economics, but I underestimated the political aspect: The populist movements like the Peronist dictatorship. They were never able to control prices.

Spiegel: India and China seem to be making more headway on their path to prosperity.

Samuelson: India simply slept for 40 years. And China is the 800-pound gorilla in the living room. We are talking about a process that is accelerating. I think – and I hope I'm right this time – it is inevitable that China will outstrip Japan in the not too distant future.

Spiegel: Do you expect China to become an even bigger economic power than the United States?

Samuelson: A sober and realistic extrapolation would suggest that China will become the dominant economy in the world if its political system doesn't get in the way – but that's a very big 'if'.

Source: Spiegel 2005.

A significant development in this area is the **elimination of cross-national trade barriers**, which has contributed to an increase in international business operations. Of special relevance in this context is the emergence of **free trade zones**, such as, for example, ASEAN (Association of Southeast Asian Nations), EFTA (European Free Trade Association) and NAFTA (North American Free Trade Area), as well as **common markets**, such as the ACM (Arab Common Market), EU (European Union), Andean Common Market and Mercosur (Mercado Commún del Cono Sur). Table 12-2 lists the world's major free trade zones and common markets.

Furthermore, in many areas, **deregulation** has opened up national markets for international competitors (for example, in the telecommunications and energy supply industries). Moreover, a tendency towards **cross-national harmonization of legal regulations** can be observed with regard to political-legal market conditions (e.g. Europe-wide harmonization of the legal market conditions concerning advertising).

With respect to **sociocultural market conditions**, the **cultural differences between various countries** play a particularly decisive role in the design of international marketing. Hofstede describes culture as the 'collective programming of the mind which distinguishes the members of one human group from another' (1980, p. 25). Hofstede developed a concept for describing the cultures of various countries (1980, 1991), which is also used in company practice. Accordingly, the following five dimensions can be applied to characterize the culture of a country.

1 **Power distance** refers to the degree of inequality among people that is viewed as being equitable. With a high power distance, the weaker members of a society expect or accept a relatively unequal

Table 12-2 List of free trade zones and common markets

Trading blocks	When established?	Explanation	Member states	Population (million), approximated	GDP (PPP) (billion US$), approximated
■ European Union (EU)	■ 1957 (Treaty of Rome)	■ Common market and monetary union with free trade of products, services, persons, and capital.	■ Austria, Belgium, Bulgaria, Cyprus, Czech Republic, Denmark, Estonia, Finland, France, Germany, Greece, Hungary, Ireland, Italy, Latvia, Lithuania, Luxembourg, Malta, Poland, Portugal, Rumania, Slovakia, Slovenia, Spain, Sweden, The Netherlands, United Kingdom	■ 488 (EU-27, 2007)	■ 14,728 (approx. 10,896 €)
■ North American Free Trade Area (NAFTA)	■ 1994	■ Free trade agreement, i.e., no assimilation of laws. Only relevant for corporations with headquarters in Canada, Mexico, or the United States. For firms from other countries, member states' import regulations are effective.	■ Canada, Mexico, United States	■ 435	■ 14,564
■ Andean Community of Nations (CAN)	■ 1969	■ Goals are to promote the member countries' balanced and harmonious development under equitable conditions through integration and economic as well as social cooperation and to gradually form a common Latin American market.	■ Bolivia, Columbia, Ecuador, Peru (Associated countries: Chile, Argentina, Brazil, Paraguay, Uruguay)	■ 97	■ 216
■ Mercado Común del Sur (MERCOSUR)	■ 1991	■ Single market without tariffs among member states. Aims at establishment of common trading policies for the rest of the world in terms of tariffs and exchange rates.	■ Argentina, Brazil, Paraguay, Uruguay, Venezuela (since Dec. 2005) (Associated countries: Bolivia, Chile, Peru, Columbia, Ecuador)	■ 261	■ 931
■ ASEAN Free Trade Area (AFTA), previously: Association of Southeast Asian Nations (ASEAN)	■ ASEAN: 1967	■ Goal is the establishment of a free trade area to act as a counterbalance towards China.	■ Brunei Darussalam, Cambodia, Indonesia, Laos, Malaysia, Myanmar, Philippines, Singapore, Thailand, Vietnam	■ 559	■ 884

■ Caribbean Community (CARICOM), forerunner Caribbean Free Trade Association (CARIFTA)	■ CARICOM 1973	■ The objectives include improved standards of living and work, accelerated, coordinated and sustained economic development and convergence, expansion of trade and economic relations with third states, enhanced levels of international competitiveness, organisation for increased production and productivity, enhanced coordination of member states' foreign and [foreign] economic policies and enhanced functional cooperation.	■ Antigua and Barbuda, The Bahamas, Barbados, Belize, Dominica, Grenada, Guyana, Haiti, Jamaica, Montserrat, Saint Lucia, St. Kitts and Nevis, St. Vincent and the Grenadines, Suriname, Trinidad and Tobago	■ 7 (2002)	■ 23
■ Southern African Development Community (SADC), forerunner Southern African Development Coordination Conference (SADCC)	■ SADC: 1992	■ The objectives are to achieve development and economic growth, alleviate poverty, enhance the standard and quality of life of the people of Southern Africa, support the socially disadvantaged through regional integration and promote and defend peace and security.	■ Angola, Botswana, the Democratic Republic of Congo, Lesotho, Madagascar, Malawi, Mauritius, Mozambique, Namibia, South Africa, Swaziland, United Republic of Tanzania, Zambia, Zimbabwe	■ 305 (2004)	■ 235 (2004)
■ Common Market for Eastern and Southern Africa (COMESA), previously: Preferential Trade Area for Eastern and Southern Africa (PTA)	■ COMESA: 1994	■ The aim is to facilitate the removal of the structural and institutional weaknesses of member states and to attain collective and sustained development by creating and maintaining a free trade area and a customs union, adopting common investment practices and by gradually establishing a payments union and monetary union with a common currency.	■ Angola, Burundi, Comoros, Democratic Republic of Congo, Djibouti, Egypt, Eritrea, Ethiopia, Kenya, Libya, Madagascar, Malawi, Mauritius, Rwanda, Seychelles, Sudan, Swaziland, Uganda, Zambia, Zimbabwe	■ 386 (2004, excl. Angola)	■ 194 (2004, excl. Angola)
■ World Trade Organization (WTO)	■ 1995	■ Previously: GATT (General Agreements on Tariffs and Trade). The Uruguay Round (1986–1994) set up an international body called WTO. Permanent institution with its own secretariat, entity of the United Nations. WTO commitments are full and permanent and legally binding under international law. WTO has statutory powers to adjudicate trade disputes among nations.	■ 150 member states (Jan. 2006)		

distribution of power. Societies with low power distances are characterized by a certain degree of egalitarianism.

2 **Individualism** describes the degree to which people prefer to act as individuals rather than group members ('me' versus 'we' societies). In an individualistic society, the focus is on people's own interests; there is little need for loyalty to a group. In collectivistic societies, the interests of the group take center stage.

3 **Masculinity**: if a country culture demonstrates a high degree of masculinity, individuals tend to be more assertive and display competitive behavior; with low masculinity, values such as modesty and care-taking predominate.

4 **Uncertainty avoidance** is defined as the extent to which people in a culture prefer structured situations, with clear rules, over unstructured ones. With a high uncertainty avoidance, members of a society feel threatened by uncertain or unfamiliar situations; cultures with a low level of uncertainty avoidance show a greater willingness on the part of individuals to take risks.

5 **Long-termism** (vs **short-termism**): with long-termism, members of the culture are very forward-looking, and value perseverance and economical behavior (e.g. thriftiness). If a culture is characterized by short-termism, its members prioritize values connected to the past and present, such as respect for tradition.

Based on extensive empirical studies conducted by Hofstede (e.g. 1980, 1994), the countries of the world can be categorized according to the cultural dimensions described above. Examples of this are shown in Figures 12-3 and 12-4, where the relative positions of 12 sample countries on the cultural dimensions are illustrated. Each country has its own position, which allows predictions about behavior in different cultures. A country's position within Figure 12-3 (which contrasts the two dimensions 'uncertainty avoidance' and 'power distance'), for example, may predict the way in which people organize themselves and how problems are approached in these cultures (Hofstede 1980, p. 320).

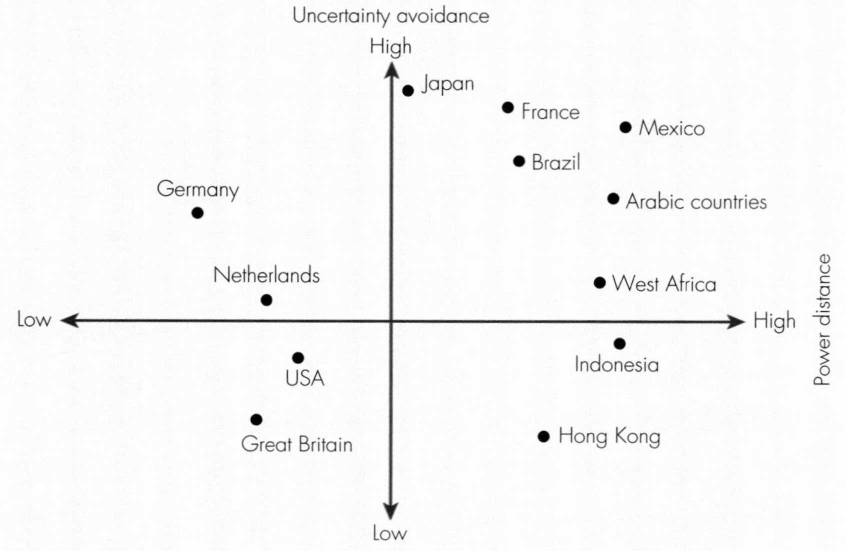

Figure 12-3 Characterization of selected countries based on the cultural dimensions of power distance and uncertainty avoidance (adapted from Hofstede 1994, pp. 6–7)

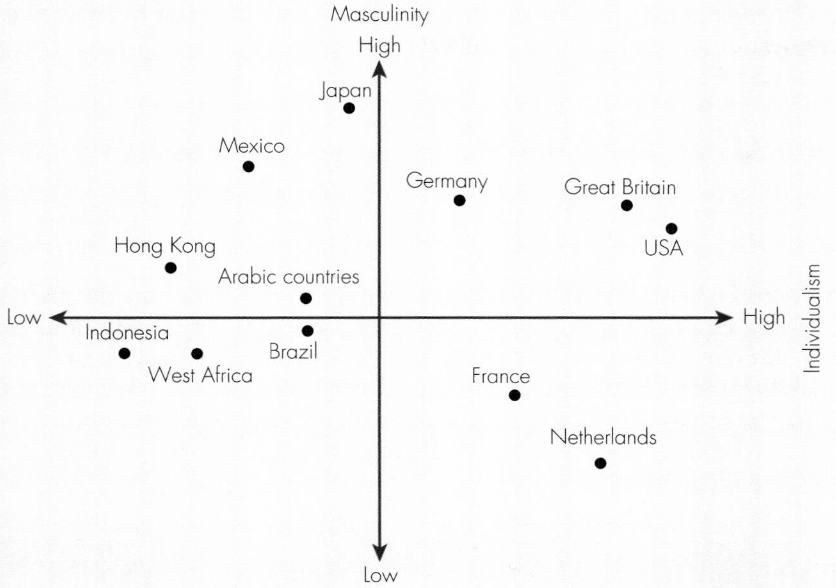

Figure 12-4 Characterization of selected countries based on the cultural dimensions of individualism and masculinity (adapted from Hofstede 1994, p. 6)

Hofstede's cultural dimensions have been used in a wide variety of studies (for a review see, e.g., Kirkman *et al.* 2006). Nevertheless, the work of Hofstede has also been criticized (e.g. Baskerville 2003; McSweeney 2002; Trompenaars 1996).

Another multidimensional approach to describing country cultures is the cultural concept developed by Trompenaars (1996), which expands the cultural dimensions used by Hofstede (power distance, individualism, uncertainty avoidance and long-termism vs short-termism) by adding three further dimensions, as noted below.

1 **Emotionality** (affective vs neutral cultures): are feelings and emotions displayed openly or kept concealed? Do people rather use affective or rational aspects to make judgements?

2 **Quality of the relationship with other individuals** (specific vs diffuse cultures): are different living situations strictly separated from one another (e.g. work and private life)? In diffuse cultures, for example, work life and family life are not sharply separated. These cultures aim at long-term relationships and loyalty to company and customers.

3 **Attitudes towards the personal environment** (self-determined vs heteronomous cultures): can individuals dominate the environment (including nature)? Do people respond to change with open minds or scepticism? Do individuals focus on themselves or others?

Lastly, the one-dimensional cultural approach taken by Hall (1976) primarily focuses on the communication behavior of individuals in various cultures. The concept differentiates between 'high-context' and 'low-context' cultures, as outlined below.

- In **high-context cultures** (e.g. in many Asian countries and Latin America), the verbal and non-verbal communication of individuals can be interpreted differently depending on the context: facial expressions, gestures and intonations are often more important than what is actually being said. Communication is more indirect, and individuals are in fact not even supposed to communicate too directly or explicitly. Much remains unspoken, but is communicated by means of non-verbal communication. Accordingly, in a high-context culture, openly expressed criticism of another person would be considered impolite.

- In contrast to this, in **low-context cultures** (e.g. the USA, Australia, Germany), communication is very explicit and direct (see Kim *et al.* 1998; Mintu-Wimsatt and Gassenheimer 2000). The information content is conveyed in the spoken word – that is, what is meant is being said. In these cultures, objections or criticisms can be communicated much more explicitly than in high-context cultures.

The cultural differences discussed here are extremely relevant with regard to designing the marketing strategy for different countries, especially with respect to designing company communications (see Section 12.4.3; Roth 1995). Moreover, cultural differences in the management style of managers, as well as the decision-making process, also need to be taken into consideration (see Newman and Nollen 1996, and Focus on Marketing 12-2). Likewise, the different approaches to communication and language also have to be taken into consideration during negotiations with foreign business partners (for more on this, see Section 12.4.4).

Focus on Marketing 12-2 Illustration of the importance of understanding cultural differences in an international marketing context

Japanese versus German business antics

[T]wo famous international companies – one Japanese, the other German – had signed a joint venture agreement to develop, produce and launch a product that had the potential to capture a new market. The joint venture would combine the marketing skills of one company with the technology and design skills of the other (my client). But, within a few days of their arrival, the Japanese engineers were in a state of shock. They found their German collaborators to be rude, inconsiderate and lazy. The Germans interrupted during meetings and presentations, and showed no interest in reaching consensus through the numerous 'pre-meeting' meetings that are an integral part of Japanese business culture. The Japanese were uncomfortable with the German way of arguing everything out in front of everyone: for the Japanese, the potential for loss of face was just too big. They also disliked what they saw as the Germans' willingness to go home, even when tasks were unfinished. As for the Germans, they were equally unhappy with the Japanese, many of whom seemed unable to speak English, the supposed common language of the team. The Germans complained that even those who could speak it didn't state their opinions clearly and frankly. The trouble is, each culture assumes their way is the 'normal' one.

Source: Pooley 2005, pp. 28f.

12.1.2 Now for Something Completely Different: Buying Behavior in an International Context

Cultural differences also exist in **buying behavior** between countries, which can be of great significance in international marketing. We will first examine the differences in the buying behavior of individuals, and then discuss the differences in organizational buying behavior.

In particular, the differences in individual buying behavior from country to country can be a result of different social and economic structures and values. A tool for deriving a typology of individuals based on these two dimensions is the lifestyle approach of Sinus Sociovision, which calls the

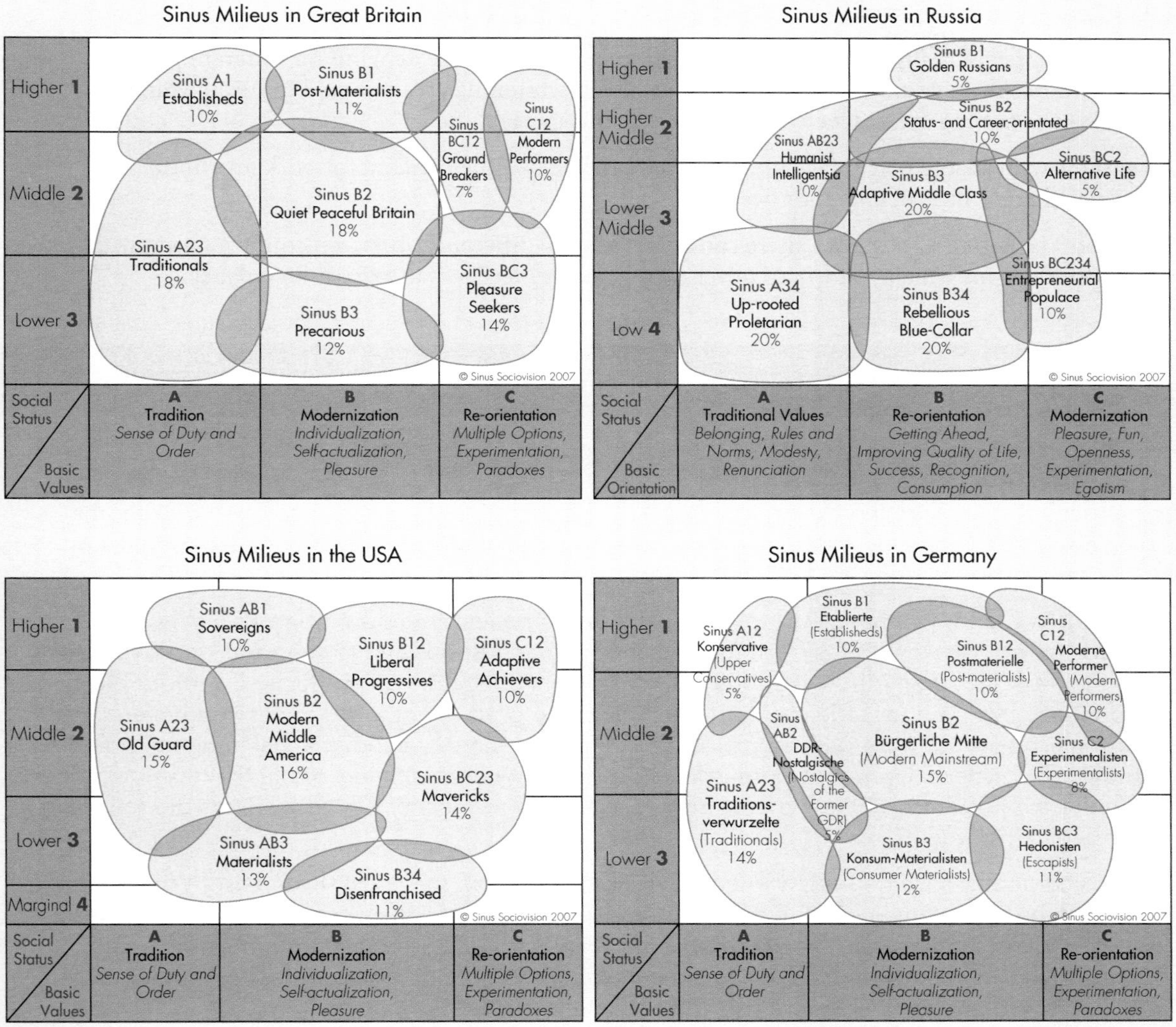

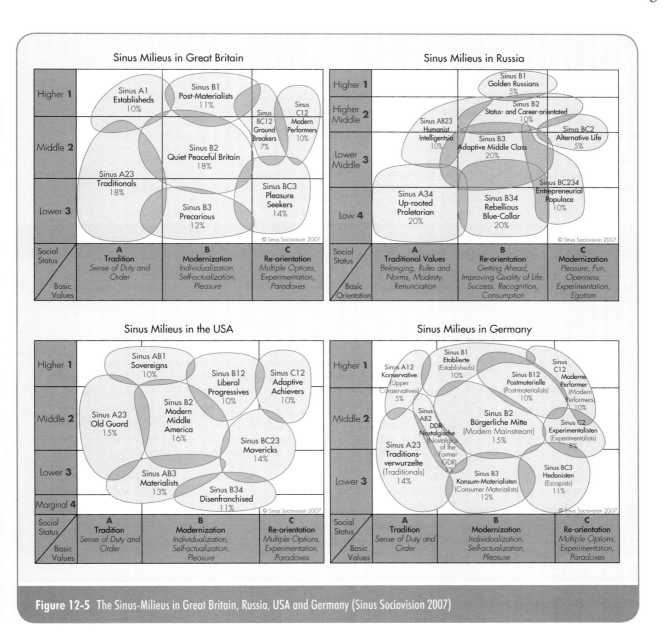

Figure 12-5 The Sinus-Milieus in Great Britain, Russia, USA and Germany (Sinus Sociovision 2007)

lifestyle types Sinus-Milieus (Sinus Sociovision 2007). As Figure 12-5 shows, considerable structural differences prevail between the various countries with regard to the existence of individual segments as well as the size of these segments.

Such differences can have relevance for international market development. For example, certain products (e.g. organic foods) are most successful in certain milieus. If these milieus do not exist in a country market or are only marginal, then, for example, the market entry of those products in that country should be critically examined.

Along with these types of differences between countries, which are ultimately based on different lifestyles, there are numerous specific differences with regard to product preferences in the various nations, as in the following examples.

- Often, Spanish customers wash their dishes by hand under cold running water. They need dish-washing liquid that performs well under such conditions.

- In Great Britain, laundry is washed at a much lower temperature than in most other European countries. Manufacturers of laundry detergents need to take this into account.
- Women's skincare is affected by climatic conditions, and therefore demand for different product features varies from country to country. For example, whitening cream is sold to Asian women, whereas self-tanning creams have no relevance in this market.
- In nations with a large percentage of Muslims there will be little demand for pork; in Hindu countries there is little demand for beef.

As Focus on Marketing 12-3 shows, there can be substantial differences between countries even with regard to products for which you would never expect such differences to exist at first glance.

Focus on Marketing 12-3 Carrefour tapping into the Chinese market

The Quarterly: How has Carrefour had to adapt to Chinese tastes?

Jean-Luc Chéreau: Take the example of fish. When I am in San Francisco and I visit a store, the fish is filleted and packed; it's dead. When I am in France, the fish is dead but it's whole; it's on ice. I can see its eyes and see if it's fresh or not. Each place has its own way of selling fish.

If you are in China, you have two ways of selling fish. The first is to display live fish. When we entered Taiwan, we went to the fresh markets in Taipei and Kaohsiung to see what kind of products they had, how they were displayed, and how customers bought those products. Carrefour decided to adopt this fresh-market style and to display the same products at lower prices in a better, cleaner environment. And we were very, very successful. Now, on the mainland, the first image customers get when they enter a Carrefour store is fresh products. When customers are in the fresh area, they recognize the fresh market they're accustomed to. And now most of our competitors are following Carrefour in this way.

But another method we neglected when we moved away from the coast: frozen fish. Why would frozen fish be important in China? Because the distance between the area where they have fresh fish and the stores in middle and western China is so vast that customers are more confident of frozen fish than of unfrozen dead fish, even if fresh. So we changed our product offering and we saw a 30 to 40 percent increase in fish sales throughout China.

The Quarterly: How have you had to adapt as you've expanded into the smaller cities?

Jean-Luc Chéreau: We also adapt the assortment. You cannot imagine the importance of local products. To give you an example, take beer. Everybody knows Tsingtao beer, but when you go to Beijing, which is only one hour by plane from Qingdao, where they brew Tsingtao beer, the number-one beer in market share is not Tsingtao; it's Beijing beer. The same goes for electrical appliances. In Nanjing, Panda is an old and famous brand, and it has 35 percent of the market share for televisions there. If you promote Panda televisions in Nanjing, you will do well.

Source: adapted from Child (2006) Lessons from a global retailer: An interview with the president of Carrefour China, *McKinsey Quarterly*, Special edition, 70–81.

Two special concepts are particularly relevant to the formation of preferences in an international marketing context.

1 According to the **country-of-origin effect**, a product's country of origin influences its image among customers in different countries (for an overview of this effect, see Clarke *et al.* 2000;

Gurhan-Canli and Maheswaran 2000; Verlegh and Steenkamp 1997). More specifically, the country of manufacture, assembly or design influences the customer's positive or negative perceptions of a product. Depending on the country of manufacture and the target country, the label 'Made in . . .' can be associated with either a positive or negative image (see Berndt *et al.* 1997). For example, cars made in Germany, red wine from France, Italian shoes and beef from Argentina all connote a positive image (see Focus on Marketing 12-4 for other examples).

2 The **ethnocentrism phenomenon** refers to the fact that certain customer groups rate the image and product quality of products from their own country as more positive than products manufactured in foreign countries (see Klein *et al.* 1998; Shimp and Sharma 1987). The result of this can be preferences for domestic products and, in the end, preferential buying of those products.

Focus on Marketing 12-4 'Made in' labels can make all the difference

Where a product has originated from can make a big difference to how consumers perceive it. Take, for example, an Italian-made shirt and a Chinese-made shirt. Both shirts are made from the same material and have been cut in the same style, but the Italian-made label will immediately give the shirt a stylish designer quality and this helps to increase the price at which the garment is sold. However, the same shirts with a 'made in China' label may be considered to be of lower quality.

Similarly, Switzerland is a good example of national brand power. Anything with 'made in Switzerland' on it is considered to be good quality, and watches are something that the Swiss are renowned for doing well.

Swiss watch standards, like Breitling, Piaget and Rolex, receive tremendous amounts of their brand equity from being Swiss-made. But, recently, more moderate price point brands, such as Swatch, Guess, Anne Klein, and even 'no name', ultra-low-price Chinese copies, have benefited from having the words 'Swiss made' stamped on them. In fact, the first three brands depend heavily on the Swiss connection to reinforce or even elevate their position as high-quality, precise and serious 'time pieces'. Even third-world counterfeit watch brands make sure that the Swiss connection is evident on their offerings.

Source: adapted from Jaworski and Fosher (2003) National brand identity and its effect on corporate brands: the nation brand effect, *Multinational Business Review*, 11, 12, Fall, 99–108.

Along with the specific characteristics of customer buying behavior described above, it is also important to consider the particulars of **organizational buying behavior in an international context**. For example, there is an increasing **cross-national centralization of organizational buying behavior**. Key motives behind this increasing centralization are the bundling of demand and the reinforcement of the position of power over the suppliers. For example, prices are often no longer negotiated on a country-by-country basis, but rather centrally negotiated. Increasingly (technical) product specifications are also harmonized across national borders.

Differences between national markets are also of consequence for **market segmentation in international marketing** (for a discussion of market segmentation in general, see Section 4.1.1, and for more on international market segmentation, see Hassan and Katsanis 1994; Hofstede *et al.* 1999). In this context, three methods can be used, as discussed below.

1 If the customer behavior is sufficiently homogeneous in several countries, a **country-as-segments** or **aggregate segmentation** approach can be applied. With this approach, national markets are the basis for segmentation and are not subdivided further. In company practice, countries of

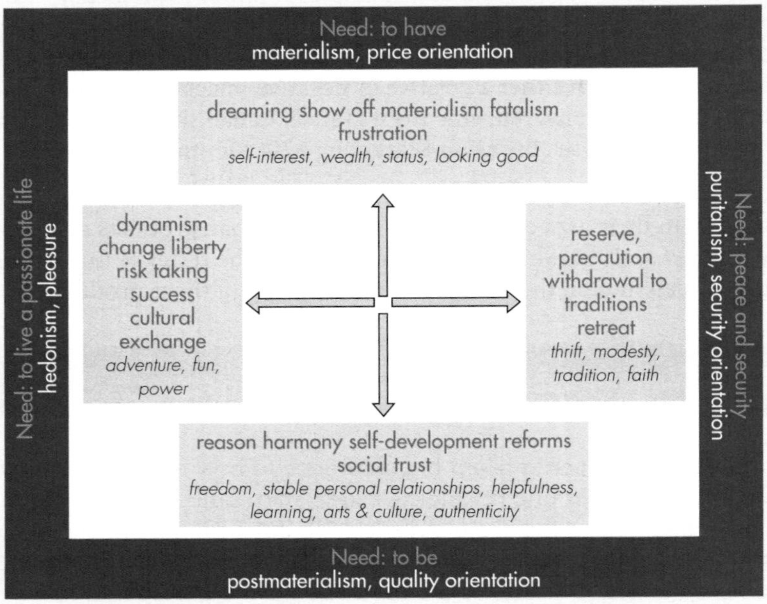

Figure 12-6a Example of the drivers of consumption and consumption preferences (GfK Roper Consumer Styles) (GfK 2007)

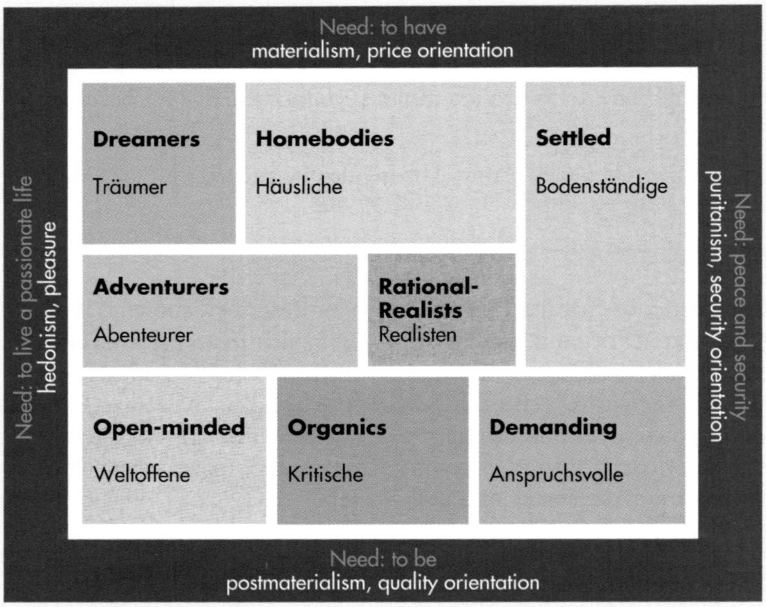

Figure 12-6b Example of a customer typology (GfK Roper Consumer Styles) as a basis for a disaggregate international customer segmentation (GfK 2007)

the same region are often clustered into segments (e.g. the European market is divided into the following segments: Central Europe, Southern Europe and Eastern Europe/Scandinavia).

2 With the **disaggregate international customer segmentation** approach, national markets are further subdivided. International market segmentation is not based on national markets as a unit, instead **customer groups** are organized in **international market segments on a cross-national basis**. Accordingly, for example, a financial services provider can develop a wealthy private customer segment on a European-wide scale. Cross-national buyer typologies, which are prepared, say, by market research institutes, can be used as the basis for developing disaggregate international customer segmentation. An example of this is shown in Figure 12-6a, where customers from 38 countries worldwide are classified into four main segments according to their value systems and preferences/according to their orientation towards the need to have vs the need to be and the need of peace and security vs the need to live a passionate life. Each of these segments describes a certain lifestyle, which is independent of nationality (lifestyle-based typology of customers; see Figure 12-6b).

In the context of disaggregate international customer segmentation, different scenarios may arise, as shown in Figure 12-7. Customer needs and preferences may be similar on a universal level (see section A in Figure 12-7) or on a regional level (see section B for Country X and Y, or D for Country Y and Z in Figure 12-7). Thus, so-called universal or global segments and regional segments can be differentiated. Examples of possible global segments are businesspeople, teenagers (the 'MTV Generation') or the global elite. As is also shown in Figure 12-7, the size of different segments varies depending on the country (see Kotabe and Helsen 2007).

3 Finally, **country-specific segmentation** can be used if the typology of the individual countries indicates that certain customer segments cannot be integrated on a cross-national basis. In this case, country-specific market segments are based solely on national markets (see segments C, E and F in Figure 12-7).

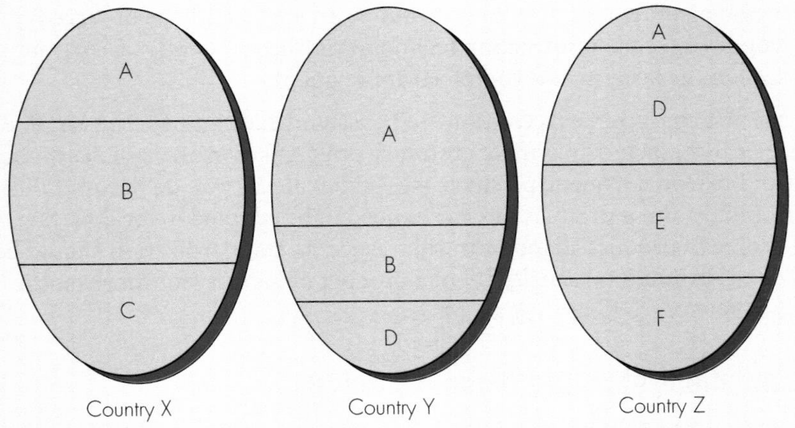

Figure 12-7 Example of different segmentation scenarios (see Kotabe and Helsen 2007)

In addition to the question of the existence of international market segments, another relevant issue concerns the extent to which social and cultural conditions, and thus customer buying behavior, across different countries of the world become more uniform. Two contrasting developments should be mentioned with regard to this: one is the **cross-national convergence of cultures**, which, for example, is promoted by the international use of media (e.g. television, the internet), as well as by tourism, workforce migration and cultural exchange activities. In many countries, similar sociodemographic developments are occurring (for example, a trend towards single-person households and a rise in the average life expectancy), too. Such developments consequently lead to a convergence of customer behavior in the various national markets. A counter-development to this is emerging from the growing **response against such cross-national convergence,** combined with a conscious return on the part of customers to regional specialities and consumption patterns.

A possible explanation for convergence is presented in Levitt's **convergence hypothesis** (1983). The author advanced the theory that markets become more similar, and that cross-cultural and cross-national segments emerge with converging needs. According to this thesis, Levitt sees reasons for the convergence of buyer demands arising from the:

- similar sociodemographic developments in many industrial nations (e.g. a trend towards families with small children, and longer life expectancy)
- intensive interaction with foreign cultures (e.g. in education), as well as
- improvements in transportation technologies (e.g. faster and less expensive long-distance flights) and communications technologies (e.g. the internet).

Companies are responding to this by **standardizing their products and services** and, increasingly, by centralizing their decision-making authorities (e.g. at company headquarters). Due to the economies of scale arising as one effect of standardization, companies are able to lower their prices. Even though Levitt's hypothesis has received academic and managerial attention, it has also been vigorously discussed and disputed ever since its emergence.

In our opinion, there can be no standard answer to the question of whether there is a trend towards a convergence of buying behavior across different countries. There are a few industries in which we can speak of **global customers**. For example, standardization of buying behavior can certainly be observed in the business-to-business sector. There, globally operating purchasing departments place priority on internationally comparable quality standards. Of course, there are also differences with regard to the culturally shaped value systems of the purchasers (Homburg *et al.* 2005), but in the course of making economically sound buying decisions, these are often secondary to economic arguments. In the business-to-consumer sector, standardization can particularly be observed in the case of durable consumer goods (e.g. cars, information technology or luxury goods). Cross-national convergences can also be seen in the fashion and youth culture segments.

In other sectors, country-specific characteristics continue to be a significant influencing variable in terms of buying decisions. Local characteristics affect customer preferences in areas such as food, beverages, and household and personal hygiene products (see Alden *et al.* 1999; de Mooij 2000; Kacen and Lee 2002). Accordingly, these product categories need to be adapted to local market requirements. Hence, the degree of product adaptation with respect to standardization should be determined by the degree of **environmental sensitivity** of a product or service (for more on the concept of environmental sensitivity see Keegan *et al.* 2002).

12.1.3 Theoretical Foundations of International Marketing

As far as **theoretical foundations of international marketing** are concerned, there are two different sets of theories.

1. **Theories that attempt to explain internationalization** focus on the question of why there is an international exchange of goods and direct investments in foreign countries at all.
2. Rather more relevant to marketing are **theories for designing concepts of international market development.** Concrete recommendations for international marketing can be derived from these theories.

Within the context of theories that attempt to explain internationalization, the evolution of marketing across national boundaries is of special interest. The EPRG model assumes such an

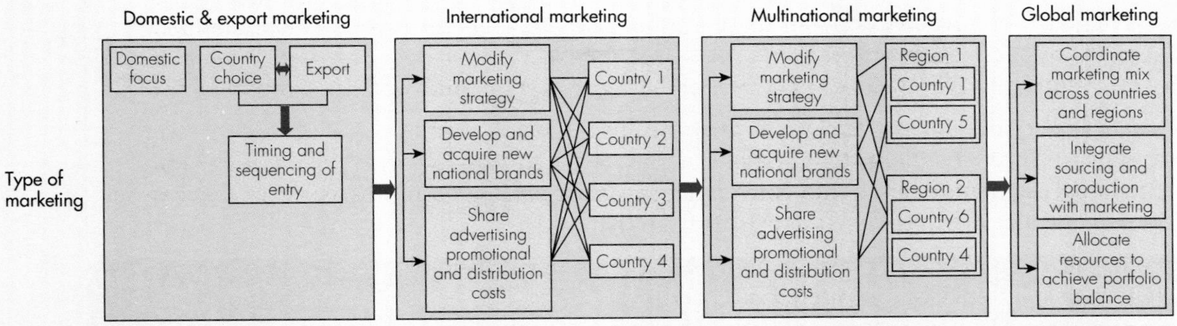

Orientation	Ethnocentric	Polycentric	Regiocentric	Geocentric
Product planning	Product development (primarily) for home country customers	Local product development based on local needs	Standardized within region, but not across	Global products with local variations
Marketing mix decisions	Made at headquarters	Made in each country	Made regionally	Made jointly with mutual consultation

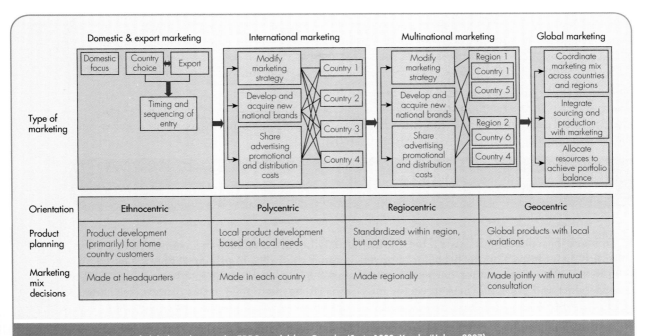

Figure 12-8 Evolution of global marketing: the EPRG-model (see Douglas/Craig 1989, Kotabe/Helsen 2007)

evolutionary perspective of internationalization of companies, describing a company's orientation towards internationalization along four different stages (see Douglas and Craig 1989, and Figure 12-8). The first stage is characterized by an **ethnocentric orientation** (see also Section 12.1.2), where marketers pay little attention to the different needs and requirements of the global marketplace. On the contrary, product development marketing activities are geared to the needs of customers located in the home country. A company in this stage operates on a domestic or export marketing level. By contrast, a **polycentric orientation** leads a company to tailor its marketing strategy and mix decisions to the respective country-specific needs. When adopting a **regiocentric approach**, a company may consolidate activities on a regional basis (e.g. product planning and manufacturing may be standardized within a region of similar and maybe geographically close countries). This is referred to as multinational marketing. Finally, a company can not only adopt a country-by-country or region-by-region perspective, it may rather be globally oriented by standardizing marketing programs when feasible, and coordinating and globally integrating country markets in order to optimize operations to be globally competitive. This approach is driven by an overall **geocentric orientation**.

Being aware of these dynamics of the evolutionary development in marketing activities helps firms to be prepared for the potential changes needed in their marketing strategy as they expand internationally. It may also provide a company with competitive advantages over time, since it can predict and pre-empt its competitors' likely marketing strategy (see Kotabe and Helsen 2007).

We will now go on to explain two important theories that deal with the **design of international market development concepts**:

1 the coordination perspective (see Backhaus *et al.* 2004), and

2 the interdependency-similarity pattern (see Homburg and Jensen 2004, 2005).

The **coordination perspective** of international marketing focuses on analyzing the cross-national coordination of market development activities (see Backhaus *et al.* 2004). The necessity for such coordination arises from interdependencies (feedback effects) between the individual national markets. In general, there are four types of feedback effect.

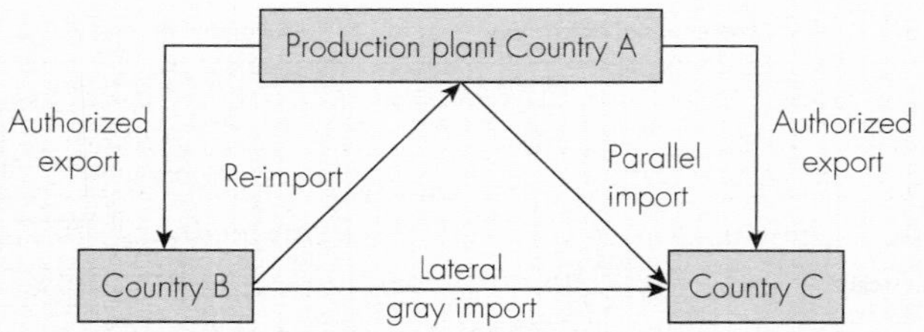

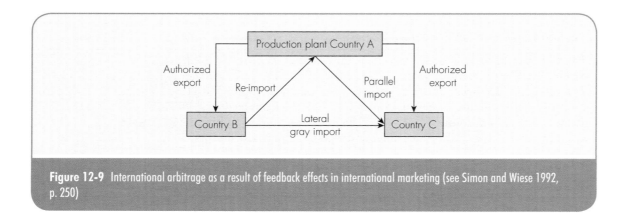

Figure 12-9 International arbitrage as a result of feedback effects in international marketing (see Simon and Wiese 1992, p. 250)

1 **Demand-based feedback** exists if the marketing activities of a company in a country have a more or less direct impact on the behavior of buyers in other countries. In principle, they are based on the exchange of information between national markets. In particular, the international availability of product and price information via the internet has to be mentioned in this context (see Dutta *et al.* 1998).

2 **Institutional feedback** refers to interdependencies between national markets that emerge as a result of political and legal market conditions. Thus, for example, problems can arise for a company if it conducts business with the governments of two hostile countries.

3 **Competition-based feedback** refers to responses on the part of competitors in one country that are triggered as a reaction to the marketing activities of the company in a different country. If, say, one firm 'attacks' a competitor in its domestic market by reducing prices, that competitor might launch a 'counterattack' in its own domestic market.

4 **Company-based feedback** exists if a company's development of a national market impacts the opportunities for developing another national market. For example, tapping into a certain national market may tax the resources of the company to such a great extent that there are fewer resources left for developing other national markets.

Next, we will focus on demand-based feedback effects. Demand-based feedback can lead to international arbitrage processes as a result of parallel imports, re-imports and lateral gray imports (see Myers 1999; Figure 12-9). Such arbitrage processes take place if the price differences between national markets are greater than the arbitrage costs associated with a cross-border product transfer (e.g. transportation costs, customs/duties, communication costs). This applies in particular in the case of products where price is high relative to transportation costs (e.g. automobiles, medication).

With regard to the European economic zone, it is particularly important to mention the currency union (see Simon *et al.* 1998). This promotes demand-based feedback effects in two respects: first, it increases the exchange of information between country markets because prices are easy to compare. Second, arbitrage costs decrease due to the common currency.

Demand-based feedback effects can have a significant impact on a company's international marketing concept and strategy. There are two main approaches to addressing feedback effects (for a similar discussion, see Backhaus *et al.* 2004):

1 coordination of marketing activities related to national markets

2 management of interdependencies.

The **coordination of marketing activities related to national markets** refers to the coordination of national marketing strategies necessitated by feedback effects between markets. Pricing decisions and decisions concerning new product developments have to be coordinated for the various markets, taking into account potential feedback effects.

The management of interdependencies comprises the ongoing monitoring of the extent of the feedback between the different markets in which the company operates. It also includes the controlled manipulation of feedback effects in order to promote the company's interests. For example, the company can attempt to prevent grey imports arising from feedback effects by implementing measures such as country-specific product differentiation and branding, warranty restrictions or limiting the product range supplied to certain distributors.

The **interdependency-similarity pattern** (see Homburg and Jensen 2004, 2005) expands the coordination perspective with an additional dimension of analysis: the similarity of cross-border customer preferences. According to this approach, international markets are characterized by two dimensions:

1 cross-national similarity of customer requirements

2 cross-national interdependency of the markets.

The concept of interdependency is closely related to the (in particular, demand-based) feedback effects discussed above. With a high degree of interdependency, the marketing activities of a company in one country have a substantial effect on the market in a different country.

The two dimensions are combined in Figure 12-10. Basic conclusions with regard to the **design of the international market development concept and strategy** can now be derived from the diagram. At the forefront here is the question of the extent to which market development should be internationally standardized or, instead, designed on a country-specific basis. We will limit our discussion in this context to product decisions and price decisions.

Since customer requirements also apply to the features of products, it is evident that the cross-national similarity of customer requirements has implications for **product decisions**. The more similar the customer requirements, the greater the pressure for product standardization. This

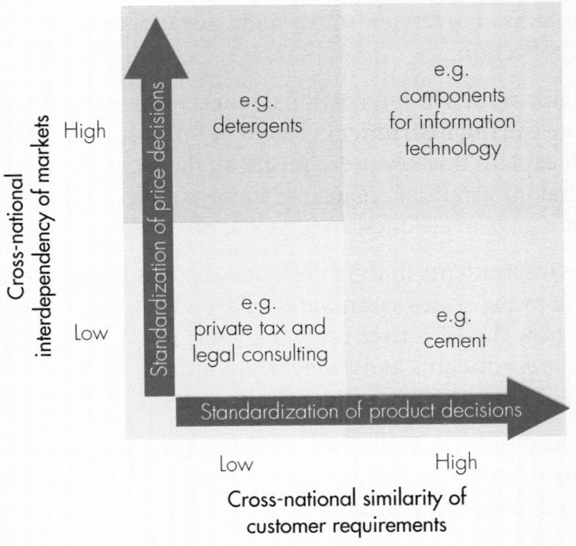

Figure 12-10 The similarity-interdependency pattern in international marketing (see Homburg and Jensen 2004)

pressure for standardization exists because customers demand internationally similar products, and because the company can decrease costs.

In the scope of **pricing**, similar customer requirements do not alone trigger any pressure for standardization. The crucial driving force here is the interdependency of the markets. If two closely connected markets offer major price differences, the consequence can be re-imports, which makes price differentiation difficult. If customers in different countries exchange price conditions with each other, price differences can easily annoy customers, but the reverse also applies: in less closely related markets, companies should not rush to standardize their prices since, in doing so, they forego the opportunity to tap into customers' willingness to pay and thus reduce their profits.

The correlation of markets has a small impact on the standardization of the product: even in extremely closely related markets, companies will not standardize their products as long as customer requirements clearly differ.

This discussion illustrates that product standardization and price standardization are driven by different forces. A simultaneous standardization of product decisions and price decisions is thus not indicated for each and every market constellation.

12.2 Specific Characteristics of International Market Research

In view of the higher level of complexity and uncertainty in international marketing (see Section 12.1.1), market research plays an especially important role in preparing marketing decisions (see Bauer 1997).

In terms of using **suitable data collection methods** (for more on data collection methods, see the Appendix), it should be noted that the various data collection methods (e.g. written questionnaires vs telephone interviews) are not accepted equally or cannot be used in all countries. For example, written questionnaires sent by mail are less acceptable in countries in Southern Europe. Consequently, the international equivalence of data collection methods is frequently not the most important criterion, but rather the selection of accepted and suitable collection methods in the countries concerned. Table 12-3 contains an overview of the main advantages and problems related to the various forms of data collection.

To achieve cross-culturally comparable results in international market research projects, however, the **cross-national equivalence of measuring instruments** has to be ensured (see Cavusgil and Das 1997; Sinkovics *et al.* 1998). We will explain this key prerequisite by the example of customer surveys in various countries (for more general information regarding 'surveys', refer to the Appendix). In principle, there are two problems of equivalence: question equivalence and response equivalence.

Question equivalence is given if the respondents in the different countries interpret the meaning of the items and anchor points in the rating scales as similarly as possible, or, ideally, identically. The example in Figure 12-11 shows how the adjectives used as anchor points on a rating scale are interpreted differently by English respondents and French respondents. In contrast to this, the adjectives presented in Figure 12-12 are interpreted identically in terms of their meaning.

Response equivalence occurs if the respondents in the different countries give the same answers under identical conditions. Problems related to response equivalence can arise, for example, as a result of differences between the countries with regard to:

- the social acceptability of answers
- communication patterns
- the general usage of language.

Table 12-3 Advantages and disadvantages of selected data collection methods used in international market research

Data collection method	Advantages	Problems
Mail questionnaire	■ Low costs ■ Geographically widely dispersed respondents can be addressed ■ Objectivity due to the elimination of (potentially country-specific) interviewer biases	■ Different countries have varying acceptance levels towards mail questionnaires (=different response rates) ■ Delays due to international mail ■ No option for the interviewee to ask questions (e.g. in the case of cultural misunderstandings)
Telephone survey	■ Procedure can be centralized (e.g. from home base country) ■ High flexibility and quick responses ■ Interviewer has option to answer questions raised by the interviewee ■ Limited interviewer bias (less than with face-to-face interviews)	■ High coordination effort (scheduling times with interviewees) ■ Problem with different time zones ■ High international phone costs arising from long interviews ■ In some countries, inadequate telephone coverage and network quality
Face-to-face interview	■ Cultural misunderstanding can be minimized if local interviewer is used	■ Often a lack of trained interviewers on-site ■ High costs (interviewer training, travel expenses, coordination) ■ Interviewer bias (potentially country-specific)

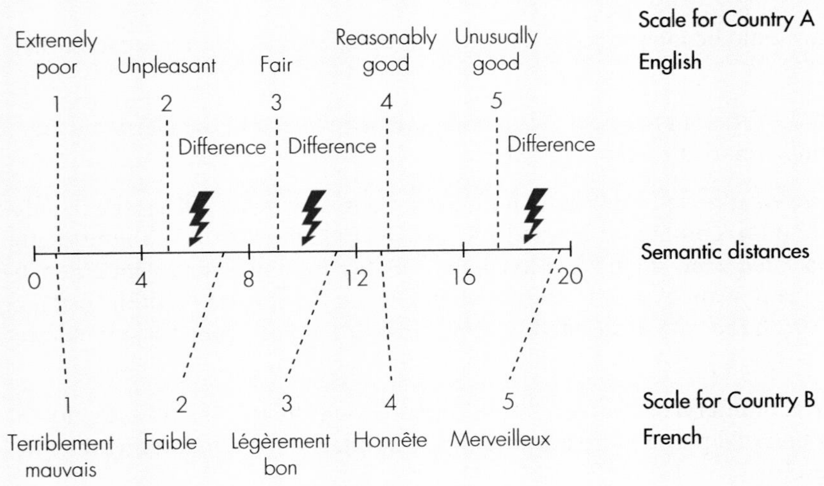

Figure 12-11 Example illustrating insufficient cross-national equivalency of measuring instruments

Example scale 1			
English adjectives		French adjectives	
fantastic	20	20	extraordinaire
delightful	17	17	superbe
pleasant	14	14	très correct
neutral	10	10	moyen
moderately poor	7	7	assez faible
bad	4	4	remarquablement faible
horrible	2	2	terriblement mauvais

Example scale 2			
English adjectives		French adjectives	
remarkably good	17	17	très bon
good	14	14	bon
neutral	10	10	moyen
reasonably poor	6	6	faible
extremely poor	3	3	très mauvais

Figure 12-12 Example of cross-nationally equivalent scale items (see Angelmar and Pras 1978; Bauer 2002)

With respect to the **social acceptability of answers**, in the USA, for example, it is very common to express and show personal affluence and success in a very positive light, whereas, in France, this is considered less acceptable. Accordingly, an empirical study on materialism in the USA would measure materialism by means of the item: 'The things I own say a lot about how successful I am in my life', while, in France, the more sensible formulation would be 'Luxury plays an important role in my life' (see Dubois and Laurent 1993).

In the area of **communication patterns**, for example, it should be noted that readiness to express criticism quite clearly varies greatly from country to country. Accordingly, in an empirical analysis of the attitudes of Japanese managers, after conducting a pre-test, the 'agree' and 'disagree' scale anchor points used in the USA were changed to 'definitely true', 'somewhat true' and 'not true at all', since the Japanese managers were not willing to express personal agreement or disagreement (see Johnson *et al.* 1993).

A number of approaches should be mentioned with regard to the design of international market research projects.

- Persons familiar with the different national cultures should be involved in the planning and design of an international market research project.
- If standardized interview/survey/questionnaire tools are used in several countries, the translation/back-translation method is recommended (see also Craig and Douglas 2000). With this method, a questionnaire is translated from language A to language B by a bilingual person and then 'back-translated' into language A again by a different bilingual person. A comparison of the original version in language A with the back-translated version can point out any potential inconsistencies in understanding.
- Thorough pre-tests (e.g. of interviews/surveys/questionnaires) conducted in advance before the project is actually initiated play a more important role in international marketing than in national market research.

The above discussion relates to the collection and use of primary data in international market research. Specific problems are also connected to the use of **secondary data** in an international context. For example, quality differences exist among different countries in terms of the accuracy of data.

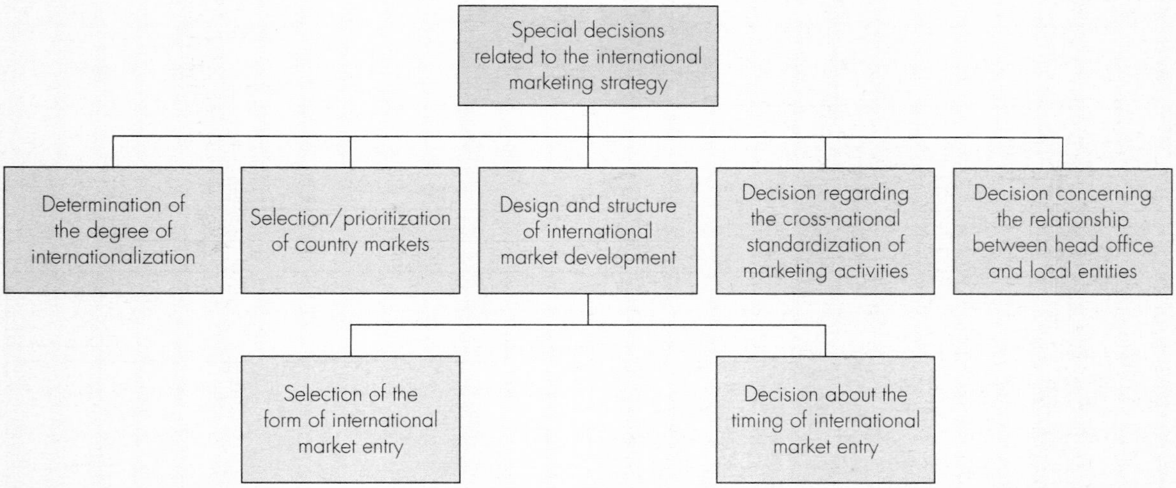

Figure 12-13 Special decisions related to the international marketing strategy

12.3 Specific Characteristics of International Marketing Strategies

The **international marketing** strategy forms the basis for designing the international marketing mix. In general, all the guiding questions concerning the marketing strategy (see Part 1) are also relevant when designing an international marketing strategy. However, there are also some **specific decisions** connected to the formulation of an international marketing strategy. Figure 12-13 provides an overview of these decisions.

A fundamental decision concerns the degree of internationalization (i.e. the extent to which a company wants to actively conduct business operations across the borders of its domestic country). In this context, we will first examine the various **motives for internationalization**. Here, we will distinguish between two main categories of motive:

1 **opportunity-oriented internationalization motives** aim to seize opportunities by entering new markets; these opportunities can be related to sales, prices or costs
2 with **diversification-oriented internationalization motives**, the company's objective is the reduction or diversification of risks.

Figure 12-14 illustrates an overview of internationalization motives.

Once a decision regarding international market entry has been made, there are two additional areas for decision-making: selection/prioritization of markets and the design of the international strategy for market development (form and timing of entry).

Market attractiveness and market entry barriers (i.e. access to markets) can be used as criteria to **select and prioritize markets**. These two aspects have to be evaluated in terms of:

- institutional
- demand-based, and
- competitor-based

factors. Examples of such criteria are listed in Figure 12-15.

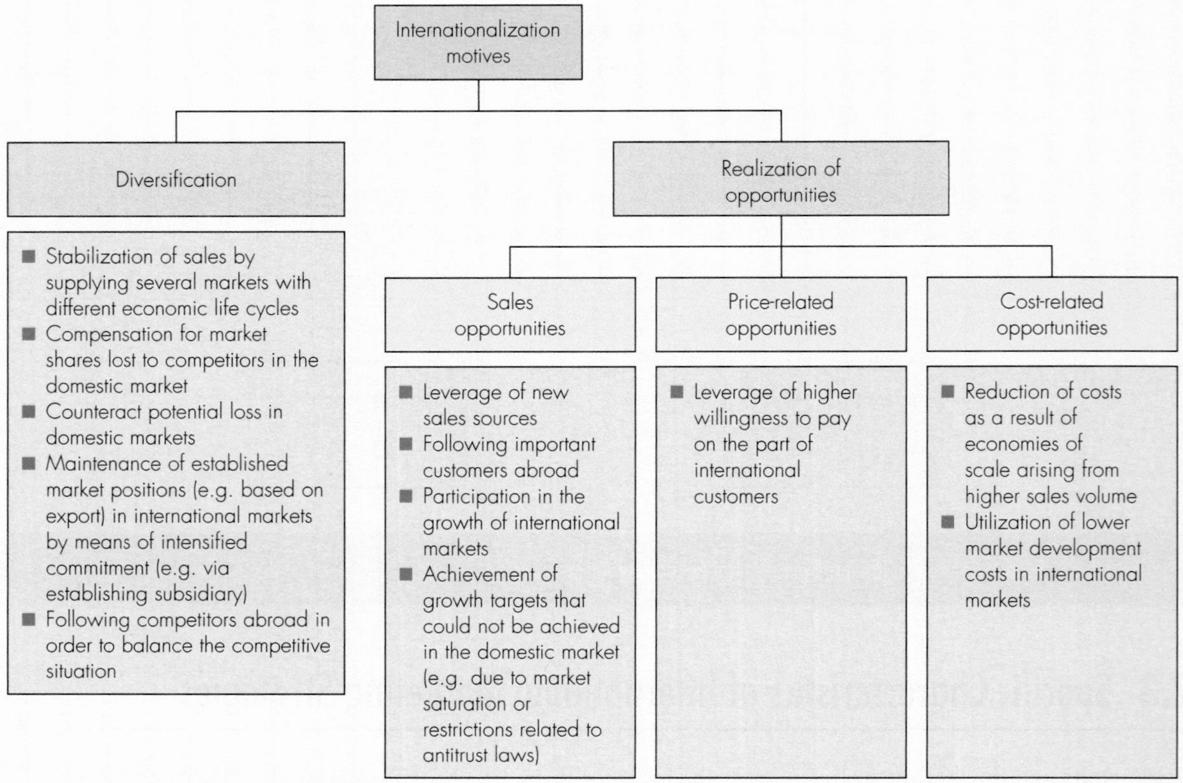

Figure 12-14 Motives for companies to internationalize

When selecting and prioritizing markets, decision-making can also be supported by **portfolio concepts** (for a general discussion of this concept, see Section 4.2). A suitable portfolio method shows a vertical axis that indicates the attractiveness of an international market, while the horizontal axis refers to the accessibility of the market to the company (which ultimately depends on the presence of market entry barriers). Figure 12-16 illustrates the use of such a portfolio with the example of a mechanical engineering company.

The highest priority should be placed on leveraging markets that demonstrate both a high degree of attractiveness and high accessibility (Field A in Figure 12-16). Less attractive, but easily accessible markets – thus demonstrating a low number of market entry barriers (Field B) – should have medium priority. In general, markets with the lowest priority are those that are less attractive as well as difficult to access (Field C).

A general statement concerning the prioritization of markets in Field D cannot be made. These markets need to be scrutinized further. Management should assess whether it will be possible to overcome the market entry barriers in an economical way in order to seize the attractive opportunities these markets offer. If this seems feasible, markets in Field D should be assigned the highest priority. On the contrary, in the case of a negative assessment, no activities should be undertaken. For example, the mechanical engineering company whose analysis is presented in Figure 12-16 decided to enter the US market despite substantial entry barriers, but opted against any development of the Indian market. The strict national regulations related to local production in India played a key role in this decision.

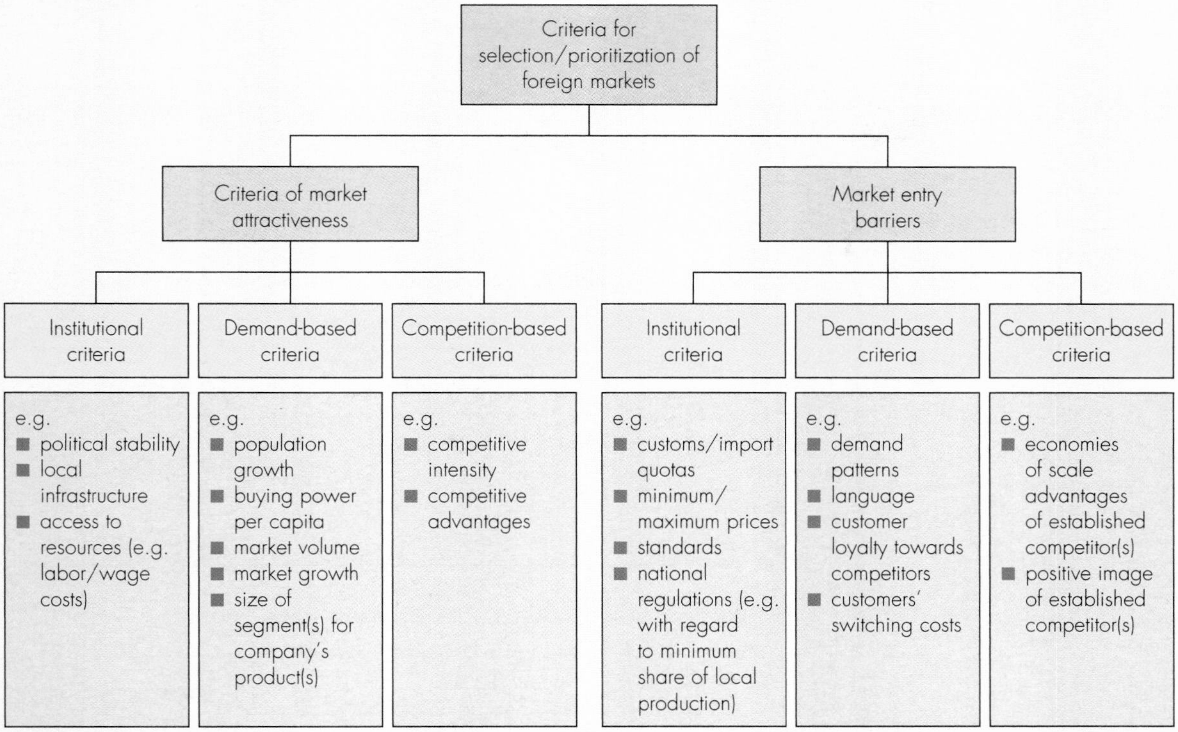

Figure 12-15 Criteria for selecting/prioritizing foreign markets (adapted from Kotabe and Helsen 2007, pp. 283ff.; Meffert and Bolz 1998, p. 141)

Decisions about the **design of the international market development strategy** concern the form as well as the time frame for entries in the selected markets. With regard to the **form of international market entry**, there are in principle a number of options to choose from, ranging from market development via direct exporting, to the establishment of a subsidiary. The decision as to what specific form the market entry should take has to be made on a case-by-case basis, taking the market conditions into account. Table 12-4 shows the basic evaluation of the various forms of market entry according to the criteria of:

- capital invested in foreign countries
- control options for the company
- dependency on cooperations (the necessity of coordinating with international partners)
- the location of headquarters (domestic country or target country).

The preferred form of the international market entry depends on the extent to which a company is already operating internationally. Frequently, a first step in a company's international expansion is exporting products, whereas establishing a foreign subsidiary usually takes place in a later phase of the internationalization process.

In addition to the decision regarding the form of the market entry, decisions also have to be made regarding the **timing of international market entries**. In this respect, different alternatives exist (see Figure 12-17), as listed below.

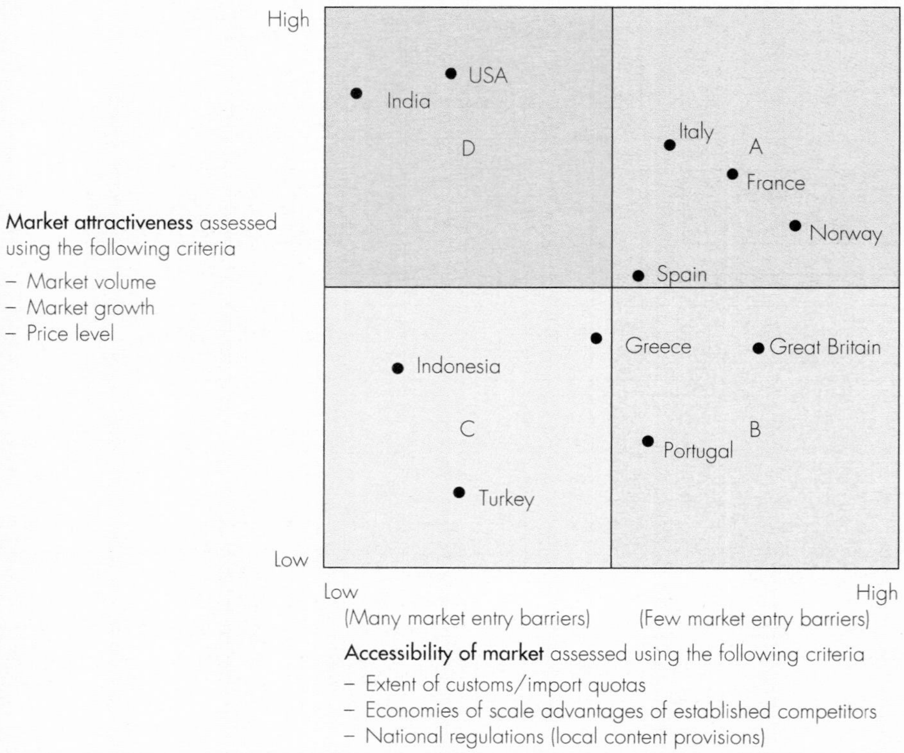

Figure 12-16 Portfolio-based selection/prioritization of international markets using the example of a mechanical engineering company

- If the company opts for a **waterfall strategy**, it enters the new international markets gradually. This internationalization process may take several decades.
- In the case of a **sprinkler strategy**, the internationally expanding company enters the targeted national markets simultaneously, with the objective of more rapid development of international markets.
- In the case of a **hybrid strategy**, the waterfall and sprinkler strategy are combined.

There are certain advantages and disadvantages associated with each of the two extreme alternatives; the most important of these are summarized in Table 12-5. The question concerning how the advantages and disadvantages should be assessed in specific decision-making situations, and which variants should ultimately be realized, has to be answered by the management on a case-by-case basis depending on the specific situation. A few situational factors that argue for the use of a sprinkler vs waterfall strategy are also listed in Table 12-5.

The advantages and disadvantages of both extreme strategies often lead to a hybrid strategy, where the waterfall and sprinkler strategy are combined (i.e. **combined waterfall–sprinkler strategy**). Companies mostly choose this strategy when some countries are perceived as being similar and therefore may be entered simultaneously (for an example, see Figure 12-18).

Another specific decision within the scope of the international marketing strategy relates to the **cross-national standardization of marketing activities** (compare Figure 12-13). In principle, this concerns determining the company's position on a continuum: at one end of the continuum

Table 12-4 Forms of international market entry (adapted from Meffert and Bolz 1998, pp. 125ff.; Kotabe and Helsen 2007, pp. 283ff.)

Form	Description	Capital invested	Control options	Dependency on cooperations	Institutional headquarters
Direct export	Sales without intermediary, primarily via agencies, representatives or branches	Medium/ low	High	Medium/low	Domestic country
Indirect export	Acquisition of orders and delivery via third-party companies acting as intermediaries	Medium	Medium/ low	Medium	Domestic country
Licensing	Transfer of usage rights for the intellectual property of the licensor to the licensee for a lump sum fee or for royalties	Medium/ low	Medium/ low	Medium	Domestic country
Contract manufacturing	Manufacturing of the entire product or individual modules by third parties on a contractual basis	Medium/ low	Medium	Medium	Target country
Joint venture	Establishment of a jointly managed company; the partner capital, knowhow and any already existing company shares are brought into the joint venture. There are three types of joint ventures depending on the distribution of capital shares, and thus the property and control rights: majority, equity and minority joint ventures	Medium/ high	Medium	High	Target country
Subsidiary	Direct capital commitment in international market, without third-party involvement. The subsidiary may perform sales, production or even independent R&D activities	High	High	Medium/low	Target country

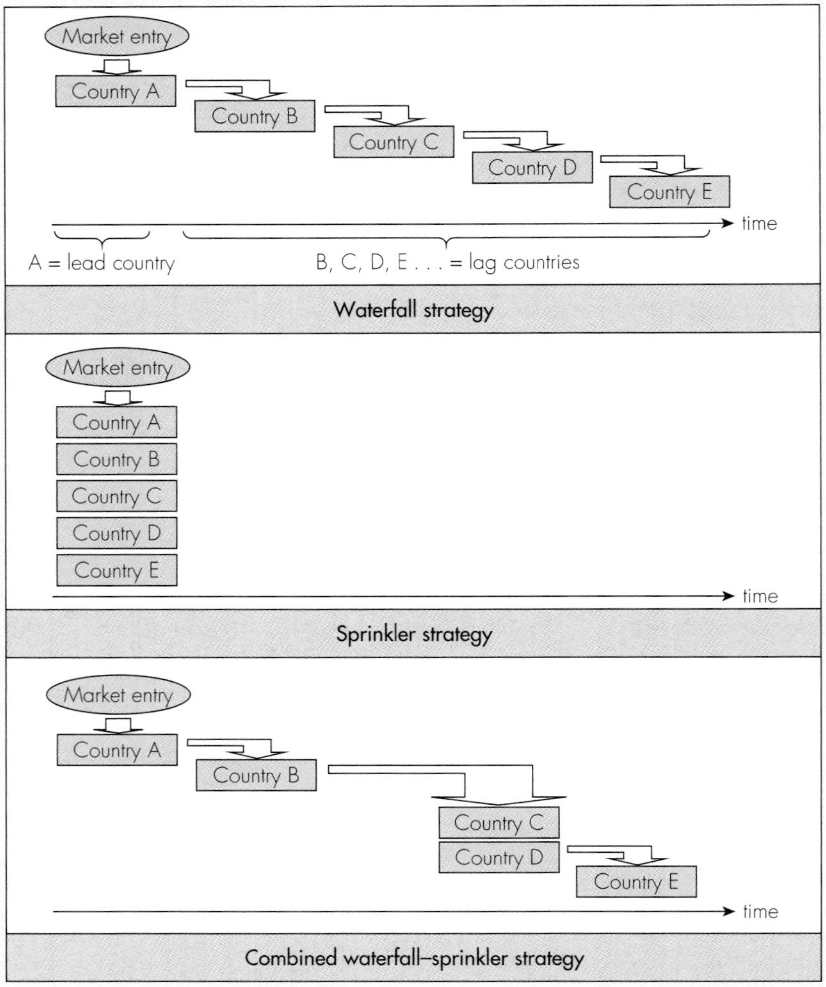

Figure 12-17 Alternatives for the timing of international market entries (adapted from Kutschker and Schmid 2006, pp. 963f.)

marketing activities are completely standardized across all countries, while the other end represents the extreme case of the total differentiation of marketing activities in the individual countries.

The primary **advantages and disadvantages of cross-national standardization and differentiation** are obvious: the main advantage of extensive standardization lies in the potential for international cost synergies. For example, extensive product standardization enables cost reductions based on experience curve effects as a result of larger production volumes (for more on the experience curve model, see Section 2.2.2). Costs can be reduced in manufacturing but also in marketing and communications.

The main disadvantage of extensive cross-border standardization is the limited flexibility available to appropriately address differences between international markets. This can have a significant adverse effect on market success. Moreover, it should be noted that demand-based feedback effects (see Section 12.1.3) tend to be promoted by a high degree of standardization. For example, the more the products are standardized across borders, the higher the risk of cross-national arbitrage (parallel imports, re-imports or lateral gray imports, see Section 12.1.3).

Table 12-5 Basic evaluation of waterfall and sprinkler strategies

	Waterfall strategy	Sprinkler strategy
Advantages	■ Successive development and expansion of financial and human resources (including personnel with marketing skills) facilitated by learning effects ■ Temporal diversification of risks ■ Marketing can be adjusted (if there are problems in a market) with respect to a later entry into other markets ■ Potential extension of product life cycle	■ Establishment of market entry barriers to thwart followers ■ Regional/geographical diversification of risks
Disadvantages	■ Risk of market entry by competitors	■ Increased short-term financial and human resource requirements ■ Major losses if the strategy fails
Situational factors favoring the use of the strategy	■ Necessity for reference markets (e.g. the USA is often a reference market for South America) ■ Longer product life cycles (since experience gathered in markets that were exploited early on can be used for further product development and upgrades) ■ Lower competitive intensity in international markets	■ Short product and technology life cycles ■ Long R&D times (since there is a higher chance of rapid recuperation)

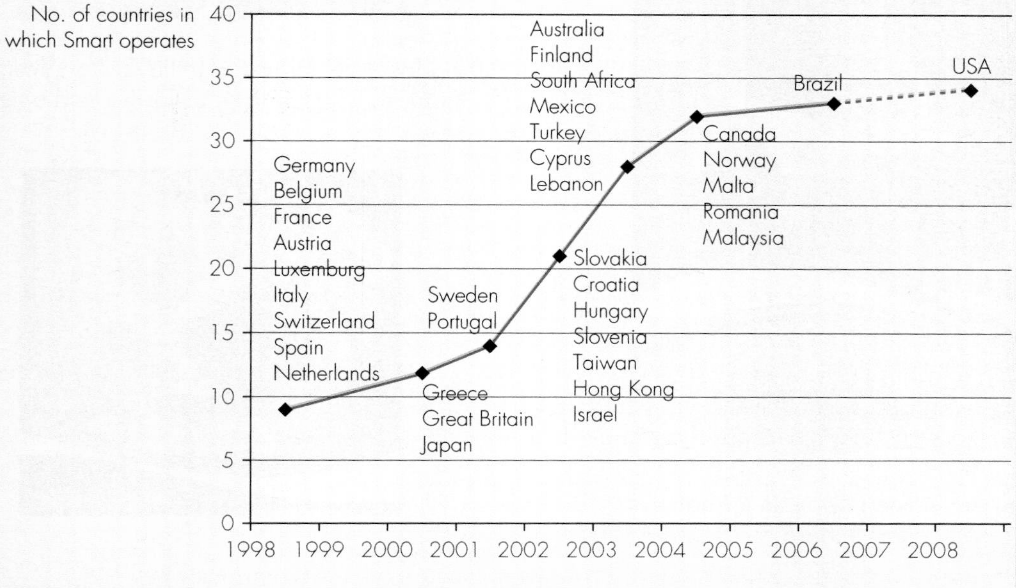

Figure 12-18 Example of a combined waterfall–sprinkler strategy used for the internationalization of the German car Smart (adapted from www.daimlerchrysler.com)

In contrast, a high degree of cross-border differentiation aids adaptation to specific local market and demand characteristics (e.g. in terms of satisfying regionally diverse customer needs). The main disadvantage of extensive differentiation is the high cost of this strategy. Accordingly, when deciding on the degree of cross-border standardization, the first priority is to weigh cost aspects against local market/customer orientation. Key here is the dissimilarity of market conditions and customer needs: the greater the dissimilarity, the more likely it is that the advantages of cross-national differentiation outweigh the disadvantages.

With regard to international marketing, the decision pertaining to the degree of cross-national standardization of marketing activities is relevant to all areas of the marketing mix. In company practice, it can often be observed that individual components of the marketing mix are largely standardized, while other components show little standardization. An example worth mentioning here is international market development applying a completely standardized product design and predominantly country-specific communication (for an example of differentiated communications, see Focus on Marketing 12-5).

Focus on Marketing 12-5 Examples of an advertising campaign adapted to different cultures

Tailoring advertising appeals to match idiosyncratic cultural characteristics: Vanilla Coke campaign 'Celebrating Romance' in Singapore.

Using local celebrities: Vanilla Coke advertising in India featuring a famous Bollywood actor.

Standardized product, adapted advertising: Vanilla Coke in the Republic of the Philippines

Source: www.moviegupshup.net, www.coca-cola.com, www.sanmiguel.com

Many studies have examined the impact on success of standardization and differentiation (for an overview, see Waheeduzzaman and Dube 2004). The relatively inconsistent findings of these studies underscore that the impact of standardization vs differentiation on success depends on situational variables (see Theodosiou and Leonidou 2003). This means that the ideal degree of standardization or differentiation of the marketing strategy depends on the specific environmental and market conditions with which the company is confronted. For example, in general, a standardization strategy is particularly successful if the customers in the various target markets are similar (see Özsomer and Simonin 2004) or if the company's management team has extensive marketing experience (see O'Donnell and Jeong 2000).

Yet another important decision in connection with the international marketing strategy is the design of the **relationship between the headquarters and the various international branches.** Here it is important to consider the allocation of roles between head office and the international subsidiary.

Models that describe the roles of the international subsidiary can be used to define the allocation of roles between head office and international subsidiaries (see, e.g., Bartlett and Ghoshal 1986, 1990). For example, Bartlett and Ghoshal use two dimensions to characterize the role of an international subsidiary:

1 the strategic importance of the international subsidiary and its markets for the company

2 the competencies and capacities of the international subsidiary.

Four role types emerge from combining these two dimensions (see the matrix in Figure 12-19). Gupta and Govindarajan (1991) have developed a similar typology, which is also shown in Figure 12-19.

A basic question regarding the role of subsidiaries relates to their degree of **autonomy** from the head office (especially with respect to designing the local market development strategy). A national subsidiary's level of autonomy particularly depends on the cross-border standardization or differentiation of the market development. With a strictly differentiated market development, a

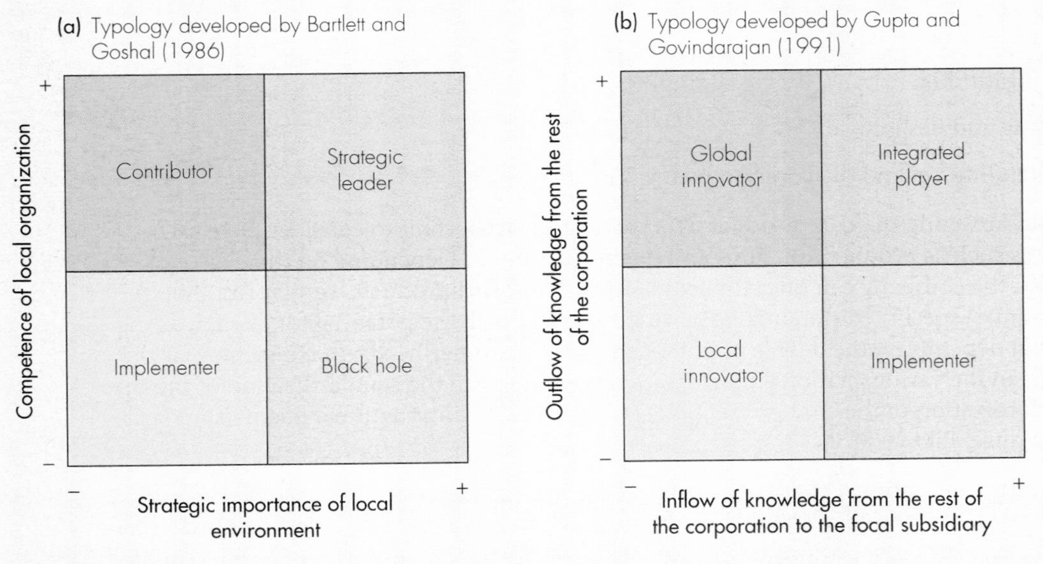

Figure 12-19 Role typologies for subsidiaries as developed by Bartlett and Ghoshal (1986) and Gupta and Govindarajan (1991)

high degree of local autonomy is practical, while local autonomy can be detrimental in the case of extensive standardization.

12.4 Specific Characteristics of Elements in the Marketing Mix in International Marketing

12.4.1 Product Decisions

Product decisions in international marketing focus on the question of the extent of cross-national product standardization. The decision in this respect is not only relevant to product decisions: the degree of product standardization has a large impact on the degree of flexibility with regard to the international standardization/differentiation of other marketing instruments. For example, international price differentiation is more difficult if products are highly standardized.

The underlying logic of the required decision has already been discussed in Section 12.3: the greater the country-specific differences of the market conditions and, in particular, the customer requirements, the more does the alignment to specific market conditions by means of differentiation outweigh the realization of cross-national cost synergies via standardization. Particularly with regard to product design, country-specific customer requirements can also arise from climatic (e.g. special technical requirements due to a tropical climate), technical (e.g. different voltages in the respective national power grids between the countries) or legal market conditions (e.g. different product standards) in the various countries.

In Section 12.3, we pointed out that the decision regarding standardization in marketing often has to be differentiated with respect to the individual components of the marketing mix. In the scope of product decisions, the most essential decision-making areas for cross-national product standardization comprise:

- the core product
- the brand (brand name/logo)
- the brand positioning
- the packaging and design
- services extending beyond the core product.

In terms of **standardizing the core product**, it is particularly important to consider physical product features such as product functions and quality attributes. Depending on the degree of standardization, the company can offer totally identical (uniform) products, similar (modified) products or country-specific (differentiated) products. In general, the potential for standardizing the core product depends on the degree of homogeneity of customer needs: the more similar the customer needs in the various national markets, the more practical the standardization of the core product. Standardization of the core product is also supported by international quality standards such as, for instance, ISO 9000.

With regard to the international **standardization of the brand**, the company has to determine whether the brand name and logo should be standardized. It should be noted that the same brand name can evoke different associations from country to country (for an example of a differentiated brand strategy see Figure 12-20). Consequently, there are numerous examples in company practice of problems related to the international standardization of brand names, such as the use of the brand name of the car make Fiat Rustica in England (problematic due to its association with 'rust')

Figure 12-20 Brand names of a haircare product by L'Oréal in different European countries (see www.loreal.com)

(see Hünerberg 1994). Logos have to be carefully considered in this context, since images and symbols can also be interpreted in different ways. For example, when exporting its beer to Africa, the producer of Carlsberg had to add a third elephant to its Elephant Beer brand logo because two elephants are a symbol of bad luck in Africa (see Jain 2000).

Within the scope of the **standardization of brand positioning**, it is important to determine the extent of the compatibility between the definitions of the target segments and the brand promises made to these segments (see Keller 2007). Standardization of the market positioning then appears to be especially practical if the values and attitudes of the target segments in the different markets correspond to a high degree.

Standardization of the packaging and design plays an especially important role in the consumer goods sector. The color, form/shape and labeling of the packaging can be standardized. It should be mentioned here that colors (see Section 12.4.3; Table 12-10) and forms/shapes can have dissimilar meanings in different countries due to cultural, religious and historical differences. Moreover, the different legal, climatic, ecological and social conditions in the various countries also have to be taken into account.

In terms of **standardizing services**, a decision has to be made with regard to whether the same warranties, technical services and/or consulting services should be offered in the respective international markets. In this context, it has to be determined whether the same information and consulting services (e.g. customer newsletter, customer training), the same technical services (e.g. installation and maintenance services) and the same business services (e.g. financing, insurance) exist in the various markets.

In general, the decision between standardization and differentiation is not a yes/no one. Rather, the question concerns the extent to which a product should be internationally standardized or differentiated. This results in the standardization profile illustrated in Figure 12-21 for products in international marketing. The figure shows several sample profiles. For instance, in the shampoo brand example presented, the product is standardized only with regard to the core product (consideration of different hair types and different climatic conditions in the various countries); the brand, market positioning, packaging, design and services (e.g. website) are less standardized.

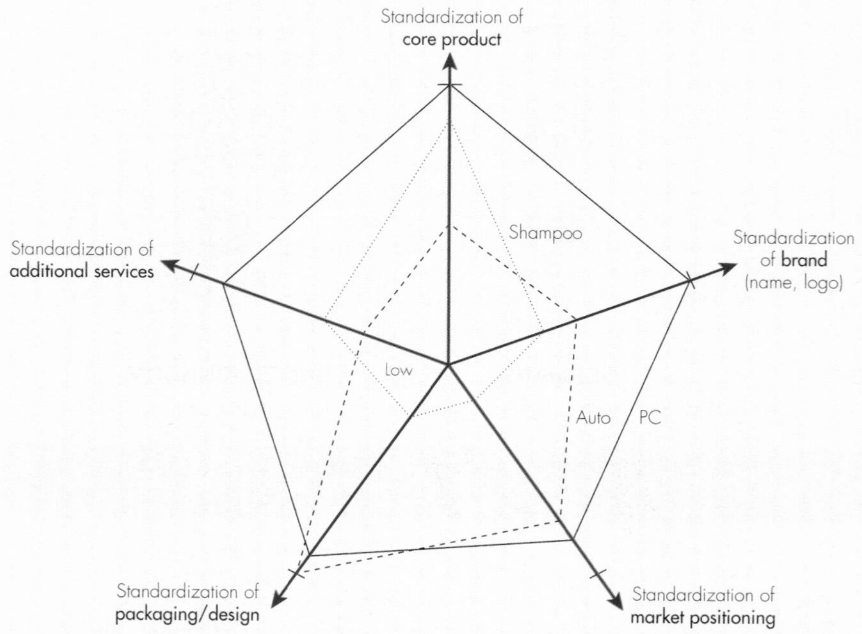

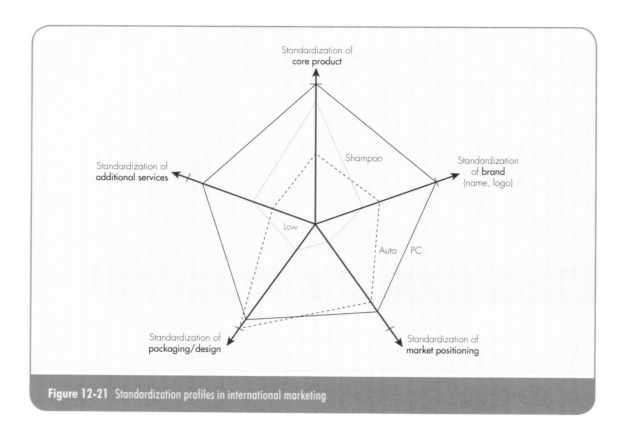

Figure 12-21 Standardization profiles in international marketing

12.4.2 Pricing Decisions

Standardization and differentiation issues also arise in international pricing. Price differentiation, which has already been presented in Chapter 6 as a main decision-making area in pricing, is relevant in both a domestic and international setting. It should be emphasized here that price differentiation in international marketing is an especially important factor. This is due to the fact that customer-related differences (e.g. willingness to pay) are frequently greater between countries than within one country. In principle, such varying degrees of the willingness to pay on the part of customers suggest that companies should use price differentiation. Furthermore, it is often easier to implement price differentiation on an international level than on a domestic level. The reasons for this are communication barriers between countries as well as arbitrage costs (arising from transportation costs, currency differences, customs/duties, import quotas and other national regulations). Against this background, many companies have developed a cross-national price differentiation (for examples, see also Table 12-6).

The question regarding to what **extent a company should practice cross-border price standardization** has to be answered on a situational basis. Major variables determining this decision include:

- the differences in customers' willingness to pay in the different countries
- the costs of obtaining international information on prices
- the arbitrage costs.

Cross-country differences in willingness to pay on the part of customers can result from different customer needs.

Table 12-6 Example illustrating international price differences (price index: European Union median = 100) (*Official Journal of the European Union* 2005)

Product	Country with lowest prices (price index)		Most expensive country (price index)	
Mineral water (Evian)	France	62	Finland	204
Soft drink (Fanta)	Spain	70	Finland	148
Butter (Kerrygold)	Ireland	90	Germany	150
Energy drink (Red Bull)	Austria	79	Finland	134
Chocolate bar (Twix)	Belgium	74	Denmark	131
Ice cream (Häagen-Dazs)	Italy	60	Greece	117
Instant coffee (Nescafé)	Greece	64	Austria	137
Cornflakes (Kellogg's)	United Kingdom	75	France	144
Rice (Uncle Ben's)	Finland	81	United Kingdom	161
Dry pasta (Barilla)	Italy	55	Ireland	114

Costs of obtaining information are affected by price transparency and language barriers. In general, these costs tend to decrease whenever customers are able to compare prices via the internet and as a result of the improved comparability of prices after the introduction of currency unions (such as the European Monetary Union).

Arbitrage costs arise, in particular, from trade barriers such as import customs and duties, as well as transportation costs. Of relevance here is not only the absolute amount of the transportation costs, but also the amount of the transportation costs in relation to the product price. Obviously, the amount of the arbitrage costs is closely connected to the concept of the interdependency of markets, which we examined in the context of the similarity-interdependency pattern (see Section 12.1.3).

Particularly with regard to the **European common market**, it can be observed that these three influencing factors are moving in the direction of an increasing harmonization of price levels in the various European countries. In light of this, the result is a harmonization of prices in the different markets, with two basic developments being conceivable: if companies do not proactively deal with price harmonization, there is the risk of prices converging towards the lowest price level of all markets concerned (see Scenario A in Figure 12-22). However, if a company influences this process, the development could be similar to Scenario B in Figure 12-22. This development is especially characterized by the fact that prices are being raised in countries that originally had a very low price level, which leads to a decline in sales in those countries. At the same time, prices are being reduced in countries that originally had a high price level. On this basis, a 'European price corridor' is materializing, with a considerably smaller range of prices than exhibited by the original price structure in the European market. The problem in terms of optimization lies in adjusting the prices in the various countries in a way that enables the emergence of a constellation that ensures profitability across all countries.

Another issue pertaining to international pricing relates to how **currency exchange rate risks** should be handled. Exchange rate fluctuations can have a substantial impact on a company's earnings and the resulting cost situation (for more on this, see Table 12-7).

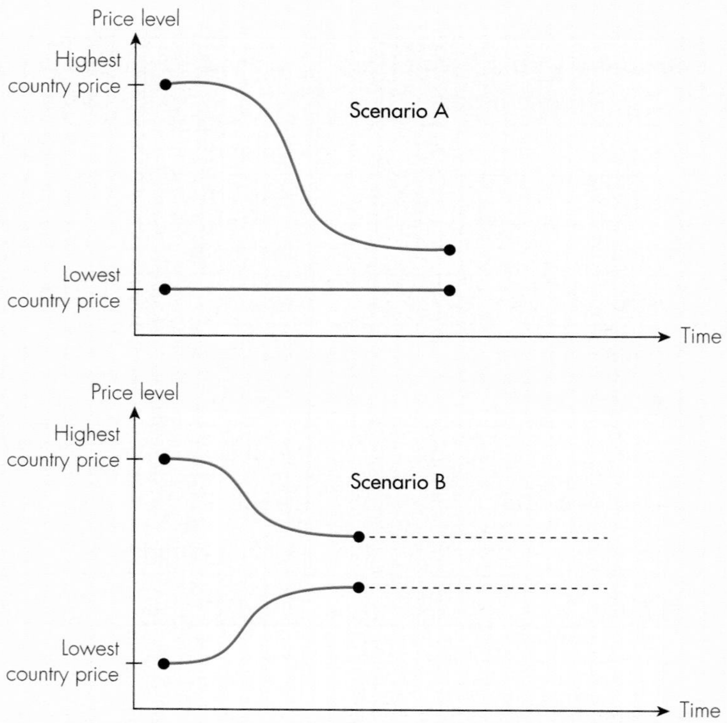

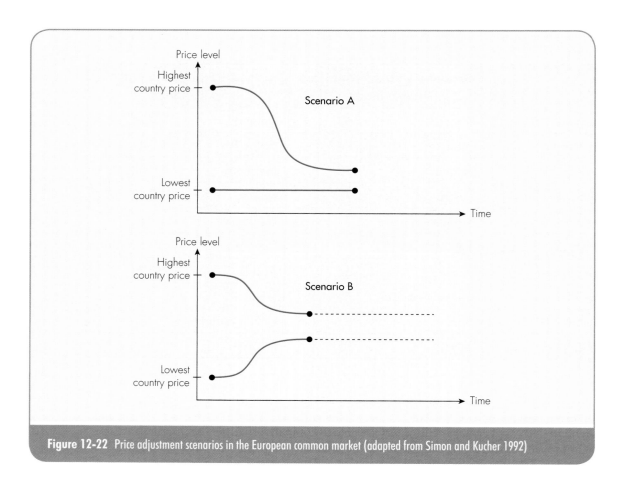

Figure 12-22 Price adjustment scenarios in the European common market (adapted from Simon and Kucher 1992)

Table 12-7 Impact of exchange rate fluctuations on prices and profit (adapted from Sander 1997, p. 52)

	Billing in domestic currency	Billing in international currency
Devaluation of international currency	Price increases from the standpoint of international customers; profit (in domestic currency) remains constant	Price remains constant from the standpoint of international customers; profit (in domestic currency) declines
Revaluation of international currency	Price drops from the standpoint of international customers; profit (in domestic currency) remains constant	Price remains constant from the standpoint of international customers; profit (in domestic currency) increases

Companies have several options to hedge currency exchange risks. In particular, the following activities can be useful:

- production in the international market
- billing in domestic currency

Table 12-8 Overview of Incoterms (see International Chamber of Commerce 1999)

Incoterm	Description	Transfer of risk from company to customer	Transfer of costs from company to customer
EXW	Ex works	Place of delivery	Place of delivery
FCA	Free carrier	Place of delivery	Place of delivery
FOB	Free on board	Ship's rail	Ship's rail
CFR	Cost and freight	Ship's rail	Port of destination
CIF	Cost, insurance, freight	Ship's rail	Port of destination
CIP	Carriage and insurance paid	Place of delivery	Point of destination
DEQ	Delivery ex quay	Quay at port of destination	Quay at port of destination
DDP	Delivered duty paid	Point of destination	Point of destination

- contractual hedge clauses
- hedging transactions (forward exchange operations and option contracts, hedging, foreign currency loans, exchange rate risk insurance).

In conclusion, it should be pointed out that the prices charged to customers in the different markets also depend on which transportation services are offered to customers. In general, the higher the end price charged to the customer, the more transportation services the company undertakes for the customer. The International Commercial Terms (Incoterms) provide a variety of standardized agreements between companies and customers. Table 12-8 lists the most commonly used Incoterms.

12.4.3 Communication Decisions

The issue of cross-national standardization is also of major relevance in international communication decisions. In principle, the cross-national standardization of communication poses a range of challenges to companies. **Barriers to standardizing communication internationally** exist, in particular, with respect to:

- the country-specific language
- the country-specific culture
- the media infrastructure in the respective country
- the country-specific legal regulations.

The **country-specific language** can act as a barrier to standardization when it comes to brand names and communication messages. Many examples of negative effects resulting from non-consideration of specific characteristics of the national language can be found in company practice. Some examples are shown in Table 12-9. Even in countries with the same language, different uses of terms/words can lead to problems (see the first example in Table 12-9).

Aspects of **country-specific culture** can also represent barriers to standardizing communication. In particular, different social behavior, diverse social norms and values, religious aspects, varying

Table 12-9 Examples of linguistic communication problems as barriers to standardization in international communications (adapted from Ricks 2006)

Situation	Misinterpretation
Use of the slogan 'You can use no finer napkin at your dinner table' in the USA and England	While the use of 'napkin' in this context is fine in the USA, 'napkin' is also used colloquially in England as a word for 'diaper'
Literal translation of the slogan 'Let Hertz put you in the driver's seat' in Spanish	Meaning: 'Hertz will turn you into a chauffeur'
Literal translation of the slogan 'Avoid embarrassment – use Parker Pens' in Spanish	Meaning: 'Prevent pregnancy – use Parker pens'

Table 12-10 Examples of different meanings of colors in an international context (Hünerberg 1994)

Color / Country	White	Black	Red	Yellow	Blue	Green
Western Europe	Birth, purity	Death, mourning	Love, danger, power, dynamism	Optimism, friendliness, sunshine	Coldness, authority	Freshness, health
China	Death, mourning		Joy and happiness, festive mood			
Japan	Death, mourning			Dignity, nobility		Future, virtue, energy
Arabic/Islamic countries				Luck, wealth	Virtue, trust, honesty	Color associated with religious connotations, fertility
Subtropical countries						Jungle, illness

interpretations of colors, as well as divergent concepts of humor can make standardization very difficult (see Alden *et al.* 1993; Müller 1996; Rinner-Kawai 1993). Table 12-10 demonstrates that the same color can evoke different associations in different countries. Table 12-11 shows examples of standardized market activities in which such cultural differences were not sufficiently taken into consideration.

International variations in the **media infrastructure** (e.g. different penetration of televisions or internet connections in private households) can indicate that the same communication tools cannot be used across all markets.

Table 12-11 Examples of specific cultural characteristics as standardization barriers in international communication

Situation	Problem	Source
In a standardized Procter & Gamble soap commercial aired in Japan, a man enters the bathroom while his wife is taking a bath	Japanese customers were irritated by the spot, since in Japanese culture the man is expected to respect his wife's privacy in the bathroom	Swasy (1993)
In a standardized Pepsodent toothpaste commercial broadcast in Southeast Asia, the advertising message emphasized the tooth-whitening features of the toothpaste	Since betel nuts are chewed in many Southeast Asian countries, yellow teeth are not considered to be as great a cosmetic flaw there as they are in Western countries	Miller and Chakravarti (1987)
Tire manufacturer Pirelli aired a standardized commercial in Brazil that depicted soccer star Ronaldo as a statue of Christ (on a hill above Rio de Janeiro, with tire tread patterns on the soles of his feet)	The commercial offended the religious sensibilities of customers in Brazil and triggered strong criticism from Brazilian church parishes	*Advertising Age International* (1998)

Due to **legal restrictions** on advertising options in some markets, not all communication messages can be standardized internationally. For example, comparative advertising is not legally permitted in all markets. Moreover, in some countries (e.g. China), advertising is subject to government censorship.

12.4.4 Sales Decisions

Compared to other components of the marketing mix, sales decisions usually tend to show a stronger degree of international differentiation, which is due to the different conditions related to sales in the various national markets. However, as a consequence of the ongoing internationalization of intermediaries and corporate customers, suppliers increasingly interact with the same intermediaries and corporate customers across country barriers. Hence, a trend towards increasing the standardization efforts of international sales activities can be observed.

The following four areas of sales decisions display specific characteristics in an international context (for more on these areas, see Chapter 7 as well as Belz and Reinhold 1999):

1 the design and structure of the sales system

2 the sales logistics

3 the structure and organization of the relationships to the sales partners and key accounts

4 the design of the sales activities.

With respect to the **design and structure of the sales system**, it should first be noted that the different national markets may necessitate a variety of sales intermediaries as well as sales channels of different depths and widths. This can hinder cross-border standardization of the sales system. Often companies must use several (different) sales channels (across the various national markets) at the same time. For example, a company can offer its products in some markets directly via its

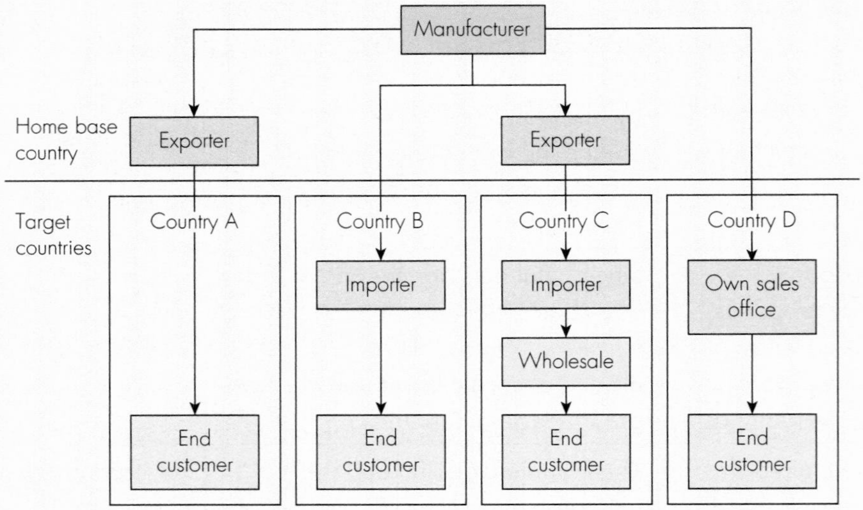

Figure 12-23 Cross-national design of the sales system of a manufacturer of electro-technical components

own foreign sales offices, while using exporters and importers in other markets (for an example of alternative sales channels, see Figure 12-23). In company practice, such an international multi-channel sales approach can be observed in many globally operating companies.

Furthermore, direct sales in international marketing (in the form of direct exports or sales personnel in foreign markets) are often more difficult to realize than in marketing restricted to one domestic market. In the case of exporting this can be due to a lack of knowledge about the conditions in the target countries (for an examination of the success factors of exports, see also Holzmüller and Stöttinger 1996). In the case of sales via the company's own sales offices, the problem lies in having to set up and maintain foreign sales offices.

Due to the difficulties involved in direct sales, sales intermediaries frequently have to be used. The primary function of the sales intermediary is to negotiate sales across national borders, so that the sales channels in international marketing display a greater depth than in domestic marketing. In this context, it is crucial to notice that the involvement of sales intermediaries makes it difficult to achieve cross-national standardization of sales activities, since the company is no longer in complete control of all sales and logistics activities.

International sales logistics concern the process of planning, implementing and controlling the efficient and effective transportation and storage of products from the point of origin to the point of consumption for the purpose of fulfilling customers' requirements (Council of Supply Chain Management Professionals 2006). As compared to national sales logistics, the distribution processes (e.g. packaging, packing, shipping and transportation) in international sales are much more complex. Decisions have to be made with regard to what markets should be supplied by which production and warehouse facilities. In addition to cost aspects, customer requirements in terms of the logistics quality (e.g. the importance of delivery time) also have to be taken into account. International marketing has also specific characteristics in its **relationships to sales partners and key accounts.** In particular, relationships to sales partners and key accounts in foreign markets can be impaired by difficult market conditions such as, for example, an initial low level of trust (see Homburg *et al.* 2002) or a lower commitment level on the part of the partner (see Schlegelmilch *et al.* 2002).

In terms of **designing the sales activities** in international marketing, there are specific characteristics related especially to **international sales negotiations** in the course of personal selling. These characteristics arise from the respective cultural backgrounds of the negotiating parties (seller and customer). Such cultural backgrounds have an effect on the typical behavioral patterns during the negotiations, such as the individual communication style or the (different) interpretation of statements made by the other party. Against this background, a thorough understanding of cultural differences is necessary in order to avoid misunderstandings (e.g. pertaining to bargaining strategies) (see Graham *et al.* 1988). With an understanding of these cultural specifics, the most suitable interaction approach and negotiating style can be specifically adjusted to the respective cultural situation.

In the case of **major cultural differences between the negotiating parties**, the following observations have become evident.

- Verbal communication is required in order to convey needs and preferences.
- In particular, negotiating strategies are deployed that are geared towards influencing the behavior and attitudes of negotiation partners. Such strategies tend not to be very successful.
- The risk of misunderstandings and misinterpretations can arise during the verbal and non-verbal exchange of information between the negotiating parties.

Another aspect that has been researched is the **impact of respective cultural backgrounds on the behavior of negotiating parties** (see, e.g., Graham *et al.* 1988). In this context, the following observations have been made on the basis of the cultural concept developed by Hofstede (see Section 12.1.1) (see Williams *et al.* 1998).

- Individualistic cultures are characterized by a low priority on interpersonal orientation and a less distinctive need for personal relationships. Accordingly, personal relationships play only a subordinate role in international negotiations with negotiating partners from strongly individualistic cultures (such as, say, the USA).
- Collectivist cultures, on the other hand, exhibit a solid interpersonal orientation and an intensive need for personal relationships. Therefore, personal relationships play a key role in international negotiations with negotiating partners from collectivist cultures (such as, say, China).

Based on the culture typology developed by Hall (1976), which differentiates between high-context and low-context cultures (see Section 12.1.1), the following phenomena could be observed during negotiations (see, e.g., Graham *et al.* 1988).

- Low-context cultures use explicit communication messages. The status of the negotiating parties has only a minor impact on the results of the negotiations.
- In high-context cultures, important information is also generally conveyed via the negotiation context. Consequently, non-verbal behavior and differences may have a substantial impact on negotiations.

Finally, a third category of research studies describes the **typical behavioral patterns and negotiating styles** of negotiating parties in specific countries (see, e.g., Adler 1986; Buttery and Leung 1998; Fisher 1980; Graham 1983, 1984; Graham and Lin 1987; Hawrysh and Zaichkowsky 1990; Lee 2000). Table 12-12 contains recommendations regarding how to approach customers in different countries.

Table 12-12 Examples of recommended and problematic behaviors in interactions with international business partners

Customer \ Customer interaction	Recommended behavior	Problematic behavior
US customers	■ Punctuality ■ Create a friendly atmosphere for conversation and discussion ■ Give positive feedback to anecdotes ■ Include local attorneys in the negotiations/ convert negotiation results into contractual stipulations	■ Religion, sexuality, race as topics of conversation ■ Overly abstract concepts instead of specific, concrete examples ■ Emphasis on academic titles
British customers	■ Search for pragmatic solutions ■ Strive for fairness ■ Wear conservative clothing ■ Be prepared for subtle humor ■ Recognize and detect discrete/only implicitly expressed criticism	■ Overly direct communication ■ Expectations of open disagreement ■ Misinterpretation of 'understatement' (a 'slight problem' may be a big one) ■ Discussion of political matters during business lunches/dinners ■ Too much emphasis on detail
French customers	■ Communicate in French ■ Elegance, eloquence and enthusiasm are important components of the communication ■ Introduce the topic by way of intellectual/ abstract/philosophical aspects ■ Accept delays on the part of the discussion partners	■ Inadequate consideration of hierarchies ■ Premature discussion of details ■ Reducing the conversation down to the facts ■ Being put off by mental leaps/ erratic conversation patterns of the French discussion partner
Russian customers	■ Be well informed about your counterparty ■ Be serious, polite and patient in negotiations ■ Clarify everything; Russians dislike uncertainty ■ Build personal relationships ■ Keep the favors that you are promising: they are serious obligations	■ Compromising too early; this is a sign of weakness ■ Overestimating a contract; delivery guarantees often do not mean a lot
Chinese customers	■ Make sure your negotiating partner has the authority to close the deal ■ Always be polite ■ Be patient; the same business takes six times as long in China as in the West ■ Build a good personal relationship and make counter-invitations ■ Document all results in detail; verbal agreements do not last long	■ Making the other side lose face ■ Being too direct; a 'no' is a no-no

Summary

In this chapter, we outlined the most important characteristics of international marketing. We highlighted the implications of differences in economic, political-legal and sociocultural structures across country markets, and the growing importance of information and communication technology in terms of new product and technology diffusion and accelerated economic growth. Here, we identified differences in international buying behavior, including a discussion on the country-of-origin effect and ethnocentrism phenomenon as factors that impact customer preferences. We looked at different customer typologies as a basis for international customer segmentation, and discussed Levitt's convergence hypothesis.

Further, we introduced internationalization theories. While the EPRG model assumes an evolutionary development of global marketing, the coordination perspective and the interdependency-similarity pattern deal with the design of international market development concepts. In this international marketing research, we explained problems of data selection methods used on an international level and pointed out ways to achieve cross-national equivalence of measuring instruments.

With respect to marketing strategic decisions, we discussed the need for a company to specify the degree of internationalization and how country markets can be selected using criteria to assess country attractiveness and market entry barriers. Further, we looked at the design of international market development strategies, and the form and timing of international market entry. We also pointed out decisions concerning the cross-national standardization of marketing activities and decisions concerning the international company structure.

Finally, we highlighted the importance of standardizing versus differentiating elements of the international marketing mix. On the product level, we discussed the pros and cons of standardizing the core product, the brand, the brand positioning, the packaging and design, and services. Concerning the standardization of pricing, we recommended making a decision on a situational basis. Here, we emphasized price adjustment scenarios and specific international pricing issues, such as exchange risk hedging. Regarding international communications, we showed how companies deal with tremendous barriers to standardization, such as language, culture, media infrastructure and habits, and legal restrictions. With regard to the design and structure of the sales system, we observed the highest degree of differentiation across country markets due to the heterogeneity of market conditions.

Case Study: L'Oréal – Worth More Than Ever

One of the best indicators of L'Oréal's position in global business was the naming of Lindsay Owen-Jones as one of the world's 100 most influential people by *Time* magazine. *Time* regarded the L'Oréal CEO's defining characteristic as the ability to stay one step ahead of his customers. This skill helped to make L'Oréal one of the world's leading cosmetics companies and the unassailable leader in Western Europe.

In 2003 the French giant withstood the lukewarm economic conditions in much of Western Europe, currency fluctuations and the downturn in international travel due to war in Iraq, fear of terrorism and SARS to match its sales targets. In fact, the company actually managed to outpace worldwide consumer spending on cosmetics and thus increased its market share in countries like the UK and Spain, and propelled its share of the combined 'Big 5' markets to over 19 per cent.

Key to L'Oréal's success was its careful attention to its substantial brand portfolio. This involved maintaining a sustainable launch program for each brand, and maximising their local appeal while keeping the brand identity coherent. This local appeal also involved L'Oréal's move into retail, opening stand-alone boutiques for some of its luxury brands.

The breadth of L'Oréal's portfolio is breathtaking. The company has a strong presence in every retail sector – selective, mass market, pharmacy and direct sales – and in virtually every product category. And ever with an eye to the future, L'Oréal entered the potentially lucrative brave new world of nutriceuticals in 2003 with the launch of the Inneov line.

With 15 global brands and some home-based power-houses, L'Oréal has leading positions in haircare, hair styling, suncare, color cosmetics, facial skincare and men's lines. It also took second place in women's fragrances and bodycare, and held third position in deodorants.
Its relative lack of attention held it back in eighth place in the bathroom products category, however, and it has a negligible position in oral hygiene through its Goupil L'Oréal division.

L'Oréal is arguably at its most influential in the haircare and styling categories, where it holds 43 per cent and 46 per cent shares respectively of the 'Big 5' markets. Where other companies have tried to globalize their brands, L'Oréal maintains a local focus, for example referring to its leading L'Oréal Paris brand as Elvive, Elsève or Elvital, according to the market.

Source: adapted from http://goliath.ecnext.com/coms2/summary_0199-277684_ITM.

Discussion Questions

1. The case highlights L'Oréal's global strategy. The company did not develop this geocentric perspective of the market when it was established, but developed it over time. Usually, companies start out to market their offerings domestically and then explore different international market opportunities.

Case Study (Continued)

(a) What are the motives for companies to internationalize? There are two different types of motive. Discuss.

(b) The fact that companies develop an internationalization strategy usually from a domestic market before they explore new international markets takes on board an evolutionary perspective. Explain a model that can help to describe this internationalization process.

2. When lauching Inneov, L'Oréal had to make decisions about the timing of its entry into target markets. What basic decisions need to be considered in this regard? Which timing strategy would you have proposed for the launch of Inneov?
3. A vital issue that arises is whether the company differentiates or standardizes its products in international markets. What are the advantages and disadvantages of differentiation versus standardization? Assess the degree of standardization for the shampoo brand Elsève/Elvital/Elvive using an appropriate international marketing tool. Under what circumstances would you recommend L'Oréal to introduce one common brand name for this brand internationally?

Key Terms

References

Adler, N. (1986) *International Dimensions of Organizational Behavior*. Boston, Mass.

Advertising Age International (1998) Brazilian ad irks church, 13 April, 11.

Alden, D., Hoyer, W. and Lee, C. (1993) Identifying global and culture-specific dimensions of humor in advertising: a multinational analysis, *Journal of Marketing*, 57, 2, 64–75.

Alden, D., Steenkamp, J.-B. and Batra, R. (1999) Brand positioning through advertising in Asia, North America, and Europe: the role of global consumer culture, *Journal of Marketing*, 63, 1, 75–87.

Angelmar, R. and Pras, B. (1978) Verbal rating scales for multinational research, *European Research*, 6, 62–67.

Backhaus, K., Büschken, J. and Voeth, M. (2004) *International Marketing*. Hampshire.

Bartlett, C. and Ghoshal, S. (1986) Tap your subsidiaries for global reach, *Harvard Business Review*, 64, 87–94.

Bartlett, C. and Ghoshal, S. (1990) The multinational corporation as an interorganizational network, *Academy of Management Review*, 15, 4, 626–645.

Baskerville, R.F. (2003) Hofstede never studied culture, *Accounting, Organizations and Society*, 28, 1–14.

Bauer, E. (1997) *Internationale Marketingforschung* (2nd edn). Munich.

Bauer, E. (2002) *Internationale Marketingforschung* (3rd edn). Munich.

Belz, C. and Reinhold, M. (1999) *Internationales Vertriebsmanagement für Industriegüter – Kernkompetenz Vertrieb, Länderselektion und Differenzierung, Minimalmarketing, Benchmarks*. St Gallen.

Berndt, R., Fantapié Altobelli, C. and Sander, M. (1997) *Internationale Marketing-Politik*. Berlin.

Berndt, R., Fantapié Altobelli, C. and Sander, M. (1999) *Internationales Marketing-Management*. Berlin.

Business Environment Risk Intelligence SA (2006) *Business Risk Service (BRS) Report 2006*. Genf.

Buttery, E. and Leung, T. (1998) The difference between Chinese and Western negotiations, *European Journal of Marketing*, 32, 3/4, 374–389.

Cateora, P.R. and Graham, J.L. (2006) *International Marketing* (13th edn). Maidenhead.

Cavusgil, S. and Das, A. (1997) Methodological issues in empirical cross-cultural research: a survey of the management literature and a framework, *Management International Review*, 7, 1, 71–96.

Child, P. (2006) Lessons from a global retailer: an interview with the president ot [*sic*] Carrefour China, *McKinsey Quarterly*, Special Edition, 70–81.

Clarke, I., Owens, M. and Ford, J. (2000) Integrating country of origin into global marketing strategy, *International Marketing Review*, 17, 2/3, 114–126.

Council of Supply Chain Management Professionals (2006) http://logistics.about.com.

Craig, C. and Douglas, S. (2000) *International Marketing Research* (2nd edn). Chichester.

de Mooij, M. (2000) The future is predictable for international marketers: converging incomes lead to diverging consumer behavior, *International Marketing Review*, 17, 2, 103–113.

Douglas, S.P. and Craig, C.S. (1989) Evolution of global marketing strategy: scale, scope and synergy, *Columbia Journal of World Business*, 24, 47–59.

Dubois, B. and Laurent, G. (1993) Is there a Euro-consumer for luxury goods?, in: van Raaij, F. and Bamossy, G. (eds) *European Advances in Consumer Research*. Provo, 58–69.

Dutta, S., Kwan, S. and Segev, A. (1998) Business transformation in electronic commerce: a study of sectoral and regional trends, *European Management Journal*, 16, 5, 540–551.

Fisher, G. (1980) *International Negotiation*. Yarmouth.

GfK AG, Lifestyle Research (2007) GfK Roper Consumer Styles, www.gfk.com.

Graham, J. (1983) Brazilian, Japanese, and American business negotiations, *Journal of International Busineses Studies*, 14, 47–62.

Graham, J. (1984) A comparison of Japanese and American business negotiations, *International Journal of Research in Marketing*, 1, 1, 51–68.

Graham, J. and Lin, C. (1987) Negotiations in the Republic of China (Taiwan) and the United States, in: Cavusgil, S. (ed.) *Advances in International Marketing*. Greenwich.

Graham, J., Kim, D., Lin, C. and Robinson, M. (1988) Buyer–seller negotiations around the Pacific Rim: differences in fundamental exchange processes, *Journal of Consumer Research*, June, 48–54.

Gupta, A. and Govindarajan, V. (1991) Knowledge flows and the structure of control within multinational corporations, *Academy of Management Review*, 16, 4, 768–792.

Gurhan-Canli, Z. and Maheswaran, D. (2000) Cultural variations in country of origin effects, *Journal of Marketing Research*, 37, 3, 309–317.

Hall, E.T. (1976) *Beyond Culture*. Garden City.

Hassan, S. and Katsanis, L. (1994) Global market segmentation strategies and trends, in: Kaynak, E. and Hassan, S. (eds) *Globalization of Consumer Markets: Structures and Strategies*. New York, 47–63.

Hawrysh, B. and Zaichkowsky, J. (1990) Cultural approaches to negotiations: understanding the Japanese, *International Marketing Review*, 7, 2, 28–42.

http://goliath.ecnext.com/coms2/summary_0199-277684_ITM

Hofstede, F., Steenkamp, J. and Wedel, M. (1999) International market segmentation based on consumer-product relations, *Journal of Marketing Research*, 36, 1, 1–17.

Hofstede, G. (1980) *Culture's Consequences: International Differences in Work-Related Values*. Beverly Hills.

Hofstede, G. (1991) *Cultures and Organizations: Software of the Mind*. London.

Hofstede, G. (1994) Management scientists are human, *Management Science*, 40, 1, 4–13.

Holzmüller, H. and Stöttinger, B. (1996) Structural modeling of success factors in exporting: cross-validation and further development of an export performance model, *Journal of International Marketing*, 4, 2, 29–55.

Homburg, C. and Jensen, O. (2004) Key-Account-Management im Export: die Perspektive der Industriegüterhersteller, in: Zentes, J., Morschett, D. and Schramm-Klein, H. (eds) *Außenhandel: Marketingstrategien und Managementkonzepte*. Wiesbaden, 551–574.

Homburg, C. and Jensen, O. (2005) Internationale Marktbearbeitung und internationale Unternehmensführung: 12 Thesen, in: Brandt, W. and Picot, A. (eds) *Unternehmenserfolg im internationalen Wettbewerb: Strategien, Steuerung und Struktur*. Stuttgart, 33–66.

Homburg, C., Krohmer, H., Cannon, J. and Kiedaisch, I. (2002) Governance Mechanisms in Transnational Business Relationships. Unpublished Working Paper, University of Mannheim, Mannheim.

Homburg, C., Kuester, S., Beutin, N. and Menon, A. (2005) Customer benefits in business-to-business markets: a cross-cultural comparison, *Journal of International Marketing*, 13, 3, 1–31.

Hünerberg, R. (1994) *Internationales Marketing*. Landsberg/Lech.

International Chamber of Commerce (1999) www.iccwbo.org/incoterms/id3042/index.html.

Jain, S. (2000) *International Marketing* (6th edn). Cincinnati.

Jaworski, S.P. and Fosher, D. (2003) National brand identity and its effect on corporate brands: the nation brand effect (NBE), *Multinational Business Review*, Fall, 11, 2, 99–108.

Johnson, J., Sakano, T., Cote, J. and Onzo, N. (1993) The exercise of inter-firm power and its repercussions in US–Japanese channel relationships, *Journal of Marketing*, 57, 2, 1–10.

Kacen, J.J. and Lee, J.A. (2002) The influence of culture on impulsive buying behavior, *Journal of Consumer Psychology*, 12, 2, 163–176.

Keegan, W.J., Schlegenmilch, B.B. and Stöttinger, B. (2002) *Globales Marketing-Management: Eine europäische Perspektive*. Oldenbourg, Munich.

Keller, K.L. (2007) *Strategic Brand Management: Building, Measuring, and Managing Brand Equity*. Upper Saddle River.

Kim, D., Pan, Y. and Park, H.S. (1998) High- versus low-context culture: a comparison of Chinese, Korean, and American cultures, *Psychology & Marketing*, 15, 6, 507–621.

Kirkman, B.L., Lowe, K.B. and Gibson, C.B. (2006) A quarter century of *Culture's Consequences*: a review of empirical research incorporating Hofstede's cultural values framework, *Journal of International Business Studies*, 37, 285–320.

Klein, J.G., Ettenson, R. and Morris, M.D. (1998) The animosity model of foreign product purchase: an empirical test in the People's Republic of China, *Journal of Marketing*, 62, 1, 89–100.

Kotabe, M. and Helsen, K. (2007) *Global Marketing Management* (4th edn). New York.

Kutschker, M. and Schmid, S. (2006) *Internationales Management* (5th edn). Oldenbourg, Munich.

Lee, D. (2000) Retail bargaining behavior of American and Chinese customers, *European Journal of Marketing*, 34, 1/2, 190–206.
Levitt, T. (1983) The globalization of markets, *Harvard Business Review*, 61, 5, 87–91.
McSweeney, B. (2002) Hofstede's model of national cultural differences and their consequences: a triumph of faith – a failure of analysis, *Human Relations*, 55, 1 (January), 89–118.
Meffert, H. and Bolz, J. (1998) *Internationales Marketing-Management* (3rd edn). Stuttgart.
Meyer, M. (1987) *Die Beurteilung von Länderrisiken der internationalen Unternehmung*. Berlin.
Miller, M. and Chakravarti, S. (1987) For Indians, a 2,000 year-old habit of chewing red goo is hard to break, *Wall Street Journal*, 12 May, 28.
Mintu-Wimsatt, A. and Gassenheimer, J.B. (2000) The moderating effects of cultural context in buyer–seller negotiation, *Journal of Personal Selling & Sales Management*, 20, 1, 1–9.
Mühlbacher, H., Leihs, H. and Dahringer, L. (2006) *International Marketing – A Global Perspective* (3rd edn). London.
Müller, W. (1996) Die Standardisierbarkeit internationaler Werbung: Kulturen verlangen Adaptionen, *Marketing – Zeitschrift für Forschung und Praxis*, 18, 3, 179–191.
Myers, M. (1999) Incidents of gray market activity among US exporters: occurrences, characteristics, and consequences, *Journal of International Business Studies*, 30, 1, 105–126.
Newman, K. and Nollen, S. (1996) Culture and congruence: the fit between management practices and national culture, *Journal of International Business Studies*, 27, 4, 753–779.
O'Donnell, S. and Jeong, I. (2000) Marketing standardization within global industries, *International Marketing Review*, 17, 1, 19–34.
Official Journal of the European Union (2005) Opinion of the European Economic and Social Committee on the Large Retail Sector – trends and impacts on farmers and consumers, C 255, 44–51.
Özsomer, A. and Simonin, B. (2004) Marketing program standardization: a cross-country exploration, *International Journal of Research in Marketing*, 21, 4, 397–419.
Pooley, R. (2005) When cultures collide, *Management Services*, 49, 1, 28–31.
PRS Group Inc. (2001) *International Country Risk Guide*, 21, 9. East Syracuse.
Ricks, D.A. (2006) *Blunders in International Business*. Oxford.
Rinner-Kawai, Y. (1993) Die Sprache der Werbung in Deutschland und in Japan – Werbeanglismus: Motivation und Auswirkungen, *Zeitschrift für Betriebswirtschaft*, 63, 9, 923–932.
Roth, M. (1995) The effects of culture and socioeconomics on the performance of global brand image strategies, *Journal of Marketing Research*, 32, 2, 163–175.
Sander, M. (1997) *Internationales Preismanagement: Eine Analyze preis-politischer Handlungsalternativen im internationalen Marketing unter besonderer Berücksichtigung der Preisfindung bei Marktinterdependenzen*. Heidelberg.
Schlegelmilch, B., Skarmeas, D. and Katsikeas, C. (2002) Drivers of commitment and its impact on performance in cross-cultural buyer–seller relationships: the importer's perspective, *Journal of International Business Studies*, 33, 4, 757–783.
Shimp, T. and Sharma, S. (1987) Consumer ethnocentrism: construction and valdiation of the CETSCALE, *Journal of Marketing Research*, 24, 3, 280–289.
Simon, H. and Kucher, E. (1992) The European pricing time bomb – and how to cope with it, *European Management Journal*, 10, 2, 136–145.
Simon, H. and Wiese, C. (1992) Europäisches Preismanagement, *Marketing – Zeitschrift für Forschung und Praxis*, 14, 4, 246–256.
Simon, H., Lauszus, D. and Kneller, M. (1998) Der Euro kommt: Implikationen für das europäische Preismanagement, *Die Betriebswirtschaft*, 58, 6, 786–802.
Sinkovics, R., Salzberger, T. and Holzmüller, H. (1998) Assessing measurement equivalence in cross-national consumer behavior research: principles, relevances and application issues, in: Balderjahn, I., Mennicken, C. and Vernette, E. (eds) *New Developments and Approaches in Consumer Behavior Research*. Stuttgart, 269–288.
Sinus Sociovision GmbH, Heidelberg (2007) http://www.sinus-sociovision.de.
Spiegel (2005) The market has no heart, *Spiegel* Special International Edition, 7, 142–146.
Swasy, A. (1993) *Soap Opera: The Inside Story of Procter & Gamble*. New York.
Theodosiou, M. and Leonidou, L. (2003) Standardization versus adaptation of international marketing strategy: an integrative assessment of the empirical research, *International Business Review*, 12, 2, 141–171.

Trompenaars, F. (1996) Resolving international conflict: culture and business strategy, *Business Strategy Review*, 7, 3, 51–68.

Verlegh, W. and Steenkamp, J. (1997) Country-of-origin-effects. A meta-analytic review, in: Arnott, D. *et al.* (eds) *Marketing: Progress, Prospects, Perspectives*. Warwick, 2136–2140.

Waheeduzzaman, A. and Dube, L. (2004) Trends and development in standardization adaptation research, *Journal of Global Marketing*, 17, 4, 23–52.

Williams, J., Han, J. and Qualls, W. (1998) A conceptual model and study of cross-cultural business relationships, *Journal of Business Research*, 42, 2, 135–143.

WITSA World Information Technology and Services Alliance (2006) *Digital Planet 2006: The Global Information Economy*. Arlington.

World Trade Organization (2006) *International Trade Statistics 2006*. Geneva.

World Trade Organization (2008) *International Trade Statistics 2007*. Geneva.

www.coca-cola.com

www.daimlerchrysler.com

www.loreal.com

www.moviegupshup.net

www.sanmiguel.com

End of Part Case Study – Amazon: International Expansion of an E-tailer

Internationalization Challenges for a Service Company

After the burst of the late 1990s dotcom bubble, the new economy experienced a consolidation process that only a fraction survived. These former start-ups of creative heads and talents are now mature stock-listed companies with thousands of employees all over the world. Recently, some of them have had to deal with a bad press, such as Yahoo!, which struggled against a takeover by Microsoft, and whose board of management was pressurized by the company's investors. eBay is another example, as it upset its top sellers with new controversial rules of procedure. Other companies, however, keep on doing very well in the online business. And it is not only firms such as Facebook and MySpace that profit from Web 2.0. Google and Amazon, for instance, have been very successful for many years now, and this has led them to export their popular business models to other countries. In this case study, we will discuss the success story of leading e-tailer Amazon and its international expansion. The case also focuses on Amazon's unique approach to service marketing, which bestows the company with a satisfied and loyal customer base. What are the secrets of Amazon's success and how can the company continue to be successful when pursuing its international expansion?

The History of Amazon and its Business Model

Amazon.com, the 'Earth's biggest bookstore', launched its website in July 1995. Back then, the book market in the USA was dominated by a small number of mega book stores, like Barnes & Nobles, offering between 170,000 and 200,000 titles. Unlike these mega stores, Amazon.com started out its business by offering books online. Its value proposition was different from that of traditional stores, as it enticed customers to 'shop at Amazon 24/7 throughout the year'. In 1999, the market value of Amazon was bigger than that of its two biggest retail competitors combined. Today, Amazon is an e-tailer with a wide variety of products. In recognition of Amazon's success in making online shopping popular, in 1999 *Time Magazine* named Jeff Bezos, CEO of Amazon.com, 'Person of the Year'. Even though Amazon was not the first store on the web, it was the first to focus on technological innovations that made online shopping faster, easier and more personal than traditional retail (Hof 2004b).

Amazon.com offers its customers more than 3 million book titles and more than 1.7 million other products since it is not limited to shelf space. It can offer the latest and greatest products like traditional sellers, but also very unique products that cannot be found elsewhere as they move too slowly (Anderson 2004; Wolf 2008). One-third to one-quarter of Amazon's book sales is supposed to come from these slow-moving items (Hayes 2007). This means that Amazon makes money on niche products that physical stores cannot afford to stock. Thus, Amazon has shifted sales from the 'short head' to the 'long tail' (see Anderson 2004 for more on the long-tail phenomenon; see also Chapter 7).

From the beginning, Bezos aimed to increase market share steadily. This was mainly done through heavy investments in research and development of technological innovations, as well as acquisitions (Hof 2006).

Consequently, Amazon was not profitable for a long time. However, Amazon endured the dotcom 'bubble' burst experienced by many e-companies and finally achieved US$5 million profit on revenues over US$1 billion in the fourth quarter of 2002. This resulted in the first full-year positive net profit (US$35.3 million) for Amazon in 2003. It has since remained profitable. However, in 2006, the growth of its profits decreased due to large investments of US$662 million in R&D (Hof 2006). At the beginning of 2008, Amazon posted a profit for the year 2007 of US$476 million on US$14.84 billion in sales. Nevertheless, until today its cumulative profits remain negative, with a deficit of US$1.58 billion in September 2007. For the year 2008 Amazon.com expects sales of US$18.75 billion (Holohan 2008).

Amazon's Product Range

Amazon.com has incorporated a variety of products and services into its portfolio, either through development or acquisition. Today, Amazon offers products including books, apparel, toys and games, electronics, videos, music, kitchenware, sporting goods, jewelry, lawn and garden items, baby products, beauty products, groceries, and much more. In addition, it provides different services to its customers, like personalized recommendations, 'search inside the book', instant order updates, wish lists, a search portal, discussion boards, and so on (see Exhibit 1 for an overview of major events in Amazon's product line expansion).

After the introduction of services like personalized recommendations, subject-area browsing and 1-click shopping, as well as instant recommendations, Amazon launched Amazon Auctions in March 1999. This was followed by the launch of a fixed-price marketplace business called zShops in September 1999. zShops did not turn out to be as profitable as expected. However, it was the basis for the successful Amazon Marketplace service launched in 2001. This service allows customers to sell used books, CDs, DVDs and other products. At the beginning of 2005, Amazon offered a wide range of products under its private label 'Pinzon'. Amazon Prime, launched in 2005, offered customers free two-day and discounted priority shipping for an annual fee of US$79. Even though this service brought many customers to the website, it also put pressure on profit margins. In 2007, Amazon announced its intention to launch its own online music store with millions of songs, free of copyright protection software, which otherwise limits what shoppers can do with the downloaded music. The songs downloaded from Amazon can be played on any personal device. One of its latest products is the e-book reader, Kindle. With Kindle, customers no longer need a computer in order to purchase reading material. Kindle directly downloads the content; books take less than one minute to download. Besides books, it also provides newspapers, magazines and blog delivery. Amazon is very pleased with demand for Kindle to date (Mintz 2008; Perenson 2008).

Two features are especially praised by customers: the ability to submit and read reviews of each product, and the 'search inside the book' function. The review feature is supposed to be the main reason for Amazon's success as a book e-tailer. Recently, users have also been allowed to comment on reviews. This has resulted in more than a thousand reviews for some products (e.g. the book *Pillars of the Earth* by Ken Follett). The feature that allows customers to 'search inside the book' permits them to search for keywords in the full text of many books. Additionally, customers can purchase a digital version of books via Amazon Upgrade. However, this service is limited to a selection of books.

This wide range of products and services, as well as being an innovator in terms of customization, has made Amazon.com a strong brand. In Interbrand's annual ranking of the world's most valuable brands, Amazon improved from number 65 in 2006 to number 62 in 2007. Its brand value has increased from US$4,707 million in 2006 to US$5,411 million in 2007 (up 15 per cent). This strong brand image provides competitive advantage in the e-tail industry and helps attract customers.

1996	– Amazon Associates Program
1997	– Personalized recommendations – Subject-area browsing – 1-click shopping
1998	– Instant recommendations – Acquisition of Sage Enterprise Inc.
1999	– Wish lists – Amazon Anywhere – zShops – Amazon Auctions – Amazon Electronics – Amazon Toys – Amazon Payments
2000	– Amazon Friends & Favorites
2001	– Amazon Honor System – Amazon Marketplace – Look inside the book – Instant Order Update
2002	– Amazon Web Services – Amazon Clothing
2003	– Search inside the book – A9.com search portal – Amazon Sporting Goods
2004	– Amazon Theatre
2005	– Amazon Prime – Amazon Pages – Amazon Upgrade – A9 yellow pages
2006	– Amazon Simple Storage Service – Discussion Boards – Amazon Connect – Amazon Elastic Compute Cloud
2007	– Unbox Online Video – MP3 Downloads – Kindle – Subscribe & Save – CreateSpace – Amazon Fresh

Exhibit 1 Major events of product line expansion

Services for Amazon's Customers

From the beginning, Amazon.com focused all its activities on the customer. This customer-centric approach has played an important role in Amazon's growth and success. The company culture promotes awareness of this approach and its application in day-to-day business. Since the early days, Bezos and his team have worked hard to satisfy Amazon's customers:

> I think somehow I am congenitally customer focused. And I think that from that comes this passion to figure out customer-focused strategies as opposed to, say, competitor-focused strategies. [. . .] a lot of our energy and drive as a company, as a culture, comes from trying to build customer-focused strategies. [. . .] in our environment there's so much rapid change on the Internet, in technology, that our customer-obsessed approach is very effective. If you're competitor focused, you tend to slack off when your benchmarks say that you're the best. But if your focus is on customers, you keep improving. [. . .] I told everyone, Be afraid of our customers, because those are the folks who have the money. Our competitors are never going to send us money. (Bezos in an interview with Kirby and Stewart 2007)

In order to achieve such a customer-focused strategy, Amazon.com personalizes storefronts for each customer (e.g. personal wish lists, shopping lists and recommendations). Amazon makes huge investments in technology in order to provide shoppers with personalized services. In addition, customers have a broad product selection to choose from, all integrated on one website: new and scarce goods, end-of-life products, as well as used and vintage items. These products are otherwise very difficult to locate and purchase. With this product range Amazon attracts around 50 million US customers to its website on a monthly basis. In January 2008, 53 million people visited the site (Siteanalytics 2008).

Amazon presents a 'search–find–obtain experience' to its shoppers like no other e-tailer (Datamonitor 2007). Looking for a specific product, customers can use subject area browsing. Amazon presents different products referring to the specific search subject. The resulting products can then be examined in more detail using the product's description, reviews and ratings. One feature customers evaluate as a very useful add-on is the customized recommendation service Amazon provides. Amazon's software detects a certain pattern in what customers want and suggests a variety of products to the shoppers based on their search and purchasing history. A chosen item can then be bought with just one mouse click. Making a payment at Amazon is very convenient as Amazon maintains its own payment system. In 2007, Amazon announced the 'Bill Me Later' payment technology as an alternative to credit cards, designed to enhance customer loyalty and increase customer purchasing power. This technology enables credit checks to allow high-value shoppers to postpone billing while receiving the ordered items immediately (Fornell 2008). After the purchase, customers can choose from different shipping options and can track the delivery status of their ordered items. Very attractive price discounts and the Amazon Prime feature add up to customer fidelity.

Customers 'want selection, low prices, and fast delivery', Bezos said in a recent interview (Kirby and Stewart 2007), and that is exactly what they get at Amazon.com. This adds up to high satisfaction for Amazon's customers. Based on the American Customer Satisfaction Index (ACSI), which includes more than 200 companies in more than 40 industries, Amazon remains the leader in customer satisfaction among e-tailers in 2007, with 88 points on a 100-point scale (Fornell 2008). These great satisfaction scores are crucial to Amazon's success, because survival in the e-commerce industry depends mainly on customer satisfaction. Switching costs are low and the next e-tailer is only one click away.

Altogether, Amazon is able to build an online experience for customers that includes greater choice, competitive pricing, ease of use, convenience and sophisticated information search. Some other steps taken by Amazon to enhance customer service are to reduce irrelevant information on product pages, decrease advertisements on the website and fully integrate the different international web pages with one another.

European Expansion

Today, in addition to its US websites, Amazon operates retail websites in the UK (www.amazon.co.uk), Germany (www.amazon.de), France (www.amazon.fr), Japan (www.amazon.co.jp), Canada (www.amazon.ca) and China (www.joyo.com), and generates almost half its revenues outside North America (Datamonitor 2007). Even more interestingly, this number is steadily increasing (Dean 2007). The international expansion of the e-tailer began in the 'old Europe' in 1998 by the acquisition of the online booksellers Bookpages.co.uk in Britain and Telebuch.de in Germany. Both markets seemed worth the effort of a conquest as they represented not only the largest online markets, but also the largest book markets in Europe. While, in the UK, the deregulation of retail book prices has led to an enormous increase in book sales, books have always played a crucial role in German culture. Moreover, German customers were also used to buying books via mail. Not surprisingly, Amazon quickly became the leading online book retailer in the UK and Germany. Having started as pure book retailers, amazon.uk and amazon.de soon began to add new product lines such as music, auctions, and so on. This European success led to the launch of amazon.fr in 2000. However, in contrast to the UK and Germany, in France the retail website was built from scratch by Amazon itself and immediately offered a wider product line, including music, video and DVD (Hammond and Chiron 2005).

Adaptation to Local Tastes

In the same year Japanese and in 2002 Canadian launches followed. In the course of its rapid international expansion, Amazon realized that it was necessary to adapt to the peculiarities of different markets, comprising legal, infrastructural and cultural aspects. Interestingly, this issue was most evident within the European Union. Although the European unification process has facilitated international activities, Amazon still had to address different selling regulations in each country. For instance, book list prices in Germany and France were fixed, which left little opportunity for discounting. Another challenge was diverse customer payment preferences, as only 38 per cent of Europeans used credit cards for online shopping. In a similar vein, Amazon had to deal with different market factors regarding both the supplier and the customer delivery side. While Germany had one single wholesaler in the book industry and another in the music and video markets, France had no wholesaler at all. Furthermore, no standard communication system, like EDI (electronic data interchange) in the USA, existed, and European vendors still used email or even faxes to deal with incoming orders. This made it hard for Amazon to forecast whether customer orders taken online could actually be fulfilled. Regarding customer delivery, Amazon had to rely on domestic postal carriers in each European country. None of these offered cross-border logistic services. Finally, cultural differences required the adaptation of local websites in terms of language, editorial content and country-specific product assortments (Hammond and Chiron 2005; see Exhibit 2).

Amazon accepted the challenge of meeting local laws and maintained a competitive offering by providing free shipping in 2001 and running legal promotional activities such as clearance sales for slow-moving items. For payment, the e-tailer allowed locally preferred alternatives such as cheques for French customers and postal orders for German online shoppers. Regarding procurement and delivery, Amazon established relationships with hundreds of publishers and distributors, and cooperated with the national postal services, both for domestic as well as international shipping.

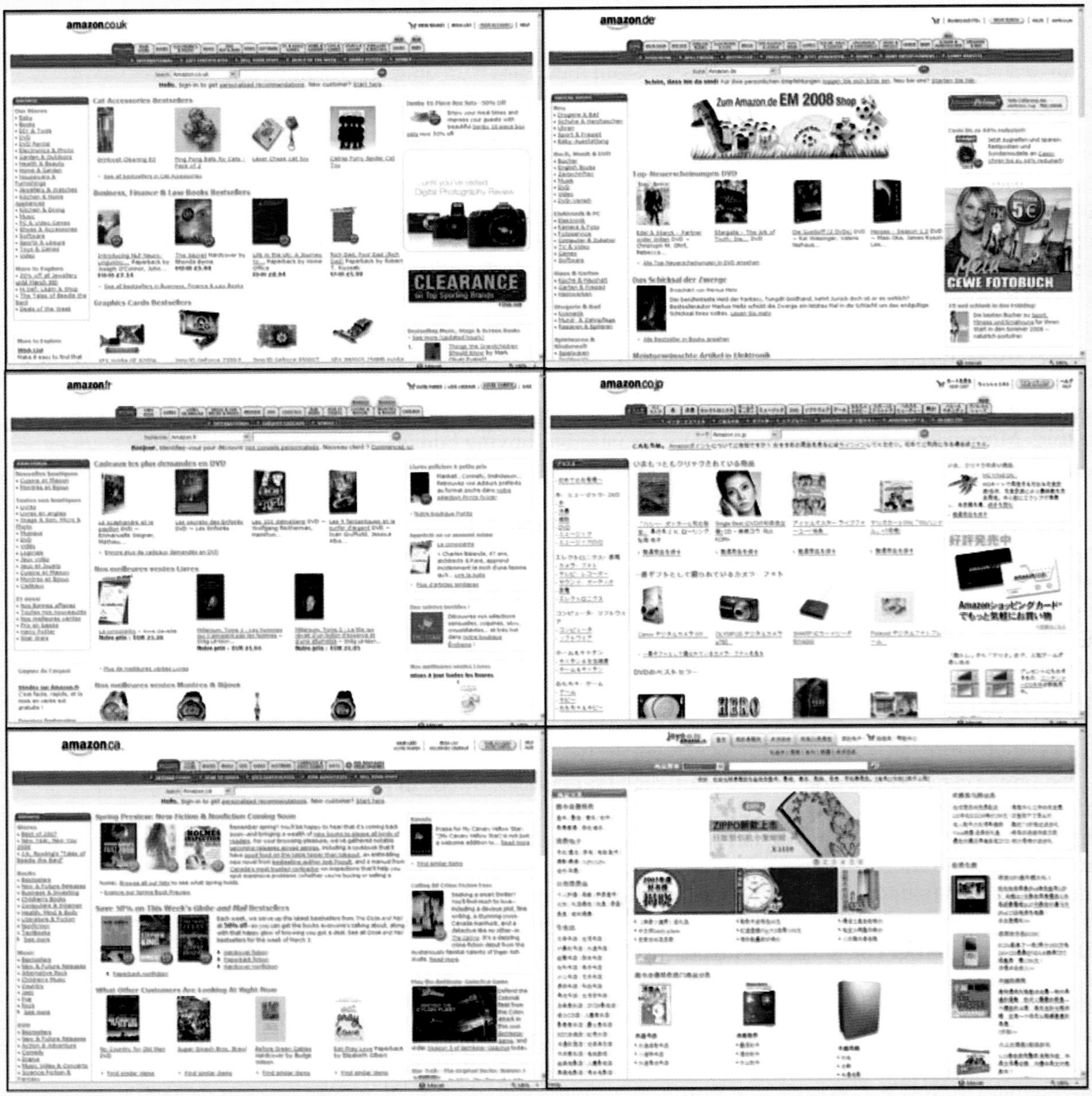

Exhibit 2 Amazon websites around the globe

Furthermore, the company set up customer service centers where native-speaker employees could meet the needs of European online shoppers. Though the online retailer was able to standardize the international websites' functionalities, such as browsing and searching, it needed to adapt content as well as product offering for every country (Hammond and Chiron 2005). Interestingly, the Canadian website also offers a Canadian product selection, which is different from the US assortment, in order to promote Canadian writers and musicians, with both English and French titles available. Canadian online shoppers can place their order, and read editorial reviews and recommendations in both English and French (Mulholland 2002).

It turned out that, for the international expansion, the major challenge for Amazon was to provide universal benefits all over the world while taking into account local habits and preferences. The universal benefits Amazon identified were better selection, more convenience and better service. As a result of Amazon's adaptation to local needs, Amazon.co.uk, Amazon.de and Amazon.fr became independently managed subsidiaries, and it was not until its cost-cutting and restructuring efforts in 2001 that the e-tailer merged marketing and branding functions at the European level (Hammond and Chiron 2005).

The Chinese Challenge

With the beginning of the new millennium, established dotcoms such as Google, Yahoo! and Amazon realized that the Chinese online market, with its enormous potential for growth, could not be disregarded. Lured by expected market growth rates, Amazon acquired the local online retailer joyo.com in 2004 for US$75 million (Hof 2004a). Although joyo.com was then the biggest online retailer in China, its rival, dangdang.com, has expanded more rapidly, and is now the leading domestic player with a market share of 18 per cent versus the 12 per cent of joyo.com (Dean 2007). However, this rival is not the only challenge for Amazon in China. The region still has comparatively primitive credit and payment systems: instead, an armada of bicycle couriers deliver cash. The transportation system is also poorly developed and Chinese shoppers still prefer to meet the seller in person (Miller 2004). Moreover, the internet itself is highly regulated in China, and is an unpredictable factor due to the way in which Chinese laws are interpreted arbitrarily (Hof 2004a). Nevertheless, maverick CEO Bezos is sticking to Amazon's expansion strategy in the region. He emphasizes that 'this business is remarkable, and it's growing so rapidly that it deserves even increased levels of investment' (Bezos, in an interview, Dean 2007). Indeed, China is now the second largest market in the world after the USA, and online shopping in the country is expected to grow by 190 per cent in the year to come. It is no wonder, then, that China remains an attractive online market although income levels are still relatively low and only about 10 per cent of the population are currently online (Datamonitor 2007).

This case was written by Silke C. Heß and Monika C. Schuhmacher, Department of Marketing, University of Mannheim.

Discussion Questions

1. How do you account for Amazon's high customer satisfaction scores?
2. What benefits occur from high customer satisfaction?
3. Review Amazon's international expansion using a timeline. Is this internationalization strategy more akin to a waterfall or a sprinkler strategy?
4. Regarding its globalization strategy does Amazon follow a standardization approach or a differentiation approach? Please discuss its entry strategies into the different countries mentioned.
5. What recommendations would you make to Amazon concerning China? Should it remain in China? Why, or why not?
6. In what way is Amazon's business different from traditional bookstores' business?

References

Anderson, C. (2004) The long tail, *Change This*, 10, 1, 1–30.
Datamonitor (2007) *Amazon.com Inc. Company Profile*, 8 June.
Dean, J. (2007) Bezos says Amazon will boost investment in China, *Wall Street Journal*, 6 June, A12.
Fornell, C. (2008) Retail trade; finance & insurance; e-commerce, *ACSI Quarterly Commentaries*, 19 February.
Hammond, J. and Chiron, C. (2005) Amazon.com's European distribution strategy, *Harvard Business School Case*, 30 June.
Hayes, B. (2007) A paradise of choice, *American Scientist Online*, 95, 1, January/February.
Hof, R. (2004a) Amazon hops on the Orient Express, *Business Week Online*, 20 August.
Hof, R. (2004b) The wizard of web retailing, *Business Week*, 20 December, 18.
Hof, R. (2006) Jeff Bezos' risky bet, *Business Week*, 13 November, 52–58.
Holohan, C. (2008) Tough love for Amazon, *Business Week Online*, 2 January, 18.
Kirby, J. and Stewart, T. (2007) The institutional yes, *Harvard Business Review*, October, 74–82.
Miller, K.L. (2004) Asian bound, *Newsweek*, 14, 16, E15.
Mintz, J. (2008) Amazon to buy Audi book seller Audible Inc., *News Tribune*, 1 February.
Mulholland, A. (2002) Amazon.ca debuts in Canada, *CTV.ca*, 25 June.
Perenson, M. (2008) Amazon Kindles interest in e-books, *Reviews & Rankings*, February, 64.
Siteanalytics (2008) http://siteanalytics.compete.com/amazon.com.
Wolf, A. (2008) Amazon's Ryder: riding herd over new technologies online and off, *Twice*, 7 January, 100.

PART 4

Marketing Implementation

This part of the book examines the implementation of marketing decisions regarding the marketing strategy and marketing instruments within a company. This perspective concentrates in particular on important company-internal aspects. The focus here is on the conditions that have to be in place for an effective and efficient realization of the market-related activities taking a company-internal viewpoint. Ultimately, this part of the book is concerned with the implementation of the marketing strategy, and the importance of having a marketing orientation.

We will discuss the following areas in Part 4:

- Chapter 13 will study aspects of the marketing and sales organization
- information systems in marketing and sales will then be discussed in Chapter 14
- subsequently, Chapter 15 will go into issues of marketing and sales controlling
- human resource management in marketing and sales will be examined in Chapter 16
- finally, market-oriented management is dealt with in Chapter 17.

Contents

CHAPTER 13

Marketing and Sales Organization

Contents

Learning Objectives

In this chapter you will become familiar with:

- the main options related to the design of organizational structures as well as the primary advantages and disadvantages of specialization
- the approaches used in company practice for combining several types of specialization (particularly within the scope of the matrix organization)
- the various methods of specialization that can be used within marketing and sales units
- the most important points of coordination in marketing and sales units (especially product management and key account management) and the main options to design coordination
- the increasing importance of teams in company–customer interfaces, and the key options to consider when designing customer support teams
- the principal approaches to coordinate the process workflow (i.e. optimization of individual processes and conditions for optimizing processes used in the company).

One of the most important aspects of the marketing implementation concerns the issue of how marketing tasks are embedded within the organization. The organizational structure of the company particularly determines which departments and employees are responsible for planning and performing the various marketing activities. The organizational structure can be characterized by two main dimensions: specialization and coordination (for alternative structures of coordination within an organization see Malone 1987).

Specialization refers to the extent to which, and how, work is divided in the company. The activities necessary to meet the company's objectives are thus allocated to individual employees and/or company business units, departments and divisions. Section 13.1 will specifically address questions related to the topic of specialization. One focus here is the specialization of the company as a whole and, in particular, the question of the role that marketing and customer-related aspects play within the scope of specialization. A second facet concerns specialization in the area of marketing and sales.

Specialization in companies requires **coordination** (see Lawrence and Lorsch 1967) – that is, aligning the activities of employees, business units, departments and divisions with the company's objectives. In Section 13.2 we will examine coordination in sales and marketing units, and present the different mechanisms for coordination.

13.1 How to Specialize: An Introduction to the Concept of Specialization

Specialization can take place at the various hierarchical levels of a company. With respect to *specialization across all hierarchical levels of the company*, the central question usually deals with how to structure the strategic business units of the company. *Specialization on the marketing and sales organization level* refers to the design and structure of marketing and sales units within the company.

We will introduce the basic types of specialization in Section 13.1.1. Section 13.1.2 will then elaborate on the organizational structures that result from these different types of specialization. Section 13.1.3 then follows with a discussion of trends with regard to specialization in company practice. These three sections primarily apply to specialization across all hierarchical levels of the company, while Section 13.1.4 specifically examines specialization within marketing and sales units.

13.1.1 Basic Types of Company Specialization

A fundamental question with regard to specialization within a firm concerns the issue of which **type of specialization** should be implemented at the highest hierarchical level of the company. This decision has far-reaching consequences, both in terms of implementing marketing activities and for the alignment of the entire company with the market.

In general, there are two types of specialization (see also Figure 13-1): functional and business-oriented specialization. **Functional specialization** is aligned with the various activities along the value chain of the company (for more on the concept of the value chain see Section 3.4.2). In this form of specialization, related or similar activities are integrated into the same organizational unit (see Figure 13-2).

A major advantage of functional specialization is that the various functional tasks can be expertly performed by qualified and experienced specialists, which can lead to a relatively high degree of **efficiency** ('things are done right'). A significant disadvantage of this type of specialization lies in the fact that the interests of particular 'objects' (e.g. the requirements of certain customer groups) may not be sufficiently taken into consideration. Therefore, such specialization can have a negative

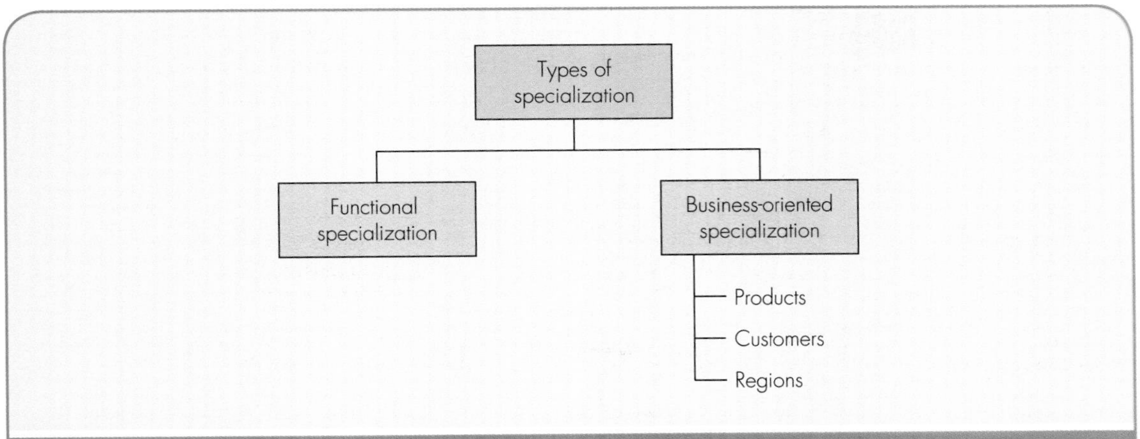

Figure 13-1 Types of specialization

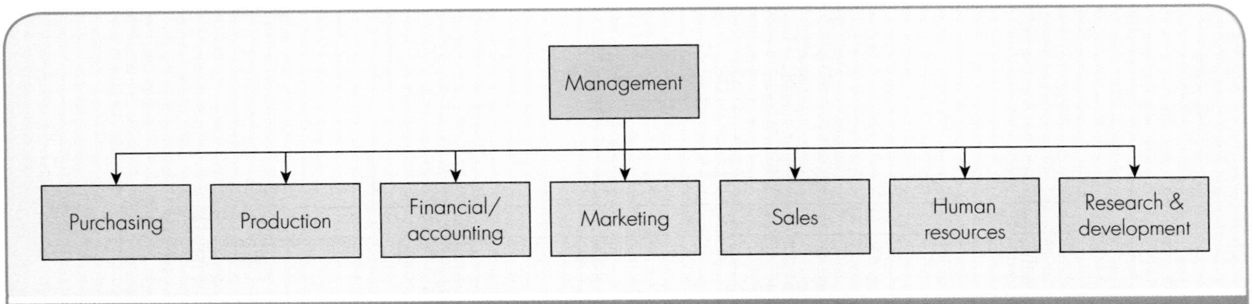

Figure 13-2 Functional specialization within a company

impact on the **effectiveness** of the company ('the right things are done'). Functional specialization is particularly appropriate for companies that achieve a majority of their sales with just a few products and develop only relatively few international markets.

In the case of **business-oriented specialization**, the focus is not on the type of task, but rather on the tasks' objects of reference. The most important objects used to organize business-oriented specialization are products, customers and regions. This organizational form does not focus on bundling certain similar activities, such as production or sales. Instead, there are separate divisions for different product lines, customer groups or geographical sales regions (see also Figure 13-3).

If business-oriented specialization is implemented at the highest hierarchical level of the company, it is generally associated with the establishment of units that have a certain degree of autonomy and are managed as responsible **profit centers**. In practice, terms such as 'division', 'group', 'subdivision', 'business unit' and 'strategic business unit' are commonly used. In our discussion on marketing strategy (see Section 2.1), we labeled these company divisions 'strategic business units'; we will thus use the term 'business unit' in what follows.

An organizational structure with *separate divisions for different product lines* is suitable mainly for companies that offer a wide and diverse product portfolio. The main disadvantage of this form of specialization at the top level of the company lies in the risk of an insufficient customer orientation.

An organizational structure with separate divisions for different customer segments requires market segmentation (for more on market segmentation, see Section 3.3). The corporate customer and

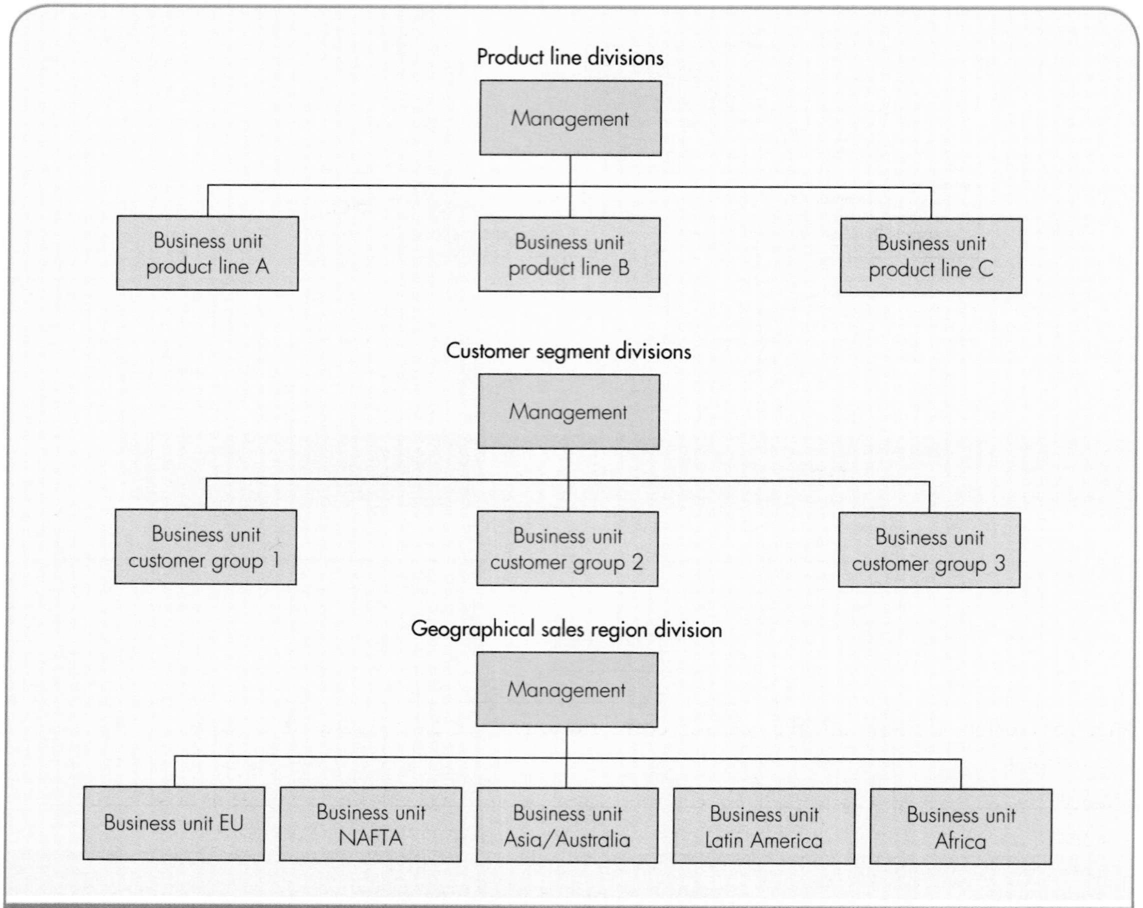

Figure 13-3 Organizational structure of business-oriented specializations within a company

personal banking business units of a bank represent examples of this type of specialization. The objective of this form of specialization is to align business activities with the specific needs and requirements of the different heterogeneous customer segments. A potential disadvantage is the loss of product-related competence and knowhow in the business units.

An organizational structure with separate divisions for different geographical regions – such as continents, groups of countries, countries or regions within countries – is primarily relevant for companies that cover a large sales territory (e.g. globally operating consumer and industrial goods manufacturers) and that are confronted with significant regional differences in terms of customer behavior. A main advantage of this form of specialization is the possibility of accounting for specific regional market characteristics. Disadvantages arise from problematic coordination between the regions – for example, in the course of serving international customers located in different country regions across the globe.

13.1.2 Combining Several Types of Specialization

In the previous section, we discussed each form of specialization separately. In company practice, especially in large companies, several types of specialization are often combined and used at the same time. In principle, there are two methods of combining various forms of specialization:

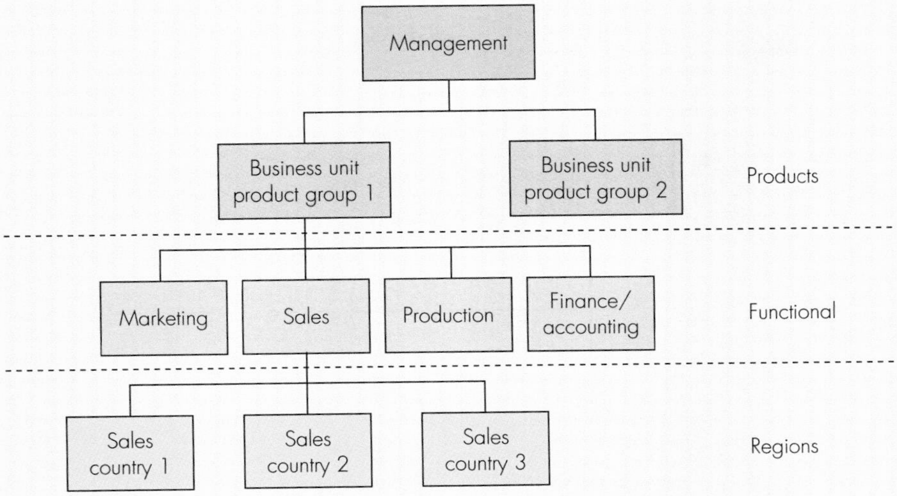

Figure 13-4 Implementation of several types of specialization at different hierarchical levels

combination across different hierarchical levels and combination on the same hierarchical level (matrix organization).

If several types of specialization are combined across different hierarchical levels, the question arises as to which types of specialization should be implemented at which hierarchical levels. Figure 13-4 gives an example that illustrates the application of three specialization criteria: products, functions and regions. At the highest level of this organization, business units are based on product groups (Business unit product group 1 and Business unit product group 2). These business units specialize according to functional criteria (marketing, sales, etc.). The functional sales department then specializes according to regions (Countries 1, 2 and 3). Such organizational structures are very common in company practice.

If two forms of specialization are combined at one level, the result is a matrix organization. A **matrix organization** aims to facilitate decision making while making full use of the competences of employees and employee teams. This organizational form combines different types of specialization and was proposed to avoid rigid structures resulting from, for example, a pure functional structure. For example, in the structure shown in Figure 13-5, both the strategic objectives of the business unit for Product group 1, as well as the strategic orientation of the functional sales department, are taken into account when making sales decisions regarding Product group 1.

Obviously, matrix organizations can be complex, in particular because units report directly to two (or sometimes more) managers in different departments. In concrete terms, this means that an employee has two supervisors from different areas in the organization ('a servant of two masters'). For example, in the structure presented in Figure 13-5, the sales employee responsible for Product group 1 receives instructions from both the head of the sales division and the manager of the business unit for Product group 1.

It is for this reason that the matrix organization requires a high degree of coordination effort in the company. In such organizational structures, competing interests frequently arise, which can be especially intense if the objectives of organizational units are not consistent. This may arise, for example, if the head of the business unit for Product group 1 in Figure 13-5 focuses on the

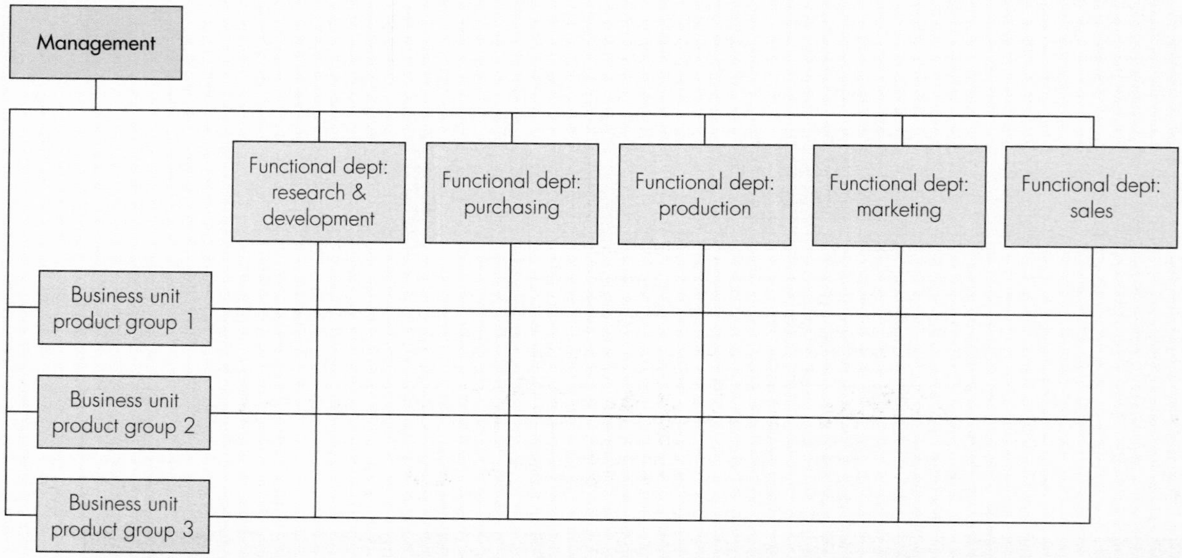

Figure 13-5 Example of a matrix organization

optimization of profits, while the sales manager's goal is to improve market share (building market share is costly and can hurt profitability, at least in the short run). Thus, a key factor in such matrix organizations is consistency with regard to both objectives and performance-based remuneration systems.

In company practice, the negative consequences of matrix organizations can easily surface. Nevertheless, this organizational form is widely practiced as it is the only alternative for companies once they reach a certain size and level of complexity. Companies with a very broad and diverse product portfolio often have to establish product-based business units. If a company also operates in many regions of the world and there are considerable synergies between the products with regard to marketing, the creation of regional business units with marketing tasks across product groups is often appropriate.

13.1.3 The Trend Towards Customer-Focused Organizational Structures

In practice, many companies tend to reinforce their customer orientation by establishing customer segment divisions (see Homburg *et al.* 2000b). Consequently, product line divisions and regional divisions are of decreasing importance for the organizational structure – without being completely abandoned (see also Figure 13-6 and Focus on Marketing 13-1).

In this section we will be taking a closer look at the challenges that arise for companies if they move from a more product-focused to a more customer-focused organizational structure (see also Homburg *et al.* 2000b). In order to make the transition from a product-focused to a customer-focused structure, firms typically have to undergo several, often major, reorganizations. Figure 13-7 portrays six organizational types that differ in their degree of customer focus.

While phase (a) in Figure 13-7 shows a functional organization – implying the lowest level of customer orientation – phase (b) comprises the implementation of separate divisions for different

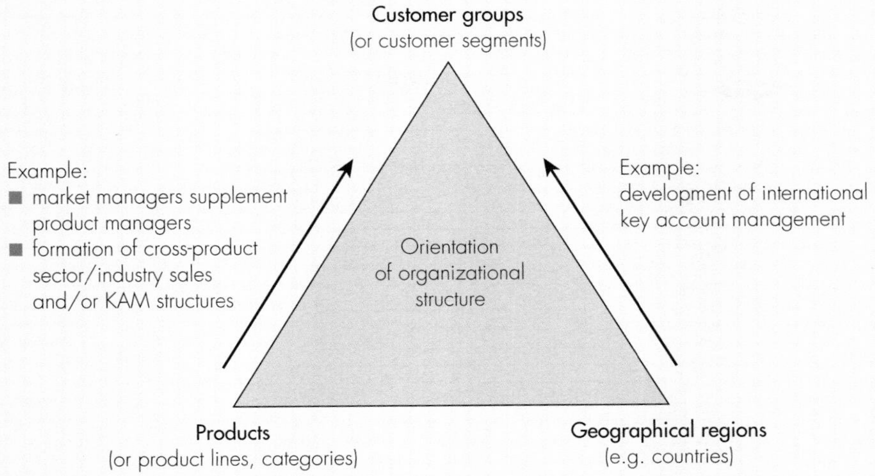

Figure 13-6 The shift towards customer-focused organizational structures (adapted from Homburg *et al.* 2000b, p. 468)

Focus on Marketing 13-1 Example of a transition towards customer-focused organization

Reinventing Motorola

It takes Motorola Inc. employees about 30 seconds after they meet Edward J. Zander to realize how different their new boss is from their last one.

The changes are just beginning. By October, Zander hopes to abandon Motorola's stovepipe divisions, which are focused on products like mobile phones and broadband gear, and reorganize operations around customer markets – one for the digital home, for example, and another for corporate buyers.

The reorganization will help Zander deliver on several new initiatives. Perhaps the most important is what the chief executive calls 'seamless mobility'. The idea is that Motorola should make it easy for consumers to transport any digital information – music, video, e-mail, phone calls – from the house to the car to the workplace.

Mastering that technology would do more than boost cell-phone sales. It also could make Motorola a key player in the digital home, helping it sell flat-panel TVs and broadband modems, home wireless networks, and gateways to manage digital content. Separately, Motorola is planning a major push to sell more services to corporations. While Motorola sells communications gear to corporate customers now, Zander sees an important growth opportunity in managing networks for those companies. 'We have to get more focused on that,' said Zander in an interview.

Source: Crockett 2004, pp. 82–83.

product lines. This stage reflects the formation of a divisional structure (see Chandler 1990), which, in contrast to an exclusively functional organizational structure, establishes responsible profit centers within the company. The divisional form helps the firm to focus better on the individual markets. Therefore, this form is more customer oriented than a purely functional organizational structure.

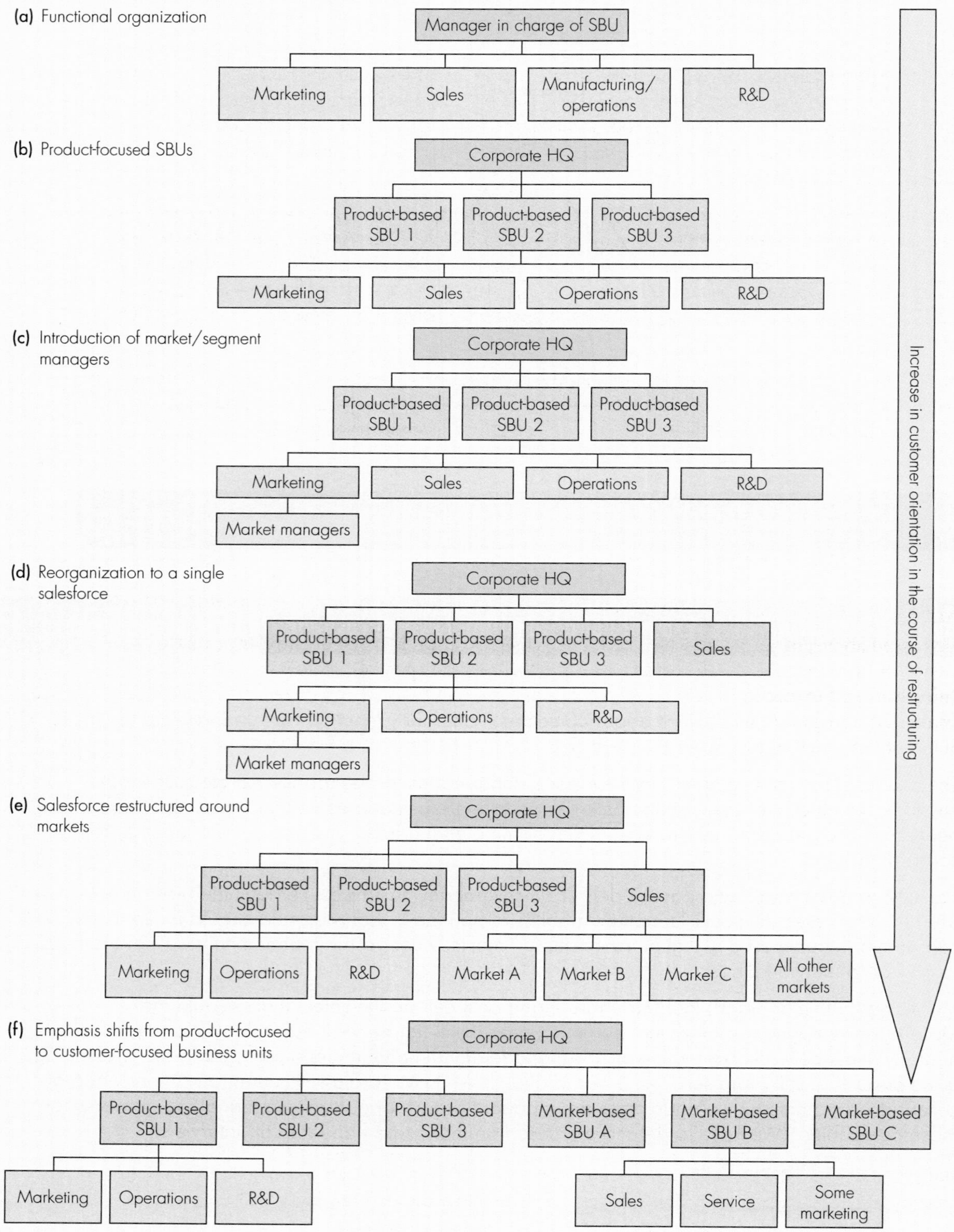

Figure 13-7 Organizational configurations in the movement towards customer-focused business units (adapted from Homburg *et al.* 2000b, p. 471)

Often a transition follows where companies with product line divisions introduce **customer segment managers** (also called market managers) (see phase (c) in Figure 13-7). These positions are implemented with the objective of coordinating the marketing activities pertaining to certain customer groups both on a cross-functional level within the respective business unit as well as (informally) between the different business units.

A possible approach to increasing a firm's customer orientation is to form a general sales unit that is responsible for the products handled in all business units (see phase (d) in Figure 13-7). In this context we speak of presenting 'one face to the customer'. With this organizational structure, the business units thus do not have any complete control over sales – a matrix organization usually exists. Accordingly, customers who purchase the products of several business units can be optimally supported.

Naturally, not every company goes through all the organizational structures presented here. Some of the evolutionary stages shown in Figure 13-7 can be skipped, and companies can transition directly from an organizational form with a relatively low customer orientation (e.g. phase (b)) to a form with a stronger customer focus (e.g. phase (d)).

13.1.4 Specialization within Marketing and Sales Units

This section examines the question of which criteria should be used to demarcate the various departments and positions within marketing and sales units. In general, the same types of specialization used at the level of the entire company can be used here too (see Section 13.1.1).

As discussed above, in **functional specialization**, categorization is based on similar or related activities. Within the area of sales and marketing, this form of specialization is very widely used because sales and marketing perform very different tasks and thus the organizational separation between marketing and sales is prevalent in company practice (see Workman *et al.* 1998). Figure 13-8 provides an overview of the various specialized areas in marketing and sales.

With a **business-oriented specialization**, a variety of different activities that are directed towards the same object (product, customer, region) are combined (also see Section 13.1.1).

In **product management organizations** product managers or category managers are assigned direct responsibility for a broad spectrum of tasks related to a certain product or product lines (see Ruekert *et al.* 1985). With category management, the tasks explicitly refer to a group of related products (i.e. a product category) (for more information on product categories, see Section 5.4.1).

Market management organizations are of major importance in marketing and sales (see Ruekert *et al.* 1985). A prevalent practice is for the company's field salesforce to specialize in particular customer segments. One example to be mentioned here is segmentation based on the medical specialization of physicians in the case of pharmaceutical sales (i.e. segments can be formed for, say, dentists and psychologists). Assignment to specific customer groups is also commonly found in the internal sales department.

Moreover, there are special forms of customer-oriented market management organizations. These forms include **key account management**, in which activities associated with very important customers are consolidated, and **customer segment management**, which coordinates activities related to certain customer segments (see Section 13.1.3 and phase (c) in Figure 13-7). Finally, **customer support teams** should be mentioned. They perform customer support activities in teams that may include employees from other functional departments. Rather than customer support being provided by one individual salesforce employee, the team is often more effective due to the multiple competences of team members. As a common characteristic, these special types of market management organizations frequently share a strong focus on coordination (see also Section 13.2).

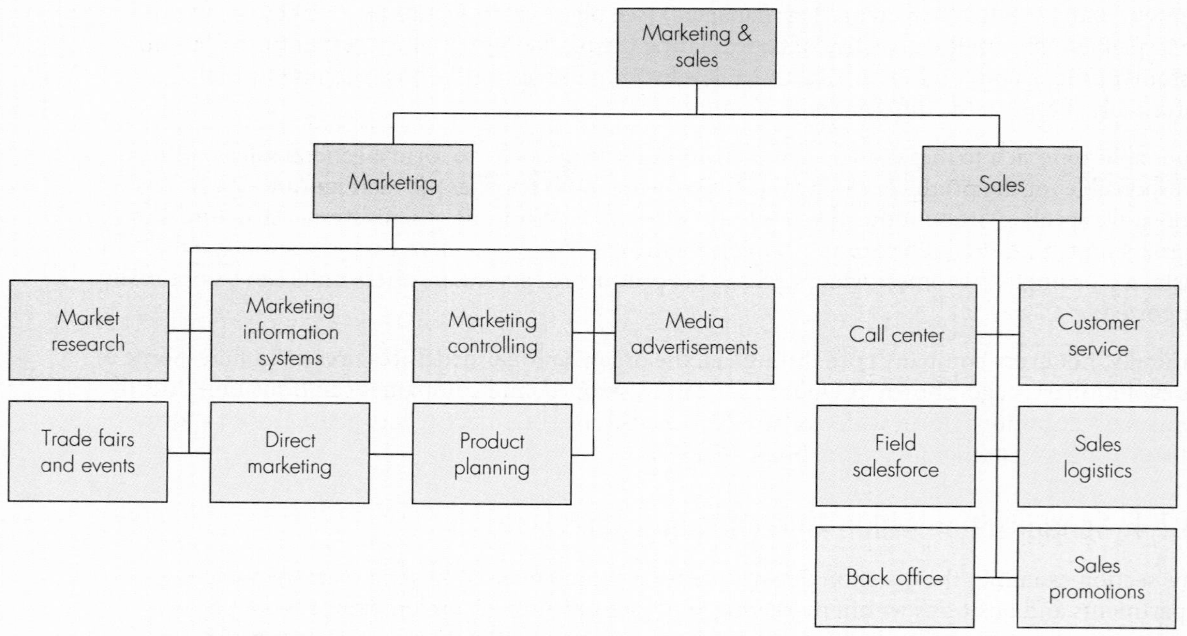

Figure 13-8 Example of the functional specialization of marketing and sales units

Organizing marketing activities according to different regions plays a key role in sales, especially field sales. This type of marketing organization is often used in connection with market management organization (see also Figure 13-9). If the sales territory of a company exceeds a certain geographical size, the regional specialization of field sales is indispensable in terms of reducing travel time alone. Along with this aspect, in the area of international marketing, familiarity with different national cultures is another main reason for implementing the regional specialization of the field salesforce. The organization of marketing activities according to different regions (e.g. European market research, Asian market research, South American market research) can also be implemented in the marketing units of companies that cover large sales territories (e.g. globally operating companies).

Finally, it should be noted that many companies also use **sales channels as objects of specialization**, particularly in the sales department. This is also due to the increasing importance of multi-channel sales systems. For example, organizational units for field sales, call center sales and e-commerce sales can be organized according to this structure.

Figure 13-9 provides a corresponding example. Functional organization is evident at the top hierarchical level. Both product management and functional organization (marketing communication and market research) elements exist within the marketing unit at the first level. At the next level, organization according to regions (Europe, Asia and Americas) is used in the product management units, while functional organization (divided into communication tools) is once again applied in the marketing communication units. At the first level below the sales unit, organization according to regions (regional sales departments for Europe, Asia and America) and market management organization exist in parallel. The entire decentralized sales organization is located here, along with global key account management, which is responsible for coordinating the support of internationally operating key accounts across regions. It is thus a form of market management organization.
A further element of market management organization emerges from the creation of target group

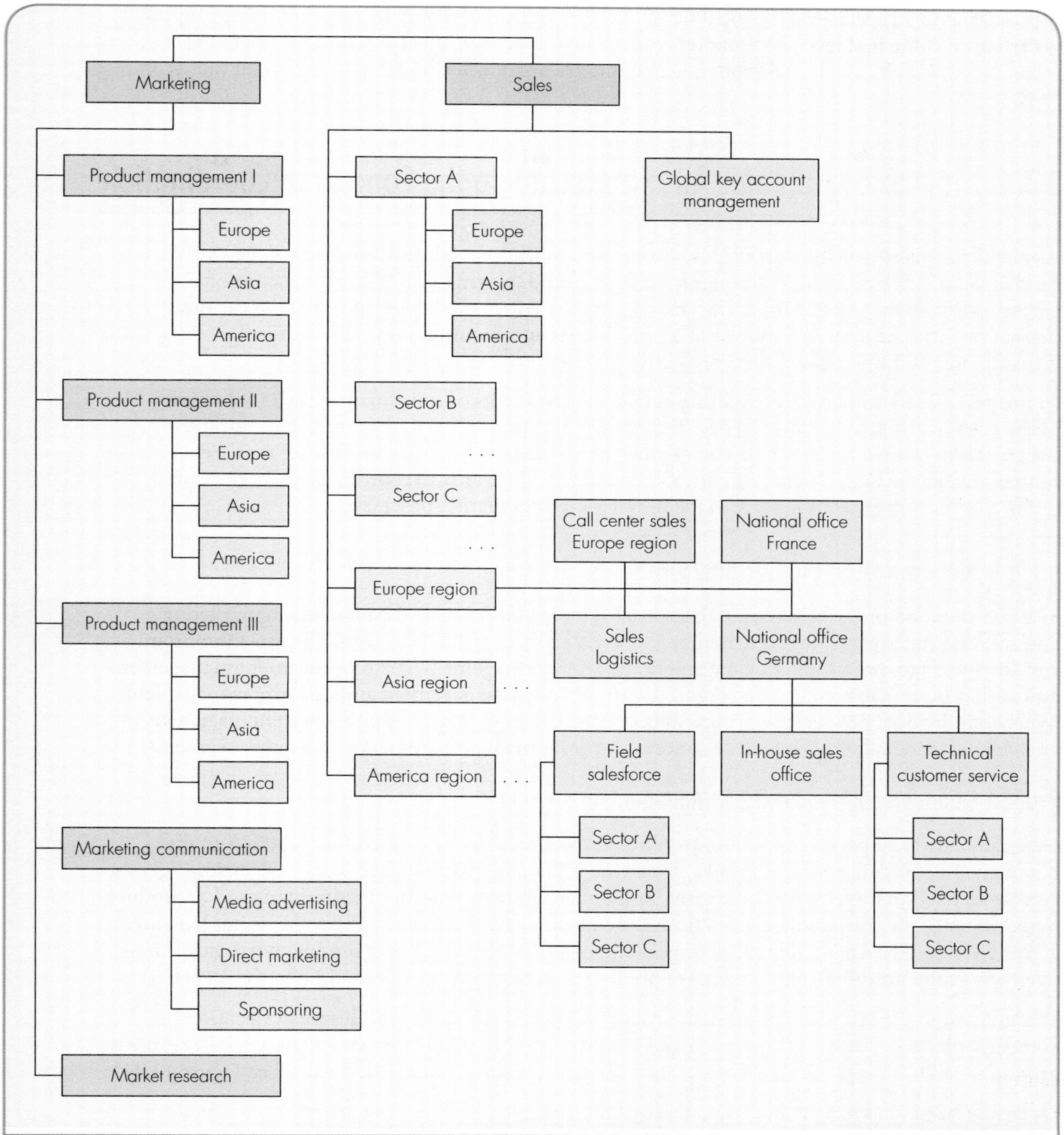

Figure 13-9 Example of the organization of the marketing activities of a globally operating chemical company

sales channels, which are in charge of coordinating market development in the various customer segments (Sectors A, B and C).

At the next level, both functional organization (centralized call centers for the region, as well as sales logistics) and organization according to regions (individual countries) exist. Within the national offices, functional specialization (field sales, internal sales department, technical customer support) is then used at the first level, and market management organization is used to some extent at the second level. Finally, the target group sales channel is organized according to regions at the second level.

13.2 How to Coordinate: An Introduction to the Concept of Coordination

As already explained at the start of this chapter, specialization and coordination are the two fundamental tasks involved in designing the organizational structure. Within the scope of specialization in the organizational structure, which we discussed in Section 13.1, the various marketing tasks are allocated to several business units and/or employees. This requires coordination of the activities of the respective business units and employees.

In this section, we will be differentiating between instruments of coordination used in the area of the **organizational structure** (see Section 13.2.1) and those used in the area of the **workflow organization** (see Section 13.2.2). The organizational structure concerns measures that are represented in the organizational chart of the company. In contrast, coordination instruments of the workflow organization refer to the design of the company's processes.

13.2.1 Coordination via Organizational Structure

The coordination of the activities of the specialized business units and employees in marketing and sales via the organizational structure is supported by **coordination sites**. The most important coordination sites are product management, category management, customer segment management and key account management (see Figure 13-10). Product management and category management focus on individual products or groups of products (categories), while key account management and customer segment management concentrate on individual customers or customer segments.

Product Management and Category Management

Generally, the focal points relevant to **product management** are the individual products of the company. In companies where brands play a vital role in the marketing concept (e.g. major consumer good manufacturers), the term 'brand management' is sometimes used instead of product management. The concept originates from the consumer goods industry and today is implemented across all industries and in almost all large companies that manage larger product portfolios (for an overview of the historical development of product management, see Low and Fullerton 1994).

With regard to the tasks associated with product management, there is widespread variation in company practice (see, e.g., Hankinson and Cowking 1997). Product management typically revolves around the following phases: analysis, planning, implementation and monitoring (see Figure 13-11).

Occasionally (and especially in companies that are largely technologically oriented), product management tasks are also undertaken by departments with a technical focus (such as, e.g., Research & Development; see the empirical findings of Johne and Rowntree 1991). Product managers are only rarely assigned to the sales department.

In **category management** product-related activities need to be coordinated within a product group. Very often, this group is tasked with considering possible cannibalization effects between the products (see Section 5.3.3) within a product category (see Zenor 1994). Category management is responsible for ensuring that product management decisions in favor of individual products within a product category will not have a negative impact on the success of other products (and thus the entire product category).

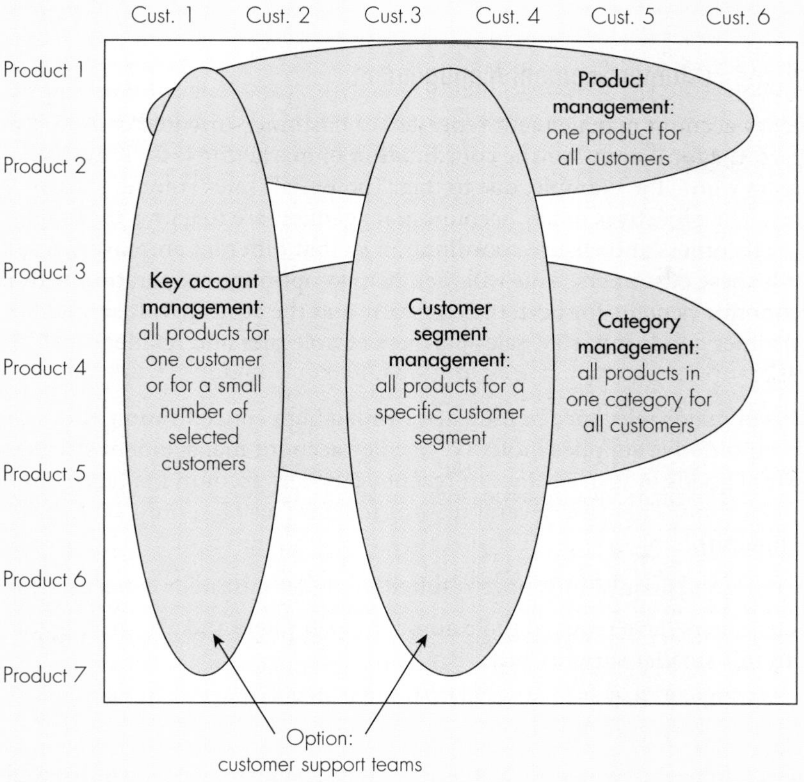

Figure 13-10 Illustration of various coordination sites

Analysis →	Planning →	Implementation →	Monitoring
■ Initiation of market research ■ Analysis of the positioning of products and brands ■ Analysis of customer satisfaction with the products ■ Analysis of customer requirements ■ Analysis of the competitor activities and products ■ Analysis of the internal resource allocation	■ Strategic planning for the product ■ Annual sales planning for the product ■ Marketing planning for the product with regard to product decisions (new variants, line extensions, elimination), pricing decisions, communication decisions and sales decisions ■ Coordination with the planning of other functional departments	■ Implementation of planned measures ■ Activities within the scope of the market launch of new products (e.g. field salesforce training, direct customer care/support, application support/user training) ■ Coordination with other functional departments in order to initiate planned activities	■ Monitoring the achievement of objectives related to potential (e.g. customer satisfaction with products/brands) ■ Monitoring the achievement of objectives related to market success (e.g. market share of products/brands) ■ Monitoring the achievement of economic objectives (e.g. profitability of products/brands)

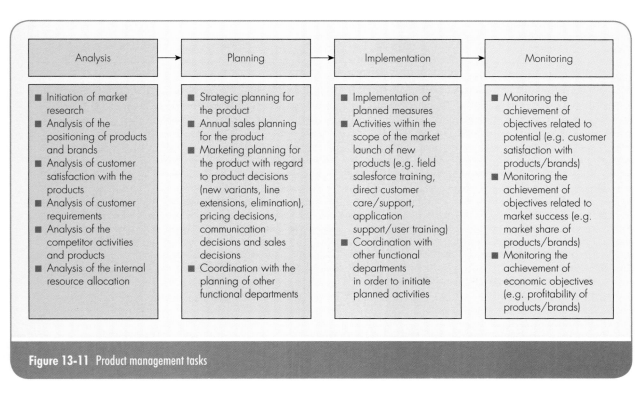

Figure 13-11 Product management tasks

Key Account Management and Customer Segment Management

As shown in Figure 13-10, key account management represents a customer-oriented coordination unit within a company. Here, the focal point for the coordination of marketing tasks is a small number of selected customers who – for example, due to their (potential) sales volume – are of great significance to the company. The objectives of key account management are to gain a thorough understanding of these key customers and ensure coordination so that different employees display a uniform approach towards these customers. This will then help to optimize cooperation with the customer, and generate economic benefits for both the company and the customer. It should be mentioned that, in the consumer goods industry, sales partners (wholesaler and retailer) are also referred to as 'key accounts'.

Key account management is of major relevance in industries with a high concentration of customers. An extreme example is the automotive supplies industry. The key account management structure is widely used in other industrial goods industries, too. In recent years, key account management *has become increasingly more important*. There are several reasons for this (see Homburg *et al.* 2002, as well as the literature cited therein).

- In many industries, mergers and acquisitions have resulted in higher customer concentration.
- In recent years, many customers have reduced their number of suppliers and are striving for closer cooperations with this smaller supplier base.
- Many companies have centralized their procurement activities internationally and expect the same high degree of cross-national coordination from their suppliers.

Similar to product management, the range of tasks in key account management can be illustrated with a phase model comprising analysis, planning, implementation and monitoring (see Figure 13-12).

A comprehensive typology of the **design forms of key account management** identifies a total of eight different design forms (Homburg *et al.* 2002) (see Table 13-1).

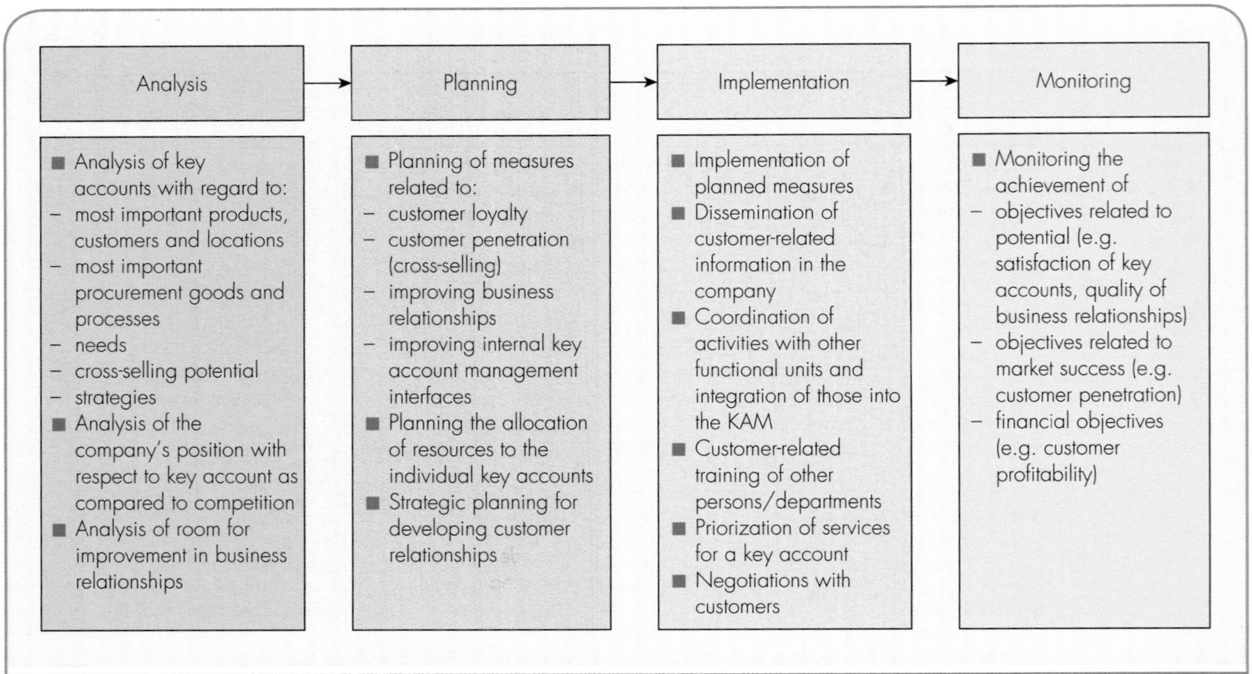

Figure 13-12 Key account management tasks (adapted from Homburg *et al.* 2006, p. 313)

Table 13-1 Typology of the alternatives for designing key account management systems (Homburg *et al.* 2002, p. 50)

KAM approach / Variable	Top management KAM (n = 37)	Middle management KAM (n = 76)	Operating-level KAM (n = 57)	Cross-functional, dominant KAM (n = 44)	Unstructured KAM (n = 38)	Isolated KAM (n = 40)	Country club KAM (n = 37)	No KAM (n = 46)
Activity intensity	Medium-high	Medium	Medium-high	High	Medium	Medium	Low	Low
Activity proactiveness	Medium	Medium	Low-medium	High	Low-medium	Medium	Low	Low-medium
Approach formalization	Very high	High	Rather high	Very high	Low	Rather low	Very low	Low
Top management involvement	Very high	Medium	Low	High	Very low	Medium-high	High	Low
Use of teams	Much	Little	Much-very much	Very much	Little	Medium	Very little	Very little
Selling center *esprit de corps*	Rather strong	Rather weak	Rather strong	Strong	Strong	Weak	Rather weak	Weak
Access to marketing and sales resources	Rather low	High	Low	Very high	Rather high	Medium	Very high	Very low
Access to non-marketing and non-sales resources	Low	Medium	Low	High	Medium	Low	Medium	Low

In view of the multitude of options regarding the design of key account management, the question arises of the success factors associated with designing it. In this context, Workman *et al.* (2003) conducted a study of the factors that influence the effectiveness of key account management. Their findings showed that the effectiveness of key account management largely depends on the team spirit of the company employees involved. According to the study, the degree to which the key account manager can access company-internal resources is another main success factor.

Another customer-oriented coordination site within a company is **customer segment management**. This differs from key account management in that the focal point for the coordination of tasks is entire customer segments that have been identified to be very important for the company. The objective of customer segment management is to align the company's activities with the needs of the customers within the respective segment (see Collins *et al.* 2006). Focus on Marketing 13-2 gives an example of customer segment management in retailing.

Focus on Marketing 13-2 Example of customer segment management

Store of knowledge

Tesco plc, Britain's largest retailer's big weapon is information about its customers. Tesco has signed up 12 million Britons for its Clubcard program, giving cardholders discounts in exchange for their name, address and other personal information. The Clubcard has helped boost Tesco's market share in groceries to 31%.

The data let Tesco tailor promotions to individual shoppers and figure out quickly how new initiatives are working. Tesco's computers often turn up counterintuitive results. Shoppers who buy diapers for the first time at a Tesco store can expect to receive coupons by mail for baby wipes, toys – and beer. Tesco's analysis showed that new fathers tend to buy more beer because they are home with the baby and can't go to the pub.

Each product is scored on 50 dimensions such as price and the size of the package. The computer looks for customers whose shopping baskets have similar combinations of scores. [The consultancy] Dunnhumby classifies shoppers in six segments. The 'Finer Foods' segment, for example, is made up of affluent, time-strapped shoppers who buy upscale products. 'Traditional' shoppers are homemakers with time to buy ingredients and cook a meal.

Tesco's recent rollout of an ethnic-food line called 'World Foods' shows how customer data can shape decision-making at almost every step of the way. The idea got its start when Clubcard records showed shoppers at a small store in the town of Slough weren't buying full meals. Many people in the town have South Asian or Arab roots.

Source: Rohwedder 2006.

Marketing and Sales Teams

In many companies, the formation of teams is essential for key account management (see Cespedes *et al.* 1989; Hutt *et al.* 1985; Marshall *et al.* 1999; Weitz and Bradford 1999). Key account management teams represent a special form of customer support teams. The major importance of teams with regard to company–customer interfaces arises from the intensive cooperation with customers (corporate clients) that can be observed in many companies. This requires a concentration of competencies that generally cannot be bundled in one single person, at the point of contact with the customer.

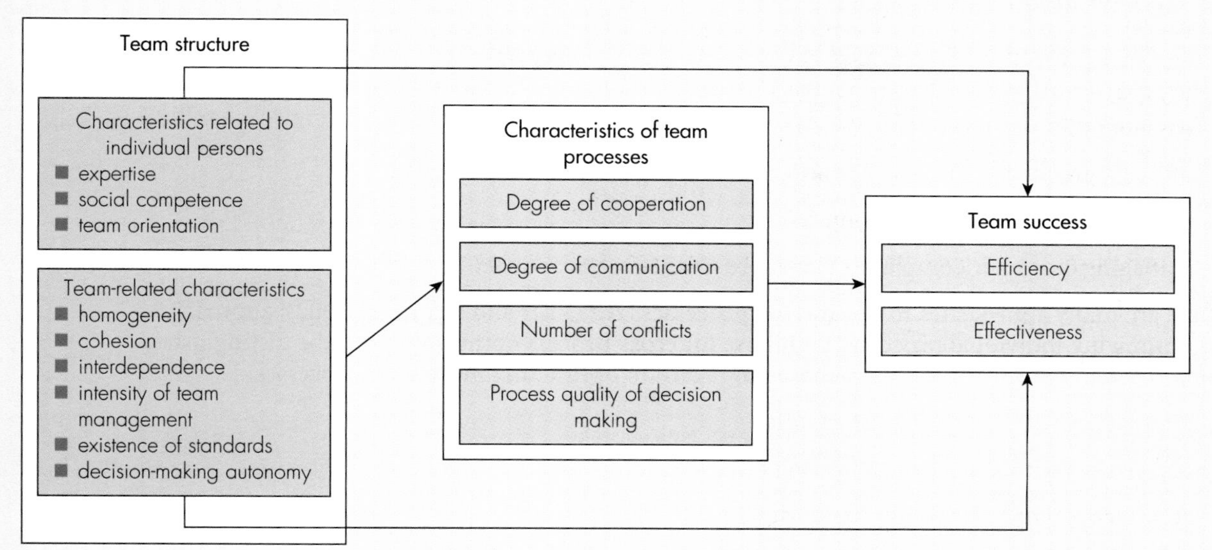

Figure 13-13 Integrative input–process–output model for illustrating the success of teams (adapted from Stock 2003)

Numerous studies have investigated the **success factors associated with customer support teams** (see Stock 2003 for an overview). In general, team success can be explained using 'input–process–output' models. The input consists of the characteristics of the team, which can be determined by management. There are two categories of these characteristics: those that concern individuals and those that concern the team itself (see Stock 2003). While characteristics concerning individuals relate to the personal aspects of team members (e.g. their expertise), team-related characteristics apply to interpersonal aspects of the team. The homogeneity of the team can be mentioned here as an example. The process components of such models refer to the characteristics of processes in the team (e.g. aspects such as communication, cooperation, conflicts and decision-making processes).

Figure 13-13 shows an integrative input–process–output model, to illustrate the success of customer support teams. Research has demonstrated that characteristics concerning individuals have a more direct impact on team success (the effectiveness and efficiency of the team), while team-related characteristics influence success more indirectly via the characteristics of team processes (Stock 2003).

13.2.2 Coordination Based on Workflow Organization

While coordination based on the organizational structure focuses on creating special coordination sites within the company, coordination based on workflow organization is concerned with designing and optimizing company processes in a way that facilitates and promotes coordination (see Gaitanides 1992). In this context, a **process** refers to a sequence of steps (combination of activities) that have to be carried out in order to complete a specific task.

With respect to activities in the marketing and sales units of companies, we differentiate between design processes and performance delivery processes. **Design processes** involve the task of developing a concept and deciding between several alternatives. Examples include the development of a marketing strategy (see Section 4) or the development of a product concept (see Section 5.3.1).

In contrast, **performance delivery processes** focus on the creation of tangible results for the customer. For example:

- responses to customer enquiries
- preparation of offers for customers (including the necessary pricing)
- administrative processing of customer orders (from order confirmation to final receipt of payment)
- physical processing of customer orders (including delivery to the customer)
- providing services to the customer
- managing customer complaints (for more on this, see Section 9.6).

There are many **approaches to optimizing processes** (see Diller and Saatkamp 2002); approaches for optimizing individual processes and those for cross-process optimization can be distinguished. There are four categories of approaches with regard to **optimizing individual processes**:

1 approaches with a focus on information
2 approaches with a focus on allocating tasks and competencies
3 approaches with a focus on process design
4 approaches with a focus on process coordination.

Figure 13-14 illustrates the respective approaches.

Approaches that focus on information aim to make the relevant process-related information available to the persons involved. **Approaches that focus on allocating tasks and competencies** concentrate on allocating process-related tasks and/or decision-making competencies to employees and departments.

Approaches that focus on process design are directed towards the design of the process flow. **Approaches that focus on process coordination** aim to improve coordination between the employees, divisions and departments involved.

In addition to these approaches, **interface management** aims to provide suitable conditions for **cross-process optimization**. In this regard, the company has to identify which interfaces are relevant for performing certain marketing activities (also see Cespedes 1993; Griffin and Hauser 1996; Gupta *et al.* 1986). Figure 13-15 provides an overview of company-internal interfaces. In addition to the relevant interfaces, the processes affected by these interfaces are also shown. Of particular significance is the aforementioned interface between marketing and sales units. The configuration of this interface causes problems in many companies. Moreover, interfaces exist between marketing and sales, as well as the more technically oriented functional departments: R&D, application engineering and production. For a number of processes, there are also interfaces with the functional department concerned with administration, such as finance, and controlling and purchasing.

Interface problems have a negative impact on the efficiency, effectiveness, speed and/or flexibility of cross-functional processes (such as those illustrated in Figure 13-15). Typical interface problems become evident when processes are slow and inefficient because functional departments are unable to coordinate tasks properly. As shown in Figure 13-15, the goal of interface management is to limit and – ideally – eliminate such problems.

Another aspect of interface management is the alignment of the **power of the individual functional departments**. Empirical studies on the internal distribution of power within companies have shown that the marketing and sales business units have a great deal of power in many decision-making areas (for more on this, see Homburg *et al.* 1999 and Figure 13-16). Interestingly, findings also demonstrate that other functional departments may, to a certain degree, impact the successful realization of marketing activities (see Krohmer *et al.* 2002).

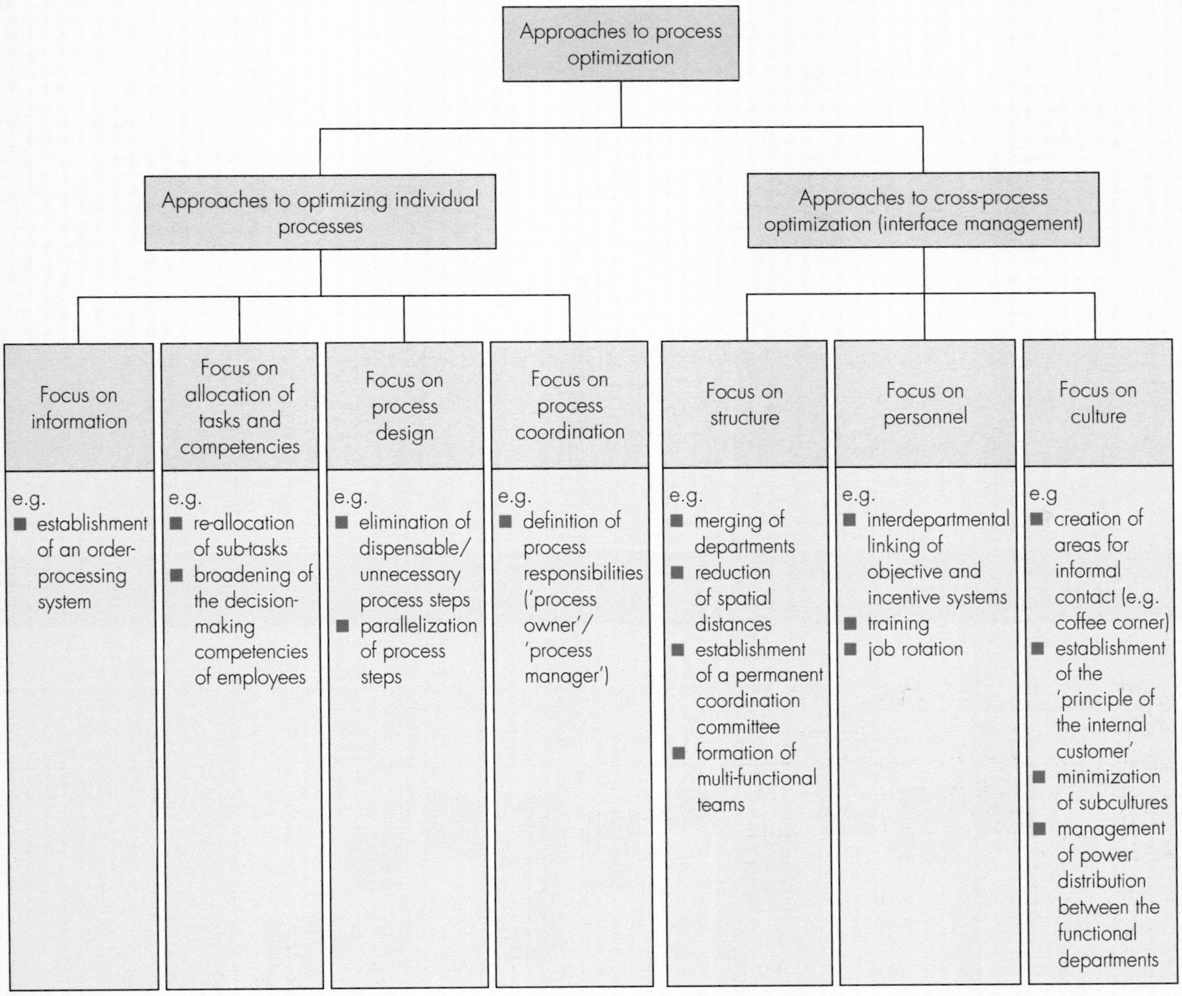

Figure 13-14 Overview: approaches to process optimization

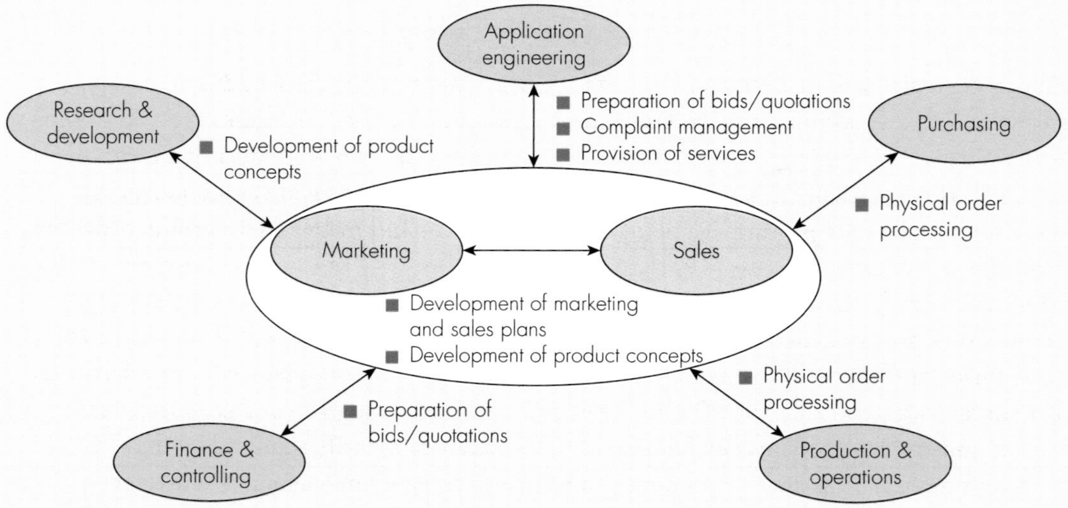

Figure 13-15 Important company-internal interfaces for marketing and sales tasks

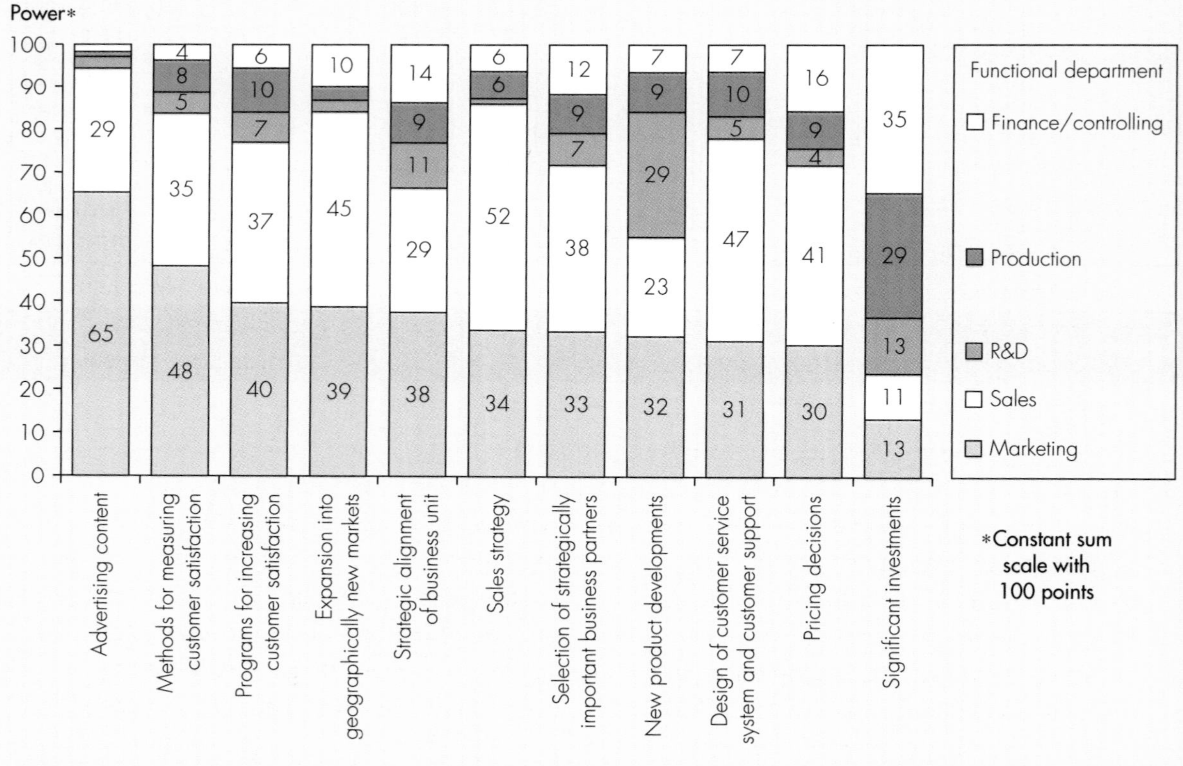

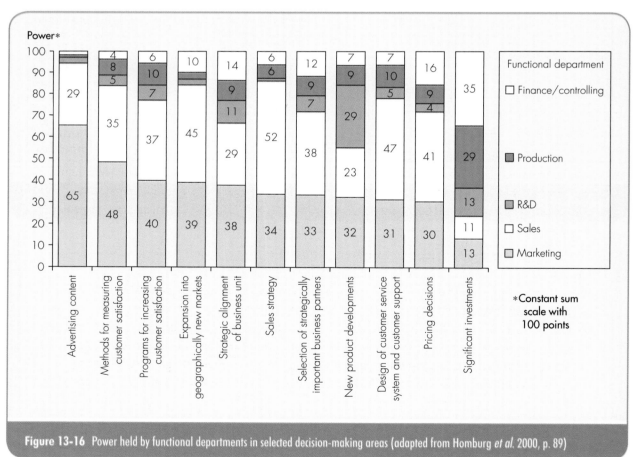

Figure 13-16 Power held by functional departments in selected decision-making areas (adapted from Homburg *et al.* 2000, p. 89)

Summary

In this chapter we discussed the design of organizational structures along the two dimensions of specialization and coordination. The first dimension – specialization – refers to the extent to which and how work is divided within the organization. Basically, there are two types of specialization: functional and business-oriented. In practice, several types of specialization are combined across different hierarchical levels, resulting in a matrix organization. A shift from a more product-focused to a more customer-focused structure is currently taking place in practice, and consequently product line divisions and regional divisions are becoming less important. Another facet of specialization concerns functional specialization in the area of marketing and sales. In general, the same types of specialization used at the level of the entire company can be used here too. The second fundamental aspect of an organizational structure refers to the coordination of the activities of the specialized business units and employees. The coordination of these activities is partly achieved by the creation of coordination units such as product management, category management, customer segment management and key account management. Coordination can also be based on workflow organization, which is concerned with the design and optimization of company processes.

Case Study: Siemens Exec Breaks Down Borders, Connects

Listening to Jack Bergen, senior vice president of corporate affairs and marketing for the $110.8 billion Siemens, you realize Bergen is no ordinary marketer. Bergen is a multi-disciplinary executive who was born to break down barriers.

Consider these facts: Siemens invests $6.3 billion in R&D annually and 75% of Siemens' revenue comes from products that didn't exist five years ago. They have more than 53,000 active patents and created 8,800 inventions in their last fiscal year. The 159-year-old company operates in 190 countries, employs 460,000 people and ranks No. 21 on the Fortune 500 list. The company has a market cap of $85.8 billion.

To break down organizational boundaries within Siemens, Bergen has instituted a City Ambassador's program. Siemens is composed of large vertical units in Information and Communication, Automation and Control, Power, Transportation, Medical and Lighting. Typically there's not much collaboration across these units, but Bergen's changing that. 'In one city we brought all the people from our 13 operating companies together in a room,' Bergen says. 'Two of the companies are at the same building, but they did not know they were in the same location.' Getting Siemens people acquainted stimulates new business. Bergen funds bonuses of $500 to $1,000 for cross divisional leads with $5,000 going to the individual whose efforts generate the most business. The program resulted in $130 million in incremental business last year for Siemens.

Case Study (Continued)

The functional barriers that Bergen is trying to obliterate are those where advertising types don't talk to PR people, and direct and online marketers don't talk with special events experts at Siemens. Bergen draws an oval with all the marketing and communications competencies surrounding a central circle containing the terms 'customers and influencers'. 'If you want funding for an advertising program,' Bergen says, 'you have to use one or more of the other competencies.' Such cross-functional thinking is transforming Siemens.

Source: excerpt from Siemens exec breaks down borders, connects (Reprinted with permission from *Marketing News*, published by the American Marketing Association, Krauss, M., 2007, 41, 2, 6).

Discussion Questions

1. Characterize Bergen's optimization approach.
2. Would you agree that his approach of 'breaking boundaries' leads to a more customer-focused organization? What are the advantages of a customer-focused structure?
3. What do you think about the following statement: 'No specialization without coordination'?

Key Terms

References

Cespedes, F. (1993) Coordinating sales and marketing in consumer goods firms, *Journal of Consumer Marketing*, 10, 2, 37–55.

Cespedes, F., Doyle, S. and Freedman, R. (1989) Teamwork for today's selling, *Harvard Business Review*, 67, 3/4, 44–54.

Chandler, A. (1990) *Strategy and Structure*. Cambridge.

Collins, S.R., Dahlström, P.W. and Singer, M. (2006) Managing your business as if customer segments matter, *McKinsey Quarterly* (web exclusive), August, 85–95.

Crockett, R.O. (2004) Reinventing Motorola, *Business Week*, 3894, 82–83.

Diller, H. and Saatkamp, J. (2002) Schwachstellen in Marketingprozessen: Ergebnisse einer explorativen Reengineering-Metaanalyze, *Marketing – Zeitschrift für Forschung und Praxis*, 24, 4, 239–252.

Gaitanides, M. (1992) Ablauforganisation, in: Frese, E. (ed.) *Handwörterbuch der Organisation* (3rd edn). Stuttgart, 3–18.

Griffin, A. and Hauser, J. (1996) Integrating R&D and marketing: a review and analysis of the literature, *Journal of Product Innovation Management*, 13, 3, 191–215.

Gupta, A., Raj, S. and Wilemon, D. (1986) A model for studying R&D – marketing interface in the product innovation process, *Journal of Marketing*, 50, 2, 7–17.

Hankinson, G. and Cowking, P. (1997) Branding in practice: the profile and role of brand managers in the UK, *Journal of Marketing Management*, 13, 4, 239–265.

Homburg, C., Krohmer, H. and Workman, J. (2000a) Machtstrukturen in Unternehmen: Bestandsaufnahme und systematische Erklärungsansätze für den Marketingbereich, *Die Betriebswirtschaft*, 60, 1, 78–96.

Homburg, C., Schäfer, H. and Schneider, J. (2006) *Sales Excellence: Vertriebsmanagement mit System* (4th edn). Wiesbaden.

Homburg, C., Workman, J. and Jensen, O. (2000b) Fundamental changes in marketing organization: the movement toward a customer-focused organizational structure, *Journal of the Academy of Marketing Science*, 28, 4, 459–478.

Homburg, C., Workman, J. and Jensen, O. (2002) A configurational perspective on key account management, *Journal of Marketing*, 66, 2, 38–61.

Homburg, C., Workman, J. and Krohmer, H. (1999) Marketing's influence within the firm, *Journal of Marketing*, 63, 2, 1–17.

Hutt, M., Johnston, W. and Ronchetto, J. (1985) Selling centers and buying centers: formulating strategic exchange patterns, *Journal of Personal Selling & Sales Management*, 5, 1, 33–40.

Johne, A. and Rowntree, S. (1991) High technology product development in small firms: a challenge for marketing specialists, *Technovation*, 11, 4, 247–258.

Krauss, M. (2007) Siemens exec breaks down borders, connects, *Marketing News*, 41, 2, 6–10. (Reprinted with permission from *Marketing News*, published by the American Marketing Association.)

Krohmer, H., Homburg, C. and Workman, J. (2002) Should marketing be cross-functional? Conceptual development and international empirical evidence, *Journal of Business Research*, 55, 6, 451–465.

Lawrence, P. and Lorsch, J. (1967) *Organization and Environment: Managing Differentiation and Integration*. Boston, Mass.

Low, G. and Fullerton, R. (1994) Brands, brand management, and the brand manager system: a critical-historical evaluation, *Journal of Marketing Research*, 31, 2, 173–190.

Malone, T.W. (1987) Modeling coordination in organizations and markets, *Management Science*, 33, 10, 1317–1332.

Marshall, G., Moncrief, W. and Lassk, F. (1999) The current state of sales force activities, *Industrial Marketing Management*, 28, 1, 87–98.

Ruekert, R., Walker Jr, O. and Roering, K. (1985) The organization of marketing activities: a contingency theory of structure and performance, *Journal of Marketing*, 49, 4, 13–25.

Rohwedder, C. (2006) Stores of knowledge: no. 1 retailer in Britain uses 'Clubcard' to thwart Wal-Mart, *Wall Street Journal*, 6 June.

Stock, R. (2003) *Teams an der Schnittstelle zwischen Unternehmen und Kunden: Eine integrative Betrachtung*. Wiesbaden.

Weitz, B. and Bradford, K. (1999) Personal selling and sales management: a relationship marketing perspective, *Journal of the Academy of Marketing Science*, 27, 2, 241–254.

Workman, J. Homburg, C. and Gruner, K. (1998) Variations in the organization and role of marketing: findings from an international field study of manufacturing companies, *Journal of Marketing*, 62, 3, 21–41.

Workman, J., Homburg, C. and Jensen, O. (2003) Intraorganizational determinants of key account management effectiveness, *Journal of the Academy of Marketing Science*, 31, 1, 1–23.

Zenor, M. (1994) The profit benefits of category management, *Journal of Marketing Research*, 31, 2, 202–213.

CHAPTER 14

Marketing and Sales Information Systems

Contents

Learning Objectives

In this chapter you will become familiar with:

- the key requirements of marketing and sales information systems
- aspects related to the design of marketing and sales information systems
- the most important components of a marketing and sales information system, and their interrelationships.

Today, marketing managers need to make effective decisions fast. An important requirement for decision making in marketing and sales, but also elsewhere in the organization, depends on the smart management of information. Information technology plays a vital role here, as it involves the design and management of computer and communication networks to provide an information system that caters to the organization's need for data storage, processing and access (Berkowitz *et al.* 2000).

For marketing and sales, information technology is especially important as it allows a better understanding of the market and customer needs. To this end, the marketing and sales information system is the basis for providing information that is relevant to all marketing and sales activities. Consequently, this system is essential for the implementation of decisions with regard to the company's marketing strategy and marketing instruments.

In Section 14.1 we discuss fundamental issues of marketing and sales information systems, including the key requirements for these systems, the design of these systems, and the characteristics of the information that serves as the basis for marketing and sales information systems. In Section 14.2, we will describe the main elements and components of marketing and sales information systems.

14.1 Basic Information about Marketing and Sales Information Systems

The **marketing and sales information system** of a company comprises the technical equipment, devices, methods and procedures that decision-makers need when collecting, systematizing, analyzing, evaluating and sharing up-to-date, accurate and relevant information (see also Greatorex 2005; Schewe 1976).

Special types of marketing and sales information systems use **customer relationship management (CRM) systems**. These systems are strictly concerned with customer information and communication. They serve to provide all relevant information in order to manage long-term customer relationships through (possibly customized) marketing, sales and service concepts (see Buck-Emden and Zencke 2004; Buttle 2004; Greenberg 2006; Peppers and Rogers 2001). They can be powerful tools in marketing and sales, as effective CRM can create profitable win-win situations for both the company and its customers (see Chapter 9 for more on the role of customer relationship management).

When designing new or modifying existing information systems, certain steps have to be followed. Figure 14-1 illustrates the *process of designing a marketing and sales information system*. The first step is to *identify the user of the information*. These are the decision-makers in companies, who make decisions on the basis of information supplied to them by the marketing and sales information system.

The *identification of the demand for information* is based on the specific requirements of the respective decision-making situation. The following questions have to be answered.

- What specific information is required by the various users of the information?
- What level of aggregation is required for the information?
- At what intervals will the users need updates?
- For what purposes will the information generated be used?

In order to identify what information is required for the company's decision-makers, the following approaches apply:

- advice on demand for information can be derived from company objectives
- job analyzes that are specific to the information users can be assessed

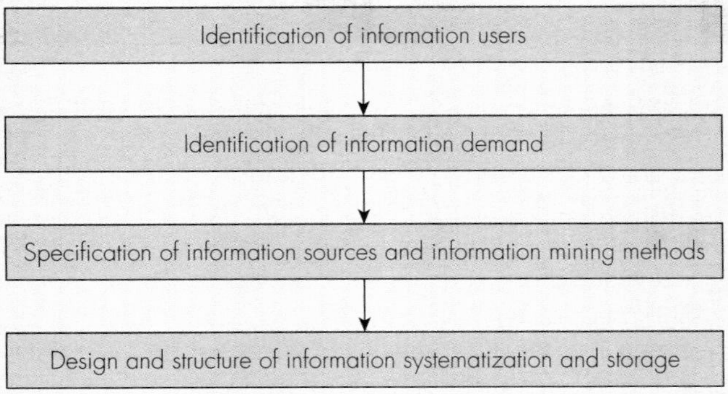

Figure 14-1 The process of designing a marketing and sales information system

- information users can be questioned (e.g. with mail questionnaires or in interviews)
- users can be observed in order to gauge their information requirements.

Once the demand situation has been evaluated, **information sources and mining methods** can be determined. Information users from marketing and sales require both company-internal information and external information about customers, competitors and the market (see Kotler and Keller 2006). Relevant information can be gathered from primary and secondary market research and generated in the course of market development activities (for additional information, see Section 14.1.2; see also the Appendix for more on the different methods of 'market research' and – more specifically – 'data collection methods'). The collection of information within the scope of market development activities comprises data that is generated automatically during interactions with customers (such as customer feedback on product features, or outcomes of order and price negotiations).

Information storage refers to the safe and secure central storage of information, as well as the provision of suitable hardware for data storage. In company practice, the main problem lies in the existence of diverse storage systems that are not coordinated in terms of data formats, access procedures and storage methods. Consequently, information users do not know what information is available, or where and how the desired information from the various sources can be retrieved, bundled and processed. The data warehouse is a central concept for resolving these problems (see Simon and Shaffer 2001; see also Section 14.2.1, as well as Focus on Marketing 14-1).

Focus on Marketing 14-1 A data warehousing success story

Standard Bank of South Africa reaps the business benefits of data warehousing
The Standard Bank of South Africa is the second largest banking group in the Republic, but has the reputation of being the most technologically advanced. The Standard Bank has over 1,000 branches or affiliated offices and 33,000 employees worldwide, and is expanding rapidly because of its attention to good customer service.

When competition from new banks and some 50 international banks that had moved into the country challenged their position, Standard Bank began a review of its customer base and product offerings. The challenge was to identify which customers were profitable and which were

Focus on Marketing 14-1 (Continued)

not, and then apply to each the appropriate service. The bank decided to restructure itself into four specialised units. This moved away from the 'one-size-fits-all' approach to one which concentrated on giving customers what they needed and could afford. This meant that managers needed to be more aware of their customers and required accurate, up to date information quickly. The challenge was that this information resided in at least 18 different source systems. It was clear that Standard Bank needed to move to a central repository of customer information. This was the only way that the correct information could be assessed and delivered rapidly and accurately to end users. To achieve this, Standard Bank created an Enterprise Data Warehouse taking the basic information from its operational systems. The data warehouse was made available to a select number of end users to test the acceptance level of the customer profiles. The bank set up the data warehouse initially on a test basis with a small group of users. It proved so successful that it was quickly extended to the whole marketing and customer service departments.

As Rogers says, 'The data warehouse has become fundamental to the bank, and because accurate and complete client information is critical to the data warehouse, data management is also critical to our success. Budgets, targets, and forecasts, supported by a five-year strategic plan, have been finalized and approved based on the segmentation undertaken in the Enterprise Data Warehouse.'

Now that the new system has been running for a while, Standard Bank has begun to realize many significant benefits by providing a true picture of the bank's customers. It enables a much more informed, personal and focused approach to working with customers.

The new system enables multiple views of customers to be displayed in order to determine true profitability and to improve staff performance and satisfaction, as it is now possible to use the system as a basis for measurement and reward. The combination of technology and accurate customer information greatly assists credit scoring, so that risk is much more manageable. The bank expects that this capability by itself will save them millions over the next two years, and is already saving money in many ways, not the least of which is by allowing the bank to dispense with a number of systems which have been made obsolete by the new one.

Source: Innovative Systems 2006.

14.1.1 Requirements of Marketing and Sales Information Systems

Irrespective of its concrete design and structure, a marketing and sales information system should satisfy the following criteria:

- a focus on user requirements
- the capability to integrate and coordinate
- profitability
- safety and security
- user acceptance.

User requirements are usually fulfilled when information is correctly reduced and guaranteed to be up to date, when access to the system is easy and fast, and when data recording is highly standardized. Furthermore, users expect that information will be represented and displayed appropriately, and that information that is needed on a continuous basis will automatically be provided (see also Chenoweth *et al.* 2006; Shin 2003).

Information needs to be shared continuously within an organization. Therefore, the marketing and sales information system should be able to integrate and coordinate in order to ensure the efficient exchange of information between different departments – for example, between marketing and sales, and the production and logistics departments (also referred to as an enterprise resource planning (ERP) system). See Focus on Marketing 14-2 for an example of the success of an integrated information system.

Focus on Marketing 14-2 ERP systems support firms' CRM capabilities

ERP systems at heart of steel firm's expansion

Greater use of enterprise resource planning software is helping Pressed Steel Products in County Durham, United Kingdom, to extend its product range and double its turnover.

Since Pressed Steel Products went live with an Epicor Vantage ERP system in 2004, the company has cut idle time by 25% and delivers 93% of orders on time.

Now the firm, which makes architectural facades, is making more use of the software's customer relationship management capabilities to allow it to link with architects and become involved with customers earlier in the design stage of the development. 'The system is now linking with the architects from the design stage and throughout the delivery, which will allow us to improve our cost estimations,' said Tamer Qaqish, IT manager at Pressed Steel Products.

The project to bring in ERP systems started in 2002, when the government-funded Knowledge Transfer Partnership scheme enabled Pressed Steel Products to work with Durham University to improve its business processes. Even as a shortlist of ERP suppliers was being drawn up, the company started to move to new business processes.

'The result was that the move to the new software was a really smooth transition,' Qaqish said. 'It is normally quite difficult for a small company with limited resources to manage the implementation of a new ERP system. But the implementation process itself can help all involved get a better understanding of fundamental business processes.'

Source: Clark 2006.

Of course, information systems do come at a cost. Systems become profitable if the added value generated by the system exceeds the necessary expenses for maintaining it. For example, if the system is too costly it could be considered to reduce the requirements of information maintenance by limiting the amount of information collected. Obviously, users' needs should be driving this optimization.

System **safety and security** (see also Simon and Shaffer 2001) particularly concerns aspects such as:

- data availability by means of appropriate storage (e.g. back-ups to protect against physical destruction of storage media)
- protection against access by unauthorized people (e.g. protection against internet/virus attacks by using firewalls and password-controlled access)
- specification of security levels for different types of information, combined with the corresponding access authorizations (e.g. definition of different information access levels for different hierarchical levels in the company)
- reliability guarantees (e.g. signing customer agreements with digital signatures).

A key success factor for implementing a marketing and sales information system is its **acceptance on the part of information users** (see Leverick *et al.* 1998). If users do not accept the system, for whatever reason, they will not use it in their decision making (Chenoweth *et al.* 2006). One reason for the lack of user acceptance is employees' concerns regarding control and monitoring. This is particularly the case when the system concerns the performance of employees. Consequently, sales representatives, for instance, might worry that an information system could provide information about their work performance and identify inefficiencies that had not been discovered before.

Another important reason for a lack of acceptance relates to employees' concerns with respect to losing their acquired rights. For instance, field sales representatives are afraid of losing power if they are asked to enter everything they know about their customers into the information system. In addition, entering the information is often viewed as an annoying duty and, in many cases, is neglected due to a lack of discipline and/or time.

Some ways to ensure high user acceptance of information systems are:

- involvement of various users in the conceptual development of the system, to orient it towards user needs
- clear and compelling communication of benefits
- project support on the part of top management
- comprehensive user training.

14.1.2 Designing a Marketing and Sales Information System

Marketing and sales information systems can be designed in a wide variety of forms, ranging from simple customer databases on stand-alone PCs to sophisticated systems with thousands of networked computers accessing a shared database. Figure 14-2 shows an example of a marketing and sales information system. It is a viable option for companies to equip their marketing and sales information system with only a selection of the components described here. The final scope of a marketing and sales information system depends in particular on company size, available financial and personal resources, as well as the size of the customer base. It is obvious that a small domestic company with only a few employees has a different demand for information system support than an internationally operating company (see Focus on Marketing 14-3).

The marketing and sales information system illustrated in Figure 14-2 has three important features (see also Buck-Emden and Zencke 2004 for a similar approach):

1. **integration of all data**, collected via the various information and contact channels during interaction with customers and sales partners, into a central database (**data warehouse**, see Section 14.2.1)
2. **support in analyzing data** (see Section 14.2.2)
3. **support of market development processes** based on completed analyzes (see Section 14.2.3 as well as Focus on Marketing 14-4 for an example).

In the following text, the marketing and sales information system illustrated in Figure 14-2 will be discussed in more detail. As shown in Figure 14-2, the marketing, sales and service departments of the company are connected to the customers and sales partners via various contact and communication channels (e.g. telephone/call center, personal contact, internet). The marketing and sales information system can integrate and coordinate these various external contacts and interactions. The term **collaborative CRM** (see Buck-Emden and Zencke 2004; Kracklauer *et al.* 2004) is used in this context. A second component of collaborative CRM is new electronic contact channels (e.g. electronic marketplaces), which are intended to enhance the interaction between the company and its target groups.

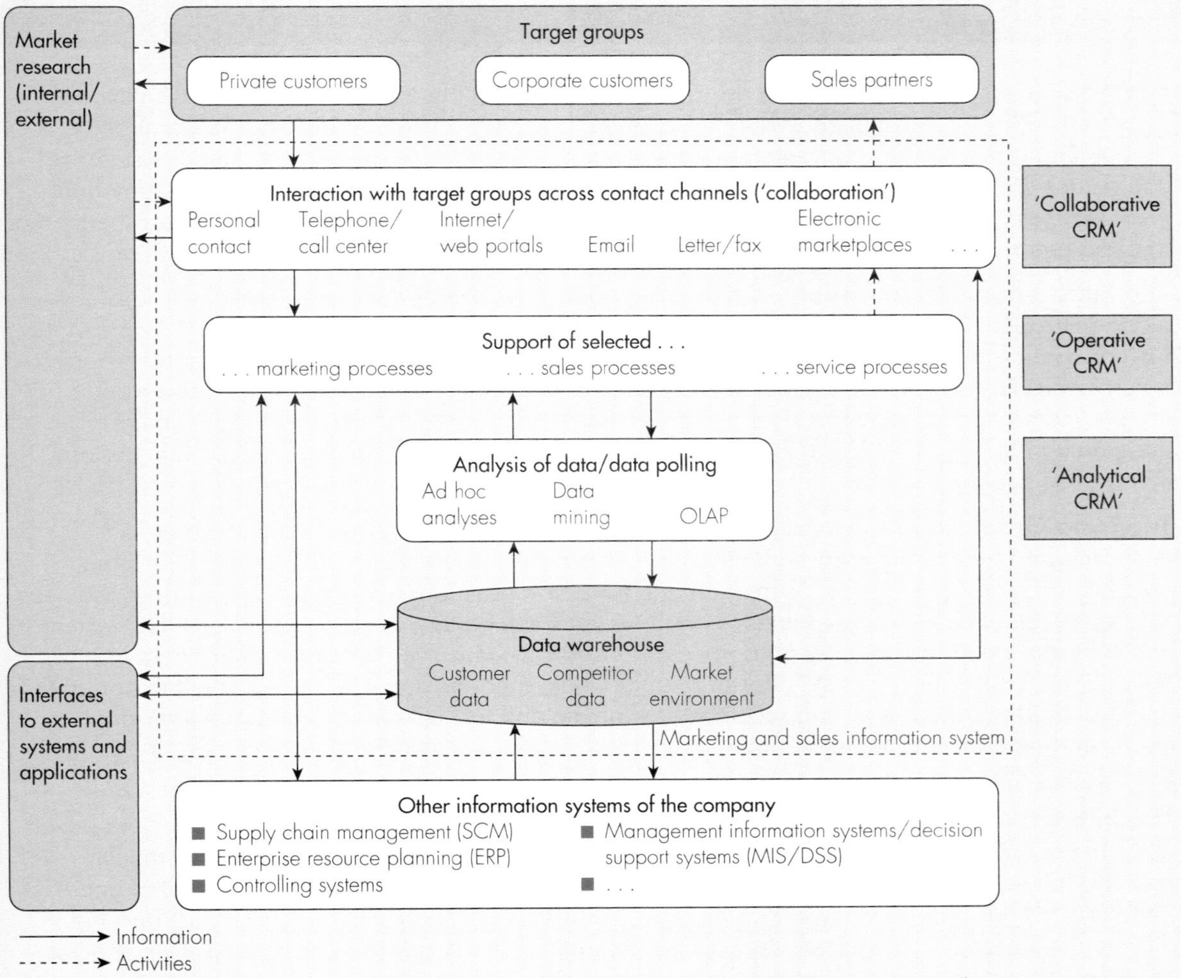

Figure 14-2 Typical structure of a marketing and sales information system

Focus on Marketing 14-3 IT requirements of different businesses

The evolution to an information enterprise

The Entrepreneurial Venture: Starting a company requires a good business model, an understanding of the market for which the goods or services are sold, and a passion to make the venture succeed. Small businesses such as a local bakery, restaurant or services provided by a sole practitioner do not require any information systems to start their business venture. For example, a local bakery orders supplies and materials without any formal requisition, purchasing or inventory management procedures.

The Automated Organization: As the activities of the organization increase in volume and complexity, manual processes begin impeding the pace of operations. To support operations,

Focus on Marketing 14-3 (Continued)

transactional systems such as enterprise resource planning (ERP) applications are implemented. For example, as the local bakery expands its operations from selling goods from its storefront to distributing its products to convenience stores and restaurants, it needs a transactional system that can record and process its sales, production runs, inventory and purchases. Without automation, these business processes would be overwhelming. In addition, business activities are now monitored through reports generated by the ERP system.

The Reactionary Organization: As the volume and complexity of activities continue to grow, managing operations requires greater monitoring and analysis. Continuing with the example of the bakery, as it expands its operations and capabilities to service a larger geographic region, more complex business questions, such as aligning production runs with product sales by geographic region and seasonal trends, need to be addressed. Managing the organization now requires integrated information sets to assist management in their ability to monitor, measure and choose a course of action.

The Data Organization: A significant shift occurs within the organization. The focus on collecting and processing data about its activities becomes subservient to the desire for a greater understanding of the business. As the demand for data and information increases, so does the need to create scalable information solutions. In the case of the bakery, the business has an ERP system that sufficiently allows it to enter and process transactions. However, growing the business into a national manufacturer and distributor of premium baked goods requires management to correctly interpret market conditions and execute their strategic and tactical plans. To do this, individuals need comprehensive information about their customers, products and operations. Organizations at this stage implement a data warehouse or create subject-matter-specific data marts.

The Information Enterprise: Organizations at this stage build an information infrastructure based upon the corporate information factory or dimensional warehousing approaches. They quickly respond to requests for information and changes to the business. Information is integrated and enables cross-functional analysis. For the bakery that's grown into a national manufacturer and distributor of premium baked goods, an information infrastructure is created that enables analysis to ensure operational efficiencies, continued financial viability, customer satisfaction and product innovation. With the information available, conventional thoughts are challenged and the business model shifts to capitalize on new opportunities.

Source: Wu 2005.

Information gathered during the interaction with target groups is compiled and stored according to category by means of **online analytical processing (OLAP)** in a central database of the marketing and sales information system (the data warehouse). This central database stores customer, company and competitor data, as well as information about the market environment (see Section 14.2.1). If necessary, information can also be stored in linked information systems (e.g. ERP system, controlling system). The information gathered, stored and secured in this way can then be retrieved later:

- within the scope of marketing and sales activities, or
- for the purpose of more in-depth analysis.

The support of marketing and sales activities, and the interactions with the target group and the marketing and sales information system (see Section 14.2.3 for a detailed discussion) is also called **operative CRM** (see Buck-Emden and Zencke 2004). For example, the system can support interaction processes by providing and recording information; this can mean processes such as the preparation of quotations, complaint management, and so on. The required information can be retrieved from the data warehouse of the marketing and sales information system, other company information systems (e.g. controlling system) or external information systems (e.g. the information system of a supplier).

If the information stored in the data warehouse is used for further analyses (e.g. to support marketing and sales decisions), it is called **analytical CRM** (see Buck-Emden and Zencke 2004). There are two methods of analysis:

1 automated analysis

2 ad hoc analysis.

Automated analyses are initiated and processed automatically by the information system. In particular, methods include OLAP (see Section 14.2.2) and data mining (see Section 14.2.2, as well as Berry and Linoff 2000; Hurtado *et al.* 2005; Simon and Shaffer 2001). **Ad hoc analyses** are individually conducted, non-standard analyzes that use statistics packages (e.g. SPSS), spreadsheet software (e.g. Microsoft Excel) or CRM software analysis modules (e.g. mySAP CRM Analytics; for more information, see Table 14-1).

Direct interaction with customers and sales partners facilitates the marketing and sales information system in generating data for subsequent **market research activities**. As a rule, market research data is also collected direct from target groups during individual market research projects. These market research projects produce both raw data and analysis results, which can be made available on a company-internal basis by storing them in the data warehouse.

Table 14-1 Overview of mySAP CRM Analytics analysis modules (Buck-Emden and Zencke 2004, p. 327)

Analysis module	Short description
Product analytics	Analysis of the products and product properties preferred by customers, as well as analysis of product profitability
Marketing analytics	Optimization of the efficiency and effectiveness of marketing measures on the basis of market analyzes, ranging from the assessment of marketing programs to the concluding success analysis
Sales analytics	Optimization of the efficiency and effectiveness of sales processes, entailing sales planning, predictive analysis of business trends and corresponding pipeline analyzes, and success analysis in sales
Service analytics	Planning and controlling service activities and processes, with success analysis
Interaction channel analytics	Analysis and comparison of the performance of the individual communication channels. Additional analytical functions for each communication channel in the following business scenarios: E-Analytics, Partner and Channel Analytics, Field Analytics, and Interaction Center Analytics
Customer analytics	Analysis of customer behavior and customer value to optimize and personalize how a company approaches customers

14.1.3 Information as the Basis of a Marketing and Sales Information System

The basis for a functioning information system is the information stored in it. Information can be collected during direct interactions between the company and its customers and sales partners, as well as in the course of market research activities (see Figure 14-2).

Information can be categorized into customer information, competitor information and market information. **Customer information** is the usual focus of a marketing and sales information system.

Of course, different industries require different information from their customers. However, six general customer information categories can be identified.

1 **Basic data** includes elementary and product-independent information about the customer (e.g. name, address, customer's bank details, segment affiliation).

2 **Decision data** provides information about the customer's approach to purchasing decisions. The first aspect here concerns how important certain criteria (e.g. price, value-added services) are to a customer's purchasing decision. Furthermore, business-to-business marketing requires information about the relevant decision-makers (see Chapter 10 for a discussion of the buying center concept in business-to-business marketing) and how the decision-making processes are structured (e.g. formalized rules for decision processes related to purchasing).

3 Ideally, **contact data** comprises all previous contacts the company has had with a customer. A differentiation has to be made between contacts initiated by the company (e.g. sending information material during direct marketing activities, outbound telephone contacts with the customer) and contact data from contacts initiated by customers (e.g. inquiries on the part of a customer, customer complaints).

4 **Buying behavior data** relates to a customer's purchase history (e.g. purchase date/time, quantities purchased, point of purchase).

5 **Data related to potential** provides information with respect to the sales potential the company can realize with a customer (e.g. quantification of customer demand, information about customer requirements, future plans of the customer, business relationships with competitors).

6 **Performance data** shows how successful the business relationship with a customer is for the company. In this context, there are success factors related to potential (such as, e.g., customer satisfaction, openness and transparency of the customer's information behavior), success factors related to market success (e.g. 'share of wallet', i.e., the portion of a customer's demand that is covered by the company and not by competitors) and economic success factors (e.g. realized price level, contribution margin provided by the business relationship) (for more information on these three categories, see Section 2.1 and Figure 2-2).

Competitor information can be collected, for example, during sales talks, by visiting and participating in trade fairs and conferences, and within the scope of market observation and research (see the Appendix for more on 'market research'). Table 14-2 lists the essential competitor information that a company should have at its disposal.

Market information refers to general market conditions, including, say the company's market share and market share history, market volumes and market growth. Similar to competitor information, market information can be gathered from market observation and research carried out by an internal market research department or by external market research agencies.

Table 14-2 Overview of essential competitor information (Homburg *et al.* 2006, p. 221)

Question	Competitor information
Who are our competitors?	Name and headquarters of company, industry sector, number of employees, key decision-makers, organizational structure, owner structure, affiliations with other companies, etc.
How are our competitors positioned in the market?	Market share, sales/profit situation, cost structure, distribution rate, image, customer satisfaction, customer loyalty, etc.
What are the resources and competencies of our competitors?	Quality and quantity of human and material resources, liquidity and other financial resources, access to additional capital, knowhow, patents, access to sales channels, relationships to customers and dealers, etc.
What strategies do our competitors pursue?	Objectives, schedules, target segments, marketing/sales budgets, etc.
How do our competitors develop the market? How do they implement their strategy?	Quality/age/width/depth of product and service portfolio, price positioning, structure of terms and conditions, customer loyalty management, logistics quality, content and scope of advertising, sales promotion and public relations, etc.

14.2 Components of Marketing and Sales Information Systems

In general, marketing and sales information systems comprise three central components (also see Figure 14-2):

1 data warehouse

2 components for conducting analyzes

3 components for providing and using information within the scope of marketing activities.

We will discuss these components in the following sections.

14.2.1 Data Warehouse

A data warehouse is the central storage location for all information (customer, competitor, market) in a marketing and sales information system. The core of a data warehouse is an integrated database for storing information (see Berry and Linoff 2000; Simon and Shaffer 2001). Employees' access to the information stored in the data warehouse can be facilitated by the following two measures:

1 implementation of a **meta database** providing information about the contents, formats and evaluation options offered by the data warehouse

2 segmentation of the data warehouse into **sub-databases** ('**data marts**') where information is stored separately according to topics (e.g. customers, products) or departments (e.g. marketing, sales).

In most cases, a data warehouse is not a stand-alone system, but rather is connected to other internal and external information systems and applications. These connections are realized via **interfaces** that enable the exchange of data with such systems and applications. The electronic exchange of information with external information systems is called **electronic data interchange (EDI)**. For example, a company that cooperates with a debt collection agency will supply this agency with relevant customer data and receive corresponding customer status reports in return.

A data warehouse should meet the following requirements (see Marks and Frolick 2001):

- data independence of the application programs
- data integrity in the event of software bugs and system failures
- data protection against unauthorized access
- concurrent database access
- user-friendliness through easy-to-learn database language
- efficient modification and querying of data.

14.2.2 Components for Conducting Analyzes

Marketing and sales information systems can also support users in conducting analyzes. In the text below, we will address three main analysis tools: ad hoc analyzes, online analytical processing (OLAP) and data mining.

Ad Hoc Analyzes

Ad hoc analyzes are individual analyzes initiated by employees. They are based on the data available in the marketing and sales information system. For example, an employee of a consumer goods company can conduct an ad hoc analysis to evaluate sales trends for a certain product.

Ad hoc analyzes can be conducted with **standard software packages** (e.g. spreadsheet program, statistics software) into which the data from the data warehouse are imported. The employee of the consumer goods company can thus export the sales figures for the product being analyzed from the data warehouse to a spreadsheet program, and then use the software to analyze the data.

Moreover, a marketing and sales information system can be designed and implemented in a way that enables ad hoc analyzes by means of **analyzing modules integrated into the system**. For example, advanced CRM systems offer the option to analyze customer data with multivariate analysis methods, and display the results in graphic form (see Figure 14-3 for an example of a screenshot).

Online Analytical Processing

Online analytical processing (OLAP) refers to a structured database inquiry. From a technical perspective, OLAP consists of a series of database queries at varying levels of detail (see Berry and Linoff 2000; Hurtado *et al.* 2005).

During an OLAP run, an OLAP server transforms and aggregates data from the data warehouse and stores them in multidimensional form. This enables multidimensional analysis of the data according to various criteria, such as product families, periods and regions. This information is tailored to the requirements of the respective specialized departments.

As illustrated in Figure 14-4, a regional manager could be interested in an overview of all products and months for a specific sales region, while a product manager might be interested in information regarding all regions and months, but for just one product. The multidimensionality of OLAP-generated data is displayed by the OLAP cube, which provides an illustration of the various layers of analysis that can be represented with OLAP (see Figure 14-4).

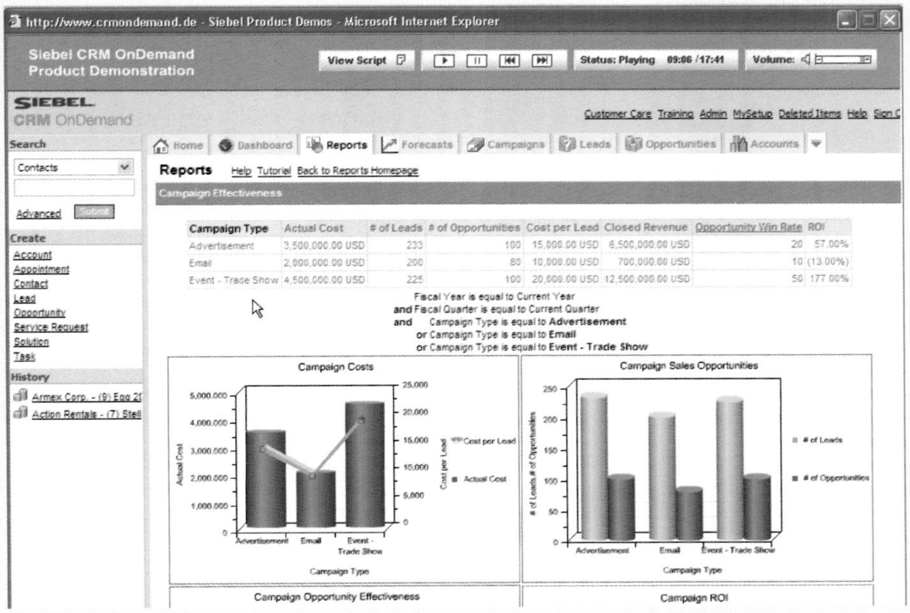

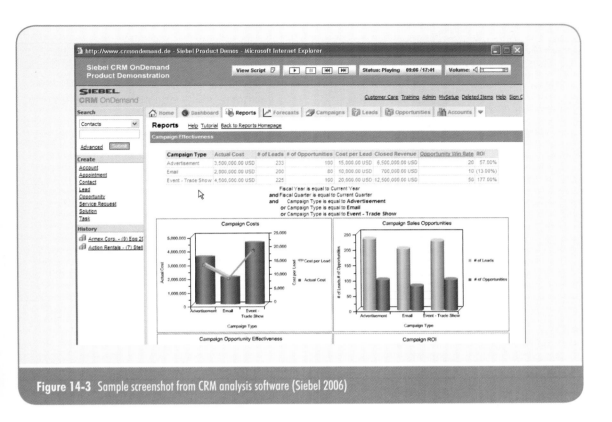

Figure 14-3 Sample screenshot from CRM analysis software (Siebel 2006)

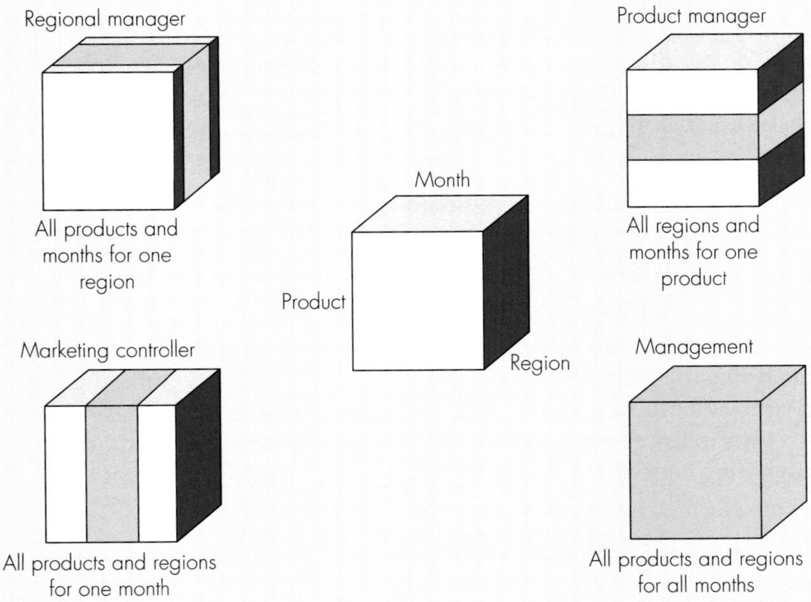

Figure 14-4 Various OLAP analysis layers (Bager *et al.* 1997, p. 284)

Table 14-3 Data mining: application examples

Industry	Applications	Exemplary findings
Financial services	Risk analysis with regard to customer relationships and financial standing	■ Assessment of the credit risk associated with a customer on the basis of socioeconomic data (credit check) ■ Identification of customer segments with high insurance risks in order to adjust insurance premiums (e.g. new drivers)
Retailers	Analysis of purchasing behavior or customer transactions in order to support decisions regarding the design of salesrooms, adjustments to the range of products or planning of order quantities	■ Product A and Product B are frequently purchased in combination, particularly by the XY customer segment ■ Product Z is purchased more often if it is placed on the right-hand side of the shelf
Pharmaceutical wholesalers	Analysis of the pharmaceuticals order patterns of individual pharmacies	■ Identification of clusters (pharmacies with similar order patterns and geographical locations) and use of findings to optimize deliveries of pharmaceuticals

Data Mining

The term **data mining** has its roots in the mining industry. In this industry, extensive technological effort is invested in mechanically mining large volumes of rock in order to extract, say, precious metals. Accordingly, data mining uses sophisticated automated methods for processing large data volumes for the purpose of identifying crucial decision-relevant information (see Berry and Linoff 2000; Cabena *et al.* 1998; Cios *et al.* 2006; Tan *et al.* 2006; Williams and Simoff 2006). In this context, multivariate methods are the preferred choice (see the Appendix for more on 'multivariate methods').

Data mining supports a wide variety of analyzes; examples to be mentioned here include target group selection, response analyzes, market basket analyzes, cross-selling/upselling analyzes and customer ratings. Table 14-3 summarizes some applications for data mining tools.

A special form of data mining is **web mining**, which is used for analyzing websites (see Berry and Linoff 2000; Lihui and Wai 2005; Shahabi and Banaei-Kashani 2003). Web mining, on the one hand, is concerned with analyzing the content of third-party websites (web content mining; e.g. investigating competitor prices). On the other hand, it is concerned with analyzing the behavior of visitors to the company's own website (web usage mining; e.g. analyzing website visitor click patterns, recording the purchasing behavior of online shop customers, logging all website hits).

14.2.3 Components for Providing and Using Information Related to Marketing Activities

Marketing and sales information systems can also include information components that support marketing, sales and service employees during interactions with customers. They can be categorized into the following components in accordance with the supported task:

- components for supporting marketing processes ('marketing automation')
- components for supporting sales processes ('sales automation', 'salesforce automation', 'computer-aided selling').

Components for Supporting Marketing Processes

Components that support marketing processes assist employees in conceptualizing, designing and conducting certain marketing activities. In this context, the term **marketing automation** is frequently used (see Buttle 2004; DeFelice 2005; Raab 2005).

The term marketing automation itself already indicates that only those activities that display a high degree of standardization can be supported. For example, it is difficult to imagine automation in the conceptualization of a new product.

The planning and implementation of a direct marketing campaign is a good example of supporting marketing processes. In this area, a marketing and sales information system can, in particular, provide tools for project planning (e.g. setting up the campaign, selecting the target group, preparing a mailing), evaluate the results of the project (e.g. number of letters sent, responses per day, orders received), as well as assist in project controlling (e.g. response analyzes, target group analyzes, project and budget planning).

Focus on Marketing 14-4 Example of a customer valuation using mySAP CRM

Customer valuation and scoring

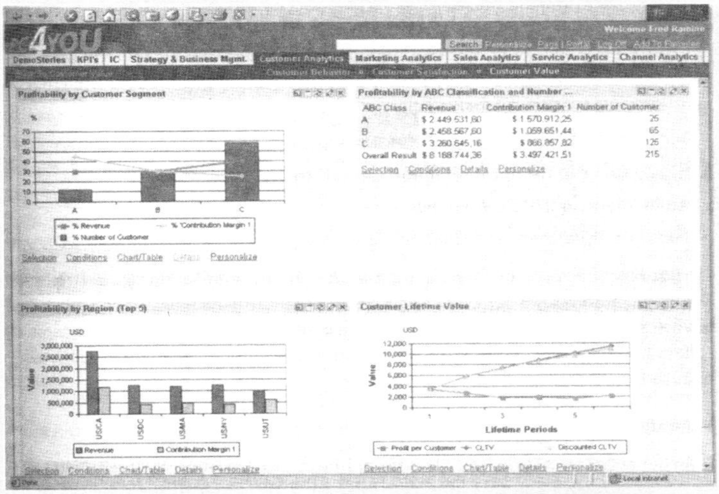

More and more companies are discovering the fact that only a relatively small number of customers actually make a significant contribution to the company result. Consequently, it is essential to make the significance of individual customers transparent to the company by applying suitable methods for ABC classification and scoring and then to consider this significance in all decision-making regarding customers. The figure (top left) shows, for example, that about 10% of customers account for a 30% share of sales and a 45% share of the company revenue.

Source: Buck-Emden and Zencke 2004, pp. 316f.

Components for Supporting Sales Processes

Components that support sales processes assist sales employees in customer acquisition and customer support by displaying existing customer-specific information. Furthermore, these components facilitate the inclusion of customer data into the company-internal information system. Frequently used synonyms for components that support sales processes include **sales automation**, **salesforce automation** and **computer-aided selling**.

In particular, components that support sales processes help employees in performing routine and administrative tasks related to sales (see Buttle 2004), which include the following processes:

- planning of appointments and customer visits (e.g. customer attractiveness rating, scheduling coordination, selection of a suitable schedule for visiting several customers, travel expense accounting)
- customer visits (support by providing data, for example, on the sales employee's notebook on-site at the customer's premises)
- management of customer data (e.g. systematic recording of customer contacts).

Table 14-4 illustrates examples of routine tasks that can be facilitated by the information system within the scope of sales activities. In addition, Focus on Marketing 14–4 provides an example of the use of a marketing and sales information system for customer valuation purposes.

Table 14-4 Selected examples of support for sales processes provided by marketing and sales information systems

Task	Support provided by the marketing and sales information system
Planning and realization of customer appointments	Scheduling coordination support, calculation and display of optimal travel routes, provision of appropriate forms for fast preparation of visit reports; post-travel activities: facilitates travel expense accounting by importing the required data from the route planner
Provision of price-related and product-related information for sales talks/customer inquiries	Display of current product price, technical product information, previous customer-related terms and conditions (e.g. A B C customer, see also Section 15.4.1) as well as customer equity (see Section 15.4.4 for customer equity) on the sales representative's laptop
Decision with regard to granting discounts during a customer-initiated telephone call	Display of information on the call center employee's monitor about the customer equity rating and the maximum possible discount for each customer equity level
Quotation preparation	Forms and standard text templates customized for quotations, display of specific contractual clauses
Giving a presentation	Visualization of products and product information with 2D or 3D graphics, calculators for preparing customized offers
Target planning and budgeting	Display of standard indicators in order to simplify the planning and budgeting process.
Customer contact management	Automated resubmission of scheduled tasks (call-back on certain date), display of customer contact history
Coordination of sales activities	Coordination and prevention of redundant work through systematic allocation of customers

Summary

This chapter provided an introduction to the role of information technology in marketing and sales. The marketing and sales information system of a company provides the data basis for the implementation of decisions related to the company's marketing strategy, as well as the marketing instruments. Marketing and sales information systems can be designed as simple customer databases on stand-alone PCs or as sophisticated systems with thousands of networked computers accessing a shared database. Although there is a wide variety of design forms, five criteria should always be met: a focus on user requirements, the capability to integrate and coordinate, profitability, safety and security, and user acceptance. The information stored in an information system can be categorized into customer information, competitor information and market information. The central components of a marketing and sales information system comprise the data warehouse, the central storage location for all information in a marketing and sales information system, components for conducting analyzes such as data mining, and components for providing and using information within the scope of marketing activities.

Case Study: Stopping the Sprawl at HP

When Randy Mott joined Wal-Mart fresh out of college in 1978, its in house tech staff had only 30 members and company founder Sam Walton had not yet become a believer in the power of computing to revolutionize retailing. But Mott and his cohorts developed a network of computerized distribution centers that made it simple to open and run new stores with cookie-cutter efficiency. Then in the early 1990s, Mott, by this time chief information officer, persuaded higher-ups to invest in a so-called data warehouse. That let the company collect and sift customer data to analyze buying trends as no company ever had – right down to which flavor of Pop-Tarts sells best at a given store. 'Information technology wasn't Mr. Sam's favorite topic. He viewed it as a necessary evil,' recalls fellow Wal-Mart Stores Inc. alumnus Charlie McMurtry, who has worked with Mott for years. 'But later, Randy got [Walton's] ultimate compliment. He said, "Man, you'd make a great store manager."'

By the time Mott took his latest job last summer, as CIO of Hewlett-Packard Co., he had become a rock star of sorts among the corporate techie set – an executive who not only understood technology and how it could be used to improve a business but how to deliver those benefits. Besides his 22-year stint at Wal-Mart, Mott helped Dell Inc. hone its already huge IT advantage. By melding nearly 100 separate systems into a single data warehouse, Mott's team enabled Dell to quickly spot rising inventory for a particular chip, for instance, so the company could offer online promotions for devices containing that part before the price fell too steeply.

Case Study (Continued)

Now, Mott, 49, is embarking on his boldest and most challenging project yet: a three-year, $1 billion-plus makeover of HP's internal tech systems. On May 17, the company announced it will replace 85 loosely connected data centers around the world with six cutting-edge facilities – two each in Austin, Atlanta, and Houston. Mott is pushing sweeping changes in the way HP operates, slashing thousands of smaller projects at the decentralized company to focus on a few corporate-wide initiatives – including scrapping 784 isolated data-bases for one company-wide data warehouse. Says Mott: 'We want to make HP the envy of the technology world.'

If it works, Mott's makeover could have more impact than any new HP advertising campaign, printer, or PC – and could turbocharge the company's already impressive turnaround. HP posted profits of $1.5 billion in its second quarter, up 51% from the year before, on a 5% increase in sales. HP shares had been slipping, but they jumped on May 17, the day of the earnings call. All told, the stock is up 65% since new CEO Mark Hurd took over in April, 2005. If Mott is successful, HP's annual spending on tech should be cut in half in the years ahead, from $3.5 billion in 2005, say insiders.

More important, a Wal-Mart-style data warehouse could help HP make headway on its most vexing problem in recent years: how to capitalize on its vast breadth. While HP sells everything from $10 ink cartridges to multimillion-dollar supercomputers, the company has operated more like a conglomerate of separate companies than a one-stop tech superstore. 'We shipped 55 million printers, 30 million PCs, and 2 million servers last year,' says CEO Hurd. 'If we can integrate all that information, it would enable us to know exactly how we're doing in Chicago on a given day, or whether the CIO of a big customer also happens to own any of our products at home.'

Source: Stopping the sprawl at HP, by: Burrows, P. (2006) *Business Week*, 29 May, Issue 3986, 54–56.

Discussion Questions

1. What is meant by the term 'data warehouse' and what is its role in a marketing and sales information system?
2. Please characterize Mott's 'Wal-Mart-style data warehouse'.
3. In which ways can HP benefit from the makeover of its internal technology systems?

Key Terms

Acceptance on the part of information users *494*
Ad hoc analyses *497*
Analytical CRM *497*
Analyzing modules integrated into the system *500*
Automated analyses *497*
Basic data *498*
Buying behavior data *498*
Collaborative CRM *494*
Competitor information *498*
Computer-aided selling *504*
Contact data *498*
Customer information *498*
Customer relationship management (CRM) systems *490*
Data marts *499*
Data mining *502*
Data related to potential *498*
Data warehouse *494*
Decision data *498*
Electronic data interchange (EDI) *500*
Information sources and mining methods *491*
Information storage *491*
Integration of all data *494*
Interfaces *499*
Market information *498*
Market research activities *497*
Marketing and sales information system *490*
Marketing automation *503*
Meta database *499*
Online analytical processing (OLAP) *496*
Operative CRM *496*
Performance data *498*
Safety and security *493*
Sales automation *504*
Salesforce automation *504*
Standard software packages *500*
Sub-databases *499*
Support in analyzing data *494*
Support of market development processes *494*
User requirements *492*
Web mining *502*

References

Bager, J., Becker, J. and Munz, R. (1997) Data-warehouse, *c't, Magazin für Computertechnik* 3, 284–291.
Berkowitz, E.N., Kerin, R.A., Hartley, S.W. and Rudelius, W. (2000) *Marketing* (6th edn). New York.
Berry, M. and Linoff, G. (2000) *Mastering Data Mining*. New York.
Buck-Emden, R. and Zencke, C. (2004) *MySAP CRM, The Official Guidebook to SAP CRM 4.0*. Fort Lee, NJ.
Burrows, P. (2006) Stopping the sprawl at HP, *Business Week*, 29 May, 3986, 54–56.
Buttle, F. (2004) *Customer Relationship Management: Concepts and Tools*. Amsterdam.
Cabena, P., Hadjinian, P., Stadler, R., Verhees, J. and Zanasi, A. (1998) *Discovering Data Mining – from Concept to Implementation*. Upper Saddle River.
Chenoweth, T., Corral, K. and Demirkan, H. (2006) Seven key interventions for data warehouse success, *Communications of the ACM*, 49, 1, 114–119.
Cios, K., Pedrycz, W., Swiniarski, R. and Kurgan, L. (2006) *Data Mining: Knowledge Discovery Methods*. Berlin.
Clark, L. (2006) ERP systems at heart of steel firm's expansion, *Computer Weekly*, 29 August.
DeFelice, A. (2005) Marketing automation, *Customer Relationship Management*, 30, 3, 854–886.
Greatorex, M. (2005) Marketing information systems, *Blackwell Encyclopedic Dictionary of Marketing*, 1–209.
Greenberg, P. (2006) *CRM at the Speed of Light, Essential Customer Strategies for the 21st Century* (3rd edn). New York.
Homburg, C., Schäfer, H. and Schneider, J. (2006) *Sales Excellence* (4th edn). Wiesbaden.
Hurtado, C., Gutierrez, C. and Mendelzon, A. (2005) Capturing summarizability with integrity constraints in OLAP, *ACM Transactions on Database Systems*, 30, 3, 854–886.
Innovative Systems (2006) http://www.innovativesystems.com/success/standard_bank_of_south_africa.php.
Kotler, P. and Keller, K. (2006) *Marketing Management* (12th edn). Upper Saddle River.

Kracklauer, A., Mills, D. and Seifert, D. (2004) Collaborative customer relationship management (CCRM), in: Kracklauer, A., Mills, D. and Seifert, D. (eds) *Collaborative Customer Relationship Management: Taking CRM to the Next Level.* Berlin, 25–45.

Leverick, F., Littler, D., Bruce, M. and Wilson, D. (1998) Using information technology effectively: a study of marketing installations, *Journal of Marketing Management*, 14, 8, 927–962.

Lihui C. and Wai L. (2005) Using web structure and summarisation techniques for web content mining, *Information Processing & Management*, 41, 5, 1225–1242.

Marks, W. and Frolick, M. (2001) Building customer data warehouses for a marketing and service environment: a case study, *Information Systems Management*, 18, 3, 51–56.

Peppers, D. and Rogers, M. (2001) *One to One B2B, Customer Development Strategies for the Business-to-Business World.* Oxford.

Raab, D. (2005) The market for marketing automation systems, *DM Review*, 15, 12, 86–87.

Schewe, C. (1976) *Marketing Information Systems, Selected Readings.* Massachusetts.

Shahabi, C. and Banaei-Kashani, F. (2003) Efficient and anonymous web-usage mining for web personalization, *INFORMS Journal on Computing*, 15, 2, 123–148.

Shin, B. (2003) An exploratory investigation of system success factors in data warehousing, *Journal of the Association for Information Systems*, 4, 141–170.

Siebel (2006) http://www.crmondemand.de/products/tour.jsp, 11 February.

Simon, A. and Shaffer, S. (2001) *Data Warehousing and Business Intelligence for E-Commerce.* San Francisco.

Tan, P., Steinbach, M. and Kumar, V. (2006) *Introduction to Data Mining.* Boston, Mass.

Williams, G. and Simoff, S. (2006) *Data Mining, Theory, Methodology, Techniques, and Applications.* Berlin.

Wu, J. (2005) The evolution to an information enterprise, *DM Review*, 15, 3, 24–59.

CHAPTER 15

Marketing and Sales Management Control

Contents

Learning Objectives

In this chapter you will become familiar with:

- the most essential functions of marketing and sales management control
- the main contents of strategic and operative marketing and sales plans
- the relevant objects and aspects of a marketing and sales management control system
- the ABC analysis, as well as (product or customer) portfolio analysis within the scope of marketing and sales management control
- the cost and profitability accounting tools and their use with respect to products (full product costing and direct product costing) and customers (sales segment analysis)
- the process of investment planning in marketing and sales, as well as its relevance with regard to value-based management
- the various types of indicators that can play a key role in marketing and sales control.

Focus on Marketing 15-1

> "Companies need to gain an understanding of their performance drivers, especially in marketing and sales. This understanding is paramount for strategy implementation especially in the area of planning and sales controlling marketing and sales activities.
>
> *Peter Angehrn, Managing Director, Head of Marketing Private Banking, Crédit Suisse*"

Marketing and sales management control plays a key role in strategy implementation: 'Management control is the process by which managers influence other members of the organization to implement the organization's strategies' (Anthony and Govindarajan 2004, p. 7; see also Focus on Marketing 15-1). Key activities include planning the organization's activities, coordinating the activities of different parts of the organization, and communicating and evaluating information. Primary tasks of marketing and sales management control include the provision of information, as well as the planning and control of marketing and sales activities. The latter topic is examined in this chapter; how information is provided for marketing and sales has already been discussed in Chapter 14.

15.1 Tasks and Roles of Marketing and Sales Management Control

We consider **marketing and sales management control** to be a function of **management support** for marketing and sales management (and possibly also for the corporate management or heads of a strategic business unit) in **controlling market-related activities.** A fundamental task in this regard is controlling the allocation of resources in a company. Here the effectiveness and the efficiency of the deployment of resources in marketing and sales is of particular relevance.

The three **central tasks of marketing and sales management control** are:

1 providing information to marketing and sales (see Chapter 14)

2 marketing and sales planning

3 marketing and sales control.

There are two different marketing and sales roles within each task area. The first role is **system design**. The objective is to provide the individuals in charge of the marketing and sales units with suggestions about designing and modifying the planning and control systems.

The second role is **system implementation**, which focuses on the use of the systems in the three areas mentioned above. The differentiation between the two roles can be illustrated by this example: the system design role concentrates on the design of the planning system in marketing and sales whereby, for example, the scope and time frame of planning activities, as well as the level of detail, are defined. In contrast, the role of system implementation concerns the introduction and maintenance of a marketing and sales plan.

In this connection, it should be noted that **marketing and sales controllers** only coordinate the use of the systems; they themselves do not use these systems. The essential information contained in a marketing and sales plan is provided by product managers, key account managers and regional sales units, as well as the market research department. The task of the marketing and sales controlling team is to coordinate this pool of information into a coherent plan.

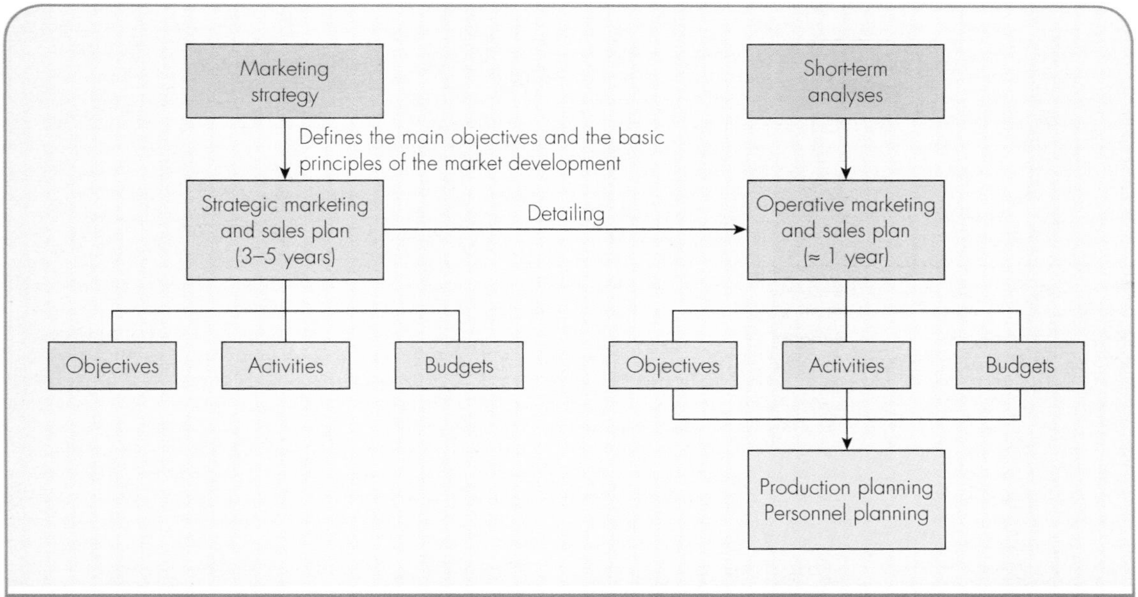

Figure 15-1 Overview of the strategic and operative marketing and sales plans

15.2 Marketing and Sales Planning

Marketing and sales planning encompasses defining the

- objectives,
- activities, and
- budget

related to marketing and sales for a clearly specified period of time. The result of this planning is the marketing and sales plan. It is crucial to differentiate between the strategic and operative marketing and sales plan (see also Figure 15-1). Major differences between these two planning levels exist with respect to the time frame and degree of detail.

The **strategic marketing and sales plan** has a long-term orientation. In company practice these plans are usually developed for a three- to five-year period. In many companies, the strategic marketing and sales plan is updated and extended on a 'rolling' basis (for example, always for the following three years). The level of detail of this planning is rather low. The strategic marketing and sales planning is derived from the marketing strategy (see Figure 15-1) (for the development of the marketing strategy please refer to Chapter 3).

Strategic marketing and sales planning thus aims at transforming (and integrating) the contents of the marketing strategy into a coherent framework of objectives, activities and budgets (see also Menon *et al.* 1999; Piercy and Morgan 1994). Figure 15-2 shows how the strategic marketing and sales plan relates to the marketing strategy, using the example of a mechanical engineering company.

Operative marketing and sales planning serves to detail and refine strategic marketing and sales planning. These plans have a much shorter planning horizon than the strategic plans. Often, operative marketing and sales plans are limited to a single business year. A distinctive characteristic of operative marketing and sales planning is its high degree of detail. For example, if sales targets for a national market have been defined in strategic marketing and sales planning, they are broken

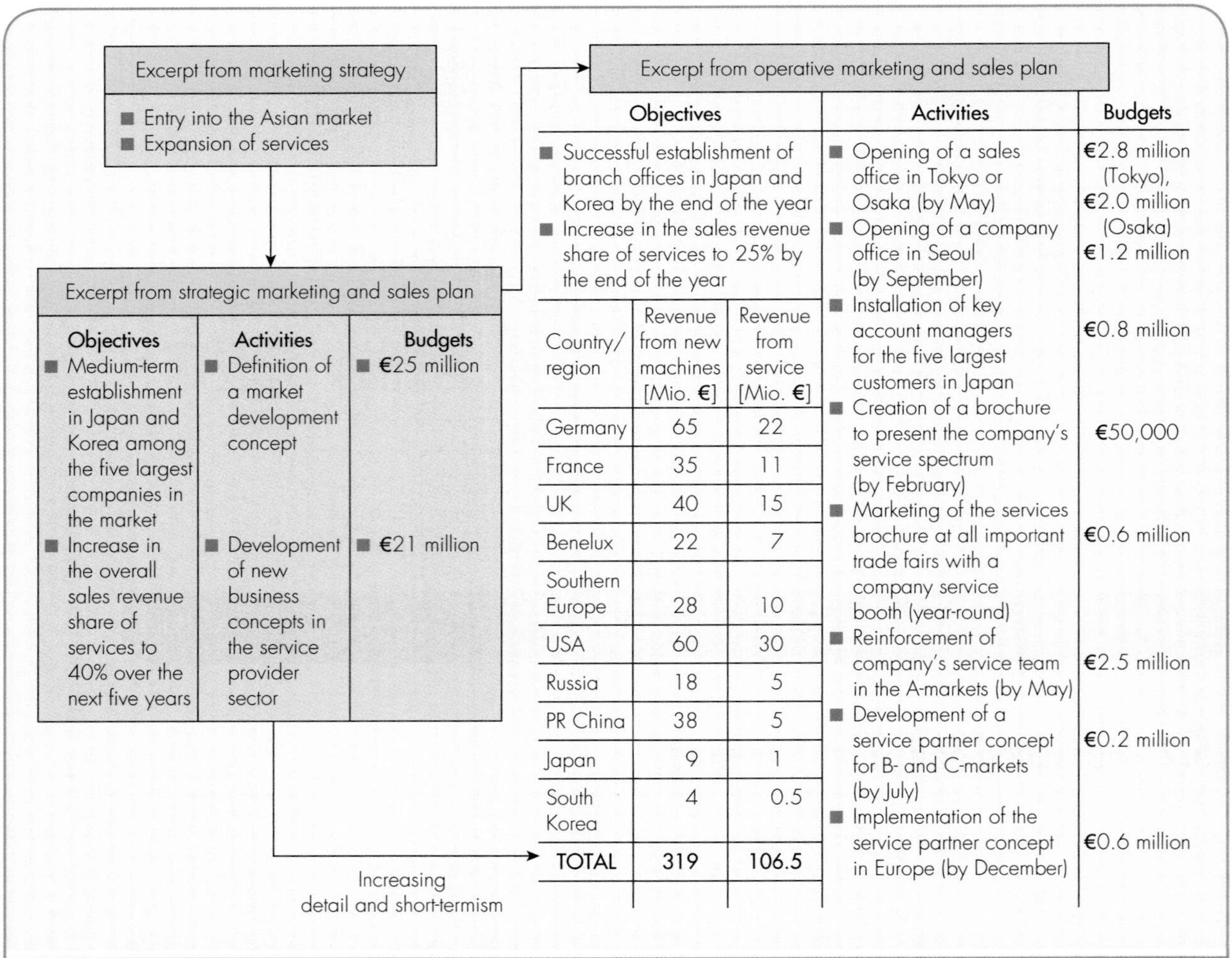
Excerpt from marketing strategy
■ Entry into the Asian market
■ Expansion of services
Excerpt from strategic marketing and sales plan
Objectives
■ Medium-term establishment in Japan and Korea among the five largest companies in the market
■ Increase in the overall sales revenue share of services to 40% over the next five years
Activities
■ Definition of a market development concept
■ Development of new business concepts in the service provider sector
Budgets
■ €25 million
■ €21 million
Excerpt from operative marketing and sales plan
Objectives
■ Successful establishment of branch offices in Japan and Korea by the end of the year
■ Increase in the sales revenue share of services to 25% by the end of the year
Country/region | Revenue from new machines [Mio. €] | Revenue from service [Mio. €]
Germany | 65 | 22
France | 35 | 11
UK | 40 | 15
Benelux | 22 | 7
Southern Europe | 28 | 10
USA | 60 | 30
Russia | 18 | 5
PR China | 38 | 5
Japan | 9 | 1
South Korea | 4 | 0.5
TOTAL | 319 | 106.5
Activities
■ Opening of a sales office in Tokyo or Osaka (by May)
■ Opening of a company office in Seoul (by September)
■ Installation of key account managers for the five largest customers in Japan
■ Creation of a brochure to present the company's service spectrum (by February)
■ Marketing of the services brochure at all important trade fairs with a company service booth (year-round)
■ Reinforcement of company's service team in the A-markets (by May)
■ Development of a service partner concept for B- and C-markets (by July)
■ Implementation of the service partner concept in Europe (by December)
Budgets
€2.8 million (Tokyo), €2.0 million (Osaka)
€1.2 million
€0.8 million
€50,000
€0.6 million
€2.5 million
€0.2 million
€0.6 million
Increasing detail and short-termism

Figure 15-2 Illustration of the interconnections between the marketing strategy and strategic and operative marketing planning, using the example of a mechanical engineering company

down into sales targets for the individual sales regions in the respective national market in operative planning. In practice, if individual customers are of major relevance to a company, operative marketing and sales planning is frequently detailed even to the level of the individual customer.

As already described, both the strategic and the operative marketing and sales plans outline objectives, activities and budgets. There is a logical interconnection between these three components – that is, activities are derived from the objectives, while budgets are derived from the planned activities. A more in-depth insight into the contents of the planning process covered by these three areas is provided in Figure 15-3 (for a more detailed discussion of the contents of such plans, see also Greenley and Oktemgil 1996).

So far our discussion has concentrated on the contents of the marketing and sales plan. We will now turn to the **marketing and sales planning process**, which concerns the development of the marketing and sales plans. In this context, three different approaches exist:

1 top-down planning
2 bottom-up planning
3 combined top-down/bottom-up planning.

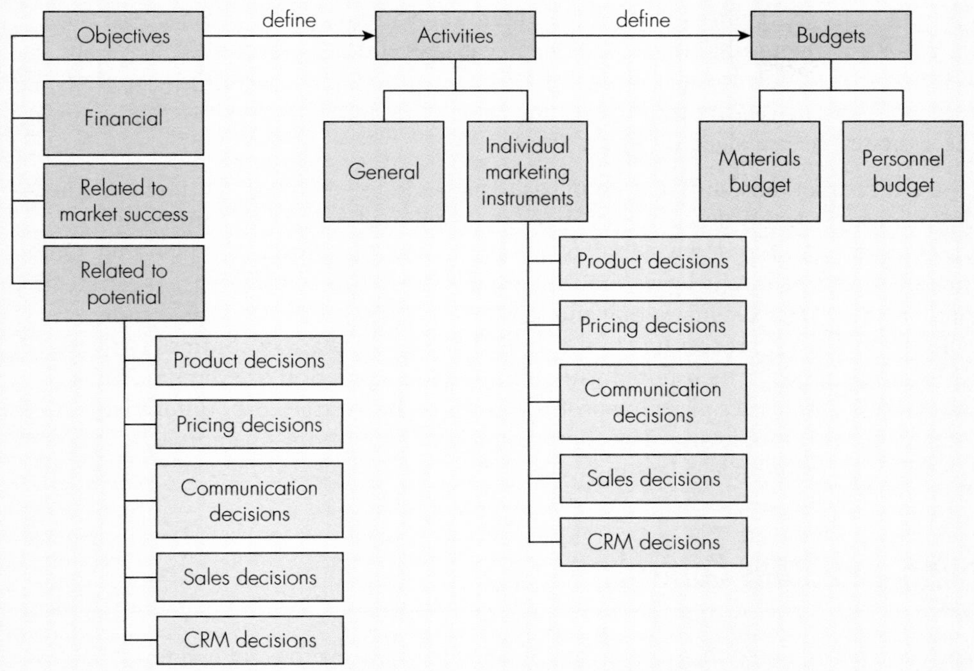

Figure 15-3 Overview of the contents of a strategic/operative marketing and sales plan

Basically these three methods differ with regard to the degree of influence they have on the content of the planning that is done at the various levels of the firm's hierarchy.

With **top-down planning** (see Dess *et al.* 2003, pp. 385f.; Drury 2005, p. 665), the planning takes place from the top to the bottom of the company hierarchy: the top-level objectives, main activities and budgets are defined by top management personnel for the lower levels of management. The plans are then successively further detailed – for example, for individual sales regions or product groups by the individuals at lower hierarchical levels. An advantage of this process is a consistent direction in marketing effort, which leads to a high degree of planning consistency. A major disadvantage, however, is that the objectives may trigger acceptance problems at the lower hierarchy levels.

Bottom-up planning is quite the opposite process (see Dess *et al.* 2003; Drury 2005). This means that the planning process originates at the lowest levels of management, and is refined and coordinated at higher levels. The ideas, concepts and suggestions are provided by the lower hierarchies and decentralized units (e.g. those responsible for product management, key accounts or sales regions). With this method, higher hierarchy levels exert less influence on the planning process than is the case with top-down planning. The particular advantages of bottom-up planning are that the planning is carried out where the relevant information (e.g. about markets and customers) is available, and that the planning and implementation responsibility lies in the same hands. Furthermore, because managers participate in the preparation of the planning they are more likely to accept the decisions that arise in this process. The disadvantages of this approach lie in the fact that the method requires coordination and the marketing effort does not exhibit the same level of consistency as a top-down approach.

Top-down/bottom-up planning represents a combination of both processes. The starting point of this approach is an objective or target specified by an upper hierarchy level, which is followed by decentralized planning (e.g. for individual product groups, sales regions or key accounts). The competent decentralized units are required to align their planning with the top-level objective. The plans are then aggregated and the results adjusted to the objectives defined by the higher hierarchy levels. This method combines the advantages of both top-down planning (consistency in planning content) and bottom-up planning (feasibility and acceptance of planning). Nevertheless, this complex process necessitates the use of significant resources.

When evaluating these three methods, differentiation has to be made between strategic and operative marketing and sales planning: the top-down approach (or the combined top-down/bottom-up approach with a predominance of top-down elements) is widely used in strategic sales planning. One reason for this is that the upper hierarchy levels should generally exert a greater influence on strategic considerations; another is that strategic marketing and sales planning is more manageable and easier to control with the top-down process due to the limited degree of detail. In contrast, both the top-down and bottom-up methods in their pure forms are usually less practical or even unrealistic for use in operative marketing and sales planning processes (especially in large corporations with a certain degree of organizational complexity). The combined top-down/bottom-up approach is more suitable for operative marketing and sales planning.

15.3 Marketing and Sales Controls

At its core, the term 'controls' refers to the comparison of an actual status with a defined target situation. This targeted situation is usually derived from marketing and sales planning. Therefore, marketing and sales controls are closely connected to marketing and sales planning. We differentiate here between strategic and operative marketing controls. Furthermore, controls also contribute to ensuring the realization of the plan (e.g. through the initiation of corresponding activities), and thus facilitate the implementation of plans (see Dess *et al.* 2003, pp. 296ff.; Drury 2005, p. 643; Innes 2004, pp. 738ff.; Kotler and Keller 2006, pp. 716ff.; Smith 2005, pp. 180ff.).

Marketing and sales controls can be geared towards:

- individual marketing activities (e.g. special price promotions, a new product launch, a product modification, an advertising measure)
- certain stakeholders (organizational units/individual persons) in the marketing and sales units (e.g. product managers, field salesforce employees, regional sales offices)
- certain sales objects (e.g. product groups/lines, customer segments, sales territories).

Here we distinguish between result (or output) controls and action (or behavioral) controls.

- **Result controls** are at the forefront of marketing and sales controlling and refer to the comparison of the target results and the results actually achieved. This type of control can be used for objectives related to potential, objectives related to market success, or economic objectives (for more on the differences between these objectives, see Section 2.1) (a corresponding overview is presented in Figure 15-3). Such measures for controlling that determine the degree of achievement of targets/objectives can be applied to the ultimate objectives set at the end of a planning period as well as to interim goals. Controlling the achievement of interim goals is particularly important in order to ensure prompt detection of deviations.
- **Action controls** compare real processes or behavior with objectives. Here the actions and behaviors themselves are the focus of control. Examples in the area of marketing and sales include controlling compliance with the visit plans (sales calls) of field salesforce employees and the adherence to schedules for new product launches.

Table 15-1 Areas and concrete examples of marketing and sales controls

What is being controlled? / Type of control	Marketing activities	Stakeholders in marketing and sales	Sales objects
Result controls with respect to objectives related to potential	Controls of the awareness of a TV spot (day-after recall)	Level of customer satisfaction with the technical customer service	Level of customer satisfaction in customer segment A
Result controls with respect to objectives related to market success	Controls of the price level realized in the market after a modification of the discount system	Number of new customers acquired by a sales employee	Level of customer loyalty in customer segment B
Result controls with respect to economic objectives	Controls of the costs of a direct marketing campaign	Controls of the contribution margin achieved by a sales territory	Profitability of key account C
Action controls	–	Controls of the adherence to schedules on the part of the market research department	–

Table 15-2 Excerpt from the marketing and sales controls report of a software provider

Target / Country		Germany	France	Great Britain	USA	Spain
Sales quantity (in number of licenses)	Planned	9,500	3,400	7,000	6,500	2,400
	Actual	9,750	3,643	6,891	7,102	2,140
Price level (index 100 = price level of previous year)	Planned	102	103	100	104	102
	Actual	97	98	99	101	98

Table 15-1 provides an overview of the various areas of marketing and sales control.

To further illustrate marketing and sales controls, Table 15-2 presents an example from a software company. Here, the sales quantities as well as the price levels achieved are controlled on the basis of individual geographic markets.

15.4 Analytical Tools Used in Marketing and Sales Management Controlling

A broad range of analytical tools can be used in marketing and sales management control. It is difficult to narrow down this range. For example, the tools used for analyzing the initial strategic situation already discussed in Chapter 3 also have relevance in marketing and sales controlling. And the data analysis methods used in market research can also be practical in the context of marketing and sales management control. Consequently, it is nearly impossible to provide a complete presentation of all the analytical tools relevant here. In view of this, we will be concentrating on those analytical tools that are primarily associated with marketing and sales management control. In the following, we will be examining:

- ABC analysis
- portfolio analysis
- cost and profitability accounting tools
- investment planning methods.

The relevance of these analytical tools with regard to the tasks of marketing and sales management control is illustrated in Table 15-3. It should be stated that all the analytical tools discussed here support the task of providing relevant information for this process. Moreover, ABC analysis, portfolio analysis and investment planning tools are also very relevant to planning, while the cost and profitability accounting tools are especially suitable for tasks in marketing and sales management control.

Table 15-3 Application of analytical tools used in marketing sales and control

Analytical tools / Area of application	ABC analysis	Portfolio analysis	Cost and profitability accounting	Investment planning
Provision of information	x	x	x	x
Planning	x	x	x	x
Control			x	

15.4.1 ABC Analysis

ABC analysis is a general tool that aims to identify 'important' and 'less important' objects (e.g. products or customers) in order to support and facilitate prioritization when allocating resources in marketing and sales. ABC analysis can be used to analyze:

- products and product groups/lines
- customers and customer segments
- markets.

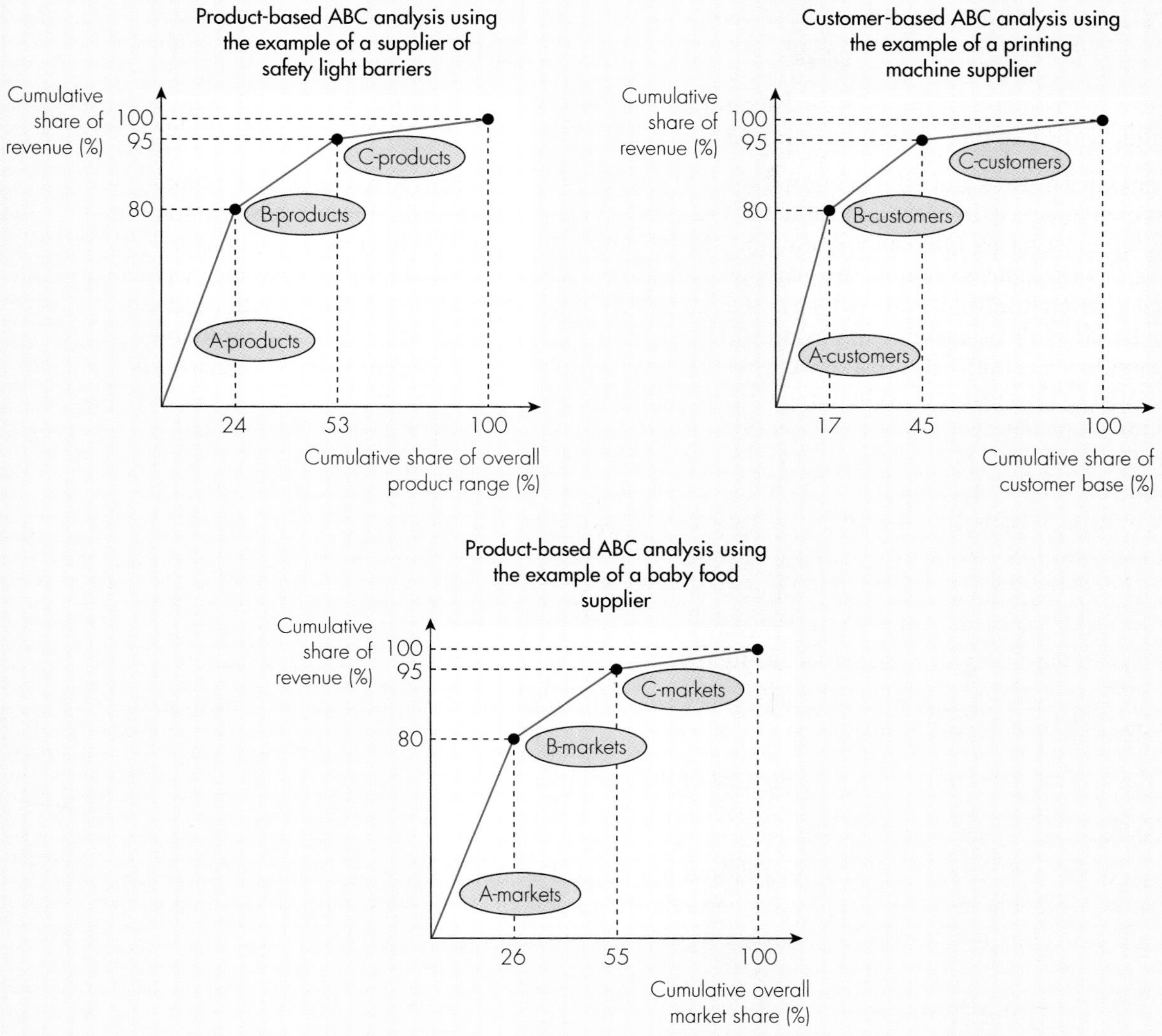

Figure 15-4 Application of ABC analysis in marketing and sales management control

In an ABC analysis, the objects being analyzed (e.g. products, customers or markets) are first arranged in descending order according to a specific criterion (e.g. sales). A key component of an ABC analysis is a two-dimensional visualization, as shown in Figure 15-4. On the horizontal axis, the objects are arranged in descending order according to the criteria being analyzed (e.g. sales). The vertical axis refers to the cumulative value of the criteria across all objects under consideration. Frequently, the result is an 80 : 20 ratio, which, for example, indicates that 80% of sales are achieved with 20% of the customers belonging to the group with the highest sales. These objects are typically assigned to the A-category. Objects with average values with regard to the category under examination are placed in the B-category (e.g. B-products, B-customers, B-markets), while the rest of the objects are allocated to the C-category.

The key **advantage of ABC analysis** lies in the fact that it shows that the different objects have different economic significance. In particular, such analyzes can facilitate decisions concerning how much expense and effort is being invested, or should be invested, into developing the objects in the C-category (C-products, C-customers or C-markets). In extreme cases, marketing activities related to these objects can even be discontinued. In company practice, this means eliminating products or foregoing customers or markets.

C-category objects and their economic assessment are associated with a widespread problem in company practice. In cost and profitability accounting (see Section 15.4.3 for more information on this topic), costs are often allocated to individual objects (e.g. products or customers) on a general basis. For example, sales costs are generally allocated to individual customers or customer segments. Such a generalized allocation can be based on, say, the production costs connected with products purchased by those customers. This would mean that, with customer-based cost and profitability accounting, a certain sales cost mark-up on the production costs of the purchased product would be allocated to the customer. When implementing this method, a customer with an annual purchasing volume of products equivalent to €1 million in production costs (e.g. an A-customer) would be subject to the same percentage-based sales cost increase as a customer that buys products with production costs amounting to €1,000 (e.g. a C-customer). This type of cost allocation poses the risk of being completely unrealistic: company practice shows that sales expenses for C-customers are generally disproportionately high, since a certain amount of customer-related sales expenses have to be incurred regardless of the purchasing volumes of the customer (see Homburg *et al.* 2006). The risk thus lies in an overly positive economic assessment of C-products or C-customers.

The restrictions of ABC analysis are the following:

- the analysis uses just one criterion (e.g. if a sales criterion is used, no information is provided about the profitability) (Ng 2007)
- the analysis does not assess the potential of the customer
- synergy effects are not included.

Due to these restrictions, ABC analysis should not be used as an isolated way of making decisions. As shown in Table 15-3, ABC analysis is particularly suitable in terms of providing information and planning recommendations in marketing and sales management control.

15.4.2 Portfolio Analysis

We have already presented a detailed description of **portfolio analysis** in our discussion of the strategic marketing perspective (see Chapter 4). In Chapter 4 we examined the use of this method for answering the question concerning the extent to which a company should invest resources in developing a specific market or a specific market segment. In the portfolio model presented there, markets are positioned in a two-dimensional system, with one axis indicating market attractiveness in the broadest sense and the other axis mapping the strength, in the broadest sense, of the company's position in the markets being analyzed. From the evaluation of these two dimensions, recommendations are derived regarding the allocation of resources.

Portfolio analysis also has some relevance in marketing and sales management control. At the strategic level this method is used more for analyzing entire markets, market segments or strategic business units. In marketing and sales controlling, individual products/product categories and individual customers/customer segments are the subject of this analysis. Accordingly, we will be discussing product and customer portfolio analyzes. Both variants are quite similar to the portfolio models presented in Chapter 4 (particularly the market attractiveness/competitive position portfolio) with regard to their structure, procedures and conclusions. In light of this, we will be limiting our discussion here to a brief description.

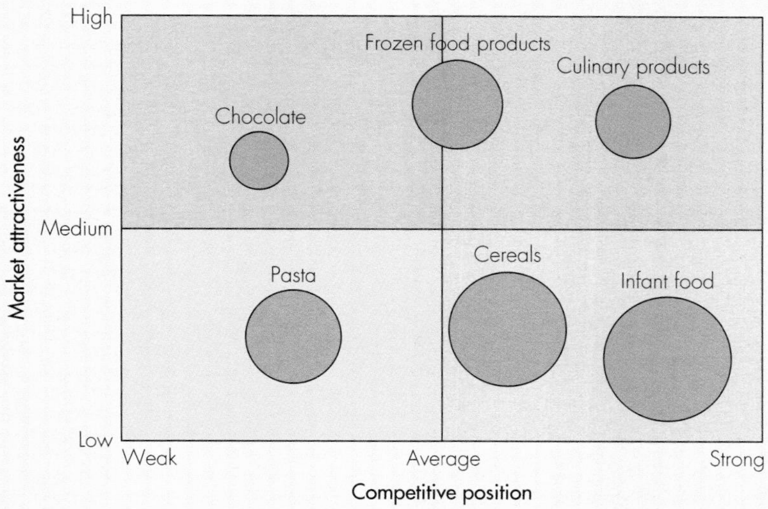

Figure 15-5 Product portfolio analysis using the example of a food company

In **product portfolio analysis**, individual products or product categories are assessed with respect to the market attractiveness and competitive position of the company. From this analysis the manager can derive recommendations for the investment in certain products and product groups (Walters and Halliday 2005, pp. 203ff.). Figure 15-5 illustrates a product portfolio analysis using the example of a food company (the size of the circles in Figure 15-5 corresponds to the sales revenue volume of the individual product groups). The market attractiveness/competitive position portfolio is used in the example; for reasons of simplification, we have only differentiated between four fields. The example shows that marketing resources should be intensively invested in culinary and frozen food, whereas it appears advisable to invest less in pasta.

Customer portfolio analysis is similar in its basic structure (see Figure 15-6). This analysis is often used for positioning individual customers in the portfolio. If the number of customers is too large for such an analysis (which is generally the case in consumer goods marketing), customer segments are evaluated instead of individual customers.

In a customer portfolio analysis, the vertical axis usually represents the degree of **customer attractiveness**. A key criterion in practice is customer demand for the company's products (i.e. the sales revenue that the company could potentially achieve with the customer, regardless of the actual sales revenue realized with the customer). Other criteria for assessing customer attractiveness include, for example:

- the estimated growth in demand
- the quality of the revenue (i.e. the price level that can be achieved with the customer)
- the potential influence of the customer on other prospective customers.

We will call the horizontal axis of the customer portfolio the **company position**. A primary criterion here is the '**share of customer**' (also called '**share of wallet**'), which refers to the percentage of the relevant customer demand that is covered by the company (i.e. the 'customer-based market share' of the company) (Kotler and Armstrong 2006, p. 20). For example, if the annual relevant demand of a customer amounts to €100,000 and the customer uses €20,000 of that for purchasing products from

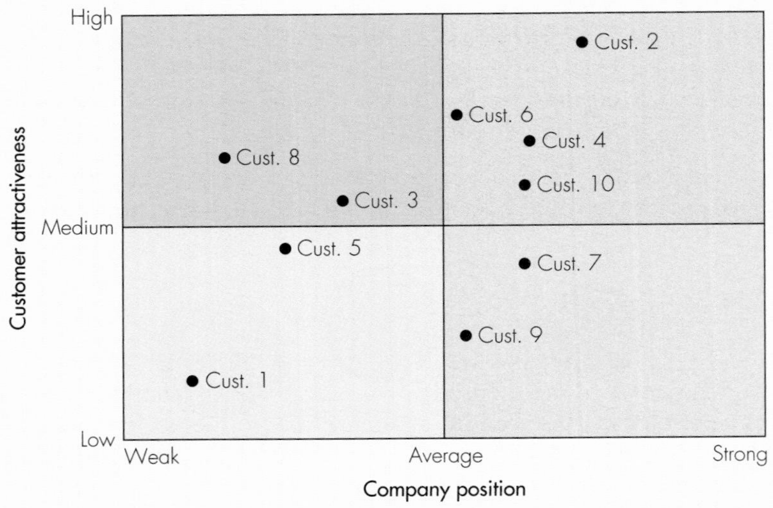

Figure 15-6 Customer portfolio analysis using the example of a supplier of transmission technology products

the company under consideration, the share of customer is 20%. Furthermore, if the company knows the share of customer of its strongest competitor, the relative share-of-customer ratio can be determined by dividing the company's own share of customer by that of the strongest competitor (analogous to the relative market share, see Section 4.2). In the example provided above, if the strongest rival has a share of customer of 40%, the relative share-of-customer ratio of the company for this customer is 0.5.

With customer portfolio analysis, customers can be classified into four categories (as illustrated in Figure 15-6; for a further example based on the BCG matrix, see Smith 2005).

The main information provided by portfolio analysis relates to the allocation of resources to various customers.

- Extensive resources should be invested in **Star customers** (high customer attractiveness, strong company position), in order to defend and strengthen the company's strong position against competitors.
- In the case of **Question Mark customers** (high customer attractiveness, weak company position), this analysis suggests a selective approach. One option is to intensively invest resources with the aim of improving the company position over the long term, in order to transform these customers into Star customers. If the company decides against this investment, it should consider withdrawing from the business relationship.
- For **Cash Cow customers** (low customer attractiveness, strong company position), the recommendation is to limit the deployment of resources so that the business relationship can be maintained at the existing level.
- Finally, with respect to **Dog customers** (low customer attractiveness, weak company position), customer portfolio analysis advises the significant limitation of the amount of resources invested in these customers. In company practice, this can even mean exiting the business relationship with these customers altogether.

As shown in Table 15-3, in marketing and sales management control, portfolio analysis is useful for providing information as well as for planning purposes. In terms of providing information, this analysis proves interesting, for example, for evaluating the structure of a company's sales revenues (categorized according to products and/or customers). A company should therefore strive to achieve a well-balanced customer profile, which ensures that Star, Cash Cow and 'Question Mark' customers make an appreciable contribution to the company's sales revenue.

However, portfolio analysis disregards synergies between products and customers and, therefore, has to be used with caution (see also Section 4.2; Nutton 2006/2007) and in connection with other analytical tools.

15.4.3 Tools for Cost and Profitability Accounting

The **tools for cost and profitability accounting** that will be discussed in this section are characterized by an allocation of costs to certain sales objects (e.g. products or customers). In combination with an allocation of revenues this helps to assess the economic results of these objects. The core question here addresses the profitability of a company with respect to individual products or customers. The tools examined here are very useful to monitor results.

Full and Direct Product Costing

Full and direct costing methods focus on analyzing the economic results of products, with the differentiation between indirect costs and direct costs being of fundamental importance. **Direct costs** are those costs that can be directly attributed to a product, including, say, material costs as well as labor costs for producing and/or processing a certain product. Conversely, **indirect costs** (also called overhead costs) arise from cross-product activities (e.g. marketing and sales) (see Drury 2005, pp. 30f.; Walters and Halliday 2005, pp. 84f.). The difference between the full and direct product costing methods lies in the fact that the full costing method allocates all costs incurred during a period (thus also including indirect costs) to the products. With respect to the allocation of indirect costs, they have to be categorized according to certain criteria. In contrast, with the direct costing method, only a portion of the total costs (in particular, the direct costs) are allocated to the products (see Drury 2005, pp. 371f.).

Table 15-4 shows a costing sheet that forms the basis for the full product costing of a manufacturing company. Particular attention should be paid to the allocation of indirect costs as a percentage increase. For example, indirect marketing and sales costs are allocated to the products by an increase of the product manufacturing costs by a certain percentage. This approach, which is widely used in company practice, demonstrates one of the main problems of full product costing, namely the issue of a causal allocation of indirect costs. Thus, the **traditional costing** method (in company practice based on, for example, direct costs, production costs or revenue) shown in Table 15-4 can be described as being somewhat arbitrary: a product with twice the amount of production costs will also be allocated twice the amount of indirect marketing and sales costs (Innes 2004, pp. 423f.). It is obvious that this cost allocation can hardly be called causal, since a product with production costs greater than those of another product does not necessarily lead to higher marketing expenses. A more causal allocation of indirect costs is possible with the activity-based costing method, which will also be described in this section.

The key indicator of the success of products within the scope of the full product costing method is the product result, which is calculated by deducting the product-related cost price from the product revenue. In contrast, the direct product costing method calculates the product contribution margin as the main benchmark for product success. The product contribution margin refers to the monetary amount that a product contributes to covering all other costs (i.e. all costs not attributed to the product) after deducting the costs allocated within the scope of direct costing from the product revenue (see Drury 2005, p. 271).

Table 15-4 Costing sheet for a full product costing, using the example of a manufacturing company

1		Direct material costs
2	+	Indirect material costs (percentage of 1)
3	=	**Material costs** (1 + 2)
4		Direct production costs
5	+	Indirect production costs (percentage of 4)
6	+	Special direct production costs
7	=	**Production costs** (4 + 5 + 6)
8		**Manufacturing costs** (3 + 7)
9	+	Indirect administrative costs (percentage of 8)
10	+	Indirect marketing and sales costs (percentage of 8)
11	+	Special direct costs of sales
12	=	**Cost price** (8 + 9 + 10 + 11)

Table 15-5 Example of direct and full product costing (figures in million €)

Product group / Economic factor	A	B	C	D	E		
Revenue	27.48	17.56	15.23	12.48	35.12	Direct costing	Full costing
– Direct costs	11.94	10.41	9.53	5.62	21.51		
= Contribution margin	15.54	7.15	5.70	6.86	13.61		
– Indirect costs	9.32	9.77	3.71	4.43	9.23		
= Result	6.22	–2.62	1.99	2.43	4.38		

Table 15-5 illustrates the full product costing and direct product costing methods with an example, demonstrating that product group B, for example, is positively assessed when direct product costing is used, but achieves a negative result when the full costing method is applied.

The contribution margin analysis method shown in Table 15-5 applies a one-stage approach, however there are also multi-stage contribution margin analyzes whose individual stages represent intermediate steps between direct costing and full costing analyzes (see Table 15-6 for a corresponding costing sheet).

These analyzes affect a number of **marketing decisions** – for example, pricing decisions: in the short term, direct costs represent the price floor for a company; in the long term, full costing analyzes have a greater impact on pricing decisions than direct costing analyzes. Such analyzes are also important for decisions regarding the product mix (e.g. when deciding whether a certain product should remain in the product mix or be eliminated from it). Here, the product contribution margin is of short-term relevance, while the results of a full costing analysis concern a long-term effect.

Table 15-6 Sample costing sheet of a multi-stage contribution margin analysis

	Revenue	
–	Variable costs per product type	
=	**Contribution margin I**	
–	Fixed costs per product type	
=	**Contribution margin II a**	■ per product group
–	Fixed product group costs	
=	**Contribution margin II b**	■ per unit
–	Fixed unit costs	
=	**Contribution margin III**	■ Sum total of all contribution margins
–	Fixed company costs	
=	**Operating income**	

Activity-Based Costing

Activity-based costing is a special type of full costing. We have already mentioned the problems associated with the use of full product costing. A main characteristic of activity-based costing is its approach to establishing a more causal allocation of indirect costs than is possible with the traditional costing approach.

The basic idea of activity-based costing is to allocate indirect costs according to the actual usage of resources in the indirect cost units. Correspondingly, activity-based costing starts with a comprehensive job/task analysis of the indirect cost units, which provides the basis for an aggregation of the identified jobs/tasks into activities. For each individual activity, a **cost driver** is specified as an allocation base (see Innes 2004, p. 425); it is important that a proportional relationship exists between the allocation base quantity and the resource utilization (i.e. costs incurred) (see Horngren *et al.* 2006, pp. 32f.). For the 'order processing' activity, for example, the number of orders represents a suitable cost driver.

Table 15-7 provides an illustration of an activity-based costing approach. For each activity, the **cost driver rate** is calculated by dividing activity costs by the total quantity of the cost driver (see Innes 2004, p. 425).

Table 15-7 Illustration of an activity-based costing procedure

Activity	Cost driver	Activity costs	Cost driver quantity	Cost driver rate
Order processing	Number of orders	€2 million	10,000 orders	€200 per order
Customer support by field salesforce employees	Number of visits	€6 million	15,000 visits	€400 per visit

Table 15-8 Example of indirect cost allocation within the scope of activity-based costing

Customer group / Activities and cost driver rates	Key accounts		Other customers	
	Cost driver quantity	Costs specific to customer segment	Cost driver quantity	Costs specific to customer segment
Order processing (€200 per order)	800 orders	€160,000	2,200 orders	€440,000
Customer support by field salesforce employees (€400 per visit)	1,000 visits	€400,000	3,000 visits	€1,200,000
Total	–	€560,000	–	€1,640,000

The allocation of costs to cost objects (e.g. products) is based on multiplying the cost driver rate by the quantity of cost driver that is used by the cost object under investigation (see Innes 2004, p. 425). This procedure is illustrated by the application example in Table 15-8. The company under consideration supplies two customer groups, namely key accounts and other customers. The costs of 'order processing' and 'customer support by field salesforce employees' activities are allocated to both customer groups on the basis of activity-based costing. For example, in the period under consideration, 800 orders were processed for the key accounts. Based on a cost driver rate of €200 per order, order processing costs of €160,000 (800 × €200) are thus allocated to this customer group.

Now, it is interesting to compare this with the cost allocation according to the traditional costing approach. Prior to implementing activity-based costing in the company described in Table 15-8, the indirect sales costs (which also included costs arising from 'order processing' and 'customer support by field salesforce employees') were allocated to the customers in proportion to the respective revenue. Consequently, since approximately two-thirds of the company revenue is attributed to key accounts and about one-third to other customers, double the amount of indirect costs were allocated to the key accounts as compared to the other customers. Activity-based costing leads to a completely different distribution of costs between the customer groups (see Table 15-8): here, the indirect cost distribution ratio between other customers and key accounts roughly corresponds to 3 : 1. In the example given, the reason for this lies in the lower number (despite the higher sales volume) of orders and customer visits attributable to key accounts. The example demonstrates that the allocation of indirect costs via activity-based costing has substantially different results as compared to the percentage increase-based allocation.

Activity-based costing can supply valuable information for a great number of **marketing decisions**. Its relevance to the product-related and price-related decisions discussed in this section in conjunction with product-related costing is obvious as well. When applied properly, it provides a better information basis than conventional costing mechanisms (see Innes 2004, pp. 433f.). Activity-based costing is particularly significant with respect to the pricing of complex (e.g. customer-specific) products.

As regards the **overall assessment of activity-based costing** in the area of marketing and sales controlling and for a wide range of marketing decisions, it can be stated that it represents a considerable improvement compared to conventional overhead costing approaches.

15.4.4 Investment Planning Methods

While cost and profitability accounting tools tend to be used retrospectively for controlling purposes, investment planning methods place a strong focus on the future. The value of an object to be analyzed is measured by the future surplus generated by this object. For marketing and sales controlling, the use of such methods is practical for analyzing the economic feasibility of new products, evaluating customer relationships and developing sales segments. Since analysis of the economic feasibility of new products has already been described in Chapter 5, we will limit the following discussion to sales segments and customer relationships.

The calculation of **customer lifetime value** (CLV) aims at the future-oriented economic assessment of sales segments (we will focus on customers in the following) across several periods (see Berger and Nasr 1998; Ching *et al.* 2004; Kotler and Armstrong 2006, pp. 19f., Rust *et al.* 2000, pp. 32–49 for more information on customer lifetime value). In extreme cases, the analysis concerns the entire (expected) duration of the business relationship with the customer. The customer lifetime value calculation is based on a forecast of the future revenues and expenditures arising for the company from one customer relationship. This time series, consisting of forecast revenues and expenditures, is assessed according to the principles of dynamic investment planning: the future revenue surplus (difference between forecast revenue and expenditure) is calculated and discounted with a discount factor, and then added up. Thus, the customer lifetime value corresponds to the net present value of the business relationship with a customer. Consequently, if we take r_t and e_t to denote the forecast revenues/expenditures arising from the business relationship in period t, the CLV can be calculated as

$$\text{CLV} = \sum_{t=0}^{n} \frac{r_t - e_t}{(1+i)^t} = r_0 - e_0 + \frac{r_1 - e_1}{(1+i)} + \frac{r_2 - e_2}{(1+i)^2} + \cdots + \frac{r_n - e_n}{(1+i)^n}$$

with i indicating the discount factor (for example, a discount factor of $i = 0.1$ corresponds to a 10% discount on the future revenue surplus per period) and n the horizon of the analysis (usually indicated in years).

Thus, the CLV calculation is based on the concept of viewing the business relationship with a customer as an object of investment. The quality of this investment is then assessed by means of the dynamic investment planning method. In this context, a positive CLV value denotes a positive economic rating for the customer relationship. Table 15-9 uses an example to illustrate the calculation of customer lifetime value. The figures shown in Table 15-9 refer to an industrial goods manufacturer that applies a five-year time horizon in order to assess its business relationship with a key account customer. The overall result is a slightly negative CLV. From an economic viewpoint, the business relationship thus appears problematic. Since the CLV (as compared to the forecast sales volume of the business relationship) is only slightly negative, the company should not fundamentally question the business relationship in this example, but rather should work towards changing the individual parameters of this economic analysis (e.g. strive to reduce costs).

Due to the future-oriented approach of the CLV, this tool is particularly relevant for planning purposes. In company practice, objects assessed by CLV analyzes frequently include individual customer relationships in the corporate customer segment, while in consumer goods industries such analyzes tend to target customer segments.

There are **advantages to using the CLV** when planning market development activities. Venkatesan and Kumar (2004) demonstrated for a computer manufacturer that prioritizing customers on the

Table 15-9 Customer lifetime value calculation using the example of the customer relationship of an industrial goods manufacturer

	Year 1 (t = 0)	Year 2 (t = 1)	Year 3 (t = 2)	Year 4 (t = 3)	Year 5 (t = 4)	Total
Revenue from selling physical products	10,000,000	9,500,000	9,025,000	8,573,750	8,145,063	**45,243,813**
Revenue from services rendered	80,000	80,000	80,000	80,000	80,000	**400,000**
Total revenue	10,080,000	9,580,000	9,105,000	8,653,750	8,225,063	**45,643,813**
Pre-production costs: technology	1,300,000					**1,300,000**
Pre-production costs: sales and marketing	220,000					**220,000**
Associated costs	100,000	100,000	300,000	100,000	100,000	**700,000**
Variable costs	6,900,000	6,417,000	5,967,810	5,550,063	5,161,559	**29,996,432**
Customer-specific sales costs	750,000	765,000	734,400	660,960	594,864	**3,505,224**
Customer-specific fixed production costs	1,800,000	1,854,000	1,909,620	1,966,909	2,025,916	**9,556,445**
Follow-up costs					250,000	**250,000**
Total expenditures	11,070,000	9,136,000	8,911,830	8,277,932	8,132,339	**44,528,101**
Annual revenue surplus	–990,000	444,000	193,170	· 375,818	92,724	**115,712**
Discounted revenue surplus (discount factor: 10%)	–990,000	403,636	159,645	282,358	63,332	**–81,029 CLV**

basis of the CLV leads to a significantly higher average future profitability of the selected customers than prioritization of customers based on other widely used metrics for customer selection (such as, say, the 'share of wallet' of the previous year's sales).

In some cases, more recent sources also use the term **customer equity** (see Blattberg *et al.* 2001; Burmann 2003; Rust *et al.* 2000; Srivastava *et al.* 1998), which is defined as the total sum of all CLVs of all customers of a company (see Kotler and Armstrong 2006, p. 21; Rust *et al.* 2004). In other words, the term refers to the overall value of the entire customer base of a company.

Summary

In this chapter, we introduced the three central tasks of marketing and sales control: providing information to marketing and sales, marketing and sales planning, and marketing and sales controlling. In marketing and sales planning, objectives, activities and budgets are defined for a specific future period of time, which results in the marketing and sales plan. The strategic marketing and sales plan refers to the long term and aims to transform the marketing strategy into a coherent framework. This is further refined in the operative marketing and sales plan, which has a shorter time horizon and thus allows a higher degree of detail. A marketing and sales control system compares this target situation with the actual status. Its reference objects are individual marketing activities, stakeholders in the marketing and sales units, and sales objects.

Next, key analytical tools in marketing and sales control were introduced. In ABC analysis, products, customers or markets are categorized into A-, B- and C-categories, thus illustrating their different economic significance for the company. Portfolio analysis identifies 'Star', 'Question Mark', 'Cash Cow' and 'Dog' products or customers. While these methods are useful for providing information and planning, cost and profitability accounting tools such as full and direct product costing methods are mainly used for monitoring results. In contrast, investment planning methods are forward-looking. Customer lifetime value (CLV) aims to assess the future revenue surplus arising from the relationship with a customer or customer segments.

Case Study: Cost and Profitability Accounting Tools/Activity-Based Costing

AIRCO is a manufacturer of industrial air-conditioner units whose management is concerned that its current traditional cost accounting (TCA) system is not accurately representing its product cost behavior. Under certain operating conditions, an activity-based costing (ABC) system can provide relevant and accurate indirect cost information that assists in making customer, product and process improvement decisions. An ABC system was successfully developed for AIRCO which indicated that its products do not consume overhead costs on a volume basis as represented by its current TCA system. Valuable product and process information was obtained.

Discussion Questions

1. What is the fundamental difference between direct and indirect costs? Why does only activity-based costing provide relevant and accurate indirect cost information?
2. How do you explain the fact that the ABC method produces different overhead costs than traditional cost accounting? Describe the basic difference between the two systems.
3. Exhibit 1 shows different cost pools (aggregation of the cost of different activities) that were identified for the manufacturing of AIRCO's products. What would be an appropriate cost driver for each cost pool?

Case Study (Continued)

Exhibit 1 Cost pools and drivers

Cost pool	Cost driver
Machines	
Data record maintenance	
Material handling	
Product changeover	
Scheduling & production preparation	
Raw material receiving & handling	
Product shipment	
Customer service	

4. Exhibits 2 and 3 show the final results for the different products of AIRCO calculated using the TCA and ABC methods. Interpret the different results. What are the possible implications for marketing decisions?

Exhibit 2 TCA final results

Output parameter	Product						
	5-ton	6-ton	7.5-ton	10-ton	12.5-ton	15-ton	20-ton
Direct labor cost ($)	342.20	342.20	342.20	410.64	410.64	410.64	410.64
Direct material cost ($)	665	665	665	1957	1957	2510	2510
Overhead costs ($)	240.41	240.41	240.41	288.49	288.49	288.49	288.49
Total product costs ($)	1247.61	1247.61	1247.61	2656.13	2656.13	3209.13	3209.13
Selling price ($)	1000	1300	1750	2560	3200	4572	5450
Profit %	–20%	4%	40%	–4%	20%	42%	70%

Exhibit 3 ABC final results

Output parameter	Product						
	5-ton	6-ton	7.5-ton	10-ton	12.5-ton	15-ton	20-ton
Direct labor cost ($)	342.20	342.20	342.20	410.64	410.64	410.64	410.64
Direct material cost ($)	665	665	665	1957	1957	2510	2510
Overhead cost ($)	174.63	404.27	160.26	172.62	1029.52	343.95	309.90
Total product cost ($)	1181.83	1411.47	1167.46	2540.26	3397.16	3264.59	3230.54
Selling price ($)	1000	1300	1750	2560	3200	4572	5450
Profit %	–15%	–8%	50%	1%	–6%	40%	69%

Source: Nachtmann, N. and Al-Rifai, M.H. (2004) *The Engineering Economist*, 49, 3, 221–236. Persistent link: http://search.ebscohost.com/login.aspx?direct=true&db=buh&AN=14353049&site=ehost-live.

Key Terms

ABC analysis *516*
Action controls *514*
Activity-based costing *523*
Advantage of ABC analysis *518*
Advantages to using the CLV *525*
Bottom-up planning *513*
C-category objects *518*
Cash Cow customers *520*
Central tasks of marketing and sales management control *510*
Company position *519*
Controlling market-related activities *510*
Cost driver *523*
Cost driver rate *523*
Customer attractiveness *519*
Customer equity *526*
Customer lifetime value (CLV) *525*
Customer portfolio analysis *519*
Direct costs *521*
Dog customers *520*
Full and direct product costing *521*
Indirect costs *521*
Investment planning methods *525*
Management support *510*
Marketing and sales controllers *510*
Marketing and sales controls *514*
Marketing and sales management control *510*
Marketing and sales planning *510*
Marketing and sales planning process *512*
Marketing decisions *522, 524*
Operative marketing and sales planning *511*
Overall assessment of activity-based costing *525*
Portfolio analysis *518*
Product portfolio analysis *519*
Question Mark customers *520*
Result controls *514*
Share of customer *519*
Share of wallet *519*
Star customers *520*
Strategic marketing and sales plan *511*
System design *510*
System implementation *510*
Tools for cost and profitability accounting *521*
Top-down planning *513*
Top-down/bottom-up planning *513*
Traditional costing *521*

References

Anthony, R. and Govindarajan, V. (2004) *Management Control Systems* (11th edn). Boston, Mass.

Berger, P. and Nasr, N. (1998) Customer lifetime value: marketing models and applications, *Journal of Interactive Marketing*, 12, 1, 17–30.

Blattberg, R., Getz, G. and Thomas, J. (2001) *Customer Equity: Building and Managing Relationships as Valuable Assets*. Cambridge.

Burmann, C. (2003) 'Customer Equity' als Steuerungsgröße für die Unternehmensführung, *Zeitschrift für Betriebswirtschaft*, 73, 2, 113–138.

Ching, W., Ng, M., Wong, K. and Altmann, E. (2004) Customer lifetime value: stochastic optimization approach, *Journal of the Operational Research Society*, 55, 860–868.

Dess, G.G., Lumpkin, G.T. and Taylor, M.L. (2003) *Strategic Management* (2nd edn). New York.

Drury, C. (2005) *Management and Cost Accounting* (6th edn). London.

Greenley, G. and Oktemgil, M. (1996) A development of the domain of marketing planning, *Journal of Marketing Management*, 12, 1, 29–51.

Homburg, C., Schäfer, H. and Schneider, J. (2006) *Sales Excellence* (4th edn). Wiesbaden.

Horngren, C., Datar, S. and Foster, G. (2006) *Cost Accounting: A Managerial Emphasis* (12th edn). Upper Saddle River.

Innes, J. (2004) *Handbook of Management Accounting* (3rd edn). Oxford.

Kotler, P. and Armstrong, G. (2006) *Principles of Marketing* (11th edn) Upper Saddle River.

Kotler, P. and Keller, K. (2006) *Marketing Management* (12th edn), Upper Saddle River.

Menon, A., Bharadwaj, S., Adidam, P. and Edison, S. (1999) Antecedents and consequences of marketing strategy making: a model and a test, *Journal of Marketing*, 63, 2, 18–40.

Nachtmann, N. and Al-Rifai, M.H. (2004) *The Engineering Economist*, 49, 3, 221–236.

Ng, W. (2007) A simple classifier for multiple criteria ABC analysis, *European Journal of Operational Research*, 177, 1, 344–353.

Nutton, S. (2006/2007) Management accounting – business strategy, *Financial Management*, Dec. 2006/Jan. 2007, 43–46.

Piercy, N. and Morgan, N. (1994) The marketing planning process: behavioral problems compared to analytical techniques in explaining marketing plan credibility, *Journal of Business Research*, 29, 3, 167–178.

Rust, R., Lemon, K. and Zeithaml, V. (2004) Return on marketing: using customer equity to focus marketing strategy, *Journal of Marketing*, 68, 1, 109–127.

Rust, R., Zeithaml, V. and Lemon, K. (2000) *Driving Customer Equity, How Customer Lifetime Value is Reshaping Corporate Strategy*. New York.

Smith, M. (2005) *Performance Measurement & Management, A Strategic Approach to Management Accounting*. London.

Srivastava, R., Shervani, T. and Fahey, L. (1998) Market-based assets and shareholder value: a framework for analysis, *Journal of Marketing*, 62, 1, 2–18.

Venkatesan, R. and Kumar, V. (2004) A customer lifetime value framework for customer selection and resource allocation strategy, *Journal of Marketing*, 68, 4, 106–125.

Walters, D. and Halliday, M. (2005) *Marketing and Financial Management: New Economy – New Interfaces*. Basingstoke.

CHAPTER 16

Human Resource Management in Marketing and Sales

Contents

Learning Objectives

In this chapter you will become familiar with:

- the aspects of human resource planning in marketing and sales, as well as its interconnections with both the marketing strategy and marketing and sales planning
- the main decisions in personnel recruitment, the requirements and qualification criteria for new marketing and sales employees, and the key methods for selecting personnel
- the general principles of the process of employee performance appraisal, behavior-based and results-oriented evaluation approaches for the various marketing and sales tasks, and the balanced scorecard in marketing and sales
- the main decisions in human resource development, as well as the most important continuing education and training measures in marketing and sales
- the key decisions regarding employee compensation
- the basic management styles and their relevance to marketing and sales.

This chapter discusses human resource management in marketing and sales. It is obvious that the successful implementation of concepts in the marketing and sales business units largely depends on the qualification and commitment of the employees working in these units. Numerous empirical studies have demonstrated that human resource management plays a significant role in company success.

Human resource management comprises two main task areas (see Figure 16-1):

1 personnel management

2 personnel supervision.

In general, **human resource management** is the effective management of people at work: 'Human resource management is the function performed in organizations that facilitates the most effective use of people (employees) to achieve organizational and individual goals' (Ivancevich 2004). It is thus concerned with the design of systems intended to support certain human resource management tasks such as human resource planning, recruitment, employee compensation and human resource development (see Figure 16-1). That we refer to 'systems' in this regard implies the existence of general rules and guidelines that apply to all employees of a company or a company's organizational units (e.g. the marketing and sales business unit). Section 16.1 discusses the design and structure of these human resource management systems.

Personnel supervision refers to the direct management of employees by their superiors. On the one hand, superiors manage and supervise by using the personnel management systems that are in place (see Figure 16-1). On the other hand, they apply the leadership styles and techniques that will be addressed in Section 16.2, following a discussion of the characteristics that are desirable in marketing and sales managers.

In principle, human resource management is more complex in marketing and sales than in other functional departments. This is because the tasks that marketing and sales units are required to perform tend to be highly versatile (e.g. advertising design and planning, product management, field salesforce) and employees are confronted with quite diverse requirements. These different job duties require different personal traits (e.g. creativity, empathy, friendliness, assertiveness), skills

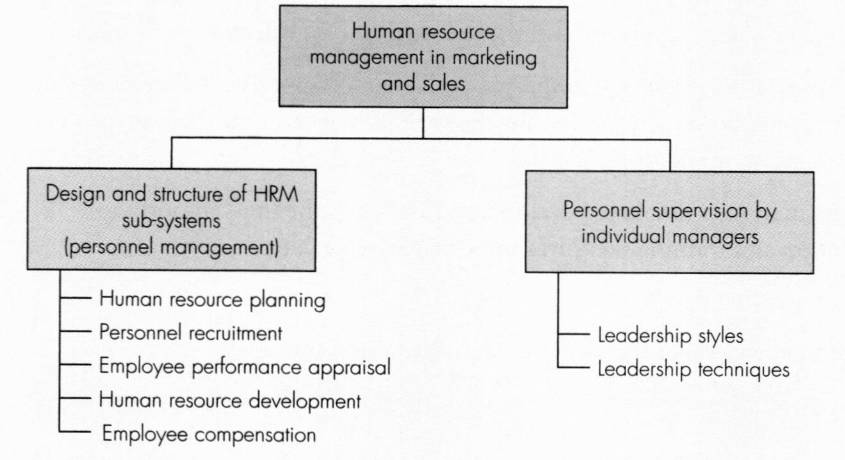

Figure 16-1 Overview of the key areas of human resource management in marketing and sales

(e.g. acquisition skills, analytic skills) and qualifications (e.g. business management or technical qualifications).

16.1 Personnel Management in Marketing and Sales

As already mentioned, human resource management concerns the design and structure of the required **systems for human resource management**. Five main systems can be distinguished (see also Bartol and Martin 1998; Oechsler 2000):

1. human resource planning (see Section 16.1.1)
2. personnel recruitment (see Section 16.1.2)
3. employee performance appraisal (see Section 16.1.3)
4. human resource development (see Section 16.1.4)
5. employee compensation (see Section 16.1.5).

16.1.1 Human Resource Planning in Marketing and Sales

In marketing and sales, human resource planning is concerned with the assessment of the workforce requirements of a company. The core question is 'How many employees, with which characteristics, skills and qualifications, are likely to be needed for which tasks at which point in time, and for which period of time, in order to effectively and efficiently fulfill the marketing and sales tasks?'

Human resource planning for marketing and sales units is usually derived from the marketing strategy as well as from the strategic and operative marketing and sales plans. For example, if new customer segments have to be addressed, this will have direct implications for the scheduled number of employees and their required personal traits, skills and qualifications. Just as in marketing and sales planning, human resource planning is differentiated into strategic and operative planning levels. Table 16-1 illustrates **strategic human resource planning** for the marketing and sales units of a computer manufacturer. Focus on Marketing 16-1 demonstrates how human resource planning can be shaped in management practice.

16.1.2 Personnel Recruitment in Marketing and Sales

Personnel recruitment in marketing and sales concerns the recruitment of employees according to workforce requirements as determined by human resource planning. The major relevance of systematic personnel recruitment in marketing and sales arises from the significant **risks** associated with **hiring mistakes**. For example:

- high training costs for new employees with insufficient qualifications
- high staff turnover rates along with the associated costs (for more information, see Jolson *et al.* 1987; Lucas *et al.* 1987)
- negative effects on customer relationships.

Table 16-2 comprises the central questions that have to be addressed in personnel recruitment for marketing and sales.

Table 16-1 Strategic human resource planning for the marketing and sales units, using the example of a computer manufacturer (in number of employees)

Units \ Years	1	2	3	4	5	Requirements		
Marketing						**Personal traits**	**Skills**	**Qualifications**
Product management	25	27	30	33	35	Strong focus on performance and conscientiousness	Excellent analytic-conceptual skills, assertiveness, ability to cooperate, ability to establish personal networks, excellent product and customer knowledge, programming skills, IT skills, English proficiency	University degree
Marketing communication	4	4	5	5	6	High degree of sociability, openness, originality	Excellent verbal and creative skills, experience in cooperating with agencies, English proficiency	University degree, continuing education
Market research	3	3	3	3	4	High degree of conscientiousness	Excellent analytic-conceptual skills, comprehensive knowledge of market research methods	University degree
Sales								
Field salesforce	85	90	92	92	95	High degree of sociability, friendliness, emotional stability	High degree of social competence, ability to establish personal networks, excellent industry knowledge, customer and product knowledge, sales techniques	University degree, vocational business training
Sales office	15	12	10	10	11	High degree of conscientiousness	Excellent PC knowledge, database application experience	Vocational business training
Technical customer service	12	15	15	16	16	Friendliness and flexibility	Excellent technological/hardware knowhow, software knowledge, customer knowledge	Vocational technical training

Focus on Marketing 16-1 Example of human resource planning

> "Continuous personal and professional development based on a training system adapted to different individual needs and ambitious employees with the audacity to take risks – these are fundamental drivers of economic performance. Another substantial pillar for sustainable growth is diversity. At L'Oréal, we strongly believe that diversity is a source of creativity and performance. By promoting the respect and value of difference through human resources development, a company can establish itself as a global corporate citizen and a preferred employer.
>
> *Dr. Andreas Reusch, Director Human Resources L'Oréal Germany*"

How a talent management plan can anchor your company's future

One of the stars of talent management in the HR profession is Libby Sartain, who now heads HR for Yahoo, Inc. Sartain presented Yahoo management with a three-year plan to recreate Yahoo's staffing as a 'talent organization'. HR is in the process of instituting a number of staffing and talent initiatives related to that plan.

One of the many reasons for this plan is that Yahoo is expecting a hiring boom and intends to obtain and keep the best talent for its organization no matter how competitive the environment becomes. Since Sartain joined Yahoo about three years ago, the organization has undergone a number of changes in its business strategy and staffing needs, including adding new business and eliminating old ones – and it has laid off employees as well. HR also needed to help change cultural issues to make employees feel comfortable seeking jobs in other sectors of the company and to train managers and involve them in recruiting and retention activities.

Another goal is to tell the world about Yahoo's excellent employment situation and opportunities by developing the brand. The talent management program will be enhanced by a combination of staffing, learning, and development into a single strategic staffing and development function. In terms of development, e.g., Yahoo assembled a list of characteristics for the process. These included the ability to integrate the workforce plan into recruiting and development.

The company sought a seamless integrated talent function to hire, develop, and retain. It included these steps:

1. Plan who and how many to hire, including filling 'gaps'.
2. Attract those you want.
3. Recruit those you want.
4. Assess correctly.
5. Develop carefully.
6. Retain only those you want.

To build the workforce plan, Yahoo started in the first year by having HR work with the finance department on budget items. It created a profiling tool to plan headcount by levels and develop job descriptions and pay ranges. In the second year, the finance department asked HR to work ahead of the budget process, and so it built a system to keep track of the progress with the workforce plan. Now, HR is starting a talent review program in high-potential areas, including identifying top talent and developing steps to retain them. At senior executive and higher levels, this means assessing development needs as well as beginning work on a succession plan. Next year, the program will add product management and business leader groups.

Source: *HR Focus* 2004.

Table 16-2 Central questions for designing the personnel recruitment process in marketing and sales

- Which are the primary target groups for personnel recruitment?
- Which communication media should be used for approaching potential new employees?
- Which information and arguments will be used to encourage potential new employees to join the company?
- Which requirement profiles will be applied to potential new employees?
- Which selection methods will be applied to test potential new employees?

Regarding **target groups for personnel recruitment**, we have to differentiate between target groups inside and outside the company (see also Ivancevich 2004). Important external target groups for personnel recruitment in marketing and sales are:

- university graduates
- employees of competitors
- employees of customers
- individuals with marketing and sales experience in other industries (e.g. in industries with similar marketing and sales tasks).

Relevant **communication media for approaching potential new employees** include:

- job ads in newspapers and magazines
- job ads in online job marketplaces
- direct approach
- indirect approach via job recruiters (called headhunters)
- recruiting events at universities

Figure 16-2 Example of a company website informing about career opportunities (www.loreal.com)

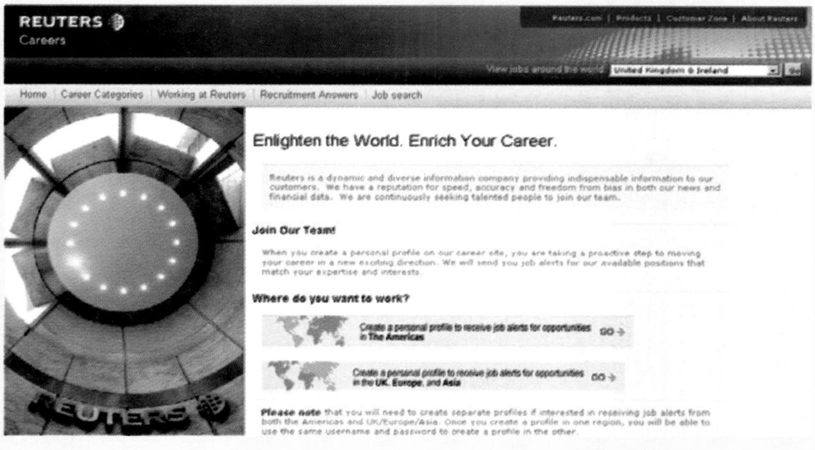

Figure 16-3 Example of a company website informing visitors about international career opportunities (www.reuters.com)

- trade fairs and exhibitions focused on establishing contact between companies and potential employees
- the company's website (see screenshots in Figures 16-2 and 16-3).

When determining the requirement profiles that should be met by potential marketing and sales employees, the tasks involved in the respective job need to be considered. Therefore, a comprehensive job analysis needs to be performed outlining the job's core duties, responsibilities and special stress factors (e.g. extensive travelling associated with salesforce jobs).

Important categories of criteria addressed in the resulting profiles are:

- expert knowledge
- analytical and conceptual skills
- soft skills
- personality traits.

(See also Figure 16-4.)

Expert knowledge comprises both general and business-specific knowledge. Expert knowledge can be acquired by means of specific training or directly on the job.

In the area of **analytical and conceptual skills**, intelligence is a key construct, generally defined as 'the global capacity to act purposefully, to think rationally, and to deal effectively with one's environment' (see Kaplan and Saccuzzo 2005). Here, general cognitive abilities play a major role. These skills can be assessed by operational intelligence, content intelligence and the knowledge of special problem-solving strategies (see Figure 16-4). Aspects of operational intelligence are processing speed (e.g. working speed), memory (e.g. short- or long-term active memory or recognition skills), creativity (e.g. creative ideas, ability to look at things from different perspectives) and processing capacity (e.g. processing of complex information, logical thinking). Aspects of content intelligence are verbal, numerical and spatial-figural thinking (see, e.g., Jäger *et al.* 1997).

Soft skills refer to a person's social competence, which is the ability to interact successfully with other people. In the context of the skills required by marketing and sales employees, this specifically concerns:

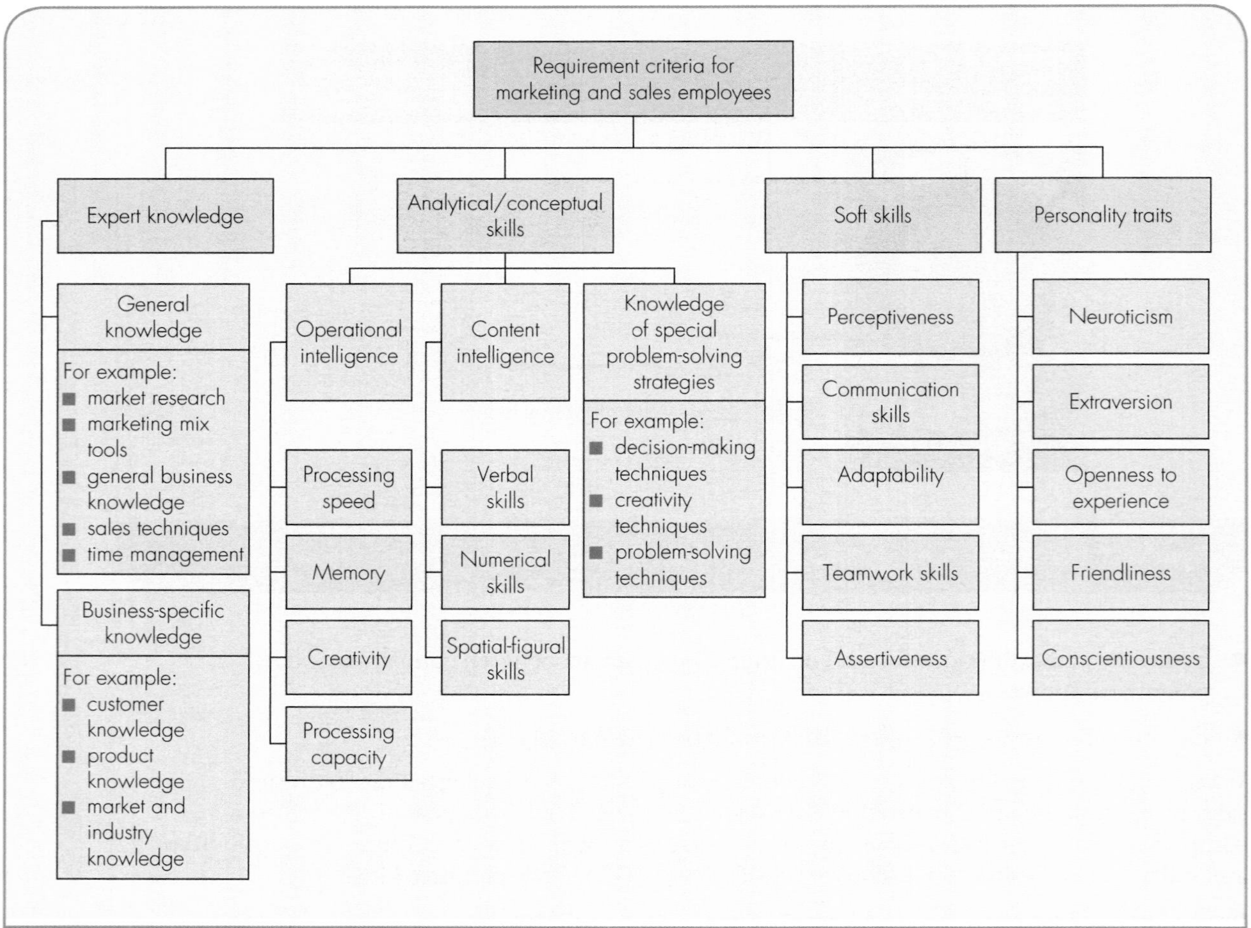

Figure 16-4 Categorization of requirement criteria for marketing and sales employees

- perceptiveness (i.e. the ability to identify with others)
- communication skills
- adaptability (i.e. the ability to interact with other persons in a flexible and situation-specific manner)
- teamwork skills (i.e. the ability to collaborate and to deal with conflicts)
- assertiveness (i.e. the ability to act confidently and in a self-assured manner).

Personality traits are relatively constant characteristics that concern the non-cognitive aspects of a person's personality structure. An individual's personality can be characterized in numerous ways. The following five traits can be used in this regard:

1. neuroticism (anxious, labile, depressed vs peaceful, relaxed, balanced, secure)
2. extroversion (sociable, talkative, active vs quiet, reserved, shy)
3. openness to experience (imaginative, intellectually curious, behaviorally flexible vs dogmatic, shallow)
4. friendliness (trusting, cooperative, sympathetic vs cynical, callous, antagonistic)
5. conscientiousness (reliable, well-organized, diligent vs lax, disorganized, lackadaisical).

In psychology, these traits are often referred to as the 'big five' (see Costa and McCrae 1992).

Figure 16-5 Example of an advertisement for a marketing and sales position detailing the job responsibilities and requirement profile

The ad pictured in Figure 16-5 provides an example of a company job advertisement that is specific in terms of the requirement profile of the potential candidate and their core duties.

A particularly intensive discussion in the literature centers on the traits that should be searched for in potential management staff. This issue is closely connected to **'great man' theories**, which are based on the premise that it is possible to make generalized statements about the typical traits of successful leaders (see Bass 1981; Stogdill 1974). This approach is likewise relevant in conjunction with the charismatic leadership concept (see, e.g., Bass and Avolio 1990, 1993; Dubinsky *et al.* 1995, as well as Hauser 1999, for an overview). However, such trait-based approaches to leadership have received plenty of criticism for their disregard of situational circumstances, and their negligence of the interaction between the traits of superiors and the traits, expectations and requirements of employees.

Table 16-3 Degree of suitability of various selection methods with respect to different selection criteria for marketing and sales positions

Selection criteria / Selection methods	Expert knowledge	Analytical and conceptual skills	Soft skills/ personality traits
Examination of the application material	+ +	0	0/+
Obtaining references	+ +	+	+ +
Job interviews (individual interviews)	+ +	0/+	+ +
Assessment center	+ +	+ +	+ +
Simulations (e.g. in-basket test)	0	+	+
Group discussion	+	0	+ +
Role plays	0/+	0	+ +
Case studies	+	+ +	+
Performance tests	+ +	0/+	0
Intelligence tests	0	+ +	0
Psychological tests	0	0	+ +
Graphological report	0	0	0/+
Suitability: + + high, + medium, 0 low			

A wide range of methods (for detailed information, see Höft and Funke 2001; Schuler 2000; Schuler and Marcus 2001) can be used for **selecting potential new employees**. Table 16-3 lists some common selection methods, along with their degree of suitability for assessing the selection criteria of interest. Some of the methods will be discussed in more detail below.

Role plays usually simulate interactive situations between (mostly) two persons in an in-house context or during customer contact. In an in-house context, for example, a simulated staff meeting can be used to assess the leadership conduct and soft skills of the applicant. Simulating a customer contact situation allows for an evaluation of the applicant's degree of customer orientation, their interactive behavior during customer contact and their ability to cope with stress (see Stock 2003).

Test procedures are standardized, routinely applicable procedures for measuring and evaluating the characteristics of the tested individual (see Sarges and Wottawa 2001; Schuler 2000). Suitable methods for assessing applicants in marketing and sales include performance tests (e.g. written test of methodical competence for a market research position), intelligence tests (e.g. for evaluating numerical cognitive abilities for a marketing control job) as well as personality tests (e.g. for evaluating degree of assertiveness for the field salesforce team). Personality tests aim to analyze the personality profile of an applicant, thus providing the basis for determining whether or not the applicant's personality matches the respective job requirements (for an example of personality

Table 16-4 Selected personality scales for identifying the personality profile of applicants, according to the California Psychological Inventory (CPI) (see Gough and Bradley 1996; Jones *et al.* 2003)

Scale	Purpose of scale
Flexibility	Identification of people who are flexible and who like change as well as variety, but are easily bored by routine and everyday experience
Self-control	Indicator for people who try to control emotions and temper, and who are self-disciplined
Sociability	Identification of people with a sociable and agreeable temperament, who are outgoing and enjoy actively participating in group activities
Tolerance	Indicator for the degree of tolerance of others' beliefs and values; fair-minded, reasonable and tactful attitude

dimensions that can be identified within the scope of such tests, see Table 16-4; for more information on personality tests, see Scholz 2000).

Assessment centers provide a structured approach to selecting new marketing and sales employees: several applicants are presented with certain challenges, while their performance in fulfilling the tasks is assessed by a group of observers (see Goffin *et al.* 1996). Assessment centers are especially well-suited to hiring management staff and young professionals. When deciding whether to conduct an assessment center or not, it should be considered that the conceptualization and implementation of an assessment center is associated with significant costs (see Cook and Herche 1992).

Within the scope of an assessment center, various tasks can be assigned to the applicants, including, say, giving lectures or presentations, participating in group discussions, solving analytical problems, and analyzing case studies (see Focus on Marketing 16-2 for an example of an assessment center).

Focus on Marketing 16-2 Example of an assessment process for call center agents

The Vodafone experience

Making its assessment centers more fun is all part of the strategy that telecoms giant Vodafone uses to ensure it picks the right recruits for its call centers. Vodafone recruited around 1,400 people for its call centers last year, and all of them participated in a Vodafone Experience or 'VE' day – an assessment center that the telecoms giant is particularly proud of.

On VE Days, candidates go through role-plays, interviews and other tools, depending on their role, but one word you won't hear is 'assessment'. 'People don't like the word,' says Andy Hill, head of resourcing; 'they get a little scared. We want to relax them and put a bit of fun into it, so we've taken the word out.'

The thinking behind the assessment model is that from the moment people see the job advertisement to the moment they join the company, they are learning more and more about Vodafone. The idea is to make the transition in the first few weeks of a new job a lot easier. Hill

Focus on Marketing 16-2 (Continued)

explains: 'When candidates meet us face-to-face, there are tours around the facility, there are presentations by line managers. It's interactive, so they get a realistic job preview. And the more engaged they become, the better the customer service they give – they become an advocate of the brand.'

Vodafone develops its assessment programs in conjunction with Reed Consulting. Julie Lowe, Reed's head of assessment services, explains that 'It's a case of designing materials that predict future performance accurately.'

There are two main stages. The first is pre-screening, which involves telephone interviews and online personality measures, and the second is VE days. The latest innovation in pre-screening is a workstyles-fit questionnaire that works as a self-selection tool. Typical questions concern the kind of culture candidates would like to work in and how they feel about hierarchy and taking ownership of issues. The results are then mapped against the culture of Vodafone and what it expects of people in their role.

Vodafone feeds back [detailed] information on how people performed into their development plans – as no one is ever a 100 percent fit.

The assessment process is constantly reevaluated, with employees being assessed regularly on their background and personality. It also tracks new hires on attrition, sickness absence, performance in training and performance in the job.

The process clearly works. As Hill says: 'We recruit fewer people than before because our assessment process has had such a positive effect on both attrition and performance. There's a key attrition measure in call centers at 13 weeks into the job. It's the first pinch-point. We've improved ours dramatically by selecting the right people at the outset.'

Source: Smethurst 2006.

16.1.3 Employee Performance Appraisal in Marketing and Sales

Employee performance appraisal refers to the assessment of the characteristics and performance of marketing and sales employees. Employee performance appraisals are essential, since they provide a substantial basis for further human resource management activities. For example, they are used for planning human resource development measures (e.g. training or promotions, see Section 16.1.4) and influence decisions on compensation (see Section 16.1.5). Moreover, it has been demonstrated that a systematic and fair appraisal of marketing and sales employees significantly boosts their motivation and performance (see DeCarlo and Leigh 1996; MacKenzie *et al.* 1993), and can contribute to lowering staff turnover rates (see Pettijohn *et al.* 1999).

When designing employee performance appraisal systems, the following questions particularly need to be addressed:

- Who is being appraised?
- Who is the appraiser?
- What aspects are being appraised?
- What are the appraisal criteria?
- To what extent will the appraisee(s) be informed about the appraisal results?

With respect to the question of who is being appraised, a differentiation can be made between the appraisal of an individual person and a team appraisal. An appraisal that targets individual persons can be conducted on various hierarchy levels (ranging from, say, a salesforce employee to the sales director). Relevant teams in marketing and sales mainly comprise new product development teams and customer support teams.

The **appraisal** is usually conducted by a direct superior (e.g. performance appraisals of field salesforce employees are conducted by the manager of a regional sales office). Moreover, it is customary for superiors to be appraised by their team, and for teams and employees to perform self-appraisals or to be appraised by their peers or customers. Such an extensive appraisal perspective is applied, for example, by the 360-degree feedback method, which aggregates the different appraisal perspectives to a cumulative result (for additional information on this method, see Gerpott 2000; Nicolai 2005). Table 16-5 provides an example of a 360-degree feedback form and Focus on Marketing 16-3 describes how such a system can be implemented company-wide.

Focus on Marketing 16-3 Example of online-based 360-degree feedback

Anonymous 360-degree feedback drives Vauxhall Strategy

In theory, the concept of 360-degree feedback provides the HR professional with one of the most enlightening and potentially effective appraisal tools. The reality, however, has meant it hasn't always delivered on these fronts. It can be cumbersome to implement such a system and its use is blighted by confidentiality and impartiality issues. The internet has gone a long way towards providing a suitable medium for easing the implementation of 360-degree feedback, but there is a lot more to it than simply migrating a paper-based system to an online environment. To maximize the benefits, what's needed is a clearly thought-out approach which links the system to a wider business and people strategy. This was the line taken by car manufacturer Vauxhall. 'We had a paper-based system, but it was difficult to administrate, rate of returns was low, results came back late and it tied up resource,' says Richard Pennington, Vauxhall's manager of planning and development. 'Our starting point was to use the new system to help us move towards a performance-driven culture – tying it in with results, business objectives, and behaviors.'

Vauxhall employed the services of performance management consultancy Getfeedback which devised an online system that embedded the 360-degree feedback facility into a wider performance management system called Performance and Development Review (P&DR). 'Having a third party involved adds a degree of trust,' says Pennington. 'Employees know the system is entirely anonymous and any comment non-attributable.' The system is accessed through Vauxhall's intranet, Socrates, and provides three tiers of access: to individual employees, to managers and to administrators – the latter is the only group who can see everything on the system.

Vauxhall will be starting the appraisal and performance management cycle when the 360-degree feedback is carried out. The system automatically reminds all those involved in the process to return their feedback and this generally takes around four weeks. Questions cover the organization's cultural priorities of 'people development', 'act as one company', 'product and customer focus', 'stretch' and 'sense of urgency'. There must be a 100 percent response from those who have been nominated to supply feedback before the system will generate a report. If you continually get no response from an individual, however, it is possible to delete them from the list. During the first six weeks of the process, employees and their managers review the previous year's performance, including the 360-degree feedback, then discuss and agree new business and behavioral objectives. If the feedback is lower than the standard in a certain area, such as communication, employee and manager will discuss how to address it and review it during their mid-period review.

Source: Weekes 2003.

Table 16-5 Example of a 360-degree feedback form (according to Slater 1997, pp. 188ff.)

Characteristics	Performance criteria	Superior	Peer	Employee
Vision	Has developed and projected a clear, straightforward, customer-oriented vision/alignment for his/her own sphere of responsibility Is forward-thinking, expands horizons, promotes a visionary approach			
Customer focus/quality orientation	Listens to customers and gives highest priority to customer satisfaction (including internal customers) Conveys and demonstrates enthusiasm for excellent performance in all job-related aspects			
. . .	. . .			

Personal characteristics such as those discussed in Section 16.1.2 (expert knowledge, personality traits, etc.) can be chosen as performance criteria on which to assess the appraisees.

With a **behavior-based approach**, the quality of the employee activities is evaluated, including aspects such as work conduct and habits (e.g. work planning, working speed, perseverance, ability to cope with stress), behavior towards peers and superiors (e.g. open-mindedness, helpfulness, cooperation), leadership style (e.g. motivation, delegation, assertiveness and control) as well as personal image (e.g. articulateness, appearance, manners). In contrast to this, the **results-oriented approach** bases the appraisal on objective outcome criteria (e.g. sales realized by a sales employee).

An approach that combines behavior-based and results-oriented appraisal techniques is the **balanced scorecard** concept (see Kaplan and Norton 2003), which is the method of choice for appraising managerial performance. This method derives a number of behavior- and results-related key performance indicators from the corporate and marketing strategy (see Section 15.5.4 for information about the use of key performance indicators in a marketing and sales controlling context) and compiles them in a scorecard (see Kaplan and Norton 2003). In this process several perspectives are taken into consideration (see Figure 16-6).

These four perspectives can be characterized as:

1 the customer perspective, which considers customer needs and requirements

2 the internal process perspective, which allows for an evaluation of the effectiveness of internal business processes in realizing the goals of other perspectives

3 the learning and growth perspective, which refers to company-internal requirements (e.g. employee qualification, information flow) that need to be met for the realization of the other perspectives' goals

4 the financial perspective, which provides information about the impact of the executed strategy on financial outcomes.

All four perspectives are interdependent: the realization of the objectives of one perspective is often a prerequisite for the realization of the objectives of another perspective.

Financial perspective

Sub-goals	Measures	Achievement ratio
Sales for current year: 70 million euros	Increased sales with existing customers, acquisition of new customers	60%
Contribution margin f. current year: 30 million euros	See above, plus cost reduction in logistics	55%
. . .	. . .	. . .

Customer perspective

Sub-goals	Measures	Achievement ratio
Customer satisfaction index for key accounts: 82	Development of a key account management program	45%
Acquisition of 5 new customers	Trade fair/customer visits, mailings	80%
. . .	. . .	. . .

Sales strategy

Internal process perspective

Sub-goals	Measures	Achievement ratio
Reduction of order processing time by 20%	Restructuring of order processing workflow	10%
Processing of incoming complaints within three days	Implementation of an IT-based complaint management system	100%
. . .	. . .	. . .

Sub-goals	Measures	Achievement ratio
Development of a knowledge management system	Essential contribution within the scope of the project team	75%
All employees are familiar with the CRM module	All employees attend and successfully complete seminars	33%
. . .	. . .	. . .

Learning and growth perspective

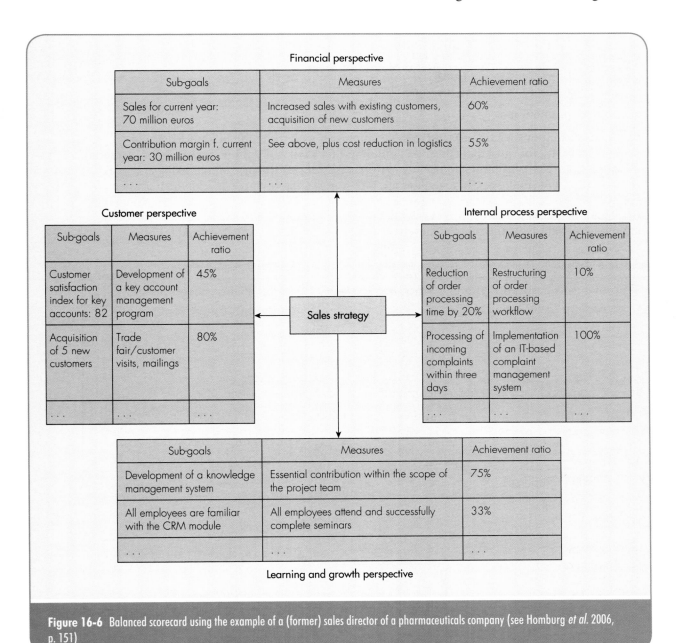

Figure 16-6 Balanced scorecard using the example of a (former) sales director of a pharmaceuticals company (see Homburg *et al.* 2006, p. 151)

A set of key performance indicators are identified to capture the balanced performance on each perspective. Thereby short- and long-term, easily quantifiable and decision-dependent qualitative, monetary and non-monetary, early and late indicators are considered (see Figure 16-6 for an example). A balanced scorecard can be defined on various organizational levels – for instance, on the corporate level, on the business unit level, on the functional level or on the individual level.

Finally, when designing an employee performance appraisal system, a decision has to be made regarding the extent to which the appraisee(s) will be informed about the results. In this context, appraisals can be conducted with or without the knowledge of the person or group being appraised. Furthermore, the results of the performance appraisal can be communicated to the respective person or group in written form or during a personal meeting.

16.1.4 Human Resource Development in Marketing and Sales

Human resource development comprises the following areas:

- continuing education/training measures
- employee promotion.

Training aims to provide both new and existing employees with the required knowledge and necessary skills. It is obvious that effective continuing education and training measures for marketing and sales employees contribute significantly to the successful performance of marketing and sales tasks on the part of employees. In the sales area, however, human resource development is often neglected (in particular with respect to non-management staff) (see Ganesan *et al.* 1993; Homburg *et al.* 2006). In addition to providing knowhow and skills, human resource development can boost employee motivation. At the company level, the design of continuing education and training

Table 16-6 Applicability of various types of continuing education and training measures in marketing and sales

Type of continuing education and training measure		Primary content: Expert knowledge	Primary content: Analytical and conceptual skills	Primary content: Soft skills/ personality traits	Example of applications in marketing and sales
Individual	Seminars	x	x	x	Seminar on the measurement and evaluation of customer satisfaction
Individual	Training courses	x	x	x	Training in conflict management
Individual	Workshops	x	x	x	Workshop on using creativity techniques
Individual	Courses	x	x	x	Courses in data-mining methods
Individual	Conferences	x			Field salesforce conference for exchanging market trends
Individual	Mentoring/coaching		x	x	Mentoring programs for new high-potential employees
Individual	Learning by observation	x	x	x	Job entrants observe how experienced sales employees serve customers
General/ autodidactic	Training manuals	x		x	Manuals instructing on product application techniques
General/ autodidactic	Videos	x		x	Videos demonstrating and teaching conversation/dialog techniques
General/ autodidactic	E-learning	x	(x)		Interactive language courses

Focus on Marketing 16-4 Example of training for salespeople

Peugeot opts for blended learning

Peugeot is set to revolutionize the training of 1,500 salespeople at its UK dealerships by switching to a blended learning approach.

The move will mark the replacement of its current two-week residential introductory sales course with just five days of instructor-led training and a significant component of online learning.

'Much of the current course involves teaching knowledge-based material, which can just as easily be taught online,' explains David Davies, Peugeot's sales training manager.

'The new programme will reduce the amount of time spent away from work and should triple the number of people able to take the course.'

The training, provided free to dealers, will now involve a mix of pre-course preparation, a two-day residential introduction course, online learning and three days of practical training.

Davies admits that the new approach calls for a change in culture. 'Managers need to accept that it is OK for staff to spend two hours learning online,' he says.

Source: IT Training 2002.

measures for marketing and sales employees is derived from human resource planning for these business units (see Section 16.1.1) while, on an individual level, it is based on the results of employee performance appraisal (see Section 16.1.3).

There is a broad spectrum of types of **continuing education and training measures**. Table 16-6 shows a corresponding overview. The various types of continuing education and training vary in their suitability to convey individual contents (expert knowledge, analytical and conceptual skills, soft skills, personality traits). Table 16-6 also provides a rating of these applications in a marketing and sales context. See Focus on Marketing 16-4 for an example of sales training.

A key issue in designing continuing education and training measures concerns the definition of the target group. In particular, a differentiation can be made between functional and hierarchy-based target group definitions. With a functional target group definition, the continuing education and training measure is geared towards employees of a specific functional department (e.g. the regional sales organization). A hierarchy-based target group definition applies a cross-functional approach to include employees on a specific hierarchy level (e.g. all middle-management employees in marketing and sales). Another decision concerns the selection of an instructor for the continuing education and training measure, from either company-internal or company-external individuals.

With respect to job training for new employees (with limited professional experience), in particular, trainee programs and learning on the job can be distinguished. Learning on the job is characterized by the immediate assumption of responsibility (and the associated motivational effects) as well as realistic conditions. In contrast, trainee programs provide the opportunity to gradually familiarize job entrants with the company.

In the context of employee promotion, a relevant set of criteria for promotion decisions needs to be defined. General characteristics (expert knowledge, analytical and conceptual skills, soft skills and personality traits) that are desirable in marketing and sales managers have already been discussed in Section 16.1.2. In company practice, these general criteria are to be supplemented by job-specific criteria (e.g. special language skills as required for an internationally oriented sales director position, or assertiveness as an indispensable personality trait for a senior position in key account management).

16.1.5 Employee Compensation in Marketing and Sales

Decisions about the employee compensation system concern the pay and benefits that employees and managers receive from a company in return for their work. In this context, decisions have to be made regarding:

- compensation level
- salary dynamics
- types of compensation
- variable compensation.

Decisions regarding **compensation level** relate to the question of where the company generally wants to position itself in the human resource market with regard to the amount of pay and benefits that employees and managers will receive. This decision is closely connected to the standards (e.g. expected performance) that the company prescribes for its employees and managers: as a rule, the higher these standards, the higher the compensation level. However, it can be observed in practice that companies can somewhat compensate for competitive disadvantages arising from the compensation level by providing other perks and amenities (e.g. job security, attractive tasks, company culture).

Decisions regarding **salary dynamics** concern the speed at which the compensation level changes over time. In this respect, there are two basic design options, which are illustrated in Figure 16-7: Model A is characterized by a rather low starting salary but a fast progression rate. In contrast, the starting salary in Model B is fairly high, whereas the progression rate is rather low. The advantage of Model A lies in the fact that it provides relatively strong material incentives to advance in the company. On the downside, companies with such salary dynamics will probably encounter

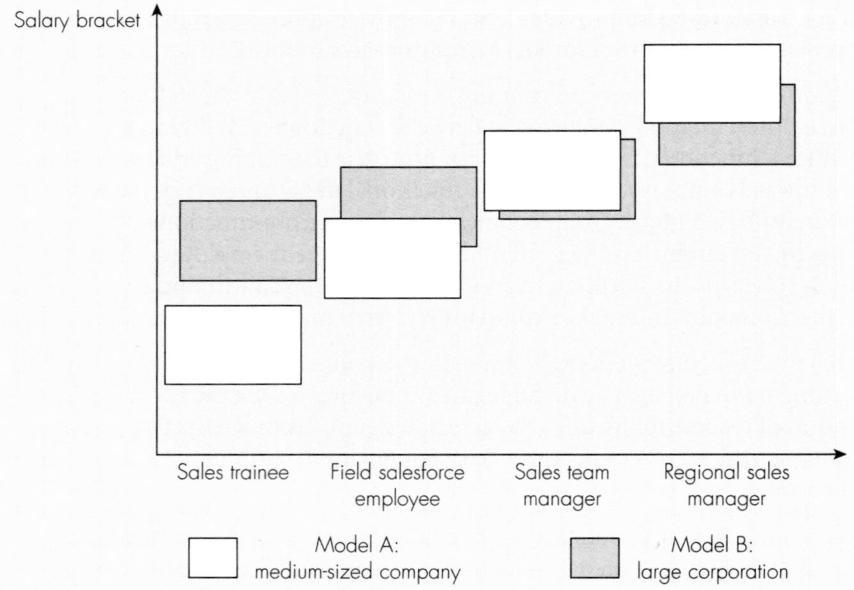

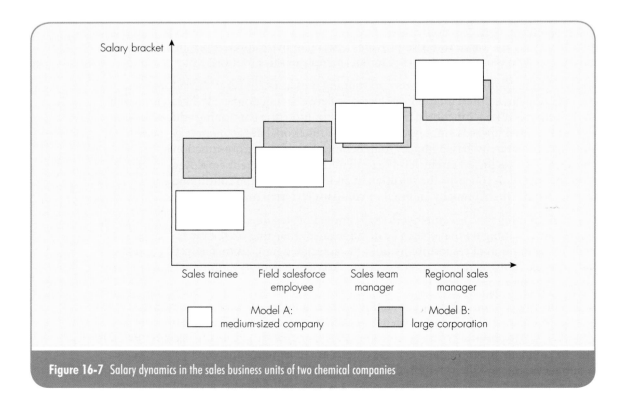

Figure 16-7 Salary dynamics in the sales business units of two chemical companies

difficulties in hiring employees. In contrast, companies deploying Model B are able to offer new employees comparably attractive salaries.

Types of compensation include monetary and non-monetary benefits. Monetary benefits can be of a direct (e.g. salary, bonus) or indirect (e.g. employee insurance plans, employee stock ownership programs) nature. Company cars (predominantly for field salesforce employees) are an example of non-monetary benefits commonly used in sales and marketing.

Decisions regarding **variable compensation** in marketing and sales are extremely important (for more information, see Dannenberg 2001; Maas 2001; Ramaswami and Singh 2003; Schröder and Schweizer 1999). Extreme alternatives include exclusively fixed or variable compensation. In the case of exclusively fixed compensation, an invariable amount of money is paid for the activities performed over a certain period of time (e.g. monthly). This occurs irrespective of the results or performance. This salary model can be practical for tasks that have no direct impact on results (e.g. for marketing control or market research jobs) (see also Becker 1995). When using this salary model, companies largely abstain from deploying compensation as a motivational tool.

If the remuneration system in marketing and sales should contain variable compensation components, several fundamental decisions have to be made. A first decision relates to the **proportion of variable and fixed compensation.** It can be assumed that the variable component has to exceed a certain minimum threshold in order to have a motivational effect.

A second crucial decision when designing a variable compensation system concerns the selection of **criteria** on which the variable compensation component is based. Please refer to our discussion of employee performance appraisals in Section 16.1.3 for a review of possible performance criteria. Here, we distinguished between behavior-based and results-oriented appraisals and the balanced scorecard was described as a frame of reference for an employee performance appraisal. In company practice, it is advisable to give equal consideration to the four dimensions of the balanced scorecard, in order to prevent an overly strong focus on optimizing particular performance indicators.

Finally, when designing a variable compensation system, the **structure of the interrelationship between results/performance** (measured on the basis of the defined criteria) and the **amount of the variable compensation** has to be specified (for additional information about results-oriented compensation systems, see also Jenkins *et al.* 1998; Joseph and Kalwani 1998; Menguc and Barker 2003). Figure 16-8 presents four basic models, each of which can be used with or without an upper limit. The different motivational effects of the various models are self-evident.

16.2 Personnel Supervision in Marketing and Sales

While the first section of this chapter focused on the design of personnel management systems, this section concentrates on the supervision of staff by their respective individual superiors. The basis of this discussion is leadership research, which deals with the effects of leadership styles on management success (see Neuberger 1985; Staehle 1999). This research discipline has its roots in psychology – mainly industrial and organizational psychology.

Leadership styles are of particular relevance within the scope of personnel supervision in marketing and sales. Generally they refer to the typical conduct that a superior normally displays when interacting with employees (see Northouse 2004). Leadership style thus describes the basic leadership conduct that superiors display towards their employees on a relatively consistent basis in different situations (see Drenth 2001). The respective leadership styles of managers play such a significant role in sales and marketing because they have a major impact on employee motivation, goal and role clarity, as well as employees' customer-oriented behavior (see Hartline *et al.* 2000). In many

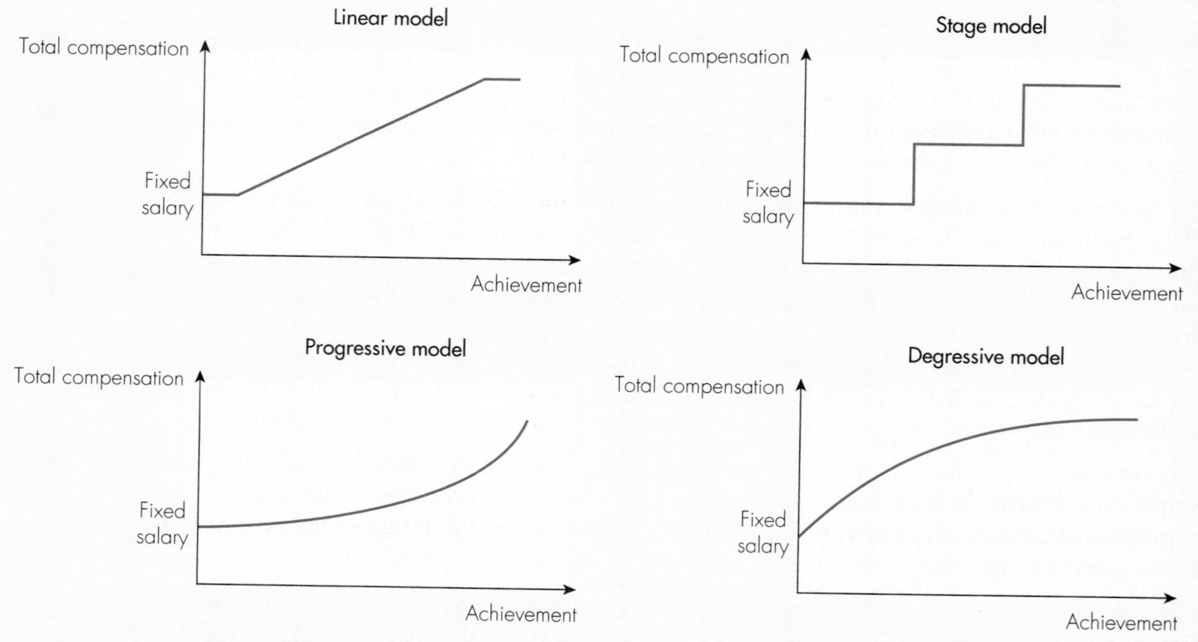

Figure 16-8 Possible distribution functions for results-oriented compensation systems (according to Homburg and Jensen 1999, p. 28)

companies, it can be observed that an inappropriate leadership style in sales and marketing can cause considerable productivity problems (see Homburg *et al.* 2006).

A well-known approach to **characterizing leadership styles** was developed on the basis of the **Iowa Studies** (see Lewin 1948). Here, leadership styles are categorized according to the decision-making authority granted to employees by the superior. Three basic types of leadership styles are distinguished, as follows:

1 With an **autocratic leadership style**, the superior strictly dictates the activities and objectives of the employees, so that individual employees have virtually no decision-making power. Neither long-term goals nor the assessment criteria used by the superior are transparent to employees.

2 Managers with a **democratic leadership style** discuss activities and objectives with their employees. To a certain extent, superiors take employee suggestions into consideration. Goals and assessment criteria are largely transparent.

3 In the case of a **laissez-faire leadership style**, the activities of employees are generally not controlled or appraised. Superiors take a more passive approach. Accordingly, this style is a form of 'non-management'.

Another well-known approach is the **Ohio State Model** (see Fleishman 1953). This model has identified two dimensions of leadership conduct: task orientation (originally called 'initiating structure') and people orientation (originally called 'consideration').

Strongly task-oriented leadership is characterized by superiors paying a great deal of attention to the fulfillment of assigned tasks on the part of employees. Task-oriented managers:

- communicate company objectives regularly and proactively to their employees
- align the activities of employees to specific performance goals
- transfer direct responsibility for achieving performance goals to employees
- focus strongly on performance when complimenting employees
- use performance-based techniques of employee motivation.

Superiors that are **people-oriented (social-emotional leaders)** prioritize their interpersonal relationships with employees. Managers who are strongly people oriented:

- show appreciation for their employees on both a personal and professional level
- take into consideration the personal and professional goals of their employees
- consider the well-being of employees when making decisions
- strive for good relationships with employees
- involve employees in the decision-making process
- create a work atmosphere in which employees can speak openly and freely with their superiors
- personally advocate and support employee interests vis-à-vis third parties.

These two dimensions have also often been used in studies examining leadership behavior in the area of marketing and sales (see, e.g., Kohli 1989; Stock 2003; Teas and Horrell 1981). For example, with new sales and marketing tasks that are not routine in nature, a performance-based, task-oriented leadership style is viewed positively by employees, since this style allows for more clearly defined objectives and more effective structuring of tasks (see Kohli 1989). Moreover, the effect that leadership style has on employee satisfaction also depends on the characteristics and traits of employees. For example, it has been empirically shown that a people-oriented, social leadership style tends to increase satisfaction on the part of experienced sales and marketing employees. Conversely, with less experienced sales and marketing employees, it is a performance-based, task-oriented leadership style that improves the level of employee satisfaction (see Kohli 1989).

Numerous studies have concluded that employee productivity tends to be highest in conjunction with a cooperative leadership style. Furthermore, these two dimensions of leadership behavior play a decisive role with regard to an employee's customer orientation.

Summary

This chapter discussed the two facets of human resource management: personnel management, which refers to the design and structure of human resource management systems, and personnel supervision, which is associated with the direct management of employees by their superiors. Crucial to effective human resource management is the planning and organization of employees according to their characteristics, skills and qualifications. The recruitment of employees is therefore based on the workforce requirements determined by human resource planning. Continuous education and employee promotion is the key to highly motivated, high-performing employees. Decisions regarding compensation levels relate to the question of where the company generally wants to position itself in the human resource market with regard to the amount of pay and benefits that employees and managers will receive. The leadership styles and techniques applied by superiors also influence employees' motivation and performance.

Case Study: Secrets of an HR Superstar

General Electric Co.'s legendary reputation in talent management owes much to one man: William J. Conaty. In his 40 years at GE, including 13 as head of human resources, he helped to shape the modern face of HR. Conaty took a department that's often treated as a support function and turned it into a high-level business partner, fostering a deep bench of talent and focusing attention on the need for continuous leadership development. Among other things, he helped manage the seamless transition from Welch to Jeffrey R. Immelt in 2001 and was critical in shaping a new vision of global leadership that emphasizes such traits as imagination and inclusiveness. At 61, Conaty is now easing into retirement, having passed the top job over to long-time HR colleague John Lynch earlier this year while agreeing to stay on to handle GE's labor union negotiations this summer. As he winds up affairs at GE, Conaty shared his advice for nurturing leaders.

DARE TO DIFFERENTIATE Relentlessly assessing and grading employees build[s] organizational vitality and foster[s] a true meritocracy, in Conaty's view. Employees must be constantly judged, ranked, and rewarded or punished for their performance.

CONSTANTLY RAISE THE BAR Leaders continually seek to improve performance, both their own and their team members'. 'The one reason executives fail at GE is they stop learning,' says Conaty.

DON'T BE FRIENDS WITH THE BOSS Too often, says Conaty, HR executives make the mistake of focusing on the priorities and needs of the CEO. That diminishes the powerful role of being an employee advocate. 'If you just get closer to the CEO, you're dead,' says Conaty.

BECOME EASY TO REPLACE Great leaders develop great succession plans. Insecure leaders are intimidated by them. 'I can go business by business and tell you where we're strongest and

Case Study (Continued)

weakest on succession. It all comes down to having an executive who doesn't want to admit someone else could do their job,' says Conaty.

BE INCLUSIVE Within every organization, there's a tendency to favor people you know. That can undermine success.

FREE UP OTHERS TO DO THEIR JOBS When it comes to the CEO, says Conaty, 'one of my jobs is to take things off his desk, not put things on his desk.'

KEEP IT SIMPLE Most organizations require simple, focused, and disciplined communications. 'You can't move 325,000 people with mixed messaging and thousands of initiatives,' notes Conaty.

Source: Secrets of an HR superstar, by Brady, D. (2007) *Business Week*, 4029, 9 April 66–67.

Discussion Questions

1. After reading the case study, which of the ideas mentioned here do you think are most important for the long-term success of an organization?
2. What might a job ad for a potential marketing manager at GE look like? (Please think of the requirement profile according to Conaty's ideas of a successful leader.)
3. What leadership style would best describe a successful GE manager?

Key Terms

Amount of the variable compensation *549*
Analytical and conceptual skills *537*
Appraisal *543*
Assessment centers *541*
Autocratic leadership style *550*
Balanced scorecard *544*
Behavior-based approach *544*
Characterizing leadership styles *550*
Communication media for approaching potential new employees *536*
Compensation level *548*
Continuing education and training measures *547*
Criteria *549*
Democratic leadership style *550*
Expert knowledge *537*
'Great man' theories *539*
Hiring mistakes *533*
Human resource management *532*
Iowa Studies *550*
Laissez-faire leadership style *550*
Ohio State Model *550*
People-oriented (social-emotional leaders) *551*
Personality traits *538*
Personnel supervision *532*
Proportion of variable and fixed compensation *549*

References

Bartol, K. and Martin, D. (1998) *Management* (3rd edn). Boston, Mass.
Bass, B. (1981) *Stogdill's Handbook of Leadership: A Survey of Theory and Research* (2nd edn). New York.
Bass, B. and Avolio, B. (1990) *Transformational Leadership Development: Manual for the Multifactor Leadership Questionnaire*. Palo Alto.
Bass, B. and Avolio, B. (1993) Transformational leadership: a response to the critiques, in: Chemers, M. and Ayman, R. (eds) *Leadership Theory and Research: Perspectives and Directions*. San Diego, 49–80.
Becker, F. (1995) Personalmanagement im Marketing, in: Tietz, B., Köhler, R. and Zentes, J. (eds) *Handwörterbuch des Marketing* (2nd edn). Stuttgart, 1989–2019.
Brady, D. (2007) Secrets of an HR superstar, *Business Week*, 4029, 9 April, 66–67.
Cook, R.A. and Herche, J. (1992) Assessment centers: an untapped resource for global salesforce management, *Journal of Personal Selling and Sales Management*, 12, 3, 31–38.
Costa, P.T. and McCrae, R.R. (1992) Normal personality assessment in clinical practice: the NEO personality inventory, *Psychological Assessment*, 4, 1, 5–13.
Dannenberg, H. (2001) *Vertriebsmarketing – Wie Strategien laufen lernen* (4th edn). Neuwied.
DeCarlo, T. and Leigh, T. (1996) Impact of salesperson attraction on sales managers' attributions and feedback, *Journal of Marketing*, 60, 2, 47–66.
Drenth, P.J.D. (2001) *Introduction to Work and Organizational Psychology* (2nd edn). Hove.
Dubinsky, A., Yammarino, F., Jolson, M. and Spangler, W. (1995) Transformational leadership: an initial investigation in sales management, *Journal of Personal Selling & Sales Management*, 15, 2, 17–31.
Fleishman, E. (1953) The description of supervisory behavior, *Journal of Applied Psychology*, 37, 1–6.
Ganesan, S., Weitz, B. and John, G. (1993) Hiring and promotion policies in sales force management: some antecedents and consequences, *Journal of Personal Selling & Sales Management*, 13, 2, 15–26.
Gerpott, T. (2000) 360-Grad-Feedback-Verfahren als spezielle Variante der Mitarbeiterbefragung, in: Domsch, M. and Ladwig, D. (eds) *Handbuch Mitarbeiterbefragung*. Heidelberg, 195–220.
Goffin, R.D., Rothstein, M.G. and Johnson, N.G. (1996) Personality testing and the assessment center: incremental validity for managerial selection, *Journal of Applied Psychology*, 81, 6, 746–756.
Gough, H.G. and Bradley, P. (1996) *CPI Manual* (3rd edn). Palo Alto.
Hartline, M., Maxham, J. and McKee, D. (2000) Corridors of influence in the dissemination of customer-oriented strategy to customer contact service employees, *Journal of Marketing*, 64, 2, 35–50.
Hauser, M. (1999) Theorien charismatischer Führung: kritischer Literaturüberblick und Forschungsanregungen, *Zeitschrift für Betriebswirtschaft*, 69, 9, 1003–1023.
Höft, S. and Funke, U. (2001) Simulationsorientierte Verfahren der Personalauswahl, in: Schuler, H. (ed.) *Lehrbuch der Personalpsychologie*. Göttingen, 135–173.
Homburg, C. and Jensen, O. (1999) Kundenorientierung als Maßstab für Vergütungssysteme, *Frankfurter Allgemeine Zeitung*, 17 May, 28.
Homburg, C., Schäfer, H. and Schneider, J. (2006) *Sales Excellence: Vertriebsmanagement mit System* (4th edn). Wiesbaden.
HR Focus (2004) How a talent management plan can anchor your company's future, October, 7–11.
IT Training (2002) Peugeot opts for blended learning, June, 12.
Ivancevich, J.M. (2004) *Human Resource Management* (9th edn). New York.
Jäger, A., Süß, H. and Beauducel, A. (1997) *Berliner Intelligenzstruktur-Test*. Göttingen.
Jenkins Jr, G.D., Gupta, N., Mitra, A. and Shaw, J.D. (1998) Are financial incentives related to performance? A meta-analytic review of empirical research, *Journal of Applied Psychology*, 83, 5, 777–787.

Jolson, M., Dubinsky, A. and Anderson, R. (1987) Correlates and determinants of sales force tenure: an exploratory study, *Journal of Personal Selling and Sales Management*, 7 (November), 9–27.
Jones, C.J., Livson, N. and Peskin, H. (2003) Longitudinal hierarchical linear modeling analyzes of California psychological inventory data from age 33 to 75: an examination of stability and change in adult personality, *Journal of Personality Assessment*, 80, 3, 294–308.
Joseph, K. and Kalwani, M.U. (1998) The role of bonus pay in salesforce compensation plans, *Industrial Marketing Management*, 27, 2, 147–159.
Kaplan, R. and Norton, D. (2003) *The Balanced Scorecard: Translating Strategy into Action*. Boston, Mass.
Kaplan, R.M. and Saccuzzo, D.P. (2005) *Psychological Testing: Principles, Applications, and Issues* (6th edn). Belmont.
Kohli, A. (1989) Effects of supervisory behavior: the role of individual differences among salespeople, *Journal of Marketing*, 53, 4, 40–50.
Lewin, K. (1948) *Resolving Social Conflicts: Selected Papers on Group Dynamics*. New York.
Lucas, G., Parasuraman, A., Davis, R. and Enis, B. (1987) An empirical study of sales force turnover, *Journal of Marketing*, 51, 4, 34–59.
Maas, M. (2001) *Praxiswissen Vertrieb: Berufseinstieg, Tagesgeschäft und Erfolgsstrategien*. Wiesbaden.
MacKenzie, S., Podsakoff, P. and Fetter, R. (1993) The impact of organizational citizenship behavior on evaluations of sales performance, *Journal of Marketing*, 57, 1, 70–80.
Menguc, B. and Barker, A.T. (2003) The performance effects of outcome-based incentive pay plans on sales organizations: a contextual analysis, *Journal of Personal Selling & Sales Management*, 23, 4, 341–358.
Neuberger, O. (1985) *Führung: Ideologie, Struktur, Verhalten* (2nd edn). Stuttgart.
Nicolai, C. (2005) 360°-feedback, *WISU*, 4, 506–514.
Northouse, P.G. (2004) *Leadership: Theory and Practice* (3rd edn). Thousand Oaks.
Oechsler, W. (2000) *Personal und Arbeit* (7th edn). Munich.
Pettijohn, L., Pettijohn, C. and Taylor, A. (1999) An empirical investigation of the relationship between retail sales force performance appraisals, performance and turnover, *Journal of Marketing Theory and Practice*, 7, 1, 39–52.
Ramaswami, S.N. and Singh, J. (2003) Antecedents and consequences of merit pay fairness for industrial salespeople, *Journal of Marketing*, 67, 4, 46–66.
Sarges, W. and Wottawa, H. (eds) (2001) *Handbuch wirtschaftspsychologischer Testverfahren*. Legerich.
Scholz, C. (2000) *Personalmanagement: Informationsorientierte und verhaltenstheoretische Grundlagen* (5th edn). Munich.
Schröder, G.A. and Schweizer, T. (1999) Anreizsysteme als Steuerungsinstrument in Sparkassen, *Zeitschrift für betriebswirtschaftliche Forschung*, 51, 6, 608–622.
Schuler, H. (2000) *Psychologische Personalauswahl: Einführung in die Berufseignungsdiagnostik* (3rd edn). Göttingen.
Schuler, H. and Marcus, B. (2001) Biographieorientierte Verfahren der Personalauswahl, in: Schuler, H. (ed.) *Lehrbuch der Personalpsychologie*. Göttingen, 175–214.
Slater, R. (1997) *Business is simple: Die 31 Erfolgsgeheimnisse von Jack Welch* (3rd edn). Landsberg/Lech.
Smethurst, S. (2006) Case study: Vodafone, *People Management*, 12, 19, 15.
Staehle, W. (1999) *Management: Eine verhaltenswissenschaftliche Perspektive* (7th edn). Munich.
Stock, R. (2003) Kundenorientierte Personalführung als Schlüssel zur Kundenbindung, in: Bruhn, M. and Homburg, C. (eds) *Handbuch Kundenbindungsmanagement: Grundlagen – Konzepte – Erfahrungen* (4th edn). Wiesbaden.
Stogdill, R. (1974) *Handbook of Leadership*. New York.
Teas, K. and Horrell, J. (1981) Salesperson satisfaction and performance feedback, *Industrial Marketing Management*, 10, 49–57.
Weekes, S. (2003) Anonymous 360°-feedback drives Vauxhall Strategy, *Personnel Today*, 19 August, 16.
www.loreal.com
www.reuters.com

CHAPTER 17

Market Orientation

Contents

Learning Objectives

In this chapter you will become familiar with:

- the various definitions of market orientation as well as an understanding of market-oriented corporate management
- the impact of market orientation on organizational performance
- the way market orientation manifests itself in corporate management, and how it can be promoted
- how market orientation is expressed in various functional departments
- the differences between external customer orientation, internal customer orientation and competitor orientation in the various functional departments
- the conflicts between marketing, sales and the other functional departments in the company that can negatively affect the implementation of a market orientation.

17.1 Definitions of Market Orientation

Market orientation comprises two concepts. First, it can be understood as market-oriented corporate management: the orientation of organizational culture, organizational structure and organizational processes towards the firm's customers and competitors. Second, market orientation refers to market-related activities. Here, market orientation refers to the degree to which the product offered by the firm and the customer-related behavior of the firm correspond to customer needs and competitive requirements. Such an understanding of market orientation embraces both an orientation towards customers and an orientation towards competitors (see also Ketchen *et al.* 2007; Li and Calantone 1998; Marinova 2004, as well as the discussion of market analysis, including buyers and competitors, in Chapter 3).

As we will show in this chapter, market orientation is not limited to the marketing and sales departments. Instead, it refers to a specific orientation of management, and to specific activities in various organizational units of the firm, including top management, marketing/sales, R&D, purchasing, operations, finance and accounting, human resources and the IT department.

17.1.1 Market Orientation of Organizational Culture

A first element of market-oriented corporate management is the market orientation of **organizational culture**. Here, market orientation can be observed at the following three cultural layers (see also Homburg and Pflesser 2000):

1. the layer of values
2. the layer of norms
3. the layer of artefacts.

Values form the basic layer of organizational culture. They represent the firm's basic objectives at a relatively high level of abstraction and are shared by the firm's employees. The following values support the firm's market orientation (Gebhardt *et al.* 2006; Homburg and Pflesser 2000):

- appreciation of employees/respect
- cross-functional cooperation/collaboration
- innovation and flexibility
- keeping promises
- openness/frankness of internal communication
- quality and competence
- responsibility of employees
- speed
- trust.

Norms are explicit or implicit rules about the behavior that is desired or undesired within the firm. They are more concrete than values and are closer to actual behavior. In terms of content, market-oriented norms are quite similar to market-oriented values, supporting the firm's market orientation. As an example, market-oriented norms can demand cross-functional cooperation to satisfy customers' needs, or the internal dissemination of market information. In business practice, the following rules can be found with regard to this:

- Important customer-related issues have priority over internal tasks as a matter of principle.
- We always make precise promises to our customers, which have to be kept.
- Customer-related information must be distributed proactively within our company.

In addition to these general rules, behavioral rules on how to act in specific situations can be formulated. The following examples of norms illustrate this.

- Recognizable expressions of customers' dissatisfaction must never be ignored, but always require a reaction from our company.
- A customer never waits longer than 24 hours for a call-back.

In contrast to values and norms, **artefacts** can be observed directly (Hatch 1993; Schein 1992; Trice and Beyer 1993). The following categories of artefacts can be distinguished:

- narratives
- language
- rituals
- arrangements.

In many companies, **narratives** report meaningful (more or less true) stories and activities within the firm. For instance, such narratives try to explain the company's success or failure. Often, they refer to the activities of top managers or the founders of the company. Usually, these narratives implicitly communicate certain values or norms (Martin *et al.* 1983).

A second category of artefacts is the **language** used within the firm. In this context, the usage of specific notions and of a specific language style is relevant. Such a style can be observed, for example, during company meetings.

Rituals constitute a third category of artefacts. They refer to regular activities that do not have a direct link to the firm's tasks and objectives, but rather have a symbolic function to communicate values and norms. As an example, awards to employees have this kind of symbolic function.

Finally, **arrangements** serve as artefacts. They comprise buildings, offices and other facilities. For instance, the design of office spaces can communicate the value of openness.

In all four categories, artefacts can appear to be signalling high or low market orientation. Some examples are shown in Table 17-1.

17.1.2 Market Orientation of Organizational Structure

A second element of market-oriented corporate management is the market orientation of **organizational structure**. In the organizational structure of the firm, market orientation can be achieved, for example, by the following approaches:

- consideration of customer-related aspects when defining organizational divisions (e.g. business units for specific customer segments; Homburg *et al.* 2000b)
- limitation of the number of hierarchical levels (Smith *et al.* 1991) – closer customer contact at higher hierarchical levels resulting in unfiltered information about markets and faster decision processes
- prominent hierarchical position of the head of marketing/sales
- existence of clearly defined contact persons and contact points for customers
- avoidance of over-specialization (over-specialization may slow down coordination and decision processes, which reduces market orientation).

Table 17-1 Examples of artefacts that demonstrate high and low market orientation

	Degree of market orientation	
Category of artefacts	**High market orientation**	**Low market orientation**
Narratives	In a machinery construction company, stories are told about a top manager who drove spare parts to a customer during the weekend, when a service technician fell ill	In an insurance company, the story is told of a salesperson who very successfully sold highly profitable policies to customers, which did not meet those customers' needs
Language	During the internal meetings of a software company the following question is commonly asked: 'How would our customers decide?'	In a transport company, it is common practice to talk of customers as 'shipments'
Rituals	In a transport company, every month one employee is awarded 'Customer Orientation Champion'	In a service company, many customer counters are closed during peak times, so that employees can have a second breakfast
Arrangements	The design of office spaces supports open communication between various departments	In a company, the customer complaint department is situated in a different location from the other marketing departments

17.1.3 Market Orientation of Organizational Processes

A third element of market-oriented corporate management is the market orientation of **organizational processes**. Here the following aspects are relevant:

- generation and cross-functional sharing of market-related information and knowledge (Kohli and Jaworski 1990; Kohli *et al.* 1993; Maltz and Kohli 1996; Menon and Varadarajan 1992; Moorman 1995; Narver and Slater 1990; Sinkula 1994)
- avoidance of excessive process standardization
- facilitation of self-coordination between employees (within and across departments)
- delegation of decision authority to employees in customer contact (empowerment; see also Conger and Kanungo 1988; Day 1994; Zeithaml *et al.* 1990)
- implementation of the principle of the 'internal customer' within the firm (Mohr-Jackson 1991; see Section 17.2 for the internal customer orientation of non-marketing functional units such as finance, R&D, operations)
- enhancement of transparency of customer-related processes.

17.1.4 Performance Implications of Market Orientation

Overall, the various aspects of market orientation illustrated above are seen to have positive performance implications. The general performance implications of market orientation are

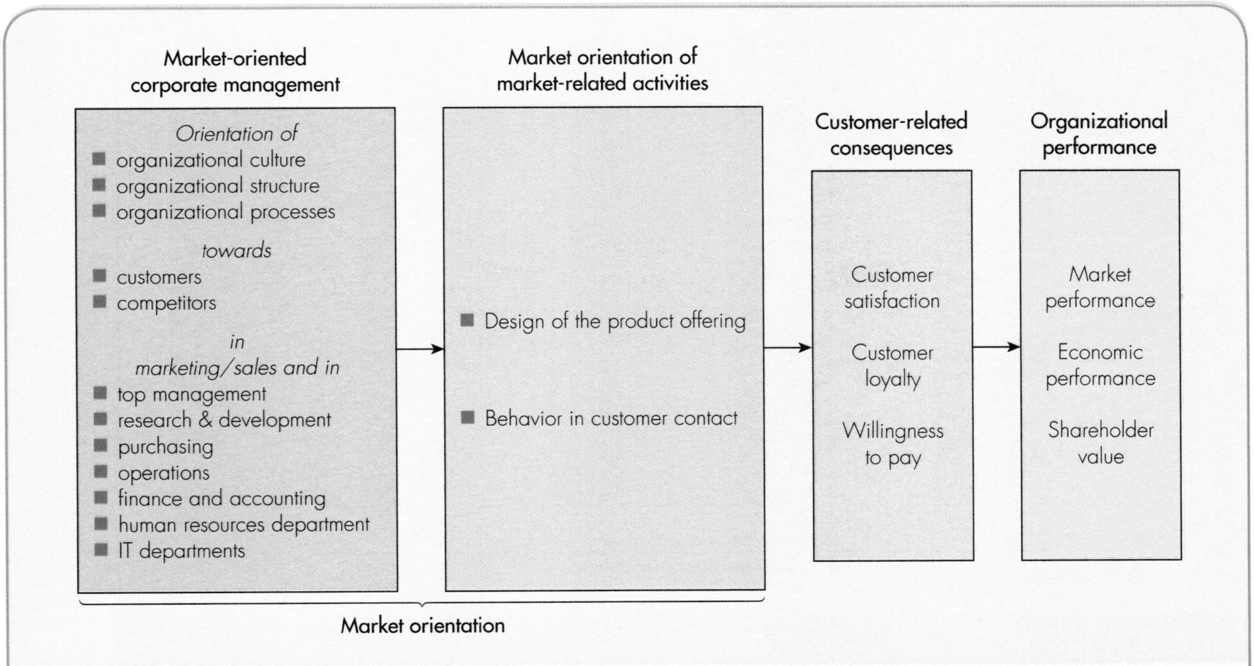

Figure 17-1 Causal chain of the performance implications of market orientation

illustrated in Figure 17-1 (see also Connor 2007; Kirca *et al.* 2005; Matsuno *et al.* 2002; Rodriguez-Cano *et al.* 2004; Slater and Narver 2000): market-oriented corporate management affects the market orientation of the firm's market-related activities (especially the design of the product offering and the behavior of employees), which then affect customers' satisfaction, loyalty and willingness to pay, finally resulting in increased performance and shareholder value for the firm (see also Matzler and Stahl 2000; Rust *et al.* 2004; Srivastava *et al.* 1998, 1999). Hence, market orientation is a basic requirement for the generation of shareholder value.

17.2 Market Orientation within a Company

We will now examine the market orientation of various company departments. We will be concentrating on the company departments that are more concerned with company-internal tasks and internal customer contact (in contrast to marketing and sales that are rather concerned with external customers and activities).

In our discussion of market orientation earlier in this chapter we dealt with the company as a whole. We will now be looking at how the various functional departments within a company cooperate and jointly undertake market-oriented activities. Each functional department can contribute to the market-oriented activities of a company in two ways (see Figure 17-2).

1. Functional departments can undertake **direct activities** for customers. Customer contact is not limited to marketing and sales. Particularly in business-to-business marketing (see Chapter 10), specialists on the company side often have direct communication with specialists on the customer side (e.g. technicians on the company side with technicians on the customer side, and financial experts on the company side with financial experts on the customer side).

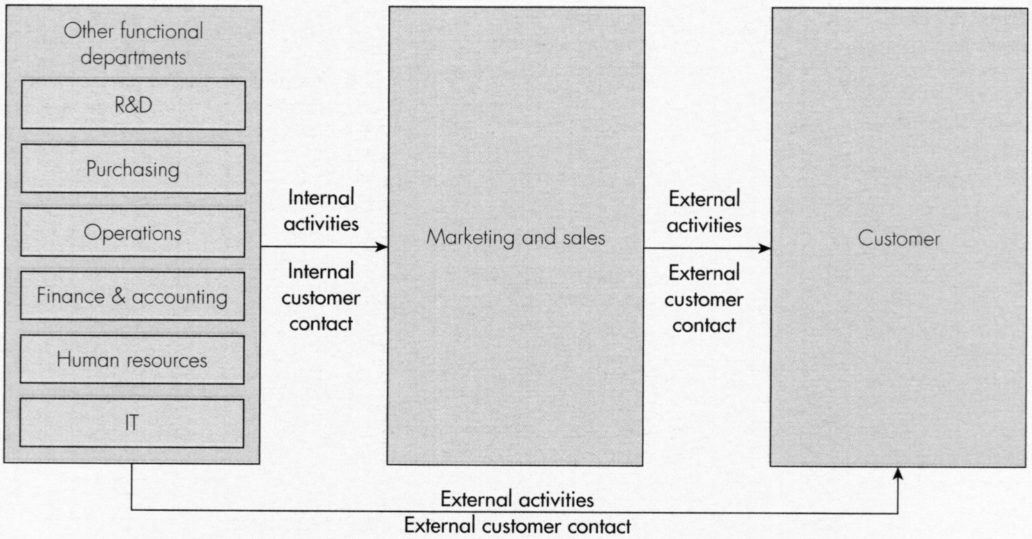

Figure 17-2 Differentiation between external and internal customer orientation

2 Functional departments can also undertake **indirect activities** for customers by supporting the functional departments that have direct contact with customers. For example, the sales department can deliver products on schedule only if it has received the product on time from logistics, and can supply products of the promised quality only if production fulfills the quality requirements.

With regard to establishing a market orientation in a company, it is therefore useful to differentiate the customer orientation concept into two aspects: orientation on **external customers** and orientation on sales and marketing as **internal customers** (concerning internal customer–supplier relationships, see also Hauser *et al.* 1996; Reynoso and Moores 1995; Vandermerwe and Gilbert 1991; for a further discussion of the concept of internal marketing, see Ahmed and Rafiq 1999; Lings 2004). Table 17-2 shows examples of how internal functional departments influence the market orientation of a company via contact with internal customers, external customers and competitors.

Before concentrating on each of these internal functional departments individually, the following section will address the topic of market orientation in top management.

17.2.1 Market Orientation in Top Management

For the following reasons, the market orientation of the top management is especially important for the market orientation of the entire company.

- Decisions of particular significance for the company are made by the top management – for example, decisions about strategies and strategic priorities.
- The experiences, mindsets and values of top management have an impact on managers at the lower hierarchy levels and their decisions (see Carpenter *et al.* 2004).

The career background of the members of the board of directors and the top management team, and especially the career background of the **chief executive officer (CEO)/chairperson of the**

Table 17-2 Points of contact of various departments with customers and competitors

Internal functional departments	Examples of points of contact with . . .		
	. . . external customers	. . . internal customers	. . . competitors
R&D	Research on customer requirements with regard to the next product generation	Target costing for new products	Analysis of competitor products
Purchasing	Joint optimization of inventory along the entire supply chain	Information from marketing and sales about expected raw material price increases	Analysis of the company's dependency on suppliers as compared to competitors' dependency on their suppliers
Operations	Resolution of quality problems	Coordination of delivery dates	Benchmarking of the company's own productivity
Finance and accounting	Preparation of financing offers for the company's own products	Implementation of a multi-stage customer contribution analysis	Assessment of the capability of a competitor to withstand a price war
Human resources	Recruitment/hiring of a new customer service representative	Creation of job rotation systems for development of young professionals	Knowledge of the remuneration level of competitor(s)
IT	Set-up of an extranet and data exchange with customers	Provision of an information infrastructure that minimizes the data interfaces between sales and production	Benchmarking of the company's own productivity

management board plays an interesting role with respect to market orientation in top management. Studies show that the career background (in particular the functional department where the top manager gained the most professional experience) has an effect on behavior: accordingly, managers from 'output'-driven departments (e.g. sales, R&D) tend to favor seeking out new market opportunities, while managers from 'throughput'-driven departments (e.g. operations, finance/accounting) put a priority on increasing efficiency in existing processes (see Hambrick and Mason 1984).

Moreover, the career background of the CEO/chairperson of the management board affects the distribution of power among the functional departments of the company: managers who come from

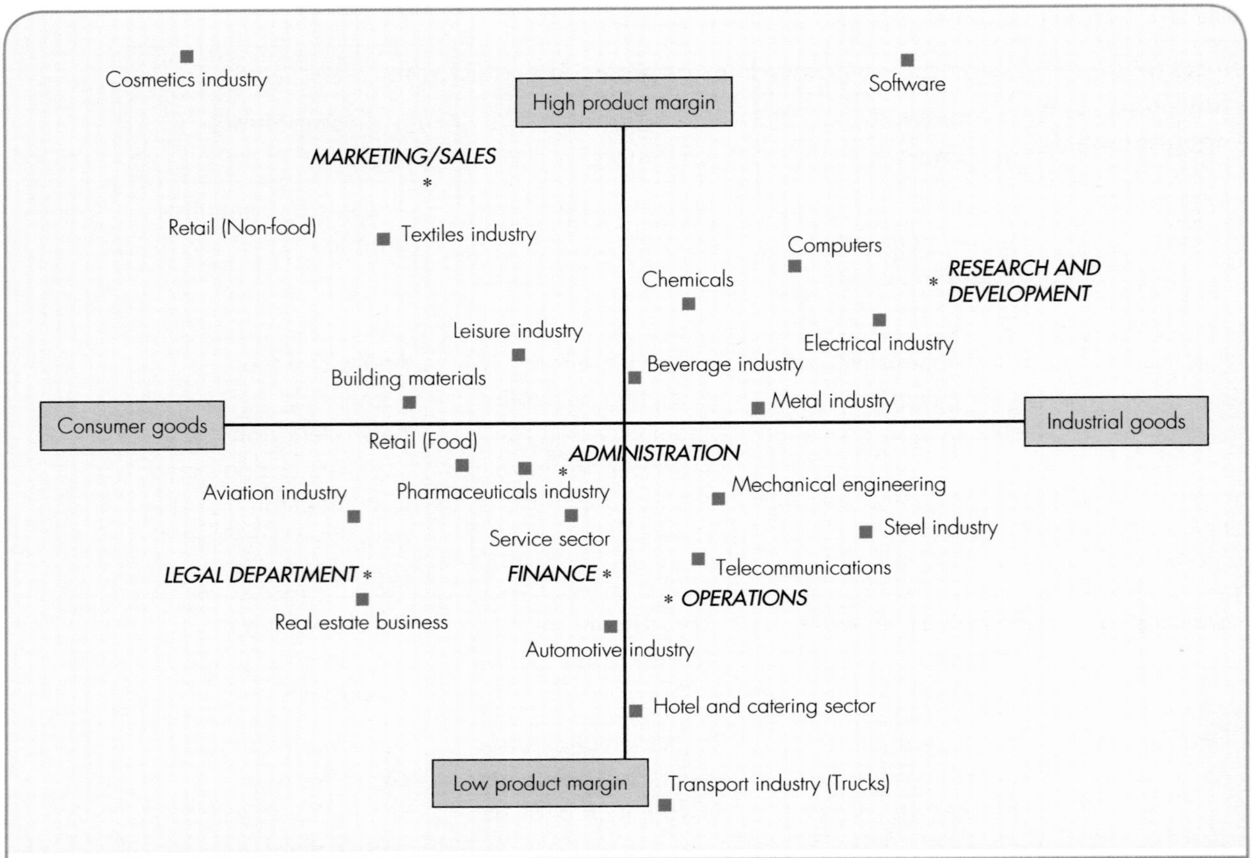

Figure 17-3 Dominant career backgrounds of the CEOs in various industrial sectors (see Workman and Webb 1999)

the same functional department as the CEO/chairperson of the management board tend to be more influential in the company (see Bunderson 2003; Enz 1988; Homburg *et al.* 1999).

This information demonstrates that a starting point for ensuring market-oriented management lies in filling board and management positions, and especially executive positions, with individuals who have extensive experience in the area of marketing and/or sales.

However, there are also industry-specific tendencies with respect to hiring CEOs/chairpersons of the management board. As the empirical findings in Figure 17-3 demonstrate, CEOs with a strong marketing or sales background are predominantly found in high-margin consumer goods industries. In contrast, the R&D department dominates in the industrial goods industries. Interestingly, managers from operations and finance/accounting dominate in low-margin industries (which have to place top priority on cost efficiency).

17.2.2 Market Orientation in Research & Development

The main tasks of the research & development department (R&D) comprise the development of new products, the modification and further development of existing products, customization of existing products, as well as the management of new product development processes.

A high degree of **external customer orientation in the R&D department** is especially characterized by the following (see Mohr *et al.* 2005; Mukhopadhyhay and Gupta 1998) factors:

- R&D strives for regular customer contact and does not conduct isolated 'laboratory work'.
- R&D integrates customers into the development process (e.g. lead users or key accounts).
- R&D knows about the most important customer requirements (needs, problems and willingness to pay). Furthermore, R&D is also aware of what the basic requirements and 'excitement factors' are for customers.
- R&D aligns the design of product features to customer requirements (see Focus on Marketing 17-1). However, if the product features exceed the needs and willingness to pay on the part of customers, we speak of 'over-engineering'.
- R&D develops the product design in a way that offers the customer a wide range of variants (e.g. by means of cost-efficient customization within the scope of production).
- R&D promptly develops solutions for existing customer problems.
- R&D takes customer needs into account only if they can be realized at a marketable price.

In this context, it should be pointed out that we are not suggesting that R&D departments should align their tasks solely on the basis of customer needs. There are numerous examples of fundamental and successful innovations that are more technology-driven than market-driven. Nevertheless, within the scope of such innovations customer aspects should also be considered (for an example, see Focus on Marketing 17-1).

Focus on Marketing 17-1 Example of customer-oriented R&D activities

Few companies would willingly gamble billions on a long shot. Yet when it comes to research and development, many do. Every year companies in the Standard & Poor's 500-stock index pour more than $100 billion into *R&D*. Sometimes it results in the kind of groundbreaking science that gave us lasers and AIDS drugs. More often it results in dead ends or intriguing innovations that nobody wants.

At Dow Chemical Co., scientists seeking a better batting average are using an approach that has been catching on in recent years, but with a twist. Before it heads for the lab, Dow solicits a wish list of products or technical characteristics from customers. If Dow can make what they want – and enough companies agree to buy it – Dow scientists will return to the lab and invent to order. The idea is similar to efforts at open-market innovation attempted elsewhere, but is designed to build in guaranteed demand.

Source: Lavelle 2004.

A **competitor orientation in the R&D department** is demonstrated, for example, by the following aspects (see Mohr *et al.* 2005).

- R&D analyzes the ongoing innovation projects being conducted by the competitor(s).
- R&D knows the company's capabilities and resources, as well as the product strategies for and the strengths and weaknesses of competitors' new products.
- R&D compares the company's own development processes with those of competitors (e.g. with respect to speed, milestones and reject rates).

An **internal customer orientation in the R&D department** towards the sales and marketing department is expressed in the following activities (see Griffin and Hauser 1996; Gupta *et al.* 1987; Workman 1993):

- R&D includes marketing and sales in the development of new products and services in the early phases; this can be accomplished by working in cross-functional teams (e.g. within the scope of quality function deployment (QFD); see Chapter 5).
- R&D maintains regular contact with marketing and sales, which improves the R&D department's level of knowledge concerning processes and tasks in marketing and sales, and sensitizes R&D to the challenges and problems of market development.
- R&D develops the product design in a way that facilitates on-site repairs by sales and customer services.

When it comes to conflicts between R&D and marketing and sales, it is difficult to align research and development tasks with a market-oriented approach. Conflicts can occur, for example (also see Lucas and Bush 1988; Mukhopadhyhay and Gupta 1998; Souder 1988),

- if R&D 'speaks a different language' to marketing and sales (e.g. if R&D thinks in terms of product features while marketing and sales focuses on customer solutions)
- if R&D has different goals to marketing and sales (e.g. if R&D primarily strives to maximize quality and innovativeness, while marketing and sales is more interested in meeting customer requirements in a way that is as economically feasible as possible)
- if there are major differences in the work styles of the different departments (e.g. if R&D managers prefer a somewhat informal culture while marketing and sales is characterized by a more formal culture).

Typical fields of conflict between R&D and marketing and sales are listed, with examples, in Table 17-3.

17.2.3 Market Orientation in Purchasing

The main tasks of the purchasing department are to procure the materials and products, in the required quality and quantity, needed for the company's production processes, and to conduct, conclude and manage negotiations with suppliers, as well as analyze and evaluate the supplier market.

An **external customer orientation in the purchasing department** is manifested in the following activities (see, e.g., Ellram *et al.* 2002; Rossler and Hirsz 1996):

- Purchasers know the requirements of the customers and take them into account when procuring materials.
- Purchasers not only consider the mere purchase price, but all the costs associated with the purchase, including the consequential costs for the company and the customers. For example, a component can have a low purchase price, but quality defects can subsequently materialize when the component is used by the customer, which can be costly for the supplier with respect to recall actions and customer satisfaction.
- Purchasers regularly seek out direct contact with customers in order to keep informed about customers' experiences and needs pertaining to components and materials.

The **competitor orientation in the purchasing department** is characterized by the following activities (see Koppelmann 2002):

- Purchasers compare their company's own purchasing policy and purchasing terms with those of competitors. This is particularly relevant in industries in which purchasing affects a substantial share of the costs.

Table 17-3 Typical fields of conflict between R&D and marketing and sales

Fields of conflict	Risks of conflict if . . .	
	. . . R&D says:	. . . while marketing and sales says:
Quality level	'We have to develop products of the highest possible quality'	'Meeting the highest quality standards won't bring us any benefit if we experience cost disadvantages or if customers hardly perceive the quality improvement'
Product features	'We should not let current requirements limit our creative potential and we have to continuously seek out innovative solutions'	'We should not fall for resource-intensive innovation gimmicks. The market is not willing to pay for that' 'We need to concentrate on innovations that the market requires. Our market research will provide the relevant information'
Product range	'Instead of giving facelifts to existing products, we should use our resources to create revolutionary new solutions'	'There is great market potential to enhance our existing products by adding new variants, which lets us realize additional revenues with less expense and risk'
Target groups	'The more innovative, the better. We need to be technology leaders and should primarily target innovative lead users'	'It is not the lead users, but everyday consumers who comprise the target group we earn our money with. Our target group is not far enough along yet for this level of innovation' 'We should not scare off the normal customers, who first have to get used to the new technology. They will not accept deep application changes and initial development problems'

- Purchasers analyze their company's dependence on suppliers as compared to competitors' dependence on suppliers.

The **internal customer orientation in the purchasing department** is expressed in the following activities (see Goebel *et al.* 2003):

- Purchasers maintain a regular dialog with marketing and sales.
- Purchasers proactively inform marketing and sales about purchase price increases, quality issues and availability problems.

The realization of a market-oriented purchasing department is difficult if conflicts arise between purchasing and marketing and sales. Such conflicts can occur, for example, if (see Goebel *et al.* 2003) the purchasing department pursues different goals from those of marketing and sales (e.g. if purchasers are primarily assessed on the basis of negotiation results and cost savings, and have no incentive to undertake market-oriented activities). Table 17-4 describes some typical fields of conflict between purchasing and sales/marketing:

Table 17-4 Typical fields of conflict between purchasing and marketing and sales

Fields of conflict	Risks of conflict if . . .	
	. . . purchasing says:	. . . while marketing and sales says:
Product range width	'We can ensure the necessary cost-effectiveness in purchasing only if we have limited product lines'	'We can only satisfy our current customers and acquire new customers if we offer a broad product range'
Product standardization	'A crucial success factor in purchasing is the procurement of standardized components to the greatest extent possible. In comparison to the competition, our level of complexity is too high'	'We have to differentiate our products from competitor products in a credible way. We can achieve that if our products feature only non-standardized elements and modules'
Warehousing	'Our goal is to purchase quantities in optimal batch sizes. Tying up capital by warehousing purchased products must absolutely be minimized. This is one of our most important areas of optimization'	'Supply bottlenecks in production and for deliveries to customers have to be avoided at all costs. Customers who do not receive their deliveries switch to competitors. High capital commitment costs thus appear to be an acceptable disadvantage'
Selection of suppliers	'We have to choose suppliers based on the purchase price they offer for the components we need. We are still too expensive as compared to the competition'	'Our purchases also have to be governed by the quality of the components procured. At any rate, we should consider the total cost – subsequent repairs and gestures of goodwill are expensive and damage our image'

17.2.4 Market Orientation in Operations

The operations department comprises the production and logistics departments of the company. In addition to production in manufacturing companies, the term 'operations' also refers to the back office and support in service companies (e.g. baggage handling by airline carriers, payment processing at banks).

The tasks in the production department are to do with converting the material and immaterial input from the procurement markets into sales: products are assembled and/or product features are enhanced. In many industry sectors, this department operates with a relatively strong market focus, examples being many service providers as well as industrial plant construction companies. In these sectors, the productive processes take place in the direct presence of and in close cooperation with the customer. The core tasks of the logistics department include order processing (receiving, preparing, converting, forwarding and documenting order data) as well as warehousing and transport (scheduling and route planning). Logistics engages in a great deal of customer contact (e.g. in the course of receiving orders, warehousing directly on the customer's premises and during the delivery).

In the literature, market orientation in the operations department is frequently discussed in connection with concepts such as **total quality management** (TQM) and **supply chain management** (see Day 1994; Min and Mentzer 2000; Wang and Wei 2005; Yam *et al.* 2005). Among other things, both concepts are based on improving performance and service quality by means of increased customer orientation in all relevant functional departments.

The **external customer orientation in the operations department** is characterized by the following (see Vollmann and Cordon 1999):

- The operations department does not isolate itself from external influences, but rather seeks out customer contact. This applies not only to the already market-oriented logistics departments, but also to the production departments.
- The operations department is familiar with customer requirements with regard to quality, price and speed, and acts accordingly.
- The operations department can respond flexibly to changes in requirements related to quantities, schedules and locations.
- The operations department can provide information at any time about the status of order processing, as well as communicate reliable deadlines and completion dates.
- The operations department is not exclusively cost and process oriented, but also takes into account the requirements and satisfaction of external customers.
- The operations department works together with customers in order to optimize the total cost along the value-added chain. In the business-to-business sector in particular, such joint efforts often offer great potential for both suppliers and customers to reduce costs and prices.

Systematic benchmarking of the department's own efficiency as compared to that of competitors is one manifestation of **competitor orientation in the operations department**. Such comparisons particularly concern relevant indicators (e.g. processing duration, quality benchmarks, complaint rates, unit costs in production, warehouse capacity) as well as the use of optimization methods (e.g. implementation of TQM measures and cooperation strategies, or the inclusion of employees in the quality circle).

The **internal customer orientation in the operations department** can express itself in the following ways (see Crittenden 1992; Hausman *et al.* 2002; Mukhopadhyhay and Gupta 1998; St John and Rue 1991):

- The operations department is not only focused on its own processes and problems but is also aware of what marketing and sales can realistically achieve (e.g. with respect to the accuracy of sales forecasts).
- With regard to direct customer contact, the operations department coordinates information given to customers (e.g. about delivery times) with marketing and sales.
- The operations department proactively and continuously provides marketing and sales with information relevant to market development (e.g. information related to production costs, capacity utilization, production bottlenecks and quality problems).
- The operations department responds flexibly to changes in requirements from marketing and sales.

The realization of a market-oriented operations department is made difficult if conflicts arise between operations and marketing and sales (see Clare and Sanford 1984; Kahn and Mentzer 1994; Krishnan and Ulrich 2001; Shapiro 1977). Such conflicts can occur, for example, if operations places top priority on optimizing cost efficiency and minimizing process complexity, while marketing and sales strives to fulfill customer needs to the greatest extent possible (e.g. through improved product quality and service levels, shorter delivery times, broader range of variants, and the customization of products and services).

Table 17-5 provides examples of such conflict situations. The goal conflicts described in the table are even more pronounced by the use of different incentives in the remuneration and bonus systems: marketing and sales employees are rewarded for sales, for improving market share and for acquiring customers. In operations, on the other hand, the minimization of production and logistics costs is at the forefront, especially if the department is managed as a cost center.

Table 17-5 Typical fields of conflict between the operations department and marketing and sales (adapted from Shapiro 1977)

Fields of conflict	Risks of conflict if . . .	
	. . . operations says:	. . . while marketing and sales says:
Capacity planning	'Why don't we have precise sales forecasts?' 'We need binding assurances from customers, and budget plans that stay on track. We need stability: production changeovers are too expensive'	'Why don't we have enough capacity?' 'We have to react more quickly to changes in customer requirements. Our response times are unsatisfactory'
Processing speed	'We have to bundle orders for production – that is the only way to keep our costs down'	'Why does it sometimes take three days to process a customer order and other times two weeks? We can't explain that to our customers'
Quality assurance	'Why does the sales department always make such unrealistic promises to customers?'	'Why isn't operations able to handle the simplest processes without any problems?'
Product range width	'The product range is too broad, which only leads to complexity costs'	'Our customers want as much variety as possible'
Product customization	'Product customization is one of the most significant cost drivers, and one we cannot afford'	'The only way to stand out from the competition and avoid a price war is to align our product range to the requirements of our customers'
Cost controlling	'We can't make quick deliveries, offer a broad product range, respond quickly and flexibly and offer high quality all at the same time – and all that at low costs, too'	'Our costs are so high that we are pricing ourselves out of the market'
Product innovations	'Product modifications are prohibitively expensive'	'New products are the fundamental basis of our success'

17.2.5 Market Orientation in Finance and Accounting

The main tasks of the finance and accounting department comprise financing and investment, cost accounting and cost control, as well as external accounting. In addition, finance and accounting has to support marketing and sales in making decisions by providing suitable information, including, for instance, customer relationship profitability analyses, budget allocation, support with investment decisions, as well as assessments of brands and customers (for more information, see also the discussion of marketing control in Chapter 14).

The **external customer orientation in finance and accounting** is demonstrated by the following aspects (see Ratnatunga *et al.* 1990):

- Finance/accounting provides the customer with adequate financing offers for the company's own products, thus facilitating the reduction of investment obstacles for the customer. A prerequisite here is that finance and accounting must possess knowledge about the customer's financing requirements.
- Finance/accounting is able to provide an accurate assessment of the creditworthiness of potential customers.

A **competitor orientation in finance and accounting** is manifest if this department analyzes the financial resources of competitors and evaluates, say, their ability to withstand a price war.

The **internal customer orientation in finance and accounting** is demonstrated as follows (see Homburg *et al.* 1998, 2000a).

- Finance/accounting ensures an information supply geared to the requirements of marketing and sales as the recipient (comprehensible, target group specific and up to date), which first and foremost concerns the information needed for efficient marketing and sales control (e.g. product profitability analysis, customer profitability analysis, customer lifetime value, determination of meaningful indicators for the effectiveness/efficiency of marketing and sales activities).
- The finance/accounting department does not task marketing and sales with excessive reporting and information requirements. This also includes reasonable deadlines, e.g. in the scope of marketing and sales planning.
- The finance/accounting department provides timely information about restrictions and reservations with regard to important investment decisions that pertain to marketing and sales.
- The finance/accounting department provides marketing and sales with suitable tools for fostering the effectiveness and efficiency of market development activities (e.g. customer portfolios).

The anchoring of a market orientation in the finance/accounting department is impeded by conflicts between finance/accounting and marketing and sales (see De Ruyter and Wetzels 2000; Ratnatunga *et al.* 1990; Table 17-6). In particular, conflicts arise:

- if the finance/accounting department and the marketing and sales department focus on different target groups (e.g. finance/accounting focuses on shareholder needs, while marketing and sales is aligned with customer needs)
- if finance/accounting has objectives that differ from those of marketing and sales (e.g. finance/accounting focuses on short-term economic success (e.g. quarterly figures), while marketing and sales centers on long-term market success (e.g. customer loyalty)
- if there are existing communication problems between finance/accounting and marketing and sales (e.g. due to insufficient knowledge of the methods utilized in the other department, department-specific language/terminology or inadequate consideration of the requirements of the other department when providing information), and/or

Table 17-6 Typical fields of conflict between finance/accounting and marketing and sales (see De Ruyter and Wetzels 2000)

Fields of conflict	Risks of conflict if . . .	
	. . . finance and accounting says:	. . . while marketing and sales says:
Goals/ motives	'The benefits associated with the suggested image campaign are much too vague. Our discounted cash flow model suggests that this is yet another careless waste of money' 'The profitability of an investment should always be the decisive factor'	'We urgently need to liven up our brand with a fresher image' 'We need the additional product line in order to withstand competitive pressure. This is the only way to guarantee our long-term success in the market'
Resources	'We really need to gain control of our costs. We can't afford to increase the marketing budget' 'We have to optimize our working capital. It is absolutely necessary to minimize warehousing costs arising from intermediate storage'	'Without additional marketing funds, we will face great difficulties in trying to realize our ambitious growth targets in an increasingly competitive market' 'We categorically need sufficient intermediate storage capacities – delivery bottlenecks have to be avoided at all costs'
Investment decisions	'The marketing and sales departments do not have any cost consciousness at all' 'Our marketing and sales people think they are top strategists – but they are completely incapable of preparing even the most basic cash flow plans'	'Our accountants are bean counters' 'Finance and accounting always interfere with our workflow by demanding complex figures and statistics. In many cases, such information is completely unnecessary and will not be acted upon anyway' 'How can you quantify the future? It is simply unrealistic to expect that it would be possible to calculate a valid return on marketing investment'

- if finance/accounting and marketing and sales have different department cultures (e.g. finance/accounting has an internal focus dominated by monetary aspects, while marketing and sales has an external focus characterized by qualitative aspects, with non-monetary factors such as, say, customer satisfaction and brand image cultivation playing key roles).

17.2.6 Market Orientation in the Human Resources Department

On one hand, the main tasks of the human resources department comprise those elements that concern the entire employment cycle of an employee, including personnel requirements planning, personnel recruitment, human resources planning and personnel layoffs (see Section 16.1). A second task area is dedicated to supporting the other functional departments with respect to human resource matters such as personnel administration, personnel controlling, employee remuneration, employee assistance, personnel supervision/motivation and human resources development.

In particular, a high degree of **external customer orientation in the human resources department** manifests itself in the following activities (see Becker and Homburg 1999; Chimhanzi 2004):

- When selecting new employees, the human resources department applies appropriate measures (e.g. assessment center, role plays) in order to evaluate whether potential employees exhibit a sufficient customer focus.
- When designing remuneration systems, the human resources department takes customer satisfaction into consideration.
- The human resources department is aware of its significant role in directly and indirectly influencing customer satisfaction through employee satisfaction, and acts accordingly.
- The human resources department measures the correlation between training measures and market success.

Indicators of a **competitor orientation in the human resources department** include the following activities:

- The human resources department periodically compares its performance with that of competitors. Relevant aspects include, for example, remuneration level, variable pay, fringe benefits, success, employee churn, employee satisfaction and development programs for young professionals.
- The human resources department is aware of the sales employees of competitors who are willing to switch employers.

The **internal customer orientation of the human resources department's** is expressed by the following activities (see Chimhanzi 2004; Glassman and MacAffee 1992).

- On the basis of the requirements of marketing and sales, the human resources department develops suitable job profiles/descriptions and job advertisements.
- The human resources department provides marketing and sales employees and managers with efficient further education, training and coaching opportunities (e.g. customer-oriented management coaching).
- The human resources department develops systems for cross-functional job rotation.
- The human resources department supports the international deployment of expatriates as well as international employee transfer by providing training courses, legal and administrative assistance and reintegration measures.
- The human resources department establishes suitable framework conditions for ensuring (permanent) loyalty on the part of marketing and sales employees. Particularly in the sales department, there is the risk that an employee will 'transfer' his or her customers to a competitor.
- The human resources department supports high-performance marketing and sales managers to stand out from the crowd.
- The human resources department develops motivational remuneration models for marketing and sales employees. Key aspects in this context include, for example, rewards based on customer satisfaction as well as bonuses for successful cross-selling across several business sectors.

The anchoring of market orientation in the human resources department is impeded by conflicts between the human resources department and marketing and sales (see Chimhanzi 2004; Glassman and MacAffee 1992; Piercy 1997; Table 17-7). In particular, conflicts arise:

- if the human resources department is strongly cost-oriented, while marketing and sales wants to expand personnel resources for market development activities
- if the human resources department attaches importance to having similar remuneration levels in different functional departments (safeguarding 'internal peace'), while marketing and sales aims to establish very high remuneration levels for its employees

Table 17-7 Typical fields of conflict between human resources and marketing and sales (see Chimhanzi 2004; Glassman and MacAffee 1992; Piercy 1997)

Fields of conflict	Risks of conflict if . . .	
	. . . the human resources department says:	. . . while marketing and sales says:
Cost savings	'We have a hiring freeze in place – we cannot afford to hire any more highly paid sales employees'	'It is precisely a crisis that offers opportunities. If we approach customers with additional sales employees right now, we will be able to carve out a significant competitive advantage'
Remuneration level	'Major differences in salary between office employees and field salesforce employees are detrimental. The generous company car arrangements made for the field salesforce are met with criticism'	'The company thrives on sales, a fact that has to be reflected in the salaries. And, if we do not provide our good sales employees with appropriate compensation, they will switch to the competition'
Employee development	'Our long-term employee development is based on versatility. All of our future managers must be familiar with more than just their own department and area of expertise. Therefore, cross-functional job rotation is an absolute must'	'Our job is not a sandbox to make experiments in. Particularly with respect to the sales department, job rotation puts valuable customer relationships at risk'

- if the human resources department pushes for cross-functional employee job rotation within the scope of long-term employee development, while marketing and sales promotes staff continuity in order to secure customer relationships.

17.2.7 Market Orientation in the IT Department

The main tasks of the IT department include provision of the physical IT infrastructure, operative technical support, the design/layout and procurement of information systems and system architecture (both company-internal as well as involving external partners along the value added chain), the design of user interfaces in various functional departments, as well as training for IT system users.

The **external customer orientation in the IT department** becomes evident when the IT department provides efficient solutions for exchanging information with customers.

- **Electronic data interchange (EDI)** is one form of continuous data exchange with customers. The key requirements to be met by such a system are safety/security, up-to-dateness and user-friendliness.
- **Extranets** serve as a data exchange platform between the supplier and customer. Extranets are used in particular in the business-to-business sector, providing customers with limited access to the databases and intranet sites of the supplier.

Competitor orientation in the IT department manifests itself in the following activities (see Fried and Johnson 1992):

- The IT department compares its own activities and systems with those of other companies, in particular with those of direct competitors. Such a comparison can apply to, say, the technical infrastructure, safety and security measures, and the user-friendliness of the information systems.
- The IT department consents to having its performance and activities assessed on the basis of market standards, and if an external offer is more beneficial and efficient, recommends outsourcing the activities to the benefit of the entire company.

An **internal customer orientation in the IT department** is characterized by the following activities:

- The IT department provides the infrastructure as well as the hardware and software required for efficiently supporting the storage, processing, provision, distribution and utilization of information in marketing and sales. This also includes the provision of systems for supporting decision-making and sales processes, as well as systems for relieving marketing and sales employees and managers from standardizable operative tasks.
- The IT department perceives itself as an internal service provider. It offers solutions that are aligned to the level of IT knowledge of the users, and does not expect the functional departments to adapt to the mindset and solutions of the IT department.
- The IT department involves the future users of marketing and sales information systems in the conceptualization, design and testing of these systems.
- In its relationship to internal customers, the IT department commits itself to service standards, and subjects itself to sanctions in the case of non-compliance. Service standards include, for instance, availability as well as the binding assurance of deadlines and completion dates.

The anchoring of a market orientation in the IT department is impeded by conflicts between the IT department and marketing and sales (see Table 17-8). In particular, conflicts arise in connection with making the decision between standard software and proprietary in-house IT solutions: standard software is more cost-efficient in terms of maintenance and less fraught with risk since it does not depend on individual programmers. On the other hand, software that has been specifically developed is often easier to use, since it contains neither more nor fewer functions than those required by the internal customer. In many companies, this conflict arises in the scope of, for example, migrating from proprietary in-house IT solutions to SAP standard software.

Table 17-8 Typical fields of conflict between IT and marketing and sales

Fields of conflict	Risks of conflict if . . .	
	. . . the IT department says:	. . . while marketing and sales says:
Communication	'The technical implementation of the features promised by marketing is often impossible or involves extremely high effort and expense'	'We want to meet the expectations of our customers and thus promise individualized solutions'
Culture/ orientation	'We are oriented towards technology and research. Accordingly, we focus on technological feasibility'	'We have a strong customer focus. Our primary goal lies in meeting our customers' requirements and needs'
Requirements/ applications	'Ensuring the intercompatibility of the individual tools is often technically impossible or involves extremely high effort and expense'	'We want all our tools to be compatible with each other in order to guarantee the best possible customer service'

Summary

In this chapter we explored the definitions of market orientation to provide the reader with a basic understanding of market orientation and market-oriented corporate management. Market orientation refers to the orientation of organizational culture, organizational structure and organizational processes towards the firm's customers and competitors (market-oriented corporate management). Furthermore, market orientation refers to the degree to which the product offering of the firm and the customer-related behavior of the firm correspond to customer needs and competitive requirements (market orientation of market-related activities). There are various positive performance implications of market orientation, including customer loyalty.

In this chapter, we also addressed market orientation in top management and in the various functional departments of the firm (R&D, purchasing, operations, finance and accounting, human resources, IT). Basically, functional departments can undertake direct activities for customers (such as giving technical advice to customers) as well as indirect activities for customers by supporting the functional departments that have direct contact with customers (e.g. the operations department meeting quality requirements promised to the customer by the sales department). This perspective results in the differentiation between two components of market orientation: the orientation of external customers (i.e. the customers in the market) and the orientation on internal customers (such as the sales and marketing department). In addition, we conceptualized competitor orientation as a third component of market orientation. We were able to show that the specific contents of market orientation differ depending on the various functional departments involved.

Key Terms

References

Ahmed, P. and Rafiq, M. (1999) The role of internal marketing in the implementation of marketing strategies, in: Bruhn, M. (ed.) *Internes Marketing* (2nd edn). Wiesbaden, 469–492.

Becker, J. and Homburg, C. (1999) Market-oriented management: a systems-based perspective, *Journal of Market-Focused Management*, 4, 1, 17–41.

Bunderson, J. (2003) Team member functional background and involvement in management teams: direct effects and the moderating role of power centralization, *Academy of Management Journal*, 46, 4, 458–475.

Carpenter, M., Geletkanycz, M. and Sanders, W. (2004) Upper echelons research revisited: antecedents, elements, and consequences of top management team composition, *Journal of Management*, 30, 6, 749–778.

Chimhanzi, J. (2004) The impact of marketing/HR interactions on marketing strategy implementation, *European Journal of Marketing*, 38, 1/2, 73–99.

Clare, D. and Sanford, D. (1984) Cooperation and conflict between industrial sales and production, *Industrial Marketing Management*, 13, 3, 163–190.

Conger, J. and Kanungo, R. (1988) The empowerment process – integrating theory and practice, *Academy of Management Review*, 13, 3, 471–482.

Connor, T. (2007) Market orientation and performance, *Strategic Management Journal*, 28, 9, 957–959.

Crittenden, V. (1992) Close the marketing/manufacturing gap, *Sloan Management Review*, 33, 3, 41–50.

Day, G.S. (1994) The capabilities of market-driven organizations, *Journal of Marketing*, 58, 4, 37–52.

De Ruyter, K. and Wetzels, M. (2000) The marketing–finance interface: a relational exchange perspective, *Journal of Business Research*, 50, 2, 209–216.

Ellram, L., Zsidisin, G., Siferd, S. and Stanly, M. (2002) The impact of purchasing and supply chain management activities on corporate success, *Journal of Supply Chain Management*, 38, 1, 4–17.

Enz, C. (1988) The role of value congruity in intraorganizational power, *Administrative Science Quarterly*, 33, 2, 284–305.

Fried, L. and Johnson, R, (1992) Planning for the competitive use of information technology, *Information Strategy: The Executive Journal*, 8, 4, 5–14.

Gebhardt, G.F., Carpenter, G.S. and Sherry, J.F. (2006) Creating a market orientation: a longitudinal, multifirm, grounded analysis of cultural transformation, *Journal of Marketing*, 70, 3, 37–55.

Glassman, M. and MacAffee, B. (1992) Integrating the personnel and marketing functions: the challenge of the 1990s, *Business Horizons*, 35, 3, 52–59.

Goebel, D., Marshall, G. and Locander, W. (2003) Enhancing purchasing's strategic reputation: evidence and recommendations for future research, *Journal of Supply Chain Management*, 41, 2, 26–38.

Griffin, A. and Hauser, J. (1996) Integrating R&D and marketing: a review and analysis of the literature, *Journal of Product Innovation Management*, 13, 2, 137–151.

Gupta, A., Raj, S. and Wilemon, D. (1987) Managing the R&D–marketing interface, *Research Management*, 30, 38–43.

Hambrick, D. and Mason, P. (1984) Upper echelons: the organization as a reflection of its top-managers, *Academy of Management Review*, 9, 2, 193–206.

Hatch, M. (1993) The dynamics of organizational culture, *Academy of Management Review*, 18, 4, 657–693.

Hauser, J.R., Simester, D.J. and Wernerfelt, B. (1996) Internal customers and internal suppliers, *Journal of Marketing Research*, 13, 268–280.

Hausman, W., Montgomery, D. and Roth, A. (2002) Why should marketing and manufacturing work together? Some exploratory empirical results, *Journal of Operations Management*, 20, 3, 241–258.

Homburg, C. and Pflesser, C. (2000) A multiple-layer model of market-oriented organizational culture: measurement issues and performance outcomes, *Journal of Marketing Research*, 37, 4, 449–462.

Homburg, C., Weber, J., Aust, R. and Karlshaus, J. (1998) *Interne Kundenorientierung der Kostenrechnung – Ergebnisse der Koblenzer Studie*. Weinheim.

Homburg, C., Weber, J., Karlshaus, J. and Aust, R. (2000a) Interne Kundenorientierung der Kostenrechnung? Ergebnisse einer empirischen Untersuchung in deutschen Industrieunternehmen, *Die Betriebswirtschaft*, 60, 2, 241–256.

Homburg, C., Workman, J. and Krohmer, H. (1999) Marketing's influence within the firm, *Journal of Marketing*, 63, 2, 1–17.

Homburg, C., Workman, J. and Jensen, O. (2000b) Fundamental changes in marketing organization: the movement toward a customer-focused organizational structure, *Journal of the Academy of Marketing Science*, 28, 4, 459–478.

Kahn, K. and Mentzer, J. (1994) Norms that distinguish between marketing and manufacturing, *Journal of Business Research*, 30, 2, 111–119.

Ketchen, D.J., Hult, G.T.M. and Slater, S.F. (2007) Toward greater understanding of market orientation and the resource-based view, *Strategic Management Journal*, 28, 961–964.

Kirca, A., Jayachandran, S. and Bearden, W. (2005) Market orientation: a meta-analytic review and assessment of its antecedents and impact on performance, *Journal of Marketing*, 69, 2, 24–41.

Kohli, A. and Jaworski, B. (1990) Market orientation: the construct, research propositions, and managerial implications, *Journal of Marketing*, 54, 2, 1–18.

Kohli, A.K., Jaworski, B.J. and Kumar, A. (1993) MARKOR: a measure of market orientation, *Journal of Marketing Research*, 30, 4, 467–477.

Koppelmann, U. (2002) *Procurement Marketing: A Strategic Concept*. Berlin.

Krishnan, V. and Ulrich, K. (2001) Product development decisions: a review of the literature, *Management Science*, 47, 1, 1–21.

Lavelle, L. (2004) Inventing to order, *Business Week*, Issue 3890, 7 May, 84–85.

Li, T. and Calantone, R.J., (1998) The impact of market knowledge competence on new product advantage: conceptualization and empirical examination, *Journal of Marketing*, 62, 4, 13–29.

Lings, I.N. (2004) Internal market orientation: construct and consequences, *Journal of Business Research*, 57, 405–413.

Lucas, G. and Bush, A. (1988): The marketing–R&D interface: do personality factors have an impact, *Journal of Product Innovation Management*, 5, 4, 257–268.

Maltz, E. and Kohli, A.K. (1996) Market intelligence dissemination across functional boundaries, *Journal of Marketing Research*, 33, 1, 47–61.

Marinova, D. (2004) Actualizing innovation effort: the impact of market knowledge diffusion in a dynamic system of competition, *Journal of Marketing*, 68, 3, 1–20.

Martin, J., Feldmann, M., Hatch, M.J. and Sitkin, S. (1983) The uniqueness paradox in organizational stories, *Administrative Science Quarterly*, 28, September, 438–453.

Matsuno, K., Mentzer, J. and Özsomer, A. (2002) The effects of entrepreneurial proclivity and market orientation on business performance, *Journal of Marketing*, 66, 3, 18–32.

Matzler, K. and Stahl, H. (2000) Kundenzufriedenheit und Unternehmenswertsteigerung, *Die Betriebswirtschaft*, 61, 5, 626–641.

Menon, A. and Varadarajan, R.P. (1992) A model of marketing knowledge use within firms, *Journal of Marketing*, 56, 4, 53–71.

Min, S. and Mentzer, J.T. (2000) The role of marketing in supply chain management, *International Journal of Physical Distribution & Logistics Management*, 30, 9, 765–787.

Mohr, J., Sengupta, S. and Slater, S. (2005) *Marketing of High-technology Products and Innovations*. New York.

Mohr-Jackson, I. (1991) Broadening the market orientation: an added focus on internal customers, *Human Resource Management*, 30 (Winter), 455–467.

Moorman, C. (1995) Organizational market information processes: cultural antecedents and new product outcomes, *Journal of Marketing Research*, 32, 3, 318–335.
Mukhopadhyhay, S. and Gupta, A. (1998) Interfaces for resolving marketing, manufacturing and design conflicts, *European Journal of Marketing*, 32, 1/2, 101–124.
Narver, J. and Slater, S. (1990) The effect of a market orientation on business profitability, *Journal of Marketing*, 54, 4, 20–35.
Piercy, N. (1997) Partnership between marketing and human resource department for implementation effectiveness in services marketing, *Academy of Marketing Conference Proceedings*, Manchester Metropolitan University, 865–878.
Ratnatunga, J., Hooley, G. and Pike, R. (1990) The marketing–finance interface, *European Journal of Marketing*, 24, 1, 29–44.
Reynoso, J. and Moores, B. (1995) Towards the measurement of internal service quality, *International Journal of Service Industry Management*, 6, 3, 64–83.
Rodriguez-Cano, C., Carrillat, F. and Jaramillo, F. (2004) A meta-analysis of the relationship between market orientation and business performance: evidence from five continents, *International Journal of Research in Marketing*, 21, 2, 179–200.
Rossler, P. and Hirsz, A. (1996) Purchasing's interaction with customers: the effects on customer satisfaction – a case study, *International Journal of Purchasing and Materials Management*, 31, 1, 37–43.
Rust, R., Ambler, T., Carpenter, G., Kumar, V. and Srivastava, R. (2004) Measuring marketing productivity: current knowledge and future directions, *Journal of Marketing*, 68, 4, 76–89.
Schein, E. (1992) *Organizational Culture and Leadership* (2nd edn). San Francisco.
Shapiro, B. (1977) Can marketing and manufacturing coexist? *Harvard Business Review*, 55, 5, 104–114.
Sinkula, J. (1994) Market information processing and organizational learning, *Journal of Marketing*, 58, 1, 35–45.
Slater, S.F. and Narver, J.C. (2000) Intelligence generation and superior customer value, *Journal of the Academy of Marketing Science*, 28, 1, 120–127.
Smith, K., Grimm, C., Gannon, M. and Chen, M.-J. (1991) Organizational information processing, competitive responses, and performance in the US domestic airline industry, *Academy of Management Journal*, 34, 1, 60–85.
Souder, W. (1988) Managing relations between R&D and marketing in new product development projects, *Journal of Product Innovation Management*, 5, 1, 6–19.
Srivastava, R., Shervani, T. and Fahey, L. (1998) Market based assets and shareholder value: a framework for analysis, *Journal of Marketing*, 62, 1, 2–18.
Srivastava, R., Shervani, T. and Fahey, L. (1999) Marketing, business processes, and shareholder value: an organizationally embedded view of marketing activities and the discipline of marketing, *Journal of Marketing*, 63, Special Issue, 168–179.
St John, C. and Rue, L. (1991) Coordinating mechanisms, consensus between marketing and manufacturing groups and marketplace performance, *Strategic Management Journal*, 12, 7, 549–555.
Trice, H. and Beyer, J. (1993) *The Cultures of Work Organizations*. Englewood Cliffs, NJ.
Vandermerwe, S. and Gilbert, D. (1991) Internal services. Gaps in needs/performance and prescriptions for effectiveness, *International Journal of Service Industry Management*, 2, 1, 50–60.
Vollmann, T. and Cordon, C. (1999) Building a smarter demand chain, *Financial Times Series*, 4, 2–4.
Wang, E.T.G. and Wei, H.-L. (2005) The importance of market orientation, learning orientation, and quality orientation capabilities in TQM: an example from Taiwanese software industry, *Total Quality Management & Business Excellence*, 16, 10, 1161–1177.
Workman, J. (1993) Marketing's limited role in new product development in one computer systems firm, *Journal of Marketing Research*, 30, 4, 405–421.
Workman, J. and Webb, K. (1999) Variations in the power of marketing between consumer and industrial firms, *Journal of Business to Business Marketing*, 6, 2, 1–37.
Yam, R.C.M., Tam, A.Y.K., Tang, E.P.Y. and Mok, C.K. (2005) TQM: a change management model for market orientation, *Total Quality Management & Business Excellence*, 16, 4, 439–461.
Zeithaml, V., Parasuraman, A. and Berry, L. (1990) *Delivering Service Quality – Balancing Customer Perceptions and Expectations*. New York.

End of Part Case Study – The Nespresso Story: Success with Coffee Based on Market Orientation

If you go to the luxury sushi-restaurant Unkai in the Grand Hotel Wien (Austria) and order coffee after your expensive sushi meal, the espresso served will have been produced by Nestlé Nespresso. In high-end restaurants in the UK guests are also being served Nespresso coffees. These coffees taste perfectly acceptable in the environment of a high-end restaurant, even though they are not provided by a traditional supplier.

Away from restaurants, among private coffee consumers a 'Nespresso revolution' is taking place – revolutionizing the multibillion-euro global coffee industry. Nestlé Nespresso pioneered the portioned coffee market to provide the highest quality coffees to be enjoyed both in private homes as well as in restaurants or offices. Nestlé Nespresso has fully understood the changing consumption preferences of global coffee consumers who demand a combination of variety (offer of a broad range of capsules with differing coffee blends) and high convenience (capsule system requires little maintenance of the coffee-machine) together with highest quality (capsule system preserves the coffee aroma and only top quality coffee blends are used).

Who is responsible for this 'Nespresso revolution'? 2,500 employees work for Nestlé Nespresso, which is headquartered in Paudex, Switzerland. They currently operate in more than 40 countries around the world. Nestlé Nespresso is a globally managed business of the Nestlé Group, the world's largest food and beverages company. While benefiting from Nestlé's expertise, Nestlé Nespresso has overall responsibility for its research and development, the supply of its raw materials as well as the production and the marketing of its super-premium coffee products.

How does the Nespresso system work? The Nespresso system consists of a coffee machine and corresponding capsules. The coffee machines can only be operated with these capsules. The Nespresso coffee machines are manufactured by an OEM (original equipment manufacturer) supplier and distributed by partners such as Krups, Miele and Siemens. In the design process, Nespresso teamed up early on with Swiss designer Antoine Cahen to design the machines. The Nespresso coffee machines are widely sold in electrical retail stores.

In its product offering, Nespresso focuses on the coffee capsules, which can only be bought directly from Nespresso – in Nespresso stores ('Nespresso boutiques'), in the Nespresso Online-Shop, or via mail-order. Nestlé had been researching the idea of capsules since 1970. Coffee starts to deteriorate the minute it has been picked, and particularly once it has been ground. By storing it in an individual hermetically-sealed alloy capsule, the quality of the coffee is prolonged for several months. For its capsules, the company uses only 'gourmet' or specialty coffee (which makes up 10%–20% of world production), of which only 10% meets its standards. Most of it (95% Arabica) comes from Latin America and grows at between 1,500m and 2,500m; the remainder (Robusta) comes from small plantations in Asia and Africa.

There are two types of Nespresso capsules available – one intended for domestic use, and another for office use. The domestic capsules cost around 0.30 euro per capsule containing around 7 grams of coffee, resulting in a kilo price of more than 40 euros. Once consumers buy a Nespresso coffee machine, they automatically become 'Nespresso club members' and receive a welcome package with a set of free coffee capsules and directions on how to order new capsules directly from Nespresso. They then get regularly informed on coffee innovations by Nespresso via direct mailings.

Exhibit 1 Nespresso coffee machine

Exhibit 2 Nespresso coffee capsules

The Nespresso company operates in two market segments: the Nespresso In-Home Division and the Nespresso Business Coffee Solutions for the out-of-home sector. The In-Home Division accounts for 85 per cent of sales, and focuses on the coffee and machine needs of customers, the Club Members. Nespresso enables Club Members to order coffee capsules and machines through the internet or via phone. At the boutiques customer service professionals are on hand to answer questions and provide their expertise to customers .

The Out-of-Home division, or Nespresso Business Coffee Solutions, accounts for 15% of sales and provides solutions for customers in five primary channels. These channels include: high-end restaurants, hotels and cafes; premium event caterers; customer care and other luxury retail; first class travel; and offices.

The success of Nestlé Nespresso is illustrated by the fact that Nespresso grew by an average of 35% between 2000 and 2007. This makes Nestlé Nespresso the fastest-growing business in the Nestlé group. Nespresso is well on course to hitting the two billion CHF revenue mark by 2010. The following milestones illustrate the development of Nespresso's success story:

In 1970, Nestlé created the Nespresso system, a technically advanced espresso machine using pre-measured ground coffee capsules that protect more than 900 coffee aromas.

In 1986, the Nespresso SA company, wholly owned by the Nestlé Group, is founded in Vevey. In partnership with Swiss manufacturer Turmix, it launches the Nespresso system in the office coffee sectors of Switzerland and Italy.

In 1996, Nestlé Nespresso SA celebrates ten years of success with 3,500 points of sale and 180,000 affiliated Club members. The system is also launched in Great Britain, Malaysia, Singapore and Taiwan.

In 1998, the company widens its range: in partnership with Alessi, it launches a machine of distinctively avant-garde design and expands its horizons with a redesigned internet site.

In 2001, the ease-of-use and ergonomic design offered by the Nespresso 'Concept Machine' launch lead to record machine sales. Nestlé Nespresso SA begins construction of a new production center for coffee capsules in Orbe, Switzerland.

In 2002, capsule production capacity is expanded 400% to meet future growth requirements and on-line orders increase 94% during the year. E-business now accounts for 30% of the company's turnover.

In 2003, at the Sintercafé Convention in Costa Rica, Nestlé Nespresso SA announces the launch of its 'AAA Sustainable Quality Coffee' program designed to promote production and supply of sustainable, highest quality coffee.

In 2004, Nestlé Nespresso SA signs an event supporter agreement with America's Cup management, making Nespresso the official coffee of the 32nd America's Cup, and also forms an alliance to be the co-sponsor of Alinghi, the defender of the 32nd America's Cup.

In 2005, sales of the revolutionary Nespresso Essenza coffee machine help establish Nestlé Nespresso as the European market leader in Espresso machines.

In 2006, Nestlé Nespresso engages George Clooney to star in a 50-second film entitled, 'The Boutique' to run in European movie theaters and television stations.

Exhibit 3 Building the brand image with George Clooney as a celebrity endorser

Exhibit 4 Nespresso sponsoring the Alinghi team of the America's Cup

'The key to our success is what we call the Nespresso trilogy: the combination of highest quality Grands Crus coffees, smart and stylish machines and exclusive customer service,' says Richard Girardot, CEO of Nestlé Nespresso. 'In addition, we have the ability to engage with and delight coffee connoisseurs around the world in a very personal way through our global network of 117 Nespresso boutiques. In 2008, we expect to continue our pattern of steady and sustainable global growth by continuing to focus on our trilogy and expanding our network of boutiques' (Nespresso 2008).

Nespresso likes to think of these boutiques as coffee destinations. Places where customers can relax, catch up with friends and enjoy the pleasures of perfect coffee. Boutique bars are located in key cities around the world. All boutiques have a special interior design that is consistent with Nespresso's corporate design and brand personality. Trained coffee specialists in the boutiques provide with advice on the various coffee variants and the machines.

Exhibit 5 New York City boutique bar

While many highly satisfied consumers contribute to the Nespresso success story, there are also some criticisms. First, the unique design of Nespresso capsules requires customers to purchase the relatively expensive coffee from Nespresso and prohibits them from purchasing coffee made by other coffee providers. Furthermore, Nespresso machines do not allow users to fine-tune the strength of a beverage (as possible with traditional pump espresso machines). Hence, customers do not have control over the amount of ground coffee used per shot – they can only choose between a long or short espresso. It is also criticized that no Fairtrade coffee is available as a Nespresso capsule. Nespresso has devised its own scheme known as 'AAA Sustainable Quality' in cooperation with the Rainforest Alliance. Finally, even though the aluminum capsules are recyclables, Nestlé has only implemented a recycling concept in Switzerland. In all other countries, customers must remove the coffee grounds from the capsule prior to recycling the aluminum.

However, even against these criticisms, the development of Nespresso is widely viewed as an important success story. It is worthwhile looking at the corporate vision and corporate culture behind this Nespresso success story. They are formulated by Nespresso as follows:

Our vision is to be preferred and respected as the leading quality coffee company for portioned coffee and become **The Icon for Perfect Coffee Worldwide.**

In order to achieve this, we have set out for ourselves the core areas which we as a Company believe strongly in:

- **Employees:** People from diverse backgrounds with the right expertise and skills are our most important asset and the source of our competitive advantage. Recruitment of these people and ongoing training and development are crucial to our Company's success.
- **Quality:** We are dedicated to achieving the highest-quality standards of our coffee, machines and services.
- **Brand:** The strength of our brand ensures the continuity of our growth and profitability. It is the responsibility of every employee to support the strength and quality of the *Nespresso* brand.
- **Consumers:** Our reason for being is to understand, anticipate and best fulfill our consumers' needs. The trust our consumers have in our Company and our behavior is vital to our success.
- **Partners:** We strive to create constructive, inspiring and professional relationships with all of our business partners and suppliers of materials, goods and services to achieve mutual value and respect.
- **Performance:** We are all committed to achieving our financial and strategic objectives while working in line with our core values.

CORE VALUES

- Trust in People
- Excellence and Perfection
- Passion, Commitment and Pride
- Pioneering Spirit
- Honesty and Ethics

CULTURAL DRIVERS

- Team Work
- Focus
- Fighting Spirit
- Open Mindedness
- Innovation

In order to implement the required skills and cultural values among Nespresso employees, the Nespresso employees regularly attend the 'Nespresso Coffee Academy', a comprehensive coffee training program developed specifically by and for Nespresso. Furthermore, Nespresso invests heavily in continuous market research with a strong focus on continuous blind tests to find out about consumers' coffee preferences.

Source: Nespresso (2008), Nestlé Nespresso poised for continued growth, Nespresso Media Center.

This case study was written under the supervision of Harley Krohmer, Universiy of Berne.

Discussion Questions

1. How do you account for Nespresso's success in the global coffee market?
2. How do you relate Nespresso's intended corporate culture (core values and cultural drivers) to the concept of market orientation?
3. How do you evaluate the concept of the Nespresso Club Membership and relate it to market orientation?
4. How should Nespresso respond to the critique formulated in the case?

End of Part Case Study – Bayer CropScience: Aspirin for Crops?

The Bayer Story in Crops

What do you know of Bayer? Of course the 'Aspirin'! But there is far more to the company than Aspirin and healthcare in general (only 40% of revenue). Bayer is also active in other fields such as materials science (35%) and crop science (20%, see Bayer 2008). The crop science part alone is a €5.8 billion business and therefore larger than most other companies. With an adjusted 22% EBITDA it is also the most profitable division of Bayer AG. Bayer CropScience is head to head with the second largest company Syngenta AG (€6.3 billion) from Switzerland (see Syngenta 2008a). Crop science products include generally four kinds of products: herbicides, insecticides, fungicides and seed treatment.

Bayer has organized this business into a stand-alone legal entity called Bayer CropScience AG (in the following called BCS). The legal entity is situated in Monheim, Germany, but achieves more than 80% of its revenues outside of Germany. The business is the combination of units from different companies. A major part of the business was AgrEvo GmbH, founded in 1994, which was a joint venture of Hoechst AG and Schering AG and in 1999 merged with the unit Rhône-Poulenc Agro into Aventis CropScience. This unit was in 2002 bought by Bayer AG and then merged into the new unit Bayer CropScience AG. In 2007 BCS had revenues of €5.8 billion and EBITDA of 22.7% achieved with 17,800 employees around the globe (see Bayer 2008). Through the different mergers, BCS has acquired roughly 11,000 patents for products, product names, process technologies etc.

The Global Fruit and Vegetable Market

Today, it is virtually impossible to get fruit or vegetables that have not been treated by crop protection products in one way or another. Main crops to be protected and treated are rice, soy, wheat, grapes, maize and horticulture vegetables (tomatoes, cucumbers, etc.). Protection means protection from insects (by insecticides), fungus (by fungicides), and weeds (by herbicides). Furthermore, there is a (growing) market for genetically treated crops. This market falls within the area of 'seed treatment'.

The crop protection market is a slow-growing market (see Exhibit 1). However, the growing world population (up to over 7 billion) and the unresolved food problems (farm land expected to be constant at 1.5 billion hectare) for large parts of this population would imply a growing demand for crops. This would imply an increased need for crop protection and therefore a growing future market (see Berschauer 2005). At the same time, agriculture and crops are still undergoing significant productivity improvements. This becomes apparent when one looks, for example, at India: India has about 1.1 billion people and an estimated 90 million farmers (see Klas 2008) with an average lot size of about 1.5 ha (see Petersen 2008). A lot of the agricultural work is still done by hand. Furthermore, the crop protection market has a significant problem with decreasing prices. International experts estimate the price decline in the market to approximate 1 to 2% p.a. (see Berschauer 2006). Those effects lead in total to only a moderate growth for crop protection.

Exhibit 1 Development of Global Crop Protection Market

Global Crop Protection Market: 2001 – 2007		
Year	**€ billion**	**% Growth**
2001	26.0	–
2002	24.5	–5.8%
2003	25.0	2.0%
2004	25.7	2.8%
2005	27.0	5.1%
2006	27.5	1.9%
2007	28.0	1.8%

Source: Prof. Homburg & Partner Estimations 2008.

The type of fruits and vegetables grown depend very much on the climate in the country. Since almost every country has a different climate, almost every country has a different agricultural approach. For example, there are already major differences between the agriculture culture of Germany and France although they are next-door neighbors. This also applies for larger countries such as Brazil or the US with very different climates (and therefore crops) in the different regions.

But the crops and the crop protection employed also depend on a country's culture and history. First of all, certain cultures favor the growth of certain crops. Since, for example, France is rather a 'wine-drinking nation' it is clear that it will grow comparably more grapes than other nations with a similar climate, such as Germany which is rather a 'beer-drinking nation' therefore also growing hops. Similar conclusions can be drawn with regard to crops like soy and rice, which play a major role in Asia, whereas wheat, rye and so on play a bigger role in Europe. As a consequence, many countries have an often 'historically grown' view on crop protection. As an example one might look at the usage of genetically altered crops which is very critically discussed in Germany whereas this is not considered critically in the Benelux countries, for example. Moreover, country-specific legal restrictions might apply to the usage of crop protection. For example, allowed levels for crop protection content in bananas are five times higher in the US than in the EU. This obviously leads to the effect that growth methods for bananas sent to the EU have to be different or other crop protection methods and/or products have to be used. Exhibit 2 shows the geographic distribution of crop protection worldwide.

Exhibit 2 Distribution of Global Crop Protection Market

Global Crop Protection Market: % Share, by Value, 2006	
Geography	**% Share**
North America	Ca. 24%
Latin America	Ca. 17%
Europe	Ca. 30%
Asia-Pacific	Ca. 24%
Rest of the World	Ca. 5%
Total	**100%**

Source: Prof. Homburg & Partner Estimations 2008.

Exhibit 3 Major Players in the Global Crop Protection Market

Global Crop Protection Market			
Company	**Revenue (€ billion)**	**Market Share (%)**	**EBITDA**
BCS	5.8	Ca. 19%	Ca. 22%
Syngenta	6.3	Ca. 20%	Ca. 20%
BASF	3.0	Ca. 10%	Ca. 19%
Monsanto	5.0	Ca. 16%	Ca. 28%
Dupont	4.7	Ca. 15%	Ca. 19%
Other	6.2	Ca. 20%	–
Total	**31.0**	**100 %**	–

Source: Summary of the homepages of the relevant companies.

Interestingly, the rather profitable international crop protection market is an oligopolistic one (see Exhibit 3). In certain areas, products are basically not easy or are even impossible to differentiate by the customer (the farmer). Products are also often 10 years or even up to 40 years old (see Scheitza 2005). Therefore, patents and low cost production methods on the one hand and strong brands and innovative sales and marketing concepts on the other hand play a very important role in the business (see Scheitza 2005). Only a few large players can obviously survive this balancing act between a commodity and specialty business type (see McDougall 2007).

How to Implement Marketing Strategies and Approaches?

We will focus on marketing implementation as discussed in Part 4 of this book. Marketing implementation issues became apparent when BCS started a major systematic price management initiative in 2005 (see Gruber 2006). The price management initiative concerned all four areas of marketing implementation: marketing organization, marketing and sales information systems, marketing and sales management control, and human resource management in marketing and sales.

As a traditional European company, BCS had a classical centralized marketing department formerly called 'marketing services'. This department was concerned with the typical communication issues such as advertising, trade shows, internet/intranet appearance, sales support, give aways, PR etc. Traditionally, BCS has also been strong in research and has therefore spent money on numerous market research studies. Proof of this is that basically every market research institute has BCS as a reference on their homepage, especially institutes well known in the agriculture market such as Kleefmann, Produkt & Markt, Frost & Sullivan and GfK (see the homepages of these companies). Logically, the centralized marketing department employed market researchers. Due to the increasing number of brands resulting from the mergers mentioned above, brand managers had to be introduced. Around the year 2004 new tasks were assigned to the marketing department. These tasks included mainly the establishment of a CRM system, the development of employees in marketing and sales, and the development of a systematic pricing approach for BCS. Furthermore, as one can easily observe from job openings and platforms (like linkedin, facebook, xing etc.), BCS has marketing managers, business development managers and market research managers in all major countries. Altogether – depending on the marketing definition – we are talking about 150 people around the globe involved in marketing, approximately thirty of them centralized. As mentioned above, one of the major new tasks was to ensure a systematic pricing approach around the globe and to half the price decline as mentioned in the introduction. For this, following a pricing project, approximately 25 'price champions' – one per country, one per business unit and several coordinating ones – were named (see Gruber 2006).

Marketing and sales management control is mainly managed by the controlling department. As a German company, the controlling department is rather centralized. Moreover, a lot of procedure, instruments, reports and so on were put in place by the parent company Bayer AG and employees have to adhere to them. Reporting was traditionally organized per country. The incentive systems were organized similarly. Therefore, good country managers were able to more easily achieve their financial goals (such as local EBIT) by negotiating either lower transfer prices or 'special prices'. However, in 2006 the system was changed to a consolidated contribution margin including the local and the business unit margin (see Hennecke 2007). This was also done in order to provide the pricing managers with a tool to exercise some governance.

In contrast to most other companies, the responsibility for certain parts of human resource management in Marketing and Sales was early farmed out to the marketing department. One of the key factors for an international company with more than 80% of the business outside of the home country is 'speaking the same language' and frequent information exchange. Interestingly, as one can see by the vitae of many marketing managers of BCS posted on the platforms mentioned above, they have typically been in sales or marketing and have worked at some time in another country. This leads to a strong local content – even in central marketing. Furthermore, there is an extended, international, at least English-speaking network of marketing managers around the globe. In addition to these framework factors the central marketing department has been carrying out extensive marketing training for all 'high potentials' around the globe. This training (called Marketing Academy) includes at least a two-week training session in different topics ranging from branding, new product development, market research, pricing etc. to team building and other soft skills (see Klein 2005). Moreover, the centralized marketing department took on the task to provide better sharing of market information in the marketing community. To accomplish this goal, several centralized intranet zones were created. As an example, nowadays every market research study that is conducted (by either central marketing, business unit, region or country) has to be classified and details as well as results have to be provided on the intranet server by the responsible unit. Additionally, 'integrated crop platforms' with all information about a certain crop were established (see Scheitza 2006). The effect of this was a marked increase in transparency which helped to prevent that the 'wheel was invented over and over again' in different units.

Final Thoughts on the Crop Protection Market

Quo vadis crop science market? As discussed above there are major influences on crops in the agricultural market. On of the unsolved problems is the need for more and better food to provide sufficient food for the world population. Increased and improved crop protection will play a major role in this. Furthermore, the use of genetically altered crops will change the picture. All major trends are summarized by the two largest players in the market in Exhibit 4.

Much, however, will depend on global climate change. In the end this will lead to the effect that certain crops cannot be cultivated in certain countries any more. The declining part of the agricultural industry in these countries will pose major challenges to the marketing and sales of corresponding crop protection products in these countries. BCS, with its local approach, has a good basis to address these problems from a global perspective. But the best insights in the markets by the local people staff to be consolidated. Ultimately, time will tell whether BCS will choose the most suitable marketing implementation approach.

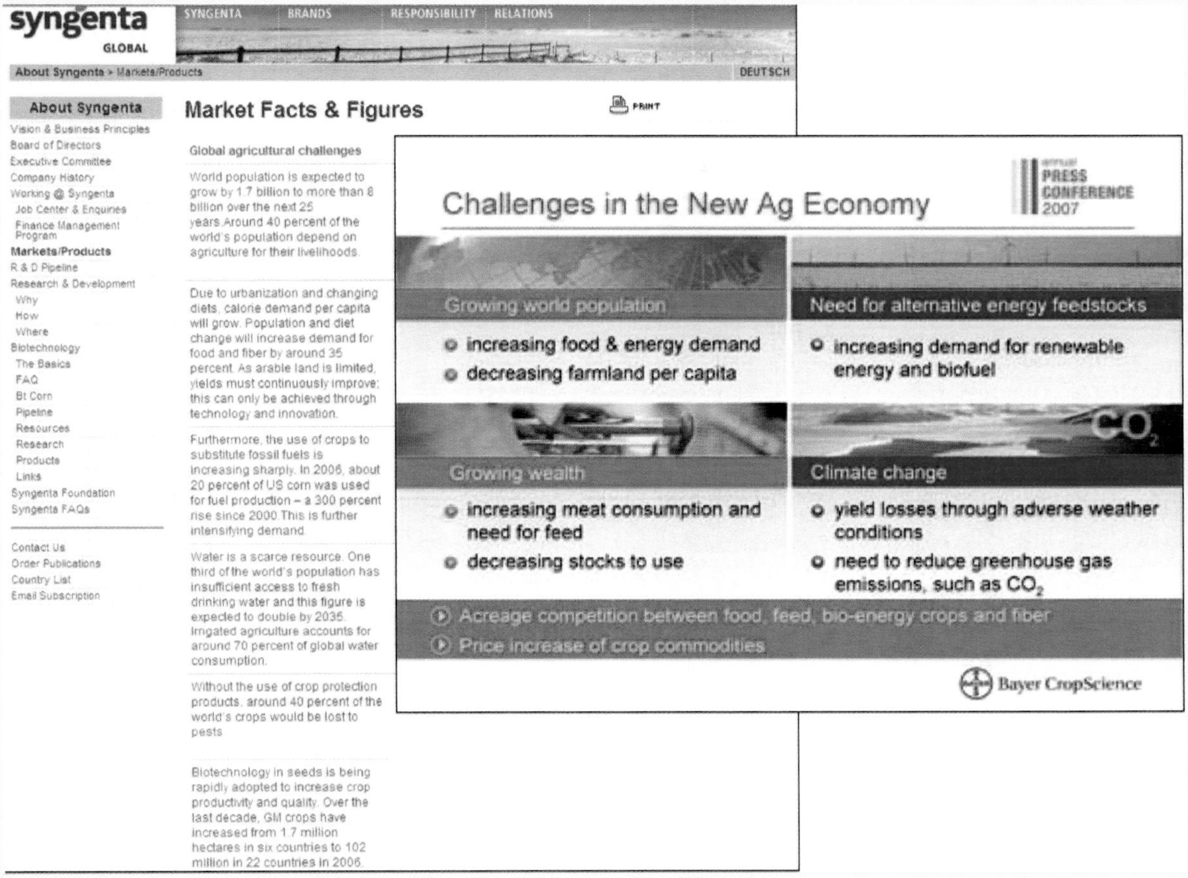

Exhibit 4 Global Trends in Agriculture Economy
Source: Syngenta AG 2008b and Berschauer 2007

This case was written by Dr. Nikolas Beutin Managing Director and Partner, Prof. Homburg & Partner, Germany.

Discussion Questions

1. What marketing implementation approach does BCS use? Describe the challenges with regard to the marketing implementation perspective of HRM, marketing and sales information systems, marketing and sales management control, and marketing organization.
2. What is the advantage of this marketing implementation approach? Discuss other marketing implementation alternatives.
3. Could the global changes in the crop market imply that a different marketing implementation approach is more suitable in the future?

References

BASF AG (2008), http://www.berichte.basf.de/basfir/copsfiles/de/2007/datenundfakten/14036_BASF_Daten_und_Fakten_2007.pdf?suffix=.pdf&id=JgNKCC2hcbcp*OT.
Bayer AG (2008), http://www.bayer.de/de/Namen-Zahlen-Fakten-2007_2008-D.pdfx.
Bayer CropScience AG (2006), http://www.bayercropscience.com/bayer/cropscience/cscms.nsf/id/DE_20061702?Open&ccm=400020870000&L=DE&markedcolor=%23003399.
Berschauer, Friedrich (2007), http://www.bayercropscience.com/bayer/cropscience/cscms.nsf/id/2007-1520_EN?open&ccm=400.
Berschauer, Friedrich (2006), http://www.bayercropscience.com/bayer/cropscience/cscms.nsf/id/Pres_Berschauer.
Gruber, Friedrich (2006), Customer Segmentation and Pricing in the CropScience Market, presented at the DVS Distribution Partner conference, 09.05.2006 in Stuttgart.
Hennecke, Ingo (2007), Systematic Pricing at BayerCropScience, presented at the DVS Pricing conference, 13.06.2007 in Duesseldorf.
Klas, Gerhard (2008), Neue Hoffnung für Indiens Bauern?, 16.03.2008, http://www.heise.de/tp/r4/artikel/27/27477/1.html.
Klein, Udo (2005), Local Implementation of Global CRM Projects, presented at the 4th Yearly CRM Meeting 2005, 19.04.2005 in Heidelberg.
DuPont (2008), http://library.corporate-ir.net/library/73/733/73320/items/280068/DD_2007_10-K.pdf.
McDougall, Phillips (2007), The Global Crop Protection Market –Industry Prospects, http://www.cpda.com/TeamPublish/uploads/McDougall_Global.pdf.
Monsanto Co. (2008), http://www.monsanto.com/pdf/pubs/2007/2007AnnualReport.pdf.
Petersen, Britta (2008), Trotz High-Tech-Boom – Indien ist ein Agrarland, http://www.bpb.de/themen/ZVOYPO,0,0,Reise_durch_den_Selbstmordg%FCrtel.html.
Scheitza, Ruediger (2005), http://www.bayercropscience.com/bayer/cropscience/cscms.nsf/id/Pres_Scheitza.
Scheitza, Ruediger (2006), http://www.bayercropscience.com/bayer/cropscience/cscms.nsf/id/DE_2006-1524?Open&ccm=400020870000&L=DE&markedcolor=%23003399.
Syngenta AG (2008a), http://www.syngenta.com/de/media/press/2008/02-07.htm.
Syngenta AG (2008b), http://www.syngenta.com/en/about_syngenta/overview.aspx.

Appendix: Theories and Techniques

This appendix serves as a source of additional and supplementary information on the theories and techniques discussed in the book. It captures basic aspects of theories in psychology and economics that help to explain consumer behavior. Additionally, it provides an overview of the main methods in market research. To obtain an overview of these topics, the appendix can also be read separately from the rest of the book. In this case we recommend that you begin with the basic key words 'consumer behavior' or 'market research', and continue with the references provided.

All terms are listed in alphabetical order.

Activation

Activation is an important construct of **consumer behavior**. Activation has been defined as a strong, excited emotion that stimulates an individual – for example in a buying situation, to act. Activation energizes the organism of a consumer and prepares it to perform. Activation is the basis for the willingness to process information, perceive ads or form attitudes on brands, products, etc.

There are two types of activation:

1. **tonic** activation – long-term general ability to perform, independent from the situation
2. **phasic** activation – short in duration, triggered by certain stimuli.

Stimuli are external factors that trigger activation. These can be:

- **emotional stimuli** – trigger activation via internal excitement, partly biologically programed (e.g. a picture of a child in need of help)
- **cognitive stimuli** – created via conflicting thoughts, contradictions or surprise, which then trigger activation (e.g. elderly people who overtly exhibit youthful behavior)
- **physic (or physical) stimuli** – activation triggered by the special physical attributes of objects (e.g. commercials with special sounds).

Activation has an impact on consumer behavior, especially on the way in which individuals process information (e.g. if customers are strongly activated they may be inclined towards impulse buying). The impact of activation on information processing can be explained by the Lambda hypothesis.

Lambda hypothesis:

- According to this hypothesis, the performance (e.g. the processing of information) of an individual improves with increasing activation, and drops off again from a certain activation level (see Figure A-1).
- In the case of over-activation, an increase in activation level leads to diminished performance.

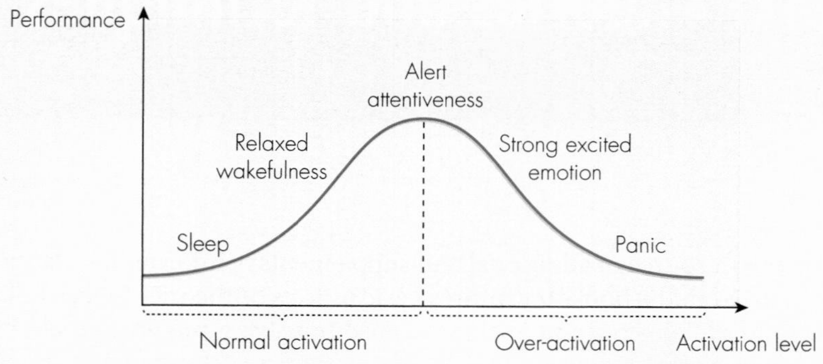

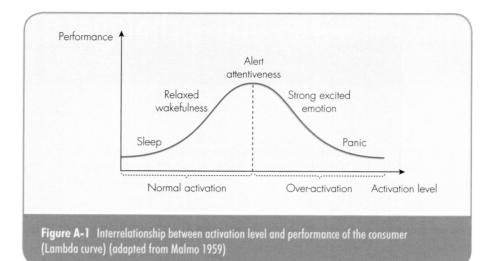

Figure A-1 Interrelationship between activation level and performance of the consumer (Lambda curve) (adapted from Malmo 1959)

- The task of marketing is thus to increase activation while avoiding over-activation, so that customers can adequately process information.

Influencing activation

- The design of the communication measures should promote the activation of consumers and therefore enhance information processing.
- Enhancing information processing can be accomplished by means of the emotional, cognitive and physical stimuli described above.
- Most marketing activities take place in the sphere of normal activation.

Attitude

Attitude is one of the main constructs explaining *consumer behavior*. An attitude is a relatively stable mindset or belief of a consumer towards a brand, product, product category, etc. This mindset is usually accompanied by evaluations or expectations. Attitudes influence how individuals behave towards objects.

There are different **types of attitude:**

- **cognitively based attitudes**, which arise from intellectually evaluated information about the object (e.g. consumer evaluation of a new product according to objective product features), **versus emotionally based attitudes**, which arise from the consumer's feelings and emotions about the object (e.g. consumer evaluation of a new product according to objective product features)
- **categorical attitudes**, which relate to categories of objects (e.g. product categories such as tobacco products), **versus specific attitudes**, which are related to a concrete object (e.g. a specific product such as the new skin cream brand)
- **attitudes based on experiences**, which result from personal experience with an object (e.g. attitude towards a spa resort based on experience from last visit), **versus adopted attitudes**, which are based on external information (e.g. attitude towards a new product after reading testimonials).

Attitudes can be **measured** as follows.

- Consumer's **physical (physiological) reactions** (e.g. pulse rate) can be recorded.
- Consumer's **behavior** can be observed (see *Observation*).
- Consumers can be interviewed about their attitudes (see *Surveys*).

Marketing can influence consumer attitudes:

- within the scope of product decisions, especially with the design and development of new products and the management of existing products and brands (see Chapter 5)
- within the scope of pricing decisions (see Chapter 6)
- in the area of the sales decision, especially the design of sales activities (see Chapter 7)
- by the way the company communicates (see Chapter 8)
- by managing customer relationships (see Chapter 9).

Cluster analysis

Cluster analysis is a *multivariate method* used in *market research* to analyze data. Cluster analysis classifies objects, e.g. customers, into distinct groups. The principal objective of cluster analysis is to reduce the complexity of a data set by combining objects into groups (clusters). These clusters are as homogeneous as possible within each other and as heterogeneous as possible compared to the other clusters. As opposed to *factor analysis*, cluster analysis reduces the number of objects, not of variables.

In market research, the main area of application of cluster analysis is **market segmentation.**

Cluster analysis can be applied to both metric and non-metric variables (see also *multivariate methods*). The **procedure for conducting a cluster analysis** consists of the following analytical steps.

1. **Selection of the cluster variables**
   - Selection of the characteristic attributes of the objects to be considered (for example, purchase intention).
2. **Creation of a distance matrix**
   - The distance matrix measures the similarities of and differences between the objects. The most common measure of difference is the Squared Euclidean distance, which adds up the squared difference between the values of two objects across all attributes.
3. **Elimination of outliers**
   - Outliers are those objects whose characteristic values are abnormal or atypical for the sample, in the sense that they are far away from all the other objects or close to only a very few other objects. They should be eliminated from the data set since they can have a major impact on results and can distort the analysis.

4. **Selection of a cluster algorithm**
   - Individual objects are either grouped together according to their similarity (hierarchical algorithms), or the group of objects as a whole is split according to their differences (partitioning algorithms).
5. **Identifying the number of clusters**
   - There is no explicit rule on how many clusters to build. The researcher has to judge how many clusters should be built and investigated. However, there are some well-established criteria for the termination of the amalgamation process (e.g. the Cubic clustering criterion and the Elbow criterion).
6. **Interpretation and labeling of the clusters**
   - Labels need to be found for the clusters formed, which describe them best in terms of their attributes and differentiate them from the other clusters.

Conjoint analysis

Conjoint analysis is an important method in market research that involves measuring preferences for different product attributes at the individual customer level. It belongs to the class of *multivariate methods*, which allows the study of a large number of variables simultaneously.

The underlying idea of conjoint analysis is that the benefit created from a product as a whole can be split into distinct utilities generated by single product attributes. In order to do this, the product is decomposed into several attributes, each potentially offering benefit for the customer. The overall objective is to find a combination of attributes that customers prefer most.

Main areas of application are in **new product development** (see Section 5.3.2) and **pricing decisions**, especially measuring willingness to pay (see Section 6.2.1).

The most important analytical steps of conjoint analysis are as follows.

1. **Definition of salient attributes and corresponding attribute levels**
2. **Specification of how data is collected from customers**
   - via profile method – with this method, customers have to evaluate hypothetical products using a full description of all attributes
   - via trade-off method – here, just two attribute pairs are compared at a time and rank ordered, which makes it easier for customers to answer.
3. **Data collection**
4. **Estimation of the utility values**
   - part worth utilities for the different attributes can be computed from the preferences customers indicate for the proposed attribute bundles; the total utility is calculated by the sum of the part worth utilities
   - the analysis also reveals which attributes are especially important for customers and which are not (see the application in Section 5.3.2).
5. **Interpretation of the resulting utility values**
   - a change in single product attributes affects the total utility of the product. Therefore, the effects of product design on the buying decision can be estimated by comparing total utilities.

Consumer behavior

Consumer behavior refers to all actions of individuals associated with the purchase or consumption of products and services. Understanding what drives customers' purchasing decisions is essential for marketing. For marketing, and especially for communication design, the understanding of consumer behavior is of central importance (see Section 8.1). This is the overall objective in consumer behavior research.

The **main constructs** examined in consumer behavior research to understand and explain consumer behavior are:

- activation (see also *Activation*)
- attitude (see also *Attitude*)
- customer satisfaction (see also *Customer satisfaction*)
- emotion (see also *Emotion*)
- environmental factors (see also *Environmental factors*)
- involvement (see also *Involvement*)
- motivation (see also *Motivation*)
- values and lifestyle (see also *Values and lifestyle*).

Apart from these basic constructs, consumer behavior also deals with the question of how individuals **process information**. Information processing involves different types of memory within the brain at different stages (see *Memory model*). Knowing how information is processed helps marketing managers to design communication in such a way that it will be easily perceived and processed.

Consumer behavior research draws on **psychological and economic theories** to explain how customers process information and make purchasing decisions. The most important theories for consumer behavior are:

- dissonance theory (see also *Dissonance theory*)
- game theory (see also *Game theory*)
- information economics (see also *Information economics*)
- learning theory (see also *Learning theory*)
- risk theory (see also *Risk theory*)
- transaction cost theory (see also *Transaction cost theory*).

Customer needs

In general, needs arise when there is a discrepancy between actual and desired states of being. Needs are human requirements that result from subjectively perceived – psychological, personal or sociological – deficiencies. Individuals' desire to meet these needs is the driving force of their motivation (see also *Motivation*).

Products create benefit for the customer by satisfying customer needs. Therefore, a careful evaluation of customer needs should, for example, be the basis for all product decisions (see Section 5.4.2). A **method to evaluate customer needs** is conjoint analysis, which helps to assess to what extent specific product attributes contribute to customer benefits (see also *Conjoint analysis*).

Needs can be distinguished into basic needs and higher needs, suggesting the idea of a hierarchical ordering (see also Maslow's pyramid in *Motivation*).

Customer satisfaction

Customer satisfaction is a key construct in marketing and *consumer behavior* research. Enhancing customer satisfaction is a key objective in customer relationship management and often referred to as a measure of marketing effectiveness.

The formation of customer satisfaction is explained by the widely accepted confirmation/disconfirmation paradigm (C/D paradigm). The basic idea of the **C/D paradigm** can be explained as follows.

- Customer satisfaction results from comparing the actual experience (perceived actual performance of a product) with a comparison standard (the expected performance).
- Customer satisfaction arises when the actual performance exceeds expectations.

According to the C/D paradigm, customer satisfaction can be **influenced** by:

- increasing performance (e.g. product quality)
- influencing perceptions about performance (e.g. appropriate communication activities)
- influencing expectations.

Establishing customer satisfaction is considered important because:

- customer satisfaction is a prerequisite for customer loyalty and ensures future revenues (see Section 9.1)
- customer satisfaction has an impact on the customer's willingness to pay; in particular, it decreases a customer's price sensitivity (see Figure A-2).

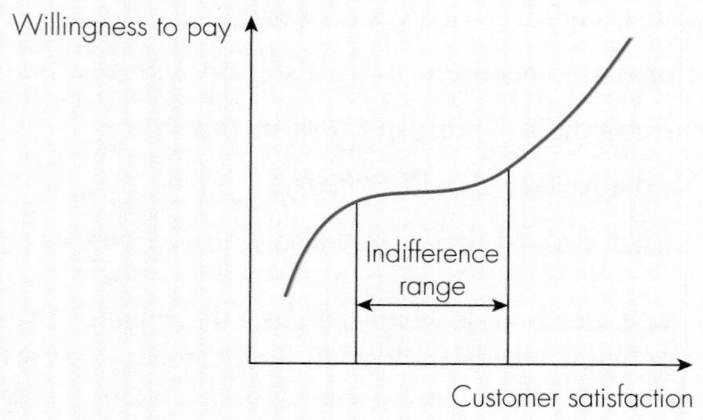

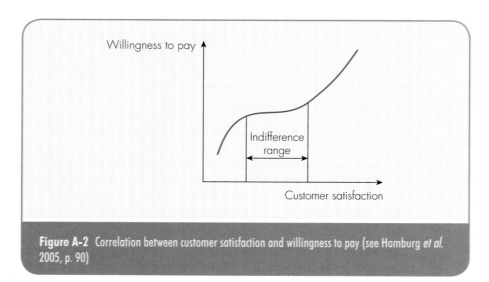

Figure A-2 Correlation between customer satisfaction and willingness to pay (see Homburg *et al.* 2005, p. 90)

Data collection methods

Data for market research can be obtained in two ways: by the use of secondary data or the collection of primary data.

Secondary data:

- is retrieved from already existing information sources
- is usually quickly available at reasonable costs
- but does not always meet the information requirements of a market research study completely.

See also *Secondary data*.

Primary data:

- is newly collected during a market research study
- is tailored to individual information requirements
- but requires much more effort and time to gather.

See also *Primary data*.

Primary and secondary data imply different methods of data collection and use (see Figure A-3).

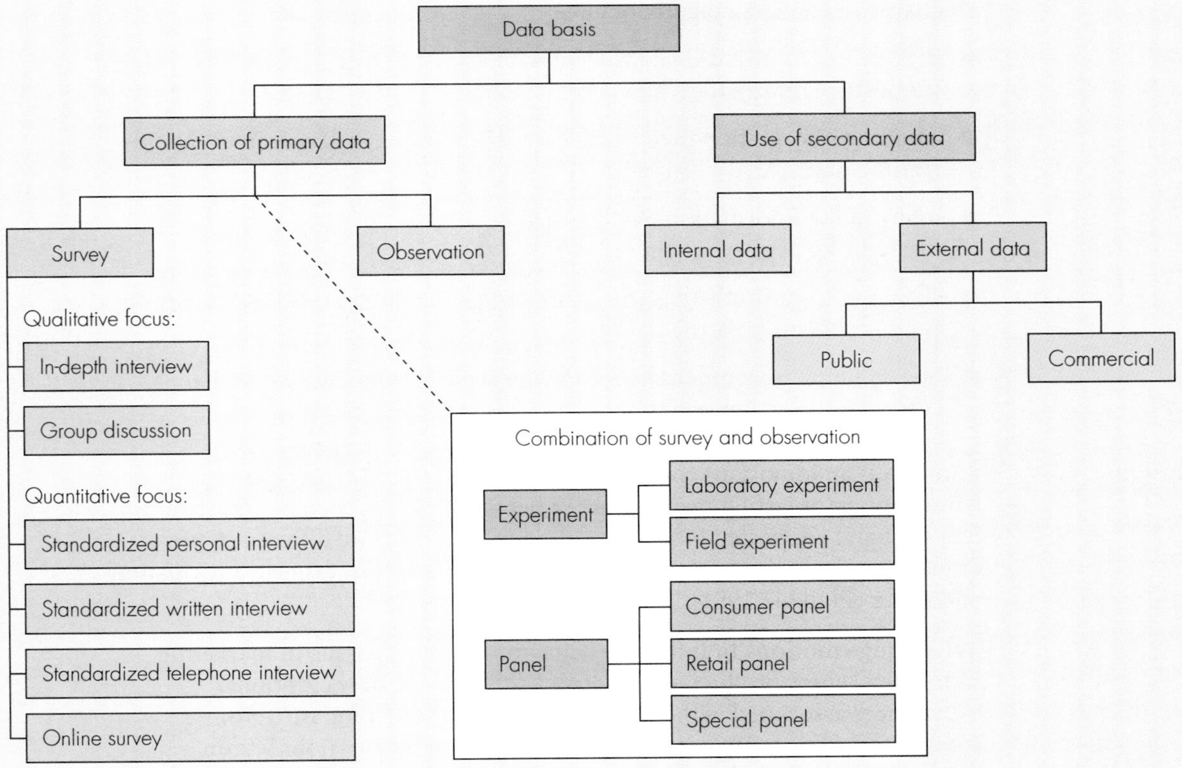

Figure A-3 Overview of the main methods for establishing a data basis for a market research study

Dissonance theory

Information processing is a core aspect of *consumer behavior*. Several psychological factors influence or control the search and evaluation of information. Dissonance theory is a psychological approach to explain how customers process information. In particular, it examines how customers deal with inconsistent and conflicting information.

Cognitive dissonance theory

According to cognitive dissonance theory customers strive for an inner cognitive (intellectual) balance; this is referred to as consonance. This balance is achieved if the consumer's cognitive elements, which comprise knowledge, experience, attitudes and opinions, are compatible with each other.

Cognitive dissonance occurs when cognitive elements are not in harmony with each other (Festinger 1957). In this situation individuals try to reduce the dissonance. For example, customers may have two attitudes about a product: one favorable from previous experience and one non-favorable with the product from recent experience. Another typical situation can occur after purchase, when customers especially notice favorable information about other brands or notice negative features of the purchased product.

It is an objective in marketing to avoid, or at least minimize, cognitive dissonance on the part of the customer, as this may have a negative impact on the establishment of customer loyalty (see Section 9.1). There are several **mechanisms for reducing dissonance**:

- seeking out information consistent with an attitude (e.g. customers search for positive information about the product)
- avoiding information inconsistent with an attitude (e.g. customers avoid reading negative test results)
- interpreting information in a dissonance-avoidance manner (e.g. discrediting negative test results)
- changing the attitude (e.g. the customer gives in to the fact that the product is not performing satisfactorily)
- taking action to compensate for the negative consequences (e.g. the customer files a complaint).

Emotion

Emotion is an important construct of *consumer behavior*. An emotion is a momentary or lasting mental state of being, which is generally (more or less strongly) connected to physical excitement. There are different **types of emotions**, such as joy, acceptance, surprise, fear, sadness, disgust, anticipation and anger (Plutchik 1991).

Triggering emotions to influence behavior is a central issue in marketing. In markets where product quality is almost identical, only emotional experiences associated with a product can help to differentiate it from competitors. An example is the targeted triggering of emotions within the scope of **communication management**. Emotion in ads often helps customers to memorize them (see Section 8.4 for information on the design of communication measures).

Emotions can be measured by different methods:

- psychobiological measurement: the intensity of the emotional excitement is recorded (e.g. pulse rate)

- measurement of subjective experience: respondents describe their emotional reactions, either verbally or in writing
- measurement of expressions: observation of body language and facial expressions.

Environmental factors

Consumer behavior is determined not only by internal psychological processes. Environmental factors – external factors such as the physical, social and cultural environment – also play an important role in explaining consumer behavior.

The **physical environment** is composed of the natural environment (e.g. nature, climate) and the human-made environment (e.g. infrastructure). Examples of stimuli of the physical environment are sounds, colors, pictures, smells and tastes. These physical stimuli often arouse emotional reactions, which can be used in marketing (e.g. a shopping environment using specific music).

The **social environment** refers to people or groups of people with whom a customer maintains regular contact (e.g. family, friends, co-workers) and to the broader social environment with which the customer has no regular contact (e.g. one's own social class, religious associations or public institutions). The social environment can influence a person's buying decision either directly or indirectly through expectations.

Basic concepts of social influence on consumer behavior are as follows.

- **Role theory** is concerned with the expectations that arise from the social role of the consumer (see Coser 1991). According to role theory, individuals perceive their own role and the associated expectations arising from the social environment, and align their behavior with these expectations.
- The **reference group** is a collection of people that individuals use as a point of comparison or aspiration for attitudes, beliefs, values and behavior. According to this concept people compare, for example, their attitudes and behavior to those of the reference group and may make adjustments to comply with the expectations of the group.
- **Opinion leaders** are persons considered as experts and highly trustworthy. Individuals rely on their advice when making decisions.

Consumer behavior is also influenced by **cultural environmental factors**. This can be the culture of a region, a country or a specific social group. In this context culture refers to values, norms, attitudes and typical behaviors shared by this group.

Experiments

Experiments are one way to collect *primary data* for *market research*. Like panels, experiments are a combination of observation and survey. In general, experiments study the behavior of consumers in a simplified environment under changing conditions.

The objective is the identification of cause–effect relationships. The general idea is to change one factor (independent variable) of the design and measure how it affects another (dependent variable). Typical applications are determining **willingness to pay** (see Section 6.2.1), measuring **communication effect** (see Section 8.5), as well as **test markets** (see also *Test markets* and Section 5.3.3).

There are two basic forms of experiment.

1. A **laboratory experiment** takes place in an artificial environment, which represents a simplified form of reality. The basic advantage of this form of experiment is that interfering factors can be controlled. Laboratory experiments are also cost effective and fast.
2. **Field experiments** take place in a natural environment. Participants usually are not aware that they are involved in an experiment. This typically leads to more valid results. However, company-external parties such as retailers have to cooperate in most cases.

In both forms of experiment, misleading effects or **biases** can occur.

- 'History' effects: exogenous events affect the dependent variable of the experiment (e.g. negative reports about the competitor's product quality during the field experiment lead to increased sales of the test product).
- 'Testing' effects: the repeated usage of a measurement tool influences the measurement result (e.g. customers participating in a brand recall test several times learn from previous rounds).
- 'Instrumentation' effects: distorted measurements can be caused when the measurement device is adjusted (e.g. observers learn to assess participants' reactions better over the course of the experiment).
- 'Selection' effects: these arise when errors occur in test group composition (e.g. a new part of a series of movies happens to be tested among fans of that series).

Factor analysis

Factor analysis is a *multivariate method* used in *market research* to analyze data. Its objective is to reduce a larger number of variables (called indicator variables) to a few basic factors. In this way, factor analysis reduces complexity in data sets with regard to the number of variables (whereas *cluster analysis* reduces complexity with regard to the number of objects).

There are two basic variants of factor analysis: **exploratory** and **confirmatory factor analysis**.

1. **Exploratory factor analysis** starts without any prior hypothesis of the underlying factors. It is the objective to identify these factors. Exploratory factor analyzes are applied in marketing research mainly in the area of **market segmentation**, to identify the main factors differentiating customers or in **product development** to identify the main product features determining customer choice.
2. **Confirmatory factor analysis** checks an a priori definition of a factor structure for consistency with the sample data. Confirmatory factor analysis is mainly applied in market research areas that work with **complex constructs** (e.g. trust, commitment, dependence), which cannot be directly measured and thus have to be measured by means of indicator variables.

Game theory

Game theory is a well-established theory in economics explaining the behavior of competitors. Its major application is for situations where several persons have to take decisions. Marketing research has adopted the principal ideas of game theory to analyze *consumer behavior* or the behavior of managers.

According to game theory, players (e.g. the companies' managers) have to choose between different strategies. The players choose the strategy that maximizes their own benefit. Knowing that this benefit will also be determined by the opponents' decisions, a player anticipates the opponents' strategies in their own decision-making.

The so-called **Nash equilibrium** is reached when no player can achieve a higher benefit by choosing a different strategy – taking into account the opponent's anticipated strategy. Diverging from this general equilibrium would lead to a worse result for the individual players. This dynamic can result in a situation in which all players are worse off than if they had collaborated (a situation described as the **prisoners' dilemma**). Game theory always asks for the consideration of competitors' reactions in decision making.

Game theory is **applied in marketing** – for example, in:

- competition in prices, especially price wars (see Section 6.3.3)
- competition in innovation
- competition in product compatibility
- competition in quality.

Information economics

To analyze how customers process information is a key aspect of *consumer behavior*. Information economics is an approach to explaining customers' search for information and the evaluation of this information. The basic concern is to determine which factors are relevant to seeking out and evaluating information about products and services.

Two conditions make information economics especially relevant for marketing.

1. The search and evaluation of information is examined in light of the fact that customers often do not have all relevant information when making decisions. For example, customers do not definitely know the quality of a product before purchasing it. This is referred to as **uncertainty**.
2. In an interaction where one party has more or better information than the other one has obtained, this is called **information asymmetry**. In a typical purchase situation customers possess less information about the product than the manufacturer.

The extent of this information uncertainty and asymmetry depends on the **characteristics of products** (see Figure A-4).

- **Search characteristics** of a product/service offer can be completely evaluated prior to purchase via a simple inspection (e.g. inspection of furniture prior to purchase).
- **Experience characteristics** can only be evaluated by using or consuming the product after purchasing it (e.g. a visit to the hairdresser).
- **Credence characteristics** cannot be fully evaluated by the buyer either before or after the product has been purchased (e.g. the services of surgeons or consultants).

Strategies for reducing information asymmetries are as follows.

- **Signalling:** signalling refers to a company sending out information that alters the belief or conveys information to customers in the market. For example, a company can send a signal by including favorable test results in its advertisements.

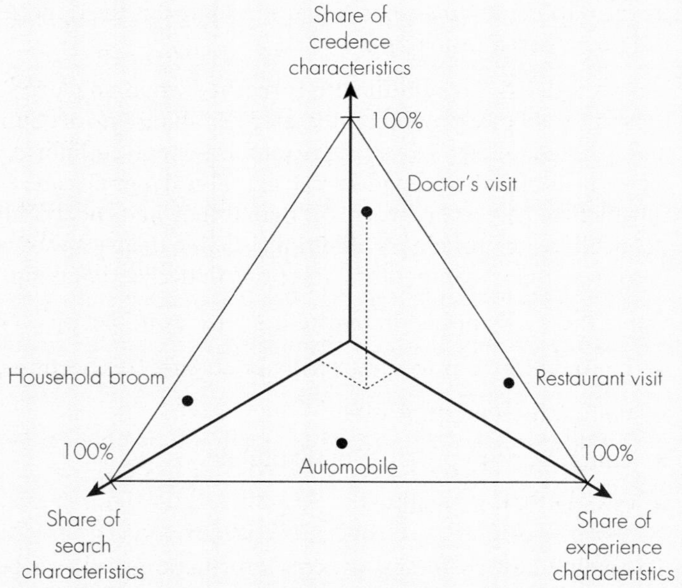

Figure A-4 Positioning of products on the basis of search, experience and credence characteristics (adapted from Weiber and Adler 1995, p. 100)

- **Screening:** screening refers to customers searching directly for information. For example, a customer can go online to obtain detailed company information.

Involvement

Involvement is a basic concept of *consumer behavior*. Involvement refers to a customer's willingness to seek out, assimilate, process and store information. It also describes the degree to which a customer is willing to engage in the purchasing decision of a product.

Involvement is important in product decisions (e.g. when considering buying habits; see Section 5.2), pricing research (e.g. when assessing customer's willingness to pay; see Section 6.2.1) and in communication (e.g. in advertising design; see Chapter 8.4).

There are different **types of involvement**.

- **Long-term involvement** is when customers demonstrate interest in an object (e.g. a product) over a long time period, **versus situational involvement**, which is a temporary interest in an object. Situational involvement diminishes after the purchase has been made.
- **Cognitive involvement** means that the customer is interested in thinking about information related to his/her goal and in cognitively processing it, **versus affective involvement** which means that the customer has special emotions/feelings related to a specific product offer.
- **High involvement** occurs in situations when the product is particularly important for the customer or is associated with risks, **versus low**

involvement, which is connected with products that are less risky for customers and less important for them. In this case, the customer exhibits somewhat passive information-seeking behavior. Highly involved customers, on the other hand, actively seek information, and the company should support this active information-seeking behavior (e.g. with adequate online information).

Learning theory

Learning theories are derived from psychology to explain *consumer behavior*. Their main objective is to explain how information is stored in and retrieved from memory. One can distinguish three learning theories: classical conditioning, instrumental conditioning and observational learning.

1. **Learning by classical conditioning** is based on innate, instinctive reflexes (e.g. blink reflex, salivation, emotions). Classical conditioning uses these reflexes by showing a stimulus that arouses the reflex (unconditioned stimulus) simultaneously with a neutral one (conditioned stimulus). After several repetitions the conditioned stimulus alone causes the same reflex. An application in marketing is emotional conditioning in communication (e.g. showing pleasant surroundings in a new product ad will provoke positive emotions when seeing the product again).
2. **Learning by instrumental conditioning** is triggered by the consequences of behavior. Individuals tend to repeat a behavior for which they were rewarded and avoid a behavior for which they were punished. This explains why customers who are satisfied with a brand remain loyal (see Section 8.4). An application of instrumental conditioning in marketing is a bonus for especially loyal customers.
3. **Observational learning** is based on the idea that individuals learn by direct experience as well as by observing others. The behavior of others is observed and imitated in similar situations. Marketing applies observational learning when using celebrities in advertisements (see Section 8.4).

Likert scale

The most common instrument used to collect primary data is the *survey* using questionnaires. When designing a questionnaire, the researcher has to consider different types of question. **Open-end questions** allow respondents to answer in their own words, and are typically used in qualitative survey methods. Quantitative survey methods mostly use **closed-end questions**, where the respondent can choose between the possible answers provided. Likert scales are a commonly used measurement scale in **quantitative surveys**. Respondents rate their accordance with a question or statement on a bipolar scale.

An example from customer satisfaction research (see Section 9.1) is shown in Figure A-5.

How satisfied are you with . . .

. . . the overall service? Extremely satisfied ☐ ☐ ☐ ☐ ☐ ☐ Not satisfied at all

Figure A-5 Example of a Likert scale

Likert scales are a popular scaling method for survey design since the cognitive effort required of respondents is relatively low. Other types of closed-end questions are, for example, rating scales and multiple-choice questions.

Market research

Market research refers to the process of gathering and evaluating information in the market (e.g. from actual and potential customers or competitors) in order to support marketing decision making. Typical market research tasks are the identification of market opportunities, monitoring the impact of marketing activities and answering specific marketing questions.

Market research projects ideally proceed through the following main steps.

- **Definition of the market research problem:** in this step, it is important to precisely define which questions will be answered by the research project and what its basic objectives are.
- **Decision on research method and data sources:** next, the researcher determines what information is necessary to answer these questions and how this information can be gathered (see also *Data collection methods*).
- **Data collection:** the next step is the execution of the data collection; here one aspect can be the design of questionnaires (see also *Likert scales*).
- **Data analysis:** in this step, statistical methods are applied to analyze the data collected (see also *Multivariate methods*).
- **Interpretation and decision:** Finally, a recommendation for action should be given based on an interpretation of the results.

Memory model

Information processing is a core process in *consumer behavior*. This process has different facets: information has to be absorbed, evaluated, stored and retrieved. The process can be explained by the memory model, as depicted in Figure A-6.

The knowledge of this information processing can be crucial for marketing (e.g. in the area of behavioral pricing; see Section 6.2.2).

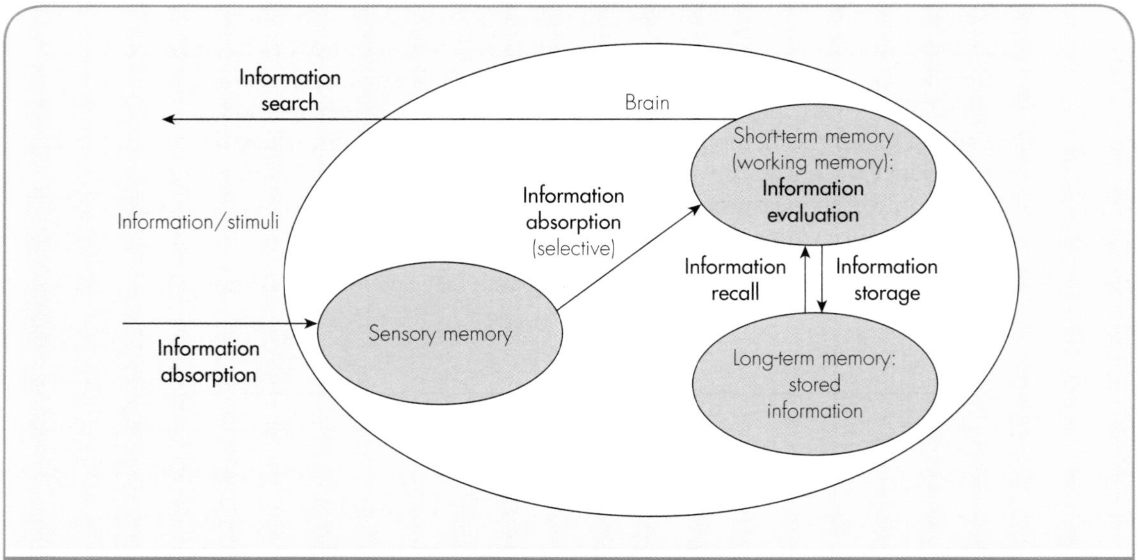

Figure A-6 Overview of information processing using a memory model (adapted from Atkinson and Shiffrin 1968)

Different **types of memory** are involved in the facets of information processing.

- The **sensory memory** retains the sensory impressions triggered by environmental stimuli for a very brief time, without interpreting the meaning.
- The **short-term memory** selectively processes only some of the information from the sensory memory.
- The short-term memory retrieves information from previous experiences stored in the **long-term memory**.

Motivation

Motivation is a key construct of *consumer behavior*. Motivation drives a person to act. It describes the driving force that is directed to achieve a goal.

Motivation is usually geared towards meeting needs (see also *Customer 'needs'*). A basic concept to aid in the understanding of the meaning of needs for marketing is **Maslow's pyramid** (see Figure A-7). Maslow suggested that needs have a hierarchical ordering (Maslow 1970). People first fulfill lower-order needs (e.g. physiological needs) before fulfilling higher-order needs.

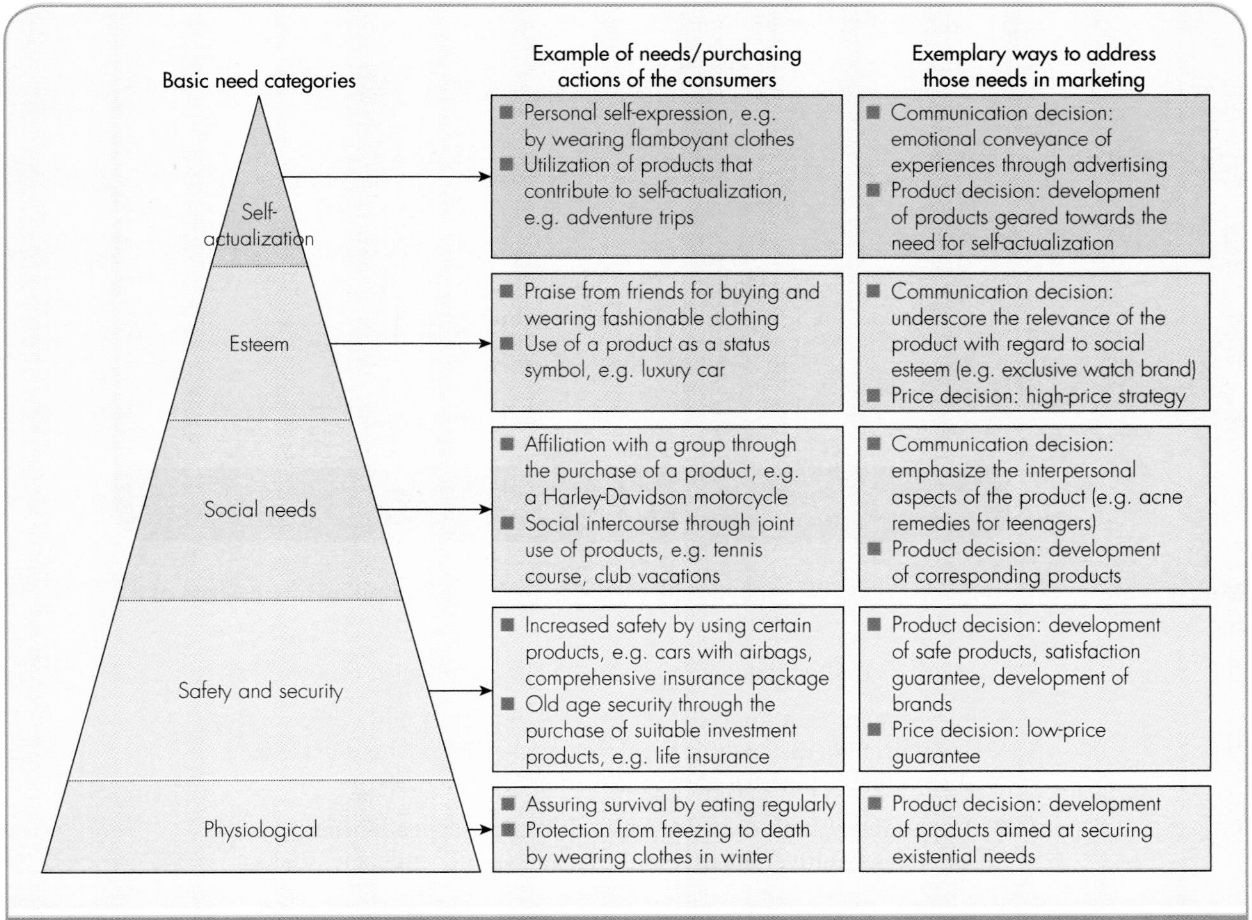

Figure A-7 Maslow's basic need categories and ways to influence them with marketing tools (Maslow 1970)

Marketing measures can influence consumer behavior by satisfying or deliberately stimulating certain needs (see Figure A-7).

Multi-dimensional scaling (MDS) MDS is a method of *multivariate data analysis* in *market research*, which can be applied to both metric and non-metric variables. The objective is to position objects in the lowest possible dimensional space on the basis of similarity relations (for detailed information, see Aaker *et al.* 2004). The positions of the objects in this space should reflect the similarity relations between the objects as accurately as possible. Identification of the similarities of objects is not based on evaluations of individual characteristics, but rather on a global similarity rating. MDS results in a visual representation of these perceptions.

Important areas of **application** in market research are positioning analyzes (see Section 5.4.2) to analyze the brand image of products, new product development and market segmentation. The result of an MDS can be the visualization of the positioning (so-called 'perceptual maps') of different brands in a given market (see Figure A-8).

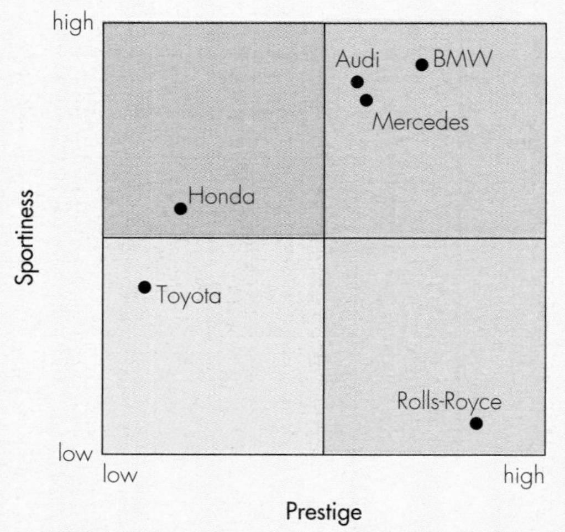

Figure A-8 Example of positioning of car brands as a result of MDS

Multivariate methods In *market research*, multivariate methods enable the simultaneous analysis of a large number of variables.

The various multivariate methods can be differentiated as follows.

- **Interdependency analysis:** all variables have the same a priori status. It entails only the analysis of interdependencies, without drawing up a directional hypothesis about those interdependencies.
- **Dependency analysis:** these methods analyze dependencies between variables. Multivariate methods that analyze dependencies make a distinction between independent and dependent variables. The **independent variable** is the cause variable and the **dependent variable** is the effect variable (e.g. price is the independent (cause) variable and demand is the dependent (effect) variable).

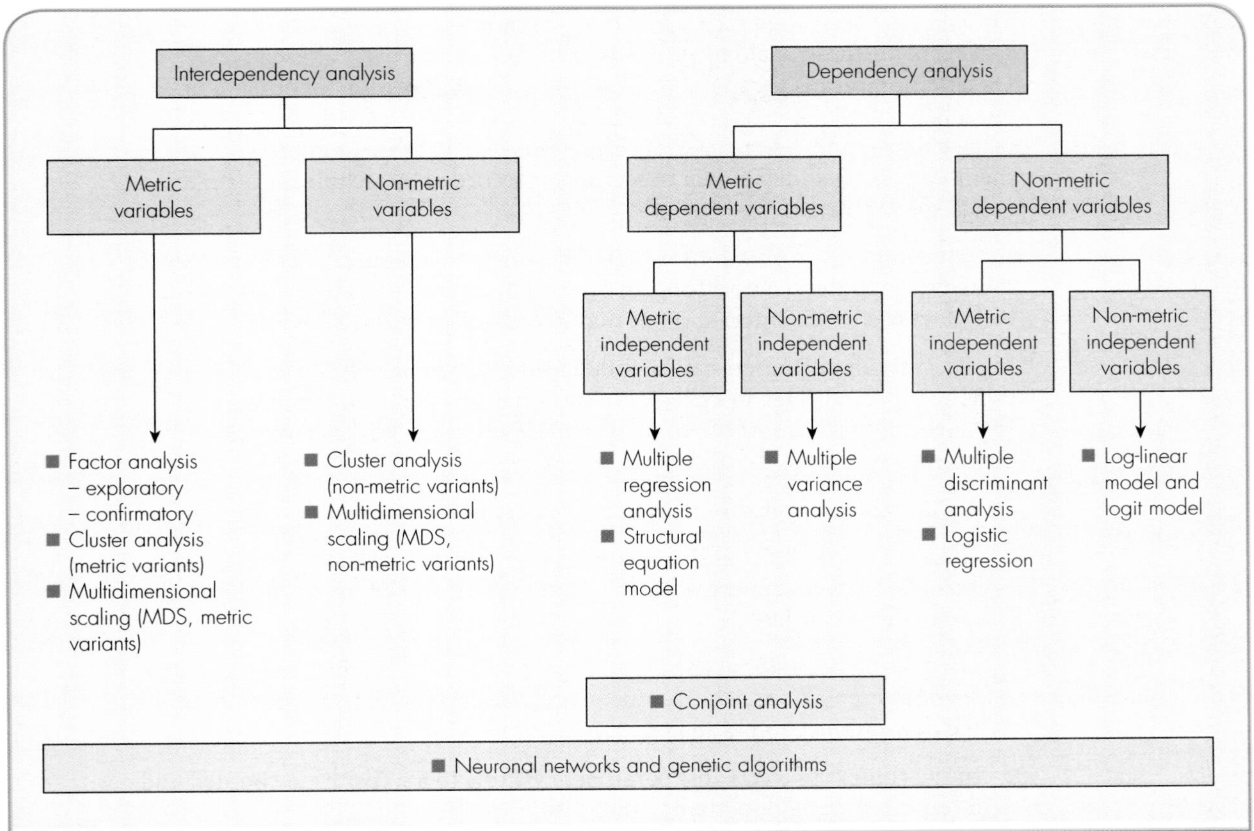

Figure A-9 Overview of important multivariate methods

Figure A-9 provides an overview of the various multivariate methods.

Which exact method is applicable depends on the types of variables under analysis. Variables can be differentiated based on the **scale of measurement**, as follows.

- **Metric variables** are measured on a scale where the distances between the scale points can be quantified (e.g. revenues, sales, income).
- **Non-metric variables** are measured on a scale where the distances between scale points cannot be interpreted. These can be nominal variables classifying objects into groups (e.g. gender types, profession, state) or ordinal variables ranking objects without quantifying the differences between them.

For the principal objective and procedure of the most commonly applied methods in marketing research see:

- *Cluster analysis*
- *Conjoint analysis*
- *Factor analysis*
- *Multi-dimensional scaling*
- *Regression analysis* and other methods of dependency analysis.

Observation

To obtain *primary data* for *market research* purposes, observations and *surveys* of customers (along with hybrid forms) are the basic alternatives. **Observation** means the methodical and systematic recording of observable facts, behavioral patterns and characteristics of certain individuals. These facts, patterns and characteristics can be reported by the customers themselves or by independent observers, or recorded by technical instruments (e.g. a video camera).

An **advantage** of observations is that they are more cost-effective than surveys; moreover, no interviewer effect can occur. This means that customers cannot be influenced by the interviewer as may occur in face-to-face interviews.

In observations customers can be influenced if they realize that their behavior is being observed. This so-called **observation effect** is a major **problem** with observations. Another problem results from the selective perception of observers.

Observations are **applied in marketing research** for a number of purposes.

- **Customer flow in retail stores** can be observed by cameras or persons to examine how customers walk through the store and adjust the presentation of objects accordingly.
- **Purchasing behavior** at the shelf can be observed to estimate the success of product innovations. The number of customers who pass the shelf, examine the new product and ultimately buy it, is recorded.
- In the context of **electronic commerce** visitors to a website are counted and, often, click-through patterns can be observed.
- **Mystery shoppers** (or silent shoppers) check service quality on behalf of the company. Mystery shoppers pretend to be clients and conduct anonymous test purchases in stores to evaluate service quality.

Panels

Panels are one method of collecting *primary data* for *market research*. Like experiments, panels are a combination of observation and survey.

Panels consist of individuals who agree to report their purchases of products/product categories over a certain time. These panels allow companies to track product and brand purchases, and thereby monitor the impact of communication measures (see Section 8.5).

There is a risk that panels do not **represent the customer base adequately**. This risk is especially high:

- if random selection is not possible
- if willingness to participate is heterogeneous
- if some members leave the panel over time (panel mortality)
- if changes in the composition of the population over time would require adjustments of the panel (panel rotation).

Another bias in panels can result from the so-called **panel effect**. This means that buying behavior changes over time as a result of participating in the panel. For example, panel members can pay more attention to a specific brand when they know that it is being examined in the panel.

Perceptual maps

Perceptual maps belong to the class of *multivariate research methods*. They are based on the assumption that products can be described by a number of attributes. Like *multi-dimensional scaling*, perceptual maps position brands, products etc. according to salient attributes. In addition, perceptual maps also plot customers' preferences in order to predict buying behavior, and therefore can be used to predict customers' choices among the positioned products.

There are two alternative models for the mapping of preferences (see Section 5.5.3).

1. The **ideal point model** is based on the ideal point concept: the ideal point is the place in the product market space that represents the highest preference score. The assumption is that, the closer its distance to the ideal point, the more a certain product will be selected. Products on the same circle around the ideal point have an equal purchase probability (see Figure A-10).

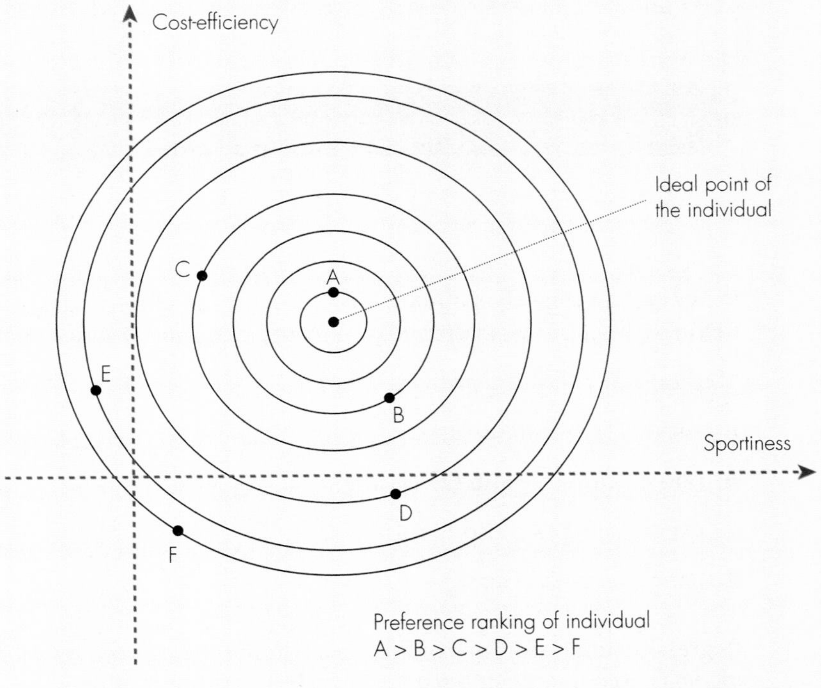

Figure A-10 Illustration of the ideal point model (according to Dichtl and Schobert 1979)

2. In the **ideal vector model**, the preference ranking of an individual is mapped via a vector in the product market space. The direction of the vector indicates the increasing preference (i.e. an alternative whose perpendicular on the vector is further in the direction of the preference maximum is preferred over an alternative that is further away from the preference maximum on the vector; see Figure A-11).

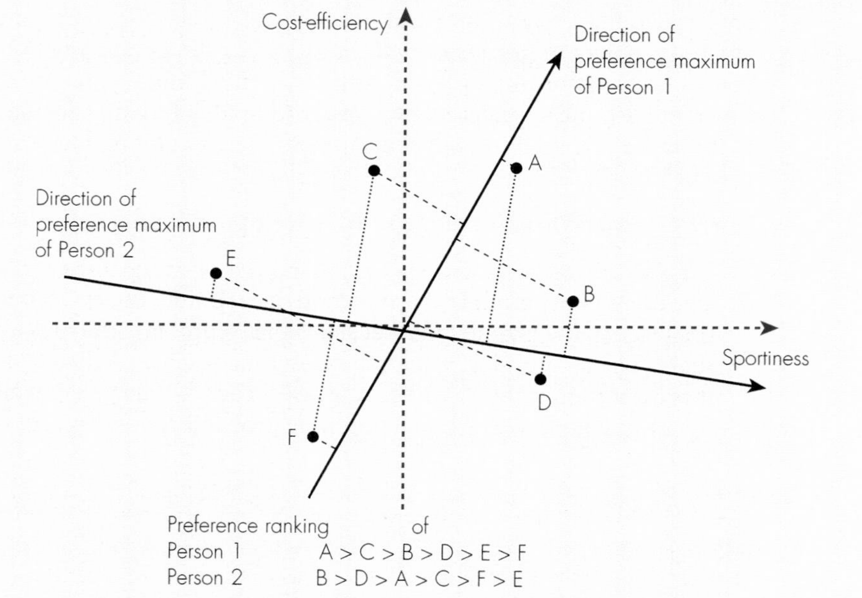

Figure A-11 Illustration of the ideal vector model (according to Dichtl and Schobert 1979)

Primary data

Primary data is newly collected for a specific market research study and tailored to the particular information requirements (see also *Data collection methods*).

Methods for collecting primary data are:

- **surveys** (see also *Surveys*)
- **observation** (see also *Observation*)
- **experiments** (see also *Experiments*)
- **panels** (see also *Panels*).

Regression analysis

Regression analysis is one of the most commonly used *multivariate analysis methods* used in *market research*. It analyzes the effect of one or several cause variables on an effect variable.

Several **different forms of regression analysis** exist: the most prevalent forms are binary regression (just one cause and effect variable is considered), multiple regression (several cause variables are considered) and logistic regression (the effect variable is non-metric).

Regression analysis has a wide range of **applications in marketing**. It is used to explain how marketing management variables affect sales, profit or other marketing objectives. Typical questions are: 'Which attributes influence customer satisfaction?', 'Which factors influence sales?' and 'Which factors determine willingness to pay for a specific product?'

Regression analysis follows **four process steps.**

1. **Model specification:** the relationship between the cause and the effect variables is specified in the form of an equation; often the relationship between cause and effect variable is depicted by a linear curve.
2. **Parameter estimation:** fitting the parameters of the equation, in a way that the resulting linear curve approximates the observed data as exactly as possible.
3. **Model validation:** examine how well the cause variables considered explain the effect variable; all cause variables are analyzed together in order to measure the overall correctness of the model.
4. **Interpretation of the results:** comparison of the parameters of the equation (regression coefficients) with regard to their impact on the effect variable; each cause variable is analyzed individually for the intensity of its impact on the effect variable.

Regression analysis is the basis for several other multivariate methods. **Variance analysis** and **discriminant analysis** are statistical tools closely related to regression analysis. These multivariate methods also consider the cause–effect relationships among variables. Variance analysis can be applied in the case of non-metric cause variables and discriminant analysis in the case of non-metric effect variables.

Logit models are used to predict probabilities for the occurrence of an event (e.g. product purchase) based on several cause variables (e.g. prior purchase). **Structural equation models** consider causal chains and can deal with complex constructs (e.g. trust, satisfaction) as cause and effect variables (see also *Factor analysis*). **Neural networks** examine indirect cause–effect relationships considering a network of other variables between the cause and the effect variable without prior hypotheses on these relationships.

Risk theory

Risk theory is one theory referred to in *consumer behavior*, which explains how customers make purchasing decisions. Risk theory is essentially based on the assumption that, when making purchasing decisions, individuals endeavour to avoid and reduce the perceived risk (referred to as risk aversion).

Perceived risk can arise from different sources such as (see Hoyer and MacInnis 2004):

- **performance risk** relates to whether a product can fulfill the desired performance requirements
- **social risk** refers to the potential damage to the customer's image or reputation that could be caused by purchasing, consuming or using a certain product
- **financial risk** is perceived as being especially high if an expensive purchase (e.g. a house or machinery) is involved
- **physical risk** (safety risk) is perceived if customers fear that consuming the product could be hazardous to their own health
- **psychological risk** is perceived if the purchase or consumption of a product is difficult to reconcile with the customer's own convictions
- **temporal risk** arises from uncertainty concerning the amount of time involved in buying or using the product.

In this connection, consumer behavior research studies have analyzed strategies that customers can use to **reduce purchase risk**, including the following (see Blackwell *et al.* 2005):

- customers can search (pro)actively for information
- customers can remain loyal to a brand or company (see Section 9.1)
- customers might imitate the choices of other specifically relevant and competent reference persons
- customers might lower their expected standards
- customers may select upscale products.

Secondary data

In contrast to *primary data*, **secondary data** are retrieved from already existing information sources (see also *Data collection methods*). This is usually more cost effective than collecting primary data, but does not always meet all the information requirements of the specific research project.

Sources of secondary data can be both **internal and external** to the company.

Company-internal data sources for secondary data can be:

- accounting documents and records
- costing documents and records (e.g. sales and distribution costs, contribution margins)
- general statistics (e.g. overall sales, sales categorized by product group, items, customers, sales representatives, regions and periods)
- customer statistics (e.g. customers categorized by type, size and region, order volumes, sales channels, complaints, reminders)
- reports and messages submitted by the field salesforce (e.g. visit and sales call reports)
- previous collections of primary data that appear relevant to the issues at hand.

Company-external data sources can be:

- statistics and other publications by official institutions
- publications by trade associations and organizations
- publications by scientific institutions
- publications by banks and special report providers
- publications from publishing houses (books, trade journals, newspapers)
- publications by advertising companies and suppliers of promotional material
- publications by competitors (annual reports, company magazines, catalogs and advertisements, competitor websites)
- information material from mailing list publishers, list brokers, special information providers/services, consulting firms and market research institutes.

Surveys

To obtain *primary data* for *market research* purposes *observations* and surveys of customers (along with hybrid forms) are the basic alternatives. Surveys can include qualitative as well as quantitative methods.

Qualitative methods generate qualitative information from a somewhat limited number of interviewees. Qualitative survey methods include the following.

- **In-depth interview:** this refers to a relatively free-form, qualitative interview in the form of a face-to-face conversation. In-depth interviews are typically applied to examine the motivations of customers (e.g. churn analysis; see Section 9.1). The complex, time-consuming analysis and the difficulty of comparing the contents of several interviews are major problems related to this survey method.
- **Focus groups/group discussions** consist of several people involved in a discussion led by a moderator. Focus groups are typically applied to generate or test new product ideas (see Sections 5.2 and 5.5.5). The main problem here is that opinion leaders can dominate the other participants. To avoid this, the moderator needs to be highly qualified, both professionally and socially.

Quantitative methods aim to collect quantitative information and therefore typically interview a large number of people. Some quantitative survey methods are:

- standardized personal interview
- standardized written interview
- standardized telephone interview
- online surveys
- email surveys.

Test markets

Test markets and test market simulators are typical examples of the application of *experiments*. **Test markets** can occur in different forms.

- Regional test markets are conducted in a geographically limited area; the structure of the area should be representative of the overall market.
- In micro test markets a small number of selected test stores are used to evaluate the effectiveness of marketing measures.
- Electronic test markets are regional test markets in which data are collected by using a combination of household and retail panels.
- Virtual shopping describes a photorealistic, computer-based simulation of a store model.

Test market simulators are experiments under laboratory conditions. In contrast to field test markets, test market simulators are significantly less costly and new product developments can be concealed from competitors. The **ASSESSOR** model is one of the most prominent test market simulators. It aims to predict the market share of new products by estimating trial rate, repeat purchase rate and purchase probability (see Section 5.3.3).

Transaction cost theory

Transaction cost theory is a key concept in economics used by marketing research to explain *consumer behavior*. It justifies the existence of organizations and addresses the efficiency of different organizational forms (Coase 1937).

Transactions are considered transfers of goods or services across a separable interface (e.g. departments, companies, markets). The basic assumption is that carrying out a transaction invokes costs. These are mainly **information and communication costs** when:

- initiating a transaction (e.g. searching information to select possible partners)
- agreeing on a transaction (e.g. negotiation, settlement, contract)
- monitoring the transaction (e.g. adherence to the agreement)
- adapting the conditions of the transaction (e.g. renegotiation).

Transactions can be carried out:

- within the **organization**
- in the **market**, or
- in a **hybrid** form.

These organizational forms of transaction invoke different costs depending on the **specificity** and **uncertainty** of transactions. Specific investments into transactions are those that cannot be used for other purposes (e.g. investments in special technologies). Uncertainty results from complex, dynamic environments (environmental uncertainty – e.g. changing prices) and possible opportunistic behavior on the part of the transaction partner (behavioral uncertainty – e.g. the transaction partner uses the dependency to achieve an advantage).

Applications of the transaction cost theory in marketing are decisions on:

- investments in long-term customer relationships
- (direct versus indirect) sales channels (see Sections 7.2 and 7.3)
- customer relationship management, especially in the business-to-business context (see Sections 10.1 and 10.2).

Values and lifestyle

Values are a basic construct of *consumer behavior*. **Values** are long-lasting convictions that a certain behavior is desirable or good (see Hoyer and MacInnis 2004). Values are endurable in nature and play a central role in personality structure.

Rokeach suggested that values are concerned with both objectives and ways of behaving (**Rokeach Value Scale** (RVS)).

- Values representing objectives are: a comfortable life, an exciting life, a sense of accomplishment, a world at peace, a world of beauty, equality, family security, freedom, happiness, inner harmony, mature love, national security, pleasure, salvation, self-respect, social recognition, true friendship and wisdom.

- Values referring to ways of behaving are: ambition, broad-minded, capable, cheerful, clean, courageous, forgiving, honest, imaginative, independent, intellectual, logical, loving, obedient, polite, responsible and self-controlled.

Values can be distinguished according to their specificity. **Societal values** are based on a cultural orientation framework (see Holt 1997), whereas **personal values and attitudes** are the conscious or unconscious evaluation criteria of the individual.

Values have a **direct** (determining objectives) or **indirect effect on behavior** (influencing emotion, involvement and attitudes). Their influence on the objectives, attitudes and motives of an individual make them applicable to many aspects of consumer behavior, including advertising, product choice, branding and market segmentation.

Lifestyle is a more comprehensive concept than values. It refers to behavioral patterns within a corridor shaped by personal and societal values (see Anderson and Golden 1984). Lifestyles reflect the way people live, their activities, interests and opinions, as well as demographic attributes (age, income, marital status, etc.). A person's lifestyle may change over time.

In marketing, lifestyles are often used for **market segmentation** (see Section 3.3.2).

References

Aaker, D., Kumar, V. and Day, G. (2004) *Marketing Research* (8th edn). New York.

Anderson, W. and Golden, L. (1984) Lifestyle and psychographics: a critical review and recommendation, *Advances in Consumer Research*, 11, 1, 405–411.

Atkinson, R. and Shiffrin, I. (1968) Human memory: a proposed system and its control processes, in: Spence, K. and Spence, J. (eds) *The Psychology of Learning and Motivation: Advances in Research and Theory*. New York, 89–195.

Blackwell, R., Miniard, P. and Engel, J. (2005) *Consumer Behavior* (10th edn). Chicago.

Coase, R.N. (1937) The nature of the firm, *Economica*, 4, 16, 386–405.

Coser, R. (1991) *In Defense of Modernity: Role Complexity and Individual Autonomy*. Stanford.

Dichtl, E. and Schobert, R. (1979) *Mehrdimensionale Skalierung*. Munich.

Festinger, L. (1957) *A Theory of Cognitive Dissonance*. Stanford.

Holt, D. (1997) Poststructuralist lifestyle analysis: conceptualizing the social patterning of consumption in postmodernity, *Journal of Consumer Research*, 23, 4, 326–350.

Homburg, C., Koschate, N. and Hoyer, W. (2005) Do satisfied customers really pay more? A study of the relationship between customer satisfaction and willingness to pay, *Journal of Marketing*, 69, 2, 84–96.

Hoyer, W. and MacInnis, D. (2004) *Consumer Behavior* (3rd edn). Boston, Mass./New York.

Malmo, R.B. (1959) Activation: a neuropsychological dimension, *Psychological Review*, 66, 6, 367–386.

Maslow, A. (1970) *Motivation and Personality*. Princeton.

Plutchik, R. (1991) *The Emotions*. Lanham.

Weiber, R. and Adler, J. (1995) Positionierung von Kaufprozessen im informationsökonomischen Dreieck, *Zeitschrift für betriebswirtschaftliche Forschung*, 47, 2, 99–123.

Index